CITY POLITICS

CITY POLITICS

Private Power and Public Policy

DENNIS R. JUDD
University of Missouri—St. Louis

TODD SWANSTROM
State University of New York—Albany

HarperCollins*CollegePublishers*

Acquisitions Editor: Maria Hartwell
Project Editor: David Nickol
Design Supervisor: Heather A. Ziegler
Text Design: Rohit Sawhney
Cover Design: Rohit Sawhney
Cover Illustration: Georgia O'Keefe, City Night, 48" x 30", oil on Canvas. The
                    Minneapolis Institute of Art, Gift of the Regis Corporation.
Production Manager: Hilda Koparanian
Printer and Binder: R. R. Donnelley & Sons Company
Cover Printer: The Lehigh Press, Inc.

City Politics: Private Power and Public Policy

Library of Congress Cataloging-in-Publication Data

Judd, Dennis R.
    City politics : private power and public policy / Dennis R. Judd, Todd Swanstrom
      p.   cm.
    Includes bibliographical references and index.
    ISBN 0-673-46962-X
    1. Municipal government--United States.   2. Urban policy--United States.
3. United States--Economic policy.   4. Sociology, Urban--United States.
I. Swanstrom, Todd.   II. Title.
JS331.J78   1994
320.8'5'0973--dc20   93-22903
                                                      CIP

93 94 95 96 9 8 7 6 5 4 3 2 1

To my mentors, Lou Gold and Phil Meranto

D. R. J.

To my mother, Beatrice Swanstrom, for teaching me to care

T. S.

We will neglect our cities to our peril, for in neglecting them we neglect the nation.

—President John F. Kennedy, Message to Congress, January 30, 1962

CONTENTS

PART TWO   NATIONAL POLICY AND THE CITIES

PART THREE   SUBURBS, SUNBELT, AND THE ECLIPSE OF THE CENTRAL CITIES

PART FOUR   THE RETURN OF THE PRIVATE CITY

PREFACE

In the summer of 1987 Dennis Judd asked Todd Swanstrom to collaborate in revising his text, *The Politics of American Cities*. First published in 1979, it had gone through three successful editions. As the two authors discussed the project, it became clear that urban politics and the scholarly literature about cities had changed so much over the past decade that an entirely new book was called for. The result is what you see before you. Though Judd's earlier text provides the foundation, *City Politics* is a new book through and through. The theory guiding the book is more comprehensive, several new topics have been introduced, and every chapter has been written to take into account the most recent research.

As with the original text, it is our intention that this book serve simultaneously as a scholarly contribution and as a textbook that covers the urban politics field comprehensively. We are convinced that a scholarly enterprise and a textbook project need not be mutually exclusive undertakings. A textbook should derive its strength from original scholarship and insight while thoroughly synthesizing the literature that defines a field of inquiry. Guided by this principle, we have combined both tasks here. *City Politics* should be useful to advanced scholars and graduate students and to students taking their first course in urban politics.

We have constructed *City Politics* around a political economy perspective. City politics can be understood as a complex interaction among the institutions, actors, and resources of both the public and the private spheres. It is true that urban life would hardly be possible without governments, which are vested with the capacity to represent the collective needs of citizens. Governments both manage the processes of democratic decision making and provide essential services. City governments, however, are particularly dependent upon marketplace institutions if they are to advance the general welfare of urban citizens. An inexhaustible variety of private institutions—defense contractors, large corporations, banks, insurance companies, retailers, real estate companies, and so on—make critical decisions that determine the well-being of urban communities. They provide jobs and housing, influence land use patterns, affect air and water pollution, and determine a multitude of other matters of great moment to urban dwellers.

The scholarly research of the last few years has advanced our understanding of how public and private institutions work out their interdependence in urban areas. Judd's text was based on the idea that politics involves such an interaction, but recently we have begun to understand what motivates public and private actors to cooperate. Put briefly (we expand on this statement in the first chapter), governments must implement policies that promote local economic growth and, at the same time, they must maintain popular support for their actions. In their turn, private actors know that their own well-being is related to the urban community's quality of life, which depends on governmental services and policies. We need to point out that this interdependence is as often expressed in a tension between the two spheres as in cooperation. There is no solution to this tension, only continual negotiation and debate. This is what makes the study of cities so fascinating. Throughout this book we examine how this interdependence is expressed in the political arena.

The interdependence of public and private institutions has been particularly obvious in recent years. During the 1980s national, regional, and local economic vitality became the ascendant issues of the day. The national government substantially withdrew from policies to help troubled cities. To cope with a combination of federal aid cutbacks and fiscal problems induced by two recessions, urban leaders scrambled to attract business investment by offering an array of local policies designed to stimulate local economic growth. Cities engaged in an increasingly heated competition, trying to outdo one another in generous tax breaks and other incentives. Issues connected to local economic vitality crowded everything else off the urban policy agenda, despite troublesome news about deteriorating public infrastructure, a rising incidence of poverty and inequality, escalating violence and crime, homelessness, racial and ethnic tensions, and a host of other social problems.

The Los Angeles riots of 1992 and the results of the 1992 presidential election made it clear that the urban agenda of the 1990s is likely to be far more complex than that of the 1980s. The riots serve as a reminder that American cities have once again become, as they were in the nineteenth and early twentieth centuries, the crucible for the nation's political and social divisions. Whereas in the 1980s attention was focused on the external economic forces affecting cities, policymakers and scholars alike are turning their attention toward the governance of cities. Politics matters. It will take a combination of new national policies and the energies of a new generation of urban leaders to keep cities from degenerating further into social chaos. In this book we document the conditions that led us to this prognosis.

As we indicate in our introductory and concluding chapters, the 1990s are like previous periods when government was called on to address mounting collective problems that cannot be solved by economic prosperity alone. The 1980s, too, can be understood better when placed in a historical context; there have been previous periods when the imperative of economic growth has outweighed all other issues. The difference between the two decades will certainly affect the nature of the interdependence of the public and private spheres and the tension and cooperation between them.

The presidential election of 1992 served as a vehicle for new policy debates that will deeply affect the cities. President Clinton has proposed a variety of important programs that may help urban leaders cope with the new urban agenda. A few examples are funds to rebuild America's public infrastructure, a public jobs program, a comprehensive national health care plan, and a program to help defense industries convert to peacetime production. Though this book goes to press too early to assess these policies (none of which have yet been adopted or implemented), we believe that our sensitivity to historical themes and our thesis that private and public purposes are always in tension will make this book extremely relevant to the new politics of the 1990s.

City Politics can be used as the basic text in courses in urban politics, urban sociology, urban planning, urban geography, and urban history. We think that the book communicates essential information about cities at the same time that it encourages students to think critically. To accomplish this goal, we offer both the political economy theme, which ties all the book's material into a coherent whole, and also substantial material comparing American city politics with urban politics elsewhere in the world. We encourage students to consider, for example, that in most nations of the world wealthy people live at the center of cities and the poor often live at the urban periphery, a fact that should serve as an antidote to any view that the American pattern of settlement is usual, natural, or inevitable.

Though our subject matter is a constantly moving target, new material included in this book will keep it relevant to the issues of the 1990s. Several features that will keep it current are:

- A historical approach that highlights the continuities in American urban politics, showing how the politics and issues of the past shed light on today's politics and problems

- A synthesis of the most recent literature on party machines that documents their successes and failures

- An analysis of the reform tradition that examines its biases and its continued relevance for urban politics today

- An analysis of suburbanization that describes the historical development of the suburbs and of suburban politics and considers the costs and consequences of governmental fragmentation and urban sprawl

- An analysis of the changing balance of power in national politics since the 1930s and the resulting enhanced influence of suburban voters in national politics

- An account of the rise of the Sunbelt and of the urban problems long associated with older industrial cities that are now affecting Sunbelt cities

- A discussion of the special relationship forged by Democratic presidents between the federal government and the central cities and the collapse of that relationship in the 1980s

- A description of the effect of the global economy on cities and the response of urban leaders

- A discussion of new approaches to economic development in central business districts, with a special focus on professional sports franchises

- An analysis of the impact on urban politics of recent immigration

- A discussion of the response of African-American mayors to urban problems and their approach to urban politics

- Substantial material on urban poverty and attendant issues of the disconnection of poor minorities from the economy, family breakdown, inadequate health care, inadequate housing, substance abuse, and crime and how these issues are treated in urban politics .

- A discussion of enclave politics as an expression of the breakdown of the urban community

- The use of 1990 census information

We are pleased to be able to thank, in print, the many people who provided valuable advice and assistance during the three years we spent on this project. The following reviewers read part or all of the manuscript and made helpful comments: John Brettling, University of New Mexico; James Button, University of Florida; David Louis Cingranelli, SUNY—Binghamton; Robert Kerstein, University of Tampa; Joel Lieske, Cleveland State University; Richard C. Rich, Virginia Tech; Pamela H. Rogers, University of Wisconsin, La Crosse; Irving Schiffman, California State University, Chico; and Robert Warren, University of Delaware. Several colleagues and friends offered advice and trenchant criticisms of parts of the manuscript, including Robert Kerstein, Paul Kantor, Richard Nathan, Norton Long, Alan DiGaetano, and Robert Fisher. David Olson and Rich Sauerzopf at SUNY-Albany and Steve Roberts at the University of Missouri–St. Louis helped with the data collection. We want to thank Maria Hartwell, Ashley Chase, and David Nickol at Harper Collins for efforts beyond the call of duty in shepherding this book through the production process. At SUNY-Albany Addie Napolitano ably helped with typing and Ellie Leggieri provided skilled secretarial assistance. At the University of Missouri–St. Louis Janet Frantzen, as always, applied her extraordinary secretarial skills to a sometimes messy manuscript and, in conspiracy with Lana Vierdag, managed to keep humor in an often hectic situation. We are lucky to know and be able to work with all of these people. In personal and professional relationships and in the cities we write about, a sense of community is essential to the good life.

Dennis R. Judd
Todd Swanstrom

CITY POLITICS

CHAPTER 1

THE POLITICS OF AMERICAN CITIES: AN INTRODUCTION

❖ THE INFLUENCE OF PRIVATISM

City politics in the United States arises from the intersection of governmental power and private resources. At both the national and local levels, governments in twentieth-century America have vastly increased their responsibilities. Even so, the growth of the public sector has not eclipsed the authority of private institutions to make critical decisions involving jobs, land use, and investment. City governments (indeed, governments at all levels) can influence, but they do not control, the many voluntary actions and decisions that taken together determine the material well-being, the social character, and the quality of life of an urban community.

Throughout our national history, cities have been conceived more in economic than in cultural, social, and political terms. Founded originally as centers of trade and commerce, America's cities and towns came into being as places where people could make money. This was true for the oldest colonial cities and for cities on the frontier. Throughout the nineteenth century the movement west across the continent placed towns at the leading edge of territorial expansion. National economic growth was promoted through penetration into unsettled land, and exploitation of the land and resources found there was made possible by the constantly expanding network of cities, towns, and villages.

America was settled as a long, thin line of urban places, scattering outward and westward from the Atlantic seaboard. The popular imagination has it that farmers came first and villages later. The historian's truth is that villages and towns came first, pulling farmers along to settle the land around and between urban settlements.[1]

Each town was its own capitalist system in miniature, held together by the independent actions of individuals in search of profit and fortune. The urban historian Sam Bass Warner suggested the concept of "privatism" to describe the politics and local culture of American cities. Privatism refers to a set of cultural values that emphasizes individual rights and aspirations. According to Warner, the tendency to value private over collective or public purposes has powerfully shaped America's urban development: ". . . [the] local politics of American cities have depended for their actors, and for a good deal of their subject matter, on the changing focus of men's private economic activities."[2] The primary goal of government was to maximize the opportunities for individual economic advancement.

The pattern of American urban development has been different from urban development almost anywhere else in the world. The great cities of Europe, Asia, and elsewhere evolved not only as places of commerce and trade, but also as centers of religious, military, cultural, and political power. Before the modern nation-state, there was the city-state, "owing no fealty to any other sovereign, temporal or spiritual, outside its own territory."[3] The English writer Charles Dickens wrote, "The city . . . as it appears throughout all ages and in all lands, [is] the symbol and carrier of civilization. . . . it is an institutional centre, the seat of the institutions of the society which it represents. It is a seat of religion, of culture and social contact, and of political and administrative organization. . . . it is the seat of commerce and transport."[4]

Rome, the historic capital of Italy, has been occupied since about 1500 B.C. When workers excavated the city's subway system after World War II, they uncovered, layer by layer, traces of the city's history reaching far into the past.[5] By the sixth century B.C. Rome had established political control over the central Roman province and was beginning to assert authority over much of the Italian peninsula. In the next few centuries it became the political and administrative center of a vast empire, reaching the height of its grandeur in the first and early second centuries A.D., when its population exceeded one million people. Even as the empire weakened and finally dissolved, the city continued to exert enormous cultural and religious influence around the globe as the seat of the Roman Catholic Church.

London, like Rome, has also presided over a global empire. The Romans founded the city they called Londinium as an administrative outpost at the far reaches of their empire. It experienced rapid growth in the sixteenth and seventeenth centuries, and during the eighteenth and nineteenth centuries it became the industrial, commercial, and political center of the British Empire. The Crown, Parliament, the Royal Navy, and vast governmental bureaucracies clustered together in London to manage an empire that circled the globe.

Paris is older than London. Sitting in the center of a huge basin drained by the Seine, for more than 2,000 years it has been a center of trade and commerce. It has also emerged as a center of religion, culture, and political power. It was designated a capital in Roman times, and from that time until the present no city in France has challenged its preeminence. Indeed, probably no other city in the world, not even Rome, so completely defines and dominates the national culture of its country.

Urban development in the United States took a completely different course. Despite its status as a global center of finance and corporate power, even New York cannot be compared to the ancient cities of the world. New York began as a Dutch colonial settlement in 1609, becoming a city, known as New Amsterdam, in 1625. By the time of the American Revolution its population was just over 50,000, making it, by far, the largest city on the eastern seaboard. Throughout the nineteenth and twentieth centuries it remained the nation's greatest financial and commercial city. However, New York never exerted political or administrative authority on behalf of a central government. It was never the center of religious authority—no city could be in a nation that had explicitly divorced religion from state power. In 1790 Congress designated Washington, D.C., as the new nation's capital, making it one of the few cities in the world to be planned solely as a national capital. Almost all the states followed that first example; most state capitals are located "downstate" or "upstate," well away from the major cities.

In other parts of the world cities had long histories as the carriers of power, culture, and civilization. In the United States, by contrast, cities had little past, and their only purpose, their reason for being, was practical. They were places of economic opportunity, or they were nothing. The French philosopher Jean-Paul Sartre observed, "For [Europeans] a city is, above all, a past; to [Americans] it is mainly a future; everything they like in the city is everything it has not yet become and everything it can be."[6] Like so many Europeans before him, Sartre was startled by the chaos and squalor of American cities, the relative absence of monumental architecture and orderly development. He recognized the cause of this difference when he said, "the American city, originally, [was] a camp in the desert. People from far away, attracted by a mine, a petroleum field or fertile land, arrived one day and settled as quickly as possible in a clearing, near a river."[7] Though containing a bit of poetic license, Sartre's version captures the essence of American city building.

Lacking a long cultural, social, and political history, valued for little more than their economic function, cities in the Unites States have generally been regarded with distrust and as threats to, rather than the seats of, civilization. John V. Lindsay, a former mayor of New York, once observed that "In the American psychology, the city has been a basically suspect institution. . . ."[8] The habit of equating cities with corrupt political power and with a breakdown of social morals is as old as the nation. Thomas Jefferson wrote, "I view great cities as penitential to the morals, the health, and the liberties of man." He even thought that democracy could not withstand the growth of cities: "I think our governments will remain virtuous for many centuries; as long as they are chiefly agricultural; and this will be as long as there shall be vacant lands in any part of America. When they get piled upon one another in large cities as in Europe, they will become corrupt as in Europe."[9]

❖ THE EXPANDING POWERS OF AMERICAN CITY GOVERNMENTS

The combination of antiurban attitudes and the tradition of privatism has had the effect of limiting the public powers of cities. City governments are far more restricted in the United States than in most other nations. Nevertheless, American cities have evolved as public corporations possessing important powers and responsibilities. The reason for this development is that forces have been at work that have made the expansion of governmental powers virtually irresistible.

Ironically, a key reason for the expansion of the public powers of cities was the desire of urban residents to expand the local private economy. The founders of cities and the business elites that made their money there recognized that in order to ensure their mutual success, they had to take steps to promote the whole city or region. In nineteenth-century America city growth and local boosterism went hand in hand. Boosters extolled their city's natural advantages—its harbor, its strategic location on a river, the proximity of rich farming and mining areas, and so forth. They boasted about its cultural attributes—its music societies, libraries, and universities. And they went further than boasting; they used the powers of city governments directly to promote local economic success.

"Internal improvements"—turnpikes, canals, and most importantly railroad connections—were the key to economic growth. Local entrepreneurs were aware that they were participating in a race in which some cities would move ahead quickly and prosper and others would fall behind and die. Municipalities were corporations that could be used to help finance transportation links that could give a city an advantage over others. After the 1850s, cities aggressively bought railroad stocks, made loan guarantees to railroad companies, and gave away land in their efforts to become linked to a growing network of rail lines. Many cities spent so much money in these efforts that they were dragged into financial disaster by the depression of the 1870s.

American cities still use their powers and resources to promote local economic prosperity; indeed, at times and for some cities, it seems that such boosterism is the main item on the public agenda. Cities float bonds to build new sports stadiums. They offer tax abatements and hand out subsidies to encourage the construction of enclosed malls. They run convention and tourism bureaus, repair fountains, plant flowers, restore historic buildings, and intensify crime control in areas used by tourists. In these and countless other ways cities in the 1990s use their public powers and resources to promote local economic prosperity.

A second reason the public powers and responsibilities of cities have grown over time is that when large numbers of people crowd together, problems arise that can be solved only through collective efforts. The tradition of privatism tended to make people believe that they need not be concerned about how their actions might affect others. However, as cities grew in the nineteenth century, sometimes exploding within a few years from small settlements to densely packed industrial cities teeming with immigrants, the consequences of unrestrained private activity became impossible to ignore. Individuals saw that they were powerless to correct or to escape the collective problems of crime, fire, and disease.

Municipal governments assumed increasingly complex responsibilities—to supply water and dispose of wastes, to fight fire and crime, to build and maintain streets and bridges. The expansion of the public sector was fueled by recurring crises that threatened not only the health and welfare of urban residents, but also local economic vitality. Riots, fires, outbreaks of contagious disease, and other calamities could easily force people to leave. Municipal institutions were used to address such problems because only government could claim the legitimacy to act in behalf of all citizens.

After the Civil War, industrial cities began to expand their responsibilities significantly not only in response to crises threatening the health and welfare of urban dwellers, but also because conditions that in the past had seemed tolerable and inevitable (such as muddy streets, polluted water, and open sewers) had come to be regarded as unacceptable. Municipal governments provided a range of new and expanded services administered by full-time employees. They built parks, adopted building codes, and paved streets. They wrote health and sanitation codes. They granted franchises and licenses for telephone service, gas and electrical service, and public transportation. Much of the infrastructure and many of the municipal responsibilities of American cities date from this period of city building.

Today, cities provide a remarkable array of services. Cities build and maintain a public infrastructure—roads, bridges, sewer lines, sewage treatment plants, water mains, parks, zoos, hospitals, and sometimes even universities. They provide police and fire protection. They collect garbage (or pay someone who does). They run public health services that inspect restaurants, vaccinate children, and test for the HIV (AIDS) virus. Through city zoning ordinances, they influence the location of homes, factories, office buildings, restaurants, and parking lots. Through local building codes, they regulate such matters as plumbing, wiring, building materials, height of structures, and architectural styles. Cities poison rats and sometimes try to scare away pigeons. These public activities and more are essential to the safety and well-being of all city dwellers. Without them, life in most cities would quickly become not only dangerous, but intolerable.

❖ THE COMPLEX TASK OF GOVERNANCE

Until the mid-nineteenth century, public and private goals were thoroughly mingled; "leadership fell to those who exercised economic leadership. All leadership, political, social, economic, tended to collect in the same set of hands."[10] Business owners, professionals, and aristocrats ran municipal affairs. They derived their authority from their social standing within the informal communities that composed the cities. However, as cities grew in size and became more complex, formal mechanisms of governance slowly replaced community norms. The popular control of political authority became possible when new generations of politicians learned to mobilize the electorate. When forced to compete in the electoral arena, members of the business, professional, and social elites often won elections, but after the Civil War they were increasingly replaced by politicians who were closer to, and often drawn from, the ranks of ethnic immigrants who were streaming into the industrial cities. Public leaders began to build their careers by mobilizing the mass electorate. At the same time, business leaders became more specialized; their responsibilities running firms that relied on national and even international markets pulled them away from local city affairs.

Increasingly, governments had to become involved not only in promoting local economic prosperity and providing routine services but in the complex task of *governance*. City governments are mechanisms for arbitrating social and political tensions among the various groups and factions that make up the local polity. Democratic procedures invest those who govern with the legitimacy to act in the name of citizens collectively. Governmental authority springs from the right to "make and apply decisions that are binding upon any and all segments of society."[11] City officials can preserve their claim to authority only so long as they seem sufficiently responsive to a large enough proportion of the urban population. Just as the currency of the economic marketplace is money, the currency of the political marketplace is votes. In a democratic system, politicians must spread the rewards of public policies around in order to construct a governing coalition. If only a few are benefited by the activities of government, there is the likelihood that significant opposition will arise.

Democratic procedures impose a "political logic" that forces public leaders to build broad coalitions. What kinds of policies must urban leaders pursue to maintain such coalitions? Since the late nineteenth century urban populations have come to expect a wide range of public services and a large, well-maintained public infrastructure. Accomplishing all of this requires a high level of public financing and a continuous governmental presence.

The fiscal resources of local government are limited, however, especially by an "economic logic" that requires cities to adopt policies to persuade businesses and investors to remain as participants in the local economy, rather than move elsewhere. Often, the policies dictated by political logic conflict with the policies dictated by economic logic. Investors and the local business community are free to move from a central city to a suburb, from one suburb to another, from one metropolitan area to another, even from one country to another, if the costs of doing business or the risk to profits are too high in a particular locality. They are interested in minimizing their tax burden, and in addition they often seek policies favorable to them that must be paid for by someone else. Local politicians simply cannot afford to resist the demands of business too much; if they do, they will be blamed if a city loses business—and the jobs provided by business. Local governments are expected to provide an adequate level of public services and, at the same time, to help preserve the health of the local economy. Thus, politicians often find themselves caught in a tug-of-war between a political logic that tempts them to try to finance and support policies that benefit a large proportion of the urban population and an economic logic that forces them to acknowledge that business is the first and most important interest group in city politics.[12]

The controversy surrounding New York City's fiscal crisis of the 1970s illustrates the tensions between the demands of democratic governance and the dictates of the marketplace.[13] In the decades leading up to the city's near bankruptcy in 1975, local political leaders, in alliance with Democratic officials in Congress and the White House, succeeded in building a broad electoral coalition that could be relied upon to deliver its votes to Democrats in local, state, congressional, and presidential contests. The coalition was held together by social programs and services that benefited a large variety of groups. The city, for example, provided assistance to neighborhood organizations, administered a generous welfare system, provided funding for neighborhood health clinics, ran public hospitals, and supported a university.

To maintain its programs and services, the city spent more money than it took in. The only way New York's growing deficits could be managed was through massive borrowing, which eventually precipitated a financial crisis. When it became clear that the city could not meet its debt obligations and it sought a federal loan to help it do so, financial and corporate lenders demanded a larger role in budgetary decisions. Two new institutions, the Municipal Assistance Corporation and the Emergency Financial Control Board, were empowered to control the city's spending, taxing, and borrowing policies. Public spending fell quickly, and the city's priorities shifted away from social and public expenditures and toward reduced taxes and a variety of subsidies for business. In other words, an economic logic, which dictated that the city would have to become a more favorable environment for business investment, eclipsed the political logic that had driven the municipal agenda for years.

Improving a city's chances of luring business and investment would seem to be an unmixed blessing, a goal that few people could question. Doing it by lowering taxes and offering expensive subsidies to business, however, has the consequence of reducing a city's capacity to supply public services and amenities. If this process goes far enough, the tension between political and economic logic can build to the breaking point and provoke a crisis of governance. In the 1990s many cities are at such a juncture.

All through the 1980s, cities tried to regenerate their local economies by lowering taxes for businesses and offering direct subsidies to investors. In New York and other cities across the country, gleaming office towers, luxury hotels, and enclosed malls sprung up. At the same time, however, cities (as well as the federal government) cut spending for housing, schools, and other public services and amenities. Partially as a result, downtown prosperity exist-

ed side by side with growing numbers of homeless people, decaying neighborhoods, and deteriorating parks, bridges, and roads. For a time, economic logic,
the idea that cities should primarily promote private economic growth,
seemed to dictate that government should not try to address social problems.
In the 1990s, however, there was rising concern about problems of social
cohesion and the health and welfare of ordinary citizens. The Los Angeles
riots of 1992 served as a reminder of the hazards of too long neglecting the
social needs of the urban citizenry.

❖ THE CHOICES CITIES MAKE

The choices available to local political leaders are sharply limited by the environment within which cities are situated. Cities do not exist in isolation. They
are part of a complex intergovernmental system, and they are subject to economic forces beyond their control. Given this situation, can they make meaningful political choices, or are they constrained to do whatever is necessary to
promote economic growth? In the past few years, this question has become
particularly urgent.

Changes in the global and national economic structure—especially the
loss of manufacturing employment in favor of service-sector jobs since the
mid-1970s—have been felt by urban communities in the old manufacturing
belt trying to cope with declining local economies and by Sunbelt cities trying
to provide public services and build the infrastructure to cope with rapid population growth. Changes in national governmental policy likewise reverberate
within metropolitan areas. Since the early 1980s, the federal government has
drastically cut many social programs of particular importance to people living
in older cities. Changes in national policy interacted with economic transformations. Reductions in urban social programs and the replacement of higher-
wage industrial sector jobs by minimum-wage service-sector jobs created the
phenomenon of divided cities; in urban areas everywhere, pockets of poverty
exist side by side with areas of affluence. Even before the recession of the early
1990s, the numbers of the homeless roaming the streets multiplied, crime escalated, incidents of racial conflict increased, and poverty spread. Cities were not
in a position to control any of these developments. They are, nevertheless,
expected to deal with the consequences.

The way a city responds to its external environment is determined, to a
considerable degree, by the nature of its internal politics. Different cities make
different choices. Sometimes these choices reflect the limited options available.
However, they also reflect a particular city's history, its size, the composition
of its population, the nature of its economy, and even the region within which
it is located.

The politics of the older cities of the industrial belt differs, for instance,
from the politics of the newer cities of the Sunbelt. The cities located at the
core of older metropolitan areas (even if they are no longer industrial) share a

distinctive history, politics, and political culture. Many of these cities were once governed by party machines that prospered on the basis of voting majorities in ethnic wards. In the nineteenth century, these cities attracted waves of foreign immigrants. In the twentieth century, they served as magnets for blacks leaving the South and for Latinos and whites fleeing rural poverty. In the past two decades, they have attracted new waves of immigrants from Latin America, the Caribbean, Asia, and elsewhere. As a result, the politics of these older cities tends to revolve not only around issues of economic prosperity, but also around ethnic, racial, and neighborhood issues.

In contrast, cities of the Sunbelt developed much later. Until the 1970s, politics in most cities of the South and Southwest was tightly controlled by business elites, who kept taxes as low as possible and provided a minimal level of public services and infrastructure. For most of its history, for example, Houston was run by a business group that met in private to make policy and slate all candidates for public office. In the 1970s, a woman, Kathy Whitmire, won the mayor's office, backed by an electoral coalition of middle-class whites, Hispanics, blacks, gays, and feminists. As in Houston, politics in other cities in the Sunbelt has begun to open up and become more participatory, a reflection of the fact that cities in that region are becoming more complex. In other words, Sunbelt cities are slowly becoming more like the older cities of the manufacturing belt.

Of course, the politics of suburbs and smaller cities and towns is different from the politics of larger cities. Their political coalitions are often rather simple, especially where the population is homogeneous. Frequently, a few "insiders" hold tight-fisted control over local elections and the day-to-day running of the suburb or town. In very small towns and cities, there may be no full-time politicians or administrators at all, and a small group of citizens— usually business owners and professionals—may, in effect, take turns holding public office. In smaller cities and suburbs political issues are likely to be defined narrowly, typically focusing on the preservation of real estate values, the quality of police services, the character of the schools, and little else.[14]

In recent years the concept of urban regimes has been used to describe the political coalitions that govern cities. This concept is based on the recognition that local politics involves more than the public sector alone; it is characterized by the collaboration of public power and private resources. Since the most important private resources in most cities are held by business institutions, they tend to be central to local regimes, though other institutions of the nongovernmental sector, most notably nonprofit organizations and ethnic, racial, and neighborhood organizations, may also exert influence. The informal coalitions that define the character of a particular community differ from city to city. Describing politics in Atlanta, political scientist Clarence Stone observed, "What makes governance in Atlanta effective is not the formal machinery of government, but rather the informal partnership between city hall and the downtown business elite. This informal partnership and the way it operates constitutes the city's regime; it is the same means through which major policy decisions are made."[15] Though we do not employ the concept of urban regimes in this book, the idea that politics involves informal alliances, not just governmental structures and public officials, accurately captures the essence of politics in all cities.

❖ A GUIDE FOR READING THIS BOOK

This book is organized historically. Without an understanding of the evolution of urban institutions and political conflicts it would be difficult to make sense of contemporary urban politics in the United States. The limited powers of American cities compared to cities elsewhere in the world, the governmental fragmentation of metropolitan areas, the economic rivalry between cities, and other facets of American urban politics have deep roots in our history and culture. Though we discuss in detail the evolution of political institutions and processes, this is a book about urban politics, not urban history, and therefore, when we present historical material, we do so for the purpose of placing contemporary urban politics in context. The politics of America's cities is dynamic. The political issues of one era fade away to be replaced by new issues for a new generation. Though the details may change, however, striking similarities and continuities remain. The present always builds upon and borrows from the past.

We make comparisons not only across time but also across space. We often compare urban development in the United States to urban development in other countries, especially in Western Europe. Such comparisons place the character of American city politics in bold relief and help dispel the illusion that the particular features of city politics in the United States are either usual or inevitable.

■ Part One. Contested Terrain: Political Conflict in Cities

The three chapters that make up Part One trace the evolution of urban politics from the constitutional era to the New Deal of the 1930s. In Chapter 2 we describe how the United States was transformed from a small nation dominated by a few commercial cities clinging to the eastern seaboard to a complex industrial world power with cities that were centers of industry, immigration, and technological change. Cities successfully incorporated a broad range of classes, races, and ethnic groups into the democratic political process. The issues that dominated city politics during this era—local economic growth, ethnic conflict, social order, and inequality—have endured as pivotal concerns in our cities to this day.

The concentration of millions of immigrants in industrial cities presented an opportunity for political entrepreneurs to accumulate power by organizing the new mass electorate. In Chapter 3 we describe how politicians seized this opportunity, building informal political organizations—the infamous "machines" that were welded together by the distribution of patronage jobs and other "spoils" and favors. Machine politicians depended on the loyal support of ethnic voters. Probably as much because of their identification with the immigrants as because of their sometimes corrupt practices, they soon became the targets of a reform movement that swept the country.

As we describe in Chapter 4, the municipal reform movement was energized by the desire of the reformers to reduce the political influence of the immigrants. The reformers were drawn from the ranks of the upper-middle classes. The reforms they accomplished made cities less democratic, but probably better run. Their reforms—notably, nonpartisan and at-large elections, professional city management, and civil service hiring—are still in use today. To understand the political effects of these "reformed" institutions and political practices, it is important to understand what motivated the reformers. At-large elections, for example, which were originally adopted to undercut the machines and reduce the voting influence of immigrants, have recently come under attack because they make it difficult for African Americans and other minority groups to win local political office.

▇ Part Two. National Policy and the Cities

The chapters that make up Part Two trace the increasing influence of the big industrial cities in national politics from the 1930s to the 1970s and the national urban policy that resulted from this influence. From 1932 to 1964 the Democrats won seven out of nine presidential elections and urban voters were key to their victories. Beginning with the New Deal, the federal government implemented national policies that greatly influenced the governance of cities and metropolitan areas.

As we show in Chapter 5, the economic calamity of the 1930s fundamentally altered the nation's politics. The Democrats became the majority national party in the 1930s, and Democratic politicians soon learned that they could secure the loyalty of urban blue-collar workers and union members, ethnic groups, and blacks by passing federal programs that helped the unemployed and destitute. A new relationship was forged between the federal government and cities that matured in the years after World War II and bore fruit during the Democratic administrations of John Fitzgerald Kennedy and Lyndon Baines Johnson.

Chapters 6 and 7 trace the federal involvement in cities. In 1949, a broad alliance composed of big city mayors, liberal Democrats in Congress, and business leaders concerned about their inner-city investments was able to persuade Congress to pass federally funded urban renewal and public housing legislation. These programs remade cities everywhere; all through the 1950s and 1960s huge clearance projects leveled the slums. Though these programs were launched with great fanfare and high hopes, within a few years they were the subject of considerable controversy. Urban renewal displaced inner-city minorities and poor people who lived in the path of the bulldozer, and because more low-income housing was torn down than was built, the renewal programs actually contributed to worsening housing conditions in the cities.

In Chapter 7 we describe the social programs of the 1960s. These programs have been identified with two "liberal" Democratic presidents, John Kennedy and Lyndon Johnson. In the 1960s, federal aid to cities mushroomed, extending far beyond urban renewal and public housing to embrace a broad range of social concerns—juvenile delinquency, crime, poverty, education, racial discrimination, and unemployment. The cultural and political conflicts of the 1960s helped fuel a backlash against urban programs. Republican presidential candidates successfully exploited deep animosities that pitted cities against suburbs, blacks against whites, the South against the North. As the suburbs and the Sunbelt grew, the political influence of central city voters in national politics waned. In 1968, a Republican won the White House, and the national government began to withdraw from the cities.

▮ Part Three. Suburbs, Sunbelt, and the Eclipse of the Central Cities

The changing political balance in the United States, discussed in the four chapters of Part Three, explains why the cities now receive little attention from the national government. By the 1980s the majority of people who lived in metropolitan areas resided not in central cities, but in suburbs. The growth of population in the Sunbelt and in Sunbelt cities also tipped the balance of national power away from the older industrial cities.

In Chapter 8 we profile suburbanization, which has been one of the most massive demographic movements in U.S. history. America's urban areas are sprawled out further and are fragmented into more separate political jurisdictions than are urban areas in almost all other Western nations. Affluent urban residents have moved from the center to the periphery, leaving the central cities to the poor, to ethnic and minority groups, and to recent arrivals. Over the past several decades, suburbs and cities have become locked in battles over issues of ethnicity, race, and inequality.

The political separation of the suburbs from the central cities occurred not simply because suburbanites wanted to segregate themselves. Private developers and financial institutions, as well as national policies, made moving to the suburbs so attractive that it was difficult for urban dwellers not to move. Suburbanization would have occurred anyway, but public and private policies greatly increased the pace and scale of suburbanization in the United States. In Chapter 8 we show how developers and financial institutions used federal home loan guarantee programs to insure that new housing would be built in the suburbs and that it would be racially segregated. Federal policies helped entrench patterns of segregation so deeply that attempts in the 1960s and since to use civil rights laws to reduce housing segregation have largely failed. Indeed, these attempts have helped fuel a political reaction against cities and minorities.

In Chapter 9 we review the consequences and costs of the extreme governmental fragmentation in America's urban areas. Most suburbs practice a "politics of exclusion"—they use zoning codes and other devices to keep property values high and to shut out unwanted groups. African Americans have been the most frequent object of these policies. Partially as a result of such policies, the disparities between cities and suburbs continue to widen. Increasingly, middle-class blacks have been able to make it to the suburbs, but they continue to live in segregated conditions. The issues of race and ethnicity, which have always been central to city politics in America, are now the issues that pit suburbs against city and suburb against suburb.

Central cities have become isolated within their own metropolitan areas and have also lost influence in the politics of the nation as a whole. In Chapter 10, we discuss the rise of the Sunbelt and the impact of this development on city politics and on the nation's urban policies. The growth of the Sunbelt and the simultaneous population loss and economic troubles in the Northeast and Midwest, combined with the growth of the suburbs, have fundamentally shifted the national balance of power. These regional shifts have undermined the New Deal coalition that gave the Democratic party its majority status. All the presidents elected from 1964 to 1992 came from the Sunbelt. In every decade since 1940, the number of congressional seats apportioned to Sunbelt states has increased, while the number allocated to the northern states has declined.

The changing political balance in Congress has eroded support for urban and social welfare legislation. In Chapter 11 we discuss the fate of national urban policy and explain why most urban programs were abandoned in the 1980s. The election of Richard Nixon in 1968 represented a backlash against the federal activism of the 1960s, but because of their majorities in Congress, the Democrats were able to protect urban programs for a decade. Beginning with the last two years of the Carter administration, however, federal funding for cities began to decline. After Ronald Reagan's decisive win in 1980, urban and social programs were slashed. Made vulnerable by ideological attacks on government and welfare, isolated by poverty and race, and voting at low rates, central city residents simply lacked the political clout to defend urban programs.

■ Part Four. The Return of the Private City

The four chapters of Part Four examine how urban fiscal crises, declining central city economies, and deteriorating social conditions have combined since the late 1970s to produce the contemporary inner-city crisis. The crisis has two principal dimensions. First, central cities face chronic fiscal problems; the taxes they raise are rarely sufficient to fund the services they are under pressure to provide. Second, the intensified segregation of the poor in central cities has produced a new crisis that in some ways can be compared to the crisis of poverty and inequality that characterized the industrial cities of the nineteenth century. In an attempt to turn their fortunes around, cities have thrown themselves into a desperate competition for economic growth.

As we show in Chapter 12, throughout American history city finances have been vulnerable to economic downturns. Today, however, worsening structural problems reduce the ability of cities to cope with fiscal stress. The concentration of poor people and immigrants in cities increases service demands while providing little in the way of tax revenues. The middle class continues to flee to the suburbs, escaping the tax burdens of cities. While many suburbanites continue to work in the city, most do not pay taxes there. Massive cutbacks in federal grants left cities especially vulnerable to the recession of the early 1990s.

In Chapter 13, we profile cities' efforts to turn their economies around and make up for federal aid cutbacks. Since the late 1970s, cities have become entrepreneurial in their attempts to promote local economic development. Mayors routinely take credit for the recent rehabilitation of downtowns. The media frequently tout the new "urban renaissance," highlighting stories about towering office buildings, luxury hotels with multistory atriums, impressive domed stadiums, and "gentrified" neighborhoods. The eagerness of cities to give tax abatements and other subsidies to lure corporations, tourists, and sports franchises is reminiscent of the railroad wars of the nineteenth century. And, as in the earlier competition, not everyone is a winner today. Though the physical appearance of cities has improved dramatically, making them better places for white-collar professionals to work in and tourists to play in, the development has, for the most part, not benefited inner-city poor and minority residents.

The tendency toward extremes of affluence and poverty is exaggerated by recent demographic changes. As we discuss in Chapter 14, the number of people immigrating to the United States has increased steadily since the 1950s, and most of the new residents have settled in urban areas. The sources of immigration have changed substantially since the early twentieth century. The new immigrants come primarily from Asia, Central and South America, and the Caribbean. During the 1980s, the number of legal immigrants reached the second highest total in American history (exceeded only by the record decade of 1900 to 1910), and the total immigrant flow, when illegal and undocumented immigrants are included, probably exceeded any previous decade in American history. This immigration flow has been accompanied by an increasing concentration of poverty in the inner cities. Extremely high levels of unemployment, crime, drug use, health problems, and family breakdown are found in urban ghettos. Extreme poverty has heightened tensions between African Americans and the new immigrants from Asia and Latin America. It is under these difficult circumstances that black and Latino mayors have come to power.* We examine their efforts to improve their local economies and, simultaneously, to address the social problems in their cities.

---

* The terms Latino and Hispanic are used interchangebly throughout this text to refer collectively to Mexican Americans, Puerto Ricans, Cubans, Central Americans, and "other Hispanics" from the Dominican Republican, Spain, or of Spanish-speaking origin.

America's contemporary urban crisis and the policies that might be brought to bear to ease the crisis are the subjects of our concluding chapter. During the twentieth century geographic avoidance behavior (moving to the suburbs) replaced politics as the characteristic way affluent urban dwellers dealt with urban problems. Recently, the affluent have devised new strategies for separating themselves from urban problems even when they live within cities. A high degree of spatial apartheid now characterizes all metropolitan areas. Enclosed malls, for example, that keep the city at bay and exclusive housing developments are segregrated by walls and elaborate security systems. As the 1992 Los Angeles riots revealed, the tensions arising from inequality and segregation can touch everyone. In our concluding chapter we examine some policies that could unite, rather than divide, central city residents and suburbanites, blacks and whites, the poor and the middle class.

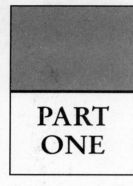

PART
ONE

CONTESTED TERRAIN

POLITICAL CONFLICT IN THE CITIES

CHAPTER
2

THE PRIVATE CITY AND LOCAL DEMOCRACY

THE POLITICAL LEGACY OF THE NINETEENTH CENTURY

❖ NATIONAL DEVELOPMENT AND LOCAL POLITICS

At the time the Constitution was ratified in 1789, the cities of the new nation were scattered along the coastline of a vast, mostly unexplored continent. Only five of these cities exceeded 10,000 in population. Over the course of the nineteenth century national development and the westward march of cities went hand in hand. By the beginning of the twentieth century a culture that had defined its character by reference to rural life and a western frontier had become industrial and urban. Urbanization occurred at such an incredible pace and scale that it created nearly irresolvable political and social tensions. The cities' economic and cultural dominance spawned a distrust and sometimes a hatred for anything "urban" that influences American culture up to the present day.

Americans have tended to use cities and their residents as scapegoats, blaming them for the tensions besetting a mobile, ethnically and racially complex society. In the 1990s the inner cities are associated with images of poverty, crime, racial and ethnic conflict, and social disorder. Throughout much of the nineteenth century the cultural representation of cities was remarkably similar to current media images. Then, as now, class, ethnic, and racial divisions provided the stuff of urban politics. To understand urban politics in the United States today, a good starting point is to study cities of the past.

Cities have always been pivotal in shaping the nation's economic and cultural development. Before the industrial revolution, America's cities prospered by presiding over a commercial economic system that relied on the exchange of agricultural and extractive products (such as furs, minerals, and lumber) for goods shipped from abroad or produced by craftworkers, most of whom lived in cities. Trappers, miners, loggers, and farmers, whether on the frontier or in rural areas of the more settled East, sold their commodities to traders and brokers and bought city-made goods, and thus they participated in a system of trade and commerce that ran through the cities.

The industrial revolution fundamentally transformed the United States and its cities, and that transformation magnified the urban-rural conflicts that already existed. The symbols and the reality of the industrial age—belching smokestacks, regimented armies of immigrant workers, spreading slums—all were concentrated in the cities. The cities—and the people who lived in them—were blamed for the changes sweeping through American life. The new industrial economy thrived on plentiful, cheap labor. The flood of foreign immigration that broke over the country in the 1840s swelled in volume for the next eighty years. Most of the immigrants settled in cities, close to the factories. From the beginning there were tensions between the so-called nativists, who mistakenly thought of themselves as the original Americans, and the newcomers. There were, as well, cultural and religious conflicts among the immigrants themselves. Often these conflicts turned violent. Successive waves of immigrants—poor, often illiterate, unfamiliar with the language and customs of their new country, unfamiliar with city life—faced miserable conditions in crowded, spreading slums.

For the first half-century after the constitutional era, commercial elites dominated the cities. However, they were unable to retain their grip in the rough-and-tumble politics of the emerging industrial city, and they were gradually replaced by a new generation of politicians who learned how to mobilize immigrant voters. In the last section of this chapter, we describe how political processes emerged in the cities to manage the enormous political tensions of the industrial era.

❖ THE URBANIZATION OF AMERICA

In the eighteenth and nineteenth centuries the Western world underwent urbanization on a scale unprecedented in history. In 1800 only London approached 1,000,000 in population.[1] Paris ranked second among European cities with 547,000. New York, by far the biggest city in America, had just over 60,000 people. A century later eleven Western cities had topped the million-mark; by 1900 London had 6,586,000, Paris 2,714,000,[2] and New York 3,437,000. In England and Wales, the percentage of the population living in towns[3] and cities increased from 25 percent to 77 percent. Commenting on the growth of cities in 1895, the *Atlantic Monthly* noted: "The great fact in . . .

social development . . . at the close of the nineteenth century is the tendency all over the world to concentrate in great cities. This tendency is seen everywhere."[4]

In the United States, urban population soared. As Table 2-1 shows, from the first national census of 1790 to the census of 1920, urban population (defined by the census as people living in cities and towns of 2,500 or more) increased in most decades at twice the rate, or faster, than the U.S. population as a whole. The only significant exception occurred between the censuses of 1810 and 1820, when homesteaders and farmers poured across the Appalachian Mountains to settle the old Northwest (now western Pennsylvania, Ohio, and Indiana).

As late as the census of 1840, nine out of ten Americans still lived outside cities and towns. In the 1840s, however, cities began to grow at breakneck speed. A flood of Irish and German immigrants began pouring into the cities, and at the same time a steady migration from farms to cities began to change the United States irretrievably into an urban nation. Foreign immigrants and rural migrants were pulled to the cities by the promise of jobs. By 1860, almost 20 percent of the American population was classified as urban: in only two decades, the proportion of Americans living in cities and towns had doubled. By the turn of the century, this proportion doubled again to almost 40 percent. Twenty years later, when the 1920 census was taken, 51.2 percent of the American people lived in urban places of 2,500 or more. In less than a century the United States had been transformed from an overwhelmingly rural to an urban nation.

Before the century of urbanization, American cities were few in number, small in size, and relatively isolated from one another. In 1800, only 322,000 of the 5.3 million Americans, about 6 percent, lived in urban places of 2,500 or more. More than half of the city dwellers lived in five seaboard cities: New York (60,515), Philadelphia (41,220), Baltimore (26,514), Boston (24,937), and Charleston, South Carolina (18,924).[5] No other cities were as large as 10,000 in population. By 1850, however, New York topped 660,000 people, and Philadelphia and Boston surpassed 100,000. By 1860 six more cities passed the hundred-thousand-mark, and by the turn of the century a total of twenty-three cities were at least this large. Indeed, by 1900 nine cities had at least 250,000 people.[6]

Because of their continued importance as financial and commercial (and later also industrial) centers, the old cities on the eastern seaboard benefited from national development. New York maintained supremacy as the hub of finance and trade. Its deep harbor was unsurpassed, and it became even more dominant in trade after 1825, the year that the Erie Canal linked the city directly to the Great Lakes. New York served as a giant funnel for trade between Europe and the United States, and after the Civil War it further consolidated its supremacy as it became a great manufacturing and immigrant city. Huge numbers of immigrants, more than 60 percent of all the immigrants who came to the United States, passed through New York, and many of them settled there. From a population of 369,000 in 1840, New York exploded to

TABLE 2-1   THE PACE OF URBANIZATION IN THE UNITED STATES, 1790–1920

YEAR	TOTAL POPULATION	PERCENT INCREASE OVER PRECEDING CENSUS	URBAN POPULATION	PERCENT INCREASE OVER PRECEDING POPULATION	PERCENT OF TOTAL POPULATION — URBAN	PERCENT OF TOTAL POPULATION — RURAL
1790	3,929,214	—	201,655	—	5.1	94.9
1800	5,308,483	35.1	322,371	59.9	6.1	93.9
1810	7,239,881	36.4	525,459	63.0	7.3	92.7
1820	9,638,453	33.1	693,255	31.9	7.2	92.8
1830	12,866,020	33.5	1,127,247	62.6	8.8	91.2
1840	17,069,453	32.7	1,845,055	63.7	10.8	89.2
1850	23,191,876	35.9	3,543,716	92.1	15.3	84.7
1860	31,443,321	35.6	6,216,518	75.4	19.8	80.2
1870	39,818,449	26.6	9,902,361	59.3	25.7	74.3
1880	50,155,783	26.0	14,129,735	42.7	28.2	71.8
1890	62,947,714	25.5	22,106,265	56.5	35.1	64.9
1900	75,994,575	20.7	30,214,832	36.7	39.6	60.4
1910	91,972,266	21.0	42,064,001	39.2	45.6	54.4
1920	105,710,620	14.9	54,253,280	29.0	51.2	48.8

Source: U.S. Department of Commerce, Bureau of the Census, *Historical Statistics of the United States, Colonial Times to 1970*, pt. 1, Bicentennial ed. (Washington, D.C.: Government Printing Office, 1975), p. 8; U.S. Department of Commerce, Bureau of the Census, *1970 Census of Population*, vol. 1, *Characteristics of the Population*, pt. 1 (Washington, D.C.: Government Printing Office, 1973), p. 42.

TABLE 2-2 POPULATION AND RATE OF GROWTH IN FIVE LARGE CITIES, 1820–1920[a]

	NEW YORK CITY[b]	PERCENT INCREASE	CHICAGO	PERCENT INCREASE	PHILADELPHIA	PERCENT INCREASE	ST. LOUIS	PERCENT INCREASE	BOSTON	PERCENT INCREASE	PERCENT INCREASE IN U.S. POPULATION
1820	137,388		—		63,802		4,598		43,298		
1830	220,471	60.5	—		80,462	26.1	5,847	27.1	61,392	41.8	33.5
1840	369,305	67.5	4,470		93,665	16.4	16,469	181.7	93,383	52.1	32.7
1850	660,803	78.9	29,963	570.3	121,376	29.6	77,860	372.8	136,881	46.6	35.9
1860	1,183,148	79.1	112,172	274.4	565,529	365.9	160,773	106.5	177,840	29.9	35.6
1870	1,546,293	30.7	298,977	166.5	674,022	19.2	310,864	93.4	250,526	40.9	26.6
1880	2,061,191	33.3	503,185	68.3	847,170	25.7	350,522	12.8	362,839	44.8	26.0
1890	2,507,474	21.7	1,099,850	118.6	1,046,964	23.6	451,770	28.9	448,477	23.6	25.5
1900	3,437,202	37.1	1,698,575	54.4	1,293,697	23.6	575,000	27.3	560,892	25.1	20.7
1910	4,766,883	38.7	2,185,283	28.7	1,549,008	19.7	687,029	19.5	670,585	19.6	21.0
1920	5,620,048	17.9	2,701,705	23.6	1,823,779	17.7	772,897	12.5	748,060	11.6	14.9

[a]These five cities were ranked as the five largest in the 1910 Census.
[b]Using the consolidated borough boundaries of 1898.
Source: Glen E. Holt, personal files; U.S. Department of Commerce, Bureau of the Census, *The Growth of Metropolitan Districts in the United States: 1900–1940*, by Warren S. Thompson (Washington, D.C.: Government Printing Office, 1947); Blake McKelvey, *American Urbanization: A Comparative History* (Glenview, Ill.: Scott-Foresman, 1973), pp. 24, 37, 73.

1.1 million people by the Civil War and to over 3.4 million by 1900. And it continued to grow. By 1920 it had a population of over 5.6 million and it was a leading global center of finance, trade, and manufacturing.

Despite the incredible pace of its growth, New York's share of the nation's total urban population fell steadily throughout the nineteenth century simply because hundreds of new towns and cities sprung up in the process of national development, and these grew as fast or faster than did New York. In 1800, 18 percent of all the nation's urban dwellers (almost one out of five) lived in New York, but by 1890 this proportion had fallen to 7 percent.[7] New York remained the largest city, but as the century progressed other cities assumed prominent places in a truly national urban network (see Table 2.2). As the continent filled in, interior towns popped up like mushrooms. One of the oldest, St. Louis (the old French settlement where Lewis and Clark outfitted their expedition in 1805), increased its population ten-fold in only twenty years, growing from only 16,000 people in 1840 to over 160,000 by the census of 1860. In the same twenty years, Chicago grew from a swampy frontier village of 4,500 to a city of more than 112,000. By the turn of the century 1.7 million people lived in Chicago, and this number soared to 2.7 million by 1920. Smaller urban settlements dotted the landscape between the larger cities. In 1840 twenty-five cities in the United States contained 10,000 people or more, but by the turn of the century there were 465 cities of this size or larger.[8]

Until at least the middle of the nineteenth century, the settlements that sprung up along the leading edge of westward movement and that gradually filled in the interior served as trading and distribution centers. It didn't take long before cities and towns began to sort themselves out into an urban hierarchy. Those located along rivers and waterways, such as St. Louis, New Orleans, Chicago, and Cincinnati, got a head start as major distribution centers, transferring goods through the Great Lakes or the inland river system to the eastern seaboard cities, or directly to Europe. With the coming of the railroads after midcentury, cities without water connections were able, for the first time, to tie themselves into the growing national economic system. Cities that had transportation advantages and were also able to make the successful transition to large-scale industrial production attracted new capital and immigrants. The large, economically complex cities formed the top tier of the urban hierarchy. The more specialized transportation and industrial centers occupied the next tier. Then came the small manufacturing, farming, or mining communities (like Oklahoma City or Moline, Illinois, which specialized in farm implement machinery) and finally the multitude of little towns that served as trading centers for surrounding farming areas.

❖ THE COMPETITION FOR URBAN GROWTH

The fortunes of individual cities were only partially determined by locational advantages. The elites that governed cities were indefatigable promoters of local economic growth. They worked hard to exploit any locational advantages that existed and equally hard to overcome any physical barriers that impeded the exchange of goods between the hinterland and their city and between their city and other commercial centers. Those cities that were able to situate themselves as centers of commerce grew, and their promoters and merchants profited. For much of the nineteenth century, the economic competition among cities was the dynamic force underlying city politics in the United States.

Especially after the national population began spilling over the Appalachians, businesses in the cities on the eastern seaboard vied with one another for a share of inland trade. Likewise, businesses in the newer cities in the interior tried to survive and flourish by beating out their nearby competitors. Cities of this era can be understood as "mercantile" not only because their economies were primarily commercial, but also because they pursued *mercantilist* policies, that is, rather than passively allowing the marketplace to decide their fate, they tried to shape patterns of trade and economic development.

Entrepreneurs in individual cities staked their fortunes on future growth. They were keenly aware that they were involved in a competition in which some cities would succeed in expanding while others would stagnate or even die. The entrepreneurial motive for city building ignited a "struggle for primacy and power" in which "Like imperial states, cities carved out extensive dependencies, extended their influence over the economic and political life of the hinterland, and fought with contending places over strategic trade routes."[9]

The building of the Erie Canal demonstrated that individual cities could gain substantial control over their own destinies. Prodded by entrepreneurs in New York City, in 1817 the New York State Legislature authorized money for the construction of the 364-mile waterway to connect the Hudson River with Lake Erie. When the canal opened in 1825, it became possible to ship huge volumes of agricultural and extractive goods from the interior through the Great Lakes to Buffalo, down the canal, and on to the port at New York, where they could be distributed along the eastern seaboard, put into manufacturing processes, or shipped to Europe. Many producers and shippers abandoned the long, circuitous, and hazardous journey down the Ohio, Missouri, and Mississippi rivers to the port at New Orleans. New York's direct connection to the heartland via the canal quickly vaulted it past all the other eastern seaboard cities in population and volume of trade. By 1860, 62 percent of the nation's foreign trade passed through New York's harbor.[10]

The lesson was not lost on entrepreneurs elsewhere. Urban leaders lobbied their state capitals for financial assistance to build canals. Pennsylvania, Maryland, Virginia, North Carolina, and South Carolina financed canal projects through the Appalachians. Between 1824 and 1840 more than 3,000 miles of canals were constructed, most of them run by state governments.[11] About 30 percent of the costs were raised through private sources, but the capacity of the states to sell bonds was essential for these expensive undertakings.[12]

Canal building was so expensive, the engineering was so complicated, and the natural barriers were often so formidable that most cities could not participate in the competition for business and trade. The railroads changed all that. In the first decades of the century, for the river towns like St. Louis, Pittsburgh, Cincinnati, and New Orleans, the steamboat had been "an enchanter's wand transforming an almost raw countryside of scattered farms and towns into a settled region of cultivated landscapes and burgeoning cities."[13] In the 1850s, the railroads became the new enchanter's wand. The rail lines became the new rivers of commerce, capable of carrying huge volumes at amazing speed over long distances. A rail connection carried the promise of economic prosperity for a city. The railroads guaranteed that America's frontier would eventually vanish and that a network of cities, towns, and villages would spread over the entire continent.

In 1840, only 2,800 miles of track existed, most of it in the urban East. No connection reached even as far west as Pittsburgh. The early steam locomotives were hazardous contraptions, blowing up with a regularity that provoked opposition to their use in urban areas. Railway companies, lacking the capital to take on bigger projects, built short lines, and each used its own peculiar gauge. At the end of each line, goods had to be unloaded from one company's cars and reloaded onto cars that fit the next company's rails.

Despite such initial obstacles, the rail network expanded at astonishing speed. Once city promoters grasped what was at stake, an integrated rail system developed quickly. By the 1850s, cities along the eastern seaboard were investing in stock subscriptions, floating bond issues, clearing rights-of-way, and building terminal facilities to persuade railroad companies to make a connection through their city. Railroad entrepreneurs quickly became adept at playing cities off against one another to get the most lucrative subsidies. For decades intercity rivalry provided the motive and much of the capital for railroad building; "the pioneer railroads in a very real sense were built by the cities [and] represented an extension of their commercial enterprise. . . ."[14]

The rail network expanded from 9,021 miles of track in 1850, to 30,626 miles in 1860, to 52,922 miles in 1870, and to 258,784 miles by the turn of the century.[15] In 1857, the newly consolidated Pennsylvania Railroad first connected Pittsburgh to Chicago. Three years later, eleven trunk lines ended in Chicago, twenty branch and feeder lines passed through it, and the city's status as the nation's largest rail terminus was soon assured. By 1869, the Golden Spike was driven at Promontory Point, Utah, completing the first cross-continental route by joining the Union Pacific line originating on the east coast to the Central Pacific line starting in San Francisco. Within another decade the outline of the modern rail system was nearly complete, a spider's web with strands reaching into every section of the country.

Cities did everything in their power to attract railroads. They gave land to the railroads, bought their bonds, and sometimes financed construction. In the 1860s, the business leaders of Kansas City, Kansas, sold bond issues to private investors, the proceeds going to a railroad company, and persuaded Congress to approve a federal land grant. As a result of its success in this venture, Kansas City prospered while its nearby rival Leavenworth stagnated (today, Leavenworth is known mainly for its federal prison).[16] Denver's board of trade raised $280,000 to finance a 100-mile spur line to obtain access to the intercontinental track that ran through Cheyenne, Wyoming.[17] Some of Denver's businesses had already moved to Cheyenne in the expectation that its position astride the intercontinental line would make it the premier city of the Rocky Mountain West. The convergence of rail lines from all directions into Denver, however, secured its status as the dominant city of the Rocky Mountain region.

No city benefited from railroad building as dramatically as Chicago, whose phenomenal growth was founded on its access to raw materials over a vast region. Corn and grain, cattle and hogs, iron ore and coal poured into Chicago through the Great Lakes and over the rails. The city became a center for steel making, manufacturing of agricultural implements and other tools and machines, slaughtering and meat packing, as well as for trade. Chicago eclipsed St. Louis as the Midwest's premier city by 1870, a feat accomplished partly through the aggressiveness of its local business community in securing railroad links. Chicago built its first railroad in 1852 and then helped finance feeder lines into the city. The city also invested in grain elevators, warehouses, switching yards, and stockyards. In contrast, St. Louis's business community held fast to a faith that the steamboats would be enough to guarantee the city's continued prosperity. By the time St. Louis began seeking rail connections, Chicago's advantage was overwhelming. It should be added that Chicago also had the great advantage of being located on the Great Lakes and it was closer to the great farming regions of the Midwest than St. Louis. However, its actions clearly gave it a greater edge over St. Louis than its locational advantage alone would have conferred.

The urban wars were important in the development of the U.S. economy in the nineteenth century. Relying strictly on private resources, the railroads would have expanded much more slowly than they did. Until the 1890s, most private corporations lacked the ability to raise the huge amounts of capital that would later become routine for them. Public subsidies helped to make the railroads "America's first big business,"[18] and thus the popular image of the nineteenth century as the age of laissez-faire is utterly false.[19] Up to 1861, excluding federal land grants, 25 percent to 30 percent of all direct investment in railroad building was supplied by governments. The cities were the biggest spenders; they contributed, in various ways, $300 million in railroad subsidies, while the states spent $229 million and the federal government $65 million.[20] It is important to add, however, that both the states and the federal government provided huge indirect subsidies in the form of land grants, which the railroads then converted to cash by selling land to settlers. Indeed, there was so much land in the hands of the railroads that they sent agents to the Scandinavian countries, Germany, and elsewhere to recruit immigrants who could buy and settle it.

After the Civil War, railroad construction became the most important single stimulus to industrial production, accounting for more than half the demand for iron in the United States in 1875.[21] "Railroads . . . both lowered the cost of transportation and stimulated the economy directly by their use of labor, capital, and iron," and created "mass markets that made mass production possible."[22] It is not difficult to understand Congress's motivation in providing huge land grants to the railroads in the Pacific Railways Acts of 1862 and 1864. As a result of land grants and direct cash subsidies, the United States laid more miles of track more quickly than did any other nation.

Most urban voters, when asked to vote for bond subscriptions and other subsidies, supported local business elites and their railroad subsidy schemes. The competition among political factions within cities was completely overshadowed by the competition among cities. As long as everyone's attention was riveted on external threats to local prosperity, a politics of consensus tended to develop around the idea of local promotion: "developmental policy was almost wholly a product of consensus-building among groups of merchant elites to support particular canal, turnpike, rail and other projects in response to merchant elites in nearby communities."[23] Most voters followed the lead of local business promoters, presumably sharing the belief that a growing economy would ultimately benefit everyone. In the years 1866 to 1873, the legislatures of twenty-nine states granted over 800 authorizations for aid by local governments to railroad projects.[24] A study of governmental aid to railroads in New York found that no community ever voted against subscribing to railroad stock.[25] The votes were usually so lopsided as to be a foregone conclusion.[26]

For many cities the fight for rail connections brought prosperity, but just as often the overheated competition between cities for railroad connections had disastrous consequences. Railroad promoters played one town against another in search of better subsidies (a process akin to the competition today among state and local governments for footloose businesses). Unplanned redundancy and overbuilding, to say nothing of outright thievery and swindling by promoters and politicians, left many cities with little to show for their financial sacrifices. The competition among cities was often so fierce that they bid up the subsidies beyond what was economically rational; cities incurred huge debts on a hope and a promise. In New York State, for example, 50 towns bypassed by a major railroad joined in a $5.7 million stock subscription to the New York and Oswego Railroad. Zigzagging across the state to link the towns, the railroad went bankrupt shortly after completing its line in 1873 because the areas it served had too few people and products to sustain a healthy business. Most of the investments made by the towns were wiped out.[27]

Then, as now, promoters exaggerated the positive effects to be expected from public subsidies, predicting rapid town growth, rising real estate values, and overflowing municipal treasuries. Profits on railroad stocks, they often promised, would eliminate the need for local taxes altogether. For most cities, however, "the direct effect on government finances was on the whole unfavorable."[28] Too many cities bought railroad stock that went bust, or the railroads brought far less prosperity than promised.

Many cities that had heavily invested in speculative railroad ventures found themselves dragged into fiscal crises. Although some cities defaulted on railroad debts in the 1860s, during the three-year depression that began in

1873 (which was itself partially brought on by the overbuilding of railroads and the overvaluing of railroad stock and local real estate), hundreds of towns and cities were forced into default. An estimated $100 million to $150 million of municipal debt was involved in railroad bond defaults in 1873—one-fifth of all the municipal debt.[29]

Municipal bond railroad defaults and revelations of political corruption associated with railroad building affected politics at all levels. Political consensus gave way to political conflict. Citizens rebelled against paying back Eastern financiers for municipal railroad bonds that had become worthless. In some cases the railroads had not even been built. Cries of debt repudiation filled the air, and some cities and states did manage to repudiate their debts.[30] From 1864 to 1888 the most common category of case before the United States Supreme Court involved railroad bonds.[31] Especially after 1872, many states adopted restrictions on local debt and limited the aid that could be given to private corporations.[32]

Financial and political abuses by railroad barons fueled a populist rebellion against big business that shook the political system in the late nineteenth century.[33] In many smaller cities consensus dissolved into conflict. In larger cities, however, consensus politics had already begun to break down. The twin processes of industrialization and immigration had already fragmented the cities into separate social, ethnic, and racial enclaves. Increasingly, the separate groups clashed with one another for control of city politics.

❖ THE BREAKDOWN OF COMMUNITY: INDUSTRIALIZATION

As dramatic as they may seem, statistics on nineteenth-century city growth cannot adequately describe the social and political dislocations brought about by urbanization. The traditional relationships that had underpinned society were overturned. As described by the urban historian Eric Lampard:

> After several thousand years of relatively stable levels of urbanization, the past two or three centuries have witnessed an unprecedented increase in both rates and levels of urbanization with repercussions and ramifications that mark the changes of the period c A.D. 1750–1850 as one of the crucial disjunctions in the history of human society. Whatever constraints had hitherto checked or moderated the growth and re-distribution of population were suddenly relaxed.[34]

In the United States the disjunctions that Lampard speaks of refer to the massive economic and technological changes brought about by industrialization. Cities changed from relatively compact communities held together by informal community norms to sprawling industrial cities characterized by social stratification and segregation, constant population change, and social and political conflict.

The lifeblood of the preindustrial merchant cities flowed along the water-front. Wharves and docks, warehouses, clerks' offices, banks, newspapers and printing establishments, taverns and breweries, and private homes all clustered close to the harbor or riverfront. Urban historians have labeled the mercantile city "the walking city," because the area of urban settlement was bounded by the distance that the inhabitants could walk within an hour or two. Typically, the city spread out about two miles from the center, but the area of dense set-tlement was only a few blocks deep. The cost and inconvenience of hauling goods on horse-drawn wooden wagons guaranteed that cities would remain compact. For the same reason, settlements without access to water transporta-tion could not amount to much. In the first decade of the nineteenth century, a ton of goods could be shipped all the way from Europe for the same amount that it cost to haul it nine miles over inland roads.[35] Inland cities without waterfronts could not conceivably compete with the port and river cities as centers of trade.

The small size of the merchant cities fostered "a sense of community iden-tification similar to that of traditional societies. . . ."[36] There were, to be sure, substantial inequalities. In colonial New England the inequality in wealth was about the same as in the slave-holding South.[37] At the time of the Revolution, about three out of four white persons in Pennsylvania, Maryland, and Virginia had come to America as indentured servants, and most of them remained at the bottom of the social hierarchy.[38] Only about 5 percent of property-own-ing white males were eligible to vote. However, the compactness of the mer-cantile cities moderated the effects of social inequality. Business establish-ments tended to be small, typically employing one or two apprentices who often lived on the premises. Individual artisans, craftworkers, and shopkeepers ran businesses in their homes or in adjoining buildings. Workers clustered together in shanties or back alleys, still within shouting distance of the better homes of wealthy merchants. In his study of colonial Philadelphia, Sam Bass Warner found that various occupational groups were highly segregated in 1774, but it was a proximate segregation: "It was the unity of everyday life, from tavern, to street, to workplace, to housing which held the town together in the eighteenth century."[39]

The economy of these cities revolved around trade and commerce: the importation and distribution of European goods; the regulation of docks and farmers' markets; the financing and insuring of ships and goods; the printing of accounting ledgers, handbills, and newspapers. Educated aristocrats, importers, bankers, wholesalers, and shopkeepers were among a city's most prominent citizens. A notch down in the social hierarchy were the craftwork-ers and artisans engaged in services and small manufacturing: shoemakers, hat-ters, bakers, carpenters, blacksmiths, potters, butchers, wheelwrights, saddle and harness makers, and boatwrights. At the bottom were the unskilled work-ers who moved goods from docks to warehouses, sailors, domestic workers, and servants.

In the years following the Civil War, the large-scale production of goods in factories quickly replaced commerce and trade as the leading source of urban prosperity. The process had actually been underway for some time, but it gained momentum from and required the emergence of an efficient transportation system capable of linking national and international markets. In the second half of the nineteenth century, the railroads revolutionized the urban system in two ways. First, even without access to water, cities could tie into the interurban transportation network. Second, truly big cities became possible. The railroads were able to bring together the raw materials, energy, and labor required for large-scale factory production. In 1850, not much more than 10 percent of workers were engaged in manufacturing, and they produced less than 20 percent of the nation's output of commodities. By 1870 industrial production exceeded the commercial and agricultural sectors in value added to the economy, and by the turn of the century manufacturing accounted for more than both of these sectors put together.[40]

Industrialization removed economic production from small shops and homes and put it in factories. Before the Civil War manufacturing establishments rarely employed more than 50 workers, and even in large cities they averaged between 8 and 20 workers. In 1832, for example, the average-sized manufacturing establishment in Boston employed 8.5 workers.[41] In the years following the Civil War manufacturing concerns became vastly larger. In agricultural implements and machinery the number of employees per establishment increased from 7.5 in 1860 to 79 in 1910. In malt liquor breweries the number of workers increased from 5 to 39, in iron and steel establishments from 54 to 426.[42]

Capital became concentrated in large firms. Limited-risk corporations[43] were relatively rare before the Civil War. By the turn of the century, there were 40,000 such firms, and though they amounted to only one-tenth of all business establishments, they produced 60 percent of value in manufacturing.[44] In 1896, twelve firms were valued over $10 million; by 1903 there were fifty firms worth over $50 million.[45] Several giant corporations were formed between 1896 and 1905, including U.S. Steel, International Harvester, General Electric, and American Telephone and Telegraph.

In the small shops of the mercantile cities the work atmosphere had been relatively informal. Within limits, artisans and craftworkers chose their working hours and manner of production. In contrast, factories imposed hierarchy and discipline. Machine-tooled, standardized parts replaced handcrafted goods. The manufacture of standardized products began in 1798, when Eli Whitney designed a musket that was built and repaired with interchangeable parts. Clocks, sewing machines, typewriters, and farm machinery were next. Huge military orders during the Civil War led to mass-produced shoes and clothing. As a result of these new processes, work became regimented and closely monitored. Factory methods of production required specialized, repetitive work and a rigid distinction between management and workers.

Especially in the larger cities, extreme class and income differences increased social tensions. The concentration of economic resources in big corporations created a class of industrial magnates who flaunted their wealth by building mansions and estates, throwing lavish parties, and constructing monuments to themselves.[46] The number of poor people in the cities multiplied, prompting the rich to found charitable societies to deal with the "dangerous classes." The number of people in middle-class occupations soared. Between 1870 and 1910, the number of clerical workers, salespersons, government employees, technicians, and salaried professionals multiplied 7.5 times, from 756,000 to 5,609,000.[47] Class differences increasingly became expressed in seg-regated residential patterns. Immigrant working-class tenement slums crowd-ed close to the downtown business district or in bottomlands near the facto-ries. Middle-class neighborhoods tended to be located farther away from the business and industrial districts. The wealthy claimed such exclusive areas as Park Avenue in New York and Beacon Hill in Boston, or lived on suburban estates beyond the middle-class sections.

Segregation on this scale changed the very idea of community. If it had once evoked images of disparate people rubbing shoulders in their daily lives, it now came to mean separation from those who were different. In the par-lance of today's cities, we speak of a bedroom suburban "community" made up of middle-class professionals, a working-class "community," a black or white "community," and so on. From the industrial city to the present time, urban politics has revolved around issues of class, race, and segregation.

❖ THE BREAKDOWN OF COMMUNITY: TRANSPORTATION

Throughout the nineteenth century, city residents tried to escape the noise, congestion, and filth of the waterfront. A series of transportation improve-ments—most of them the products of the technological advances made possi-ble by industrialization—allowed the cities to expand the outward boundaries of settlement and, in the process, to achieve a greater degree of population segregation.

When the omnibus was introduced to the streets of New York City in 1828, it represented a genuine breakthrough in urban transportation. Urban transportation had changed little for hundreds of years. The wealthy owned or rented carriages; everyone else walked or, rarely, rode a horse. From the 1830s until the Civil War, dozens of omnibuses careened down the streets of all the major cities. Basically an enlarged version of the long-distance stagecoach, the omnibus was pulled by a team of two to four horses and typically carried up to a dozen people. Omnibuses were crowded and uncomfortable, cold in the winter, hot in the summer, and slow, barely moving faster than a person could walk. The coaches swayed and lurched over cobblestones and rutted unpaved streets.[48] A newspaper of the time complained that "During certain periods of the day or evening and always during inclement weather, passengers are packed in these vehicles, without regard to comfort or even decency."[49]

Nevertheless, those who could afford the fares—merchants, traders, lawyers, artisans, managers, junior partners—crowded into the omnibuses. The omnibus ran on a fixed schedule and route, picking up and dropping off passengers at frequent intervals, and the fixed fare, typically a nickel, was a small fraction of the cost of renting a hackney coach. Therefore, the omnibus was more convenient and less expensive than any alternative mode of traveling except walking. By encouraging in some urban dwellers the "riding habit,"[50] the omnibus signaled the beginning of the end of the walking city.

Omnibuses allowed some of the upper and upper-middle classes to expand their choice of residential location. For the first time the workplace could be located at some distance from the home. American cities began to take on their present form, the center being abandoned by the affluent classes. The omnibus, the first mass transportation device used in American cities, facilitated a process of spatial segregation and differentiation that is still occurring in urban areas.

Other transportation innovations had a similar impact. Steam railroad lines, for example, were constructed in Boston in the late 1830s and in several other large cities over the next twenty years. Steam engines were suited for constant speed rather than for frequent stops and starts, they were expensive to build and operate, and they were fearfully loud and prone to blowing up. They did not, therefore, compete with omnibuses on crowded urban streets, but, rather, they facilitated commuting from the area of dense settlement in the city center to smaller towns and villages a few miles away. The 40- to 75-cent fares were out of reach of all but the wealthy (the average laborer made about $1.00 a day; sometimes skilled workers made as much as $2.00 a day).[51] Even so, by 1848 one-fifth of Boston's businessmen commuted daily by steam railway[52] (though in other cities the proportion was much lower).

After 1852, with the development of a steel rail that could be laid level with the surface of the street, horse-drawn streetcars quickly replaced the omnibuses on main thoroughfares. Though they, like the omnibuses, tended to be crowded and uncomfortable, horsecars represented a significant advance in mass transportation. Because the cars were pulled on rails, thus reducing friction, the horsecars were able to carry twice as many passengers and travel almost twice as fast as the omnibuses.

The horsecars "contributed to the development of the world's first integrated transportation systems."[53] In the bigger cities the lines radiated out from the center like spokes on a wheel. Because horsecars could travel 6 to 8 miles in an hour, middle-class residential settlements spread as many miles and more from the city center. The horsecar lines sometimes extended well beyond built-up areas, serving hospitals, parks, cemeteries, and independent villages.[54] Wherever they reached, land speculators and builders bought up property in the usually realistic expectation that development would occur.

Frank Julian Sprague revolutionized urban transit when he installed the first electric streetcar system in Richmond, Virginia, in 1888.[55] Sprague's accomplishment was to devise a wheeled carriage that rode atop an overhead cable. This device trolled along the wires, pulling the car as it went. The "troller" gave the trolley car its name.[56]

Trolley cars had so many advantages over horsecars that despite the expense of installing overhead wires, traction companies and cities rushed to convert. In 1890, 60 percent of streetcars were still pulled by horses. Twelve years later the figure was less than 1 percent.[57] Trolleys traveled almost twice as fast as horsecars. Areas 6 to 8 miles from the city center could now be reached in half an hour, making it possible for people to live 10 miles or more from work. And electric streetcars were infinitely cleaner than the horsecars they replaced. City residents had always complained about "An atmosphere heavy with the odors of death and decay and animal filth and steaming nastiness."[58] The trolley allowed cities to remove thousands of horses, together with their tons of manure, from the streets.

Both the horse-drawn streetcars and the electric trolleys led to a greater degree of segmentation of activities within cities. Until the 1870s, warehouses and factories in multistory buildings dominated downtown areas, with crowded financial and retailing districts close by and even mixed in with wholesaling and storage facilities.[59] In the last third of the nineteenth century, distinct downtown shopping and financial districts became separated from industrial and warehouse areas. The middle class developed a new shopping habit, riding the streetcars downtown to shop in the new chain and department stores. The first chain retail company, the Great Atlantic and Pacific Tea Company, was organized in 1864, and in the 1870s the A&P stores expanded to several cities. Frank W. Woolworth opened his five-and-dime store in Lancaster, Pennsylvania, in 1879, and by the 1880s Woolworth's became a familiar marquee in downtown areas.[60] The middle class's habit of shopping in downtown stores for major purchases persisted right up until the 1950s, by which time the streetcar system had been largely dismantled in most cities.

While distinct residential and business zones developed within the cities, new residential communities proliferated just beyond city boundaries. Between 1890 and 1910 the nation experienced its first suburban boom. In most large metropolitan areas suburbs grew almost as fast as the central cities in the 1890s and often faster than the cities after the turn of the century. Chicago's population grew by 29 percent between 1900 and 1910, but the population of its suburbs increased by 88 percent. In the St. Louis, Philadelphia, Boston, Pittsburgh, and New York urban areas, the suburbs also grew at a faster pace than did the central cities.[61]

❖ THE BREAKDOWN OF COMMUNITY: IMMIGRATION

Industrialization set off waves of foreign immigration and a restless internal population movement that eventually destroyed the informal urban community of the mercantile era. The industrial economy depended upon a constantly expanding pool of cheap labor. Millions of foreign immigrants were pushed out of their homelands by war, civil unrest, and hardship and pulled to American shores to find work. They worked on the railroads, in meat packing, in steel making, in coal and lead mining, and in factories of every kind. An unprecedented migration from farm to city was simultaneously set in motion.

Between 1830 and 1896, developments in farm machinery cut in half the average time and labor required to produce agricultural crops. Over this period, for example, the time required for wheat harvesting was reduced by 95 percent and labor costs fell by one-fifth.[62] The new machinery increased the capital investment required for farming, and thus small farms became less practical. A rising numbers of unemployed farm laborers and young people streamed into the cities.

Between 1820 and 1919, 33.5 million foreign immigrants arrived on American shores (see Table 2-3). Almost three-fourths of them, 24 million in all, settled in the cities. By 1870, more than half the population of at least twenty American cities were foreign-born or children of parents who had immigrated (see Table 2-4). The census of 1920 showed that about 58 percent of all the residents of cities of over 100,000 in population and almost half (48 percent) of the nation's entire urban population were first- or second-generation immigrants.[63] In just the two decades between 1900 and 1920, 14.5 million immigrants entered the country.[64] The immigrant flood slowed to a trickle by the mid-1920s, a result of immigration restriction laws passed by Congress in 1921 and 1924.

Immigrants passed through the port cities of the eastern seaboard and many of them stayed in those cities and contributed to their phenomenal growth. From midcentury on, increasing numbers fanned out to the growing cities in the interior, went on to mining camps, or joined railroad construction gangs. Most of the immigrants, however, settled in cities. In 1920, more than 80 percent of the Italians, Irish, Russian, and Polish immigrants were urban, as were 75 percent of the immigrants from the United Kingdom.[65] A lesser proportion of German immigrants, about two-thirds, lived in towns and cities, reflecting the fact that in the middle decades of the century many of them had settled in rural areas of the Midwest. A smaller proportion of the Scandinavians settled in urban places than any other group. Many of them were lured into immigration by railroad agents sent to the Scandinavian countries in search of buyers for land secured through government land grants. Enough Scandinavians settled in rural areas in Wisconsin, Minnesota, the Dakotas, and throughout the Midwest that only 55 percent were classified as urban in the census of 1920.

Sixty percent of all the European immigrants between 1820 and 1919 flowed through New York harbor. Between the turn of the century and World War I, approximately two-thirds of all U.S.-bound immigrants were processed through New York's Ellis Island, making it (together with the Statue of Liberty) an enduring symbol of America's immigrant history. Though clustered in large numbers in a few northeastern and midwestern cities, immigrants spread out to all the cities that supplied industrial jobs. As shown in Table 2-4, by 1870 immigrants made up 40 percent, and immigrants and their American-born children accounted for at least 72 percent, of the populations of eight cities of more than 500,000 people. In New York City first- and second-generation immigrants made up almost 80 percent of the population. In Chicago an astounding 87 percent of the population was com-

TABLE 2-3 DECENNIAL IMMIGRATION TO THE UNITED STATES, 1820–1919

	1820 TO 1829	1830 TO 1839	1840 TO 1849	1850 TO 1859	1860 TO 1869	1870 TO 1879	1880 TO 1889	1890 TO 1899	1900 TO 1909	1910 TO 1919
Total in millions	0.1	0.5	1.4	2.7	2.1	2.7	5.2	3.7	8.2	6.3
Percentage of total from:										
Ireland	40.2	31.7	46.0	36.9	24.4	15.4	12.8	11.0	4.2	2.6
Germany	4.5	23.2	27.0	34.8	35.2	27.4	27.5	15.7	4.0	2.7
United Kingdom	19.5	13.8	15.3	13.5	14.9	21.1	15.5	8.9	5.7	5.8
Scandinavia	0.2	0.4	0.9	0.9	5.5	7.6	12.7	10.5	5.9	3.8
Canada	1.8	2.2	2.4	2.2	4.9	11.8	9.4	0.1	1.5	11.2
Russia					0.2	1.3	3.5	12.2	18.3	17.4
Austria-Hungary					0.2	2.2	6.0	14.5	24.4	18.2
Italy					0.5	1.7	5.1	16.3	23.5	19.4

Source: From N. Carpenter, "Immigrants and Their Children," *U.S. Bureau of the Census Monograph*, no. 7 (Washington, D.C.: Government Printing Office, 1927), pp. 324–325.

TABLE 2-4 PROPORTION OF IMMIGRANT POPULATION IN CITIES OF 500,000 OR MORE, 1870 AND 1910

		PERCENT FOREIGN-BORN	PERCENT FOREIGN-BORN OR NATIVE-BORN WITH AT LEAST ONE FOREIGN PARENT[a]
New York	1870	44.4	80.0
	1910	40.4	78.6
Chicago	1870	48.3	87.0
	1910	35.7	77.5
Philadelphia	1870	28.4	51.1
	1910	24.7	56.8
St. Louis	1870	36.1	65.0
	1910	18.3	54.2
Boston	1870	35.1	63.2
	1910	35.9	74.2
Cleveland	1870	41.8	75.3
	1910	34.9	74.8
Baltimore	1870	21.1	38.0
	1910	13.8	37.9
Pittsburgh	1870	32.3	58.2
	1910	26.3	62.2
Mean for all 8 cities (each counted equally)	1870	40.0	72.0
	1910	32.0	72.3

[a]Native-born with foreign parents is unavailable in the 1870 Census. The figures for 1870 are estimated by adding 80 percent to the number of foreign-born. In all cases, this should yield a safely conservative estimate.
Source: U.S. Department of the Interior, Superintendent of Census, *The Ninth Census* (June 1, 1870), vol. 1, *Population and Social Statistics* (Washington, D.C.: Government Printing Office, 1872), p. 386; U.S. Department of Commerce, Bureau of the Census, *Thirteenth Census of the United States Taken in the Year 1910*, vol. 1, *Population 1910* (Washington, D.C.: Government Printing Office, 1913), p. 178.

posed of the foreign-born and their American-born children. A huge migration from rural areas to the cities in the latter years of the nineteenth century brought down these proportions somewhat, but the volume of immigration was accelerating as well, so that by 1910, in most cities, the proportion of first- and second-generation foreign-born was about the same as it had been in 1870 (see Table 2-4). By the census of 1920, just before Congress passed legislation restricting immigration, 58 percent of the population of all cities with over 100,000 people were first- or second-generation immigrant.[66]

The ethnic composition of the immigrant tide changed substantially over the decades. As shown in Table 2-3, during the 1840s and 1850s Irish and German immigrants made up more than 70 percent of all immigrants. By the 1880s, however, Irish and Germans accounted for only about 40 percent of the flow of immigrants, and after the turn of the century their proportion fell to about 8 percent. Similarly, as a proportion of all immigrants, immigration from the United Kingdom gradually declined decade by decade, then plummeted after the turn of the century.

The immigrant tide reached flood proportions after the depression of 1873–1879 had run its course. The volume of immigration doubled from 2.7 million in the 1870s to 5.2 million during the 1880s. After declining somewhat in the 1890s, the number of immigrants soared to more than 8 million in the first decade of the twentieth century and another 6.3 million from 1910 to 1920. In the 1890s, Jews from Russia and Austria-Hungary, together with Catholics from Italy, made up 42 percent of immigrants, and their proportion of all immigrants rose to more than 60 percent from 1900 to 1920.

The Irish and then the Germans set off the first big surge of nineteenth-century immigration. Famine and disease pushed the Irish to American cities. Irish peasants subsisted primarily on potatoes and vegetables grown on tiny, rocky plots of ground and in strips of soil along the roads, the only usable land not claimed by English landlords. When a potato blight swept through Europe in the 1840s, its effects were more devastating in Ireland than elsewhere. Between 1845 and the mid-1850s, up to a fourth of Ireland's peasants starved to death. Many of the survivors streamed into Liverpool and bought or bartered passage on ships heading for America.

As soon as they arrived, the Irish encountered intense hostility. Irish workers could rarely read or claim a skilled occupation. They took menial, temporary, low-paying jobs—moving goods on the waterfront, building streets and roads, working in slaughterhouses and packinghouses. Because of their poverty and their religion and perhaps their peasant origins as well, they became etched in the public mind as dangerous, alcoholic, criminal, and dirty. Anti-Catholic and anti-Irish riots broke out from time to time. Irish churches, taverns, and neighborhoods were attacked by mobs whipped up by a rhetoric that spoke of "an invasion of venomous reptiles . . . , long-haired, wild-eyed, bad-smelling, atheistic, reckless foreign wretches."[67] Protestant Yankees were in a position to hire, promote, and fire. Even as late as the 1920s, want ads in Boston frequently added "Protestant" as a qualification for employment.[68] The Irish clustered on the lowest rungs of the social and economic ladder well into the twentieth century.

The Germans encountered far less antipathy. A large proportion of German immigrants were wealthy or from middle-class origins. They were escaping war and political turmoil, not poverty and starvation. They brought with them music and literary societies and a commitment to formal education.

Although the Germans nominally faced a greater language barrier than did the Irish, the Irish brogue—and even more, the widely used Gaelic—sounded just as foreign to American ears as did the German language.

Important variations existed among the different immigrant groups as they strove to catch up to the native Yankee Protestants. In late nineteenth-century Boston, for example, there was an immigrant "pecking order."[69] The Irish and Italians competed for the lowest wages and lowest-skill jobs. Only blacks were below them. German and recent British immigrants frequently entered middle-class occupations right away. A few with exceptional education or a needed skill achieved real success quickly. The Russian and eastern European Jews, who came in the 1890s and later, placed emphasis on formal education and business. Though discrimination kept them out of corporations and larger business enterprises, they occupied their own niche as jobbers, middlemen, and small shopkeepers.

The various immigrant groups crowded into densely packed communities near the waterfront and factories. In the 1840s and 1850s, real estate speculators and landlords shoehorned them into deteriorated houses and into attics and basements, into unused warehouses and factories. Rents were so high that a large proportion of urban dwellers in cities receiving large numbers of immigrants made money by renting extra space in their own living quarters.[70] Even so, there was still a shortage of housing. Narrow, three- and four-story buildings divided into tiny living quarters sprung up in alleyways and on back lots. On vacant lots and behind and between buildings, immigrants crowded into sheds and shanties.

In New York as early as the 1850s, and in other cities somewhat later, the first tenement districts began to spread. With a larger proportion of the middle class leaving the city center, it became possible to raze older structures and replace them with buildings designed to crowd as many people as possible into the available space. The population density in post–Civil War tenement districts was remarkably high. The tenement—the name given to any low-cost multiple-family rental building—became a cultural symbol for urban slums. Indeed, by the twentieth century multistory buildings of any kind came to represent city living and the suburbs became identified with free-standing houses and low-density subdivisions.

The dense clustering of immigrants into slum districts led native-born Protestants to conclude that the immigrants were dangerous and morally deficient. In spite of the obvious problems caused by overcrowding, however, the clustering of the various immigrant groups into separate communities was crucially important for assimilating them into city life. For some groups ethnic traditions and social and religious practices smoothed the transition to city life in America. Thus, although the Lower East Side of Manhattan became the most densely crowded residential district in any American city during the 1890s, its disease, death, crime, and alcoholism rates remained extremely low. The customs and life-styles of the eastern European Jews who settled there accounted for this anomaly. Jewish families insisted on personal cleanliness and careful preparation of food. By 1897, over half of New York's bathhouses were Jewish.[71] Jewish children were imbued with the idea that education was the sure road to success. Orthodox Jews did not tolerate heavy drinking, and suicide and crime were nearly nonexistent among Jewish youth.

In contrast, rates of crime, alcoholism, and disease ran high in the Irish wards. The Irish tended to be the hardest hit by the periodic epidemics that swept through the cities. The Irish populations were virtually decimated, for example, by the yellow fever epidemics that swept Memphis in 1873 and 1878. No other group was affected as much.[72]

❖ MUNICIPAL GOVERNMENT AND THE EXPANSION OF CITY SERVICES

All city residents, whether native born or immigrant, were subjected to the dislocations arising from the frenetic pace of urban growth. In comparison with life in cities today, conditions of life for most city residents in the latter half of the nineteenth century ranged from squalid to barely tolerable. Epidemics sometimes swept through the cities. Streets turned to seas of mud in winter and to dust bowls in summer, and in every season they were littered with refuse and piles of steaming horse manure. A Swedish novelist commented that Chicago in 1850 (when it still had only 30,000 people) was "one of the most miserable and ugly cities," where people had come "to trade, to make money, and not to live."[73]

Urban dwellers complained about the conditions of daily life, but there was no guiding philosophy about what municipal governments should do to improve things. In the American political tradition, government has generally been viewed as a necessary evil, or at best a nuisance. The American Revolution, fought to throw off an oppressive imperial power, guaranteed that government institutions would be distrusted for a long time. The ideal of limited government was founded on the assumption that individual freedoms would be preserved not by the intervention of government, but by its weakness.

The political culture of American cities seemed to express perfectly this ideal of privatism. Cities sprang up on the coastlines, on rivers, and along the frontier because their founders and residents could make money trading goods. Cities existed to protect and promote local economic vitality. As a consequence, urban leaders could easily persuade their fellow citizens to use local government to support schemes to promote the local economy, but it was much more difficult to sell the idea of raising taxes to support municipal services.

In the compact mercantile cities, voluntarism had been a principal means of providing essential services. Thus, for instance, volunteer night watchmen tried to enforce the law; even in big cities, full-time, paid, uniformed police forces were rare until nearly midcentury. Volunteer fire gangs answered the fire alarm. Individual property owners often swept the streets and collected refuse. Even when city life became increasingly unpleasant, city dwellers were reluctant to acknowledge that municipal government might do better than the community's volunteer efforts.

After the Civil War, the cultural distrust of government was given new voice by the hard-edged conservatism of the new generation of industrial elites. The new conservatism was built on the philosophical assumption inherited from the Revolution that American democracy required citizens who were free to develop their moral capacities and individual talents without external restraint. This idea, so central to the democratic ideal of the constitutional period, was reinterpreted after the Civil War to mean that the main expression of political liberty was material success. This philosophy bore striking similarity to the Puritan notion that interpreted material success as a sign of spiritual worthiness.

Social Darwinism provided the logic and the language needed to apply this principle to government action. In 1859, Charles Darwin, in *The Origin of Species,* revolutionized theories about processes of nature. Darwin's idea was that the "struggle for existence" weeded out the weakest individuals and species, those unable to adapt to changing conditions in nature, resulting in the "survival of the fittest." The Social Darwinists applied this idea to society. They suggested that society, like nature, provided a competitive environment in which the fittest survived *if no one intervened to save the weak.*

The Darwinist idea provided a convenient justification for the adverse consequences of industrialization (unemployment, poverty, starvation), a rationale by which conservatives could "reconcile their fellows to some of the hardships of life and to prevail upon them not to support hasty and ill-considered reforms."[74] The conservatives explained that reforms designed to mitigate the effects of capitalism could only upset the natural social processes that resulted in progress for the human species. They "suggested that all attempts to reform social processes were efforts to remedy the irremediable, that they interfered with the wisdom of nature, that they could lead only to degeneration."[75] They maintained that any attempts to help the weak individuals of society would endanger the welfare of all. "Let it be understood," wrote the influential American Social Darwinist William Graham Sumner, "that we cannot go outside of this alternative: liberty, inequality, survival of the fittest; not—liberty, equality, survival of the unfittest."[76]

Social Darwinism glorified the business leaders who accumulated large amounts of capital, for these were (it was clear by their success) the individuals who contributed most to societal progress.

> As conservatives employed it, the Darwinian revelations supported all their traditional premises. In nature, the fittest rise to positions of dominance, the less fit are eliminated. Thus the species slowly improves through natural selection, so long as no extraneous influence interferes. "Fitness" was defined in terms of material success, because nature is incapable of recognizing another standard.[77]

According to Sumner, those who held great wealth had demonstrated by their success their superior ability to preside over economic institutions: "the aggregation of large amounts of capital in few hands is the first condition of the fulfillment of the most important tasks of civilization."[78]

One measure of the influence of the materialistic ethos was the great popularity of "success" literature between the 1860s and the turn of the century. Especially in the 1880s, following the worst depression after the Civil War, dozens of books extolled the virtues of hard work, thrift, moral habits, discipline, and cleanliness as the main ingredients in the attainment of wealth. The titles of some of the bestsellers are revealing. P. T. Barnum published *The Art of Money Getting* in 1882 and two years later followed it with *How I Made Millions. The Secret of Success* (1881), *How to Succeed* (1882), *The Royal Road to Wealth* (1882), *Success in Life* (1885), and *Danger Signals: The Enemies of Youth from the Business Man's Standpoint* (1885) were other popular books. Poverty was widely acclaimed as the greatest teacher of virtue; climbing out of poverty was a test of character. Andrew Carnegie, the self-made steel magnate, enthusiastically praised poverty: "Abolish luxury if you please, but leave us the soil upon which alone the virtues of all that is precious in human character grow; poverty—honest poverty."

Rural life was promoted as the teacher of moral habits and industry. By playing on the twin themes of poverty and rural beginnings, the literature offered hope of success to nearly everyone. The Unitarian minister, Horatio Alger, bound these themes together into a literary formula. Beginning with his first successful book, *Ragged Dick,* his writings were wildly popular. He wrote 106 rags-to-riches stories between 1868 and 1904 (the last books were written by others using his name). His stories invariably described a poor boy who, through perseverance, hard work, honesty, religious probity, and a little luck, achieves moderate financial success.

The success literature flooded the schools, with the express purpose of teaching immigrant children proper "American" values and personal habits. *McGuffey's Readers*, which dominated the schools from the later 1830s through the 1890s, were full of stories and poems based on success themes. A philosophy that romanticized individual progress and denigrated public measures to ameliorate life's travails could obviously be applied to mean that all governments, including city governments, should do as little as possible.

Even in this political atmosphere, however, the scope of municipal government vastly increased in the latter half of the nineteenth century. There were at least three reasons why city governments took on new public responsibilities. First, new public services were provided in cases when urban dwellers of all classes felt threatened by imminent catastrophe or crisis. Second, the entrepreneurs who promoted cities organized public services when the absence of services threatened the continued economic vitality of the city. Third, by the late nineteenth century the growing middle class became intolerant of urban conditions that had heretofore been considered normal or inevitable, and it demanded new levels of services and amenities.

Urban conditions that threatened all city dwellers sometimes goaded governing elites to organize and finance new municipal services. Epidemics were feared in all cities. During the summer of 1793, 10 percent of Philadelphia's population died from yellow fever.[79] The city's economy came to standstill, and a third of the population and virtually all wealthy people fled for the summer months. Outbreaks of yellow fever or cholera occurred in Philadelphia, Baltimore, and New Haven in 1793; in New York City, Baltimore, and Norfolk, Virginia, in 1795; and in Newburyport, Massachusetts, Boston, and Charleston, South Carolina, the next year.[80] Nearly a dozen cities were hit in 1797; three-fourths of Philadelphia's population fled and 4,000 people died (about 7 percent of the population).[81]

The threat of contagion prompted cities to invest in waterworks, drain swamps, and regulate the keeping of animals and the dumping of refuse. Philadelphia was goaded by its epidemics to construct the first municipal waterworks in the nation's history. Begun in 1799 and operational by 1801, it piped water to the city from the upper Schuylkill River. Philadelphia's system was constantly improved by the merchant elites that ran the Watering Committee. By the 1840s, however, these elites began to withdraw from political activities, partly because competition for political office had become more intense. Without their guiding hand on the Watering Committee, the water supply system became less and less adequate.[82]

New municipal services tended to lag behind the need for them because they always constituted a minimal response to a crisis; "municipal authorities, loath to increase taxes, usually shouldered new responsibilities only at the prod of grim necessity."[83] New services were provided as cheaply as possible and to as few urban residents as seemed necessary. The object, after all, was to resolve a crisis as efficiently and quickly as possible. Planning for the future was extremely rare. Epidemics brought about the formation of boards of health in New York, Baltimore, and Boston in the late 1790s, and most cities had organized them by the Civil War.[84] In the periods between outbreaks of contagion, however, these boards lapsed into complete inactivity. When an epidemic hit, they would take charge of organizing a quarantine of affected areas and houses, bury the dead, clean up the streets, and regulate the water supply. Once the crisis had passed, they would, once again, recede from view.[85]

A positive philosophy about the responsibility of government to provide for the general welfare did not exist. In the absence of such a philosophy, urban services were supplied and were expanded by fits and starts, in response to an imminent threat or emergency. The result was that services tended to be minimal and, generally, available only to some urban dwellers. Essential as they were to basic health, water systems, for instance, were chronically inadequate. Most urban dwellers got their water from these systems through street hydrants and hand pumps. Only wealthy people who could afford to pay for the service had water piped into their homes. In 1860, about one-tenth of Boston's residents had access to a bathtub and one-twentieth of the homes had indoor water closets.[86] Few cities made attempts to supply clean water until the 1850s, and as a result devastating outbreaks of yellow fever, typhoid, and cholera continued to make their rounds, particularly in the inland cities like New Orleans and Memphis that lagged farthest behind in providing uncontaminated water. Several water systems were built in the 1850s; by the Civil War seventy towns had waterworks, owned by eighty different private companies.[87]

In part, the water supply problem could be solved only through the development of adequate technology. Even Philadelphia's relatively sophisticated system delivered its water with only the heaviest silt filtered out.[88] Pumps frequently failed; in the winter pipes froze. People found dirt, insects, and even small fish in their water. During the first decade of the twentieth century, when modern filtration techniques were developed, death rates in New York, Boston, Philadelphia, and New Orleans were cut by one-fifth.[89]

Epidemics also prompted cities to provide sewer facilities. In 1823, Boston began installing the nation's first sanitary sewers. Other large cities followed suit, but slowly. By 1857, New York City, by then nearing the million-mark in population, provided sewers under only one-fourth of its streets, and most of these were storm rather than sanitary sewers.[90] Taxpayers resisted the high cost of laying underground pipes and installing costly pumps. Though most of the big cities had constructed sewers by the 1870s, these were usually paid for by the property owners who subscribed, leaving vast areas, always the neighborhoods inhabited by the poor, without service.

The sewage was usually not drained away from the cities but collected in community cesspools, which had to be dug out frequently. Even when sewers drained waste away from the city, the benefits were somewhat doubtful. Serious typhoid epidemics occurred in the cities along the Merrimac River in Massachusetts during the 1880s because residents were drinking sewage-polluted water. Boston Harbor was called "one vast cesspool" in 1877, because of Boston's habit of dumping wastes directly into the harbor.[91] Most other towns followed the same practice. Until the 1920s, crowded residential districts were dotted with outdoor privies, and water bearing a burden of horse manure and other refuse coursed along open street gutters.

A sense of crisis eventually led cities to finance and organize professional police forces. It is instructive just how reluctant the cities were to take on this task. In the mercantile cities informal community norms had kept crime and violence in check. Long after cities had grown too big for community customs and traditions to govern behavior, urban leaders clung to the notion that informal governance would continue to be adequate. In the early nineteenth century most cities remained "a community in which every citizen was closely bound to other members of the community by familial, recreational, economic, and social ties. The social hierarchy was clear; a series of institutions supported that hierarchy; and the community was so compact that it was difficult to escape the vigilance of the dominant class."[92]

The governance of these communities was informal. Merchants, landowners, and bankers took turns serving in municipal offices. When confronted with a new problem, they would typically organize a committee to decide what to do. Philadelphia's waterworks, for instance, were built by merchants who formed a Watering Committee that raised money through private donations and individual subscriptions to the service. Prominent merchants led the committee until 1837.[93]

As community norms broke down and as municipal services became more complex, formal public institutions increasingly replaced part-time, informal governance. This trend is particularly clear in the case of law enforcement. Until at least midcentury, the law enforcement function in most cities was met irregularly with night watches and constables. In 1845 Boston became the first city to provide uniforms for its officers. The same year, when its population numbered more than 400,000, New York replaced its force of part-time policemen with full-time officers. The police, none of whom received any training, went about the jobs in streetclothes, completely without supervision.[94] Eight years later the city's police finally received uniforms and some training. Until the late 1830s, Philadelphia relied on posses, militia, and night watches to enforce the law. They worked part-time and did not wear uniforms.[95]

As cities grew in size and complexity, this means of enforcing the law became obviously inadequate. During the 1830s and 1840s, rioting directed against Irish immigrants and free blacks broke out regularly in Philadelphia. The riots indicated the degree to which informal community was being fragmented by ethnic and racial divisions. Almost all cities experienced rising levels of violence. In frontier cities the connection between rapid population growth and social instability was particularly apparent. In the early years more than half the residents of San Francisco, St. Louis, and New Orleans were transients. A constant stream of river men, wagoners, and traders moved in and out of these cities. Saloons proliferated; gambling and prostitution flourished. Violent crimes became such a fact of everyday life in San Francisco in the 1850s that vigilante committees were organized. These committees were funded by local merchants who found the vigilantes cheaper than a police force, but soon the vigilantes seemed almost as dangerous as the criminals they were supposed to catch.[96]

New York's police forces were in constant turmoil for many years. There was considerable resistance to the idea of creating a professional police force because the two political parties that contended for power in the city considered the police an important source of patronage jobs. After the 1857 mayoral election, the new mayor fired everyone in the police force and installed people loyal to his own party. The former policemen refused to quit their jobs, and so for several months the city had two competing police forces. In June of that year a full-scale riot broke out between the two groups.[97] Similar confusion repeated itself again in 1868, when the newly elected Democratic governor removed all of the city's police commissioners, who were Republicans. The commissioners refused to vacate their offices. Finally, the state legislature resolved the dispute by assuming the power to appoint the police commissioners.

These events illustrate one reason it took so long to build modern, professional police forces. Political factions feared that, as a quasi-military organization, the police might be used by one faction against another. This fear was not completely irrational. Well into the twentieth century, police departments were prolific sources of patronage jobs, and their political loyalties and political debts, as well as their ethnic prejudices, affected their work.

The idea that crisis provoked the expansion of city services begs an important question: What gave rise to a sense of crisis? Objective conditions, however dire, may be adjusted to, may be considered normal, or may seem beyond anyone's control. In the cities of the nineteenth century, urban leaders felt a sense of crisis when *the economic vitality and existence of the city they lived in seemed threatened.* Local business leaders had a stake in preserving, rather than abandoning, the city. As a consequence, they preferred to invest their energy to meet the latest "crisis" threatening their city, and incidentally their own economic future, rather than picking up stakes and moving elsewhere.

Even if it may be said that a sense of crisis provided the original motivation for supplying and expanding an array of city services, it was often the case that once a service existed it tended to become regarded as normal and routine. This was especially the case with services, such as water systems and fire departments, that required building a permanent infrastructure or investing in expensive equipment.

The origins of modern bureaucracies can be found in the breakdown of informal community and the provision of services through formal public institutions during the latter half of the nineteenth century. Part-time politicians could not organize and supervise complex urban services. As the scope of municipal services broadened, the number of paid city employees multiplied. Where volunteers once joined firehouse gangs and even cleaned streets, salaried, full-time employees took their place.

Milwaukee's volunteer fire department gave way to paid professionals in the 1850s, when new steam pumps proved too complicated for volunteers to maintain and operate.[98] Public works employees were hired to maintain the streets when it became too difficult to find volunteers for the task. In the same decade, the provision of health services became too complex for volunteers when the Milwaukee city council required vaccination for smallpox and when it provided funds to build a sewer system. Gradually, the day-to-day administration of services was put in the hands of salaried employees: "Politics became a full-time business and professionals moved in to make careers of public office."[99]

In the last three decades of the nineteenth century, a growing middle class began to demand integrated water and sewer systems,[100] and by the 1890s there was popular pressure to improve services of all kinds. From 1840 to the 1870s, assistance to railroads had been the largest single cause of municipal debt. In striking contrast, over the last thirty years of the century, the cities went into debt mainly to finance the expansion of new services and to build infrastructure.[101] Cities ran up debts at a feverish pace to finance improved water systems, sewers, paved streets, parks, and other improvements.[102] Because of rising standards of public health, new technologies, even when very expensive, were quickly adopted. The creation of integrated sewerage systems is instructive. Complete systems of separate sanitary and storm sewers were not completed in most cities until late in the nineteenth century. Laying sewer pipe was a huge public works project for any city. Nevertheless, the number of miles of sewer pipe laid increased four-fold from 1890 to 1909.[103]

By the late nineteenth century, American cities, in general, provided more and better services than did European cities. American cities had more miles of sewer and water mains, more miles of paved streets, more street lamps, better mass transportation, and more fire departments with better equipment.[104] City dwellers in the United States used more than twice as much water per capita as their counterparts in England, and many times more than city-dwellers in Germany.[105] This was due, no doubt, to the fact that flush toilets and bathtubs were far more widespread in American cities.[106] The building of integrated sewer systems and the adoption of new water filtration technology dramatically reduced typhoid mortality rates.[107]

The cities also vastly expanded public health efforts. Using the new science of bacteriology, health inspectors examined children in schools, checked buildings for ventilation and faulty plumbing, and inspected food and milk.[108] Death rates fell sharply in the big cities, by 20 percent or more in New York, Chicago, Cleveland, Buffalo, and other cities in the 1890s[109] and just as sharply again in the first decade of the twentieth century.[110]

American cities invested heavily in basic urban infrastructure. City governments placed themselves at the cutting edge of technology, building such engineering marvels as the Brooklyn Bridge and New York's Croton aqueduct system. The Parks Movement and the City Beautiful Movement, both supported by urban elites and the middle class, swept the country, resulting in new and improved parks, ponds, formal gardens, bandstands, ball fields, broad tree-lined avenues, ornate public buildings, and other amenities. Urban dwellers came to expect a level of municipal services that was previously unheard of. The squalor of the nineteenth-century American city began to yield to the relative safety, cleanliness, and health of the twentieth-century American city.

❖ THE FIGHT FOR CONTROL OF URBAN GOVERNMENT

The new functions being taken on by cities tended to be added piecemeal—a water board added here, a health commission there, perhaps a police commission and a harbor board next. The precedent for the board system can be found in the committee system of the mercantile city. For example, when a water system was needed, the merchant elite that controlled the mayor's office and board of aldermen would organize a committee to build the system; an epidemic would prompt them to create a health board. City governments were modest in their powers and undertakings, but complicated, nevertheless, in their governmental structure.

Until at least midcentury, most powers were still lodged in city councils rather than mayors' offices or administrative units. As the sense of community of the mercantile city broke down, replaced increasingly by the ethnic complexity and geographic segregation of the industrial city, trade-offs, logrolling, and partisan wrangling replaced the relative political consensus that had prevailed among councilors in years past. Such a disorganized politics also brought with it high levels of political corruption. Aldermen often sold their votes to paving contractors, restaurant or brothel owners, or utility companies in exchange for contracts, licenses, and franchises.

The widespread graft and corruption incensed middle- and upper-class voters. Their remedy was to approach state legislators with requests for charter reform or for special legislation to take powers out of the hands of city councils. Over the last three decades of the nineteenth century, city councils lost more and more of their authority. State legislatures intervened to take budgetary and supervisory authority from elected councils and to give these powers to mayors or to full-time boards and commissions that were independent of aldermen. In the 1870s and 1880s, state legislative committees took over financial or administrative control of the police departments of Detroit, Baltimore, Boston, St. Louis, Kansas City, and New York. Fights for political control within cities often ended up in the state house. Reformers, citizens' committees, party leaders, and mayors all became accustomed to trying to persuade legislatures to pass special legislation favoring their cause. Legislatures became, in effect, referees among the contending interests trying to control city politics.

Legislative interference took many forms and sprang from a variety of motives. In 1869, the boss of New York City's machine, William Marcy Tweed, paid $600,000 in bribes to state legislators to get a new city charter passed.[111] Two years later (and, ironically, just before Tweed was arrested for bribery), the legislature helped Tweed consolidate his control over the city's budget by creating the Board of Estimate and Apportionment. The board, composed of the mayor, comptroller, the president of the Department of Taxes and Assessments, and the president of the Board of Aldermen, was required to submit the city's budget to the aldermen for review, but could then make its own decisions.[112] Two years later, following investigations and a series of trials involving financial corruption under Tweed, the legislature passed still another charter giving the mayor, rather than the Board of Aldermen, the authority to appoint department heads, though the board still held the power to veto appointments. In 1884, this power, too, was removed.[113] In each case, giving more power to the mayor and taking it away from the aldermen, the reforms were adopted as part of a crusade to fight corruption.

Boston's aldermen also progressively lost their authority to make key decisions. In 1885, the Boston city charter took all authority to supervise city departments out of the hands of the council and gave the mayor the power to nominate and fire executive officials. In the same year, to make the police department more independent of the council, the legislature created a police commission, whose members were appointed by the governor. And finally, the legislature imposed a limitation on Boston's tax rate. In the 1890s Boston's council lost its power to veto mayoral appointments to administrative departments, and by the late 1890s the council had lost all control over the city budget.[114]

In cities elsewhere the story was similar. In 1891, the Indiana legislature gave the city controller in Indianapolis the authority to draft the budget; the council could lower but not increase appropriations. This new charter also gave the mayors of Cleveland and Indianapolis the authority to remove executive officials, a feature that was also adopted in new charters in other states:

New Orleans in 1896 and Baltimore in 1898.[115] In most states mayors gained the right to veto legislation. Budget authority passed out of the hands of municipal legislators and into the hands of comptrollers or independent boards. In 1892, New York's legislature mandated a Board of Estimate and Apportionment, modeled on New York City's, for all cities over 50,000 in population. In other states commissions or boards were created to take over functions such as public parks, education, libraries, health, and public works.

Why were state legislators so willing to give more powers to mayors and to special boards and commissions? Whereas aldermen and city councilors came from and represented neighborhoods, the members of boards and commissions often were "bastions of the city's elite."[116] They were businessmen, bankers, lawyers, and other men of professional and social standing. The men of wealth and social prestige, who had deserted electoral politics in the industrial city, now found a new niche. They refused to run for office against the new breed of immigrant saloonkeepers and party loyalists. Instead, they were appointed by governors, legislative committees, and mayors to sit on boards and commissions. These boards were "protected from popular control, insulated from the undue influence of the city's aldermen, and dominated by those perched proudly on the top rung of the urban social ladder."[117]

Mayors also tended to come from prominent, even upper-class, backgrounds. Mayors had to win citywide election and thus had to appeal to a broad cross-section of the urban electorate. Citywide campaigns were expensive, and in the late nineteenth century candidates for mayor paid most of their own campaign costs.[118] What was an advantage, even a requirement, for an alderman—to come from the neighborhood, be close to individual constituents, meet people in saloons and beer halls, speak the language of immigrants, accentuate ethnic identity, be one of the people—became a liability for someone running for citywide office. In the first years of the twentieth century (as we discuss in the next chapter), party machines were able to centralize power, and machine mayors were able to win elections even without personal wealth and social standing. In late nineteenth-century America, however, the powers of city government were up for grabs. The immigrants, by virtue of their numbers, were able to elect their representatives to boards of aldermen. Middle- and upper-class elites, by being able to persuade state legislatures to amend city charters and vest more authority in mayors and administrators, were nevertheless able to keep their grip on important levers of power.

According to the urban historian Jon Teaford, this arrangement amounted to an "unheralded triumph" because it allowed city governments in the late nineteenth century to accomplish two difficult but essential tasks. The first task was to broker among the various interests that contended for power within the cities. Without formal representation in politics, immigrants would never have considered city governments legitimate, and the level of social turmoil in cities would probably have been higher than it was.

The second task of governance was the building of the modern city, with its panoply of services and amenities. The transformation would have been much more difficult without the development of institutions of professional management; these were the independent boards and commissions. There was a price to be paid, however, for such advances: Local democracy was, to a considerable degree, undermined.

> Through its control of executive offices and independent commissions, the upper middle class was usually the dominant force within city government, and America's municipalities proved especially effective in providing services for this class, with its devotion to flush toilets, public libraries, and suburban parks. No other group, however, proved more hostile in its attacks on the existing system of municipal rule. Though often effective, city government was, according to upper-middle-class critics, almost always dishonorable.[119]

❖ THE POLITICAL ISOLATION OF THE CITIES

If upper- and middle-class urban dwellers often thought that city governments were corrupt, rural America thought that cities, in general, were entirely beyond redemption. Until the mid-nineteenth century, cities were largely ignored by the rurally dominated state legislatures. As long as cities were ruled by patricians and businessmen, they were allowed to run their affairs without interference. This laissez-faire attitude gave way when rural interests became convinced that the industrial cities, and even the whole nation, might soon be governed by immigrants and Catholics.

State and federal court decisions consistently upheld the powers of the states to interfere in the cities' affairs. In 1819, in the *Dartmouth College* case, the United States Supreme Court held that cities were created by the states and that their charters could therefore be amended or rescinded at will.[120] The definitive interpretation, however, was offered in a decision handed down in 1868 by Judge John F. Dillon, when he was chief justice of the Iowa Supreme Court:

> Municipal corporations owe their origin to, and derive their powers and rights wholly from, the legislature. It breathes into them the breath of life without which they cannot exist. As it creates so it may destroy. If it may destroy, it may abridge and control. Unless there is some constitutional limitation on the right, the legislature might, by a single act, if we can suppose it capable of so great a folly and so great a wrong, sweep from existence all of the municipal corporations of the state, and the corporations could not prevent it. We know of no limitation on the right so far as the corporations themselves are concerned. They are, so to phrase it, the mere tenants at will of the legislature.[121]

Dillon was convinced that all ambiguities about the authority of states to control cities had to be swept aside, once and for all. His missionary zeal was fired by a conviction that cities were governed by riffraff: "men the best fitted by their intelligence, business experience, capacity and moral character, for local governors and counsellors are not always, it is feared—it might be added, are not generally—chosen."[122] In 1872, Dillon published his *Treatise on the Law of Municipal Corporations*. Originally 800 pages long, by the time the fifth edition was published in 1911, it had grown to five thick volumes.[123] It became the bible on municipal law in the United States, and thus the dictum that cities are absolutely controlled by the states became enshrined in textbooks as "Dillon's rule."

Inspired by a similar distrust of cities—or, rather, of immigrants—state legislators took steps to ensure that no matter how fast and big cities grew, their representatives to the state house would never be able to exert a majority voice in state legislatures. Most rural legislators would probably have agreed with a delegate to the New York state constitutional convention of 1894, who said, "the average citizen in the rural district is superior in intelligence, superior in morality, superior in self-government to the average citizen of the great cities."[124] A distrust of cities was hardly new. Maine's constitutional convention of 1819 had, decades earlier, established a ceiling on the number of representatives who could represent towns in the state legislature. In 1845, the Louisiana legislature limited New Orleans to 12.5 percent of the state's senators and 10 percent of the state's assemblymen (New Orleans's population then accounted for 20 percent of the state's total.)[125] By the end of the century, every state had ensured that no matter how large the cities became, rural legislative districts would continue to hold a controlling majority in state legislatures.

The underrepresentation of cities in state legislatures had huge consequences. If their influence in state legislatures had grown in step with their populations, cities would have been able to secure state financial support for the expansion of city services. They received practically none. They also would have been able to assert a political voice in national politics. Rural elites firmly controlled the party caucuses that nominated governors, congressmen, senators, and presidents. Immigrants and labor unions had no effective means of influencing governmental policies at the state or national levels (and, as we have seen, they had a restricted influence in local politics as well). Underrepresentation of the cities resulted in indifference to the problems faced by big cities in state legislatures, governors' offices, Congress, and the White House. Traffic congestion, slum housing, disease, poverty—none of these problems interested rural and small-town legislators or a Congress and president beholden to state party leaders who represented rural constituents.

Underrepresentation of cities throughout the federal system had profound and enduring consequences, for it allowed governments at all levels to wash their hands of the devastating effects of industrialization and urbanization. In the late nineteenth century, powerful populist movements were pushing for the recognition of labor unions' right to organize. In the first twenty years of the twentieth century, reformers were pushing states to adopt universal health insurance, workers' compensation, and relief programs for widows, children, and the elderly. A ground swell of opposition to child labor swept the country; nevertheless, the federal government did not adopt child labor legislation until 1916, and it was struck down by the Supreme Court two years later. Partially because urban dwellers had so little political voice, these and other reforms were delayed until the New Deal of the 1930s, and some, such as national health care programs, have never been adopted.

The federal courts finally moved against legislative malapportionment in the 1960s, more than forty years after the 1920 census showed that a majority of Americans lived in urban places. In the 1962 case of *Baker v. Carr* a group of Knoxville, Tennessee, residents challenged the fact that the Tennessee legislature had not been reapportioned since 1901.[126] Their lawyers argued that citizens living in urban areas were being deprived of "equal protection of the law," as guaranteed by the Fourteenth Amendment to the U.S. Constitution. The important court decision that decided this case, as well as others, came on June 15, 1964, when the United States Supreme Court, in *Reynolds v. Sims,* ruled that state legislative apportionments must follow a "one man-one vote" principle.[127] Within a few years, for the first time in the nation's history, state legislative and congressional districts were apportioned to equalize population among legislative districts.

The social conditions in the cities would have been addressed sooner and more effectively if these judicial decisions had come decades earlier. It would be unrealistic to expect that cities could have addressed problems associated with inequality and poverty with their own resources. To persuade the states and federal government to help, voters in the cities would have had to gain influence in state and national politics. The American political system was structured to reduce such influence. Such a circumstance arose because in the United States the people who lived in cities had long been regarded as "strangers in the land."[128]

CHAPTER 3

PARTY MACHINES AND POLITICAL ENTREPRENEURS

❖ MACHINES AND MACHINE-STYLE POLITICS

The image of the rotund, cigar-smoking machine politician handing out buckets of coal to poor widows and cutting deals in smoke-filled rooms is part of the lore of American urban politics. Though machine-style politics exists throughout the world, the city-based machine appealing across economic classes on the basis of ethnicity was unique to the United States. Americans, however, have long been ambivalent about their political machines; they have viewed them as both beneficent and evil. As President Theodore Roosevelt observed in his *Autobiography,* "A leader is necessary; but his opponents always call him a boss. An organization is necessary; but the men in opposition always call it a machine."[1]

Defining political machines is difficult because they differ so much in organization and style. A suburban political organization may be run by a small clique of well-dressed businesspeople, a stark contrast to the usual image of machine politicians, but we can still label it a "machine" if it is a stable organization that depends primarily or entirely on material incentives to build and maintain political support. Such incentives may come in many forms: a patronage job, a government contract, a zoning variance, a fixed parking ticket, an expedited business license. A political organization that extensively and regularly uses such material incentives to maintain support engages in what we call machine-style politics.

However, something more than machine-style politics is needed if we are to apply the term "machine" to a political organization.[2] A machine is a hierarchical organization controlled by a single leader, a "boss," or by a well-organized clique. Many cities, suburbs, and rural counties are run by factional machine-style politics, with various politicians having their own bases of support. In some local governments a hierarchical structure centralizes power into one or a few hands. A full-fledged political machine is characterized by both machine-style politics and a well-defined hierarchy.

At some time in the past most of America's big industrial cities had machine-style politics. From 1870 to 1945, seven of the nation's largest cities had no machine politics at all, but twenty-three of them did. Seventeen had boss rule and a disciplined, hierarchical party organization at some point in their history.[3] In most cities that had party machines, factional machine-style politics existed for some time before machines emerged. With only two or three exceptions in the big cities, the classic machines flowered in the first few years of the twentieth century. Boss rule peaked sometime in the late 1920s and early 1930s. In 1932, the year that Democratic candidate Franklin D. Roosevelt won the presidency, ten of America's thirty biggest cities were ruled by machine bosses. Today, the urban political machine is pretty much extinct. The death of Chicago boss Richard Daley in 1976 marked the end of the era of big-city machines.[4]

A study of the classic party machines will help answer an important question: Would blacks, Hispanics, and the other recent immigrants to American cities benefit if they were to build machines in the 1990s?[5] We will return to this question at the end of this chapter. Before we can hope to answer it, it is first necessary to consider what history can teach us about the classic party machines.

❖ THE ORIGINS OF MACHINE POLITICS

The rise of the machines was made possible by the confluence of two factors: the emergence of a mass electorate, and industrialization. When the Constitution was ratified in 1789, only about 5 percent of adult white males were eligible to vote, but by the presidential election of 1840, 80 percent of adult white males went to the polls, the highest rate in any major democracy.[6] The spread of universal male suffrage coincided with the explosive growth of cities. From the 1830s to the 1920s, more than 30 million immigrants came to the United States, most of them pouring into the cities. As soon as they were citizens, if they were male, they could vote. A new breed of enterprising politicians took advantage of this circumstance. The mass electorate could be mobilized on the basis of feelings of ethnic solidarity and the promise of material rewards. Politicians who managed to gain control of local government could command important resources that could be distributed to loyal supporters. Between 1870 and 1900, municipal work forces grew even faster than the population of cities.[7] During this period, local governments spent more money than either state governments or the federal government.[8] The growing resources of city governments provided machine politicians with the glue they needed to piece together local party organizations.

Deeply rooted in the social life of immigrant wards, machine politicians formed personal relations with voters that created bonds of loyalty and obligation. Social and political relationships were closely connected. Most large American cities went through a "friends and neighbors" or "local followings" style of politics, in which local leaders, often pub owners, entered politics on the basis of their extensive social networks. In the immigrant neighborhoods pub owners were often sought out as reliable sources of information and advice. Saloons were central in the day-to-day life in the wards and, more than any other institutions, served as neighborhood centers. There was an astonishingly large number of them in the cities. In 1915, there was a saloon for every 515 residents in New York, and the number was greater in Chicago, with a saloon for every 335 persons, and in San Francisco, with a saloon for every 218 residents.[9] In working-class districts the ratio in most cities was at least a pub for every 50 males.[10] In late nineteenth-century Chicago, half the city's total population entered a saloon every day.[11]

A large proportion of machine politicians got their start as pub owners. Of New York City's twenty-four aldermen in 1890, eleven were pub owners. Pub owners made up a third of Milwaukee's city councilmen in 1902 and a third of Detroit's aldermen at the turn of the century.[12]

Party machines combined two apparently contradictory qualities: informality and hierarchy. Precinct captains, who were responsible for getting out the vote in each election district, knew each voter personally, often as a friend and neighbor. To secure a following at this level, a politician had to be known not only as a person involved in politics, but as someone who participated in community life. At the same time, machine politicians climbed the political ladder only if they could put together coalitions with other politicians that were sufficiently strong to elevate them far beyond their own neighborhoods.

Most machine politicians had backgrounds and personalities that offended silk-stocking elements. Schooled in rough-and-tumble political competition, they often were men of incredible energy, hot tempers, and inflated egos. At the least, they loved what they were doing; they felt no alienation from politics. Far from being a part-time avocation, as it had been for the merchant elites of the preindustrial cities, politics was everything the machine politicians knew and did—it was their social life, their profession, their first love. They pursued political power, not social prestige.[13] George Washington Plunkitt, a sachem in the Tammany Hall organization in New York, advised against what he called the "dangers of the dress suit in politics." "Live like your neighbors," Plunkitt admonished aspiring politicians, "even if you have the means to live better. Make the poorest man in your district feel that he is your equal, or even a bit superior to you."[14]

Personal relations with voters, then, served as the springboard for a politician's career. Successful political machines were able to unite the various politi-

Figure 3.1 The Organization of Machine Politics

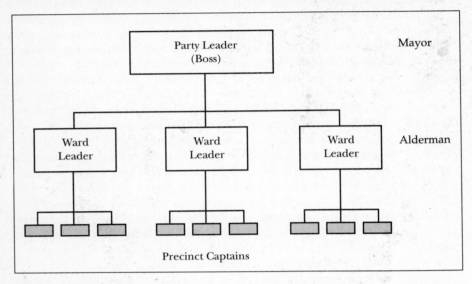

Precinct Captains

The organization of local political machines, or parties, parallels the formal structures of government but is also separate from them. Like the mayor, the party leader or boss controls the entire city, or perhaps county. The alderman represents a ward in the city council or board of aldermen. The alderman may or may not serve as ward leader of the party. Each ward consists of many precincts or election districts. Precinct captains are responsible for delivering the vote in their precinct.

In principle, power flows from the bottom up: precinct captains elect the ward leaders, and the ward leaders elect the party boss. In fact, power flows from the top.

cians, with their followings, into a disciplined hierarchical organization. This structure was once described by Frank Hague, the Jersey City boss, to columnist Joseph Alsop: "He [Hague] was talking in the dining room of one of the local hotels. He took the squares on the tablecloth to illustrate precincts and wards, tracing them out with his finger, and he explained the feudal system of American politics, whereby the precinct captain is governed by a ward lieutenant, the lieutenant by a ward leader, and each ward leader by the boss."[15]

As shown in Figure 3-1, at the bottom of the pyramid of a centralized machine was the precinct, headed by a precinct captain. The precinct captain's job was to deliver the vote for the party's slate; in the typical precinct the captain was responsible for keeping track of 400 to 600 voters. The best precinct captains knew most, if not all, of their voters by name. The captain was chosen by and worked for the ward leader (usually an alderman or party committeeman), who would supervise thirty to forty precinct captains. The ward leaders ran the party committee that represented the ward. Finally, the ward leaders reported to the citywide boss, who was usually the leader of a ward.

Ostensibly, the system was democratic—with the voters choosing the precinct captains, the precinct captains choosing their committeeman and the voters electing an alderman, and the ward leaders selecting a party chairman, the machine boss. In fact, however, centralized machines were invariably autocratic simply because those at the top controlled so many resources that they could dispense or withhold. Precinct captains, in fact, were chosen by aldermen; aldermen served as the chairs of the ward's party committee, unless an alderman preferred that a committeeman supervise the precinct captains. Party control was top down, not bottom up.

The whole structure was held together by the glue of material rewards. Bosses and individual aldermen had at their disposal patronage jobs in police, fire, sanitation, and streets departments—and sometimes in private industry. Special construction projects, such as levee construction or road building, could give a boss control over hundreds of permanent and temporary jobs. The best jobs went to party workers who performed well. Precinct captains usually held low-level jobs arranged through the machine, perhaps serving as supervisors on street crews. Ward leaders generally were rewarded with higher-paying administrative positions in city government. Aldermen and other elected officials typically owned lucrative insurance companies, ran their own construction firms, or owned saloons. The most menial jobs were passed along to some of the loyal voters who turned out faithfully on election day.

An understanding of the patronage ladder can be gained by examining the machine of Richard J. Daley, mayor of Chicago from the mid-1950s until his death in 1976. In the early 1970s, the Cook County Central Committee had about 30,000 positions available for distribution. Most of these jobs were unskilled; 8,000 were available through Chicago's departments and commissions, including street cleaners, park supervisors, and the like.[16] The jobs ranged from $3,600-a-year elevator operators and $6,000-a-year stenographers to $25,000-a-year department directors. Individual ward committeemen controlled as many as 2,000 jobs. (Richard Daley had begun his career as committeeman of his ward.) There were fifty wards in the city of Chicago, with an average of 500 to 600 jobs available in each of them.[17]

The number of jobs available for distribution by precinct captains and ward committee members was determined by the vote on election day. A precinct captain in Chicago was expected to know all the voters in the precinct and to be known by them. "When a man is given a precinct, it is his to cover, and it is up to him to produce for the party. If he cannot produce for the party, he cannot expect to be rewarded by the party. 'Let's put it this way,' [one alderman said,] 'if your boss has a salesman who can't deliver, who can't sell his product, wouldn't he put in someone else who can?'"[18]

Alderman Vito Marzullo of the Chicago machine was a successful salesman for the Chicago organization. Every week he scheduled a formal audience with his constituents. Flanked on each side by a precinct captain, he heard their complaints.

> A precinct captain ushered in a black husband and wife. "We got a letter here from the city," the man said. "They want to charge us twenty dollars for rodent control in our building." "Give me the letter, I'll look into it," Marzullo replied. The captain spoke up. "Your daughter didn't vote on November fifth. Look into it. The alderman is running again in February. Any help we can get, we can use."[19]

In the course of hearing his constituents, Marzullo exclaimed, "Some of those liberal independents in the city council, they can't get a dog out of a dog pound with a ten-dollar bill. Who's next?" Marzullo then arranged to have a traffic ticket fixed, agreed to recommend someone for a job at an electric company, refused to donate money to the Illinois Right to Life Committee ("Nothing doing. . . . I don't want to get into any of those controversies. People for it and people against it."), agreed to try to find a job for an unemployed truck driver, gave $50 to a welfare mother. Responding to several more requests, he offered to "see what I can do."[20]

During the Daley years, the Chicago machine took the form of a political pyramid. It was rooted in the precincts, where the voters lived. Ward committee members directed the captains of the precincts within their wards, and the committee members in turn reported to the Cook County Central Committee. Although most of the city machines at the turn of the century were similarly organized, some were directed from the top with an iron hand, as in Daley's Chicago, while others were little more than loose confederations of individual politicians who could deliver the vote in their own neighborhoods. Whatever the structure of the individual machines, they all showed these qualities: They were rooted in neighborhoods, they were held together by material incentives, and they delivered the vote by manipulating these incentives.

❖ JAMES PENDERGAST: A POLITICAL ENTREPRENEUR IN ACTION

The career of one machine politician, James Pendergast of Kansas City, Missouri, illustrates the process and structure of machine politics.[21] In 1876, at the age of 20, Pendergast, an Irishman with a short, thick neck and massive arms and shoulders, moved to Kansas City. With only a few dollars in his pocket, he rented a room in the West Bottoms ward, an industrial section on the floodplain of the Missouri River. The residents of West Bottoms worked in the meat packinghouses, machine shops, railroad yards, factories, and warehouses of the area. Blacks, Irish, Germans, and rural migrants lived in crowded four- and five-story tenements and tiny shanties. Overlooking this squalid area of dirt streets and open sewers was Quality Hill, from which the wealthy elite presided over the town. Pendergast held jobs in the packinghouses and in an iron foundry until 1881, when he used racetrack winnings to buy a hotel and a saloon. He named the saloon Climax, after his lucky horse.

Three factors contributed to Pendergast's success in First Ward (West Bottoms) politics. First, he was Irish, like the majority of his constituents. Second, most of the politicians of the First Ward made their money from gambling, prostitution, and liquor, and Pendergast's new business made him a member of this group. Third, as a successful saloonkeeper, Pendergast was in a position to meet the people of his ward. By staying out of factional fights within the Democratic party in his ward and simultaneously making himself a trusted friend of politicians and ward residents, he soon found himself being promoted for an alderman's seat, which he won in 1892.

During his first term as alderman, Pendergast established himself as a champion of the working class, successfully fighting against salary reductions for fire fighters, securing a city park in the West Bottoms, and opposing an attempt to move a fire station out of his ward. He won support from reform elements by favoring lower telephone rates and by proposing a better garbage collection system. Within his ward, he served his constituency. On payday he cashed payroll checks and settled credit agreements; he posted bond for men who had been arrested for gambling. His generosity cost money, but his business flourished: "Men learned that he had an interest in humanity outside of business and that he could be trusted, and they returned the favor by patronizing his saloon and giving him their confidence."[22] Thus, Pendergast's politics and social life became one and the same. It even seemed that politics was merely an extension of his personality, rather than a calculated activity:

> He had a big heart, was charitable and liberal, . . . no deserving man, woman or child that appealed to "Jim" Pendergast went away empty handed, and this is saying a great deal, as he was continually giving aid and help to the poor and unfortunate. . . . Grocers, butchers, bakers and coal men had unlimited orders to see that there was no suffering among the poor of the West Bottoms, and to send the bills to "Jim" Pendergast.[23]

Building on his solid support in the West Bottoms, Pendergast extended his influence into other areas of the city. In 1892, he opened another saloon in the Second Ward. In that saloon he employed twenty-two men to run gambling tables, and in his West Bottoms ward he continued to employ a large gambling staff. Gambling operated on a large scale in Kansas City. Opening his own operations in the North End enabled Pendergast to form alliances with the politicians of that ward, and he soon became as influential in the Second Ward as he was in the First. By working with aldermen with similar interests, he was able to secure police protection for gambling and liquor operations by paying off individual police officers and by influencing the choice of a police chief in 1895.

Pendergast's political influence began to grow. The politicians and the people of the North End supported him. His "generosity" to his West Bottoms constituents was extended to the Second Ward:

> The North Siders went to Pendergast for more than jobs. They went to him when they were in trouble and needed someone to soften the stern hand of justice. Many of them got fuel and other supplies from his precinct captains when they were down and out. Others ate his turkey and trimmings at the free Christmas dinners. . . , beginning with fifty guests and growing into the hundreds as the number of drifters increased year after year.[24]

By delivering the voters of his two wards, Pendergast was able to forge alliances with other politicians in the city. In 1900, he dominated the city's

Democratic convention and named the mayoral nominee. After his candidate won the election, Pendergast was given control of a large number of patronage jobs. He appointed his brother, Tom, to the position of superintendent of streets. More than 200 men and 30 teams of horses were employed by the streets department, and large orders for gravel and cement went to favored suppliers and contractors. Positions in the fire department also became available to Pendergast and his Democratic coalition. One of Pendergast's men was appointed as the city's deputy license inspector, an important job because saloons and other business establishments needed licenses to operate. Finally, and perhaps most important of all, by 1902 Pendergast had named 123 of the 173 patrolmen on the police force. Thus, he pyramided his ability to control politics in two wards into alliances with men who needed his support within the Democratic party or on the board of aldermen. He became Kansas City's most powerful politician.

The Pendergast machine, like the party machines in other cities, operated on the basis of exchange relationships. The boss distributed material rewards and expected loyal support in return. Some machine politicians made this relationship explicit, but the most effective ones never had to; after helping their constituents with the rent, the bosses could simply advise their constituents to "vote your conscience." Pendergast expressed it in this way: "I've been called a boss. All there is to it is having friends, doing things for people, and then later on they'll do things for you."[25] Pendergast's ward always elected him by at least a 3-to-1 margin, and without discernible vote fraud. It never occurred to him that he would need to steal an election.

Machine politicians like Pendergast were supreme pragmatists. Pendergast went out of his way to ascertain and fulfill the needs of his constituents. This was not true of all political machines. Though all machines provided something to their supporters, a great many of them delivered less than the James Pendergast story might suggest.

Several scholars have agreed that machines fulfilled several positive functions for their constituents and for cities. The Pendergast story could be used to support three claims that have been made in behalf of machines, namely, (1) they centralized power and "got the job done"; (2) they served as vehicles of upward mobility for immigrants; and (3) they helped assimilate the immigrants into American life. In the next three sections we investigate these claims.

❖ DID MACHINES CENTRALIZE POWER AND "GET THE JOB DONE"?

It has often been asserted that political machines arose in the late nineteenth century to fill a void left by the absence of effective local governments. City governments were characterized by an extreme, often chaotic division of responsibilities among many separate officials, boards, and authorities. The mayor often had little authority; government was generally run by committees appointed by the city council and by the mayor, state legislature, governor, and other appointed and elected officials. "As a consequence, when the people or particular groups among them demanded positive action, no one had adequate authority to act. The machine provided an antidote."[26] Parallel to the official governmental structure, the argument goes, machines built a centralized, extralegal structure that was able to consolidate power in order to accomplish needed tasks.

If it were true that machines arose only to fill a vacuum created by the inability of fragmented governments to make decisions, then we would expect to find that machines emerged *before* reformers were able to change local governments to make them more efficient and streamlined. In the big cities, the reformers achieved their aims of concentrating more power in the hands of mayors and civil service administrators in the last two decades of the nineteenth century, and the reform movement redoubled its efforts during the Progressive Era from 1900 to the 1920s. Centralized political machines emerged at about the same time that the institutions of local government were centralized.[27]

It is clear that machines found it was easier to build coherent, pyramidal organizations when local government had been centralized than when government was fragmented and chaotic. In 1913, for example, reformers in Jersey City persuaded the voters to fuse legislative and executive functions into one five-member commission. By controlling the city commission, the machine mayor, Frank Hague, was able to accomplish something he had not been able to do before: consolidate his power over a faction-ridden Democratic party and become the uncontested boss of Jersey City.[28]

No doubt in some instances machines did consolidate power in circumstances where no other institutions could do it, and in other instances machine leaders utilized reforms to their advantage. In either case, it is important to ask an essential question: What did the machines use their power for?

In the late nineteenth and early twentieth centuries, all big cities invested substantial amounts of money in infrastructure—paving streets, laying water and sewer lines, laying trolley tracks, stringing electric power lines, building public harbors, and constructing parks and public buildings. A study of cities from 1890 to 1940 found that there was no difference between machine and nonmachine cities in the overall level of public expenditures.[29] Even cities with factionalized politics, such as Los Angeles, were able to invest hugely in infrastructure.[30] It may be possible that the centralization of the machines was not actually necessary to "get the job done." The political support for reducing disease rates through better water and sewer services, for better roads and public transit, for new public utilities and better parks was sufficiently strong that these services were bound to expand, however badly the government of a city was organized.[31] In any case, most infrastructure was built through specialized bureaucracies, not by party politics.

Often enough, corruption canceled out any benefits that might have accrued from the informal centralization of power. Corruption could make the price of "getting the job done" astonishingly high. Probably the most notoriously corrupt machine in American history was led by William Marcy "Boss" Tweed, who ran the Tweed Ring in New York City from 1868 to 1871. In three years Tweed diverted $30 million to $100 million of public funds to the machine's private use. Under his regime the machine's "take" of 10 percent on construction contracts quickly escalated. A courthouse construction project originally estimated to cost $250,000 ended up costing taxpayers $14 million, of which at least 90 percent was the cost of payoffs, bribes, and fake contracts.[32] Tweed's rule has been called the politics of "rapacious individualism" because everyone in the machine seemed to be after personal wealth; rather than commanding a stable hierarchical organization, Tweed had to buy loyalty directly, and therefore his authority was fragile and short-lived.[33] From 1869 to 1870 the city's debt increased from $36 to $97 million. By 1871, when Tweed was arrested, the city was bankrupt.

Corruption was a basic method used by bosses to build and maintain their organizations. During the machine era, the major types of graft in American cities involved the handing out of lucrative franchises, the setting of highly profitable utility rates, the control of the city's police power (involving tavern and liquor regulations, gambling, and prostitution), and the control of public works (construction and maintenance, including roads, public buildings, and parks).

Control over the police force was a central feature of Abraham Reuf's regime, which ruled San Francisco just after the turn of the century.[34] Soon after his hand-picked candidate for mayor entered city hall in October 1901 (Reuf himself was an attorney who never held public office), Reuf let it be known that the city's laws against prostitution would be strictly enforced. He pointed out to the brothel owners the wisdom of having an attorney who could effectively represent their interests. The owners agreed to pay him a fourth of their profits, half of which Reuf shared with the mayor. This arrangement allowed the brothels to continue their operations without fear of prosecution. In his role as an attorney, Reuf also "advised" saloons in the red-light district to pay premium prices for a low-quality whiskey supplied by one of Reuf's clients. In return for police protection, the saloon owners followed Reuf's advice.

In 1905, Reuf agreed to become the attorney for the French Restaurant Keeper's Association of San Francisco, for an annual retainer of $5,000. The restaurant owners decided to retain Reuf after a decision by the city's police commissioners to revoke the liquor license of one of their establishments. Reuf, on behalf of his new clients, persuaded the mayor to remove one of the commissioners and replace him with someone sympathetic to the owners, thus assuring renewal of the restaurants' liquor licenses.

Illicit businesses commonly forged alliances with political machines. The exchange relationship was mutually beneficial; the businesses were free to operate under the "enlightened" attitudes of the police, and the machines raked in needed funds. During the prohibition era of the 1920s, several machines flourished by selling police protection to speakeasies and bootleggers.

Urban machines centralized decision making for legitimate enterprises as well. Government authorities routinely made important decisions affecting businesses and entrepreneurs. Reuf's largest attorney's fees came from businesses seeking franchises and favorable utility rates. Like other growing cities of the late nineteenth century, San Francisco invested heavily in new municipal services, and entrepreneurs were competing to supply these services. The mayor, the city council, or a utilities commission could, in a single stroke of a pen, enrich one business owner and impoverish others with the award of a monopoly contract to build electric trolley lines, install streetlights, supply gas, or install telephones. The temptation to make decisions secretly in smoky rooms was overwhelming. The chairman of the public utilities committee of the San Francisco Board of Supervisors told a group of businessmen in January 1906:

> . . . it must be borne in mind that without the city fathers there can be no public service corporations. The street cars cannot run, lights cannot be furnished, telephones cannot exist. And all the public service corporations want to understand that we, the city fathers, enjoy the best of health and that we are not in business for our health. The question at this banquet board is: "How much money is in it for us?"[35]

Actually, there was plenty of money for everyone. In a fight between two telephone companies to secure an exclusive franchise for service in San Francisco, Reuf collected a $1,200 monthly "attorney's fee" from one company while secretly accepting a $125,000 bribe from the other. Of course, Reuf awarded the contract to the higher bidder. Keeping $63,000 for himself, he distributed the remainder of the $125,000 to the supervisors, using a loyalty test: $6,000 each to those who had received no independent bribes (showing they were not trying to resist Reuf's control), $3,500 to those voting correctly despite bribes to do the opposite, and nothing to those who would not cooperate.

Reuf's position as an important "adviser" to Mayor Schmitz ended when Reuf was indicted and tried for corruption. His downfall was facilitated by too much success. After seeing how lucrative politics in the city could be, other members of the city administration began to solicit their own bribes, and before long their greed provoked legal investigations.

Although most machines were less recklessly corrupt than Reuf's, virtually all of them took graft. The temptation was overwhelming. The machines governed the cities during a period of explosive growth in population, services, and construction. Not only that, in many cases corruption was engineered from the top of the business world by tycoons eager to expand their empires. They found it convenient to work with bosses who could make decisions expeditiously behind the scenes. Big business paid bigger bribes than anyone else. As a result, national corporations quickly gained the monopolies they sought, and they were able to negotiate contracts on favorable terms. The franchises usually extended for periods of fifty to a hundred years, and some had no terminal dates at all.[36] In the 1880s and 1890s, national financial syndicates made millions of dollars by gaining control of street railway franchises. In 1890, there were thirty-nine street railway companies in Philadelphia, nineteen in New York City, twenty-four in Pittsburgh, nineteen in St. Louis, and sixteen in San Francisco.[37] By the turn of the century, only one or two major street railway companies operated in most cities.

It needs to be said that then, as now, corruption was hardly unique to machine governments. In any case, the extent and style of corruption varied from one machine to the next. During the 1930s, Boss George Cox was credited with bringing "positive and moderate reform government to Cincinnati."[38] In the years when Richard J. Daley was boss, Chicago was known as "the city that works." Daley was popular with voters because they felt that he was responsible for the efficient delivery of city services.[39]

❖ WERE MACHINES VEHICLES OF UPWARD MOBILITY?

One influential interpretation of machines argues that they succeeded partly because they provided "alternative channels of social mobility for those otherwise excluded from the more conventional avenues of 'advancement.'"[40] Job discrimination against immigrants in the nineteenth century was widespread. "Irish need not apply" was written on many an employment notice. Local politics was "like a rope dangling down the formidable slope of the socioeconomic system" which poor immigrants could use to pull themselves up.[41]

There is evidence to support the thesis that machines aided the upward mobility of immigrants. Though surely not a typical example, politics was pivotal to the rise of the Kennedy clan in Boston from poverty to wealth and national power. President Kennedy's grandfather on his mother's side, John "Honey Fitz" Fitzgerald, rose from ward heeler to become mayor of Boston. Kennedy's grandfather on his father's side was a respected ward politician and saloonkeeper, whose contacts helped the early career of JFK's millionaire father, Joseph P. Kennedy, who made a fortune in bootleg liquor.[42]

The thesis that the machines aided the upward mobility of immigrants is based on the notion that machines operated in a highly competitive environment and had to work tirelessly to incorporate new groups of voters into their coalition by offering them jobs and other favors. In their early years, most machines did in fact work to mobilize new voters and expand city governments in order to meet the patronage needs of their growing organizations and to secure the necessary votes to win office.[43] Once they had achieved a winning coalition, however, many machines became complacent. They continued to reward their supporters, but stopped reaching out to new groups.

Most of the big city machines created in the nineteenth century were Irish-dominated, and they stayed that way well into the twentieth century. In a classic study of six Irish machines, Steven Erie concluded that they were consistently biased in favor of the Irish and "turned their backs on later-arriving immigrants."[44] Between 1900 and 1930, for example, the Irish machine cities of New York City, Jersey City, and Albany, New York, added nearly 100,000 municipal jobs; close to two-thirds of the new jobs went to the Irish, even though they made up only about one-third of the city's population. Police forces were an especially well-guarded Irish domain. As late as 1970, 65 percent of police officers in Albany were of Irish descent.[45]

Later-arriving immigrants to American cities found themselves shut out of the benefits of machine rule. In New York City, Jews and Italians were excluded by the Irish-dominated machine called Tammany Hall. Though Jews and Italians represented 43 percent of New York's population in the 1920s, only 15 percent of the city's aldermen and assemblymen were Jewish and only 3 percent were Italian in 1921.[46] Fiorello LaGuardia, elected mayor in 1933, was able to smash the Tammany machine by assembling a coalition of disgruntled Jews, Italians, and other excluded groups. LaGuardia was a master at ethnic politics. "[H]alf Jewish and half Italian, married first to a Catholic and then to a Lutheran of German descent, himself a Mason and an Episcopalian, he [LaGuardia] was practically a balanced ticket all by himself."[47]

Blacks were also excluded by the Irish machines. In many cities "submachines" run by black bosses were built, but they were subordinate in every way to the needs of the white machine bosses.[48] In Chicago, William Dawson, congressman from 1942 until his death in 1970, was the boss of the huge black submachine in the South Side ghetto. Dawson reliably delivered huge pluralities for machine candidates from the black wards, but loyal black voters received relatively little in return. Though blacks made up 40 percent of Chicago's population in 1970, for example, they held only 20 percent of city government jobs, mostly menial positions.[49] A study of a typical ward in Chicago in the 1970s found that the machine consistently overrewarded middle-class voters and underrewarded loyal lower-class voters.[50] As in New York, the machine in Chicago was finally overturned by disaffected groups: In 1983 a charismatic black politician, Harold Washington, assembled a coalition of poor people, blacks, Hispanics, and white liberals to defeat the machine's mayoral candidate.[51]

Given the pressures on machine politicians, the tendency toward "ethnic particularism" was understandable.[52] The more ethnic groups in a machine's coalition, the greater the interethnic squabbles over the distribution of patronage and the thinner the distribution of rewards. As a consequence, "Once minimal winning coalitions had been constructed, the machines had little incentive to naturalize, register, and mobilize the votes of later ethnic arrivals."[53] For entrenched machines, a constantly expanding electorate only provided more opportunities for challengers.

Even for the Irish, the machines did not serve as broad avenues of upward mobility. The limited resources of city governments constrained what machines could accomplish. While it is true that city governments expanded rapidly in the late nineteenth century, government employment still amounted to a small proportion of the jobs available in industry. In 1900, Tammany's vaunted patronage army made up 5 percent of New York City's work force. From 1900 to 1920, local government expanded, with machines controlling 20 percent of the urban job growth.[54] Nevertheless, private industry was the primary avenue of upward mobility.

Though they received a disproportionate share of government jobs, the Irish were late in catching up with other ethnic groups. Scandinavians, Germans, and Jews, for example, participated relatively little in machine politics yet were assimilated into the American middle class faster than the Irish, who finally achieved parity with these groups in the 1960s and 1970s. Ironically, the preoccupation of the Irish with public-sector employment may have slowed their rise into middle-class occupations. Patronage jobs were overwhelmingly blue collar, and they were distributed not to further the upward mobility of immigrants, but to maintain the party organization. Especially at the bottom of the patronage ladder, jobs were deliberately kept low paying in order to maximize the number of jobs available for distribution.

❖ DID THE MACHINES HELP THE IMMIGRANTS ASSIMILATE?

Though the machines did not appreciably contribute to the economic success or upward mobility of their constituents, they nevertheless were instrumental in assimilating millions of impoverished immigrants into a culture which was generally fearful of and hostile to every new immigrant wave. Ethnic, racial, and class tensions were potentially explosive in cities. The political machines accomplished the task of assimilation to a surprising degree.

The machines helped to create a sense of community and belonging for the immigrants. Machine politicians organized picnics, patriotic gatherings (always Fourth of July celebrations), baseball teams, choirs, and youth clubs. Machines were themselves important community social institutions, the Democratic Club being a place where men played cards and checkers or just talked.[55]

With the material resources at their disposal already devoted to their core constituency, machine politicians learned to satisfy immigrants that arrived later with largely symbolic benefits. In New York City, Tammany leader "Big Tim" Sullivan ruled the Lower East Side even though as early as 1910 it was 85 percent Jewish and Italian.

> He and his Irish lieutenants distributed coal, food, and rent money to needy Jews and Italians on the Lower East Side. Tammany's police department opened up station houses as temporary shelters for the homeless. Sullivan expedited business licenses for ethnic shopkeepers and pushcart peddlers. He shamelessly "recognized" the new immigrants with symbolic gestures and donned a yarmulke to solicit Jewish votes. Sullivan solicited Italian votes by sponsoring legislation to make Columbus Day a holiday.[56]

Many immigrants felt like outsiders in the dominant Protestant and middle-class culture of the United States. One of the secrets of the machines' appeal was that they promised to tolerate the immigrants' "strange" practices and defend them from the dominant culture.[57] This was a benefit that machine politicians could deliver at little cost. While working-class communities in American cities were not economically independent, they were, for the most part, socially independent. Immigrants built their own social institutions, churches, clubs, and mutual aid societies. Machine politicians generally supported such activities because they could use them for campaigning and political organizing.[58]

Machine politicians appealed to and were supported by immigrants also because they represented to the immigrants the possibility of success in this strange new country. Nearly all machine politicians came from lower-class, immigrant origins. One study of twenty bosses found that fifteen were first- or second-generation immigrants, thirteen had never finished grammar school, and most had gone into politics at a young age, serving as messengers or detail boys at rallies and meetings.[59] Machine leaders, therefore, were symbols of "making it" in America. Immigrants may not have read the Horatio Alger stories, but in machine bosses they could see men who had risen out of poverty. Aspiring politicians often accepted this interpretation of themselves, too; they viewed themselves as examples of what could be done with hard work and a little luck along the way. These symbols of upward mobility were sources of pride and hope for the masses of poor immigrants who were living and working under incredibly difficult conditions. The symbols exceeded the substance, however, especially for later-arriving southern and eastern European immigrants. Irish politicians would shrewdly pick a few prominent men from excluded groups and put them in prominent places on the ballot to demonstrate their evenhandedness. Such symbolic gestures worked quite well, even though little of the bread-and-butter patronage went to these ethnic groups.

The immigrants paid a price for assimilation on these terms. Machines never attempted to address the collective aspirations of ethnic groups. The immigrants were encouraged to "cast their ballots on the basis of ethnicity rather than policy considerations."[60] Immigrants gave their votes to party politicians not as an act of consciousness about group goals, but because it was easy to do and there were no plausible alternatives. The vote was a minimal commitment by the immigrant, but a sufficient one for the machine. Commensurate with the level of commitment, constituents could hardly expect miracles in return.

The operating principles and structures of the urban machines mandated that they be conservative organizations. To deal with constituent requests effectively, machine politicians had to learn the art of manipulating public and private institutions in the urban environment. The emphasis was on pragmatic exchange, not on societal change. Additionally, machine politicians benefited from existing political arrangements. It made little sense for a ward committeeman who could deliver his ward to rock the political boat.

As a consequence, machines were hostile to political organizations and movements that tried to rally working-class people with appeals based on ideology and issues of social justice. Such organizations threatened their continued control of the immigrant vote. Until the 1930s, most machines vigorously opposed labor unions. In the first years of the twentieth century, Irish machine politicians ordered the police to attack labor organizers in Lawrence, Massachusetts, and in New York City.[61] In Pittsburgh's 1919 steel strike, the machine likewise ordered police to harass strikers.[62] Especially after Franklin D. Roosevelt's presidential election in 1932, some of the big city machines formed alliances with the moderate trade unions. The relationship, however, was never an easy one. The machines expected the unions to stay out of city politics as much as possible and focus strictly on state and national politics and on labor-business relations.

On balance, then, the immigrants' potential as a political force was stunted by the machines. Working-class immigrants shared a common need for such reforms as widows' pensions, factory legislation governing safety and working conditions, maximum hours and minimum wages for women and children, and workers' compensation.[63] On some occasions machine politicians supported these reforms, as well as regulation of utilities, legalization of boycotting and picketing by labor unions, and regulation of insurance companies. Selective support for reform measures did not, however, transform machine politicians into crusading reformers. Machine politicians serving in the state legislatures rarely sponsored a coherent reform agenda of their own. Rather, they backed individual reform items proposed by nonmachine reformers who wanted to address a particular social problem. Machine politicians were willing to enter into temporary coalitions to support legislative action at the state level, but they were never permanent partners in reform coalitions. Their support for reform was piecemeal and circumstantial; so long as reform did not harm their interests or embroil them in too much controversy, they sometimes went along with it. Machine politicians could be quite capricious, however, for immediate political circumstances often took precedence over principle. They were as likely to oppose reforms as to support them.

Machine politicians did not have political programs; they did not consider how things should be or what problems should be addressed. They generally regarded reformers as "goody-goodies," or "goo-goos," who were only in politics for a few thrills. ("Goo-goo" also stood for "good government," often the reformers' rallying cry.) Much of this bias was no doubt rooted in the social differences between upper-class reformers and lower-class immigrant politicians. Still, the politicians' excessive respect for pragmatic as opposed to idealistic motivation translated into an orientation toward the status quo, for important political change usually requires an attack on politics as usual.

❖ THE SOCIAL REFORM ALTERNATIVE

Defenders of political machines argue that there were few alternatives to the machines' style of politics, that in the face of the vast economic and political resources held by corporations and wealthy elites, the machines milked the system on behalf of their constituents as effectively as they could, and that to criticize them is to engage in utopian fantasies.

Alternatives, however, were available. In the first two decades of the twentieth century, social reformers won elections in cities across the country. Social reformers were intent upon improving the quality of life for immigrants and workers, and they campaigned for support from both the working-class immigrants and the middle class.[64] Mayors Tom L. Johnson of Cleveland, Ohio (1901–1909), Samuel "Golden Rule" Jones of Toledo, Ohio (1897–1903), and Brand Whitlock of Toledo (1906–1913) all won election by fighting against high streetcar and utility rates and for fair taxation and better social services. Their campaigns became models for like-minded reformers elsewhere. Jersey City, Philadelphia, and Cincinnati elected mayors who led similar reform crusades. These three mayors all attempted to raise more municipal revenue by increasing taxes on businesses and wealthy property owners and negotiating new streetcar and utility franchises. Machine politicians and the business community bitterly fought reform in these cities, as they had earlier in Cleveland and Toledo.[65]

The administration of Hazen S. Pingree, mayor of Detroit from 1890 to 1897, provides the best example of what machines might have accomplished in American cities. Born in Maine to a poor farmer and itinerant cobbler, Pingree did not seem destined to become a political reformer. After fighting in the Civil War, Pingree moved to Detroit where he worked as a leather cutter in a shoe factory. Saving his meager earnings, he was able, with the help of a partner, to purchase the outdated factory. Modernizing the machinery and shrewdly adjusting production to meet changing styles in footwear, in a short time Pingree became independently wealthy. He was picked as the Republican candidate for mayor in 1889, largely because he was the only member of the exclusive Michigan Club who could be persuaded by its members to run. The conservative businessmen who controlled Republican politics trusted him, as a member of the club, to pursue a program of low taxes and municipal government economy.

Pingree turned out to be an astute campaigner. Unlike the typical reform or business candidate, he campaigned in the ethnic wards, kicking off his campaign by drinking red-eye whiskey in an Irish saloon. Pingree successfully wooed German and Polish voters, who felt ignored by the Irish-dominated Democratic machine. He attacked the Democratic machine as corrupt and advocated an eight-hour work day for city employees. His willingness to seek the ethnic vote was the foundation on which he built his electoral success.

Pingree's programs, and the strategies he used to implement them, reveal how much could have been accomplished in other cities. When Pingree took over city hall, Detroit had one of the worst street systems in the nation. Many of the streets were made of wooden blocks, which would catch fire in the summer and sink into the mire in the winter. The paved streets were almost impassable with ruts and potholes. Pingree quickly realized that collusion between the Democratic machine and paving contractors was at the heart of the street problem. He launched an aggressive campaign against this arrangement, appealing to his business supporters by pointing out that the prosperity of the city depended on good streets. His insistent efforts led the city council to adopt strict paving specifications for the city. As a result, by 1895 Detroit had one of the nation's best street systems.

It wasn't long before Pingree came to recognize that the local business establishment was as much a problem as the corrupt political machine. He challenged what he thought was the unnecessarily high cost for the ferry ride across the Detroit River to Belle Isle Park. The company dropped its rate from 10 cents to 5 cents after the mayor threatened to revoke its franchise or put into operation a municipal ferry service. In a related campaign, Pingree found that private companies had located along the Detroit River waterfront, often on municipal property, choking off public access to water and recreation. He soon cleared away waterfront areas for public use.

Above all, it was Pingree's fight with the Detroit City Railway Company over streetcar service that turned him into a true social reformer willing to use public authority to limit private power when it benefited the city as a whole. At a time when other street railways throughout the nation were converting from animal to electric power, the Detroit company refused to modernize. In April 1891, the company's employees went on strike, furnishing a perfect opportunity for Pingree to fight for modernization and lower fares.

The three-day strike culminated in a riot in which workers and citizens tore up the tracks, stoned the streetcars, and drove off the horses. Pingree not only refused the company's request to bring in the state militia, but called privately owned public services "the chief source of corruption in city governments."[66] Pingree's stance initiated a protracted, bitter fight to regulate the streetcars. This conflict vaulted him to national prominence.

Many business leaders had supported the 1890 strike, feeling that the street railway was so badly run that it was hurting local business. The business community was mainly interested in better service, but Pingree pressed further, advocating lower fares and municipal ownership. Such a position ran afoul of business leaders when the company passed into the hands of a wealthy eastern entrepreneur. The new owner's first action was to pack the company's board of directors with prominent Detroit business leaders. The company then demanded a franchise renewal on favorable terms. Pingree countered with a suit to terminate the existing company in favor of municipal ownership. At that point, his former colleagues took action to bring him around to their point of view. The company bought Pingree's own attorney away from him and proceeded to offer bribes to city council members, including a $75,000 bribe to Pingree himself. The Preston National Bank dropped Pingree from its board of directors; he lost his family pew in the Baptist church; he and his friends were shunned in public. For Pingree, the lesson he learned in all this was that business supported reform only on its own terms. He also began to form an analysis about what was wrong in city politics.

In 1891, Pingree began attacking the tax privileges of the city's corporations. The railroad, he observed, owned more than one-fifth of the property value in the city but paid no taxes at all because of the tax-free status granted to it by the state legislature. Shipping companies, docks and warehouses, and other businesses escaped local taxation by claiming that their principal places of business existed outside the city. The city's biggest employer, the Michigan-Peninsula Car Company, paid only nominal taxes. In questioning these privileges, Pingree was confronting the combined wealth and power of the city's business elite. Although he was unsuccessful in equalizing the tax burden, Pingree was able to modify some of its worst features, especially the practice of assessing, for tax purposes, real estate owned by wealthy people at rates far below value. Pingree earned the special enmity of the city's elite by successfully campaigning for a personal property tax on home furnishings, art objects, and other luxury items.

On April 1, 1895, Detroit began operating a municipal electric plant to supply power for its streetlights. This ended a five-year running battle between Pingree and the private lighting interests. Pingree had used two issues to win his battle. His main argument against the private control of electricity was that it cost too much. Pingree gathered voluminous information on the costs of power in other cities, and he established that Detroit's service was overly expensive and unreliable. His argument was persuasive, but not sufficient. Corruption became the issue that tipped the scales in his favor. In April 1892, Pingree walked into a city council meeting waving a roll of bills and dramatically accused the Detroit Electric Light and Power Company of bribing council members. As usual, the mayor had the room packed with his working-class supporters. With Pingree's followers whipped into a dangerous mood, the council members hastily capitulated.

Pingree used similar tactics in his fights with the gas and telephone interests. To force the Detroit Gas Company to lower gas prices, he first initiated a campaign to educate the public on the high price of Detroit's gas, which, he claimed, was more than a third higher than the price charged by the same company in five other cities. When his attempt to force lower prices was stalled in the courts, he got the public works board to deny permits to excavate streets for the purpose of laying gas lines. When the gas company attempted to excavate anyway, Pingree had the owners arrested. "Possession is a great point," argued Pingree. "Let them get their gas systems connected and then they could float their $8,000,000 of stock in New York City and become too powerful for the city to control. Detroit would be helpless in the hands of corporations as never before in her history."[67]

Pingree continued his campaign, encouraging users not to pay their full gas bills. As public resistance against the Detroit Gas Company mounted, investors' confidence in the company plummeted, initiating a plunge in the company's stock values. Even after Southern Pacific Railroad magnate Samuel Huntington became the company's principal investor, it was impossible to hold stock prices, and Huntington negotiated an agreement to lower the price of gas from $1.50 a cubic foot to $0.80.

In his fourth term as mayor, Pingree took on the Bell Telephone Company. Again, the issue was high prices and inadequate service. This time he helped organize a competing phone company that charged less than half

Bell's rate. The new Detroit Telephone Company soon attracted twice as many customers as Bell. In response, Bell initiated a rate war and began to improve its equipment and service. By 1900, when Michigan Bell bought out Detroit Telephone, Detroit had the lowest telephone rates and the most extensive residential use of any large American city.

No other American city accomplished such a broad program of social reform as Detroit. During his last two terms, Pingree traveled around the country making speeches and gathering information. He wrote prolifically. He inspired reformers elsewhere, and his national prominence helped him win reform campaigns in his own city. After winning four terms as mayor of Detroit, Pingree went on to win election twice as governor of Michigan, where he continued to fight for social reform.

Pingree recognized the necessity of building a broad-based political coalition. He so assiduously courted ethnic voters that by his fourth term he had even won the dependable Irish away from the Democratic machine. In effect, Pingree put together his own machine, filling patronage jobs with his own supporters and firing his opponents. However, "he absolutely refused to tolerate dishonesty or theft."[68] Unlike Detroit's machine politicians, who regularly exploited ethnic hostilities to win votes in their wards, Pingree appealed to the unity of interests of working-class Poles, Germans, and Irish and the middle class. In short, he was aware that to accomplish reform it was necessary to "recruit a coalition of power sufficient for his purpose."[69] A great many political machines had likewise constructed coalitions sufficient to bring about the social reforms that would have benefited their immigrant constituents. However, they were more interested in furthering their own careers than in achieving reform.

❖ MACHINE POLITICS IN CONTEMPORARY CITIES

While boss-controlled political machines are now rare, machine-style politics is ubiquitous in cities of all sizes. Cities are once again magnets for millions of immigrants and minorities. In this context it is hard to avoid asking the question: Would recent immigrants and ethnic and racial minorities benefit if they were able to build political machines?

As vehicles of class compromise, the classic machines brokered a deal in which poor immigrants and economic elites each gave up something and each got something in return. Corporate elites gave direct power over local government to working-class ethnic politicians who controlled patronage armies, supported in part by income from bribes and contributions paid by the wealthy. In return, machine politicians essentially promised to leave corporate elites alone in their pursuit of private wealth. Machine politicians generally supported a limited role for government in urban development. The compromise involved a recognition of distinct spheres of influence—a clear separation between market and government. This compromise was important in managing the tension between capitalism, with its attendant inequalities, and popular democracy.[70]

In the end, political machines and their ethnic supporters gave up a great deal and got relatively little in return. Rather than passing out favors and low-paying jobs, machines could have, like Pingree, attacked the practices that inflated the cost of urban services and infrastructure. They could have forged an alliance with labor unions to pursue a program designed to modify dangerous working conditions, long hours, child labor, and low pay. Instead, the machines actively undercut the ability of immigrants to identify and organize around common objectives.

There are a number of reasons to believe that today's city residents can expect even less from machines. The classic urban machines prospered in rapidly growing industrial cities.[71] These cities required massive expenditures on roads, bridges, sewers, streetcar systems, schools, and parks. The resulting government jobs, contracts, and franchises were traded for the political support necessary to maintain the party organizations. Like the industrial city decades ago, contemporary cities still hold large numbers of needy people. A potential electoral base exists to support machine organizations. What cities now lack are the resources necessary to bind machines together. Advances in transportation and communications have freed business from reliance on the inner cities. The exodus of industry and the middle class to the suburbs has deprived the cities of critical tax sources and borrowing power.[72]

Even if they possessed sufficient resources, it would be extremely difficult for today's politicians to assemble the patronage and other material rewards necessary to build true machine organizations. City services have been bureaucratized and merit employment systems have been put in place so that patronage can no longer be regularly delivered on the basis of personal or political relationships. Even in the city of Chicago when it was ruled by the Daley machine, decisions on the distribution of city services relied heavily on "technical-rational criteria" that were "largely devoid of explicit political content."[73]

The urban machines that lasted beyond the 1920s relied heavily on intergovernmental political relationships and federal aid for their survival.[74] After the New Deal, many machines skillfully used federal programs to expand their resource base.[75] Those days are past. Since the late 1970s, the federal government has sharply cut grants to cities. Adding to their fiscal problems, central cities have generally been in a period of population and fiscal contraction.

All this does not necessarily mean that the political control of cities is "a hollow prize."[76] There are important policies that minority mayors could implement to advance the interests of their constituents. For example, affirmative action hiring and city residency requirements for city jobs can favor city minority residents over nonminority workers who live in the suburbs—and who often take central city jobs. Minority contractor set asides can help to insure that a percentage of jobs on public projects go to minorities.[77] City agencies can be made to be more sensitive to poor and minority constituents. In Chicago during the administration of Harold Washington from 1983 to

1987, capital improvement programs were designated for neighborhoods; loan programs were put in place to assist businesses owned by minorities and women; the city made a commitment to purchase 25 percent of its services from minority-owned and women-owned businesses; and job training and recruitment programs were put in place to reach out to unemployed people.[78]

City governments are still capable of making decisions and commanding resources that affect the lives of city residents. City politics, however, will not likely proceed again on the basis of simple trade-offs and favors for individual constituents. If cities are, once again, to become the locus of strong political organizations, those organizations will have to attend to national political issues far more than the machines of the past ever did.

**CHAPTER
4**

DEMOCRACY VERSUS EFFICIENCY: THE REFORM LEGACY

❖ THE REFORM IMPULSE

In 1902 George Washington Plunkitt of Tammany Hall pontificated that reformers "were mornin' glories—looked lovely in the mornin' and withered up in a short time, while the regular machines went on flourishin' forever, like fine old oaks."[1] At the time Plunkitt delivered himself of that poetic homily, he was essentially correct. Through the last quarter of the nineteenth century, reform movements sprang up in many cities as the reformers attempted to dismantle the party organizations that thrived on immigrant votes. These movements tended to be short-lived and sporadic, lacking an organizational base or sustaining cause, exactly as Plunkitt observed. Reformers were often successful in persuading state legislatures to take budgeting and the administration of some services out of the hands of aldermen and city councils and put them under the control of boards dominated by a "better class" of people. They were not able, however, to undercut the electoral influence of the immigrants. Aldermen from the wards still made important decisions over such matters as streetcar and utility franchises, construction contracts, and overall tax policy. Plenty of patronage jobs and plenty of money, the stuff of machine politics, were bound up in these decisions.

To many middle- and upper-class Americans, cities seemed to be in the hands of criminals who plundered the public for their own personal gain. Although reformers in Cleveland, New York, Chicago, and other cities sometimes did throw machine politicians out of office, often by prosecuting them in the courts, the politicians always made a comeback as soon as the reform fervor died down. Members of the upper and middle classes generally shared Englishman James Bryce's view that "the government of cities is the one conspicuous failure of the United States."[2] Upper-class Anglo-Saxon Protestants regarded politics as untouchable and unclean:

> The privilege seeker has pervaded our political life. For his own profit he has willfully befouled the sources of political power. Politics, which should offer a career inspiring to the noblest thoughts and calling for the most patriotic efforts of which man is capable, he has . . . transformed into a series of sordid transactions between those who buy and those who sell governmental action.[3]

The reformers' concern about political corruption was entwined with their more generalized fear of the corrupting moral influence of foreign immigrants—the so-called Great Unwashed. Americans had been nurturing a fear of the immigrants for more than half a century. An 1851 issue of the *Massachusetts Teacher* asked:

> The constantly increasing influx of foreigners . . . continues to be a cause of serious alarm to the most intelligent of our people. What will be the ultimate effect of this vast and unexampled immigration . . . ? Will it, like the muddy Missouri, as it pours its waters into the clear Mississippi and contaminates the whole united mass, spread ignorance and vice, crime and disease, through our native population?[4]

In late century, while upper-class Victorians expressed their emotional repression by draping piano legs in cloth lest these provoke erotic thoughts and by wrapping their women in bustles and corsets, they observed the Irish and German immigrants drinking beer on Sundays and read newspaper accounts of prostitution, gambling, and public drunkenness in the immigrant wards. Protestant zealots secured city and state statutes abolishing prostitution, gambling, and Sunday liquor sales. To teach immigrant children middle-class versions of dress, speech, manners, and discipline, reformers passed laws requiring school attendance and raised the upper age limit for mandatory schooling. Truant officers were hired to search for wayward youth.

The vicious reaction against immigrants further aggravated class, racial, and religious tensions. Immigrants were compared to the Goths and Vandals who invaded Europe in the second century A.D. In his book, *Our Country,* the Reverend Josiah Strong accused the immigrants of defiling the Sabbath, spreading illiteracy and crime, and corrupting American culture and morals. Gathered into the cities, he said the immigrants provided "a very paradise for demagogues" who ruled by manipulating the "appetites and prejudices" of the rabble.[5]

The spatial segregation of social classes within the cities exacerbated middle- and upper-class nervousness about the immigrants. By the turn of the century, all large cities contained overcrowded immigrant ghettos near their centers, with middle- and upper-class neighborhoods on their peripheries. Economic activities were still concentrated in downtown districts, so the more affluent city residents could hardly escape seeing, on their way to work and shop, the drab tenements, dirty streets, and littered alleys where the immigrants lived.

To a considerable degree, municipal reform arose from class tensions. Most reformers were members of the upper class or exceptionally well-educated members of the middle class. The reforms they advocated were designed to enhance the influence of the "better classes" and to undercut the immigrants' electoral influence in city politics. Where they were successful, they also undermined local democracy. As we shall see, we still live with the effects of their reforms.

❖ THE REFORM ENVIRONMENT

The municipal reform movement was an important component of the reform period labeled by historians as the Progressive Era. A sharp reaction to the social problems spawned by industrialization swept the country in the first decades of the twentieth century. The corruption of city government seemed matched only by the corruption of big business. Excesses of wealth existed side by side with grinding poverty in the immigrant wards. Newly developed mass media brought a heightened awareness about these conditions to upper-class and educated middle-class readers. By the turn of the century, falling paper prices and technical advances in rapid printing made it possible to produce high-quality mass-circulation newspapers and magazines. During the 1890s, newspaper circulation doubled and then tripled. A multitude of new periodicals appeared. All that was required to develop a mass audience was a way to popularize the press. "Muckraking" was such a technique. Crusading journalists investigated and reported "inside stories" exposing corruption in city machines and targets far beyond the cities. They wrote about organized vice. They also wrote about pervasive corruption in the national government, big business, the stock market, and the drug and meat packing industries.

Beginning with its September 1902 issue, *McClure's* magazine printed a series of seven articles by Lincoln Steffens, telling lurid stories of municipal corruption in the nation's big cities. In October, *McClure's* carried an article by Ida Tarbell exposing corporate corruption and profiteering by John D. Rockefeller's Standard Oil Company. The stories were an instant success, revealing a nearly insatiable appetite in the public for sensational accounts of wrongdoing in business and government. A new mass circulation formula was discovered. Over the next few years *Munsey's, Everybody's, Success, Collier's, Saturday Evening Post, Ladies' Home Journal, Hampton's, Pearson's, Cosmopolitan,* and dozens of daily newspapers carried stories that appealed to the popular feeling that political, economic, and social institutions had become corrupted. Big business was accused of producing unsafe and shoddy goods, fixing prices, and crushing competition. There were exposés of fraudulent practices in banking; heart-wrenching accounts of women and children working at long, tedious, and dangerous jobs in factories and sweatshops; stories about urban poverty, prostitution, white slavery, and business-government collusion to protect vice.

An outpouring of popular books played on the same themes. Steffens collected his *McClure's* articles together into a best-selling book, *The Shame of the Cities,* published in 1904. Other popular titles included *The Greatest Trust in the World,* an exposé of price-fixing and collusion in the steel industry; *The Story of Life Insurance;* and *The Treason of the Senate,* which detailed systematic bribery of U.S. Senators. Several important novelists entered the field. In *An American Tragedy* Theodore Dreiser stood Horatio Alger on his head by describing the corrupting influence of greed on a self-made small-town boy. In *The Financier* Dreiser's theme was the ruthless drive for power and wealth, using the Chicago streetcar magnate Charles Yerkes as his model. Upton Sinclair's *The Jungle* dealt with a Lithuanian immigrant's fight to survive in corrupt and chaotic Chicago. Eventually his wife becomes a prostitute, his children die, and he becomes a socialist revolutionary. Sinclair vividly portrayed the nauseating conditions in Chicago's meat packing industry. His book catalyzed a crusade that resulted in the creation of the U.S. Food and Drug Administration in 1905. Dreiser's *Sister Carrie* and David Graham Phillip's *Susan Lenox* both played on the theme of how the impersonal forces of urban life victimized young women.

Whether focusing on specific ills or on generalized conditions, the literature produced by the "muckrakers"—an epithet applied to them in 1906 by President Theodore Roosevelt, referring to a character in John Bunyan's 1645 book *Pilgrim's Progress* who was too busy raking muck to look up and see the stars—was influential in building popular interest in reform. Although investigations by reform organizations were often dull and unexciting to the average citizen, the muckrakers' stories provided a feeling of drama and urgency.

In this environment a multitude of organizations sprang up to regulate business practices, improve working conditions, impose standards on the professions, and reform government. Business leaders organized the National Civic Federation in 1900, mainly as an attempt to reduce union agitation by sponsoring workers' compensation and other minor social insurance schemes.[6] The National Child Labor Committee, organized in 1904 to fight for child labor legislation. In 1910 the National Housing Association brought together housing reform groups from many cities to agitate for building codes. A large number of public officials' associations and municipal research bureaus came into existence specifically to promote municipal reform: the National Association of Port Authorities, the Municipal Finance Officers Association, the American Association of Park Superintendents, the Conference of City Managers, the National Short Ballot Association. Groups such as these multiplied in the first ten years of the century.

Though government corruption had provoked campaigns to "throw the rascals out" in a few cities during the 1870s and 1880s, the issues had usually been local and the remedies specific to the situation. Several developments in the 1890s transformed reform into a national movement promoting change in local government structures. In response to widespread government corruption and social and physical deterioration in the immigrant wards, citizens' groups sprang up in most cities to agitate for improved public services and honesty in government. The problems faced by the reformers varied little from one city to another. Like-minded reformers from different cities soon began to exchange advice and information about their efforts. These informational networks subsequently led to the formation of national reform organizations.

In 1894, delegates to the First Annual Conference for Good City Government met in Philadelphia to create the first national municipal reform organization, the National Municipal League. The delegates to the conference were united in the belief that democratic institutions in the cities were corrupted by machine politicians and their immigrant constituents. There was, however, little agreement about the measures that could be taken to change this condition. "We are not unlike patients assembled in a hospital," one of the participants put it, "examining together and describing to each other our sore places."[7] After the formation of the National Municipal League, the nationalization of reform proceeded quickly. Within two years there were 180 local chapters affiliated with the League and, by the turn of the century, all large cities had member organizations. In their yearly meetings reformers from all over the country got a chance to compare notes. By its November 1899 meeting, the members of the National Municipal League reached agreement on a model municipal charter containing the elements making up the reformers' ideal of "good government." The charter was meant to serve as a blueprint for reform in cities everywhere.

To abolish the machines, the model charter recommended that ward elections be abandoned in favor of at-large elections, so that all city councilors would represent the entire city as a unit rather than each alderman or councilor representing an individual ward. It also recommended nonpartisan elections, which would abolish the party label on election ballots. It recommended that most administrative positions be placed under civil service appointment procedures so that party officials would not be able to use public jobs for patronage. The League also thought that local elections should be held at different times than national and state elections so that national parties would have no influence on local affairs.[8]

All of these measures sought to undercut the basic organizing feature of machine politics: the political party. But besides eliminating the machines, the reformers wanted to streamline local government operations to make them more efficient. The model charter recommended that a small, unicameral city council replace the bicameral councils then existing in most cities (many city governments had been modeled on the national government, with its two legislative chambers). It also encouraged reformers to implement strong mayor governments, giving the mayor the power to appoint top administrators and to veto legislation. The supposition behind this reform was that with power centralized in the hands of the mayor, voters would be able to hold the mayor accountable for the city's overall governance. Thus, individual city council members would no longer be able to escape responsibility by blaming each other. The League also encouraged city reformers to seek "home rule" charters from their state legislatures so cities could be governed without special legislative actions by the state legislatures.

The municipal reformers shared a conviction that it was their responsibility to educate and instruct the lower classes about good government. These reformers placed their faith in rule by educated, upper- and middle-class Americans and, increasingly, in administration by trained professionals. These convictions underlay all of the specific reforms advocated beginning in the 1890s and implemented over the ensuing decades.

❖ THE CAMPAIGNS AGAINST MACHINE RULE

The municipal reformers' principal target was machine politics. For this reason, a great number of strategies designed to accomplish "good government" attempted to weaken and dismantle party control over elections. Some reformers went so far as to question the wisdom of universal suffrage, arguing that illiterate immigrants in the cities hopelessly corrupted elections. Semiofficial sanction even existed for this view. The Tilden Commission, appointed by the New York legislature to investigate the Tweed Ring scandals in New York City, recommended in 1878 that suffrage be restricted to those who owned property.[9] The commission's report was reprinted in an 1899 issue of the National Municipal League's magazine *Municipal Affairs* and was read with approval by those reformers who shared the view that a debased, ignorant electorate accounted for the city's problems. The rationale for disenfranchising the masses was stated by the first president of Cornell University, Andrew D. White, who wrote in an 1890 issue of *Forum* magazine that:

> A city is a corporation; . . . as a city it has nothing whatever to do with general political interests. . . . The questions in a city are not political questions. . . . The work of a city being the creation and control of the city property, it should logically be managed as a piece of property by those who have created it, who have a title to it, or a real substantial part in it, . . . [and not by] a crowd of illiterate peasants, freshly raked in from the Irish bogs, or Bohemian mines, or Italian robber nests.[10]

Although taking the vote out of immigrant hands appealed to some reformers, late in the nineteenth century it was hardly feasible to attempt such a drastic remedy. To wage an all-out campaign on this issue would surely have invited a strong counterattack from many groups, including many who supported reform causes. From the constitutional period until the Jacksonian voting reforms of the 1820s and 1830s, most states restricted the vote to owners of property. The abolishment of these restrictions had been hailed as a triumph for democratic reform. It seemed unlikely that property qualifications could ever again again be attached to the vote. The 1912 charter of Phoenix, Arizona, restricted voting in municipal elections to taxpayers, but the state courts invalidated this restriction as unconstitutional.[11] Even before Phoenix's attempt, it was clear that the reformers would have to find less direct methods to reduce the influence of immigrant voters.

Most reformers did not oppose voter participation by the immigrants per se. Rather, they were convinced that elections were run in a corrupt fashion and that machine politicians victimized their immigrant constituents. Without doubt, municipal elections were chaotic and corrupt. Few election laws existed, and those that did exist were rarely enforced. Nominating procedures were not regulated at all. To select candidates for public office, political parties held city conventions or ward caucuses according to their own changeable rules, often on short notice, and often at locations known only to insiders. It was not unusual for caucuses to be held in the backrooms of saloons owned by ward bosses. Corruption was so pervasive in big city elections that few results could be trusted.

> This was the period of massive voting frauds. In the elections of 1868 and 1872, 8 percent more people voted in New York state than were registered. In 1910, when the New York City vote was challenged and recounted, 50 percent of the votes were found to be fraudulent. In New Jersey, glass ballot jars had to replace the wooden boxes to prevent vote stuffing. In Pennsylvania and Michigan, gangs of mobsters moved from polling place to polling place beating up the opposition and voting at will. Indeed so numerous were the instances of fraud that practically all voting statistics from this period are suspect.[12]

There were few legal constraints on the election process. Fictitious and repeat voters, false counting, and stuffed ballot boxes were regular features of city elections. A ruse commonly employed by the machines on election day was to vote "repeaters" several times under various names. A Philadelphia politician once boasted that the signers of the Declaration of Independence were machine loyalists: "'These men,' he said, 'the fathers of American liberty, voted down here once.' 'And,' he added with a sly grin, 'they vote here yet.'"[13]

Politicians sometimes completed the ballot for voters or accompanied them into the voting booth. "Farmer Jones," a member of the Chicago machine in the 1890s, revealed to an inquiring reformer how he guaranteed voter loyalty.

> [The reformer asked,] "When you got the polling stations in your hands, what did you do?"
> "Voted our men, of course."
> "And the negroes, how did they vote?"
> "They voted as they ought to have voted. They had to."

"... how could you compel those people to vote against their will?"
"They understood, and besides," said he, "there was not a man voted in that booth that I did not know how he voted before he put the paper in the judges' hands."[14]

The most direct and effective means of securing electoral loyalty was simply to buy the vote. The 1896 election in the First Ward of Chicago was conducted thusly:

> The bars were open all night and the brothels were jammed. By ten o'clock the next morning, though, the saloons were shut down, not in concession to the reformers, but because many of the bartenders and owners were needed to staff the First Ward field organization. The Bath, Hinky Dink and their aides ran busily from polling place to polling place, silver bulging in their pockets into which they dug frequently and deeply.
> The effort was not in vain, and outcome was gratifying.[15]

When peaceful means of guaranteeing election results failed, machine politicians sometimes resorted to intimidation and violence. Tom Pendergast, who inherited his brother Jim's Kansas City Democratic organization after Jim died, regularly used coercion to control elections. In the summer of 1914, Pendergast's organization used a mixture of bribes and violence to get out the vote for a proposed railway franchise. He "used money, repeat voters, and toughs to produce North Side majorities that pushed the franchise to victory."[16] Workers in his organization distributed liquor and money in black and Italian neighborhoods. They "paid men to vote under assumed names; and election judges who questioned some of those dragged off the streets and out of flop houses to vote were intimidated and abused, both verbally and physically."[17] In 1934, four persons were killed by gangsters on election day. Two years later, an attempted assassination and massive voter fraud led to an investigation that eventually resulted in 259 convictions for election fraud and criminal behavior.

The Chicago ward boss John Powers intimidated voters and threatened landlords, merchants, and other business owners with loss of licenses unless they supported him in his 1898 campaign for alderman.[18] "Hinky Dink" Kenna and "Bathhouse John" Coughlin of Chicago's First Ward defended their loyal lower-class constituents but routinely harassed opponents. During the 1920s, organized crime and politics in Chicago became almost synonymous. Assassination and "hits" were visited upon meddling politicians who stood outside the inner circle of men controlling and protecting illegal liquor, speakeasies, prostitution, and gambling.

Ed Crump, the boss of Memphis, Tennessee, won his first mayoral election in 1909 by watching the polls himself. He personally interfered with the use of marked ballots by a machine he was opposing, in one case by hitting a voter in the face.[19] In Pittsburgh's state and city elections of 1933, the Democrats and Republicans—both rightly fearing fraud by the other party—mobilized opposing armies of poll watchers. The state police were called in to keep the peace, and lawyers and judges stood by to provide quick court action.[20]

In the late 1890s the reformers introduced several measures to control election fraud. The key reforms aimed at individual voters included:

- *Voter registration and literacy requirements.* These requirements reduced repeat voting and stopped the practice of importing voters for an election. By 1920, almost all states had imposed registration laws.

- *Australian ballot.* This was a ballot that could be marked only by the individual voter and cast in secrecy. Before its introduction in the 1880s, ballots were printed by the parties and often cast publicly. They were even handed already marked to voters. Use of the Australian ballot became universal after the turn of the century.

- *Nonpartisan elections.* Reformers fought hard to remove party labels of any kind from many state, and most municipal, election ballots. Where they succeeded, voters had only one clue as to how they should vote: the printed name of the individual candidate.

The effect of these reforms was to reduce voting participation by immigrants and less educated voters. Twenty-five percent of the white males of voting age in the United States in 1900 were first-generation immigrants, and two-thirds of the immigrants had come from non-English-speaking countries. In the cities the proportion of foreign-born immigrants was much higher, often comprising well over half of all voters. Before reform they might ask for help in filling out the ballot or even cast a premarked one. When they showed up to vote, their eligibility was assured. Now they had to register to vote in writing, often months before an election. And when they went to the polling station, they now faced an election judge, a secret voting booth, and a printed ballot they might not be able to read. Machine politicians frequently got around the problems of the secret ballot by controlling polling places, but these actions exposed them to the possibility of criminal prosecution.

The effect of reforms in the southern states was even more extreme, for voters did not receive help from precinct captains or ward committeemen in registering to vote or in looking over a sample ballot. In the South there was an explicitly racist motive for adopting the Australian ballot, as revealed by a Democratic campaign song popular in Arkansas in 1892:

> The Australian Ballot works like a charm,
> It makes them think and scratch,
> And when a Negro gets a ballot
> He has certainly got his match.

Illiteracy among southern white males varied between 8 percent and 19 percent; for black males it varied between 39 percent and 61 percent. The

Australian ballot drastically reduced voter participation by both blacks and poor whites even before other hurdles for voters were erected in the South, such as poll taxes and literacy tests—liberally supplemented by Ku Klux Klan violence.

By 1905, voter registration laws had been placed on the books in most states.[21] From 1905 to 1920, states and localities set up election boards, made it illegal to vote more than once, and tried to define the legitimate uses of campaign funds. Although enforcement of all these laws was sporadic—the machines continued to control prosecutors and the courts in many places—the existence of new laws provided the basis for investigations and prosecutions when the middle- and upper-class public became aroused about corruption.

In a further attempt to weaken party control of elections, many reformers backed devices designed to open up the political process by taking nominations out of the hands of party caucuses. Wisconsin adopted the first statewide primary law in 1903, and twelve other states followed suit in the next ten years.[22] The popular election of U.S. senators had already been implemented in twenty-nine states by 1909; state legislatures still selected senators in the rest. The opposition to such undemocratic procedures finally forced the U.S. Senate to propose the Seventeenth Amendment, which provided for popular election of senators in all states. A wave of state laws also implemented the initiative, the referendum, and the recall, all devices to allow voters to bypass public officials.

Within the cities, once electoral reform was accomplished reformers focused their attention on the structure and operations of machine politics. It was obvious that machine politicians derived their strength from the ethnic neighborhoods and that the overall unity of the machines was furthered by the immigrants' ability to identify a party label on the election ballot. The reformers' two most popular strategies—nonpartisan ballots and at-large elections were frontal assaults on machine politics.

Municipal reformers felt that party labels encouraged bloc voting and blind loyalty to a political organization. They wanted a more "rational," educated voter who could "accumulate and carry in his head the brief list of personal preferences and do without the guidance of party names and symbols on the ballot."[23] The reformers asserted the it was the responsibility of citizens to educate themselves and vote for the best candidates strictly on their merits, not on the basis of party loyalty.

The proposal to remove the party label from election ballots reflected the reformers' conviction that the public interest overrode the preferences of particular ethnic groups or political factions. Reformers generally agreed that the public interest could be defined by one principle: public services should be provided as cheaply and efficiently as possible. To the reformers, cities had no other responsibilities. They asserted that, just as business firms produce a product as cheaply and efficiently as possible, cities should—and could—do the same. Party symbols created the impression that there were political differences when, according to the reformers, everyone had the same fundamental interest. The only legitimate question was which candidate was most qualified to help the city provide services at lowest cost. As Brand Whitlock, the famous reform mayor of Toledo, Ohio, put it:

> It seems almost incredible now that men's minds were ever so clouded, strange that they did not earlier discover how absurd was a system which, in order to enable them the more readily to subjugate themselves, actually printed little woodcuts of birds—roosters and eagles—at the heads of the tickets, so that they might the more easily and readily recognize their masters and deliver their suffrages over to them.[24]

Just as the reformers intended, the nonpartisan ballot made it harder for immigrants to vote as a bloc. Even recognizing their alderman's printed name could be hard for illiterate voters. Recognizing the party symbol on the ballot had been infinitely easier than reading the names of candidates.

Nonpartisan elections affected candidates as well as voters. Working-class candidates had few personal resources to expend on political activities. The party organization supplied campaign money and workers and freed working-class candidates from the necessity of holding a normal job, which would have denied them time for participation in politics. Few politicians in the cities could have started or stayed in politics without a party organization's help. If there were no party organization to pool resources and facilitate coalitions among politicians, people of wealth and social standing could more easily dominate local elections. This result was, in fact, the objective of the nonpartisanship crusade—to make politics once again a calling appropriate to the educated and cultured classes.[25]

Another plank in the reform platform, the proposal to replace wards with at-large elections, was designed to break the link between neighborhoods and machine politicians. Andrew White complained that "wards largely controlled by thieves and robbers can send thieves and robbers," and "the vote of a single tenement house, managed by a professional politician, will neutralize the vote of an entire street of well-to-do citizens."[26] The remedy was to have all of the city council candidates campaign for the votes of all city residents. The entire city would constitute the one and only election district. In this way no candidate could be elected by the voters of one particular neighborhood or ethnic group. Gone would be the politics of trade-offs, logrolling, and compromise among legislators representing their own neighborhoods, ethnic groups, and wards. "Special interest" politics would supposedly give way to "public interest" politics. One observer sympathetic to these reform ideas thought that "enlightened" politics was virtually impossible so long as elections were held in wards:

> [F]or decades the election of councils by wards had superimposed a network of search for parochial favors, of units devoted to partisan spoils, and of catering to ethnic groups that time and again had either defeated comprehensive city programs or loaded them with irrelevant spoils and ill-conceived ward projects. The ward and precinct were the heart of machine control, and the councils so elected were usually also infested with corruption, however acceptable the councilors may have been to the voters of their wards.[27]

Small wards potentially gave even relatively small ethnic and racial groups leverage at the ballot box. Lithuanians, for example, might be able to send a Lithuanian alderman to the city council, even though they constituted a tiny proportion of the city's total population. Small wards multiplied the points of access through which groups and individuals could influence public officials.

Citywide, at-large elections exerted an opposite effect. If the whole city is one big electoral district, candidates representing ethnic and racial groups clustered in specific neighborhoods are handicapped, for they are forced to appeal to a complex array of political and social groups in many different areas and neighborhoods to be elected. Because they are able to raise the funds required to reach a large and diverse audience, wealthier politicians representing middle- and upper-class areas and business groups have a campaign advantage in citywide elections. Campaigns covering an entire city are costly and time consuming for individual candidates. In such a system, wealth and social prominence are important ingredients of political success.

These effects were well known to reformers, which explains why the National Municipal League's model city charter of 1899 recommended at-large elections and nonpartisan ballots. Every subsequent model charter of the League contained these two features, and over the years the League carefully compiled annual statistics to track the adoption of these reforms across the nation.

There were other reform proposals for undercutting machine rule. Civil service was particularly important. Aimed at the machines' practice of rewarding loyal supporters with patronage jobs, civil service was proposed as a system that provided supposedly objective standards for hiring municipal employees. Written and oral civil service examinations were to be the sole basis for hiring decisions, and a system of tenure and seniority was supposed to make employees safe from political firings. The rise of modern public bureaucracies began with these reforms.

In the first two decades of the twentieth century, nonpartisan, at-large elections and civil service reforms were implemented in cities throughout the nation. Reformers were least successful in the big cities with complex electorates, where middle- and upper-class voters did not constitute an electoral majority. Smaller cities, however, especially those in the Midwest and the West, almost always adopted reform items in their new charters. In these communities, lower-class ethnic voters were invariably outnumbered, and therefore when reform charter proposals were put before the voters, they usually passed. This fact, together with the aggressive promotion of reform by the National Municipal League, made it difficult for voters to resist the clarion call of reform, even though there was substantial popular recognition that many reforms were antidemocratic. In many states the reformers bypassed the voters entirely by persuading state legislatures to abolish ward elections for all cities in the state.

In the bigger cities, campaigns to adopt nonpartisan, at-large elections and civil service were nearly always coupled with an antimachine, anticorruption rhetoric. Such rhetoric handed victory to the reformers in several big cities. Nonpartisan, at-large elections were instituted in Los Angeles (1908), Boston (1909), Akron, Ohio (1915), and Detroit (1918).[28] In smaller towns and cities,

where machines did not exist, reform was sold as a way to streamline government and make it efficient. The residents of smaller cities viewed government
as, at best, a necessary evil that should provide such essential public services as
water, sewage disposal, streets, and perhaps libraries and community centers.
"Consensus" politics—which, of course, excluded the ethnic and racial
minorities that might be present—characterized politics in small towns then as
it does now.

The electoral rules preferred by the municipal reformers are much in evidence in contemporary cities. Before 1910, nonpartisan elections were almost
unknown. By 1929 they were utilized in 57 percent of the cities of over 30,000
population.[29] By the 1960s many states required their cities to use nonpartisan
elections; these included Minnesota, California, Alaska, and most of the western states. In ten more states nonpartisan ballots were used in 90 percent or
more of the cities (the exceptions usually being cities above a specified size). In
the West, 94 percent of cities used nonpartisan elections. The eastern seaboard
was the only region of the country where more cities used partisan than nonpartisan elections. Among the nation's cities with over 500,000 people today,
85 percent use partisan elections. Reforms generally go together; most cities
with nonpartisan elections use at-large rather than district or ward elections.

Reformed electoral systems were originally designed to reduce electoral
influence by ethnics and minority factions. There is plenty of evidence that the
reformers' intentions were generally realized. Before the adoption of nonpartisan and at-large elections, working-class candidates, many of them socialists,
were elected to city offices in dozens of cities.[30] At-large elections made it
much more difficult for this kind of candidate to win. In the 1909 Dayton,
Ohio, elections, socialists elected two aldermen and three assessors from
wards; these candidates received only 25 percent of the city vote. Before the
1913 election, Dayton implemented citywide elections and abolished ward
boundaries. In 1913, the socialists received 35 percent of the popular vote and,
in 1917, 44 percent, but because all candidates were elected at-large, in neither
year were the socialists able to elect a single candidate. Similarly, in 1911,
Pittsburgh changed to at-large elections, with the result that upper-class business leaders and professionals pushed lower- and middle-class groups out of
their previous places on the city council and the school board.[31]

St. Louis provides an excellent example of these two electoral systems at
work. The members of the city's Board of Aldermen are placed in office
through partisan elections in each of the city's twenty-eight wards (see Figure
4-1). Members of the St. Louis Board of Education, in contrast, are elected by
placing their names on a nonpartisan ballot, and all are elected at-large.

In a city that in 1970 was 41 percent black and that had been largely abandoned by the middle class, with few exceptions race had effectively replaced
ethnicity as the basis of neighborhood identification. Ten blacks sat on the
city's Board of Aldermen after the 1977 municipal elections (and eleven by
1991). All of them represented predominantly black wards located in the
north-central part of the city. All of the eighteen majority white wards elected
white aldermen. (As in many cities, alderman is an official term in the St.
Louis city charter and does not refer exclusively to males.)

Figure 4.1 Racial Composition of Municipal Wards in the City of St. Louis, 1977

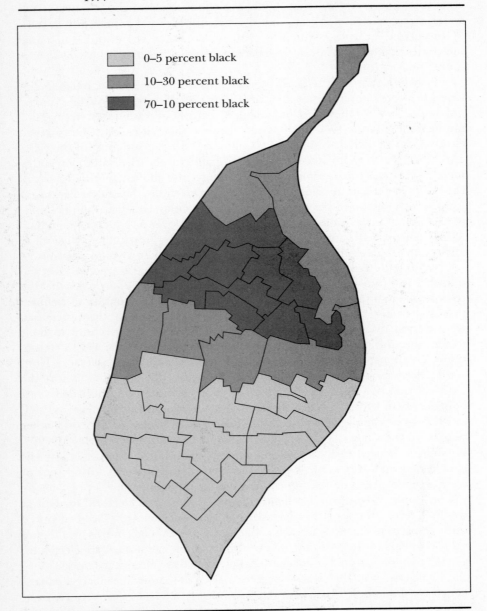

0–5 percent black

10–30 percent black

70–10 percent black

Because the school board candidates ran at-large, the composition of the school board was entirely different. In the 1977 election, all five seats on the ballot went to white, middle-class candidates. In a city where 70 percent of the public school enrollment was black, not a single African-American candidate was able to win office in the racially tinged election. Not only were the three black candidates overpowered by the electoral power of the white majority, but three other would-be black candidates were excluded from the ballot through the stringent enforcement of candidate filing rules.

The impact of nonpartisan, at-large elections is readily apparent from the St. Louis case. In the late 1970s the highly concentrated black minority was excluded from effective participation in the governing of the local schools, even though more than two-thirds of the students in the city school system were black. The ward representation used to elect aldermen, in contrast, assured that blacks would be represented in city hall. The interests of the black minority, when they diverged from those of the white majority, could be articulated in the Board of Aldermen, but not in the Board of Education.

❖ "EFFICIENCY AND ECONOMY" IN MUNICIPAL AFFAIRS

In their attempts to dismantle machine politics, reformers aimed to change the institutional structure of local government as well as to reduce the influence of the immigrants. Early in the municipal reform movement, the catchwords for good government became efficiency and economy. When he addressed the delegates to the First Annual Conference for Good City Government in 1894, Theodore Roosevelt urged them to go beyond their moral outrage at the way things were being run to find ways of streamlining and improving government: "There are two gospels I always want to preach to reformers. . . . The first is the gospel of morality; the next is the gospel of efficiency. . . . I don't think I have to tell you to be upright, but I do think I have to tell you to be practical and efficient."[32]

Actually, the reformers did not need such advice. Municipal reformers were hard at work searching for a theory of good government that would show them how to govern cities. If they succeeded at "kicking the rascals out," they needed to know what to do with their inheritance.

By the late 1890s, the municipal reformers had managed to develop such a theory. The reformers held that there was a public interest that could be defined objectively and that, if implemented, would benefit all citizens equally. There were four components of the public interest as they defined it. First, there must be strict budgetary controls to ensure that taxes would be kept as low as possible and public services would be delivered at the lowest possible cost. Second, the day-to-day administration of city government should be strictly separated from "politics." Third, flowing logically from the second, experts with training, experience, and ability should run city services. Fourth, government should be run like a business and the principles of scientific management, then being applied in business organizations, should also be applied to government. Implementing efficient government services was, in sum, simply a question of science and mechanics.

The reformers derived their ideas about how to run government from the scientific management movement that swept the country in the first two decades of the twentieth century. As businesses became larger, accountants, engineers, and corporate managers were busily inventing the structure of the modern corporation. There was considerable interest in discovering ways to elicit the highest possible output from work forces through the coordination and management of workers' time and movement. If science could invent efficient machines, it was thought, then surely it could also discover how to make workers more efficient. What emerged from this search for efficiency was a quasi-military model for business organizations.

In 1911, Frederick Winslow Taylor became world famous with the publication of his book *The Principles of Scientific Management.*[33] Basically, Taylor wanted to apply military discipline and hierarchy to the factory. He said that the movements of individual workers could be studied in order to discover how to organize work tasks to achieve the maximum output with a minimum expenditure of each worker's energy. Taylor promised that his efficiency principles would bring progress, prosperity, and happiness to society by increasing material wealth. By applying the new science of management, Taylor said, it would be possible to achieve harmony and cooperation between owners and workers because both had the same interest in maximizing output. There was even a spiritual side; principles of efficiency would allow each man to develop "his greatest efficiency and prosperity."[34] The essence of the Taylor catechism was that "In the past, the man has been first; in the future the system must be first."[35]

Taylor and his disciples spread their message across the country that "soldiering" (slow work) and inefficiency could be stamped out both at work and at home. Popular magazines featured articles on efficient housework—describing, for instance, how a housewife could sequence the daily chores and arrange appliances and furniture so as to minimize wasted movement in the household. The efficiency movement quickly achieved the status of a secular religion; its gospel of progress through efficiency swept the country.

The efficiency ideal seemed appealing because it promised social betterment without a change in class relationships. To its advocates, it was the perfect revolution, a panacea for hostile employer-worker relations, disastrous economic panics, and poverty and want. Efficiency societies sprang up in all the major cities; efficiency experts were in demand as speakers.[36] Taylorites invaded the factories to implement the gospel of efficiency. They also applied their so-called scientific principles to government operations. Efficiency and scientific management—"business methods"—soon became the model for municipal reform. The appropriateness of efficiency principles to government seemed obvious to the reformers: "The rising prestige of technicians in industry and the increasing demand for new public works and municipal services strengthened the desire for more technical efficiency in local government."[37]

In 1912, Henry Bruerè, the first director of the privately funded New York Bureau of Municipal Research, published a popular book applying efficiency principles to municipal management.[38] Bruerè took the position that much of the mismanagement in New York City "formerly attributed to official corruption and to popular indifference was really due to official and popular ignorance of . . . orderly and scientific procedures."[39] What these procedures amounted to were elaborate accounting and reporting devices designed to codify the responsibilities of city officials, the actions taken by them to carry out their duties, the costs of equipment and personnel, and other details. Bruerè invented a scoring system so that the efficiency of various cities could allegedly be rated and compared. Cities were to be rated on the basis of such questions as: "Is a record kept of all city property?" "How often are the treasurer's books audited?" "Twenty questions on the protection of milk supply." "Is the location of houses of prostitution known and recorded?"[40] In all, Bruerè and his aides used 1,300 standardized questions to rate cities from the "worst governed" to the "best."

In 1913, Bruerè was given the opportunity to make New York City efficient. In November of that year, John Purroy Mitchell, one of Bruerè's closest confidants, was elected New York's mayor. Mitchell appointed Bruerè to the office of City Chamberlain (the mayor's policy adviser). Bruerè immediately launched an attack on Tammany Hall's patronage system. He managed to push through the first large civil service system in the nation. It was explicitly designed as a Taylorite approach to municipal reform.

Bruerè assigned the task of designing the details of the civil service system to Robert Moses, a young staff member at the New York Bureau of Municipal Research. Moses carried out his assignment with the enthusiasm of a Taylorite zealot. He proposed a system in which all municipal employees would be constantly observed at work by trained efficiency experts who would rate each worker's efficiency according to an elaborate mathematical scheme. Various functions and responsibilities of each employee were codified and "given a precise mathematical grade. These grades would . . . be used as a basis for salary increase and promotion."[41] To implement his system, Moses had his assistants draw up rating forms, which he distributed to supervisors. The idea was that each day the supervisors would hand a scorecard to each employee with the employee's mathematical rating. City workers would be paid, promoted, or fired on the basis of the ratings.

Such a system, if implemented, would have fallen of its own weight. There was no way to insure objective ratings. The amount of time required to rate employees would have resulted in a truly enormous civil service administrative staff. Instead of spending the prodigious amounts of money required to hire hundreds of specially trained supervisors, Moses tried to rely on the existing city employees. The 50,000 city employees steadfastly refused to use the reporting forms. They objected that the system was hopelessly time-consuming and unwieldy—and arbitrary and capricious to boot.

The civil service reform attempted during Mitchell's mayoral tenure illuminates the values, assumptions, and foibles of the municipal reformers. As Taylor had put it, "The natural laziness in men is serious, but by far the greatest evil from which both workmen and employers are suffering is the systematic *soldiering* which is almost universal."[42] Reformers were taking on the for-

Figure 4.2   Weak Mayor Government

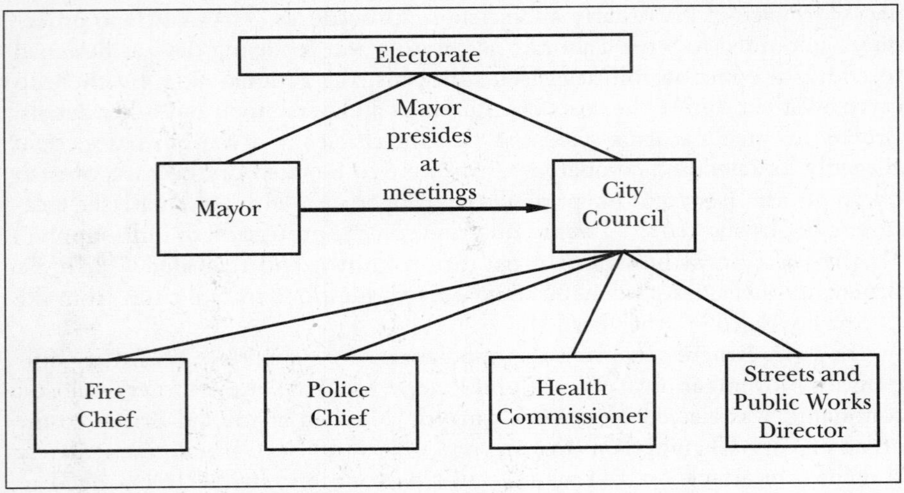

midable task of remaking human beings. Such an ambition could only be based on a distrust of people as they were. The human element was lacking.

Mayor Mitchell, while trying to reorganize city departments and implement civil service procedures, tried to reduce all "unnecessary" programs and expenditures. He instituted cutbacks in school expenditures, asked teachers to work without salaries in the summers, tried to close down special schools for the retarded, and reduced park and recreational expenditures.[43]

New York's civil service proposals proved too draconian even for most reformers. Suitably modified, however, the reform agenda made sense. There was little doubt that more careful administration and well-trained city workers could save money—and result in better service besides. Cities across the country adopted a modified version of efficiency principles through civil service systems. Not only the cities but the federal government and the states entered the field. President Taft appointed a Commission on Economy and Efficiency, and President Wilson later created the Bureau of Efficiency. Between 1911 and 1917, sixteen states established efficiency commissions. These commissions generally recommended more streamlined budgeting procedures, more centralized power in the governor, and the consolidation of state agencies as well as civil service reform.[44]

❖ THE BUSINESS MODEL

With efficiency and scientific management supplying the rationale, it was predictable that the organization of municipal government would be compared with the structure of private business. Reformers pointed out that municipal governments, unlike business firms, were not organized in such a way that decisions could be made efficiently. A history of reform sympathetic with this view described the problem in these terms: "The reformers, who tried to get good men into office, found . . . that, even if they elected a mayor or council, they were intolerably handicapped by the existing systems of municipal government. [Due to] the principles of separation of powers and of checks and balances . . . there was no single elective official or governing body that could be held responsible for effecting reform."[45]

Reformers claimed that the "weak mayor" form of government, which existed in most cities, left too much authority in the hands of a multitude of politicians—aldermen or councilors—as well as specialized boards and commissions. No one person could be held accountable for overall governmental policy. The reformers used organizational charts like the one shown in Figure 4.2 to demonstrate this fact.

It was supposed that businesses, in contrast, were organized with clear lines of authority and responsibility. In businesses there was a separation between policy-making, which was located in a board of directors, and administration, which was left in the hands of professional executive officers. Applied to cities, this model would still leave policy-making to elected officials, who represented their constituents, just as a board of directors in a business presumably represents the interests of the stockholders. But policies would be implemented by administrators, the equivalent of the professional executive officers, applying "scientific" principles of cost accounting and personnel management.

The business model required a strong executive with sufficient power to run the company—or the government. Reformers sought charter reforms to reduce the number of elected officials and expand the mayor's power to appoint most city officials and to veto legislation passed by the council. The mayor would preside at the top of a hierarchical chain of command with clear lines of authority and accountability; the "weak mayor" form was to be replaced by a "strong mayor" form of government, as represented in Figure 4.3. This was the form recommended by the National Municipal League in 1899. The league's model city charter recommended a small city council of five to nine members elected at-large, together with a strong mayor with broad appointive and veto powers. In the first decade of the twentieth century, municipal research bureaus began to design organization charts, which had previously not been applied to government, in order to promote governmental reorganization along these lines.

Now that the reformers felt confident that they knew what to do if they gained control of cities, they attempted to persuade state legislatures to grant them broad "home rule" charters. In contrast to the latter decades of the nineteenth century, when municipal reformers often went to state legislatures to request special legislation to bypass elected officials, they now wanted cities to have full authority to set their own tax rates and decide how and where to provide services. They argued that trained administrators should replace elected and appointed boards and commissions. At its state constitutional convention in 1875, Missouri became the first state to write a general home rule charter for its cities—though the legislature retained control of St. Louis's police budget. Ultimate legal power was still held by the state, but Missouri's cities

Figure 4.3 Strong Mayor Government

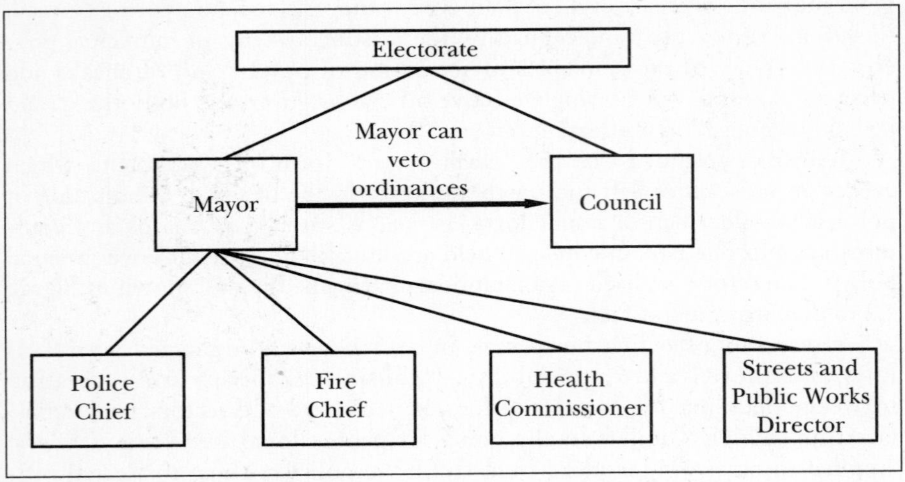

would not have to seek approval for their every action, as long as they stayed within their broad charter powers. Cities could hire new sanitation workers and firefighters, for example, or build a new street without consulting the legislature. The general charter spelled out the range of services to be provided, not such details as salary levels, the location of firehouses and streets, and the number of city employees. The home rule movement, pushed hard by the National Municipal League and other organizations, was quite successful. By 1925, fourteen states had granted home rule charters to their cities. Today, virtually all cities have such charters.

❖ COMMISSION AND MANAGER GOVERNMENT

Galveston, Texas, set up the first municipal government derived explicitly from the business model. In 1894, Galveston's business and professional leaders initiated a campaign to elect business leaders to the city government. In 1895, a coalition of city council members and business leaders secured a charter amendment from the Texas legislature that replaced ward with at-large elections. That reform did not result in the sweeping changes its sponsors had hoped for. Over the next few years, some business leaders were elected to the city council, but they continued to be outvoted by a nonbusiness faction.[46]

The press of emergency, rather than political strength, finally handed the government over to the coalition of business and corporate leaders. On September 8, 1900, hurricane-driven waves breached the seawall protecting Galveston, and the inrushing sea washed over the town, killing 6,000 of the town's 37,000 residents. Half of the property in the city was destroyed. To rebuild the city, prominent businessmen organized the Deepwater Committee and set out to gain full control of the government.

If "a municipality is largely a business corporation," as reformers maintained,[47] it follows that it should be run as such, with the voters being viewed as stockholders and a board of directors responsible to the stockholders. On this principle, the Deepwater Committee drafted an outline of a commission form of government and asked the state legislature to approve it. It was promptly enacted.

The Galveston plan created a five-member commission that exercised the legislative powers previously assigned to the city council and also the administrative authority normally assigned to professional supervisors. Each of the commissioners headed a separate department of government. Such a concentration of authority seemed appropriate in an emergency. Initially, the commission was even given jurisdiction over criminal and civil law enforcement in the city, though this power was subsequently struck down by a state court. Even without that power, however, the commission's authority was considerable. Behind the leadership of five aggressive businessmen, Galveston initiated a vigorous rebuilding program and in the process reduced its debts and restored and improved public services.

The success of Galveston's commission form of government captured the attention of reformers all across the country. Commission government spread like wildfire. Its appeal was obvious: It seemed to streamline government; it held the potential for attracting business and civic leaders back into active government service; and it was a concrete organizational plan around which reformers could rally in challenging machine politics and the urban party bosses. Galveston's performance so impressed business leaders in other Texas cities that they pressed the Texas legislature to allow them to install commission government. By 1907, seven major cities in the state had imitated Galveston's charter, including the large cities of Houston, Dallas, and Fort Worth.

In 1908, Des Moines, Iowa, adopted a charter that became a model for reformers around the country. Besides a five-member commission, Des Moines adopted initiative, referendum, and recall; nonpartisan and at-large elections; and a civil service system. This package of items, labeled the Des Moines Plan by reformers, caught on rapidly. There were twenty-three adoptions of commission government in 1909 and sixty-six in 1910.[48] In September 1915, there were at least 465 cities governed by a commission. By 1920, about 20 percent of all cities with populations of more than 5,000 had adopted it.[49] During these years, a few states made commission government compulsory for their cities, and in most states it became an option for cities that wanted it.

The Des Moines Plan was promoted as a cure-all, sure to bring less taxation, more efficient public services, and a "better class of men" to government. In city after city it was promoted as a means of making government more businesslike. Accordingly, chambers of commerce and other organized business groups became the strongest backers. The Commercial Club successfully pushed Des Moines's new charter in 1907, though, interestingly, the first commissioners voted into office represented a working-class slate—much to the dismay of the business group.[50] In Pennsylvania the Pittsburgh Chamber of Commerce organized a statewide convention of business organizations to plan a lobbying campaign aimed at the state legislature to require cities above a minimum size to adopt commission government. The coalition of bankers, merchants, and manufacturers secured the legislation in 1913.[51] The pattern was similar elsewhere: business leaders trying to transform government into a businesslike operation.

Commission government was not, however, without its problems. To its critics, its worst feature was that it did not fit the business model faithfully enough. A commission was not truly like a board of directors because commissioners engaged in both policy-making and administration. Because each of the commissioners headed a separate department, leadership was often fragmented, with the commissioners refusing to cooperate with one another or to follow the mayor's lead. All the commissioners were "first among equals." This feature was the chief complaint of the secretary of the National Short Ballot Association, Richard S. Childs. Noting that commission government was "an accident, not a plan" (referring to the Galveston emergency that brought it into being), he addressed the problem of having five coequal executives: "The theory that the commission as a whole controlled its members in their departmental activities became neglected—the commission could not discipline a recalcitrant member."[52] Commonly, Childs asserted, commissioners would ignore one another's performance ("You attend to your department and quit criticizing mine") or exchange favors and support ("I'll vote for your appropriation if you'll vote for mine").[53] It sometimes seemed like a replay of machine politics.

Before long, other municipal reformers began to notice these problems. They responded with a new idea that would place all administrative power in the hands of a single appointed, trained administrator—a city manager. According to this plan, a mayor and a city council would be responsible for policy-making, but a professional, specially trained for the job, would be responsible for coordinating all administrative functions: "The reform leaders realized that technical ability could not be expected of elected officials, and they hoped that a strong mayor could appoint trained technicians and administrators as department heads."[54] Chief among these technicians would be the city manager, appointed either by the mayor or the council. In 1913, the National Municipal League issued a report (written by Childs) recommending that the idea of commission government be abandoned in favor of the city manager plan. A manager would bring to government administrative unity, expertise, clear accountability, and formal training in management.[55] Only six years later, in 1919, the League amended its model charter to recommend city manager government. The city manager movement, because of its persuasive logic and "pure" business analogy, quickly eclipsed the commission government movement in the 1920s. The commission form became a failed experiment used by few cities.

Between 1908 and 1912, several midwestern cities hired city managers. The idea caught on in earnest when Dayton, Ohio, changed its city charter, though the ward system remained. As in Galveston, an emergency served as the catalyst for a new government form. In 1913, John H. Patterson, president of the National Cash Register Company, persuaded the Dayton Chamber of Commerce to draft a new charter for the city. The chamber established the Bureau of Municipal Research to promote the idea. The Committee of One Hundred, a group well funded by the business community, sponsored a slate of candidates for city office who were pledged to changing the city charter. By organizing a well-run campaign ward by ward, the business slate put several of its candidates on the city council, but they still were outnumbered by Democratic politicians. Two months later, the Miami River flooded the town. The municipal government was slow in organizing emergency services. Patterson turned his factory into a shelter for flood victims. Overnight, he became the town's leading citizen. When requested by local business leaders, the state governor appointed Patterson to head a new charter reform commission. The commission successfully persuaded the voters to adopt its recommended charter.[56]

The results were spectacular. The new government improved public services, retired most of the city debt, instituted new budget-making procedures, enforced a uniform eight-hour day for city employees, and established civil service. The Dayton Plan soon became the most popular reform model for good government. Though rarely instituted in the big cities, it became common in smaller cities around the nation. In the five years before 1918, 87 cities adopted manager charters, and 153 did so between 1918 and 1923. During the next five years, 84 more cities were added to the list.[57]

The commission and then the manager plans achieved great popularity because it seemed they might be able to fulfill the reformers' desires to find an objective, nonpolitical, efficient way to run government. Analogies to business organizations almost always supplied the principal supporting arguments for structural reform. The *Dallas News* promoted the manager plan in 1930 by asking, "Why not run Dallas itself on a business schedule by business methods under businessmen?... The city manager plan is after all only a business management plan. The city manager is the executive of a corporation under a board of directors. Dallas is the corporation. It is as simple as that. Vote for it."[58]

❖ THE CLASS BIAS OF MUNICIPAL REFORM

The commission and manager movements elicited support from the middle and upper classes not only because they promised to save taxpayers' money, but also because they placed political handicaps in the way of the Great

Unwashed. Reform was inspired by class antagonisms. Changes in electoral rules and in the structure of city government were designed to undercut the voting power of lower-class groups. As pointed out in a sympathetic history of the city manager movement, in "machine-ridden" cities that adopted the plan

> there were differences in nationality or religion that intensified their social and political disagreements; . . . and each of them established the city manager plan through a concerted effort, organized by commercial or reform organizations, to take the city government away from the politicians, to give it to businessmen, and to make it conform to business ideals and standards.[59]

In "faction-ridden cities," the change to manager government resulted in "the election of men who had never before taken part in municipal affairs and who had promised to end politics in the business of city government."[60]

Analysis of the social class backgrounds of reformers reveals, especially in the big cities, a uniformly upper-class bias. Studies of the origins of reform movements show that business and upper-class elements normally championed reform, while lower- and working-class groups usually opposed it. For example, the New York City Bureau of Municipal Research, founded in 1906, was initially financed by Andrew Carnegie and John D. Rockefeller.[61] The U.S. Chamber of Commerce provided office space and paid the executive secretary of the City Managers Association for several years.[62] Civic clubs and voters' leagues generally contained names from elite social directories. Professional people involved in reform tended to be the most prestigious members of their professions, and many of them had upper-class origins.

George Mowry has traced the backgrounds of more than 400 prominent reformers of the Progressive Era, and his data show that most were upper class.[63] Many of the prominent reformers were wealthy industrialists, including names like McCormack, du Pont, Pinchot, Morgenthau, and Dodge. Most had a college education in a day when this fact marked a select social strata. Even more striking, most of the women and social workers had gone to college. In a sample of 400 reformers, a majority were lawyers, many of them politicians. Almost one-fifth were newspaper editors or publishers. Most of the remainder were engaged in business, medicine, real estate, or banking. Most of them were native-born Americans of British ancestry, Protestant, and urban.

Other studies confirm these results. A California sample of forty-seven reformers found that fourteen of them were engaged in banking, real estate, or business; seventeen in law; and fourteen in journalism.[64] In Baltimore the reform group was overwhelmingly white, Anglo-Saxon, Protestant, university-graduated, and engaged in professional practice or business. Studies in Ohio, Chicago, Pittsburgh, and Kansas City reported similar findings.[65]

The Progressive reformers these studies report on constituted a more complex group than the municipal reformers. The municipal groups contained a greater proportion of local business leaders, and in most cities commission and manager charters were advocated primarily by business organizations.[66] Samuel P. Hays has catalogued overwhelming business dominance over municipal reform in Dallas, Des Moines, Pittsburgh, and several other cities.[67]

These groups were keenly aware of their political interests. The expectation that new forms of government would result in the election of a "better" class of citizens, meaning businessmen or their favored candidates, was usually fulfilled. In Galveston and Austin, Texas; Dayton and Springfield, Ohio; Jackson, Michigan; Des Moines, Iowa; and other places, business leaders dominated politics after reform.[68] More than any other reason, this fact explains why business leaders were at the forefront of the municipal reform movement.

Opponents of the commission and manager plans were just as aware of their political interests. Machine politicians, socialists, and trade unionists opposed the plans because they rightly perceived that centralized electoral systems and decision-making processes would make it more difficult for working-class candidates to win public office.[69] In big cities, coalitions of immigrants and working-class groups generally were successful in opposing key elements of the reform agenda. In smaller cities, however, especially when the immigrants and working-class groups constituted a minority of the electorate, they could not effectively resist reform. In Oakland, California, socialists polled nearly 50 percent of the vote in the 1911 city elections.[70] With the vociferous assistance of the *Oakland Tribune,* local business leaders then led a successful reform movement to secure commission, at-large, nonpartisan government. Running at-large, the socialists were unable to win any seats on the commission in the next city elections. Still not satisfied, the business coalition mounted a successful campaign in 1928 to replace the commission with a council-manager government.[71] The manager was much easier to control than the various elected commissioners. In 1938, voters in Jackson, Michigan, prodded by the chamber of commerce, instituted a council-manager charter. The new mayor and councilors were members of the chamber of commerce and of Protestant reform groups. The new officials celebrated with a reception in the Masonic hall and, once in power, dismissed most of the Roman Catholic city employees.[72]

Reformers were not apolitical. The "structural reformers"—so-called because of their fixation on changing electoral rules and government organization charts—championed their crusades as virtuous undertakings. Their political objective, however, was clear: By putting wealthier people in charge of local government, they could ensure that cities would keep taxes and spending low. The contrast to the "social reformers," such as Hazen Pingree in Detroit, is striking. The agenda of social reform encompassed restructuring of tax burdens so that wealthy property owners and businesses would pay their fair share; attempts to secure lower public utility rates; and efforts to extend housing regulation, recreation, and public health and jobs programs for less privileged people. A delegate to the 1913 meeting of the League of Kansas Municipalities, after listening to his colleagues orate about the necessity of treating the city as a business, protested that "a city is more than a business corporation" and that "Good health is more important than a low tax rate."[73]

The vast social chasm dividing municipal reformers from the rest of the urban populace, however, made such utterances anathema to most reformers.

Even when reformers achieved the structural changes they sought, the result was not always what they anticipated. In many cities the balance of electoral power was weighted sufficiently against upper-class and business reformers that structural change did not always translate into political change. When the Des Moines Committee of One Hundred, representing the business community, succeeded in persuading the voters to adopt commission government in 1908, they were appalled when working-class candidates were elected as the first commissioners.[74] Chicago long ago adopted nonpartisan primaries and elections for aldermanic candidates. To this day, however, the Democratic organization easily communicates with loyal voters through year-round personal contacts and hard work on election day.

Blacks gained representation early in Chicago, because the city's fifty ward boundaries could not be easily drawn so as to exclude them. Before its downfall in the 1930s, to fend off challenges from the Democratic party the Republican machine tried to consolidate its electoral strength in the black community by slating a black candidate for a seat on the city council.[75] As a result, the first black was elected to the Chicago city council in 1915, decades before this was accomplished in most other cities. In 1920, a black became a ward committeeman in the Republican machine, a position that ensured some patronage jobs. In 1928, Chicago's Oscar de Priest became the first African American elected to Congress from a northern state. In contrast, Adam Clayton Powell of New York City was elected in 1944, and Charles Diggs of Detroit was elected in 1954. Fifteen of Chicago's fifty aldermen in 1976 were blacks; and two Chicago blacks were congressmen, four were state senators, and several were state representatives.

Chicago is an unusual case because despite nonpartisan elections its party machine persisted. In most cities where the reformers were successful, ethnic, minority, and neighborhood groups have been systematically underrepresented. Until the 1970s, for example, Los Angeles virtually excluded blacks from formal representation.[76] City councilors were selected by nonpartisan ballots from large districts that were carefully drawn to ensure that blacks would remain a minority of the voters in all districts. Civil service was strictly enforced so that a political organization based on patronage could not be started. As a result of all these factors, nearly all officeholders were white, Anglo-Saxon Protestants.

❖ DID REFORM KILL THE MACHINES?

It has often been assumed that the party machines died out because the reformers were successful in changing the rules of the game under which local politics was conducted. A large number of machines had short lives, only a decade or so, before they went into slow decline or machine politicians suddenly lost their grip on elective offices. Between 1909 and 1918, machines fell apart in Dayton, Ohio; Detroit and Grand Rapids, Michigan; Los Angeles; Portland, Oregon; Milwaukee, Wisconsin; Minneapolis, Minnesota; San Francisco; and Seattle, Washington. In each case a variety of reforms were put through. In each case, civil service systems changed hiring rules.[77] Most of the machines that survived this era of reform were dead by the middle of the 1950s, if not before, including New York's Tammany Hall. By World War II, it would have been impossible to find a city left completely untouched by municipal reform: Voter registration was universal and civil service hiring was nearly so; at-large, nonpartisan elections were used in most cities. Even in the big industrial cities, where reform was generally less successful, election rules were at least partially reformed. Boston, New Orleans, and Pittsburgh had switched to at-large elections; Memphis and Detroit had adopted both at-large and nonpartisan elections. Denver, New Orleans, Philadelphia, Cleveland, and Pittsburgh also became nonpartisan before World War II.[78]

Nevertheless, these reforms did not lead inexorably to the demise of the machines, and, therefore, they did not immediately or invariably restructure politics so that ethnic voters lost influence: "the adoption of structural reform was not sufficient to eliminate or preclude the appearance of machine politics."[79] Machines were often adept at adjusting to the new rules and institutions. Machines in fifteen cities actually seem to have been helped by the reformers' centralization of power in the hands of mayors or city managers.[80] In those cities the reformers accomplished their goal of making someone accountable to voters, but the voters did not use their power as the reformers hoped. After the adoption of city manager government in Cleveland in the 1920s, the city's machine was able to appoint a party hack as manager because it still controlled the city council, which was elected by wards.[81] Richard J. Daley built his powerful machine in Chicago, beginning with the 1953 election, despite the fact that the city's elections were nonpartisan and the vast majority of its employees were civil service.

The machines died, in most cases, because they were unable to adapt to national transformations that affected cities and their populations. Two developments were particularly important. First, the immigrant base of the machines began to erode. After the turn of the century Irish and German immigration dropped sharply; the bulk of new immigrants came from Italy and eastern Europe. The Irish and, secondarily, the Germans had been the mainstay groups for most machines, and, as their numbers declined, machines found that their support gradually eroded. In Boston, for example, the Irish and Germans accounted for 31.9 percent of ethnics in 1890, but only 20.4 percent by 1930; in New York City, their share of the total ethnic population fell even more.[82] In New York City, Fiorello LaGuardia put together a coalition of Italian and Jewish voters to defeat Tammany Hall's candidate in 1933. James Michael Curley, Boston's longtime boss lasted longer than most other bosses, but was finally defeated for re-election in 1949.[83]

The second devastating blow to the machines occurred when their immigrant constituents began to improve their economic position. As the immigrants began to join the ranks of the middle class, they needed petty favors and patronage less. After World War II, the immigrants and the children of immigrants joined the mass movement to the suburbs. Precinct captains saw their constituents moving out of the city, and sometimes they moved, too. Machines were not generally successful in reaching out to immigrants or to blacks and poor whites who moved into the cities during and after World War II.[84]

After the war, a new generation of politicians came to power by mobilizing the business community, labor, and the middle class behind programs of urban revitalization. In this cause they were helped by the federal government, which supplied the funds for public housing and slum clearance (we discuss these programs in Chapter 8). In Chicago, Richard Daley rebuilt the machine by adding the middle class, business, and blacks to the machine's base in the old immigrant neighborhoods. Daley aggressively sought federal funds for the city. Few machine leaders in other cities, however, had the vision to follow his example.

❖ THE REFORM LEGACY: REPRESENTATION AND LOCAL DEMOCRACY

Interest in local election rules has been rekindled over the past two decades because of clear evidence that at-large elections frequently result in the underrepresentation of racial and ethnic minorities. The social science research showing this relationship has been consistent and persuasive.[85] In 1982, over the strenuous objections of the Reagan administration, Congress amended the 1965 Voting Rights Act to make it easier for minorities to challenge local election practices. Congress passed the amendments, contained in Section 2 of the Act, in explicit reaction to a 1980 United States Supreme Court decision that required litigants to demonstrate an *intent* to discriminate before an election rule could be declared invalid.[86] In Section 2, Congress specified that challenges to local election rules could meet a much easier standard than before: They would be considered illegal if they merely had the *effect* of underrepresenting minorities in elected positions.

On June 30, 1986, the Supreme Court handed down a landmark decision, *Thornburg v. Gingles,* interpreting the 1982 amendments.[87] This case came to the Court after the U.S. Justice Department brought suit against the state of North Carolina, arguing that several multimember state legislative districts in North Carolina violated the voting rights of blacks, since in those districts white candidates invariably won all seats. The Court ordered North Carolina to create single-member districts and laid down some standards for deciding when at-large and multimember district systems would be considered suspect: where litigants could show that it would be possible to create at least one single-member electoral district that would give a minority group an electoral majority; when it could also be demonstrated that the minority group seeking more representation was politically cohesive; and where it could be shown that whites had previously voted as a bloc to prevent minority candidates from being elected.[88]

At-large and some district systems have since been successfully challenged all across the United States. In 1986, a federal court ordered several Alabama counties to institute single-member districts for electing county commissioners.[89] In a 1987 lawsuit filed against the city of Springfield, Illinois, a federal judge ordered the city to expand the number of electoral districts from five to ten. Since only 10.8 percent of the city's population was African American, the expansion to ten districts was necessary if any one of them was to contain a majority of black voters.[90] (Interestingly, a different federal judge did not require this solution in a similar suit against the Springfield Park District.[91]) In the same year, the city of Danville, Illinois, expanded its city council to fourteen members elected from seven wards, after a federal judge threw out its previous system, in which a three-member commission and a mayor were all elected at-large.[92]

The extensive litigation arising from the 1982 amendments to the Voting Rights Act has produced an extraordinary amount of conflict and confusion about local election rules. The numerous court decisions have called into question the electoral systems of hundreds of cities, counties, townships, and special districts. To preempt court action, some local governments have voluntarily redrawn district and ward boundaries so as to facilitate minority representation. Frequently, this requires devising districts with tortuously meandering boundaries.[93] For several years it was unclear whether there was some upper limit to the number of districts that a local government might have to draw to achieve the equitable representation of minorities. By 1987, however, it seemed likely (despite the city of Springfield case) that, under normal circumstances, the number of districts already existing would be left alone.[94]

Another question that arose was whether the minority population or the voting age minority population would be counted in the districts drawn to give minorities better representation. Most courts decided that a majority voting age population was required.[95] Could two or more minority groups be combined to constitute a district where the combined minorities would make up the majority of voters? Only, the courts have said, if it can be shown that the groups are politically cohesive—and research makes it clear, for example, that blacks and Hispanics do not generally vote similarly.[96]

The principle that electoral districts should always be drawn so as to guarantee the representation of ethnic and racial minorities has been applied at all levels of the political system. In 1991, minority representation was at the forefront of the political infighting over congressional reapportionment required as a result of the decennial census of 1990. In that year, there were thirty-seven blacks and Hispanics in Congress. As a result of redistricting in 1992, 19 additional blacks and Hispanics were elected to Congress. In Texas the Democrats, who made up a majority of the state legislature, took on the task of creating one black-majority congressional district in Dallas and two Hispanic-majority districts in Houston and San Antonio. A similar process took place in several other states as well.

In June 1991, the Supreme Court ruled that judicial elections in Louisiana and Texas violated the 1982 Voting Rights Act because large election districts diluted the electoral strength of minorities. A flurry of lawsuits ensued that challenged election procedures for state and local judges. Traditionally, nearly all state and local judges have been elected at-large, and this perhaps explains why, as of 1985, only 3.8 percent of judges in state courts were black and only 1.2 percent were Hispanic.[97]

The multitude of court challenges over the past decade has resulted in an ongoing revolution in local electoral practices. In 1981, about two-thirds (66.5 percent) of cities used at-large election systems. By 1986, a space of only five years, the proportion had fallen to 60.4 percent.[98] The impetus for this revolution has been energized by recent research demonstrating that changing from at-large to district elections has improved the representation of blacks and Hispanics.[99] Even many existing ward and district systems will have to be redrawn. In St. Louis, for example, black leaders threatened to go to court to force a redrawing of the city's wards. Presently, eleven of the twenty-eight aldermen are black. It would be possible to redraw wards to give blacks majorities in half of them.[100]

After the period of municipal reform that we have discussed in this chapter, it took more than half a century for questions about representation and local democracy to resurface as a political issue. The years since the Voting Rights Act of 1965 may be properly regarded, therefore, as the first reform period since the Progressive Era to focus specifically on local electoral politics.

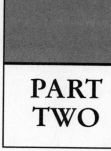

PART
TWO

NATIONAL POLICY AND THE CITIES

CHAPTER 5

NATIONAL POLITICS AND THE CITIES

❖ THE CHANGING POLITICAL BALANCE

In 1912, a Harvard political scientist wrote that "before many years have passed, the urban population of the United States will have gained numerical mastery."[1] His judgment was based on a simple calculation of demographic change. Though an increasing number of city dwellers were beginning to move to suburbs in the early years of the twentieth century, the volume of migration to the cities still vastly exceeded the suburban movement.[2] Until the depression of the 1930s, the cities continued to burst their seams.

In the thirty years from 1890 to 1920, more than 18 million immigrants poured into America's cities. These new urban immigrants came mainly from Italy, Poland, Russia, Greece, and eastern Europe. They were overwhelmingly Roman Catholic and Jewish. They made up the preponderance of the work forces in the iron and steel, meat packing, mining, and textile industries. Few spoke English, and many were illiterate even in their own language. To so-called native Americans (who were themselves simply the descendants of earlier immigrants), the immigrants and the cities they poured into seemed on the brink of overwhelming the nation's politics and culture. The distrust of cities became amplified into a political reaction against immigrants and their cultures.

The nativist reaction ultimately failed to keep the cities from gaining a voice in national political institutions. In the election of 1928 ethnic populations in the cities began to align with the national Democratic party, whose presidential candidate, New York Governor Alfred E. Smith, was the first Catholic nominated by a major party. With Franklin D. Roosevelt's landslide victory in the presidential election of 1932, the fate of the Democratic party became linked to voters in the cities. For the first time in the nation's history, the politicians representing urban voters began to wield influence in national politics. Attention to the problems of the cities was guaranteed when the national political parties began to win or lose elections on the basis of urban votes.[3] From the Roosevelt presidency until its decline and collapse by the 1980s, the New Deal coalition, which relied on loyal Democratic voters in the South as well as ethnics, blue-collar workers, and blacks in the industrial cities in the North, formed the basis of the national Democratic party's electoral success in Congress and in presidential elections. Modern American liberalism, as expressed in the New Deal programs of the 1930s and the Great Society programs of the 1960s, can be traced to the pivotal position of city electorates in national politics.

✦ THE POLITICAL ISOLATION OF THE CITIES

Before the 1930s, neither of the major national political parties had ever paid much attention to the cities. The cities were invisible in national politics because they did not fit into the coalitional structure of the national Republican and Democratic parties. Following the Civil War, each of the parties appealed to distinct sectional interests. The Republicans, the triumphant party of Abraham Lincoln, emerged from the war as the dominant national party controlling Congress and the presidency. Between 1860 and 1928, the Republicans won fourteen of eighteen presidential contests and controlled both houses of Congress the majority of the time. Representing eastern finance, industry, and commerce, they enacted high tariffs on foreign imports, gave land to the railroads for westward expansion, and financed canal and river improvements. Republicans opposed taxes on business, encouraged private exploitation (mineral, grazing, homesteading) of federal lands in the West, used troops to quell strikes, and generally promoted a laissez-faire ideology protecting business from regulation.

The Republican party encompassed other political interests as well. It was popular in the middle- and working-class electorates in the North because of the outcome of the Civil War and because it presided during a period of general economic expansion tied closely to frontier development and industrial growth. In the prairie states and in the West, "cattle barons, lumber kings, the mineral exploiters, the land speculators, and the humble homesteaders"[4] identified their prospects with the party. By identifying with the ideas of competitive individualism, the Republicans appealed to all those elements that hankered after the "main chance": "Thanks to a deep-rooted American ideology of individual enterprise, even the small farmers generally remained faithful to the party. . . . They, too, were entrepreneurs, after a fashion."[5] The Republicans' business philosophy fit well with the post–Civil War climate that stressed exploitation of natural resources and glorification of unfettered individual enterprise.

After the Civil War, the Democrats became the party of protest. Southerners joined with a loose coalition of groups opposed to economic domination by eastern banks and corporations, the railroads, and "big money." The worst problem with the Democrats' coalition was its instability, for its major issues arose from the insecurities of small farmers about credit and prices, the bitterness of the South, and the tension between business and labor. The party prospered during hard times but lost support when the economy improved. Its only secure base was in the South, where the Republican party—the party of Lincoln—was virtually absent.

In the presidential race of 1896, near the end of a three-year economic depression, the Democrats campaigned on a program advocating government intervention to protect the common man against the "money interests" symbolized by the industrial magnates Andrew Mellon, Andrew Carnegie, James Fisk, and J. P. Morgan. With William Jennings Bryan of Nebraska as its presidential candidate, the party advocated lower tariffs as a means of forcing industrial enterprises to compete with foreign producers by reducing prices. Bryan called for a paper currency backed by silver as well as by gold. Such a move would have increased the amount of money in circulation, thus inducing inflation and easing credit. Heavily indebted small business owners and farmers would have benefited. The Democrats also proposed a graduated federal income tax, government takeover of land grants previously ceded to railroads, and public ownership of telegraphs and telephones. The Democrats lost mainly because these positions failed to appeal to workers in the cities, who felt that tariffs and tight money protected their jobs. They did, however, help to create a party with specific alternatives to the pro-business policies of the Republicans.

Several events between the elections of 1896 and 1932 gradually broadened the electoral base of the Democratic party. In 1900, Bryan was once again the Democratic nominee. This time he fashioned an appeal specifically designed to build support among the urban working class. He assailed trusts and monopolies, claiming that they were crowding out smaller businesses and entrepreneurs. He urged the direct election of senators, opposed government injunctions against strikes, and advocated the creation of a Department of Labor. Bryan saw the possibility of forging a coalition between western farmers, southerners, and industrial labor against big business's control of the nation's money supply, credit, and economic policies. The American Federation of Labor (AFL) endorsed Bryan when he again ran as the Democrats' choice in 1908.

In 1912, the Democrats won the presidency for the first time in the twentieth century. President Woodrow Wilson immediately pushed a distinctively Democratic legislative agenda. The Underwood-Simmons Act lowered tariffs for the first time since 1857 and put wool, lumber, paper, wood pulp, steel rails, and sugar on a free trade list. The prices of these commodities quickly dropped. A graduated income tax was adopted, shifting federal revenues from reliance on excise taxes and tariffs, which consumers paid in higher prices, to direct taxation on earnings. The Federal Reserve Act of 1913 reformed the banking system. It spread the money supply more evenly across the nation by establishing a dozen regional banks to receive federal deposits, and it increased the money supply by the issuance of notes that did not have to be backed by full value in gold reserves. The Clayton Act and the Federal Trade Act outlawed some unfair business practices (such as price fixing), established boards for voluntary mediation between management and labor, created an eight-hour work day for railroad workers, and provided federal administrative assistance to states and companies to set up workers' compensation programs. The Federal Farm Loan Act extended limited credit to farmers. Additionally, the Wilson administration sponsored child labor and women's hours laws, exempted labor unions from antitrust legislation, and encouraged employers to negotiate with organized labor.

Despite these programs, urban ethnic voters did not immediately rally to the national Democratic banner. Many of the urban party machines (as in Chicago until 1932) were Republican, but, whatever their party affiliation, machine leaders had little connection to the national or even the state party organizations. In most states party leaders came out of the governor's mansion and state legislature. Machine politicians paid little attention to national candidates and issues. Machine politicians had gotten into politics through their local precincts and wards. Theirs was a politics of ethnicity and trade-offs, not of abstract political issues. The machines were peculiarly local organizations, a product of the segregation of ethnic voters from the rest of American society.

There was little pay or respect for ethnic politicians who were elected to the state legislature. It was often a kiss of political death to be sent away to a small, conservative upstate or downstate town like Albany, New York, or Springfield, Illinois, away from friends, family, and "boodle." When Tammany Hall sent Al Smith at the age of 30 to the state legislature, he had scarcely been outside New York City. He felt exiled:

> Al Smith went to Albany unprepared to be legislator—or even to sleep away from home. . . . overcome by the intricacies of the legislative process, he sat day after day in the high-ceilinged chamber in silence.
>
> As he sat there staring down at the desk, a page boy would deposit another pile of bills on it. The wording was difficult enough for the expert. It might have been designed to mock a man whose schooling had ended in the eighth grade, who had never liked to read even the simple books of childhood, who, he had once said, had in his entire life read only one book cover to cover: The Life of John L. Sullivan.[6]

Before Al Smith, no Tammany politician had ever done much in Albany.

Voters, too, felt isolated from national political issues. Their political activity was motivated by their personal loyalties and by their pocketbook. When precinct captains took them to the polls, they voted for the local party organization, not for a cause. What in their background would excite them about national issues and candidates—tariff policy, child labor legislation, William Jennings Bryan, Woodrow Wilson? The upshot was that although many cities were dominated by powerful party organizations, the leaders of these organizations and their voters had only occasionally become important in gubernatorial contests and had rarely been noticed in presidential elections. The rise of the cities in national politics began only when nativist Protestant elements launched a national assault on the city machines and their immigrant constituents. In doing so, they created issues that an urban electorate could easily understand.

Though Wilson had sponsored several programs in response to labor pressure and though Bryan had earlier advocated a Labor Department and laws against strike injunctions, the national Democratic party had not transformed itself into anything resembling an urban working-class party. Far from it. Its center was still to be found in the country, not the city. When the urban wing of the party began to grow in strength, a potentially devastating split developed along urban-rural lines. By the 1920s, the party was bitterly divided.

❖ A NEW URBAN CONSCIOUSNESS

The cleavages within the Democratic party mirrored the urban-rural conflicts that obsessed the nation. Rural Democrats feared that the urban wing of their party might someday command a majority. A similar concern preyed on the minds of native Protestants. What would happen to political and religious traditions if the barbarous hordes from Europe took over? The ever-present nineteenth-century nervousness about the "strangers in the land" escalated into a national phobia in the twentieth century.

Prohibition constituted a direct assault on the cities. Proposed to the states by Congress in 1917 and ratified in 1919, the Eighteenth Amendment prohibited the sale, use, and distribution of alcoholic beverages. Small-town Methodists and Baptists—joined in their crusade by upper- and middle-class Protestants in the cities and in the new suburbs—hoped to reduce poverty, improve workers' efficiency and family life, and end immorality and crime by forcing the immigrants to abstain from alcohol. Prohibition became the compelling political issue of the 1920s, for it represented a frontal assault upon the cultural values and customs of the immigrants:

> [Drinking] was associated with the saloonkeepers who ran the city machines and who used the votes of the whiskey-loving immigrant . . . with the German brewers and their "disloyal" compatriots who drank beer and ale. . . . The cities, which resisted the idea that "thou shalt not" was the fundamental precept of living, were always hostile to prohibition. The prohibitionists, in turn, regarded the city as their chief enemy, and prohibitionism and a pervasive antiurbanism went hand-in-hand.[7]

To rural and urban Protestants, the sins of liquor were indistinguishable from the sins of the immigrants. Southern and western newspapers reflexively connected crime, national origin, and liquor. When it was not legitimate to attack foreigners directly, it was easy to attack them through the surrogate liquor issue, allowing "prohibition partisans to talk about morality when in reality they were worried about cultural dominance and political supremacy."[8]

Prohibition was intimately connected to religious conflict. To Protestant Americans, the Roman Catholic church was evil incarnate. It signified ostentatious authority—the robes, the ceremony, and the architecture bespeaking a menace to the simplicity and informality of small-town life. Worse was the fear of papal imperialism. Like the right-wing groups of the 1950s obsessed by the specter of an international Communist conspiracy poised to subvert American politics, fundamentalists of the early twentieth century were haunted by the fear of a Roman Catholic church intent on subverting civil authority around the world.

Feeding on such fears, the Ku Klux Klan attracted millions of members. Revived in Atlanta in 1915, the Klan enjoyed spectacular growth during the 1920s in both the North and the South. Klan membership mushroomed in California, Oregon, Indiana, Illinois, Ohio, Oklahoma, Texas, Arkansas, and throughout the South. At its peak in 1924, 40 percent of the Klan's membership resided in Ohio, Indiana, and Illinois. Half of its membership was located in cities of more than 50,000, with chapters of hundreds of members in such cities as Chicago, Detroit, Indianapolis, Pittsburgh, Baltimore, and Buffalo.[9] The Klan was a powerful political force until at least the mid-1920s. It helped elect a member of the Senate; governors in Georgia, Alabama, Oregon, and California; and seventy-five members of the House of Representatives.

Though the Klan found its strongest support among lower-middle-class fundamentalist Christians, its basic message appealed to a wide audience. In 1916, Madison Grant, curator of New York City's Museum of National History, published *The Passing of the Great Race,* in which he worried that Aryans might be overwhelmed by dark-skinned races. His book was elevated to the status of a scientific work, along with Lothrop Stoddard's *The Rising Tide of Color against the White World-Supremacy* (1921).

Congress responded to the rising xenophobia with the Emergency Quota Act of 1921 and the National Origins Act of 1924. Both laws received support from an array of groups, including intellectuals, labor leaders, southerners, western farmers, and other major nonimmigrant groups. The Emergency Quota Act reaffirmed exclusion of Orientals and established a national origins quota of 3 percent of each nationality's proportion of the U.S. population as recorded in the 1910 census. The law succeeded in cutting immigration from 805,228 in 1920 to 309,556 in 1921–1922.[10]

The National Origins Act of 1924 further reduced the origins quota to 2 percent and established the 1890 census as the baseline for calculating the quota. Changing the baseline census year was a move designed to reduce the quotas for those nationality groups that had flooded into the country after

1890. The number of Italian and eastern European immigrants allowed into the country fell dramatically. Italian immigration was reduced by 90 percent; British and Irish immigration, in contrast, by only 19 percent.[11] Total immigration declined from 357,803 in 1923–1924 to 164,667 in 1924–1925.

In debates on these two bills members of Congress reviled the foreign-born of the cities in language not unlike that found in Ku Klux Klan pamphlets. This assault helped make immigrants aware of how deeply national politics could in fact affect them. In the 1920s they began to express their concerns.

❖ THE URBAN WING OF THE DEMOCRATIC PARTY

The prosperity of the 1920s was a serious blow to the Democratic party. The Democrats' coalition could be held together only by shared grievances. The party was composed of an unlikely combination of eastern and northern urban ethnics; western farmers and prohibitionists; and southern, dry, Klan-saturated fundamentalists.

The fragility of this coalition was revealed by the 1924 Democratic convention, held in Madison Square Garden in New York City. The Democrats treated the first radio audience of a national convention to a futile 103-ballot performance. The galleries booed the speeches of southerners and westerners, especially when William Jennings Bryan asked the convention not to condemn the Ku Klux Klan by name. The resolution to condemn the Klan brought forth such heated oratory that police were brought onto the convention floor in case a free-for-all broke out. Delegates shouted and cursed each other. When the final vote on the resolution to condemn the Klan was taken, it lost by one vote, $542\frac{3}{20}$ to $541\frac{3}{20}$. Demands for a recount were drowned out when the band struck up "Marching Through Georgia." After sixteen days, the convention finally nominated a presidential candidate neither the agrarians nor the city factions wanted.

The delegates from the towns and farms of the South and West were disoriented and frightened by the crowds and the din of New York City. They found New Yorkers unfriendly and rude, and the city seemed all too easy to get lost in. Delegates who "wandered downtown to Fourteenth Street to gawk at Tammany Hall with its ancient Indian above the door reacted as if they expected to see an ogre come popping out. Almost all delegates were dismayed by the New York traffic, the noise and hustle."[12] Their antagonisms toward the city were reaffirmed every day the convention dragged on through the muggy July heat. Small-town reporters filled their hometown newspapers with vivid accounts of the horrors of the city.[13]

Despite these divisions, only four years later the Democrats nominated Al Smith, the four-term governor of New York, for the presidency. Smith projected everything anathema to the city haters. He was a self-made Catholic graduate of Tammany Hall. He said "foist" instead of "first" and wore a brown derby, which only accentuated his bulbous nose and ruddy complexion. He proudly reminisced about his past: swimming in the East River and working at the Fulton Fish Market as an errand boy. Considering the divisive conflicts within the party, how could he have been nominated? Once he had been nominated, why did the party not simply come apart?

The southern and western factions had little choice but to stay within the Democratic fold. In spite of their differences, the Democrats had come to share, however crudely, a class interest. The party had symbolically become— mostly by default because the Republicans took a probusiness stand—the "little man's" party. Those who opposed Republican policies could never hope to have a voice in national presidential politics unless they aligned with the Democrats.

The time was ripe for compromise. Few Democrats thought that Smith could win, but no candidate was available who was capable of bridging the gap between the disparate factions that made up the party. In addition, Smith had acquired broad political support. As the four-term governor of New York, he had gained national prominence as a progressive governor who had created state parks and beaches, sponsored workers' safety legislation, and financed public improvements throughout the state. He had reorganized state government, making New York the model for progressives who believed in efficiency principles. Admired by progressives for his record as governor and supported by Democratic organizations with ethnic constituencies, his nomination could be denied by antiurban delegates, but only at the cost of another fiasco like 1924—multiple ballots and a guaranteed loss for the presidential nominee. There was even reason to believe that Smith might have a chance. In his victorious gubernatorial run in 1924, he had received 100,000 more votes than the losing Democratic presidential ticket in New York.

In 1928, the Democrats gave the nomination to Al Smith. Though he lost the election, his candidacy marked the beginning of the Democratic party's political ascendancy in the big cities.

> The election of 1928 marked a significant change in the attitude of the urban masses. Both in 1920 and 1924, the twelve largest cities in the United States had, taken together, given a decisive majority to the Republicans; now the tables were turned, and the Democrats came out ahead. This, as later elections were to prove, marked the beginning of a long-term urban trend.[14]

For the Roman Catholic ethnics in the cities, Smith's campaign sharpened their perception of the national issues of Prohibition, ethnicity, and religion. Smith campaigned with his brown derby and his theme song, "The Sidewalks of New York." Protestants shuddered at the idea of a Catholic in the White House. Smith's equivocal stand on Prohibition made drink the main issue of the campaign. Blue-blood upper-class Protestants found him beneath them. The campaign highlighted the issues of race, religion, culture, and social class so clearly that never again would the ethnics be unmindful of their stake in national politics. The election of 1928 brought a Democratic electoral plurality to the cities of the nation (see Table 5-1). Since then, the major cities have normally voted heavily Democratic, and until the 1980s they were a mainstay of the Democratic party's electoral strength.

TABLE 5-1 THE REVOLT OF THE CITY: VOTING IN THE LARGEST TWELVE CITIES	
YEAR	NET PARTY PLURALITY
1920	1,540,000 Republican
1924	1,308,000 Republican
1928	210,000 Democratic
1932	1,791,000 Democratic
1936	3,479,000 Democratic
1940	2,112,000 Democratic
1944	2,230,000 Democratic
1948	1,481,000 Democratic

The cities in this table include New York, Chicago, Philadelphia, Pittsburgh, Detroit, Cleveland, Baltimore, St. Louis, Boston, San Francisco, Milwaukee, and Los Angeles.
Source: Reprinted from the table on page 49 in *The Future of American Politics,* 3rd Revised Edition by Samuel Lubell. © 1951, 1952, 1956, 1965 by Samuel Lubell. Reprinted by permission of Harper & Row, Publishers, Inc.

Al Smith's candidacy broke new ground for a recognition of the role of cities in American politics. What cemented the relationship between the cities and the Democratic party was the Great Depression and Franklin Delano Roosevelt's New Deal.

❖ THE DEPRESSION AND THE CITIES

The Great Depression came as a shock to Americans and to their public leaders. The 1920s had been a decade of prosperity and optimism, especially for the burgeoning middle class. Business leaders and politicians sold the idea that the potential for sustained economic growth was limitless. A strong undertow of poverty ran below the surface, in the immigrant slums and on farms alike, but on the surface the signs of prosperity prevailed. It was an age that extolled mass consumption and complacency. The discontents of the industrial order seemed long past.

The symbolic beginning of the Great Depression occurred on October 24, 1929. On that day—Black Thursday—disorder, panic, and confusion reigned on the New York Stock Exchange. Stock prices virtually collapsed. For several months prices had sagged, then risen, then sagged again, with each trough lower than the previous and each peak less convincing. When the bottom fell out, "the Market . . . degenerated into a wild, mad scramble to sell, . . . the Market . . . surrendered to blind, relentless fear."[15] In one morning, eleven well-known speculators committed suicide. From Wall Street the economic catastrophe rippled outward, with consequences that would fundamentally alter American politics.

Over the next three years the nation sank steadily deeper into economic stagnation. In 1929, the unemployment rate stood at 3.2 percent. Within a few months, the number of unemployed exceeded 4 million, representing 8.7 percent of the labor force.[16] By 1932, more than 12 million workers, 23.6 percent of all workers, could not find jobs. In the depths of the depression, during the spring of 1933, about 13 million workers were unemployed, more than 25 percent of a labor force of 51.5 million.[17]

The depression dragged on for a decade. Unemployment levels remained above 20 percent in both 1934 and 1935 and dropped below 15 percent only in 1937. Most of those who managed to find work made less than before. From 1929 to 1933, the average income of workers fell by 42.5 percent.[18] Weekly wages dropped from an average of $28 in 1929 to $17 by 1934, and workers faced the everpresent threat of layoffs. Many jobs were reduced from full-time to part-time status, and employers cut wages and hours to meet payrolls. For example, the payroll of the nation's largest steel company, U.S. Steel, was cut in half from 1929 to 1933, and in 1933 it had no full-time workers at all.[19] Steel mills operated at only 12 percent of capacity by 1932.[20]

The productive capacity of business seemed irreparably damaged. In the three years following the stock market collapse, national income fell by 44.5 percent. By the summer of 1932, stocks had fallen 83 percent below their value in September 1929.[21] By the end of 1932, 5,096 commercial banks had failed. Farm income declined from $7 billion in 1929 to $2.5 billion in 1932.[22] For many farmers, whose incomes had been sharply dropping throughout the 1920s the depression was the final blow.

The statistics only hinted at the extent of human suffering. Between 1 million and 2 million men rode the rails and gathered in hobo jungles or camped in thickets and railroad cars. Others lived in "Hoovervilles," clusters of cardboard, scrap wood, and scrap metal shacks in empty lots and city parks. Those who had been chronically poor in the 1920s were now hungry and destitute. They stood in bread lines, ate from garbage cans, or went begging from door to door. One-quarter of all homeowners lost their homes in 1932, and more than 1,000 mortgages a day were foreclosed in the first half of 1933.[23] By March 1933, when Franklin D. Roosevelt was inaugurated as president, 9 million savings accounts had been lost.[24]

Never before had the nation faced such an economic catastrophie, nor was there a tradition of federal government assistance for the unemployed and destitute.[25] Unemployment and poverty were certainly not new. In the period from 1897 to 1926 unemployment levels in four major industries fluctuated around the 10 percent level,[26] and poverty was a chronic condition of industrialization and immigration. What made this depression unique was its depth, persistence, and pervasiveness. In earlier depressions, including the panics of the 1870s and 1890s, production and employment declined much less severely and the recovery began within a year or two.[27] The depression of the 1930s lasted for over a decade, it touched all classes, and its effects were felt by rich and poor alike. The measure of the crisis of the 1930s was not just unemployment and poverty, but the breakdown of economic institutions.

No one knew how to respond. President Herbert Hoover firmly resisted intervention by the federal government and instead launched two national drives to encourage private relief. Late in 1930, he appointed the President's Emergency Committee for Employment. Its main task was to encourage state and local committees to expedite public construction and to coordinate the public and private giving of relief. In August 1931, he formed the President's Organization on Unemployment Relief, whose job was to help organize private unemployment committees in states and communities.

Despite Hoover's undying opposition to federal intervention, two major programs were funded during his administration. First, the Federal Home Loan Bank Act supplied capital advances to a small number of mortgage institutions so that they could forbear rather than foreclose on mortgages in default. A few banks were saved by this program. Second, the Emergency Relief and Construction Act extended $300 million in loans to state and local governments so they could continue to provide relief to indigent people.

Hoover was hardly alone in opposing an expanded federal role. Until 1932, most governors took a "we'll do it ourselves" attitude toward solving unemployment and its associated problems.[28] Two governors refused to work with the President's Organization on Unemployment Relief, even though federal funds were not involved.[29] The officials of financially strapped local governments were also skeptical of federal aid. In July 1931, the socialist mayor of Milwaukee wrote to the mayors of the largest one hundred cities asking them to come to a conference with the purpose of requesting a national relief program. He got no response at all from several of the major cities, and several mayors criticized the idea on the premise that federal aid would constitute "an invasion of community rights."[30]

In the 1932 campaign, the Democrats accused Hoover of doing too much rather than too little. The Democratic nominee, Franklin Delano Roosevelt, promised to balance the budget while accusing Hoover of having presided over "the greatest spending administration in peace times in all our history."[31] It was apparent that the weight of the past lay heavily on both political parties. Against a cultural tradition that extolled individualism and free enterprise, there was great reluctance to expand the powers of government—especially the federal government—to meet the crisis. Nevertheless, when Roosevelt was inaugurated on March 4, 1933, he set in motion a concentrated period of reform that vastly increased the powers of the federal government in areas of business regulation, farm policy, and social insurance. Why did Roosevelt break so thoroughly from tradition?

Roosevelt's change of heart was motivated by the pervading sense of crisis that ushered him into the White House. Between his election in November and his inauguration in March, the nation passed through the worst months of the depression. The economy teetered on the brink of complete collapse. In February 1933 some of the nation's biggest banks failed. "People stood in long queues with satchels and paper bags to take gold and currency away from the banks to store in mattresses and old shoe boxes. It seemed safer to put your life's savings in the attic than to trust the financial institutions in the country."[32] Roosevelt wondered if there would be anything left to salvage by the time he assumed office. By inauguration day, thirty-eight states had closed their banks, and on that day the governors of New York and Illinois closed the nation's biggest banks.[33] The New York Stock Exchange stopped trading. The Kansas City and Chicago Boards of Trade closed their doors. "In the once-busy grain pits of Chicago, in the canyons of Wall Street, all was silent."[34]

It was also one of the harshest winters on record. In desperation, people overran relief offices and rioted at bank closings. Relief marchers invaded state legislative chambers. Farmers tried to stop foreclosure proceedings and blockaded roads. Amid marches, riots, arrests, and jailings, politicians feared a revolution.

The first one hundred days of Roosevelt's administration were characterized by frenetic activity.[35] On March 9th, Roosevelt signed the Emergency Banking Act. The act extended financial assistance to bankers so they could reopen their doors and gave the government authority to reorganize banks and to control bank credit policies. It received a unanimous vote from a panicked Congress, sight unseen. A flurry of legislation followed: the Civilian Conservation Corps (March 31), the Agricultural Adjustment Act and the Federal Emergency Relief Act (May 12), the Tennessee Valley Authority (May 18), the Federal "Truth in Securities" Act (May 27), the Home Owners' Loan Act (June 13), the National Industrial Recovery Act (June 16), and more than a score of other bills.

Most of the legislative onslaught was designed to stimulate, regulate, and stabilize the most important economic institutions of the economy. But the benefits filtered down. After the Emergency Banking Act was passed, depositors gained confidence and redeposited their savings. Under the National Housing Act (adopted in 1934), home buyers could secure long-term mortgages from banks whose loans were guaranteed by the federal government. Foreclosures on farms and homes were sharply reduced when the government, through the Farm Credit Administration and Home Owners' Loan Corporation, agreed to buy up defaulted mortgages.

New Deal programs affected many people's lives by salvaging their savings, houses, and farms. Nevertheless, the New Deal's attempts to reform the economy were designed more to bring stability to financial institutions than to fight poverty and destitution. Home lending and farm credit programs primarily helped the nation's important economic institutions and secondarily aided the heavily mortgaged middle class.

The other side of the New Deal included its public works and relief programs. These programs assisted millions of unemployed and penniless people. They vastly expanded the Democratic coalition by bringing into the fold the same elements that had identified with Al Smith. For millions of families the New Deal meant the difference between hunger and having food, between unemployment and finding a job. Between 1933 and 1937 the federal government administered public works programs for several million people and supplied direct relief to millions more.

The earliest of the public works programs was the Civilian Conservation Corps (CCC), established on March 31, 1933. In all, more than 2.5 million boys and young men were employed by the CCC. In 1935 alone, 500,000 men were living in CCC camps. They planted trees, built dams, fought fires, stocked fish, built lookout towers, dug ditches and canals, strung telephone lines, and built and improved bridges, roads, and trails. Their contribution to conservation was enormous: the CCC was responsible for more than half of all the forest planted in the United States up to the 1960s.[36]

The Civil Works Administration (CWA) was much larger and broader in scope. Established in November 1933, it employed 4.1 million by the third week of January 1934.[37] In a few months it employed almost a third of the unemployed labor force. Although the CWA lasted for less than a year— Roosevelt ended it in the spring of 1934 because he thought it was too costly—it enabled many families to survive the bitter winter of 1934. The CWA was "immensely popular—with merchants, with local officials, and with workers," and its demise was resisted in Congress.[38]

The Public Works Administration (PWA) enjoyed a longer run, and its impact was more lasting. In six years, from 1933 to 1939, the PWA built 70 percent of the new school buildings in the nation and 35 percent of the hospitals and public health facilities.[39]

The Federal Emergency Relief Act (FERA), signed on May 12, 1935, was never as popular as public works, for it undercut the cherished principles of work and independence by making relief money directly available to the destitute. Roosevelt himself viewed the Federal Emergency Relief Administration with distaste, thinking that it would sap the moral strength of the poor. Though Roosevelt constantly sought ways to cut its budget and though its benefit levels were extraordinarily low, it was mandated by the want and the civil disorder that prevailed in Roosevelt's first term. In the winter of 1934, 20 million people received FERA funds.[40]

The FERA was treated as an embarrassing necessity. Despite its importance and scope, it received little publicity. The government's response was understood to be an emergency measure, comparable to helping victims of such catastrophes as floods, earthquakes, and tornadoes. Congressional debate on the FERA received little coverage by the media. When the act was passed on May 9, 1933, the *New York Times* mentioned it on page 3 only in a column listing legislation passed by Congress. When it was signed by President Roosevelt on May 12th, it made page 21 of the *Times,* but only in reference to the appointment of the administrator. In a culture that extolled individualism, competition, and hard work, people were ill at ease with the idea of relief.

Franklin Roosevelt often expressed doubts about relief and public works programs. He preferred economic recovery to government spending. But his response to the economic emergency broadened the base of the Democratic party. Public works and relief created a loyal following among middle- and working-class people who were benefited. By the 1936 election, and for decades thereafter, voting in small towns split between the Republicans on the "right" side of the tracks and the working class and poor on the other.

The most reliable new Democratic following could be found in the cities. Urban ethnics, especially if they were union members, learned to vote. The loyalty of black voters to the Republican party was broken by New Deal programs. Before the 1936 election, a prominent black publisher counseled, "My friends, go turn Lincoln's picture to the wall. That debt has been paid in full."[41] In the 1936 election blacks gave Roosevelt 75 percent of their votes.

The Great Depression revolutionized the group composition of the party system in the United States. Both parties became class-oriented, a fact that shifted the center of gravity for the Democrats to the northern cities, where large numbers of the working class and poor were concentrated. Additionally, so many people benefited through New Deal programs that the voting coalition supporting the party broadened sufficiently to ensure that the Democrats would become the ascendant national party. In 1936 the Gallup poll found that 59 percent of farmers favored Roosevelt (Agricultural Adjustment Act, Farm Credit Administration, Farm Mortgage Corporation, abolition of the gold standard); 61 percent of white-collar workers (bank regulation, Federal Housing Administration, savings deposit insurance); 80 percent of organized labor (government recognition of collective bargaining, unemployment insurance, work relief); and 68 percent of people under 25 (Civilian Conservation Corps, National Youth Administration). Among lower-income groups, 76 percent favored Roosevelt, compared with 60 percent of the middle class.[42] In contrast, upper-income groups identified overwhelmingly with the Republican party.

❖ THE CITIES IN THE INTERGOVERNMENTAL SYSTEM

The depression years constituted a turning point for the influence of the urban electorate in national politics. Presidential candidates and a large number of Senate and House members knew that they needed the votes of people living in cities. To secure urban votes, they promised legislation. Another development also enhanced the influence of urban political representatives: the forging of a direct relationship between federal policymakers and city governments. Three elements stand out as key facilitators of this development: (1) the crisis in the cities; (2) the intransigence of the states; and (3) the forging of an alliance among city officials for the purpose of securing a federal response to their problems.

By the time of Roosevelt's election, the cities had exhausted their resources. In the 1920s, they had borrowed heavily to finance public improvements and capital construction. They were already seriously in debt when the onset of the depression confronted them with rising unemployment and poverty. Local officials could not avoid seeing the misery and want on their streets. Faced with a manifest emergency, they provided relief funds as rapidly as they could, but it was not enough. Municipal governments simply lacked the financial resources to cope with the emergency.

During the 1920s, counties and municipalities financed a multitude of new public improvement programs. The government activity represented a response to the automobile, to middle-class demands for improved public education, and to public demands for parks and recreational facilities. The auto imposed heavy new costs on local governments. Cities invested in traffic signals, police cars, garbage trucks, school buses, snowplows, roads, and bus and airline terminals. The cities also increased spending for education, constructing new public school buildings, especially high schools, and public libraries. Park and stadium construction also increased substantially.

Local governments made heavier investments in these areas than did either the state or federal governments. During the 1920s, counties and municipalities spent 55 percent to 60 percent of all public funds in the nation, and their total debts mounted to $9 billion.[43] From 1923 to 1927, while the states increased expenditures by 43 percent, spending by the largest 145 cities rose by 79 percent, and cities of 100,000 or more increased their budgets by 82 percent.[44] In these latter cities expenditures for work relief and welfare shot up 391 percent from 1923 to 1932, while the states in this period increased their public welfare budgets by only 63 percent. In the last year of the Hoover Administration, the thirteen cities with populations above 100,000 spent $53 million more than all the states combined for public welfare. Federal grants as a percentage of all public expenditures actually declined from 2 percent to 1.3 percent over the decade of the 1920s.[45] The thirteen biggest cities incurred 50 percent more debt during this period, and many of them were hard-pressed, even at the beginning of the depression, to pay for government services and public improvements.[46]

The depression placed unprecedented responsibilities on city officials at the very time that fiscal resources were drying up. Cities could not expand tax revenues to keep pace with increased responsibilities. State-imposed debt limitations did not allow cities to borrow for day-to-day services. Cities were allowed, in principle, to borrow for capital improvements, but this option soon evaporated. By 1932, because of their high debt loads, cities found it impossible to sell long-term bond issues to investors. In 1932 and 1933, many states and municipalities, including Mississippi, Montana, Buffalo, Philadelphia, Cleveland, and Toledo, were unable to market any bond issues at all.[47] Temporary loans with high interest rates replaced long-term notes.

Two-thirds of the revenue for city budgets derived from property taxes, and these declined precipitously between 1929 and 1933. As assessments on deteriorating property plummeted, property tax revenues fell by 20 percent during the four-year period.[48] At the same time, the rate of tax delinquency increased from 10 percent to 26 percent in cities of over 50,000 in population.[49] Tax losses resulted in an actual reduction in the budgets of the largest thirteen cities between 1931 and 1933, from $1.8 to $1.6 billion.[50]

The cities' attempts to help the unemployed plunged them into fiscal crises. Municipal governments lacked sufficient resources to treat the depression's symptoms, yet many mayors saw this as their principal mission. Detroit's experience revealed the impossibility of the task. In the fall of 1930, Frank Murphy won a surprise victory in a special mayoralty election on a campaign promising unemployment relief.[51] His efforts to provide relief by expanding public jobs and welfare in Detroit attracted national attention. He appointed an unemployment committee, operated an employment bureau, sponsored public works projects, raised private donations for poor relief, and consulted with private firms about rehiring workers. Detroit did more than any other city for its unemployed, but its compassion was costly. With over 40,000 families receiving relief and one-third of the work force unemployed, it was spending $2 million a month for relief in 1931, far more than second-place Boston.[52] The burden soon brought financial disaster to the city.

By the spring of 1931, Detroit faced municipal bankruptcy. To avoid default on its debts and payroll, Murphy curtailed the city's health and recreational services and slashed the fire and police department budgets. Only an emergency bank loan allowed Murphy to meet the June 1931 payroll. Even these efforts were insufficient. Under pressure from the New York banks that held most of Detroit's bonds, Murphy was forced to cut relief expenditures in half during 1932. Thousands of families were dropped from the relief rolls as it became obvious that Detroit could not single-handedly solve the problems caused by the depression.

The mayors of other cities were learning the same lesson. Finally, their sense of desperation galvanized them to take action. In the spring of 1932, Murphy invited the mayors of the major cities to a conference. In June representatives from twenty-nine cities met in Detroit with a single purpose in mind. Murphy stated the cities' case succinctly: "We have done everything humanly possible to do, and it has not been enough. The hour is at hand for the federal government to cooperate."[53] New York City's mayor likewise pleaded for assistance:

> The municipal government is the maternal, the intimate side of government; the side with heart. The Federal Government doesn't have to wander through darkened hallways of our hospitals, to witness the pain and suffering there. It doesn't have to stand in the bread lines, but the time has come when it must face the facts and its responsibility.
>
> We of the cities have diagnosed and thus far met the problem; but we have come to the end of our resources. It is now up to the Federal Government to assume its share. We can't cure conditions by ourselves.[54]

The mayors' demands for federal assistance marked a turning point. Historically, there had been no direct relationship between cities and the federal government. Many local officials felt it was illegitimate to ask the federal government for help, and others feared any aid, lest it lead to a loss of local autonomy. Only a few months before, most of the mayors had declined to attend the mayors' conference suggested by the mayor of Milwaukee.[55] Desperation finally overcame tradition.

The situation was made worse by the fact that state governments refused to respond to the cities' plight. While municipal governments' expenditures for jobs and relief skyrocketed, the states cut expenses: "As tax revenues dwindled and unemployment increased, economy in government became a magic word."[56] State officials were more concerned with balancing budgets than with alleviating human suffering. As state tax revenues declined, public works and construction programs were slashed. Whereas in 1928 the states had spent $1.35 billion for public works projects, mainly in the form of road building, this spending was reduced to $630 million by 1932 and to $290 million for the first eight months of 1933.[57] These budget cuts, which reduced public payrolls, aggravated the unemployment crisis.

Other government expenditures were likewise reduced. Per capita spending for highways and education declined only slightly from 1927 to 1932,[58] but in some states budgets were cut drastically. Tennessee, for example, failed to provide funds for its rural schools for much of 1931.[59] Beginning in 1932, several states slashed their budgets: Arizona by 35 percent; Texas, Illinois, and Vermont by 25 percent; South Carolina by 33 percent. State educational institutions, especially universities, were hard hit. During 1933, education budgets were curtailed by 40 percent in Maryland, by 53 percent in Wyoming, and by more than 30 percent in several other states.[60]

Relief spending by the states went up in the early years of the depression, from $1.00 per capita in 1927 to $3.50 four years later.[61] But the overall amount of relief spending was small and failed to come close to what was needed. The overall statistics, in any case, mask the tremendous variations among the states. From mid-1931 to the end of 1932, relief spending by the states increased from $500,000 to $100 million, but nearly all of the money was provided by a few states, especially New York, New Jersey, and Pennsylvania.[62] When the New Deal began, only eight states provided any money at all for relief.[63]

Local officials petitioned the states for help, and their pleas sounded increasingly desperate as the depression wore on.[64] Except for the very few states that provided relief to the unemployed, no response was forthcoming. The mayors of Michigan's cities, led by Frank Murphy, became so discouraged about the possibility of receiving help from their state government that they appealed for federal assistance. Their fears that such aid would compromise local autonomy were overcome by the corruption and conservatism of their state's government.[65]

State governments were slow to respond to the needs of their cities because their legislatures were controlled by rural representatives. In state after state, legislative districts were drawn up to ensure that rural counties would outvote cities in the state legislative chambers. In Georgia, each county was represented equally in the legislature, regardless of its population.[66] Louisiana provided that each parish would have at least one representative in the state senate and house, no matter what its population. Rhode Island applied this standard to each town.[67] Without exception, all the states made sure that representatives from rural areas would continue to hold legislative majorities.

There were important political stakes in this pattern of underrepresentation. If cities were allowed to gain majorities in legislatures because of their
growing populations, political alignments and party structures would fundamentally change. Incumbent rural legislators would lose their positions, and a
shift in legislative power would inevitably result in new governmental policies.
Underrepresentation of urban areas resulted in indifference to urban problems. Traffic congestion, slums, inadequate park space, and smoke pollution
did not interest rural and small-town legislators. Governors, too, tended to be
insensitive to urban problems. Governors' and legislators' national confer-
ences persistently ignored the depression. At the 1930 governors' conference
in Salt Lake City, for example, the major topics of discussion included such
weighty matters as the essentials of a model state constitution, the need for
constitutional revisions, constitutional versus legislative home rule for cities,
and the extent of legislative control of city governments.[68] The 1931 conference studiously ignored the economic crisis. The cities had nowhere to go but
to the federal government.

The federal response to the depression was designed to deal with a national, not an urban, crisis. Conditions in many rural areas were even worse than
in the cities. There was grinding poverty in the Appalachian region and
throughout the South; families lived in one-room hovels, children walked
around with distended bellies caused by malnutrition, and parents could not
afford to clothe their children to send them to school. A drought from the
Midwest to the Rockies turned much of the plains into a vast dust bowl; in the
winter of 1934, New England's snow turned red from the dust clouds blowing
from Texas, Kansas, and Oklahoma.

Not only was there compelling need in rural areas, but Roosevelt and his
advisers distrusted city politics and culture. For example, Roosevelt's first
public works program, the Civilian Conservation Corps, was based on his
feeling that the moral character of unemployed youth in the cities would be
improved by living in the country.[69] Roosevelt felt "small love for the city."[70]
One of the president's closest advisers confessed that "since my graduate-
school days, I have always been able to excite myself more about the wrongs
of farmers than those of urban workers."[71] In its first two years, the New
Deal accomplished a comprehensive farm policy of guaranteed price supports,
crop allotments to reduce supplies and increase prices, and federally guaranteed mortgages. In contrast, it produced its first program specifically for the
cities, the Wagner-Steagall Housing Act, in 1937, and that program provided
slum clearance and public housing on a very limited scale.

Despite the deep-seated antagonism to the cities, city officials were able
to develop close relationships with politicians and administrators in
Washington, D.C. The New Deal's first relief and recovery programs depended on the states for their administration. But federal programs were later
enacted that put local officials directly in charge. The three major public
works programs—Public Works Administration, Civilian Works
Administration, and Works Progress Administration—were administered by
federal officials in cooperation with both state and local officials. The Federal

Emergency Relief funds were channeled through the states, but local relief agencies actually administered the funds. Local officials found themselves testifying to congressional committees about programs that affected the cities. By 1934, a southern mayor observed: "Mayors are a familiar sight in Washington these days. Whether we like it or not, the destinies of our cities are clearly tied in with national politics."[72]

The New Deal transformed American politics. Local officials learned to petition the federal government for help. This learning process took two forms. First, it became legitimate to seek federal assistance. Second, local officials formed an enduring urban lobby organized specifically to represent cities in the federal system. It was the coming of age for cities in American national politics.

Through the United States Conference of Mayors (USCM), formed in 1932, mayors met annually to discuss their mutual problems. The USCM financed a permanent office in Washington to lobby for urban programs. Together with the International City Management Association, the National Municipal League, the American Municipal League, and other organizations representing local public officials, cities developed the capacity to lobby federal administrators, Congress, and the White House. In the 1950s and 1960s, these lobby organizations began to flex their muscles in Washington.

❖ CITIES IN NATIONAL POLITICS

By the mid-1930s, the nation had completed one political cycle and entered another. For the century and a half since the nation's founding, the conflict between rural America and the cities steadily worsened. Overall, the cities seemed to be the losers. Cities had little or no influence in state houses and in Washington. It seemed unlikely that this situation would change. State legislatures were careful to apportion seats in their legislatures to guarantee rural control. Cities were the losers in a cultural sense as well. Rural America reacted to the cities by imposing rural Protestant morality. Though ethnic community life and the party machines provided some buffer against the attacks, racism and xenophobia ran rampant.

The Great Depression changed the role of the federal government in the United States. The federal government asserted powers to regulate the economy and to assist its citizens during times of need. Urban working-class people were affected by government recognition of collective bargaining. Section 7a of the National Industrial Recovery Act and the Wagner Labor Act encouraged workers to organize. Unemployment compensation, job protection, and factory regulations were important political reforms that the party machines had never sought. Craft and industrial unions became important political forces and participants in the New Deal coalition.

In northern states, urban working-class whites and blacks became the mainstay of the Democratic party. Though it was a long way from their collective vote to Congress and the White House, the potential for political influence was obvious, and it soon was felt. Prohibition was repealed in 1933. Even in the 1930s, long before civil rights legislation was possible, the Roosevelt Administration took steps to ensure that blacks received some appointments to federal posts and a share of the benefits from job and relief programs.

The first urban programs also were passed. Through the 1937 Housing Act, the federal government undertook slum clearance and built public housing. In the late 1930s, federal policymakers expressed a concern about urban problems. The National Resources Committee, composed of federal administrators and experts appointed by the president, published a report in 1937 entitled *Our Cities: Their Role in the National Economy.*[73] The committee asserted that slums and urban blight threatened a hoped-for economic recovery and recommended federal action to improve the economic performance of cities. In 1941, the National Resources Planning Board prepared a report entitled *Action for Cities: A Guide for Community Planning.* The report recommended that cities devise local plans to combat blight and that the federal government provide assistance for this purpose.[74] In 1944, a federally assisted highways bill was enacted; unlike previous highways legislation, cities got their fair share of construction grants. In 1949, Congress passed a massive program to build public housing and clear slums in the inner cities.

The cities' new position in the federal system was only partially assured when they learned to vote Democratic. It was further enhanced when city officials became convinced that they could rightfully lobby for their interests in Washington. It is true that between 1953 and 1961, when a Republican president served in the White House, urban interests were able to push through only one significant new program, the Interstate Highway Act of 1956. From 1959 to 1961, President Eisenhower even eliminated public housing requests from the federal budget. After the election of John F. Kennedy in 1960, however, the urban lobby groups found a receptive environment, and it did not take long for them to exploit it.

CHAPTER
6

THE NATIONAL EFFORT TO "SAVE THE CITIES"

❖ THE "SAVE THE CITIES" AGENDA

In 1937, the prestigious National Resources Committee, appointed by President Franklin Delano Roosevelt, issued the first major national study of cities in the United States. Entitled *Our Cities: Their Role in the National Economy,* the report identified the interests of cities with the interests of the nation as a whole and called upon government to aid cities:

> From the point of view of the highest and best use of our national resources, our urban communities are potential assets of great value, and we must consider from the point of view of the national welfare how they may be most effectively aided in their development.
>
> The prosperity and happiness of the teeming millions who dwell there [in cities] are closely bound up with that of America, for if the city fails, America fails.[1]

It is understandable why national officials would tie the fate of the cities to the health of the nation. The industrial economy had developed in the cities, and, therefore, if the cities declined, it seemed to logically follow that the nation's economy would suffer as well.

After World War II, the physical stock of the older industrial cities deteriorated rapidly. All the nation's cities contained at their centers run-down business districts and block after block of dilapidated housing. Landlords and owners invested little or no money in repairs and renovation, and the construction of new housing had slowed to a crawl. The apparent solutions to the problems of housing and slums lay beyond the financial capacity of local public institutions. The slums that plagued the nation's cities were seen as a national problem, and local officials and business elites who were concerned about deteriorating business and residential districts looked to the national government for help.

City officials used their pivotal position in the New Deal coalition to push Democratic politicians at the national level for assistance. After years of hearings and lobbying, a broad alliance of urban officials, liberal Democratic members of Congress, and inner-city business interests were finally able to push the 1949 Housing and Urban Redevelopment Act through Congress. Using federal funds made available by the legislation, a generation of activist mayors built their political careers on a vision of civic renewal that entailed the massive clearance of inner-city slums and the construction of public housing. These programs so occupied cities in the 1950s and early 1960s that it could be said they were the only political game in town. Ironically, though they were meant to help the cities, these programs ultimately increased racial segregation and exacerbated racial tensions in urban areas.

❖ THE SEARCH FOR URBAN POLICY

The first positive federal response to the problems of urban America came in 1892, when Congress appropriated $20,000 to investigate slum conditions in cities with populations over 200,000.[2] In his subsequent report to the Congress, the Commissioner of Labor noted, among other observations, that there was a higher incidence of arrests and saloons in the nation's slums than anywhere else in the country. This conclusion, obviously, fell short of a national commitment to solve the problems of the cities.

Federal assistance for the construction of urban housing can be traced to the entry of the United States into World War I. In 1918, Congress authorized direct federal loans to local realty companies.[3] At a cost of $69.3 million, 8 hotels, 19 dormitories, 1,100 apartment units, and approximately 9,000 houses were constructed to house wartime shipyard workers in 27 cities and towns.[4] Later in the same year, Congress approved the nation's first public housing program to accommodate additional defense plant workers. The U.S. Housing Corporation was created to manage the program. In the brief three months of the program's existence, the Housing Corporation built about 6,000 single-family dwellings, plus accommodations for 7,200 single men, on 140 project sites scattered around the country.[5] At the conclusion of the war, all of these federally owned housing units were sold to private owners and the government removed itself from the housing business.

The first public housing and slum clearance programs in peacetime were initiated as a result of the economic conditions of the Great Depression. In 1932, the last year of the Hoover Administration, Congress created the Reconstruction Finance Corporation (RFC) and authorized it to extend loans to private developers for the construction of low-income housing in slum areas.[6] Only two projects were actually ever undertaken, with over 98 percent of the money spent in three slum blocks of Manhattan to construct Knickerbocker Village, with its 1,573 apartments.[7] This program had two contradictory purposes. On the one hand, it was supposed to help revive the construction industry; on the other hand, it was supposed to be a means of supplying low-income housing. In the case of Knickerbocker Village, the first goal won out. Eighty-two percent of the slum families who initially moved into the apartments were soon forced to move back to the slums they had left because of the escalating rents charged by the owners.[8]

Franklin D. Roosevelt introduced a great number of national programs designed to stimulate the economy and end the depression. One of the first of these, the National Industrial Recovery Act of 1933, included a minor provision authorizing "construction, reconstruction, alteration, or repair, under public regulation or control, of low-rent housing and slum clearance projects."[9] The Housing Division of the Public Works Administration (PWA) was charged with implementing this provision. At first the PWA tried to entice private developers into constructing low-income housing by offering them low-interest federal loans. This strategy conformed with one of the major purposes of the program, which was "to deal with the unemployment situation by giving employment to workers . . . [and] to demonstrate to private builders the practicability of large-scale community planning."[10] But contractors and home builders did not find low-interest loans sufficiently attractive, and only seven projects ever met specifications and were approved. As a result, the PWA decided to bypass the housing industry altogether and finance and construct its own federally owned housing. The U.S. Emergency Housing Corporation was created for this purpose in 1933, and it claimed the right of eminent domain to force the sale of slum property for clearance and construction.

Federal court decisions in Kentucky[11] and Michigan[12] stopped federal administrators from using eminent domain to take over slum land for clearance, so they tried another tack. The Emergency Housing Corporation decided to make low-income housing grants to local public housing authorities. Local authorities could be chartered by the states, and previous court cases made it clear that the states could use eminent domain to accomplish a variety of public purposes. With federal money available, city officials lobbied their state legislatures to allow them to create local housing authorities to receive the funds. By the end of the PWA public housing program in 1937, twenty-nine states had passed enabling legislation allowing local governments to create and operate local public housing authorities, and forty-six local housing agencies had come into existence.[13] These authorities built almost 22,000 public, low-income housing units in 37 cities.[14]

For all the effort to get the PWA program off the ground, the eventual results were questionable. More low-income units were torn down through slum clearance than were ever built. Local public housing authorities were closely tied to the housing industry in their communities, with the result that a substantial proportion of PWA funds were used to help owners sell slum properties to local housing authorities at inflated prices.[15] These properties were then slated for clearance, even though no new housing units were planned to replace them.

Despite its problems, the PWA experience provided the administrative model for future housing programs. It was accepted that if federal grants were made available for public housing in the future, local public housing agencies would become the recipients of the funds and federal agencies would not try to build public housing units themselves. The Public Housing Act of 1937 (also called the Wagner-Steagall Public Housing Act after the names of its legislative sponsors) succeeded the PWA program. Like its predecessor, its main objectives were to build low-income housing and to eradicate slums. The Act adopted the principle that housing programs would be implemented through federal grants-in-aid to local housing authorities. Under the Act public housing would be built and administered by local agencies, not by the federal government, and private realtors and contractors would handle land sales and construction. Its stated purposes were:

> to provide financial assistance to the states and political subdivisions thereof for the elimination of unsafe and unsanitary housing conditions, for the eradication of slums, for the provision of decent, safe, and sanitary dwellings for families of low income and for the reduction of unemployment and the stimulation of business activity, to create a United States Housing Authority, and for other purposes.[16]

The Public Housing Act of 1937 was "designed to serve the needs of those of low income who otherwise would not be able to afford decent, safe, and sanitary dwellings."[17] However, the absence of substantial profits for realtors, builders, and banks for constructing public housing projects meant that they persistently opposed public housing. As far as they were concerned, government-owned housing competed with the private housing market. Its only redeeming virtue was that public housing provided jobs in the construction industry. But this benefit failed to outweigh the unpopularity of providing housing subsidies to the bottom third of the population. Such subsidies were not nearly as popular as the massive FHA insurance programs designed to make home ownership more affordable to the growing middle class.[18] Realtors, home builders, and financial institutions liked the FHA program because it funneled money directly into the housing industry.

Opposition to public housing was led by the National Association of Real Estate Boards (NAREB), which promoted the idea that housing was an entirely private industry which government should leave alone. As Walter S. Schmidt, president of NAREB, explained:

> Housing should remain a matter of private enterprise and private ownership. It is contrary to the genius of the American people and the ideals they have established that government become landlord to its citizens. There is a sound logic in the continuance of the practice under which those who have the initiative and the will to save acquire better living facilities and yield their former quarters at modest rents to the group below.[19]

Though funding for public housing was bitterly opposed by real estate interests, a broad coalition supported it, including the National Public Housing Conference, the American Federation of Labor (AFL), the Congress of Industrial Organizations (CIO), the Labor Housing Conference, the National Association of Housing and Development Officials, the Urban League, the National Association for the Advancement of Colored People (NAACP), and the National League of Cities. Senator Robert F. Wagner of New York, one of the cosponsors of the 1937 housing bill, defended that legislation by pointing out that it was not intended as a program that would interfere with the private housing market:

> The object of public housing in a nutshell, is not to invade the field of home building for the middle class or the well-to-do which has been the only profitable area for private enterprise in the past. Nor is it even to exclude private enterprise from major participation in a low-cost housing program. It is merely to supplement what private industry will do, by subsidies which will make up the difference between what the poor can afford to pay and what is necessary to assure decent living quarters.[20]

Accordingly, the 1937 legislation contained specific limitations on the costs and quality of rental units and a restriction that occupancy be strictly limited to low-income families.[21] To prevent the government from competing with the private housing market, a requirement also was added that the number of new housing units constructed could not exceed the number of slum dwellings torn down.

The U.S. Housing Administration (USHA) was authorized by the 1937 Act to extend up to $800 million in long-term (sixty years), low-interest loans to local public housing agencies. The loans could cover up to 100 percent of the cost of financing slum clearance and the construction of low-income housing units. The USHA was also authorized to make grants and annual subsidies to local housing agencies for the operation and maintenance of housing units after they were built. In practice, most local projects were financed through a combination of federal (USHA) loans covering 90 percent of the development costs, plus an annual subsidy to cover a portion of the cost of operations.

Federal annual operating subsidies ranged from an average of 30 percent of operating costs in the prewar years to 16 percent during World War II.[22] Local public housing authorities derived their nonfederal revenues from rents, tax-exempt bond issues, and contributions from local governments.

The USHA and its successor agencies, the Federal Public Housing Authority (1942 to 1946) and the Public Housing Administration (1946 to the present), completed a total of 169,451 low-income public housing units under the authority of the 1937 Housing Act.[23] Most of the units were placed under construction before the United States entered World War II.

World War II was the third national emergency (the others were World War I and the depression) recognized by Congress as requiring the production of publicly built and financed housing. In addition to 50,000 units constructed during the war under 1937 Housing Act authorizations, 2 million more housing units were provided through temporary and emergency programs to house workers who streamed into cities to take jobs in defense industry plants. Of these, around 1 million units were privately built with federal financial assistance.[24] Another 1 million were completed under programs that left ownership in the hands of the federal government. As soon as the war was over, these government-owned units were sold on the private market.

❖ THE STRUGGLE OVER PUBLIC HOUSING

The concerns about inner-city slums that had been expressed during the Great Depression were voiced again following World War II. A broad coalition of interests pressed for congressional action. Local public officials and business leaders were alarmed by the condition of downtown business districts and nearby residential areas. Public housing administrators, labor unions, social workers, and liberal Democrats were concerned about the plight of the poor and argued that slum residents had a moral right to adequate housing. In addition, they said, slums bred disease, crime, and delinquency and were, therefore, detrimental to the moral fiber and social fabric of the city. It was noted, for example, that though Cleveland's slum areas contained only 2.7 percent of the city's population, they accounted for 7.8 percent of the juvenile delinquency arrests and 21.3 percent of the city's murders in 1932.[25] Improving the physical environment of slum residents, it was argued, was a good thing to do not only because it gave poor individuals immediate aid, but also because it would help families and individuals begin to improve their lives, thus lowering the level of social disorder.

Local business elites had their own reasons for favoring slum clearance. They were not concerned so much about the conditions of life for slum dwellers as for their own real estate investments. The "blight" of commercial and residential areas, they said, threatened the economic vitality of the central cities. They reasoned that falling rents and increasing vacancy rates formed a downward spiral with less and less maintenance in slum areas. Not only did this drag down all inner-city property values, but it threatened the fiscal health of city governments as well. Deteriorated property yielded little in property taxes. Much more public money had to be expended for the provision of basic municipal services than could be recovered in tax receipts. For example, the blighted areas of Atlanta during the 1930s absorbed 53 percent of the city's expenditures for public services while providing only 5.5 percent of its real property tax revenues.[26] Similarly, Chicago's 1933 tax assessment of $1.2 million in one blighted area was $2 million less than the cost of providing municipal services—and less than half the potential taxes had been collected by 1936.[27]

The U.S. Savings and Loan League voiced support for the redevelopment of blighted areas: "Our people have studied the problem of slum clearance for some years and agree that it is an appropriate field for public action ... we think it appropriate for ... land assembly [to proceed] in the slum areas of our cities."[28] Even the National Association of Real Estate Boards (NAREB) favored urban development, so long as it was implemented through private institutions and involved slum clearance rather than public housing.[29] Private business interests—primarily the real estate and organized housing trade associations—were deeply concerned over the adverse economic impact and attendant capital loss on property owned in blighted areas. As owners and investors in urban real estate, business interests in the cities "had a tremendous stake in the maintenance of residential and commercial property values."[30] Blight threatened this stake.

Though they favored federally subsidized slum clearance, conservative interests were united in their opposition to public housing. NAREB spearheaded the lobbying against federally subsidized public housing. Although its headquarters were in Chicago, NAREB maintained a well-staffed office in the nation's capital—the "Realtors' Washington Office"—from which it exerted pressure on Congress and federal administrators. The executive vice-president of the association was Herbert U. Nelson, a fervent backer of right-wing causes and a strident critic of popular democracy. He was fond of labeling his opponents Communists and subversives. NAREB described itself as a "trade and professional association, [operating] to improve the real estate business, to exchange information and, incidentally, to seek to protect the commodity in which we deal, which is real property, and to make home ownership and the ownership of property both desirable and secure."[31]

Throughout the 1940s, though NAREB and its allies promoted federally subsidized urban redevelopment, the issue remained subordinated to their venomous opposition to public housing programs. This unwavering opposition derived its force from Nelson's ideological stand against the evils of "socialism"—defined as publicly subsidized housing—and was supported by the real estate industry's interest in preventing government competition with privately owned slum housing.[32] The association pressed its opposition to public housing all across the country—on Capitol Hill, in state houses, in city halls, and in communities and neighborhoods. Between 1939 and 1949, it was instrumental in stalling congressional legislation. The blind hatred that

NAREB held for public housing led it to adamantly oppose the 1949 Housing Act, even though this legislation also made federal funds available for slum clearance, which NAREB favored.

The U.S. Savings and Loan League was the second most powerful housing industry group. In 1949, the league represented 3,700 associations, which included in their membership most of the nation's savings and loan institutions. These financial institutions issued long-term mortgage loans for the construction and purchase of homes. Although originally established to serve the working class as an alternative to conventional banking institutions, over the years savings and loan institutions acquired a middle- and upper-class bias in their policies.

The National Association of Home Builders (NAHB) was another important housing industry group. In 1949, this organization represented approximately 16,500 companies, for the most part small, local construction companies.

The three big groups of the housing industry were joined by an array of industry, trade, and financial associations that also opposed public housing, including the U.S. Chamber of Commerce, the Mortgage Bankers Association of America, the Producers Council, the National Economic Council, and the National Association of Retail Lumber Dealers.[33]

As early as 1935, the National Association of Real Estate Boards had begun promoting its own scheme for federally subsidized urban redevelopment. The proposal called for massive slum clearance, but, of course, no public housing. The NAREB proposal was similar to the provisions eventually passed under Title I of the 1949 Housing Act, which provided subsidies for slum clearance.[34]

In the preamble to the 1949 Housing Act, Congress declared a national commitment to rebuild the cities, eliminate slums and blight, and provide decent housing for the nation's citizens.

> The general welfare and security of the Nation and the health and living standards of its people require housing production and related community development sufficient to remedy the serious housing shortage, eliminate substandard and other inadequate housing through the clearance of slums and blighted areas, and the realization as soon as feasible of the goal of a decent home and suitable living environment for every American family, thus contributing to the development and redevelopment of communities and the advancement of growth, wealth, and security of the nation.[35]

During the eight years that elapsed between the first introduction of a housing and slums bill into Congress and the enactment of the legislation in 1949, the housing industry got most of what it wanted, but to get federal subsidies for slum clearance, it was forced to accept public housing. The 1949 legislation received the endorsement of business, real estate, and housing interests because of the key provisions that allowed local authorities to supervise redevelopment; because of joint federal-local subsidies to "write-down" the costs of land below market rates, so that it could be sold at reduced prices to private developers; and because urban renewal and slum clearance relied on private developers to convert the cleared land to new uses. A lot of money could be made on slum clearance.

A broad coalition of interest groups was successful in protecting the public housing component in the 1949 legislation. As might be expected, many church-affiliated welfare organizations (for example, the National Conference of Catholic Charities and the National Council of Jewish Women), civic organizations (including the League of Women Voters and the Citizens Union of New York City), and other groups (for example, the American Council on Education and the American Association of Social Workers) expressed support for public housing.

Perhaps the most influential single organization favoring public housing was the National Public Housing Conference. Formed during the early years of the depression, this group became a kind of brain trust for public housing policy. It was largely responsible for the research and staff work that underlay the development of the 1937 Housing Act. Unlike the real estate lobbies, it was not a federation of local groups, nor was it a mass-based organization. It was an elite group of individuals interested in housing policy, and it included some of the more influential local housing administrators, government officials, and academic experts on housing problems and policies. The Public Housing Conference maintained close connections with the federal government's housing administrators and thus was able to partially offset the housing industry's opposition to public housing.

A second source of support for public housing was organized labor. The AFL and the CIO both maintained housing committees and participated in the Washington-based Labor Housing Conference. Of all the pro–public housing groups, only the unions carried the substantial political clout attendant to mass-based organizations. Labor's solution to urban housing shortages and to the social evils of slum living was the construction of public housing on land made available anywhere in metropolitan areas.

Organized labor led the way in criticizing the real estate industry's redevelopment proposals. A booklet of the period published by the United Auto Workers accused realtors and developers of promoting their own narrow economic interests under the cover of slum clearance:

> Climbing on the "slum clearance" band wagon, they [the real estate and building trade associations] are trying to hoodwink the public into buying city slum areas at a high price and turning such areas over to them at a fraction of such cost to the public. Not a word of "subsidy" here. Not a word of rehousing the families who now live in the slums. . . . With sanctimonious faces they piously prate the high standards of American living and of the fire that burns in American breasts for home ownership (supplied by themselves). . . . To the shields of "private enterprise," "homeownership," and "the high standard of American living," with which they have so successfully covered their operations, they have suddenly added that shiny new shield of "slum clearance.". . . without government assistance, they would not now be operating and there would be little or no private house building in the postwar period.[36]

The National Association of Housing Officials (NAHO) was a third powerful group working on behalf of the public housing cause. This group was formed during the depression years and was responsible for educating supporters of public housing through its publication, the *Journal of Housing*. It, too, attacked the urban redevelopment proposal advocated by the real estate industry. Reflecting the basic values that drew the pro–public housing coalition together, NAHO insisted that the social goal of providing adequate housing was far more important than urban economic development itself.

Local government officials and the organizations representing them were interested in federal subsidies in any form, and therefore they lobbied for both slum clearance and public housing. The U.S. Conference of Mayors, the National League of Cities, and the American Municipal Association all lined up behind a program of federally subsidized development. They were instrumental in knitting together a coalition sufficiently broad so that the legislation before Congress would not be sabotaged by the bickering among the various interest groups. Perhaps the best indicator of the unlikely nature of the political alliance that supported the 1949 Housing Act is to be found in its unofficial title—the Wagner-Ellender-Taft Act. The three senators whose names were identified with the legislation spanned the spectrum of American political philosophy. The conservative Republican presidential aspirant, Robert A. Taft of Ohio, the New Deal big-city liberal, Robert F. Wagner of New York, and the segregationist southern Democrat, Allen J. Ellender of Louisiana united to see their bill through five rounds of hearings, four years of controversy, three redraftings, and two changes of leadership in Congress.

The housing bill was introduced in the Senate (S. 1592) in 1945 and approved there in April 1946, only to die in the House Banking and Currency Committee—killed by "very potent private lobby groups" opposing public housing.[37] The bill (now S. 866) again passed the Senate in April 1948, despite the fact that as a result of the 1946 elections the Republicans had become the majority party in that chamber. Again, the bill was killed in the House. This time it succeeded in getting the approval of the House Banking and Currency Committee, with the aid of a heavy dose of public pressure and political arm twisting applied by President Truman, labor unions, and other groups. The Rules Committee, however, refused to let it go to the House floor for a vote, so it died in the committee just before the opening of the Republican national convention in July 1948.

The general elections of 1948 returned Democratic majorities to both houses of Congress. In the battle over the bill (now S. 1070) in the Senate, supporters of public housing were put to the test. In the most devious of several obstructionist moves, Senator John W. Bricker (Republican from Ohio) introduced an amendment prohibiting racial segregation in the public housing program, thus hoping to place northern liberal Democrats on the horns of a dilemma. Such liberals as Hubert H. Humphrey (Democrat from Minnesota) and Paul Douglas (Democrat from Illinois) determined the ultimate fate of the bill in the Senate by voting against the open-housing amendments they had so recently advocated at the Democratic national convention in 1948. With a stipulation requiring integration, public housing would never have survived the opposition by southern Democrats, and the liberals knew it.

The political coalition that passed the bill in the Senate included both Republicans and Democrats, liberals and conservatives. On the key votes in the Senate, the bill received majority support from both sides of the aisle and got yes votes from such members as the maverick liberal Senator Wayne Morse of Oregon and the conservative Senator Joe McCarthy of Wisconsin. In the House, a threat by the Democratic leadership to reduce the authority of the Rules Committee (which was dominated by southern Democrats) succeeded in persuading the committee to let the bill (H. 4009) go to the floor. Despite intensive lobbying efforts by the realtors and their allies, the public housing title was retained by a razor-thin five-vote margin, and the entire bill was then passed by a bipartisan majority. Thus, northern Democrats, urban Republicans, and a few southern Democrats who decided to cooperate with the president came together to enact the nation's first comprehensive urban redevelopment policy.[38]

Title I of the Act empowered the Housing and Home Finance Agency (HHFA) to assist local efforts at blight and slum removal. Through this agency the federal government offered grants-in-aid to help local urban renewal agencies absorb the cost of the "write-down" on land that had been cleared of slum buildings. The write-down was the difference between the local agency's cost of assembling and clearing the site and the price subsequently paid for the land by private developers.

In addition to the $500 million authorized for the write-down subsidies, the HHFA was authorized to extend loans to local urban renewal or public housing agencies for land assembly and site clearance. The Act gave private developers preference over local governments in redeveloping the clearance sites. Tenants and slum dwellers displaced by renewal programs were supposed to be supplied with "decent, safe and sanitary dwellings." The redevelopment effort was required to be "predominantly residential" in character and was to conform to "general plans for the development of the locality as a whole."

Title III, Low-Rent Public Housing, authorized (but did not appropriate money for) the production of 810,000 government-subsidized housing units over the next six years. This amounted to 10 percent of the estimated national need for new low-cost dwellings. Congress authorized annual subsidies to local public housing agencies of up to $308 million. A temporary revolving loan fund of $1.5 billion was established to finance initial construction.

The 1949 housing statute established occupancy preferences for veterans and families displaced by Title I (clearance) activities. Per-room and per-unit cost limitations were imposed to prevent "extravagance and unnecessary" amenities. Rent levels and tenant eligibility requirements were regulated to minimize competition with the private housing market and to ensure that public housing benefited only the neediest families.

❖ URBAN RENEWAL AND ITS PROBLEMS

The stated objectives of the national legislation that funded urban renewal generally conflicted with the political preferences and economic interests of local elites. They were more interested in enhancing land values through commercial revitalization. The 1949 Housing Act was designed specifically to clear slums and to construct low-income housing. Amendments to the legislation, adopted in 1954, allowed communities to use 10 percent of project funds for nonresidential, commercial revitalization. In 1960, this proportion was raised to 30 percent.

In actual practice, right from the beginning half or more of all funds were diverted away from low-income housing to commercial development. This was made possible by the way federal administrators interpreted the legislation. Any renewal project that allocated 51 percent or more of its funds to housing was designated by the federal administrators as a "100 percent housing" project. By manipulating this definition, local authorities were able to allocate as much as two-thirds of their funds for commercial projects, despite the "predominantly residential" language in the legislation.

Thus urban renewal was turned into a political pawn of the larger downtown businesses.[39] Local political and economic elites were far more concerned about the economic decline of central business districts (CBDs) than they were about slum residents. Business leaders and politicians were convinced that slums were responsible for the steady decline in downtown property values and retail activity. As a consequence, they were interested in slum clearance, but not in low-cost housing for residents displaced by clearance.

In the abstract, housing for low-income people might seem worthwhile, but few local politicians felt they could afford to tolerate it in their own neighborhoods. Site selection was of paramount concern, for example, to Chicago's politicians in the 1950s.[40] The Chicago experience was duplicated in cities across the country. Public housing had failed to develop strong grass roots support in local communities. Quite the opposite. Local chapters of the National Association of Real Estate Boards organized opposition to public housing projects in city after city. In often vitriolic campaigns, the opponents of subsidized housing played on fears that public housing might be used to promote racial integration. Between 1949 and the end of 1952, public housing programs were rejected by referenda, many of them sponsored by NAREB, in Akron, Houston, and Los Angeles and in almost forty other cities. Social and political realities at the local level made public housing a volatile issue. Local officials were acutely aware that "there could hardly be many votes to be gained in championing the cause—and perhaps a great many lost."[41]

In contrast, slum clearance and economic redevelopment were good politics. Seizing on redevelopment as a way to secure federal funds, enterprising mayors could simultaneously advance their political fortunes and improve the public image of the city. To implement big clearance and redevelopment projects, an alliance had to be forged between the mayor and other local officials on the one hand and the business community on the other. In most cities, the alliance was organized by corporate executives, but there were other crucial participants as well. Real estate and merchant interests in central business districts, metropolitan newspapers, and frequently the construction trades unions lent their support. For many years, this political alliance constituted a "new convergence of power" that completely dominated the politics of most large cities.[42]

The model for this kind of alliance was established years before Congress finally approved the urban renewal legislation. In 1943, the financier Richard King Mellon organized the Allegheny Conference on Community Development in Pittsburgh. The members, most of whom were corporate executives, teamed up with the mayor they helped to elect in 1945, David Lawrence, to revitalize Pittsburgh's central business district, called the Golden Triangle. Philadelphia followed Pittsburgh's example with the Greater Philadelphia Movement in 1948. By the end of the 1950s, scarcely a large city in the United States lacked a renewal coalition. Richard J. Daley, first elected mayor of Chicago in 1953, rebuilt the Democratic machine in that city by aggressively launching the revitalization of Chicago's Loop and lakefront. In contrast, Boston's machine met its demise at the hands of a political coalition dedicated to renewing the city. The candidate selected by the New Boston Committee defeated long-time machine boss James Michael Curley in the 1951 mayoral race, then backed the massive clearance of Boston's Italian West End and the construction of a large governmental center. Ultimately, Boston's renewal program took 10 percent of the city's land area.[43] In 1950, St. Louis's Mayor Joseph Darst received widespread national publicity when his city became the nation's first to secure federal funding for a massive urban renewal program. Raymond Tucker, who replaced him in 1953, was even more aggressive in pushing clearance projects. A former St. Louis mayor recalled that renewal united political and business leaders behind a common cause:

> About a year ago, a group of distinguished citizens of our community were called into the Mayor's office and there charged by Mayor Darst with the responsibility of giving leadership to a program to take advantage of the Housing Act of 1949, Title I, and the State Act of 1945. It was suggested that an urban redevelopment corporation be organized. There was much fine publicity on the part of the metropolitan press—they not only gave considerable space but they also subscribed to the extent of better than a quarter of a million dollars to the debentures and stock of that corporation. So, we salute the press on this occasion. I should add that many other fine business institutions, sixty-nine in number, subscribed a total in excess of $2,000,000 toward the capital structure of the corporation. It is a distinguished list. There's the May Department Stores, Stix, Baer and Fuller, Scruggs, Vandervoort and Barney, the Anheuser Busch Company, Ely Walker Company, the Falstaff Company, the First National Bank, . . . and others.[44]

A similar alliance came together in New Haven, Connecticut, where the young Democrat Richard Lee hung his mayoral aspirations and his political future on the prospect of a successful urban redevelopment program. He won the 1952 election and several terms thereafter by leading a broad coalition that sponsored federally funded redevelopment. Lee's political capital derived from a coalition of government officials and local notables, particularly business leaders. It took shape in the formation of the Citizen's Action Committee (CAC), an advisory board required by the federal legislation, which included "businessmen concerned with traffic and retail sales, trade union leaders concerned with employment and local prosperity," and "political liberals concerned with slums, housing, and race relations." This group was characterized by Mayor Lee as the political alliance that ran New Haven. He described it as

> the biggest set of muscles in New Haven. . . . They're muscular because they control wealth, they're muscular because they control industries, represent banks. They're muscular because they head up labor. They're muscular because they represent the intellectual portions of the community. They're muscular because they're articulate, because they're respectable, because of their financial power, and because of the accumulation of prestige they have built up over the years as individuals in all kinds of causes.[45]

The fact that this group was brought together by an entrepreneurial mayor did not mean, however, that they had been co-opted into a supporting role against their better judgments and own interests. One CAC member, a conservative banker, noted that the city's chamber of commerce had an abiding interest in seeing the city revitalized economically: "[I]f we are going to have a city, and it's going to be a shopping area . . . something had to be done. . . . Here's a dream that we've had for a long time and we're happy to see it culminated."[46] A second banker, in an outburst of economic parochialism, said,

> If taxes are going to remain high and there is going to be a social program in the United States . . . why, there's only one thing to do and that is to devise ways and means so that we can share in it. That's pretty selfish. I'm not interested in building a highway through Montana . . . or a TVA down South, and I'd like to see some of those dollars come back to Connecticut so that we can enjoy some more benefits.[47]

Local labor leaders were as supportive of urban renewal as was the business community. A union official pointed out that urban renewal created construction jobs and had the added appeal of seeming to help the less well-off:

> [E]verybody feels—that is, most everybody feels—that they benefit one way or another by a prosperous community, even if it just means a better economic atmosphere . . . the building trades benefit directly from the program, and so they are enthusiastic towards it and have even made contributions to the CAC committee itself. . . . On the other end of the scale from the conservative building trades, the more sophisticated trade union leaders . . . have been completely taken with the program because of the concern of the program leaders for the human relations aspect of it.[48]

The programs financed by the 1949 Housing Act were perfect vehicles that mayors could use to secure their personal political futures. Mayors and business leaders tended to view urban renewal through the same lenses. Mayors universally associated the economic fortunes of their cities with the health of the central business districts, and downtown businesses identified their own economic fortunes with the future of the central cities. The full-scale flight of the middle class to the suburbs was seriously undermining the economic viability of inner cities. Against this background, it was almost certain that federal renewal dollars would be used to help business and that business's interests would be seen as indistinguishable from the interests of cities. As one businessman described it,

> They believe in the free enterprise system and have gone into this work, not to lose their money; they certainly hope to get their money back. And they hope to earn a modest profit. I point out, however, that a good many of them have a selfish motive. They want to maintain downtown values where their businesses are centered.[49]

Since the central business district was the center of activity where the local business establishment held heavy real estate and business investments, it was only logical that businesses would seek to protect their investments through revitalization of their immediate environment. The need for political visibility and campaign contributions from wealthy donors ensured that elected officials would favor sites near the CBD for renewal. Those areas were generally the oldest in the cities and were therefore susceptible to being "blighted," a designation applied to a specific area by an Urban Renewal Authority, and the first step in a process that led to condemning and clearing property. Chicago's Loop, for instance, was bordered by a semicircle of slums and blight extending out, on the average, for five miles.

The separate elements of the renewal coalition needed one another. Local officials needed the financial support and public prestige the business community possessed. The business community, in turn, depended on the resources of the public sector. Governmental authority was a necessary ingredient for a successful redevelopment effort. Public authority was, in the first instance, called upon to apply for federal funds through an officially constituted urban renewal agency. The government's power of eminent domain, which allowed it to condemn "blighted" property for a "higher" public use, was critical for land assembly, because individual property owners could not otherwise be compelled to sell. Finally, the unique ability of local renewal agencies to receive the necessary write-down subsidies and loans from the federal government made local officials and agencies indispensable to business leaders who wanted urban redevelopment. "This strange coalition"[50] was thus a mutually reinforcing alliance of formidable power.

❖ THE RENEWAL STEAMROLLER

As a result of their successful efforts to secure federal backing for urban renewal, the renewal coalition "engineered a massive allocation of private and social resources" in the cities.[51] The public funds invested in clearance and write-down subsidies leveraged investments by private entrepreneurs. By

1968, $35.8 billion had been committed by private institutions in 524 renewal projects.[52] In addition, the huge federal expenditures on the interstate highway program, funded through the National Defense Highway Act of 1956, also provided hundreds of thousands of jobs and considerable profits to construction firms building highways through urban areas.

The massive clearance of neighborhoods associated with urban renewal and highway building was controversial. While business leaders talked glibly about benefiting all the residents of the city through the provision of jobs and increases in taxes, it was painfully apparent that viable neighborhoods were often destroyed in the process. In Boston, block after block of well-kept bungalows and row houses, grocery stores, barber shops, bakeries, and taverns—all the elements making up historic, safe, thriving Italian neighborhoods in Boston's West End—were leveled. "Blight" was such a loose term that it could be, and often was, applied to viable neighborhoods.[53] Most of the community turbulence dating from the early 1950s was related to the massive destruction of neighborhoods caused by urban renewal and highway construction projects. According to one scholar, "development issues . . . dominated the neighborhoods" in the 1950s and 1960s in four cities he studied.[54]

Considering the intensity and frequency of protest, it seems surprising that neighborhoods won so few victories. The reason for this poor record was that the groups that opposed renewal were small and often quite parochial. Neighborhoods acted as interest groups protecting their own turf. The various neighborhoods were so diverse that it was difficult for them to form stable alliances with one another. As a consequence, the renewal coalition usually outlasted protests originating from a single neighborhood. By astutely selecting renewal and redevelopment sites, urban renewal administrators could pursue a politics of divide and conquer.

Atlanta provides an excellent example of this process. Beginning in 1952, Atlanta's Metropolitan Planning Commission became concerned about the movement of blacks into neighborhoods close to the business district. In its report of that year, entitled *Up Ahead,* the commission maintained that "from the viewpoint of planning the wise thing is to find outlying areas to be developed for new colored housing." The commission recommended "public policies to reduce existing densities, wipe out blighted areas, improve the racial pattern of population distribution, and make the best possible use of central planned areas."[55] The actual goal, thinly disguised by this verbiage, was to move blacks into areas further from the downtown area.

Atlanta's organization of big corporations, the Central Atlanta Improvement Association, backed faithfully by the white-owned newspapers, assiduously promoted clearance. Special care was taken to obtain the backing of the Chamber of Commerce, which represented smaller businesses. The Atlanta Real Estate Board was brought on board by promises that renewal would help to maintain segregated housing patterns. Promises were made that no public housing would be constructed on urban renewal land. Support from some leaders of the black community was obtained by promises to make land available for the construction of black housing subdivisions farther from the CBD and by a commitment to build single-family housing for blacks to be subsidized by federal funds available under Section 221 of the 1949 Housing Act.

In 1957, newspapers began to criticize Mayor William Hartsfield for not providing positive leadership on redevelopment proposals. The mayor, who had been lukewarm about the proposals for downtown renewal, soon reversed himself in the face of media criticism and pressure from the business community. After one especially tense meeting with business leaders, he stated that he would "go to the extent of rooting the entire government out if they feel we have been remiss in the face of federal opportunities to make progress."[56] Perceiving that his own future was tied to the renewal issue, Hartsfield became an avid supporter of Atlanta's redevelopment program.

In 1960, Atlanta elected a new mayor, a well-known businessman named Ivan Allen. He vigorously promoted the comprehensive renovation of downtown Atlanta. Peachtree Street became the location of several million dollars' worth of hotel construction. Eventually, most of downtown Atlanta was cleared. By the 1980s, historic downtown had been replaced by a huge enclosed mall called the Peachtree Center, all of it surrounded by acres of parking lots and empty land where buildings once stood.

The political muscle of the renewal coalition and how far the coalition was willing to go to promote redevelopment are revealed by the years of controversy over the Yerba Buena Center in San Francisco.[57] The idea of a large convention hotel and recreational center located in the heart of San Francisco originated in 1953, when the San Francisco board of supervisors approved an area south of Market Street for possible redevelopment. The center was envisioned as "the blockbusting wedge to expand the city's financial district southward across Market Street."[58] It was easy for proponents to build support for such a concept. San Francisco contains scores of corporate giants, including Standard Oil of California, Southern Pacific, Transamerica Corporation, Levi Strauss, Crown Zellerbach, Del Monte, Pacific Telephone and Telegraph, Bethlehem Steel, and Pacific Gas and Electric. Among the many financial institutions located in downtown San Francisco are Bank of America, Wells Fargo, Crocker National Bank, Bank of California, Aetna Life, John Hancock, and Hartford Insurance. During the 1960s, the buildings that housed these institutions changed San Francisco's skyline. Between 1960 and 1972, twenty-three high rises were constructed in downtown San Francisco.[59]

In late 1955, influential business leaders formed the Blyth-Zellerbach Committee to promote plans for the redevelopment of the wholesale and market area just east and south of the financial district. This area, with its market stalls, narrow passageways, and constant bustling activity, concerned business and political leaders, who worried about the impact it might have on the future downtown business district, which they envisioned as an expanding agglomeration of corporate, cultural, and tourist facilities. Motivated by this concern, they formed the San Francisco Planning and Urban Renewal Association in 1959. This was a broader group than the Blyth-Zellerbach Committee. Working with the San Francisco Redevelopment Agency, business leaders were able to have detailed input in the redevelopment plans.

The San Francisco Redevelopment Agency assumed a pivotal role in redevelopment beginning in April 1959, when Mayor George Christopher appointed M. Justin Herman as the agency's executive director. Herman became the "chief architect, major spokesman, and operations commander for the transformation of whole sections of the city."[60] Under his leadership the redevelopment agency hired several hundred professionals and dozens of consultants and applied for millions of dollars in federal urban renewal subsidies. Herman believed in his mission so zealously that he interpreted any criticism of his projects as an attempt by parochial interests to stand in the way of progress. He was vicious with his critics. In 1970, he was quoted as saying, "this land is too valuable to permit poor people to park on it."[61] He was cited in a major publication in 1970 as "one of the men responsible for getting urban renewal" renamed

> "the federal bulldozer" and negro removal. He was absolutely confident that he was doing what the power structure wanted in so far as the poor and the minorities were concerned. That's why San Francisco has mostly luxury housing and business district projects—that's what white, middle-class planners and businessmen envision as ideal urban renewal. . . . Also, with Herman in control, San Francisco renewal never got slowed down by all this citizen participation business that tormented other cities.[62]

These sentiments were shared by federal officials, who generally admired Herman's vision and skills.

One of the most important allies of the San Francisco Redevelopment Agency was the San Francisco Convention and Visitors Bureau, dedicated to promoting the city and mobilizing public support for downtown investment. As the representative of the city's tourism industry, the bureau represented hotels, retail stores, transportation and tour agencies, restaurants, athletic teams, banks, hotel and exhibit suppliers, entertainment unions, and the media. The bureau, which employed a staff of forty by the early 1970s, was principally responsible for hotel bookings for groups; for billboard, magazine, and newspaper advertising and brochures describing San Francisco; for group tour promotions; for liaisons with travel agencies; and for the promotion of special events, such as the Chinese New Year celebration, the Japanese cherry blossom festival, Columbus Day, and St. Patrick's Day. Supported by a hotel tax, the bureau operated on an annual budget of more than $1 million.

Another important member of the downtown coalition was the Hotel Employers Association, which represented the biggest hotels in San Francisco. The purpose of this group was to promote the full occupancy of hotels through a healthy tourism and convention business.

The Building and Construction Trades Council also joined the redevelopment coalition. At first distrustful of redevelopment, the unions fell in line when it became obvious that construction jobs would be generated by the reconversion of downtown property. In fact, the Building and Construction Trades Council became an unqualified backer of just about any kind of new construction that would increase employment.

The *San Francisco Chronicle* and *Examiner* were untiring backers of the Yerba Buena Center. They supplied editorial support and ample space for information about renewal plans. Both newspapers are located in the downtown area and had a direct economic interest in development. They were owned by influential business leaders who shared the business perspective on the downtown. Radio and television stations also were loyal to the cause. The economic motivation for such support was illustrated by a quote from an editorial of KPIX Television Area Vice-President Louis S. Simon: "Although I am president-elect of the Convention and Visitors Bureau, vitally interested in this subject, I am speaking today solely on behalf of KPIX and our Editorial Board."[63] All of the local television and radio stations aired frequent editorials denouncing opponents of the project and predicting financial disaster for San Francisco if the Yerba Buena Center were not constructed.

Considering the power of the coalition pushing the project, it is surprising that Yerba Buena became embroiled in a heated controversy that eventually doomed the project. Resistance to Yerba Buena came from tenants who lived in the Milner Hotel, located in the heart of the construction area. Represented by legal services attorneys, the tenants filed a petition with HUD asking for an administrative hearing on the redevelopment agency's relocation plan. HUD denied the request on the ground that no displacement had yet taken place.

During the summer of 1969, the residents of the proposed renewal area held a meeting at the Milner Hotel and formed an association called the Tenants and Owners in Opposition to Redevelopment. Taking their case into federal court, the tenants were able to secure an injunction against the Yerba Buena Center that cut off all federal funds, subject to a revised plan to relocate the area's residents. The judge who heard the case concluded that the secretary of HUD "had not been provided with any creditable evidence at all" in regard to the redevelopment agency's plan to relocate residents into suitable housing. He indicated that "the record shows that at this point there is no adequate relocation housing in San Francisco that meets the requirements of the 1949 Housing Act and is available for persons yet to be displaced from the project area."[64] Under pressure from the court to revise its relocation plans, the redevelopment agency eventually agreed to increase the hotel tax in San Francisco in order to finance the construction of low-income housing for tenants who would be displaced by the Yerba Buena Center. Court battles over this plan, however, plus the escalating costs of the Center, eventually doomed it.

❖ REDEVELOPMENT AND RACE

Justin Herman's attitudes toward the poor were shared by urban renewal administrators and their allies across the country. In the core areas of the cities issues of poverty and race were inextricably linked. As a result, most urban renewal programs had racial (or racist) overtones. The African Americans who moved to the cities in the twentieth century were housed in the most run-down areas of the inner cities. The oldest and most dilapidated housing was generally located near central business districts and, therefore, black populations were frequently displaced by clearance projects. The "black residents of the inner cities [and] black businesses were among the prime victims of federally-sponsored urban renewal programs" referred to as "black removal."[65] The program was appropriately described by critics as "Negro clearance," a phrase that derived from the fact that over three-fourths of the people displaced by urban renewal in the first eight years of the program, and 66 percent of those displaced through 1961, were black or (less often) Puerto Rican.[66]

Redevelopment of the CBD and areas near it made the city's downtown more attractive to prospective investors and suburban shoppers. Simultaneously, it removed black and lower-class neighborhoods from the immediate environs of the CBD. In its quest to protect CBD property values and to secure an attractive environment for the city's commercial activity, the urban renewal coalition extracted social costs that fell disproportionately on poor people and on African-American slum residents. Black tenants were forced into other parts of the city by clearance projects—usually to dilapidated housing in a slightly more distant slum, or to public housing constructed on cleared land still surrounded by slums. Economic and racial barriers left them no other choice but to move to another area much like the slum they left behind: "Given the realities of the low-income housing market . . . it is likely that, for many families, relocation [meant] no more than keeping one step ahead of the bulldozer."[67] Thus, a new game was added to the harsh realities of urban life—"musical slums."

Not only were the poor displaced, but they were forced to pay higher rents when the supply of low-rent housing units dwindled. With only 5 percent of the new housing units within the economic reach of low-income families, there was a 90 percent decrease in the supply of low-income housing within redevelopment areas during the first ten years of the program's operation.[68] Slum dwellers, who were initially supposed to benefit from the urban renewal program, were often the biggest losers. In the first fourteen years of the program's operation, "urban renewal demolished the homes of 177,000 families and another 66,000 single individuals, most of them poor and most of them black."[69] Less than one-fourth of the housing units were replaced, and many of these were too expensive for those who were displaced.[70] Only $34.8 million of the urban renewal funds—less than 1 percent—were used for relocation assistance, placing a disproportionate share of the cost of the program on the slum residents who were forced to move.[71]

❖ PUBLIC HOUSING: URBAN RENEWAL'S STEPCHILD

Public housing was kept in the 1949 Housing Act because the advocates of urban renewal could not get their program passed without it. It was obvious even to the most conservative members of the urban renewal coalition that the families and individuals displaced by clearance would have to find new housing. The 1949 Housing Act had called attention to this obvious fact. Public housing was part of the solution. The legislation required that people dis-placed by clearance be given priority in moving into public housing projects. However, public housing was not politically feasible in any city unless it was tied to urban renewal, and thus "the necessity of public housing as a compan-ion to these [urban redevelopment] efforts was accepted as a fact of life."[72] Public housing was reluctantly accepted as a necessary evil by supporters of renewal, but this lukewarm support meant that over the years far less low-cost housing was built than Congress had originally targeted. By the end of 1961, clearance had eliminated 126,000 housing units. The 28,000 new units that replaced them could house less than one-fifth of the 113,000 families and 36,000 individuals who were displaced by clearance.[73] Most of the cleared land was slated for commercial uses rather than housing. Public housing accounted for only 6 percent of the construction started and only 1 percent of additional construction planned in urban renewal areas as of April 1, 1961.[74]

Because public housing was tied closely to slum clearance, most public housing tenants in the central cities were black. Their status as slum dwellers gave blacks "the dubious privilege of eligibility for public housing."[75] Nonwhites accounted for 38 percent of all public housing tenants in 1952, but by 1961 this percentage had risen to 46 percent nationwide. In individual proj-ects segregation was the norm. Whites who were eligible for public housing or who had been victims of slum clearance had housing options in the private market that were unavailable to blacks. Blacks, therefore, tended to take over public housing in the cities by default—the supply of low-income housing units was shrinking—and, as a result of racial discrimination, they were kept out of many of the neighborhoods that they could afford.

Public housing never got over its stepchild status. In most European countries, housing constructed and administered by governments in the years following World War II was available to middle-class families as well as to the poor, and much of this housing was considered as good as, or sometimes bet-ter than, what could be found on the private market. As a consequence, there was widespread political support for a public role in housing.[76] In the United States, by contrast, it was regarded as a welfare program for people who had failed. It passed Congress amid intense criticism from the real estate lobby and its allied groups, who labeled it socialistic and un-American. Many local com-munities built it only as the price to be paid for getting on with urban renewal. The legacy that public housing carried was simply too negative to allow it ever to be a successful program.

Public housing "was born with profound defects, and the hostile environ-ment in which it grew aggravated its congenital ailments."[77] There were three nearly fatal restrictions built into the program. The first, and perhaps most important, restricted eligibility to those who could not afford any other kind of housing. The real estate lobby would have tolerated no other policy. The insidious result of such a policy was to concentrate those poor families togeth-er that, for whatever reasons, were unable to improve their circumstances. Rising incomes meant eviction. Already, in the 1950s, the concentration of families in poverty meant that public housing projects were prone to high levels of violence and juvenile crime. Over the years, public housing tenants were increasingly made up of "broken families, dependent families, and welfare families."[78] If the families whose incomes went up had been able to stay in their apartments and pay higher rents, the tendency to worsening social pathologies might have been moderated,[79] and the rental income they paid would have helped to make public housing more economically viable.

A second built-in flaw relates to restrictions on siting of public housing units and the racial segregation that inevitably followed from such restrictions. Public housing projects were almost always built on slum land that had been cleared for that purpose; almost never were they built outside ghetto areas or, heaven forbid, in the suburbs. This meant that almost all projects were surrounded by slums, and most of these areas were inhabited by blacks. From the beginning, most public housing projects were segregated by explicit policy in all but a few northern states.[80] By the time President John F. Kennedy signed an executive order forbidding the practice in 1962, it could have little practical effect, since by then the overwhelming majority of public housing tenants in large cities were African American anyway. Public housing policy had the perverse effect of reinforcing and intensifying the racial segregation that already existed in the cities.

A third fundamental flaw of the public housing program flows from cost and design restrictions that guaranteed that many of the units would be uncomfortable and undesirable. Public housing served as a constant reminder to its tenants and to everyone else that this was a grudging welfare program. To save money on site preparation and construction costs, cities built clusters of high-density, high-rise buildings. The African-American writer James Baldwin might have been describing almost any of these projects when he referred to those in Harlem as "colorless, bleak, high and revolting."[81] Of course, big American and European cities are full of high rises that command steep rents from affluent clientele, but such structures, especially when built cheaply, "were not suitable for poor people with big families."[82] It was difficult for parents to supervise children (even if suitable play facilities were available). The architecture was a virtual invitation to vandalism and crime: Elevators were often broken and stuck; laundry rooms were many floors removed from tenants' apartments; dark hallways and stairwells were poorly lighted even when there were bulbs available.

The Cabrini-Green projects north of Chicago's Loop began as two-story brick row houses built to house war workers in World War II. All of the occupants were white. In 1958, fifteen high-rise buildings went up, and another eight were constructed in 1962. These 19-story monstrosities loomed over the surrounding neighborhoods. Almost all the tenants were black. In New York City, high-rise public housing is often over 20 stories in height. The Pruitt-Igoe project in St. Louis, completed between 1954 and 1959, was composed of 2,762 apartments in 33 eleven-story buildings on a 57-acre site. By the time the last building was completed, it was already a community scandal.[83] By 1973, it had become an international symbol for the failure of American public housing. In that year, photographs that made *Life* magazine's

"The Year in Review" showed the shocking spectacle of one of the buildings imploding from hundreds of charges of carefully placed dynamite. As a monument to a policy failure, the episode could hardly have been more dramatic and fitting: Explosives experts got the opportunity to hone their demolition skills on buildings that had been constructed, complete with awards to the architectural firm, little more than fifteen years before.

Perhaps the most unfortunate legacy from this period of public housing is that the "projects" became enduring symbols of welfare for blacks. They stand as stark symbols of racial segregation, crime, and poverty in the inner cities, and as such they overwhelm a different, more complex lesson that can be learned, which is that not all public housing has been a failure. The two- and three-story town houses constructed in the 1930s were often pleasant places with satisfied tenants. Town house projects built in the 1960s and after have often been quite successful—and of course not in the news. The legacy and the enduring reality of the high-rise projects tend to overwhelm the success stories.

❖ THE LEGACY

By the early 1960s, there was widespread opposition to federally assisted urban renewal. Liberal critics viewed urban renewal as a "federally financed gimmick to provide relatively cheap land for a miscellany of profitable, prestigious [private] enterprises."[84] Conservatives were also appalled by the results of the program. At its inception and through its early years business leaders and politicians expected a miraculous reversal of central city decline. The optimism soon turned into frustration. Redevelopment took too long. By the later 1960s, it took an estimated four years to plan a clearance and renewal project and then an additional six years for completion. Often, by the time a project was completed, the original goals had been abandoned.[85] Blighted neighborhoods and slums grew faster than the renewal projects could eliminate them.

In 1965, rent supplement programs were enacted as an alternative to public housing for the poor. Through direct housing aid, the poor would presumably be able to choose their own housing on the private market. The Housing and Urban Development Act of 1968 required that a majority of housing units constructed on redevelopment sites be for low- and moderate-income families.[86] Such tinkering with the urban renewal and public housing programs was designed to provide more benefits for the poor. The improvements, in the end, were modest. Low-income housing continued to be replaced on far less than a one-to-one basis; indeed, only 51 percent of the new units built in urban renewal areas after 1968 were for people of low or moderate incomes.[87]

Both public housing and urban renewal met their effective demise in the 1970s. The inability of either to slow significantly the decay of the nation's inner cities weakened their bases of support. They had persisted in the face of bitter criticism because everyone felt that something should be done, but there was no agreement on what would work. In 1974, urban renewal was merged into the Community Development Block Grant program. Public housing was allowed to decline under the Nixon administration, from 104,000 starts in 1970 to only 19,000 starts by 1974.[88] A few years later, it was essentially abandoned when the Reagan Administration eliminated publicly constructed low-income housing in favor of programs to subsidize landlords and a few experiments in housing vouchers.

The urban renewal and public housing programs exacerbated racial tensions and helped shape contemporary attitudes and stereotypes about African Americans. In the 1950s, national policies were instrumental in reshaping urban areas. On the one hand, through its Federal Housing Administration and Veterans Administration loan programs, the federal government helped millions of middle-class Americans flee the cities for the suburbs. As we discuss in Chapter 8, racial discrimination was rampant in these loan programs, so much so that African Americans were generally shut out of the suburbs until the mid-1960s. This meant that middle-class blacks in search of good housing could only find it in inner-city neighborhoods adjacent to black areas. The movement of a black family onto a white block became a symbol of neighborhood decline. Realtors eagerly exploited whites' fears by blockbusting likely areas—selling to a black family, spreading fear among whites that the neighborhood was about to change; buying property from panicked whites at bargain basement prices; then selling it to middle-class blacks looking for a nice neighborhood at higher prices. Inevitably, the white middle class learned to associate blacks' presence with residential change.

Racial transition at the edge of black areas was accelerated by urban renewal and public housing policies. By reducing the supply of inner-city housing, clearance projects exponentially increased the pressure on existing housing at the margins of ghetto areas. African Americans in poverty were forced to cluster together in densely packed, run-down areas where rents were cheap, or they were forced to move into high-rise public housing projects that were even more segregated from the rest of society than the slums they left. White families moving to the suburbs were pursuing the American dream. Black families who could not make the move found, all too often, the nightmare of the bulldozer. The conflicts engendered by such policies helped to define the urban politics of the 1960s.

CHAPTER 7

SOCIAL PROGRAMS AND THE URBAN CRISIS

❖ A NEW AGENDA

The urban renewal and public housing programs floundered because they could not reverse or even effectively treat the causes of central city decline. The problems of cities went far beyond the quality of their housing and physical infrastructure. By the late 1960s it was obvious that the urban crisis resulted from a long-term dual migration that was fundamentally reshaping urban areas. For most of the twentieth century a stream of migrants from depressed rural areas poured into the old industrial cities. Millions of blacks leaving the South were joined by Mexican immigrants and by white families fleeing the poverty of Appalachia and other depressed areas. They crowded into the inner-city neighborhoods being vacated by white families moving to the suburbs. In every decade since the 1920s, the suburbs surrounding the older cities grew at a faster rate than the cities. In the decades after World War II white flight from such cities as St. Louis, Pittsburgh, Chicago, and Boston was so rapid that these cities slipped into precipitous population decline even though large numbers of city-bound migrants continued to arrive. Year by year, the numbers of minorities and poor in the cities escalated and new suburban subdivisions sprang up, seemingly without end. The cities were becoming more and more different from the suburbs. Within the cities, and between central cities and their surrounding suburbs, racial segregation and tensions intensified.

In the 1960s, the problems of racial segregation, discrimination, and concentrated poverty emerged on the nation's political agenda as the main ingredients of an "urban crisis." The National Commission on Urban Problems (1958), the National Commission on Civil Disorders (1967, called the Kerner Commission after its chairman, Illinois Governor Otto B. Kerner) the President's Task Force on Suburban Problems (1967) President Nixon's Commission on Population Growth and the American Future (1972) and a host of state and city task forces decried the segregation of the poor, the aged, and the nonwhite in central cities. The urban crisis, defined primarily in terms of issues of race and segregation, constituted the pivotal domestic political issue of the 1960s. To a considerable extent the national Democratic party staked its future on solving the problems of race and poverty in the cities. The actual results of the social and urban policies of the 1960s were mixed, but by the mid-1970s there was a widespread perception that many of the programs had failed. Republicans linked Democratic social policies with the economic recession of the 1970s. Even after twelve years of Republican presidential leadership, in the 1992 campaign George Bush still tried to get mileage out of the phrase "tax and spend." The perception that the urban programs of the 1960s failed has had enduring consequences for American national politics.

❖ THE MAKING OF THE "URBAN CRISIS"

In the nineteenth century, cities were viewed as dangerous outposts within American civilization, the places where foreign immigrants clustered and potentially threatened cultural and political control by native, Protestant, rural populations. In the twentieth century, this anti-urban legacy was given renewed vigor when millions of blacks, Hispanics, and poor whites moved to the cities. As much as ever, the cities seemed different from and at odds with the rest of the nation, but increasingly "the rest of the nation" was not only rural, but suburban as well.

Two periods of migration and immigration created the crisis of segregation, race, and poverty in America's cities (see Table 7-1).[1] The first wave crested in the two decades before the Great Depression. Between 1910 and 1930, 700,000 Mexicans moved into Texas, New Mexico, Arizona, and California, and more than 1 million blacks left the southern states for Chicago, Detroit, Cleveland, New York City, Pittsburgh, Philadelphia, and other cities of the industrial Midwest and Northeast. The second, bigger wave washed over the cities during World War II and did not ebb until the late 1960s. From 1940 to 1970 up to 5 million blacks, 1.6 million Appalachian whites, and 700,000 Mexicans moved into America's inner cities. Since the 1970s, a new group of immigrants, originating chiefly from the Caribbean, Latin America, and Asia, has arrived.

TABLE 7-1 RURAL TO URBAN MIGRANT STREAMS IN TWENTIETH-CENTURY AMERICA

MIGRANT GROUP	PRINCIPAL MIGRATION PERIOD	APPROXIMATE NUMBER OF MIGRANTS[a]	ORIGIN	DESTINATION
Appalachian whites	1940–1970	1,600,000	Southern Appalachian Mountains (Kentucky and West Virginia)	North central states
Mexicans	1910–1930	700,000	*Mesa Central* primarily, also *Mesa Del Norte*	Texas and southwestern states
	1950–1970	700,000	*Mesa Central* primarily, also *Mesa Del Norte*	Texas and California
Blacks	1910–1930	1,250,000[b]	Mississippi delta, black belt, Atlantic coastal plain	Illinois, Ohio, Michigan, New York, and Pennsylvania
	1940–1970	5,000,000[b]	Mississippi delta, black belt, Atlantic coastal plain	Cities everywhere

[a]These figures are approximate. The data for the Mexican migration, for example, are obscured by contract labor, two-way migration, and illegal entrants.
[b]U.S. Bureau of the Census, *Historical Statistics of the United States: Colonial Times to 1970* (Washington, D.C.: Government Printing Office). In Greenberg's original table, he lists 1 million blacks, 1910–1930, and 3.5 million blacks, 1940–1965.
Source: Adapted from Stanley B. Greenberg, *Politics and Poverty: Modernization and Response in Five Poor Neighborhoods* (New York: Wiley, 1974), p. 19.

Like the European immigrants who preceded them, more recent migrants to cities were pushed by crisis and pulled by opportunity. Poverty and unemployment in the South were the push; jobs in the North were the pull. Beginning in southern Texas in the late 1890s and sweeping eastward through Georgia by 1921, boll weevil infestations wiped out cotton crops, forcing black sharecroppers off the land. During the same period, an abrupt decline in European immigration occasioned by World War I, combined with the rapid expansion of armaments industries, produced labor shortages in the northern industrial cities. Between 1910 and 1920, 450,000 blacks moved out of the South, followed by another 750,000 in the 1920s.[2] With the outbreak of World War II, employment opportunities again opened up in the North. After the war, the mechanization of southern agriculture, in particular the widespread adoption of the mechanized cotton picker, threw hundreds of thousands of sharecroppers and farm laborers out of work. The lure of northern cities was overwhelming.

The northward movement lasted for at least three decades. Even against the background of the European immigration of an earlier time, its volume was astonishing. It was "one of the largest and most rapid mass internal movements of people in history—perhaps *the* greatest not caused by the immediate threat of execution or starvation."[3]

Mexicans were driven into the southwestern states by bloody and protracted violence during and following the Mexican Revolution and by the unrest that followed from 1910 to the mid-1920s. Although the revolution released millions of peasants from their feudal relationship with landholders, it left them without the means to sustain an independent livelihood. Bloody confrontations between the Mexican government and landowners recurred from the turn of the century until 1926, driving the newly liberated peasants into Texas, Arizona, and California. During and after World War II, employment opportunities in the southwestern states induced still more Mexicans to cross the border. Five and a half million Mexican Americans lived in the American Southwest by 1970, the great majority in towns and cities.[4] Hispanic immigrants from several other Latin American countries streamed into the southwestern states in even larger numbers in the 1980s, pushed by political repression and poverty and pulled by the availability of jobs.

The southern Appalachian Mountains and the Cumberland plateau of Virginia, West Virginia, and Kentucky were the source of a massive movement of desperately poor rural white families. In his moving book, *Night Comes to the Cumberlands*, Harry Caudill described the grinding poverty that forced families and entire communities to pick up and leave their marginal farm plots and shabby towns. Many families could trace their roots in Appalachia back several generations back. An entire genre of country music—bluegrass—was inspired by the homesickness for the hills and hollows left behind. In the 1950s alone, a quarter of the population deserted the Cumberland plateau, settling in cities and towns of Kentucky, Tennessee, Maryland, Virginia, and the industrial belt of the upper Midwest.[5]

❖ THE ORIGINS OF THE RACIAL CRISIS IN AMERICAN CITIES

The isolation of the cities from the suburbs was an accomplished fact by 1960. What made the isolation assume the dimensions of a national crisis was the extreme segregation of blacks. By the 1960s, millions of blacks were crowded together into spreading slums in the older industrial cities. Blacks of all social classes were shut out of the suburbs by discriminatory real estate and lending practices and by the intimidation and violence that awaited them if they tried to move into a white suburban neighborhood. In 1967, the Kerner Commission warned of "two nations, one black, one white, separate and unequal." It might well have said "two nations: one city, one suburban."

Between 1910 and 1930, about 1 million blacks—one-tenth of all blacks living in the South—moved to cities in the Northeast and Midwest. In 1910, 89 percent of the nation's black population resided in the South, but by 1930 this proportion had declined to 79 percent. From 1890 to 1910, the black population of the South increased by 29 percent, but, over the next twenty years, the rate of growth fell to only 8 percent. Blacks were moving out of the South in large numbers. Between 1910 and 1930, the black population outside the South shot up by 134 percent.[6]

Nearly all the African Americans leaving the South left poverty-stricken rural areas and settled into densely packed neighborhoods in northern cities. Only 10 percent of the nation's African Americans lived in cities of 100,000 or more in 1910. This percentage increased to 16 percent in 1920 and to 24 percent by 1930.[7] The biggest cities lured most of the migrants. The proportion of blacks living in cities smaller than 100,000 declined from 1910 to 1930, while the proportion increased substantially in cities of over 100,000.[8] Thus, the Great Migration, as it came to be labeled by historians, had two principal components: blacks were becoming northern *and* urban. In several of the largest cities, black populations multiplied by a factor or three or more in the two decades from 1910 to 1930 (see Table 7-2).

Few cities of the North had many black residents in 1910; in most cases, blacks constituted 2 percent of the city's population or less. By 1930, heavily industrial Gary, Indiana, was 18 percent black, and East St. Louis, Illinois, was 16 percent black. In big cities, percentages ranged from almost 5 percent in New York City to just over 11 percent in St. Louis and Philadelphia (these proportions had roughly doubled in twenty years). Blacks in northern cities were concentrated in well-defined ghettos. In north Harlem, New York City, about one-third (36 percent) of the population was black in 1920, but this proportion increased to 81 percent by the 1930 census.[9]

There were many reasons for the migration to northern cities, but the basic factors were employment opportunities in the North and dissatisfaction with southern life. The North was a "promised land" that offered an escape from the violent racism of the South and the opportunity for economic advancement.

TABLE 7-2 GROWTH OF BLACK POPULATION IN SEVERAL CITIES, 1910–1930						
CITY	1910	1920	1930	PERCENT INCREASE 1910–1930	PERCENT OF TOTAL POPULATION	
					1910	1930
New York	91,709	152,467	327,706	257.3	1.9	4.7
Chicago	44,103	109,458	233,903	429.3	2.0	6.9
Philadelphia	84,459	134,229	219,599	160.0	5.5	11.3
St. Louis	43,960	69,854	93,580	112.9	6.4	11.4
Cleveland	8,448	34,451	71,889	751.0	1.5	8.0

Source: U.S. Bureau of the Census, *Negroes in the United States, 1920–1932* (Washington, D.C.: Government Printing Office, 1935), p. 55.

The *Chicago Defender*, founded in 1905, circulated widely throughout the South. By May 1917, when the publisher of the *Defender* launched "The Great Northern Drive" to persuade blacks to move from the South, it had already reached a circulation of 100,000. Its great popularity south of the Mason-Dixon line was a result of the message it carried. The *Defender*'s editorials exhorted blacks to come north to the land of opportunity, where they could find employment and, if not equality, at least an escape from harassment and violence. Its columns of job advertisements added to the "promised land" vision. At the same time, the *Defender* attacked conditions in the South. Lynchings and incidents of discrimination were regularly highlighted in lurid detail. Moving out of the South was portrayed as a way to advance the cause of racial equality for all blacks.[10]

The *Defender* was only one of many voices encouraging blacks to leave the South. Blacks who had already moved wrote letters to relatives and friends describing their new life in glowing terms. Despite pervasive job and housing discrimination in the North, they found conditions preferable to what they had left behind. Throughout the South blacks lived under a cloud of terror. From 1882 to 1930, there were 1,663 lynchings in the states of the Cotton Belt alone—Alabama, Georgia, Louisiana, Mississippi, and South Carolina. During the same period 1,299 blacks were legally executed.[11] Legal systems in the South were so completely rigged that the difference between lynching and legal murder could be merely technical. Blacks who failed to obey the racial caste system, even inadvertently, could expect immediate retribution in the form of beatings or worse. Failing to step off the sidewalk, failing to say "sir" or "ma'am," or looking a white person in the eye could be cause for punishment.

The opportunities for leaving such conditions improved markedly in proportion to the labor shortages in northern factories after 1915. Factory owners found themselves with lucrative armaments contracts, but too few workers. They sent labor agents into the South in search of labor. A free train ticket was often offered in exchange for a labor agreement. By the spring of 1916, the Great Migration was on.

Southern white employers and planters took steps to prevent the exodus of their cheap labor. Magazines, newspapers, and business organizations decried the movement, as in this October 5, 1916, editorial in the *Memphis Commercial Appeal:*

> The enormous demand for labor and the changing conditions brought about by the boll weevil in certain parts of the South have caused an exodus of negroes which may be serious. Great colonies of negroes have gone north to work in factories, in packing houses and on the railroads. . . .
>
> The South needs every able-bodied negro that is now south of the line, and every negro who remains south of the line will in the end do better than he will do in the North. . . .
>
> The negroes who are in the South should be encouraged to remain there, and those white people who are in the boll weevil territory should make every sacrifice to keep their negro labor until there can be adjustments to the new and quickly prosperous conditions that will later exist.[12]

States and communities went to considerable lengths to discourage migration. Jacksonville, Florida, passed an ordinance in 1916 levying heavy fines on unlicensed labor agents from the North. Macon, Georgia, made it impossible for labor agents to get licenses and outlawed unlicensed agents. The mayor of Atlanta talked to blacks about how "dreadfully cold" the northern winters were.[13] In some communities, police were sent to railroad stations to harass blacks near the stations, keep them from boarding trains, or even drive them off the trains.

But the promised land beckoned, and the exodus continued throughout the 1920s. What the new arrivals found was opportunity—but not equal opportunity—and persistent discrimination. Whenever blacks attempted to move into white neighborhoods, they were harassed and often violently assaulted. They were the last hired and first fired. Everywhere in the North, they were kept in the most menial occupations. Job opportunities were limited not only by employers but even more so by labor unions, which generally prohibited blacks from membership. Because the North was more heavily unionized than the South, there were actually fewer opportunities in some occupations, especially for skilled laborers.[14] In both union and nonunion shops, white workers often refused to work alongside blacks. To maintain labor peace, employers in such situations voluntarily agreed to hire only white laborers or to limit black employment to the less desirable jobs.

The difficulty of adjusting to urban life added to the problems faced by blacks. Hardly any of them had previously lived in an urban environment. Many had never even participated directly in the cash economy. Sharecroppers had often worked under contracts that contained provisions that they buy only from the planters' stores and then with scrip and credit rather than cash. Some of them had never seen U.S. currency. As was the case with previous immigrant groups, they were often cheated, overpaying for food, housing, and other necessities.

These conditions, amplified by segregation in dilapidated, overcrowded ghettos, led to astonishing levels of social pathology. The arrest rate for blacks in Detroit in 1926 was four times that for whites. Blacks constituted 31 percent of the nation's prison population in 1923, though they made up only 9 percent of the total population. The death rate in Harlem between 1923 and 1927 was 42 percent higher than in New York City as a whole, despite the fact that Harlem's population was much younger. Its infant mortality rate was 111 per 1,000 births, compared with the city's 64 per 1,000. Tuberculosis, heart disease, and other illnesses also far exceeded the rates for the city's general population.[15]

Blacks moving into northern cities were often surprised to find intense racism and discrimination. They quickly learned that southern whites were not so peculiar in their racial attitudes. Many restaurants and stores in the North refused to serve blacks, though the policies of segregation were not as rigidly enforced as they were in the South. Banks typically refused them loans. Cemeteries, parks, bathing beaches, and other facilities were put off limits or divided into "white" and "colored" sections. Many dentists, doctors, and hospitals refused to treat blacks. Worse, the violence that had plagued blacks in the South followed them everywhere they went. On July 2, 1917, a riot in East St. Louis took 46 lives, 39 of them blacks.[16] In the "Red Summer" of 1919, more than 20 cities experienced race riots, all of them initiated when white mobs attacked blacks. The cause of Chicago's riot that summer was a black youth's swimming across the no-man's-land separating a colored beach from a white beach. Whites stoned the boy to death and then terrorized blacks throughout the city for days. From July 1, 1917, to March 1, 1921, Chicago experienced 58 racial bombings.[17] Unemployed blacks were forced out of Buffalo by city police in 1920. In 1925, blacks who attempted to move into white neighborhoods in Detroit were terrorized by cross burnings, vandalism, and mob violence.

In all cities, restrictive covenants were attached to property deeds to keep blacks from buying into white neighborhoods. Deeds with these restrictions were filed in the office of the county clerk or the register of deeds and were enforced by the courts. Chicago, with more than eleven square miles covered by restricted deeds in 1944, was typical of northern cities.[18] Neighborhood improvement associations were formed in new subdivisions and, by legal prosecution and social persuasion, forced home owners to accept and abide by racial restrictive covenants.

In the thirty years between 1940 and 1970, up to 5 million southern blacks moved to northern cities. From Texas, Louisiana, and Arkansas, blacks streamed into cities of the West, especially to California; from the middle South, they moved to St. Louis, Chicago, Detroit, Cleveland, and other cities of the Midwest; and from Mississippi and eastward in the Deep South, they moved to Washington, D.C., New York, Boston, and other cities in the East.

In 1940, 77 percent of the nation's blacks still lived in the southern states (compared with 87 percent in 1910). By 1950, only 60 percent of the nation's blacks lived in the South, and in the next two decades the South's share declined to 56 percent (1960) and to 53 percent (1970).[19] Nearly all of the northward-bound migrants ended up in cities. According to the 1970 census, 90 percent of all the blacks who lived outside metropolitan areas were located in the South.

A movement of this magnitude would have created a crisis under any conditions, since most of the migrants were of rural origin and predictably found the adjustment to city life difficult. But the crisis was made worse by the same factors that had plagued earlier black migrants: housing and job discrimination, racism, and extreme segregation. All of the problems faced by northern blacks in the 1920s still existed after World War II. Further, whites were leaving the cities by the millions every year, seeking their own "promised land"—the suburbs. While the cities were becoming increasingly black, the suburbs remained nearly all white. Table 7-3 shows that racial segregation between cities and suburbs had become pronounced by 1950 and worsened over the ensuing decades.

For most of the twelve cities shown in Table 7-3, the fastest growth in black population occurred in the two decades from 1950 to 1970. Northern migration was prompted by the employment opportunities in northern industry during World War II, but many white families stayed in the cities until the suburban housing boom following the Korean War. Thus, although the proportion of black residents climbed during the 1940s in all cities except St. Louis, the increase understated the extent of the migration. With the white flight from the central cities that occurred later, black proportions of central cities' populations shot up dramatically by 1970—to over 72 percent in Washington, D.C., to 47 percent in Cleveland, and to over 41 percent in St. Louis. In the 1990s, these proportions rose only modestly in most cities and actually fell sharply in Washington, D.C., reflecting the middle-class gentrification of poor neighborhoods and the immigration of Asians, Hispanics, and other groups.

❖ THE CIVIL RIGHTS CRUSADES

The movement to northern cities did not end racism and discrimination. The worst and most symbolically crude racism continued to exist in the South. Against a background of white resistance to demands for change, the civil rights movement departed from a politics of accommodation to a politics of confrontation. At first centered in the South, its political effects would soon be felt in northern cities.

The Great Depression was a crisis of such proportions that it propelled governments into action. The crisis of the 1960s brought about even greater government involvement, but this crisis was more one of social disorder than

TABLE 7-3 PERCENTAGE OF BLACKS IN CENTRAL CITIES AND SUBURBAN RINGS IN TWELVE SELECTED SMSAs, 1940–1990

	CENTRAL CITY						SUBURBAN RING					
	1940	1950	1960	1970	1980	1990	1940	1950	1960	1970	1980	1990[a]
All 12 SMSAs	9.0	13.7	21.4	30.8	32.6	32.9	3.9	4.4	4.4	6.0	7.4[b]	8.7[b]
New York	6.4	9.8	14.7	23.4	25.2	28.7	4.6	4.5	4.8	6.4	6.8[b]	11.0[b]
Los Angeles–Long Beach	6.0	9.8	15.3	21.2	16.4	14.0	2.3	2.7	4.1	7.4	9.6	6.7
Chicago	8.3	14.1	23.6	34.4	39.8	39.1	2.2	2.9	3.1	4.1	5.6	8.7
Philadelphia	13.1	18.3	26.7	34.4	37.8	39.9	6.6	6.6	0.3	7.1	8.1	10.8
Detroit	9.3	16.4	29.2	44.0	63.1	75.7	2.9	5.0	3.8	4.0	4.2	5.4
San Francisco–Oakland	4.9	11.8	21.1	32.7	24.1	22.1	3.6	6.8	6.8	9.4	6.5	5.7
Boston	3.3	12.3	9.8	18.2	22.4	25.6	0.9	0.8	1.0	1.6	1.6	2.9
Pittsburgh	9.3	18.0	16.8	27.0	24.0	25.8	3.6	3.5	3.4	3.6	4.0	4.5
St. Louis	13.4	5.3	28.8	41.3	45.6	47.5	6.7	7.3	6.3	7.7	10.6	11.0

TABLE 7-3 *(Continued)*

	CENTRAL CITY						SUBURBAN RING					
	1940	1950	1960	1970	1980	1990	1940	1950	1960	1970	1980	1990[a]
Washington, D.C.	28.5	35.4	54.8	72.3	76.6	65.8	13.7	8.7	6.4	9.1	16.7	19.4
Cleveland	9.7	16.3	28.9	39.0	43.8	46.6	0.9	0.8	0.8	1.1	7.1	9.1
Baltimore	19.4	23.8	35.0	47.0	54.8	59.2	11.9	10.2	6.9	6.2	9.1	11.0

Source: Adapted from Leo F. Schnore, Carolyn D. André, and Harry Sharp, "Black Surburbanization, 1930–1970," in *The Changing Face of the Suburbs*, ed. Barry Schwartz (Chicago: University of Chicago Press, 1976), p. 80. Reprinted by permission. The figures here were transposed to yield data on black percentages. 1980 data from U.S. Bureau of the Census, *Census of the Population, 1980,* suppl. reports, *Standard Metropolitan Statistical Areas and Standard Consolidated Statistical Areas* (Washington, D.C.: Government Printing Office, 1981), p. 3, Table 1.

[a]Except for St. Louis, Baltimore, and Washington, D.C., figures for 1990 refer to the Consolidated Metropolitan Statistical Areas (CMSAs) that are not strictly comparable to earlier years. See U.S. Bureau of the Census, *Statistical Abstract of the United States, 1991,* 111th ed. (Washington, D.C.: Government Printing Office, 1991), Tables 37, 38, 40.

[b]This figure includes data from the Nassau-Suffolk SMSA, which was deleted from the New York City SMSA in 1971. They are included to maintain comparability across time periods.

of heightened social problems. Widespread poverty, racial segregation, juvenile delinquency and crime, bad schools, and a host of other social problems were discovered in the 1960s only in the sense that they were no longer "out of sight, out of mind." They had existed for a long time and were no worse and little different by the advent of the Kennedy Administration than they had been under Roosevelt, Truman, or Eisenhower. What made them seem worse was their greater visibility. Martin Luther King, Jr., understood the task of creating visibility during the civil rights demonstrations in 1963: "I saw no way," he later commented, "of dealing with things without bringing the indignation to the attention of the nation."[20] By creating a crisis of social order in the South, King and other civil rights leaders transformed an invisible social fact into a political crisis.

The struggle for racial equality entered a new phase in the summer of 1955, when a coalition of black ministers launched a boycott against segregated buses in Montgomery, Alabama. The boycott, which ended the "back of the bus" policy in Montgomery, brought Martin Luther King, Jr., to the attention of the national press. Until the Civil Rights Act of 1964 and the Voting Rights Act of 1965, his philosophy of creative nonviolent protest dominated the civil rights movement. What made civil disobedience so effective was that it challenged laws and customs of doubtful constitutionality and morality while calling attention to the bigotry and brutality that infected state and local legal systems throughout the South. The 1954 Supreme Court decision *Brown v. Topeka Board of Education* held out the prospect of a broad assault against Jim Crow segregation laws. That decision, which struck down separate schools for blacks and whites, fundamentally altered the strategies for achieving equality. The National Association for the Advancement of Colored People (NAACP) had challenged segregationist laws in the courts for many years and had won some victories. By the mid-1950s, emboldened by the *Brown* decision, civil rights leaders began to turn to direct action to challenge segregation and discrimination.

Until the mid-1960s, civil rights protesters focused mostly on the South. Certainly the worst abuses existed there, a legacy of the racist legislation that preoccupied southern legislators from the 1880s through the first twenty years of the twentieth century. In 1881, Tennessee passed a law requiring railroad companies to segregate their cars. Following this—perhaps the first Jim Crow law after the Civil War[21]—a system of legal segregation evolved that touched every aspect of life. By the early years of the twentieth century, most railroad cars were segregated. In 1906, South Carolina required segregation in restaurants and eating establishments and later in all forms of transportation. A few years later the state required that textile factories designate separate work rooms for whites and blacks and provide separate drinking glasses, toilet facilities, stairways, doors, and tools.[22] Parks, zoos, fishing areas, bathing and boating areas, phone booths, textbooks and schools, taxicabs, orphanages, churches, courtrooms, drinking fountains, lavatories, waiting rooms, even courtroom bibles—all were segregated by state law throughout the South.[23] Most of these laws still existed in the 1950s.

There was little that blacks could do to challenge the system. Poll taxes and literacy requirements kept most blacks from voting. Between 1916 and 1936, black registration in eight southern states increased only 3.3 percent, from 5 percent to 8.3 percent. In Mississippi, registration dropped.[24] The NAACP and other organizations were declared illegal in some states. In any case, political activity of any sort by African Americans brought forth violent repression—arrests, intimidation, and even murder.

With the election of John F. Kennedy in 1960, the civil rights movement picked up momentum. When it was located in and focused primarily on the southern states, the movement had limited exposure and effectiveness. Until civil rights became a national commitment, southern resistance would be hard to break.

❖ THE FEDERAL ROLE UNDER TWO DEMOCRATIC PRESIDENTS

The federal role in the cities expanded vastly in the 1960s under the leadership of two Democratic presidents. This federal activism represented a radical departure. During the administrations of presidents Kennedy and Johnson, the social problems of cities—juvenile delinquency, crime, poverty, inadequate education, racial conflict, and joblessness—became central concerns. The decision to place the urban crisis at the center of the Democrats' political agenda arose from two developments—the growing strength of the civil rights movement and a calculation that the party's electoral fortunes could be improved by appealing to black voters.

When President John F. Kennedy was sworn in on January 20, 1961, his administration was already committed to an enhanced role for the cities. Even before his campaign, Kennedy had concluded that the problem of the cities was "the great unspoken issue in the 1960 election."[25] Not only did Kennedy feel that the election would be decided by the votes delivered in key cities in a few industrial states, he also felt that the problems of urban residents were worthy of special attention on their own merits. During the 1960 campaign, the Democrats played the city issue with scarcely a whisper from the opposition. The Republicans, in fact, tried to avoid such issues. "If you ever let them campaign only on domestic issues," confided presidential nominee Richard M. Nixon to his aides, "they'll beat us."[26] President Kennedy "emerged as an eloquent spokesman for a new political generation. In presidential message after message Kennedy spelled out in more detail than the Congress or the country could easily digest the most complete programs of domestic reforms in a quarter century."[27]

Martin Luther King, Jr., turned the civil rights issue into a national crisis in Birmingham, Alabama, in the summer of 1963. The combination of King's nonviolent demonstrations, Police Chief "Bull" Connor's fire hoses and attack dogs, and the television networks' attention to spectacle made civil rights the nation's most pressing moral and political problem.

What started in Birmingham spread across the South and into northern cities. During the course of the summer, there were 13,786 arrests of demonstrators in 75 cities of the 11 major southern states.[28] In such cities as Detroit, Chicago, and New York, blacks actively demonstrated for their rights. In the ten weeks that followed Birmingham, the Justice Department counted 758 demonstrations across the nation. These demonstrations, and the civil rights movement in general, became the most dramatic news items of 1963. Newspapers, television, and every other news media deluged the American public with tales of King and his movement.

The pressures applied by the civil rights movement were reinforced by the electoral strength of blacks. As John C. Donovan observed in his book *The Politics of Poverty,* "The greatest strength of the Negro communities lies in its voting power, in its numbers, and in their strategic location."[29] In the South the black population was geographically diffused and systematically denied the power of the vote. In their move to the North, African Americans gained the franchise and concentrated their voting strength in the big cities. The cities of the large key states holding the majority of electoral college votes—Illinois, California, Massachusetts, Ohio, Michigan, New Jersey, New York, Texas, and Pennsylvania—contained substantial black populations by 1960. Kennedy campaigned hard for blacks' votes. The 68 percent margin black voters gave him was critical to his narrow victories in several states. In 1956, the Democratic candidate, Adlai Stevenson, a liberal from Illinois, had received 61 percent of blacks' votes.[30] If Kennedy had not done better, he would have lost the election: "It is difficult to see how Illinois, New Jersey, Michigan, South Carolina, or Delaware (with 74 electoral votes) could have been won had the Republican-Democratic split of the Negro wards and precincts remained as it was, unchanged from the Eisenhower charm of 1956."[31]

During the New Deal years, the Democratic party established a national political coalition based on the urban constituencies of northern cities and Democratic voters in the one-party South. African Americans, who in 1936 had shifted from the Republican to the Democratic party, were an important voting bloc in the new coalition, but they were able to exert little influence on the party and received few tangible benefits. In the 1950s, some members of the Democratic party began to respond to the growing black voting population in the North and the rise in civil rights activity in the South. It was clear that southern Democrats would not abide forceful action on behalf of blacks. This could be discerned in the presidential election results: In 1960, though Kennedy won the South, he did so with only 51 percent of the popular vote. In northern cities he carried large enough pluralities to tip key industrial states into his column. As the Democrats' nominee in 1956, Stevenson had carried only 49 percent of the southern vote. Clearly, the cities were more solid for the Democrats than the South.[32] By the middle of 1963, Kennedy finally realized that the civil rights issue was so divisive that he would have to make painful choices about where to seek votes.

The northern wing of the party, led by congressional leaders from the unionized, industrial states, by big city mayors, and by industrial-state governors, favored an activist president in the Roosevelt mold, a president who would use the national government to address problems of poverty, jobless-ness, and urban decay. The northern wing had pressed hard for the urban renewal and public housing programs funded by the 1949 Housing Act. At the same time, a Democratic president had to be mindful of placating House and Senate members from the southern wing of the party. Because most of them ran virtually unopposed election after election (Republican candidates never had a chance in the "solid" South), southern Democrats tended to have the most seniority in Congress. Since committee appointments were assigned on the basis of seniority, they chaired the most powerful committees in both legislative chambers. In January 1961, they chaired 12 of 18 Senate committees and 12 of 21 House committees. Howard Smith of Virginia, a rabid segrega-tionist, chaired the House Rules Committee. In that capacity, he could pre-vent any bill from going to the House floor for debate or vote, since bills approved by other committees had to come through Rules before proceeding further. Southerners could also find ready allies among conservative Republicans, making life very difficult for a Democratic president.

Caught between these two poles, and having won the 1960 election by the slimmest of margins, President Kennedy was inclined to be cautious about civil rights. He was convinced that civil rights was a political mine field that could endanger his entire domestic agenda. During his first two years in office, he generally dodged the civil rights issue as best he could; partially as a result, he was able to push through some of his key bills. One of the first pieces of legislation introduced by the President and approved by Congress was the Juvenile Delinquency and Youth Offenses Control Act, signed into law in June 1961. This legislation funded a few small programs designed to provide education and job training to inner-city youth. In 1962, Congress passed the Area Redevelopment Act, which provided grants and loans for depressed areas of the country. The focus of the legislation was Appalachia, where, dur-ing the 1960 campaign, Kennedy had seen wrenching poverty in town after ramshackle town. In 1962, Kennedy also persuaded Congress to pass the Manpower Development Training Act, to train unemployed workers for new jobs. A significant number of grant-in-aid programs were enacted to help states and communities build sewage facilities and build and repair infrastruc-ture. When, however, Kennedy proposed the consolidation of several housing and urban programs into a cabinet-level department of urban affairs, the legis-lation was buried in Congress because Kennedy's choice as the first secretary, Robert C. Weaver, was black. Despite promising during the campaign that he would sign an executive order outlawing racial discrimination in housing, Kennedy delayed the order until after the 1962 congressional elections and then had Robert Kennedy, the attorney general, issue a limited order as quiet-ly as possible.[33]

By the summer of 1963, it became clear that the administration could no longer avoid dealing with civil rights head-on. The brutal treatment of civil rights demonstrators throughout the South was being televised into the living rooms of millions of American homes. During the week of May 25, 1963, civil rights demonstrations occurred in thirty-three southern and ten northern cities. By mid-June one hundred twenty-seven civil rights bill had been introduced in the House of Representatives. Whether it wanted to or not, the Administration was being drawn into the nation's most significant and divisive internal conflict since the Civil War.

On June 11, Kennedy overruled his political advisers and announced he would propose a civil rights bill. Among other features, the bill threatened to cut off federal funds to state and local governments practicing discrimination, permitted more federal intervention in school desegregation cases, and provided for the desegregation of public accommodations. When Kennedy was assassinated on November 22, the bill had just reached the House Rules Committee.

The assassination created an emotionally charged atmosphere that the new president, Lyndon Baines Johnson, adroitly exploited. Opinion polls indicated overwhelming public support for civil rights legislation. In the House, Republicans joined with northern Democrats to move Johnson's strengthened bill out of the Rules Committee. The House approved the legislation by a vote of 290 to 130. On June 6, 1964, the Senate mustered the necessary two-thirds vote to overcome a filibuster by southerners, and the legislation passed.

The Civil Rights Act of 1964 was far-reaching. It outlawed discrimination in public accommodations, effectively striking down the South's Jim Crow laws that denied blacks equal access to bus stations, restaurants, lunch counters, theaters, sports arenas, gasoline stations, motels, hotels, and lodging houses. It outlawed racial discrimination in the hiring, firing, training, and promoting of workers. It barred discrimination in the administration of federal grants. A year later, Congress passed the Voting Rights Act, which not only outlawed literacy tests and other discriminatory voting restrictions, but provided that federal registrars could replace local registrars in counties where there had been a history of discrimination against black voters.

Taking advantage of the post-assassination atmosphere, President Johnson also pressed for a program to redress economic inequalities.[34] Kennedy's advisers had persuaded him that the time had come for his administration to devise a program to attack poverty and unemployment. In June 1963, Kennedy had told Walter Heller, the chairman of his Council of Economic Advisors, to appoint a task force of officials who would be responsible for proposing a program to attack poverty. Although Kennedy's commitment to a program was almost certain by the time of his assassination, it was not clear how prominent it would have been on his legislative agenda or how large it would have been.

On being told about the proposed antipoverty program only two days after assuming office, President Johnson said, "That's my kind of program. It will help people. I want you to move full speed ahead."[35] The idea of an ambitious, highly visible program appealed to Johnson's desire to be perceived as a second Roosevelt, as a president who would go down in history as the one who completed the social agenda left unfinished in the 1930s. In his first State of the Union address of January 10, 1964, President Johnson announced that he would seek a "total effort" to end poverty in the United States. Using a grandiose military analogy, he said, "This Administration here and now declares unconditional war on poverty in America, and I urge this Congress and all Americans to join me in that effort."[36] When Johnson signed the Economic Opportunity Act on August 8, he had two big legislative victories, the civil rights act and his "war on poverty," to carry into the presidential campaign.

The 1964 campaign provided the setting for an unusually sharp national debate over the federal government's role and responsibilities. The Republican nominee, Barry Goldwater, was one of the few non-Southerners to oppose the civil rights act in the Senate. He attacked the welfare programs funded through the Social Security Act of 1935 and even questioned the immensely popular old-age insurance program set up by that legislation. The Republican party platform warned that "individual freedom retreats under the mounting assault of expanding centralized power."[37] Lyndon Johnson, in contrast, called for a Great Society that would eliminate poverty and treat other social ills through federal action on civil rights, the cities, health care, welfare, education, and employment.

Johnson won the election by a landslide, winning 61 percent of the popular vote and sweeping 486 electoral college votes to Goldwater's 53. The President's coattails were long; Democrats commanded a 289 to 146 majority in the House to go along with a 67 to 33 majority in the Senate. The Democrats' landslide set the stage for a period of legislative activism not seen since Roosevelt's fabled Hundred Days in 1933. Between 1964 and 1966, Congress authorized 219 new programs. Among these were the major social commitments of the 1960s. In 1965, Congress passed the Medicare program for the elderly and the Medicaid program for welfare recipients. The Elementary and Secondary Education Act provided federal grants to schools. Food stamps, an experimental program tried during the Kennedy years, became permanent in 1966. New and expanded educational and job-training assistance was made available for the mentally and physically handicapped. The public housing and urban renewal programs were expanded, and a new "model cities" program to treat the problems of cities was initiated. In 1966, Congress also created a new cabinet-level department, the Department of Housing and Urban Development (HUD), to administer urban programs.

Most of the new programs fit within the general rubric of "human resources." Fiscal year 1965 marked the beginning of a dramatic upswing in outlays for social programs, particularly in the areas of health, education, and employment training. Grants-in-aid to state and local governments within these fields rose from 14 percent of federal domestic aid in 1960 to 33 percent of such aid in 1970. Similarly, the proportion of assistance outlays for housing and community development nearly quadrupled, rising from 3 percent to 11 percent of the domestic budget from 1960 to 1970.[38] While aid to urban areas shot upward 590 percent from 1961 to 1972, total federal aid spending increased by 405 percent. Aid to nonurban areas rose by only 182 percent during this same period. By far the largest increment in spending was in the new programs associated with community development and housing, which were distinctly urban in orientation.

There was a sharp increase in the number and size of federal grants committed to cities and states during the 1960s. In 1960, 44 separate grant-in-aid programs were available to state and local governments.[39] Four years later, a Senate subcommittee report compiled by the Library of Congress identified 115 grant programs and a total of 216 separate authorizations for new spending under these programs.[40] An analysis done by the Legislative Reference Service in 1966 counted a total of 399 authorizations.[41] By 1969, the count was approaching 500, and it reached about 530 a year later before leveling off (see Figure 7-1).[42] The number of programs declined in the 1970s, but mainly because many of them were folded into block-grant consolidations.[43]

Figure 7-1   Growth of Grants-in-Aid Authorizations, 1962–1986

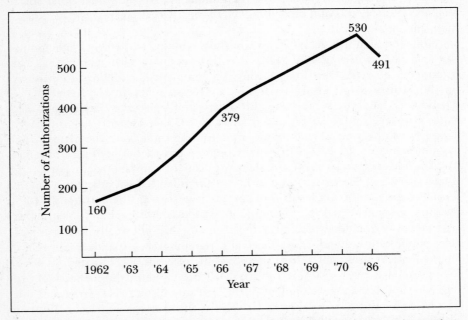

The number of grants-in-aid programs to state and local governments is somewhat less then the number of authorizations.

Source: Adapted from U.S. Congress, Senate, Committee on Governmental Operations, *Intergovernmental Revenue Act of 1971 and Related Legislation*, hearings before the Subcommittee on Intergovernmental Relations, Senate, 92nd Cong., 1st sess., 1971, p. 379; and Michael D. Reagan, *The New Federalism* (New York: Oxford University Press, 1972), p. 55; and the Office of Management and Budget, *Catalog of Federal Domestic Assistance*, 1986 (Washington, D.C.: U.S. Government Printing Office, 1986).

The amount of money spent through federal grants increased exponentially. In 1950, only $2.2 billion in grants were allocated to states and local governments. By 1960, this amount had gone up to $7 billion, and, by 1970, the national government was spending $24 billion for grants-in-aid. When President Nixon left office in 1974, the amount had gone up to $43.3 billion. Federal grant-in-aid spending rose rapidly until the late 1970s, amounting to more than $89 billion by 1980. The proportion of local budgets that came in the form of grants from federal and state governments also increased sharply. From a little over 10 percent in 1950, the proportion of local budgets that originated from state and federal governments increased to over 26 percent of municipal revenues by 1978, before falling in the 1980s.

The explosion in federal spending was accompanied by an attempt to achieve national purposes. Not since the closing of the frontier in the 1870s had the national government attempted so clearly to define a domestic agenda. In giving away land to states and railroads, in establishing a post office and financing internal improvements, and in following an aggresive military policy toward the Indians, the federal government in that period had declared its intention to open up the West and secure its territory.[44] Now the president and Congress again tried to formulate overall national policies and to assert the right of the federal government to extend its authority. The declared national purposes embraced the goals of eliminating poverty, erasing racial discrimination, providing equal opportunity in education and jobs, and developing cities and communities. This assertion of purpose was particularly direct in the case of the Civil Rights Act of 1964, in which the government served notice that its new civil rights statutes would override state and local racial practices. The preambles to the grant program legislation of Kennedy's New Frontier and Johnson's Great Society articulated many new purposes. For example, from the Manpower Development and Training Act of 1962:

> It is in the national interest that current and prospective manpower shortages be identified and that persons who can be qualified for these positions through education and training be sought out and trained, *in order that the nation may meet the staffing requirements of the struggle for freedom.*[45]

Or the Economic Opportunity Act of 1964:

> The United States can achieve its full economic and social potential as a nation only if every individual has the opportunity to contribute the full extent of his capabilities and to participate in the workings of our society. *It is, therefore, the policy of the United States* to eliminate the paradox of poverty in the midst of plenty in this nation.[46]

Or the Demonstration Cities and Metropolitan Development Act of 1966 (the so-called Model Cities legislation):

> The Congress hereby finds and declares *that improving the quality of urban life is the most critical domestic problem facing the United States.*[47]

Imagine these kinds of statements of intention introducing hundreds of pieces of legislation, ranging from rent supplements to federal school aid to crime control, and the complexity of the new system of grants becomes readily apparent. Hardly an economic or a social problem escaped attention, and each program carried with it complicated methods of implementation. Recipient institutions were subjected to close scrutiny and control. After all, it makes no sense to announce a national purpose unless the money is going to be used carefully, according to prescribed guidelines and standards.[48]

❖ THE CONFLICTS ENGENDERED BY FEDERAL ACTIVISM

The Democratic landslide victory of 1964 did not lay to rest the debate over the federal government's role. The honeymoon following the election lasted scarcely two years. In the 1966 congressional elections, the Republicans took back many of the seats they had lost to Democrats two years earlier. The Ninetieth Congress, which sat from January 1967 to the end of 1968, was much less willing to approve new programs. By the 1968 presidential election, the Democrats were clearly on the defensive.

The 1964 landslide masked a development that would soon undermine the Democrats' ability to win presidential elections. The issue of race was tearing apart the coalition that the Democrats had fashioned in the 1930s. Johnson lost throughout the deep South. Goldwater received 87 percent of the popular vote in Mississippi, almost 70 percent in Alabama, and substantially more than 50 percent in Louisiana, Georgia, and South Carolina. After 1964, Republican candidates began to win elections in the South for the first time since Reconstruction.

In 1968 the Republicans capitalized on white resentment of blacks' civil rights gains. The Democratic candidate, Hubert Humphrey, carried only one southern state, Texas. Across the South, he garnered only 31 percent of the vote, running behind both Republican Richard Nixon (34.5 percent) and Georgia governor and third-party candidate George Wallace (34.6 percent), who ran as an avowed segregationist. In 1976, Jimmy Carter of Georgia carried the South, but the Democratic presidential candidates since then have received less than 40 percent of the southern vote. The party's share of state and local offices fell from 80 percent in 1970 to 60 percent by 1982.[49]

Over the years, the Republicans have learned to manipulate the issue of race with great skill. In 1968 the Nixon campaign made law and order its main theme. This had been Goldwater's theme, too, but he had handled it crudely and ineptly. In Goldwater's depiction of blacks in Johnson's America, they were rioting. In his campaign film presenting the image of the American past he would like to restore, blacks were shown picking cotton.[50] Nixon's spot ads were less blatant—though they were not subtle, either—and more effective. One of his campaign spots showed scenes of urban riots, with a Nixon voice-over calling for "some honest talk about the problem of order."[51]

The message worked in the North as well as the South. Working-class whites in semiskilled and unskilled occupations gave Humphrey only 38 percent of their votes, less than two-thirds the 61 percent proportion cast for John Kennedy in 1960. Black voters, on the other hand, abandoned the Republicans. Nixon won 32 percent of the black vote in 1960, but his share fell to 12 percent in 1968.[52] One of the president's closest advisers, John Erlichman, told civil rights administrators that "Blacks are not where the votes are, so why antagonize the people who can be helpful to us politically?"[53]

In the campaigns of 1980 and 1984, the Republicans virtually wrote off the African-American vote. Richard Wirthlin, Ronald Reagan's campaign strategist, advised before the 1980 election that the "Reagan for President 1980 campaign must convert into Reagan votes the disappointment felt by Southern white and rural voters. . . ."[54] Reagan carried only 10 percent of blacks' votes in 1980 and slightly fewer in 1984. In 1984, however, three out of four southern whites voted for him. The Reagan White House actively worked to undo civil rights guarantees, slashing the budgets of civil rights enforcement units and slowing or stopping enforcement.[55]

Race was inserted directly and overtly into the 1988 campaign. An independent group backing George Bush ran an ad repeatedly featuring Willie Horton, a black convict who had raped a woman while on a prison furlough program in Massachusetts. The Democrats' candidate, Michael Dukakis, had been the state's governor at that time. George Bush derived political capital by conveniently distancing himself from the ad while running his own television spots denouncing the Massachusetts furlough program.[56] After winning the election, Bush consistently opposed new civil rights legislation.

It is impossible to divorce the issue of race from social welfare and urban programs, a lesson the Democrats learned very early. In the 1930s, southern Democrats in Congress often expressed their concern that New Deal programs might be used to upset traditional racial relationships in the South. Later, they fought to make sure that the public housing programs would not be used to promote racial integration. As long as the programs advanced by Democratic liberals in the North could be divorced from racial politics, southerners were willing to go along. The possibility of doing so ended with the civil rights politics of the 1960s.

Several of the programs of the Great Society became identified as programs that primarily benefited inner-city blacks. Even though this was true for very few programs—most, including those funded under the antipoverty act, distributed funds broadly to urban and rural areas across the country—perceptions mattered. When he was thinking of backing an antipoverty program, John Kennedy seemed aware of the necessity of building a broad base of support. He told one of his advisers that he was "in favor of doing something with a poverty theme . . . I think it's important to make clear that we're doing something for the middle-income man in the suburbs, etc. But the two are not inconsistent with one another. So go right ahead with your work on it."[57] The War on Poverty, Model Cities, and several other programs, however, were billed as programs to solve the problems of inner cities, and they became perceived as such.

The War on Poverty and Model Cities programs attracted a great deal of attention because they were sold with grandiose promises about what they would accomplish. The War on Poverty, in particular, became the lightning rod for political conflict. These programs attracted so much attention that it is sometimes difficult to remember that many other programs of the 1960s proved to be durable, popular, and politically secure, for instance, the Head Start early school program funded through the War on Poverty, food stamps, Medicare, and Medicaid.

The War on Poverty and the Model Cities program shared two features that made them controversial. Both programs required that new institutions be set up to receive the federal program dollars; these were the community action agencies, in the case of the War on Poverty, and the Model Cities agencies. Second, these agencies were instructed to encourage the participation of community residents in designing and running the programs. The idea was to create new institutions in the cities that would be capable of mobilizing the energies of people who lived in the communities; an early program guide distributed by the Office of Economic Opportunity said that to qualify for funding, local antipoverty programs should involve the poor from the very first "in planning, policy-making, and operation."[58]

The way citizen participation was used by federal administrators soon made local politicians nervous, then it made them angry. Policymakers in the Johnson Administration were convinced that most local power structures had systematically excluded blacks. They thought that if the money was actually going to get to the poor, especially in the inner-city black ghettos, it would be necessary to keep it out of the hands of local politicians. Community action and Model Cities agencies were devices to forge a direct link between program administrators at the national level and local leaders with the incentive and motivation to design truly innovative programs.

These programs were, in a sense, a means of fomenting a revolution in local power structures. According to two scholars, Frances Fox Piven and Richard A. Cloward, many of the Great Society programs were formulated to preserve and strengthen the Democratic party's electoral advantage in the industrialized states holding the largest blocs of electoral college votes.[59] Rather than work through local politicians who had repeatedly shown an unwillingness to mobilize the votes of inner-city blacks, federal administrators tried to work directly with organizations and leaders in black communities. The new urban programs offered material inducements similar to those offered by the old-style party machines at the turn of the century. The expectation was that blacks would vote Democratic in return.

A great many Great Society programs bypassed state and local governments. In the 1960s, a multitude of new agencies were established to receive and spend federal dollars. Of all of the community action funds spent by the Office of Economic Opportunity by 1968, only 25 percent was given to public agencies at all, the remainder going to private organizations such as universities, churches, civil rights groups, settlement houses, family services agencies, United Way programs, and newly established nonprofit groups.[60] Likewise, only 10 percent of the funds distributed through programs administered by the Department of Health, Education and Welfare were limited to governmental units.[61]

A few programs received a great deal of mass media attention when political activists associated with them became embroiled in political fights with mayors and local government bureaucracies. In Syracuse, San Francisco, and the state of Mississippi, local administrators of antipoverty programs led protest actions against mayors, welfare departments, and school boards, demanding that programs be implemented that responded to complaints from the black community. Though such protests happened in only a few places, local authorities were upset when they saw federal monies flowing into their jurisdictions to groups and organizations over which they had little control. Only in unusual circumstances would a mayor be inclined to encourage the creation of new organizations to represent minority communities and poor people. Such organizations might encourage complaints about all sorts of things—police brutality, the hiring of teachers, welfare policies, public housing maintenance; the list could be endless.

Governors, mayors, and members of Congress complained to the President and to federal administrators. The antipoverty program became such a headache to Lyndon Johnson that he suspected that it was being run by his political enemies, people loyal to the Kennedy family.[62] In June 1965, the U.S. Conference of Mayors passed a resolution urging that mayors be given control over all antipoverty funds flowing through their cities. Through 1965 and 1966, the mayors continued to vent their displeasure, both collectively and individually. The experiences with the War on Poverty chastened federal administrators enough that by the time the Model Cities program was implemented in 1967, they rapidly responded to mayors' complaints and gave the mayors the right to veto programs in their cities.

The War on Poverty and the Model Cities programs continued to receive congressional support mainly because funds flowed into a large number of congressional districts, thus making it possible for representatives of both parties to tell their constituents that they were effective at delivering federal largesse. To broaden the base of political support, the Johnson Administration quickly abandoned its initial plan to restrict the antipoverty effort to a few "demonstration" projects. In the first year, 650 projects were funded, and, by 1967, the number of programs reached 1,100. The same thing happened with the Model Cities program. Like the War on Poverty, Model Cities was promoted with grandiose rhetoric; it was supposed to involve an unprecedented "concentration and coordination of Federal, State, and local public and private efforts."[63] Initially, the number of cities that would receive money for "demonstration" programs was supposed to be as low as five.[64] By the time the interests of powerful congressional leaders were accommodated, the number of cities increased to fifty. By the time the bill was passed in 1966, however, the number of cities awarded programs had mushroomed to seventy-five, and a year later another seventy-five cities were added in a second round of funding.[65]

Though expanding the number of programs broadened the political support sufficiently to guarantee congressional support for these programs, it also virtually eliminated the possibility that each program could have much impact. The funding for individual programs did not match the inflated rhetoric used to promote them. Although it was often portrayed as a massive, radical program,[66] the War on Poverty was actually very small. The community action agencies received, collectively, $94 million in 1965 that they could spend at their discretion. Model Cities money was likewise spread thin. The combination of overblown promises and limited accomplishments became an enduring and damaging legacy of the Great Society.

❖ THE BACKLASH AGAINST FEDERAL ACTIVISM

In 1964, when Lyndon Johnson proposed the first legislation in his War on Poverty, he announced to Congress that his objective was "total victory."[67] Clearly, the War on Poverty never achieved that objective. Neither, however, was it a total failure—as conservative critics have loudly proclaimed. The overall result was decidedly mixed.

Conservative critics have contended that the expanded social programs of the 1960s and 1970s not only failed to solve the problem of poverty, but actually increased poverty and attendant social problems by providing incentives for people not to work and support a family.[68] In fact, however, the poverty rate was cut in half during the period of expanded social programs, falling from 22.2 percent of the population below the poverty level in 1960 to an all-time low of 11.1 percent in 1973.[69] During the 1980s, a period of generally declining expenditures on programs for the poor, the poverty rate rose steadily, and, by 1992, it reached the level it had been at before the social programs of the 1960s. When the income Americans receive from all sources, including government programs for the poor, is included, the reduction in the poverty rate in the 1960s and 1970s was dramatic, falling from 18 percent in 1960 to somewhere between 4 and 8 percent by the second half of the 1970s.[70]

Evaluations of specific federal programs to attack urban problems show mixed results. Often the programs were overly complex and administrators ran into severe implementation problems.[71] But some programs worked. Perhaps the best example is Head Start, a federal program to enhance the skills of poor children before they enter school. One study found that children who participated in Head Start were 45 percent less likely to be held back in school than were similar children not enrolled in the program. This produced a substantial savings for local school districts.[72] Medicare and Medicaid improved health care substantially for the elderly and the poor. In 1963, 19 percent of poor persons had never visited a doctor; this fell to only 8 percent by 1970. From 1965 to 1975, the infant mortality rate of the poor fell by 33 percent.[73] Because of such successes, most of the poverty programs became sufficiently popular that they endured despite conservatives' complaints. Two programs—

Community Action and Job Corps—took most of the political heat. The first was ended by 1974; the second barely survived as a small program.

To understand the reasons for the backlash against the Great Society programs, it is necessary to examine politics and perceptions of the programs, not their objective effects. One reason for the backlash was the overly narrow political base supporting some of the programs (particularly Community Action and Job Corps). The overwhelming (and erroneous) popular impression was that most of the programs benefited only blacks in the inner cities. In any circumstances, this perception would have created a political problem for the Democrats, but the seriousness of the problem was magnified by another, more important reason for the backlash—the political and social tensions focusing on the war in Vietnam and racial divisions that escalated all through the decade.

The war in Vietnam took much of the money that would otherwise have been available to fund social programs. The war's greatest impact on the programs, however, was that it caused a split within the Democratic fold. Johnson tried to build support for his Vietnam policy by labeling dissenters unpatriotic and even un-American. He substantially succeeded among white, blue-collar workers, but dissent continued to escalate. Demonstrations became more frequent and more confrontational. By the time Johnson announced, in March 1968, that he would not run for reelection, the Democrats were in disarray. At the Democratic national convention in Chicago that August, delegates hurled epithets at one another, and reporters were assaulted. On the streets outside the convention, Chicago police beat demonstrators by the hundreds, all in full view of television cameras.

Beginning in 1964 racial antagonisms in northern cities intensified. On July 16, within hours of the fatal shooting of a 15-year-old boy by an off-duty police officer, rioting broke out in Harlem. During the summer in Rochester, New York, it took 400 state troopers and 1,300 national guardsmen three days to put down disorders. Riots or violence broke out in Philadelphia; in Jersey City, Paterson, and Elizabeth, New Jersey; and in Dixmore, Illinois, a black suburb of Chicago. A major riot broke out on August 11 in the Watts area of Los Angeles. Like so many riots in the next few summers, this one was ignited when a crowd of blacks gathered to protest police actions in arresting a black youth. A total of 329 major incidents occurred from 1965 through 1968, with 220 deaths.[74]

In July 1967, in the midst of the third consecutive summer of urban rioting, President Johnson established the National Commission on Civil Disorders to investigate the causes of the riots and to recommend policy responses. Chaired by Governor Otto Kerner of Illinois and Mayor John V. Lindsay of New York, the commission undertook an ambitious investigation. A staff of more than thirty professional researchers compiled materials while the commission visited cities and conducted hearings. In March 1968, the Kerner Commission delivered its report.

The commission blamed the riots on white racism: "the most fundamental is the racial attitude and behavior of white Americans toward black

Americans. . . . [W]hite racism is essentially responsible for the explosive mixture which has been accumulating in our cities since the end of World War II."[75] The commission said that segregation, poverty, violence directed at blacks, and the widespread feeling of powerlessness among blacks were the main causes of the riots. The commission recommended the enactment of special housing, education, employment, and welfare programs. Failure to remedy the problems it identified would "make permanent the division of our country into two societies; one largely Negro and poor, located in central cities; the other, predominantly white and affluent, located in the suburbs and in outlying areas."[76]

The Kerner Commission's analysis of the riots and its recommendations sparked bitter controversy between whites and blacks, suburbs and cities, the South and the North, rural areas and urban areas. The riots provoked fear and resentments. The national consensus on civil rights and the political support for the Great Society social programs rapidly eroded. The congressional elections of 1966 and the presidential election of 1968 revealed a political backlash against social legislation. In 1966, the Republicans gained four seats in the Senate, and they raised their proportion of the membership in the House from less than one-third to 43 percent.

In the 1970s and 1980s, a struggle over urban policy ensued, one that the Democrats lost. Republican candidates used civil disorders and urban riots as ammunition in their election campaigns. They claimed that social programs not only had failed, but had contributed to a breakdown of "law and order." They campaigned on the premise that the federal establishment had become overreaching and dangerous. Even in the 1990s, the social programs of the Great Society still serve as useful ammunition for politicians on the campaign trail. After the Los Angeles riots in 1992, President George Bush's press secretary, Marlin Fitzwater, declared that the social welfare programs of the 1960s and 1970s were partly to blame.[77] When asked to name the specific programs he had in mind, he replied, "I don't have a list with me," but went on to add, "the basic structures of these communities were formulated in the '60s and '70s on the basis of the social welfare efforts that didn't work." Trying to blame the riots on the Great Society programs struck historian Arthur Schlesinger, Jr., as "pathetic." "What can they be smoking over at the White House these days?" he asked.[78] Whatever it was, it seemed to be extremely addicting. In the first presidential debate of the 1992 campaign, President Bush repeatedly invoked the well-worn slogan "tax and spend." Democratic candidate Bill Clinton retorted, "President Bush is running against Lyndon Johnson, Jimmy Carter, everybody but me in this campaign." In 1992, for the first time in a long time, it was not a winning strategy for the Republicans.

PART THREE

SUBURBS, SUNBELT, AND THE ECLIPSE OF THE CENTRAL CITIES

CHAPTER 8

SUBURBANIZATION AND THE ROOTS OF THE URBAN CRISIS

❖ THE U.S. PATTERN OF URBAN DEVELOPMENT

The antiurban bias that runs through the fabric of American culture gained renewed strength in the twentieth century when, in one of the "great population migrations in American history,"[1] millions of middle- and upper-class households, overwhelmingly white, moved out of central cities to low-density, largely single-family areas in the suburbs. In the 1920s, for the first time in the nation's history, suburban population growth exceeded that of central cities,[2] and the suburbs have continued to grow faster than the central cities in every decade since. In the 1970s, for the first time, more Americans lived in suburbs than lived either in cities or in small towns and rural areas. During the 1980s, population continued to sprawl in ever-widening suburban arcs around the core cities.

Population movement out from the center is a common feature of urban development all over the world. With the aid of transportation breakthroughs, such as automated rail systems and the automobile, urban areas in the advanced Western countries have been spreading out for at least a century.[3] There are, however, several characteristics that set the experience in the United States apart: lower population densities, higher rates of home ownership, an unusual pattern of class segregation, and autonomous suburban governments.

American urban areas, most of them containing detached, single-family homes with large yards, are much more spread out than most cities in other developed nations. This means that the population densities are much lower.[4] In exchange for this low-density living, Americans tolerate longer commutes to work than people elsewhere.[5]

American suburbs are composed overwhelmingly of owner-occupied houses; core cities and suburbs in other countries have a higher proportion of rental units. In the United States, high-rise, multiunit buildings are equated with the central city, and only recently have such buildings become common in the suburbs. Suburbs elsewhere in the world, in contrast, frequently contain high-rise buildings and town houses.

In the United States the incomes of urban dwellers tend to rise as the distance from the core city increases. A disproportionate number of poor people are clustered in and near the center, while more affluent people tend to live farther out. This is not the case in most other countries, where the wealthiest people continue to live in fashionable neighborhoods in the historic cities. In Paris, Rome, Barcelona, Vienna, Rio de Janeiro, Mexico City, and Tokyo, for example, the richest residential areas are near the center; the suburbs tend to be reserved for those (including some of the middle class) who cannot afford to live in the most exclusive areas. In addition, the differences between core cities and suburbs are often more extreme in the United States than elsewhere. Even in Great Britain, whose settlement pattern most closely resembles that of the United States, central cities tend to hold both the poor and a significant number of affluent people. The contrast between New York and London is revealing: "In contrast to New York the emergent pattern [in London] was not one of a succession of waves of immigrants arriving at the center and driving the previous ethnically distinct waves outwards, but, rather, a continuous process of inflow from around Britain, into available space both in the inner areas and newly developing suburbs. . . ."[6] It would be accurate to regard the American pattern as not only exceptional compared to elsewhere, but even peculiar.

A final difference in the pattern of suburbanization is that suburbs in other countries are generally components of regional governmental units, and these are in turn tied directly to the national government. American suburbs are divided into autonomous governmental units, which make taxation, spending, and land use decisions independently from the central cities and the national government. The political separation of central cities from suburban jurisdictions is a characteristic of all urban areas in the United States.

What is the cause of the American pattern of suburbanization and the closely related problem of central city decline? Conventional wisdom holds that suburbanization was the inevitable result of changing technology and consumer choice. The automobile made it possible for middle-class households to choose to live far from work, and the latest construction methods and conveniences made it possible for them to build new homes in low-density suburbs. The difference of the American pattern from other countries, however, suggests that there is more to the story than changing technology and individual tastes. In the pages that follow, we show that rather than being an inevitable outcome of anonymous forces of technology and the market, the pace and shape of suburban growth in the United States was shaped and sustained by both public policies and private institutions.

❖ THE STAGES OF SUBURBAN DEVELOPMENT

Suburbanization in the United States has passed through four distinct stages. During each period, a sorting out process occurred that lowered population densities and increased the separation of urban dwellers of different incomes, family characteristics, and ethnic and racial backgrounds.

■ Railroad and Streetcar Suburbs: 1815–1918

In Chapter 2 we referred to early American cities as "walking cities." Cities were compact, and population densities were high. Homes were rarely located more than a mile or two from places of work, and nearly everyone walked to work. Most people lived in row houses built right up to the street, with no front yards. The street was a place of lively community where rich and poor, merchant and laborer, home life and business life mingled. Outlying areas less convenient to work and the waterfront were mostly reserved for the lower orders of society.[7] To be sure, the very wealthy sometimes created rural or suburban retreats, but large-scale suburbanization as we know it today, with people living on the outskirts and commuting to jobs, awaited the industrial city. As soon as changes in production methods and the invention of new forms of transportation made it possible, the upper and upper-middle classes began to escape the congestion of downtown in large numbers.

The enthusiasm with which wealthy Americans in the nineteenth century embraced the suburban ideal can, in part, be explained by the antiurban bias that pervaded American culture. Thomas Jefferson is well known for his suspicion of city life. "The mobs of great cities," he wrote, "add just so much to the support of pure government, as sores do to the strength of the human body."[8] The enthusiasm for the suburbs was also nourished by the Romantic movement, which idealized nature and advocated a balance between humanity and nature that was, Romantic writers argued, being destroyed by cities and technology.

Later in the century suburbanization was also driven by changes in the location of production and in the division of labor within families. In preindustrial cities, most production took place in the home and women and children participated in the artisan production process. Industrialization brought with it the factory, which massed large numbers of workers under one roof, subjecting them to the strict discipline of capitalist managers. As work and residence separated, the home gradually became viewed not as a place of production open to outside relations and extended kin, but as a haven from the world of work. Especially among the middle and upper classes, the family became the center of emotional life, a sphere controlled by women apart from the grime and disorder of crowded cities. The emerging cultural ideal situated the family in a single-unit house with a large front yard that acted like a moat separating the intimacy of the home from the streets of commerce and competition. As one urban historian put it, "The growth of suburbs was to build into the physical environment that division between the feminine/natural/emotional world of family and the masculine/rational/urban world of work."[9]

In 1814, Robert Fulton began the first steam ferry service between Manhattan and Brooklyn, providing a chance for those who could afford it to live apart from the hustle and bustle of Manhattan. Brooklyn thus became the first commuter suburb.[10] The nineteenth century witnessed a succession of transportation improvements that made it possible for people to live farther and farther from the city center: the steam ferry, the omnibus, the commuter railroad, the horsecar, the elevated railroad, the cable car, and the electric trolley.

Railroads were best used for travel between cities, not for commuting, but they did enable a small elite to live in pristine isolation from the problems of industrial society. Commuter tickets on railroads were far too expensive for ordinary workers; railroad suburbs, which prospered in the mid-nineteenth century, were thus restricted to the wealthiest classes. In many ways, railroad suburbs, like Chestnut Hill outside Philadelphia, Bronxville outside New York, and Forest Park outside of Chicago, achieved the epitome of the suburban ideal. Winding lanes, in contrast to the grid-patterned streets of cities, made these suburbs look like "scattered buildings in a park," the homes integrated with nature, with no hint of the grimy factory on which this suburban wealth was based.[11]

In a pattern that repeats in every stage of urban history, transportation improvements were planned not so much for moving people as for capturing the increased land values that resulted from opening up new suburban land for development. Some railroads lost money on day-to-day operations, but that did not prevent railroad entrepreneurs from amassing fabulous fortunes through suburban land speculation.[12]

Horse-drawn streetcars became widespread after 1850, providing less expensive transportation for growing numbers of urban residents and expanding the commuting distance for workers up to three miles from downtown.[13] The real breakthrough in the scale of suburbanization came with the electric trolley in the 1890s. By tripling the radius of cities, the electric trolley increased the amount of land that could be developed for residential use by 900 percent. Its introduction was followed by a near frenzy of speculation in land.

Henry E. Huntington was one of the most astute rail entrepreneurs to profit from land speculation. As much as any single person, he was responsible for establishing the extreme urban sprawl of southern California. Son of one of the founders of the Southern Pacific Railroad, in the 1890s Huntington failed in his bid to take over that railroad and turned his considerable wealth toward developing a local rail system in the Los Angeles area. In 1901 he formed the Pacific Electric Railway Company. Recognizing that the first few years of intraurban transit were bound to be unprofitable, Huntington shrewdly bought up huge tracts of land in the western San Gabriel Valley through which his rail lines would be built. When conditions were ripe, he subdivided and sold the land, reaping huge profits. By 1911, he was able to make a deal with the president of the Southern Pacific which essentially gave him monopoly control over local rail transit in the Los Angeles area. By 1921, his Pacific Electric system was carrying over 250,000 passengers daily on over 1,000 miles of track.[14]

The building of the streetcar suburbs quickened the movement of population beyond central cities. No one considered this movement a threat to the cities, because they were still experiencing rapid population growth and economic development (see Table 8-1). Between 1900 and 1920, for example, New York City grew by 2.18 million people, compared to a population increase of only 190,000 in its surrounding area. In 1920, New York's population was 5.6 million people; its suburban ring's was 379,000. In the first two decades of the twentieth century, even though in several urban areas suburbs grew at a faster rate than the central cities, the vast majority of people living in urban areas still lived in the core industrial cities.

Industrial and manufacturing facilities remained near water and rail transportation links in the city centers. Between 1904 and 1914, St. Louis lost some industry to its suburbs (its share of industrial employment fell from 95 to 90 percent of the area's manufacturing establishments), as did Baltimore (96 to 93 percent) and Philadelphia (91 to 87 percent), but these cities were the exception rather than the rule.[15] The old industrial cities overwhelmingly dominated the economies of their urban areas. Railroad and streetcar suburbs prospered, but they were still dependent economically on the central cities.

▪ The First Automobile Suburbs: 1918–1945

The automobile ultimately came to be regarded as an expression of American values of privacy and individualism. When it was first introduced in the late nineteenth century, it was mainly an expensive plaything for the rich. Henry Ford changed that. In 1908 Ford introduced the Model T, a car for the masses that was dependable and easy to operate. Through the introduction of the moving assembly line in 1913, Ford was able to reduce the cost of a Model T from $950 in 1910 to $290 in 1924. Car ownership skyrocketed. American car production increased from 63,000 in 1908 to 550,000 by 1914. After World War I, car production took off, reaching 2.27 million in 1922 and 4.45 million in 1929.[16] The construction of adequate roads lagged seriously behind car ownership, but this problem was eventually solved when automobile owners successfully pressed for massive state and federal funding, mainly through gasoline taxes.

The automobile gave the rapidly expanding upper-middle class the opportunity to move to the suburbs. Whereas streetcar suburbs had sprung up along the rail lines like the spokes on a wheel, the automobile made it possible to develop the areas in between. Vast new tracts of land were opened to land

TABLE 8-1 METROPOLITAN AREA POPULATION, 1900–1940 (INCREASES IN POPULATION EXPRESSED AS PERCENT GROWTH AND NUMBER OF PEOPLE ADDED)

DISTRICTS	1900–1910		1910–1920		1920–1930		1930–1940	
	CENTRAL CITY	OUTSIDE CENTRAL CITY	CENTRAL CITY	OUTSIDE CENTRAL CITY	CENTRAL CITY	OUTSIDE CENTRAL CITY	CENTRAL CITY	OUTSIDE CENTRAL CITY
New York City[a]	38.7% (1,329,681)	60.9% (91,636)	17.9% (853,165)	35.2% (98,692)	23.3% (1,310,398)	67.3% (424,785)	7.6% (524,549)	18.2% (193,291)
Chicago	28.7 (486,708)	87.7 (122,226)	23.4 (512,185)	79.1 (210,797)	24.9 (673,292)	73.9 (419,906)	0.6 (20,370)	10.4 (104,214)
Boston	19.6 (109,693)	23.4 (161,273)	9.0 (61,968)	21.2 (179,148)	4.4 (33,128)	21.2 (267,344)	-1.3 (-10,372)	3.1 (47,741)
St. Louis	19.4 (111,791)	90.6 (67,357)	12.5 (85,868)	26.4 (37,412)	6.7 (56,643)	71.3 (165,344)	-0.7 (-5,912)	15.7 (74,896)
Cleveland	46.0 (176,492)	46.5 (16,698)	40.1 (227,978)	140.0 (75,171)	11.8 (95,007)	125.8 (164,128)	-2.7 (-24,135)	13.0 (38,824)

TABLE 8-1 (*Continued*)

DISTRICTS	1900–1910		1910–1920		1920–1930		1930–1940	
	CENTRAL CITY	OUTSIDE CENTRAL CITY	CENTRAL CITY	OUTSIDE CENTRAL CITY	CENTRAL CITY	OUTSIDE CENTRAL CITY	CENTRAL CITY	OUTSIDE CENTRAL CITY
Los Angeles	206.1 (214,932)	553.3 (100,232)	80.7 (257,475)	107.6 (156,692)	114.7 (661,375)	157.9 (661,548)	21.3 (263,918)	30.1 (324,138)
Mean for all metro districts	33.6	38.2	25.2 (5,385,116)	32.0 (2,236,795)	20.9 (5,851,909)	46.4 (4,819,770)	4.4 (1,498,186)	13.6 (2,086,607)
Non-metro population increase	16.4		9.6		9.5		7.2	
Total U.S. population increase	21.0		14.9		16.1		7.2	

aIncludes growth of population in New York City proper and in satellite areas of New York State. New Jersey population is excluded.
Source: U.S. Bureau of the Census, *The Growth of Metropolitan Districts in the United States, 1900–1940,* by Warren S. Thompson (Washington, D.C.: Government Printing Office, 1947), especially Table 2.

speculation and suburban development, and the upper-middle class invested much of its new-found wealth in suburban real estate. Total national wealth doubled in the ten years from 1912 to 1922, and from 1915 to 1925 average hourly wages climbed from 32 to 70 cents.[17] The value of residential land and improvements doubled in the 1920s.[18]

In the 1920s suburban growth began to compete with the growth of the industrial cities. For the first time in the nation's history, in most urban areas the total number of people moving to the suburbs exceeded the population increase in the central cities. Table 8-1 documents this development. In all metropolitan districts in the nation, almost 5 million people were added to the suburbs in the 1920s; in the same decade the central cities grew by nearly 6 million people. However, if the New York and Chicago regions are not counted in the totals, an interesting statistic emerges: The population of the suburbs grew more than the city populations in all the other metropolitan areas.

The unprecedented growth of suburbs did not seem to represent a threat to the vitality of cities. The new automobile suburbs were still dependent on their central cities; most people who lived in the suburbs worked in the city. While the proportion of factory employment in central cities declined in every city of more than 100,000 residents between 1920 and 1930—the new assembly line production techniques required lots of land rather than vertical buildings, and this land was in the suburbs, central business districts continued to thrive with new office employment and retail sales. Almost all white-collar people worked and shopped in the old downtowns. Employment soared in most central cities, with downtown office space tripling in the 1920s.[19]

The Great Depression sharply slowed suburban development, but it even more drastically applied the brake to central city population growth. The depression signaled the twilight of the city-building era in the older cities. The data in Table 8-1 reveal that Boston, St. Louis, and Cleveland all lost population in the 1930s. So did Philadelphia, Kansas City, and the New Jersey cities—Elizabeth, Paterson, Jersey City, and Newark. San Francisco, which had grown by 27 percent in the 1920s, was no bigger by the census of 1940 than it had been in 1930. A great many small manufacturing cities of New England and the midwest declined in population—Akron and Youngstown, Ohio; Albany, Schenectady, and Troy, New York; Joplin, Missouri; and New Bedford, Massachusetts.

The depression affected the suburbs as well as the cities, since most upper-middle- and middle-class people lacked the means to buy a new suburban home. The growth rate of New York's suburbs declined from 67 percent in the 1920s to only 18 percent in the 1930s. Chicago's suburban expansion slowed from 74 percent to 10 percent, Cleveland's from 126 percent to 13 percent, and Los Angeles's from 158 percent to 30 percent. All through the 1930s, the effects of the depression lingered. With the coming of World War II, materials needed for housing construction were commandeered for the war effort. As a result, suburban growth came to a near standstill.

▪ Bedroom Suburbs: 1946–1965

The standstill in housing construction resulting from the depression and the war created a huge backlog of the demand for housing. To this situation was added a rapidly increasing population. After reaching a low point during the depression, the birthrate began to rise in 1943 and then took off in the postwar baby boom, as 16 million GIs returned to civilian life.[20] By 1947, 6 million families were doubling up with relatives or friends because they could not find a home of their own.[21] The housing industry geared up to meet the demand, increasing single-family housing starts from only 114,000 in 1944 to 1,692,000 by 1950.[22] Almost all of this new construction took place in the suburbs.

Utilizing mass production methods and sophisticated marketing techniques, big companies began to dominate the housing industry. While big corporations accounted for only 5 percent of all houses built in 1938, they increased their share of the market to 24 percent by 1949. A decade later, they produced 64 percent of all new homes.[23] These builders concentrated overwhelmingly on the suburbs. Their preferred method was to buy large tracts of land on the outskirts of cities and to create whole new communities in a new landscape by bulldozing everything to an even surface and constructing houses quickly using standardized production techniques.

In earlier decades, suburbanization was mainly an upper- and middle-class phenomenon, but now it filtered down to include working-class families. For most families, owning their own home in the suburbs became a better economic bargain than trying to stay in their old neighborhoods. Federally insured home loans, cheap energy, and new efficient building technologies made it cheaper to build a new house in the suburbs than to rehabilitate a home or rent an apartment in the city. The home ownership rate increased from 43.6 percent in 1940 to 62.9 percent in 1970.[24]

The population of the suburbs exploded. The data in Table 8-2 provide a glimpse of the magnitude of the population changes that occurred in the forty years between 1940 and 1980. During the 1940s, the core cities grew by just over 6 million people, a 14 percent rate of growth. The suburbs surrounding these cities, in contrast, grew by 9 million people, a 36 percent increase. The rate of growth in the suburbs was actually much faster than these statistics suggest because most suburban subdivisions were built after 1946, when wartime conditions finally ended. In the 1950s, central cities grew by an average of 11 percent for the decade; the suburbs that surrounded them grew by 49 percent. In this one decade alone suburban populations increased by 19 million, but the core cities grew by only 6 million. Most of the central city growth, moreover, occurred in midsize and smaller central cities. Most of the big cities in the industrial belt that ran from New England through the Great Lakes states actually lost population. Attempts to reverse this trend by annexing suburbs were prevented by state laws that made such annexation effectively impossible without the approval of the suburbs involved.

TABLE 8-2 METROPOLITAN AREA POPULATION, 1940–1990 (INCREASES IN POPULATION EXPRESSED AS PERCENT GROWTH AND NUMBER OF PEOPLE ADDED)

DISTRICTS	1940–1950		1950–1960		1960–1970		1970–1980		1980–1990		1990
	CENTRAL CITY	OUTSIDE CENTRAL CITY	CENTRAL CITY	OUTSIDE CENTRAL CITY	CENTRAL CITY	OUTSIDE CENTRAL CITY	CENTRAL CITY	OUTSIDE CENTRAL CITY	CENTRAL CITY	OUTSIDE CENTRAL CITY	PERCENT OF POPULATION IN LARGEST CENTRAL CITY
Frostbelt											
New York City	5.9%	23.2%	-1.4%	75.0%	1.5%	26.0%	-10.4%	0.4%[a]	+3.5	+0.6[a]	65.6
Chicago	6.6	31.2	-2.0	71.5	-5.2	35.3	-10.8	13.6	-7.4	+7.4	45.9
Boston	4.0	11.5	-13.0	17.7	-8.1	11.3	-12.2	-2.6	+2.0	+3.5	22.7
St. Louis	5.0	33.8	-12.5	50.8	-17.0	28.5	-27.2	6.3	-12.4	+7.3	16.2
Cleveland	4.2	41.6	-4.2	67.3	-14.3	27.1	-23.6	0.4	-11.9	+0.0	27.6
Detroit	13.9	54.8	-9.7	79.3	-9.5	28.5	-20.5	7.8	-14.6	+2.5	23.5
Pittsburgh	0.8	8.9	-10.7	17.2	-13.9	4.4	-18.5	-2.2	-12.8	-5.8	18.0
Minneapolis	6.0	76.2	-7.5	115.7	-10.0	55.9	-14.6	20.6	-0.7	+22.8	14.9
Sunbelt											
Atlanta	9.6	57.8	47.1	33.9	2.0	68.6	-14.1	45.8	-7.3	+42.5	13.9
Dallas	47.4	73.7	56.4	27.0	24.2	61.8	7.1	47.9	+11.2	+48.5	39.4
Denver	29.0	73.4	18.8	121.8	4.2	63.7	-4.5	59.9	-5.1	+23.4	28.8
Phoenix	63.3	86.3	311.1	-0.3	32.4	72.0	30.9	92.1	+24.5	+61.2	46.3
Los Angeles	31.0	69.8	25.8	66.6	13.6	20.0	5.0	0.7	+17.4	+19.2	39.3
Miami	44.8	157.2	17.0	161.7	14.8	45.0	3.6	37.1	+3.4	+25.1	18.5

TABLE 8-2 METROPOLITAN AREA POPULATION, 1940–1990 (INCREASES IN POPULATION EXPRESSED AS PERCENT GROWTH AND NUMBER OF PEOPLE ADDED)

DISTRICTS	1940–1950		1950–1960		1960–1970		1970–1980		1980–1990		1990
	CENTRAL CITY	OUTSIDE CENTRAL CITY	CENTRAL CITY	OUTSIDE CENTRAL CITY	CENTRAL CITY	OUTSIDE CENTRAL CITY	CENTRAL CITY	OUTSIDE CENTRAL CITY	CENTRAL CITY	OUTSIDE CENTRAL CITY	PERCENT OF POPULATION IN LARGEST CENTRAL CITY
Mean for all SMSAs	14.0	35.9	10.7	48.6	6.4	26.8	0.1	18.2	2.3	12.3	
Number added	(6,021,074)	(9,199,931)	(6,251,181)	(19,081,702)	(3,849,814)	(15,974,243)	(80,054)	(15,631,197)	(451,423)	(3,335,814)	
Non-metro population increase	6.1		7.1		6.8		15.1		3.9		
Total U.S. population increase	14.5		18.5		13.3		11.4		9.8		

[a]Nassau and Suffolk counties were deleted from the New York City SMSA in 1971. They have been included here for purposes of comparability. The actual Outside Central City figure for the revised New York City SMSA is –1.4.

Source: U.S. Department of Commerce, Bureau of the Census, *Census of Population, 1950*, vol. 1. *Number of Inhabitants*, pt. 1 (Washington, D.C.: Government Printing Office, 1952), p. 69, Table 17; *Census of Population, 1970*, vol. 1, *Characteristics of the Population*, pt. A, p. 180, Table 34; *Census of Population, 1980*, suppl. reports, *Standard Metropolitan Statistical Areas and Standard Consolidated Statistical Areas*, p. 2, Table B, p. 6, Table 1, p. 49, Table 3; *State and Metropolitan Areas Data Book, 1991*, Table D.

Only in the South and in the West were cities still booming: Atlanta went from 331,314 people in 1950 to 487,455 by 1960; Phoenix from 106,818 to 439,170 in the same decade. But the suburbs surrounding most of these cities were growing as well. The exceptions were cities like Jacksonville, Florida; Oklahoma City; and Phoenix, Arizona; and they were exceptions only because they were able to annex new subdivisions before the subdivisions were able to incorporate as separate municipalities.

In the 1960s, the nation's central cities, on the average, grew by 6 percent, but this statistic hides huge variations. Central cities all across the manufacturing belt suffered massive population losses; St. Louis, for example, lost 17 percent, Cleveland 14 percent, and Minneapolis 20 percent. In the same decade the nation's suburbs added 16 million people. Cities in the South and West continued to grow, some of them (like Phoenix) very rapidly, but a slowdown was evident in the older cities even outside the industrial belt. Denver, for instance, grew by only 4 percent and Atlanta by 2 percent. Both of these cities, like their counterparts in the northern industrial states, were already ringed by suburbs and therefore they found it hard to annex new housing subdivisions that were springing up beyond their borders.

The suburbs of the 1950s and 1960s were by no means all cut from the same cloth. There were working-class, blue-collar subdivisions, even a few areas populated by blacks, and, of course, enclaves of the wealthy. However, most suburban homes of that period were built for white, middle-class families. Individual suburbs tended to be remarkably uniform, with row after endless row of houses that looked as if they had been produced by a cookie cutter. Suburbia came to be portrayed in the popular media as a place of look-alike streets and people, where bored couples with small children spent their free time watching television and picking crabgrass out of their lawns, where the men commuted to office jobs leaving behind frustrated housewives to care for the children in culturally sterile environments. This image of suburbia was captured in three bestselling novels published during the period: *The Man in the Gray Flannel Suit* (1955), *The Crack in the Picture Window* (1956), and *The Split Level Trap* (1960). Though the cultural criticisms of suburbia undoubtedly traded on stereotypes, they struck a responsive chord.[25]

Leaders of central cities were not concerned with the cultural shape of suburbs, but were increasingly alarmed that the suburbs represented a threat to the vitality and even viability of the central cities. It was not only that the suburbs were growing faster than the cities. They were also pulling affluent whites out of the cities, leaving behind a segregated population made up of blacks, the poor, and other minorities. Increasingly, suburbanization was understood in racial terms; the phrase "white flight" started to be heard, suggesting that suburbanization was motivated in part by racism, a suggestion for which there is abundant evidence.[26] The riots of the mid-1960s heightened the fears connected to race. In 1967, when The National Commission on Civil Disorders described a stark dichotomy between cities and suburbs, the suburbs had already evolved into enclaves that were far removed from life in the central cities.[27]

■ Enclave Suburbs: 1965–Present

Suburbs have gradually been transformed from wholly dependent satellites of cities, places where people lived but not where they worked, to increasingly self-sufficient enclaves. Though historically suburbanization was primarily a residential movement, at least since 1948 jobs have decentralized even faster than population.[28] Retailing moved out at a slower pace than did manufacturing and wholesaling because retailing is directly dependent on a nearby critical mass of buyers. By the early 1960s, however, such a critical mass had been established, and before long huge regional shopping malls began to spring up to cater to the shopping and entertainment needs of suburban consumers.[29] Suburbanites no longer needed to go downtown, and a historic link between cities and suburbs was severed. Downtown retailing went into a tailspin from which it has never fully recovered.

The suburbanization of manufacturing employment was made possible by technical innovations that freed factories from a dependence on rail connections. Electrification made single-story plants on suburban land more economical than multistory buildings which housed belt-driven machinery driven by water or steam power. In addition, manufacturers left cities because they viewed them as hotbeds of union organizing and unrest.[30] Through accelerated depreciation of assets, which allowed manufacturers to take tax deductions when they abandoned inner-city factories, and investment tax credits, which allowed manufacturers to take tax credits for new plant and equipment, the federal government subsidized the flight of industrial jobs to the suburbs.[31] By 1970, a majority of the manufacturing jobs in metropolitan areas were located in the suburbs.

The service sector was the last to suburbanize. Central business districts offered advantages to firms desiring face-to-face relations with clients and benefiting from the concentration of business services in downtowns. Advances in communications, however, made proximity less of an advantage than before. Routine service employment, what are called "back office" functions, such as copying and secretarial services, were the first to leave expensive downtown office space. In 1975, for the first time, office construction in the suburbs exceeded office construction in central cities. Higher level and higher paid corporate services, on the other hand, such as legal assistance, corporate consulting, accounting services, and investment services, continued to locate in the downtowns of large cities, partly for prestige reasons. Although many corporations are still headquartered in central cities, many have moved out to the suburbs, in whole or in part, in the past thirty years. Suburbs have begun to develop their own office complexes, or "outer cities," that duplicate many of the characteristics of central business districts.

The effect of these developments was that the suburbs became more independent of their core cities than in the past. Cross-commuting became common; by 1980, twice as many people commuted from suburb to suburb as commuted from suburb to central city.[32] The historic urban form, in which a city is surrounded by dependent suburbs, began to break down and be replaced by the "polynucleated metropolis," characterized by several nodes of concentrated land use (residential, retail, recreational, industrial, service) usually around freeway interchanges and airports.

Suburbanization has now progressed to the point where it is called exurbanization or even counterurbanization.[33] The urban agglomerations in suburbia have been given a variety of odd and often confusing labels such as "urban villages, technohubs, suburban downtowns, suburban activity centers, major diversified centers, urban cores, galactic city, pepperoni-pizza cities, a city of realms, superburbia, disurb, service cities, perimeter cities, and even peripheral centers."[34] But whatever the label, what these centers have in common is that they have recently sprung up as places where jobs, housing, light industry, retail malls, and recreation are concentrated, usually near freeway interchanges or airports.

As the suburbs became economically more complex, they also began to house a more diverse population. The new generation of suburbanites was far less uniform than the generation that preceded it. Though still more prosperous than the people left in the central cities, the new inhabitants of the suburbs differed from the inhabitants of the bedroom suburbs in being younger, often married with no children, or single.

As documented by the data in Table 8-2, through the 1970s and 1980s many old core cities continued to empty out. A large number of them, in fact, experienced more massive population losses than ever before. St. Louis lost an astonishing 27 percent of its population between 1970 and 1980 and another 12.4 percent between 1980 and 1990. Chicago, Cleveland, Detroit, and Pittsburgh also suffered population hemorrhages. Even Denver and Atlanta, though in the Sunbelt, experienced population decline. In some cases entire metropolitan areas in the manufacturing belt either stopped growing or slipped into decline. The suburbs outside of Boston, for example, fell in population in the 1970s and those surrounding Pittsburgh lost population in both the 1970s and the 1980s. In contrast, most central cities and their suburbs in the Sunbelt were booming.

In all regions of the country, however, suburbs became more complex. Added to the traditional single-family housing developments were condominium, town house, and apartment developments, each targeted to a particular demographic group or family characteristic, such as single people or smaller families. Developers were particularly keen to appeal to the two fastest growing segments of the American population: young singles and the elderly.

As they became more diverse, the suburbs became "urbanized." Many of the problems of the central cities migrated, with people, to the suburbs. In response to the perception that the city and its problems had followed them, an increasing number of suburbanites moved to defended enclaves—communities complete with walls, gates, guards, and elaborate security systems. In the 1990s, many suburban residential areas are becoming narrowly defined enclaves of like-minded people engaged in "geographical avoidance behavior" that has enabled them to avoid all contact with central cities and their residents.[35]

❖ THE ENTREPRENEURIAL SHAPING OF SUBURBIA

While many suburbanites moved out of the cities to escape crime, crowding, noise, and the presence of minorities, the families who made the suburban move exercised less choice about it than is commonly supposed. Most home building after World War II occurred outside the cities, but the preference of home buyers was only one of several factors that determined this situation. The availability of relatively inexpensive land in outlying areas encouraged real estate developers and builders to promote construction outside the cities. In their attempt to market the new subdivisions, developers virtually invented the images that came to be thought of as the American Dream, with the suburban house at its center. The suburbs were created first by decisions of entrepreneurs and only second by the choices of suburbanites themselves.

Developers influenced the character of the suburbs by selecting the clientele that could best supply profits—chiefly the middle to upper classes—and by anticipating the tastes and preferences of these consumers. Realtors, developers, and financial institutions aggressively marketed the suburbs because new housing construction maximized their profitability.[36] To market the houses they built, entrepreneurs promised not only a home but a whole way of life. They were more than house builders; they were also "community builders."[37]

One of the first and most influential community builders was Jessie Clyde Nichols. Born on a farm outside of Kansas City, Kansas, Nichols attended the University of Kansas and later studied economics at Harvard. In 1900, Nichols took a trip to Europe where he admired the beauty and grandeur of European cities. He saw no reason why, by combining beauty with business, cities in the United States could not surpass and be even more majestic than cities in Europe. After a stint in Texas, Nichols returned to Kansas City where, in 1905, he began buying up land southwest of downtown. Nichols was determined to make a living constructing and selling high class residences laid out in a beautiful and efficient manner.

Nichols was different from the typical small-time real estate operator, or "curbstoner," who bought a few small parcels of land on the edge of the city, divided them into lots, and hoped to make a speculative profit. Nichols believed in a scientific approach to land development. In a speech before a real estate convention in 1912, Nichols attracted national attention by criticizing those land developers who went for the quick sale and the quick profit. Instead, he advocated a long-term approach to control the market. He shocked his contemporaries by arguing that planning was not only compatible with private profit, but could actually increase profits over the long run. As he put it later in a landmark article on suburban shopping centers, "good planning is good business."[38]

Nichols put his principles into practice by developing the Country Club District outside of Kansas City, considered by many at the time the most beautiful suburb in the nation. Nichols appealed to his wealthy clientele with extraordinary esthetics—he modeled the suburb's shopping center, the first in the nation, on the architecture of Seville, Spain. Nichols also applied the latest in household technology, such as piped gas and electric service, in a period when servants were becoming less common. Nichols's suburban houses promised to provide a secure haven far from the stresses and tensions of city life. Husbands could go off to work in the city secure in the knowledge that their wives and children were safe in the idyllic environment of the Country Club District.

Nichols's major innovation to achieve control over the marketplace (and to promise such control to his clientele) was the self-perpetuating deed restriction, which guaranteed that owners would be forced to follow requirements laid down by the developer indefinitely, unless a majority of owners in the home owners' association voted to change the restrictions at least five years before the expiration of the twenty-five-year term.[39] The deed restrictions specified minimum-lot sizes, minimum cost for houses, set-backs from the street, and even the color and style of houses. Nichols carefully segregated houses according to price and style. By signing their deeds, buyers automatically promised to resell only to whites.[40]

Nichols became a prominent national spokesman for planned suburban development. He was a leader in the National Association of Real Estate Boards (NAREB), and in 1935, he founded the Urban Land Institute (ULI), which is influential in the housing industry to this day. In his lifetime he saw the private planning he pioneered become public policy through local subdivision regulations, zoning laws, and federal loan guarantee programs.

Nichols' projects were limited to the upper classes. Privately planned suburban development became affordable to most typical middle- and working-class families only after World War II. The Levitt family of Long Island in New York pioneered in producing standardized tract housing offered at the lowest possible price. In the late 1930s, Levitt & Sons succeeded as a medium-sized developer of plain tract housing for upper-middle-class families leaving New York City for Long Island, but the company's big break came during World War II when it won contracts to build thousands of houses for the U.S. Navy around Norfolk, Virginia. It is here that the Levitts worked on the mass production techniques that revolutionized home building. Within a few years after the war, William J. Levitt, along with his father Abraham and his brother Alfred, became the largest home builder in the United States.

Unlike Nichols, Levitt did not set out to build homes or to build communities; he simply drifted into building houses. Caring little for school, Levitt dropped out of New York University after his third year because, as he put it in a *Time* magazine cover story, "I got itchy. I wanted to make money. I wanted a big car and a lot of clothes."[41] After kicking around in several jobs, in 1936 Levitt and his father decided to build a house on a Long Island lot they had been unable to sell. They made a profit. From this small beginning, Levitt launched his amazing career.

The Levitts quietly began buying up land from Long Island farmers and mass producing inexpensive but well-designed homes. The basic method was to lay a concrete slab for a foundation on top of which were placed preassembled walls and a roof. The Levitts broke down the complex process of building a house into twenty-six operations, each of which was assigned to a separate contractor. Since each contractor did the same job over and over again, it was possible to achieve incredible speed.[42] Levitt avoided unions and used piecework incentives to speed up the process even more.[43] At the Levitt lumberyard, one man was able to cut parts for ten houses in one day.[44] By 1950, the firm was producing one house every sixteen minutes.[45] By preassembling as many components as possible, Levitt reduced the amount of skilled labor necessary on the job site, and by purchasing directly from the manufacturers, Levitt eliminated middlemen's fees. Overall, Levitt was able to cut costs on each house by about 17 percent so that a typical house could be built for about $6,000 rather than the $7,000 it otherwise would have cost.[46]

Using these methods, between 1947 and 1951 the Levitts converted 4,000 acres of potato farms in Hempstead, Long Island, into "the biggest private housing project in American history."[47] Ultimately housing 82,000 residents, Levittown, as it came to be known, was a huge success. With the huge pent-up demand for inexpensive housing from World War II, in the first years people lined up and camped out for days waiting to purchase one of the homes. The basic Cape Cod model sold for $7,990. With federal guarantees for the loan and no down payment required for veterans, an ex-GI could buy a Levitt house for only $56 a month.[48]

Like Nichols, Levitt believed in controlling the market in order to guarantee rising real estate values. Restrictive covenants required the grass to be cut each week (if not done, one of Levitt's men would cut it and send a bill), disallowed fences (but allowed hedges), and forbid clothes to be hung out on an ordinary clothesline. Also, Levitt refused to sell to blacks, arguing that economic realities required him to recognize that "most whites prefer not to live in mixed communities."[49] In 1960, not a single black lived among Levittown's 82,000 residents.[50]

Architectural and social critics said that the Levitt projects were little more than mass-produced uniformity and boredom, and some writers even imagined the emergence of a suburban personality that conformed to the housing styles. "Levittown" entered the critics' language as an epithet for all mass-produced subdivisions in the suburbs.

In the mid-1950s, Levitt decided to build two more Levittowns, one in Pennsylvania and one in New Jersey. Opened in October 1958 and finished in 1965, Levittown, New Jersey, exhibited several new features. Fearing that the unfavorable image of sterile uniformity would damage sales, the company provided several different house styles and floor plans. The idea of mixing styles was offered by William Levitt's wife and was implemented by him over the objections of his executives.[51] Levitt did not offer a change from a standardized model to provide more esthetically pleasing suburban residential areas. Levitt was motivated by a crucial economic reality: In order to sell houses, he needed to ensure that they would continue to be appealing to the aspiring middle class.

Levitt attracted purchasers by other means as well. Long-term financing with low monthly payments was made possible through the firm. He also offered his clientele a preselected community. His firm attempted to exclude people who did not conform to certain middle-class attributes. Prospective customers would be screened, for example, for clothing and appearance. All homes were expressly designed for families with young children. Advertisements stressed that it was a planned community with schools, churches, swimming pools, and parks. In all of these respects, the Levitt company carefully selected the residents of its communities.

Levitt's fortunes began to change in 1968 when he sold his development company to the International Telephone and Telegraph Corporation (ITT) for $60 million in ITT stock. The stock, which he used as collateral for loans, plunged to $15 a share. Because of a clause in his sales contract, Levitt was forbidden to renew his building activities for ten years, except in cities where ITT had no interest. Levitt invested $20 million in a project in Iran, but the new government took it over after the 1979 revolution. In 1987, at the age of 80, Levitt was forced to declare bankruptcy and was evicted from his New York City offices.[52]

The careers of Nichols and Levitt demonstrate the power of private developers in shaping the suburbs. Entrepreneurs did not try to satisfy consumer tastes so much as they helped to mold those tastes. The needs and motives of developers largely determined the type of communities that resulted.

Because developers were constrained to specialize, and thus limit, their housing alternatives, segregation on the basis of incomes and life-styles was a natural result of subdivision development. These observations hold for contemporary suburbs as well. Whether a developer builds luxury single-family homes, row houses for young middle-class home buyers, or condominiums for singles, the character of the community that results will have already been determined before the first person moves in. Suburbanites can choose their environment before they move, but once they have decided where they are going to live, they "are very largely *prisoners* of that environment with but little opportunity of changing it."[53]

For some time after World War II, the suburban home, complete with a patio, barbecue grill, and a tree in the yard, occupied center stage in the American Dream. An ad typical of the 1950s reads:

> Babylon—An early American Waterside Village—Recreated! For the person who has reached that position in life where they desire complete comfort and relaxation. . . .[54]

Most advertisements in the 1950s promised exclusion, social class segregation, and residential status. A "success" theme, designed to appeal to the striving middle class, appears repeatedly in the advertisements, as in this appeal for upward climbers to settle in Birchwood Park, a Long Island suburb:

> When you settle at East Hempstead you are "on the right side of the tracks" in more ways than one. It's the hub of Long Island's most desirable residential section.[55]

Another advertisement labeled one of its home models, "The Cadillac— Split Level Plus. . . . A most worthy addition to the 'Bluebloods of Distinctive Homes.'" For "living on a higher plane," said the builder, "you must get a 'Cadillac'!!"[56] Still another builder pleaded to "Let us show you how to make your most elite dreams come true."[57] Developers touted the features of new developments that would appeal to family-oriented, status-seeking, upward-striving young executives. For example, one subdivision advertised that:

> The Cedar Hill Ranch Home, frankly, wasn't designed for the man in the street. There are many homes costing less that ably satisfy his needs. The size and appointments of Cedar Hill were fashioned for the family who considers anything less than the best inadequate. . . . Yes, Cedar Hill was definitely designed *for the family accustomed to finer things.*[58]

The intertwining of social status and racial segregation was often suggested by code phrases, such as "get out of the jungle" of the city.[59]

Starting in the late 1960s, some developers began to promote projects designed for clienteles other than young, family-centered couples. Around many cities, and especially in Florida, Arizona, and southern California, developers began to construct condominiums and apartments for the growing market of retired and older adults. Naturally, suitable images were required to sell these projects. The following are typical:

> Jefferson Village: The first totally-electric condominium community for people 52 or over. Now that the children have moved out, is your house too large for you? Then consider the comfort of living in a full country apartment, provided for by a full staff of electric servants.[60]

Or,

> Retirement: *Where* you live it determines *how* you live it. The "second life-time" of retirement can be a delight or a delusion. It often depends on where you decide to live it.[61]

By the late 1970s, young singles had joined the elderly as a group targeted for special attention by suburban builders. Over the past two decades, the proportion of the population that is young and unmarried has increased dramatically (just as it has for those over 65). Anyone who has seen television ads for beer would be able to anticipate how builders would attempt to tap into this new market:

> Your move—make it to Woodhollow—pick of the young professionals . . . great word association: Woodhollow and Young Professionals. Lawyers . . . nurses . . . teachers . . . engineers . . . anyone with success in mind.[62]

And,

> . . . for smart young pace setters who like being together . . . for professionals who enjoy being adult and young at the same time. It's Cypress Village, where you share much more in common with your neighbors."[63]

The promise often made to young singles, with varied shades of explicitness, was sex and companionship:

> Today's young people are constantly seeking to fill their needs, whether
> working, playing or relaxing with a special kind of excitement. The Village
> gives you the opportunity to fill these needs.[64]

Developers took no chances that young people might miss the point of their
advertisements:

> . . . a play pen for kids. Big Kids. It's our clubhouse. Top of the knoll. Sort of
> an adult playground. The kind of place you go with that certain someone. It's
> roomy and comfortable. A lounge for relaxing . . . cocktails and snapping logs
> in the fireplace. The games we play are rated M.[65]

Through advertising, home styles, and sales and lending practices,
builders, realtors, developers, and financial institutions encouraged racial,
social class, and age segregation in the suburbs. They did not rely on market
forces to sort out various groups into distinct communities. Instead, they took
strong measures to ensure that class and racial segregation would be the norm.

For the first half of the twentieth century, restrictive covenants were commonly attached to mortgage deeds; indeed, they were the norm in exclusive
subdivisions. When a home buyer purchased a house, the deed might come
with a covenant that restricted the subsequent sale of the home. Typically,
blacks were the chief target, although sometimes Jews and "consumptives"
(anyone with tuberculosis) might also be named. By the 1920s, the suburban
subdivisions of most major metropolitan areas were blanketed with restric-
tive-covenant deeds.

The real estate industry accepted as a fundamental law of economics the
principle that the value of property was connected to the homogeneity of
neighborhoods. From 1924 until 1950, Article 34 of the realtors' national code
(circulated to realtors everywhere by the National Association of Real Estate
Boards) read: "A Realtor should never be instrumental in introducing into a
neighborhood a character of property or occupancy, members of any race or
nationality, or any individual whose presence will clearly be detrimental to
property values in the neighborhood."[66] In addition, most local real estate
boards were guided by written codes of ethics prohibiting members from
introducing "detrimental" minorities into white neighborhoods. The textbooks and training materials used in real estate training courses were careful to
point out that realtors were ethically bound to promote homogeneous neighborhoods. The leading textbook used in such courses in the 1940s compared
some ethnic groups to termites eating away at sound structures:

> The tendency of certain racial and cultural groups to stick together, making it
> almost impossible to assimilate them in the normal social organism, is too
> well known to need much comment. But in some cases the result is less detri-
> mental than in others. The Germans, for example, are a clean and thrifty peo-
> ple. . . . Unfortunately this cannot be said of all the other nations which have
> sent their immigrants to our country. Some of them have brought standards
> and customs far below our own levels. . . . Like termites, they undermine the
> structure of any neighborhood into which they creep.[67]

Any realtor found breaking the code by selling to members of the wrong groups was subject to expulsion from the local real estate board. Even brokers who were not affiliated with the national association felt compelled to accept the realtors' guidelines because most of their business depended on referrals.

In 1948, in the case of *Shelly v. Kraemer,* the United States Supreme Court ruled that racially restrictive covenants could not be enforced in the courts.[68] Realtors and developers immediately sought a means of continuing their practice of encouraging segregated neighborhoods. The device that replaced restrictive covenants was the common interest development (CID). The number of CIDs, which include cooperative apartments, condominiums, and single-family housing developments, exploded from about 1,000 in the early 1960s to 130,000 by 1988.[69] By the late 1980s, about 40 million Americans lived in some form of CID.[70] By the next century, CIDs will have become the principal new form of home ownership in many, perhaps most, metropolitan areas.

Common interest developments are called "common interest" because the residents not only own their own home, but also share in the cost and mainte-nance of services and amenities held "in common" with other residents. By thus privatizing streets, services such as garbage collection, and amenities such as parks, swimming pools, and tennis courts, residents are able to enjoy a higher standard of living than people living in public municipalities.

CIDs are often referred to as the "new walled communities" or "gated communities."[71] These walled communities are carefully planned as remark-ably segregated environments. Many of them are developed and marketed to appeal to people on the basis of particular shared interests or life conditions. There are, for example, communities that exist exclusively for retirees, golfers, singles, even nudists. Calling such specialization "positive ghettoism," one developer said, "I think it's fantastic. . . . Think of a community where all the people interested in the performing arts live with other people like themselves, or people who are interested in horticulture live with other horticulture hob-byists. Or fine arts or culinary interests . . . it's the us-against-them idea."[72]

Most CIDs are not so narrowly specialized as those named by the "us-against-them" developer, but the promotional literature promises exclusivity, security, and, very often, extreme segregation:

> . . . the new Southwinds Ocean House offers apartments of 3,000 sq. ft. with all the advantages of a single family home. A resident manager and security gate ensure care-free living. You may laze by the pool/gazebo, exercise in the lap pool, or stroll the miles of sandy beaches at your doorstep.[73]

> Sailfish Point is an idyll celebrating your achievements. Its numbers add up to a lifestyle without compromise. . . . Jack Nicklaus designed our par 72 mem-bership only golf course to stimulate and challenge but not intimidate. . . . Yachtsmen delight in our private sea-walled marina. . . . The St. Lucie Inlet puts boaters minutes from deep-sea fishing and blue-water sailing. . . . Natural seclusion and security are augmented by a guarded gate and 24-hour security patrols.[74]

It is illegal for housing developers to discriminate overtly on the basis of race. Other kinds of exclusions are, however, legal, and they often enforce a homogeneity that goes beyond that which is stated as the developer's goal. Gated communities have achieved a high level of racial segregation. These defended enclaves serve as an efficient means to go well beyond the level of segregation that the housing market itself might achieve. They reflect the priorities and policies of realtors, developers, financial institutions, and, as we discover in the next section, of the federal government as well.

❖ NATIONAL POLICIES TO PROMOTE THE SUBURBS: HOUSING

The builders' practice of designing and marketing segregated suburban communities was powerfully reaffirmed, even required, by the housing policies of the national government. Suburban development after the 1930s was fundamentally shaped by two programs, the Federal Housing Administration (FHA) loans established by the National Housing Act of 1934 and the Veterans Administration (VA) loans made available to returning GIs by the Serviceman's Readjustment Act of 1944. Millions of Americans were able to purchase their first suburban home because of the liberal financing features of the FHA and VA programs.

The Roosevelt Administration implemented policies that would have a profound impact on the spatial development of metropolitan America. Through the National Housing Act, the Administration attempted to revive the moribund construction industry. Second only to agriculture as an employer, the housing industry had experienced a devastating retrenchment. Before the stock market crash of October 1929, 900,000 new housing units were being built a year. In 1934, only one-tenth of this number, 90,000 units, were constructed. Throughout the 1930s, housing starts lagged far behind the demand for new housing.[75] In Chicago, only 131 new housing units were constructed in all of 1933, compared with 18,837 in 1929 and 41,416 in 1926.[76] Across the nation, 63 percent of the workers in the housing industry were unemployed. The housing problem was exacerbated by foreclosures on mortgages. Millions of families lost their homes through foreclosures, and millions more were faced with hardship in meeting their mortgage payments. They looked to the federal government for assistance.

The National Housing Act of 1934 created the Federal Housing Administration (FHA) and the Federal Savings and Loan Insurance Corporation (FSLIC). The FSLIC insured individual accounts up to $5,000 (it has since risen through a series of steps to $100,000). It was hoped that such insurance would instill confidence in potential savers and investors, so that people would put their savings into banks instead of under their mattresses. This would enable savings and loan institutions to invest more capital in the floundering housing market.

By far the most important part of the 1934 Housing Act is Section 203, the basic home mortgage insurance program under which the bulk of FHA insurance has been written up to the present day. Fully 79 percent of all FHA-insured units from 1934 to 1975, about 9.5 million units representing a face value of more than $109 billion, were insured under Section 203.[77] The purpose of the program was to finance the acquisition of proposed, under construction, or existing one- to four-family units. The Housing Act provided for FHA insurance of 80 percent of the value of the property. (Through the Housing and Urban Development Act of 1974, this amount subsequently was increased to 97 percent of the first $25,000 and 80 percent of the remaining value.) The low risk involved for the lending institution permits the mortgagee to pay a low down payment, with the remaining principal and interest spread out over a twenty-five or thirty-year period.

Various groups viewed the 1934 Housing Act with totally different goals in mind. Title I of the Act provided FHA insurance for loans used for "permanent repairs that add to the basic livability and usefulness of the property."[78] Social welfare liberals saw Title I as a means of eliminating substandard living conditions in the central cities by providing low-interest, low-risk loans. City officials hoped Title I would be a catalyst to entice affluent people to stay within the city limits and remodel their homes rather than move to new homes in the suburbs. Downtown business interests wanted Title I to bolster the value of the central business districts. Most banks, savings and loan institutions, realtors, and contractors focused Section 203 of the Act as a way to finance new construction beyond the city. In lobbying for the Housing Act, they had agreed to Title I only as a compromise to facilitate quick congressional action.

A conflict was developing between those who wanted to revitalize the inner city and those who wanted to promote construction on the urban fringe, between social welfare liberals on the one hand and banks, savings and loan institutions, realtors, and contractors on the other.

New construction under FHA came to mean housing outside the cities. Very little money was ever appropriated under Title I. Section 203, in contrast, assisted millions of people to move to the suburbs following World War II. The VA loans had much the same impact as the FHA. Together with the FHA, the no-down-payment policy of the VA helped increase the federally insured share of the mortgage market from 15 percent in 1945 to 41 percent by 1954.[79]

Table 8-3 shows how much the FHA eased the task of buying a home. In the 1920s, down payments of 30 to 50 percent were standard. Savings and loan institutions allowed a maximum of eleven years for loans to be repaid. Banks were not so generous; six years was the norm, often with a balloon payment due at the end. In the 1960s, conventional mortgage loans typically required only 25 percent down and were amortized over a twenty-year period. Under the FHA, a home buyer could get a thirty-year mortgage with only 5 percent down and could obtain a much larger loan. The VA allowed financing with no down payment at all.

TABLE 8-3 RELATIVE BURDEN OF LOAN TERMS, 1920S AND 1960S[a]

DECADE AND LENDER	TERMS	PERCENT OF ANNUAL INCOME	
		DOWN PAYMENT	ANNUAL PAYMENT
1920s			
Savings and loan association	60 percent of house value loaned for 11 years at 7 percent; fully amortized	100	20
Bank or insurance company	50 percent of house value loaned for 5 years at 6 percent; unamortized	125	7.5 plus 125 in 5th year
1960s			
Conventional lender	75 percent of house value loaned for 20 years at 7 percent; fully amortized	62.5	18
FHA	95 percent of house value loaned for 30 years at 7.5 percent; fully amortized	12.5	20

[a]For a house equal to approximately two and one-half times the purchaser's annual salary.
Source: Henry J. Aaron, *Shelter and Subsidies: Who Benefits from Federal Housing Policies,* Studies in Social Economics (Washington, D.C.: Brookings Institution, 1972), p. 77. Copyright © 1972 by the Brookings Institution. Reprinted by permission.

TABLE 8-4   USE OF FHA- AND VA-INSURED LOANS IN THE UNITED STATES, 1950–1988

YEAR	PERCENT OF PRIVATE HOUSING FINANCED THROUGH FHA OR VA	TOTAL NUMBER OF HOUSING STARTS (IN THOUSANDS)
1950	34.7	1,952
1952	28.0	1,504
1955	40.7	1,646
1960	26.4	1,274
1965	16.3	1,510
1970	30.5	1,469
1973	12.0	2,045
1975	14.9	1,160
1980	20.7	1,292
1983	13.3	1,703
1984	9.1	1,750
1988	12.3	1,376

Source: U.S. Department of Commerce, Bureau of the Census, *Statistical Abstract of the United States: 1992* (Washington, D.C.: Government Printing Office, 1992), p. 710; and *Historical Statistics of the United States to 1970,* Part 2 (Washington, D.C.: Government Printing Office, 1975), pp. 369, 641.

The FHA loan guarantee program had a huge impact on the home credit market. Between 1935 and 1974, more than three-fourths of the total FHA insured home mortgages went for new housing.[80] The proportion of all homes that were owner occupied increased from 43.6 percent in 1940 to 62.9 percent in 1970.[81] Table 8-4 shows how much the FHA and VA programs influenced the housing market. About one-third of all homes purchased in the 1950s were financed through FHA or VA. The proportion of government-financed loans gradually declined until the late 1960s, increased for a brief period, and declined again in the 1970s. By 1972, however, FHA had helped almost 11 million families become home owners.[82] In 1984, the FHA-VA share of home loans fell below 10 percent for the first time since World War II, though it later rebounded above that figure.

Almost all of the new homes bought with FHA-VA loans were built in the suburbs. Throughout the 1940s and 1950s, the FHA exhibited an overwhelming bias in favor of the suburbs; in its first twelve years it did not insure a single dwelling on Manhattan Island. In part, the FHA's suburban bias reflected a preference for less dense, single-family neighborhoods, as found in the suburbs, over more dense, multiunit neighborhoods as found in the cities. But the FHA suburban preference went far beyond a simple matter of geography; FHA administrators actively promoted the idea that housing, and therefore neighborhoods, should be segregated.

FHA mortgage insurance programs depended on private-sector lending institutions for implementation. Even if the FHA had been willing to insure mortgages in the central cities, it would have found doing so difficult. From the beginning, the FHA absorbed the values, policies, and goals of the real estate and banking industries.[83] Indeed, the staff of the FHA was drawn from the ranks of those industries, and it was only logical that the FHA's philosophy would parallel theirs. Thus "FHA's interests went no farther than the safety of the mortgage it secured."[84] FHA insurance was designed to encourage lending institutions to make home loans. Mortgage finance was typically made available only in "economically sound" areas, where depreciation of housing values seemed unlikely.

FHA administrators shared the real estate industry's view that racial segregation was preferable to integration. In fact, when it issued its underwriting manual to banks in 1938, one of its guidelines for loan officers read:

> Areas surrounding a location are [to be] investigated to determine whether incompatible racial and social groups are present, for the purpose of making a prediction regarding the probability of the location being invaded by such groups. If a neighborhood is to retain stability, it is necessary that properties shall continue to be occupied by the same social and racial classes. A change in social or racial occupancy generally contributes to instability and a decline in values.[85]

The FHA's belief that the entry of a nonwhite family into a white neighborhood inevitably led to declining property values was based on reports by real estate analysts. A revealing glimpse into how sensitive FHA administrators were to the issue of race can be gained by reading the language of a 1933 report submitted to the agency by one of its consultants, Homer Hoyt, who was a well-known sociologist and demographer at the time. Hoyt's opinion was that:

> If the entrance of a colored family into a white neighborhood causes a general exodus of the white people it is reflected in property values. Except in the case of Negroes and Mexicans, however, these racial and national barriers disappear when the individuals of the foreign nationality groups rise in the economic scale or conform to the American standards of living. . . . While the ranking may be scientifically wrong from the standpoint of inherent racial characteristics, it registers an opinion or prejudice that is reflected in land values; it is the ranking of races and nationalities with respect to their beneficial effect upon land values. Those having the most favorable effect come first in the list and those exerting the most detrimental effect appear last:

1. English, Germans, Scotch, Irish, Scandinavians

2. North Italians

3. Bohemians or Czechoslavakians

4. Poles

  5. Lithuanians

  6. Greeks

  7. Russian Jews of lower class

  8. South Italians

  9. Negroes

  10. Mexicans[86]

Many FHA administrators advised developers of residential projects to draw up restrictive covenants against nonwhites in order to obtain FHA-insured financing.[87] "This federal policy did more to entrench housing bias in American neighborhoods than any court could undo by a ruling. It established federally sponsored mores for discrimination in suburban communities in which eighty percent of all new housing [was] being built and fixed the social and racial patterns in thousands of new neighborhoods."[88] Between 1946 and 1959, less than 2 percent of all the housing financed with the assistance of federal mortgage insurance was purchased by blacks.[89] In the Miami area, only one black family received FHA backing for a home loan between 1934 and 1949, and there is "evidence that he [the man who secured the loan] was not recognized as a black" at the time the transaction took place.[90]

When the United States Supreme Court ruled in 1948 that racial covenants could not be enforced in courts of law, the FHA was forced to change its policies. To bring its policies into compliance with the court's decision, in 1950 the FHA revised its underwriting manual so it no longer openly recommended racial segregation or restrictive covenants. The FHA, however, did nothing to reverse the effects of its previous policies. Federal administrators continued to favor racial segregation, and as a result they took no actions to discourage realtors or lending institutions from discriminating against blacks. Until at least the mid-1960s mortgages continued to be insured mainly in areas where minorities were excluded.

Federal agencies also worked with the housing industry to promote common interest developments. Beginning in the early 1960s, builders and federal administrators cooperated in promoting residential condominiums and planned unit developments, which cluster housing within open space and privatized services and amenities. When in 1961 the FHA agreed to insure loans for condominiums in multiunit buildings, the housing industry went through a virtual revolution. Builders were now encouraged to move beyond the single-family suburban subdivisions and into suburban multiunit housing. The revolution also entailed the building of large developments carefully separated, often by walls and gates, from nearby developments that might be marketed to a different clientele.

Despite the fact that restrictive covenants could not be used to promote racial segregation, suburban development continued to segregate African Americans from whites. Realtors commonly refused to work with black home buyers, or they steered them to particular neighborhoods. In the 1960s, civil rights activists finally succeeded in calling attention to the problem, and in 1968 Congress passed legislation barring racial discrimination in housing. Provisions of the Civil Rights Act of 1968[91] proscribed discrimination by lenders through "either denying the loan or fixing the amount, interest rate, duration, or other terms of the loan." The statute also mandated that each of the federal regulatory agencies involved with the real estate industry take affirmative steps to enforce both the spirit and the letter of the law.[92]

Federal bureaucracies, however, were slow to change. Criticism escalated.[93] In response, the Federal Home Loan Bank Board (FHLB), which was responsible for regulating the nation's savings and loan institutions, issued new federal regulations on discrimination in lending. This was significant in that in 1973 the nation's savings and loan associations held more than $186.8 billion in outstanding home mortgages, nearly three times the amount held by the second largest source of home mortgage money, the commercial banks.[94] The new FHLB regulation recognized that "refusal to lend in a particular area solely because of the age of the homes or the income level in the neighborhood may be discriminatory in effect since minority group persons are more likely to purchase used housing and to live in low income neighborhoods."[95]

The practice of redlining derives its name from the red line drawn on maps to designate neighborhoods considered poor investment risks. By categorically refusing to make loans for properties within certain areas, regardless of an individual's credit worthiness, financial institutions can devote more time (and money) to loan applications from areas that seem to promise a lower risk to their capital. Part of the rationale for redlining derives from the fact that the neighborhood in which a property lies—its location on the social, economic, and cultural map of in an urban area—largely accounts for the value of the property. From the point of view of a central city home owner, on the other hand, redlining often has disastrous effects on future home values.

Redlining was practiced blatantly in the past, and although it is now illegal, it persists informally. Such behavior would be of little consequence were it limited to a few financial institutions or to specific periods of tight capital. But the individual decisions of lenders in different institutions and over time add up to a mutually reinforcing network of investment practices that end in the self-fulfilling prophecy of urban decay through disinvestment. The severe deterioration of housing stock in St. Louis in the 1960s and 1970s, for example, was related to redlining. Three savings and loan institutions with more than $1 billion in assets made less than $100,000 in loans on city residential property during 1975. Altogether, "only 5.6 percent of the mortgage money lent by St. Louis banks and savings and loan institutions in recent years had gone to finance property in the city."[96] Similarly, in the District of Columbia fewer than 12 percent of the real estate loans made by savings and loan institutions between 1972 and 1974 went for properties in the city. If condominiums and large home loans (over $100,000) are excluded, the figure drops to 7 percent. Most of the lending capital of financial institutions located in the city was used to finance housing in outlying areas.[97]

Racial bias in lending has resulted in serious underinvestment in the housing stock of black neighborhoods. In the nation's capital, for example, eleven areas (88 percent black, on the average) containing 69 percent of the district's population accounted for only 36 percent of the home loans made between 1972 and 1974. Half of those loans went to neighborhoods with rapidly increasing white populations. According to a study by several Washington-based public interest groups, economic class had little effect on the degree of racial bias. In four moderate- to middle-income areas dominated by owner-occupied and one- to four-unit housing structures, only 7.7 percent of the city's mortgage money was made available. Those areas contained 28 percent of the city's population and were 92 percent black.[98]

Such information as this has been collected under the provisions of the Equal Credit Opportunity Act of 1974[99] and the Home Mortgage Disclosure Act of 1975.[100] The Community Reinvestment Act of 1977 (CRA)[101] states that financial institutions "have a continuing and affirmative obligation to help meet the credit needs of the local communities in which they are chartered. . . ." Federal regulatory agencies are obligated to assess the CRA records of lenders, but rarely do they initiate any action based upon these evaluations. CRA does permit, however, third parties to file challenges to lender applications based on poor CRA performance. Using extensive data on redlining, community groups across the country have filed challenges that could result in costly delays in applications by lenders before federal regulators. Rather than engage in extensive litigation and suffer these delays, lenders have generally been willing to enter into negotiations with community groups. According to one estimate, approximately $18 billion in urban reinvestment commitments have been negotiated in more than seventy cities across the country.[102]

The success of community groups with CRA is encouraging, but it is extraordinarily difficult to remedy deepseated patterns of housing segregation that were created by the actions of public and private institutions operating for decades under the premise that segregation was desirable. Lenders continue to discriminate in the 1990s. A 1992 study by the Federal Reserve Bank of Boston found that minorities were roughly 60 percent more likely to be turned down for a mortgage, even after controlling for 38 factors affecting creditworthiness, such as credit history and total debt.[103] The policies designed to revise those continuing patterns of discrimination and segregation are weak, especially compared to the effects of decades of policies that enforced these patterns in the first place.

❖ NATIONAL POLICIES TO PROMOTE THE SUBURBS: TRANSPORTATION

Americans depend upon the automobile for urban travel more than people in any other country. Though other advanced industrial nations, such as Germany, Britain, and Japan, embraced the automobile, they also maintained modern systems of mass transit as workable alternatives. In West Germany, for example, between 1950 and 1974, at the same time that automobile travel increased fifteen times, public transit use more than doubled.[104] In the United States, by contrast, between 1950 and 1977, as the volume of automobile traffic on urban roads more than tripled from 182 to 666 million vehicle miles, urban mass transit ridership declined by over half. As shown in Table 8-5, public transit accounts for only 3 or 4 percent of commuting trips in most metropolitan areas of the United States.[105] The United States now has a one-dimensional urban transportation system.

The extreme form of suburbanization in the United States would not have been possible without the triumph of the automobile over mass transit. "Automobility" enabled Americans to implement Henry Ford's solution to urban problems: "We shall solve the problems of the city by leaving the city."[106] This strategy was not fully implemented, however, until after World War II, when a combination of highway subsidies by governments at all levels and the dismantling of trolley lines made reliance on the automobile inevitable.

In the early period of the automobile, cars were built much faster than highways. Between 1910 and 1920, the number of cars increased 1,600 percent, but the number of miles of paved roads increased by only 82 percent.[107] Mass production methods reduced the cost of cars, but highways were expensive, and there was conflict over who would pay for them. The method of paying for them finally agreed to was to place a tax on gasoline, so that the users of highways would pay for them. By 1929, all 48 states had enacted gasoline taxes, and such taxes are still the main source of highway funds in the United States. Over time, the National Highway Users Conference, which is made up of 2,800 lobbying groups, has pressured successfully for the creation of trust funds earmarked for highways.[108] By 1974, forty-six of fifty states had earmarked highway trust funds, thus guaranteeing a steady source of revenue for highway construction, free from the uncertainties of the political process.[109] In addition, local taxes have paid for the feeder roads and local streets that make car travel so convenient.

Highway subsidies were pushed through by a powerful coalition led by the nation's largest auto, oil, and tire companies. The beginning of this coalition dates to June 28, 1932, when Alfred P. Sloan, Jr., president of General Motors, called together representatives from several companies to form the National Highway Users Conference. The purpose of the conference, which was chaired by Sloan until 1948, was to unite the petroleum-related industries against the railroads and the urban transit companies.

While the conference lobbied for highway legislation, General Motors, Standard Oil of California, and Firestone Tire Company set out to buy up electric streetcar lines and replace them with buses. GM took the lead in this effort in 1932 when it formed the United Cities Motor Transit Company as a subsidiary. United Cities bought up electric streetcar companies, tore up the tracks, replaced the trolleys with buses, and then sold the bus companies to firms that agreed to use only GM products. The first cities successfully con-

TABLE 8-5 PERCENTAGE OF WORKERS USING PUBLIC
TRANSPORTATION IN SELECTED METROPOLITAN AREAS,[a] 1980

METROPOLITAN AREA	PERCENT OF WORKERS USING PUBLIC TRANSPORTATION
New York	28
Chicago	16
Washington, D.C.	15
Boston	13
Philadelphia	12
San Francisco	11
Pittsburgh	11
Minneapolis–St. Paul	9
St. Louis	6
Denver	6
Los Angeles	5
Salt Lake City	5
Dallas	4
Phoenix	2

[a]CMSAs (consolidated metropolitan statistical areas) or SMSAs (standard metropolitan statistical areas).
Source: Adapted from U.S. Bureau of the Census, *State and Metropolitan Area Data Book, 1986* (Washington, D.C.: Government Printing Office, 1986).

verted to buses were Kalamazoo and Saginaw, Michigan, and Springfield, Ohio. Many others followed: "In each case, General Motors successfully motorized the city, turned the management over to other interests and liquidated its investment."[110]

GM established two semi-independent holding companies that could be used to pool funds contributed by petroleum-based corporations. The GM-created Omnibus Corporation and the National City Lines systematically dismantled streetcar companies in the nation's largest cities, including New York, Philadelphia, Baltimore, Salt Lake City, and Los Angeles. By 1949, through National City Lines, buses had replaced streetcars in forty-five cities. The capitalization required for all this was large, with GM, Standard Oil of California, Firestone Tire, and some suppliers raising $9 million to purchase streetcars. In most cases, the new bus system operated under contractual agreements stipulating that only gasoline or diesel fuel could be used in any of their vehicles. This ensured that the systems could not revert to electric trolleys in the future.[111]

In 1949, GM was convicted in federal court, along with Standard Oil and Firestone, of conspiring to eliminate electric transportation and monopolize the sale of buses and parts. The judge administered a slap on the wrist, levying a fine of $5,000 on the company and convicting and fining one of its executives the sum of $1. Even before this symbolic gesture, the damage to mass transit was already done. By 1955, Roger M. Keyes, GM's executive in charge of bus sales, pronounced the effort a success: "The motor coach has supplanted the interurban systems and has for all practical purposes eliminated the trolley."[112] Only 5,000 streetcars were still in service, compared to 40,000 in 1936, when National City Lines began its assault on the electric railways. Tragically, many cities, such as Los Angeles, are now spending huge sums of money to bring back fixed rail transit.

The first commitment to federal highway building in urban areas came through the Highway Act of 1944. The Act allocated 25 percent of all federal highway grants-in-aid for the construction of urban roads. Before this time, no such provision had existed. Federal highway programs had been designed by the Department of Agriculture to make it easier for farmers to get their products to railway terminals. In fact, under the provisions of the original 1916 Highway Act, the states were prohibited from spending any federal highway aid money in urban areas. At the time, this reflected not only the realities of rural-dominated legislatures, but also the fact that urban streets were better developed than the dirt roads in rural areas.

During the Great Depression, road construction, which consumed huge quantities of unskilled labor, could be used to provide relief for the urban unemployed and to supply necessary public improvements. Congress temporarily lifted the ban on the use of highway funds in urban areas to provide public works in the cities. Once put to work on urban roads and freed from the oversight of the Department of Agriculture, the Bureau of Public Roads (BPR) was quick to make the cause of urban highways its own.

In 1944, the BPR recommended constructing a national system of superhighways that would link all the major metropolitan areas in the country and address the growing problem of traffic congestion in urban areas. No additional funding was provided at the time so that the system languished until the 1956 National Defense Highway Act. During this period, urban planners debated highway engineers on how the new system should be built. Urban planners wanted to design highways in the context of a larger planning effort to shape regional development and revitalize declining central cities. Highway engineers believed that the new interstate system should be designed with one basic goal in mind: moving people and goods in the most efficient manner possible. This basically meant that highways should be built wherever there was the most traffic; the goal should be to relieve congestion.

The 1956 National Defense Highway Act represented the triumph of the engineers. Federal funding of a new 42,000-mile interstate system was justified partly on military grounds—to aid the movement of troops and supplies and to help evacuate American cities in case of a nuclear attack. The main rationale, however, was that freeways would stimulate the economy by creating a modern and efficient transportation system for the country. The Clay Committee, appointed by President Eisenhower, recommended the Act on the grounds that it was necessary to relieve traffic congestion in urban areas. The Clay Report asserted that suburbs were superior to cities and recommended the new freeway system should aid the decentralization of American urban areas.[113]

The 1956 legislation placed federal gasoline taxes and new excise taxes on tires and heavy vehicles into a Federal Highway Trust Fund. Congress changed the grant-in-aid formula from a federal contribution of 50 percent to a 90 percent federal, 10 percent state share for construction of the interstate system. The federal government agreed to distribute the funds for the 41,000-mile system on the basis of need. Since costs in built-up urban areas were greater, urban areas would get the most funds. The interstate highway program, the largest construction project in American history, was to have a dramatic effect on cities.

The 1956 Act was written so that the funds would be administered by state highway departments for projects approved by the federal government. As one historian put it, "Since federal and state road engineers controlled the program, they had few incentives to include urban renewal, social regeneration, and broader transportation objectives in the programming."[114] It is interesting to note the difference between how federal funds were spent on housing and highways. Public housing was built by local public authorities and local governments were given the power to veto any projects planned for their jurisdiction.[115] By contrast, interstate highways were built by state highway departments that were given the power of eminent domain to force private owners to sell their property. Local governments could not refuse to participate in the program. Moreover, most city governments favored the program; they thought the new highways would help revitalize central cities. They could hardly have been more wrong.

Laying wide swaths of concrete had different effects in crowded cities than in the open countryside. As the famous highway builder Robert Moses said in a speech before the National Highway Users Conference in 1964, "You can draw any kind of picture you like on a clean slate . . . but when you operate in an overbuilt metropolis, you have to hack your way with a meat axe."[116] The meat axe approach turned out to be terribly destructive. To build his highways Robert Moses displaced 250,000 people in the New York City area alone.[117] Since the highway engineers wanted to cause the least disruption to private commercial land values, highways were routed through neighborhoods, especially those with the cheapest housing occupied by poor people and minorities.[118] The program was justified not only as highway building but as slum clearance. According to one estimate, the uncompensated loss to city residents who were displaced averaged 20 to 30 percent of one year's income.[119]

Interstate highways had a destructive impact on cities. They not only took land off the tax roles, but the highways damaged surrounding property and cut cities off from their waterfronts. By separating the South Bronx from the rest of the city, the Cross-Bronx Expressway in New York helped turn the South Bronx into one of the worst ghettos in the country. Scholars estimate that the unsightliness of the Fitzgerald Expressway in Boston reduced surrounding property values by about $300 million.[120] The residents of cities began to protest; "freeway revolts" arose to stop freeway construction in cities around the country.[121] One of the first successes came in 1959, when San Franciscans successfully prevented the completion of the Embarcadero Freeway. If they had not succeeded, a freeway would today run along the shores of the San Francisco Bay, thus cutting the bay off from the tourist development that has helped make San Francisco's economy healthy. Protests forced highway planners to become more sensitive to aesthetic and social considerations, but not until after irreversible harm had been done to hundreds of urban neighborhoods.

The interstate system benefited many interests, most of all the corporate interests involved in automobile-related industries. In addition, suburban land values climbed, and some central business districts benefited for a while from increased accessibility by commuters. Over the long run, however, the freeways made it easier for commuters to move farther out into the suburbs. At the same time that city officials were using urban renewal to make the city attractive to businesses and the middle class, the interstate program was making it easier for them to leave.

The final price tag for construction of the interstate system was $123 billion.[122] While highway building received huge subsidies year in and year out, urban mass transit was starved. Unlike Europe, where gas taxes were used for mass transit, federal gas taxes in the United States were not allowed to be used for that purpose until 1975. Funding for urban mass transit has gradually increased, but remains small. Senator Gaylord Nelson of Wisconsin estimated that 75 percent of government expenditures for transportation in the United States in the postwar period went for highways; only 1 percent went for urban mass transit.[123]

❖ SUBURBAN WALLS

To a considerable extent, racial and social segregation was fated by the actions of private entrepreneurs who saw it in their interest to package segregation as an essential component of the suburban ideal. The effect of entrepreneurial decisions is everywhere apparent: housing styles, design, and function preselect the clientele with appropriate income, life-style, and values. This explains the persistence of old suburbs. One study of suburbs that existed continually from 1920 to 1960 found that most of them had changed little in socioeconomic composition over the forty-year period.[124] Their original physical features continued to select new residents.

The suburbs were promoted as ways to achieve instant social status, to escape the problems of the cities, and to live in a segregated social environment. Thus the suburbs became sharply differentiated from the cities, both symbolically and in reality. The symbol of exclusion became actualized by entrepreneurs' selection of clientele.

> The plain fact is that now as before, the main force in our process of urban development is the private developer. The primacy of the bulldozer in transforming rural land to urban uses, the capacity of the private company to build thousands of homes on quiet rolling hills is a predominant fact of American urban life.[125]

Obviously, segregation came about not only because entrepreneurs encouraged it. Many and perhaps most suburbanites actively wished to segregate themselves, and they considered the move from the cities to the suburbs as an improvement in their lives.

Suburban growth was also pushed by the federal government's housing and highway programs. The credit policies of the FHA, the transportation policies of the Bureau of Public Roads, and the economic interests of real estate developers all worked in harmony to open up the urban fringe for development. The tracts of cheap, open land that appealed to the developers could not have been rapidly exploited without the development of the urban highway system, which connected the central business districts to the urban fringe. The credit policies of the FHA meant that the new home buyers would be forced to go to these suburban developments in order to satisfy their desire for quality housing. Any incentives to renovate housing in the central cities were correspondingly undercut.

It is clear that the extreme degree of suburbanization in the United States, as compared with other developed nations, occurred not simply as an expression of a desire by city residents to escape the core cities. There can be no doubt that market forces were at work, but the image of suburbia and the options available to buyers were controlled by public and private institutions alike.

In the next chapter we will discuss the political consequences of the extreme metropolitan fragmentation that suburbanization in the United States has created. The suburbs have become hostile and indifferent to the cities and toward the people who live in them. The walls between suburbs and cities affect the lives of urban residents in fundamental ways, creating advantages for some and limiting the opportunities and life chances of others.

CHAPTER 9

THE POLITICS OF METROPOLITAN FRAGMENTATION

❖ SUBURBS AGAINST CITIES

In all the industrialized nations jobs and population have decentralized. Nevertheless, the United States is unique not only because of its extraordinary urban sprawl, but also because such a large proportion of its urban dwellers live within separate governmental jurisdictions that are independent of the central cities. Throughout the twentieth century, local governments proliferated as suburbanites formed new towns and cities beyond the boundaries of the older core cities. In 1987, there were 83,237 local governments in the United States.[1] In many metropolitan areas there are more local governments than there are nation states in the world. "The degree of local government fragmentation in the United States as a whole is unique among the urban-industrial societies,"[2] and such fragmentation is central to the character of American urban politics. It mirrors the fragmentation of American society. Though suburbanization has sometimes been depicted as a homogenizing process that assimilates diverse groups into the great American melting pot, suburbanization has actually been a stratifying process, separating people by such characteristics as class, status, ethnicity, and race.

Even before the suburbanization of the twentieth century, better-off native-born Americans separated themselves from recently arrived immigrants. Residence became a primary indicator of social status. The habit of creating social status by residence bred fears that status would be compromised if "undesirable" racial and ethnic groups invaded the "better" neighborhoods. Spatial separation accentuated class and racial differences. The squabbles among neighborhoods of the nineteenth century translated into conflicts among suburbs and between central cities and suburbs in the twentieth century. Political separation in the form of independent suburban municipalities became a way for the privileged to protect their wealth and status by walling themselves off in their own enclaves. When race became a dominant feature of the political and social life of cities in the twentieth century, the suburbs became even more defensive of their separate status.

❖ THE MOTIVE TO SEPARATE FROM THE CITIES

For native-born Americans political separation promised an escape from the alleged corruption, anarchy, and immorality of the industrial cities. Those who fought for the separation of suburban towns from late nineteenth-century Boston, for example, based their cause on "the ideal of small town life: the simple informal community, the town meeting, the maintenance of the traditions of rural New England. They held out to their constituents the idea of the suburban town as a refuge from the pressures of the new industrial metropolis." Suburban life could be free from "Boston's waves of incoming poor immigrants."[3]

At the edges of all the big cities the incorporation of municipalities proceeded rapidly from the 1890s to the Great Depression. In 1890, Cook County, whose principal city is Chicago, had 55 governments; by 1920 it had 109. Similarly, the number of general-purpose governments in the New York City area grew from 127 in 1900 to 204 in 1920. There were 91 incorporated municipalities in the Pittsburgh area in 1890 and 107 by 1920.[4] During the 1920s, new suburbs were created by the score.

In the first three decades of the century, popular literature exuded an intellectual and sentimental reaction against the city. Cities had few defenders and a host of critics. Academic writers promoted the idea that "our great cities, as those who have studied them have learned, are full of junk, much of it human."[5] A Boston University professor called city life "a self-chosen enslavement" and indicated that "the psychological causes of urban drift are socially most sinister."[6] Cities were thought to nurture every conceivable sort of evil, as evidenced by such titles of sociological research as *The Social Evil in Chicago; Five Hundred Criminal Careers; The City Where Crime is Play; Family Disorganization; Sex Freedom and Social Control;* and *The Ghetto.*[7]

A "back to nature" movement, built on a romanticized version of rural and semirural environments, swept the country. Boy Scouts, Campfire Girls,

Woodcraft Indians, and other organizations sought to expose children to the healthy influence of nature study. Children's literature was filled with stories of adventure in "natural" settings. Adults, too, were thought to be purified and rejuvenated by visits to the countryside. Bird watching and nature photography became major pastimes. Tourism to national parks boomed, especially after automobiles became more widely available to the middle classes.

Inevitably, the yearning for nature became linked to suburban images. Wealthy urban residents had no intention of giving up the amenities and advantages of urban life. Instead, they attempted a fusion of both worlds—the urban and the rural—in the suburbs. Magazines and newspapers of the day were filled with articles on the advantages of suburban life as an amalgam of city conveniences and rural charm. In 1902, one magazine writer claimed that suburban living could "offer the best of chances for individualism and social cooperation."[8] The next year *Cosmopolitan* carried an article hailing the "new era" of suburban living.

> The woeful inadequacy of facilities of communication and transportation which formerly rendered every suburbanite a martyr to his faith have, in great measure, been remedied; and moreover, residents in the environs have now reached the happy point where they consider as necessities the innumerable modern conveniences of the city house which were little short of luxuries in the suburban residence of yesterday.[9]

Advertisements for suburban property just after the turn of the century stressed the presence of springs, orchards, and forests; activities such as bathing, fishing, and shooting; the healthfulness of the environment; and houses that had such modern conveniences as hot water, gas lighting, and telephones.[10] "A Country Home with All City Comforts," promised one advertisement, alongside another that talked of crops of oats and hay, orchards, trees and shrubbery, fruit trees, and other accompaniments of the rural environment.[11] Most of the advertisements carried drawings or photographs of wide expanses of lawn, trees, and meticulously tended gardens.

The shaping of a suburban ideal was closely linked to efforts to form separate suburban governments. Political separation from the industrial cities, however, was not always easy. Local governments are not mentioned in the U.S. Constitution; legally, they are creatures of the states. In the early part of the nineteenth century, the incorporation of a local government was viewed as a privilege bestowed by state legislatures. In their fights to persuade state legislators to allow them to incorporate their own governments, people who had moved beyond the limits of the industrial cities claimed that smaller cities were closer to the people and were therefore the best possible expressions of democracy.[12]

Gradually, over the nineteenth century, state legislatures made it so much easier for suburbanites to incorporate new towns and cities that incorporation shifted from a privilege to a right.[13] Through general incorporation laws, any group of suburbanites who had migrated beyond the boundaries of the city government could, if a majority of them approved, form a separate local government. "By the early twentieth century suburbanites had begun carving up the metropolis, and the states had handed them the knife."[14] By 1930, every state legislature in the country had adopted liberalized incorporation laws which put the decision of whether suburbanites would or would not be annexed by the central city firmly into the hands of those who had already fled the city.

In the early years, even though they had the right to separate, many people who moved beyond city boundaries nevertheless sought annexation with the city. Some chose annexation in order to receive public services that otherwise were hard to get. Others were coerced into joining by the city. Los Angeles, for example, used its monopoly over water supply to force consolidation on neighboring communities, including Hollywood, Venice, Lordsburg, Sawtelle, Watts, Eagle Rock, Hyde Park, Tujunga, and Barnes City. After the Metropolitan Water District was formed in 1927, however, Los Angeles lost its monopoly over water and could no longer force its thirsty neighbors to join the city.[15] Subsequently, Los Angeles, the archetype of the fragmented metropolis, led the way in the proliferation of suburban governments through the Lakewood Plan, which enabled suburbs to avoid the need to consolidate by contracting to have services provided cheaply by county government.[16] In other urban areas, special service districts enabled suburbanites to receive services without being annexed.

Suburbanites sought to form separate governments not only to gain control over their own services, but also to enforce ethnic or racial segregation. At the turn of the century, residents of Oak Park outside of Chicago feared the expansion of the Slavic population into neighboring Austin. Their motive for incorporating, according to one author, was that "Slavic persons with little aversion for alcohol were rapidly settling the Austin area, and the native American Protestant population of Oak Park feared the immoral influences that might accompany these foreigners."[17] Between 1899 and 1902, Austin joined the City of Chicago and Oak Park formed a separate suburban government.

On occasion, greed or economic self-interest supplied a sufficient motive to incorporate a new suburb. E. J. "Lucky" Baldwin was a notorious gambler and entrepreneur in California in the early twentieth century. He got his nickname by making a fortune gambling on mining stocks,[18] and he was the defendant in a number of seduction and paternity suits that culminated in spectacular trials. Baldwin wanted to build a racetrack, but he knew that he would be opposed by Southern California's foes of sin, led by the Anti-Saloon League. Accordingly, Baldwin decided to form his own suburban government, called Arcadia, free from outside interference. He imported his own employees as residents and gave them free watermelons on election day. Not surprisingly, they approved incorporation unanimously and elected a city council composed of Baldwin and his employees. Baldwin realized his dream when Santa Anita raceway opened on December 7, 1907.[19]

Suburban governments sometimes provided industrialists with havens from taxes and regulation. Efforts to incorporate almost always succeeded when they were led by industry.[20] In 1907, meat packing companies incorporated National City on East St. Louis's northern border to avoid being taxed by East St. Louis. A few years later Monsanto Chemical Company created the city of Sauget on East St. Louis's southern border for the same purpose. In the 1950s, a group of industrialists tried to form a separate suburban jurisdiction in Los Angeles County in order to avoid having to pay for the services of a growing suburban population. When they found that the area did not include the requisite 500 residents for incorporation, they redrew the boundaries to include 169 patients of a mental sanatorium, which put them over the top. Appropriately named "Industry," the newly incorporated suburb deprived the surrounding municipalities of badly needed tax revenue. In 1977, for example, Industry's tax base was $309,970 per capita, compared to only $1,512 per capita in the adjoining city of La Puente.[21]

American political evolution put the choice of whether suburbanites would join the central city or form their own governments entirely in the hands of the suburbanites themselves—"leaving the parent who had spawned the child helpless in determining their joint future."[22] Abandoned by a growing proportion of their wealthiest residents and economic enterprises, the industrial cities became more and more impoverished.

❖ THE ECONOMIC EFFECTS OF SUBURBAN AUTONOMY

Racial and economic segregation between central cities and suburbs became well established in the 1950s. For the six standard metropolitan statistical areas (SMSAs) in the Northeast and Midwest shown in Table 9-1, the median central city family income was 95 percent of the income of suburbanites in 1950. Ten years later, city residents earned only 88 percent as much as people living in the suburbs. By 1980 the gap had widened still further, so that city residents earned only 75 percent as much as people living in the suburbs.

The six SMSAs in the South and West listed in Table 9-1 show a similar pattern, except that the city-suburban disparities developed about a decade later than in the Northeast and Midwest. There are two principal reasons for this lag. First, many of the Sunbelt cities annexed new housing subdivisions in the 1950s and 1960s and thus were able to capture some of the wealth that otherwise would have been located beyond the central city limits. Second, much of the growth in these areas did not occur until after 1960. The lag notwithstanding, it is apparent that the racial and economic differences between central cities and suburbs commonly associated with northern and midwestern metropolitan areas have also developed in the urban areas of the South and West. As late as the 1970 census, central city residents of Sunbelt cities made 92 percent as much as their suburban counterparts, but their incomes compared to suburban wage earners fell to 85 percent by 1980.

A study of city-suburban disparities in fifty-five metropolitan areas, measured by income, unemployment levels, number of dependent persons, and educational attainment, found that central cities lost considerable ground relative to the suburbs in the 1970s, and the gap continued to widen in the 1980s.

TABLE 9-1   INCOME OF CENTRAL CITY RESIDENTS COMPARED WITH
REST OF METROPOLITAN AREA RESIDENTS IN 12 SELECTED AREAS

SMSAS	CENTRAL CITY FAMILY INCOME AS PERCENTAGE OF INCOME OUTSIDE CENTRAL CITY			
	1950	1960	1970	1980
Northeast and Midwest				
New York City	95	93	89	87
Chicago	97	92	86	77
Philadelphia	96	90	85	77
Detroit	99	89	83	69
Washington, D.C.	89	79	74	69
Boston	92	86	80	70
Average of six SMSAs in Northeast and Midwest	95	88	83	75
South and West				
Los Angeles–Long Beach[a]	98	98	96	92
San Francisco–Oakland[a]	100	95	89	85
Dallas–Fort Worth[a]	103	101	97	90
Houston	102	98	96	90
Atlanta	91	87	79	64
Anaheim–Santa Ana–Garden Grove[a]	—	—	96	89
Average of six SMSAs in South and West	99	96	92	85

[a]Ratio is for first-named central city only.
Source: Adapted from James Heilbrun, *Urban Economics and Public Policy*, 3rd ed. (New York: St. Martin's Press, 1981), p. 248, citing U.S. Bureau of the Census, *Census of Population*, 1950, 1960, 1970, 1980. Reprinted by permission.

The study also found a dynamic effect: The greater the disparity between a city and its suburbs, the more rapidly the city declined, because jobs and population were attracted out to the suburbs.[23] The main reason for the increasing disparity between central cities and suburbs is that the suburbs have tended to draw wealthy people out of the cities. In every phase of suburbanization the people who have moved out to the suburbs have had higher incomes, on average, than those who stayed in the cities (see Figure 9-1). The long-term effect of this movement is that local governments with the greatest needs have the least resources, and vice versa. In 1981 per capita taxes were 37 percent higher in central cities than in suburbs.[24] Cities need to levy higher tax rates to make up for their lower tax bases.

Figure 9-1   Impact of Migration on Average Family Income in Central
Cities, 1970–1974

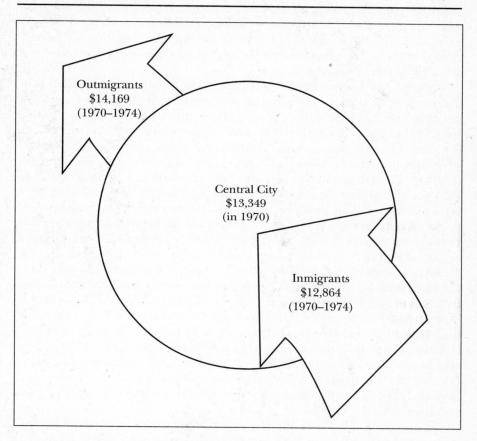

Outmigrants
$14,169
(1970–1974)

Central City
$13,349
(in 1970)

Inmigrants
$12,864
(1970–1974)

Source: Based on Vincent P. Barabba, "The National Setting: Regional Shifts,
Metropolitan Decline, and Urban Decay," in *Post-Industrial America:
Metropolitan Decline and Inter-Regional Job Shifts*, eds. George Sternlieb and
James W. Hughes (New Brunswick, N.J.: Center for Urban Policy Research,
Rutgers—The State University of New Jersey, 1975), p. 60; as cited in William
Gorham and Nathan Glazer, eds., *The Urban Predicament* (Washington,
D.C.: The Urban Institute, 1976), p. 20.

The fiscal problems of central cities are exacerbated by the fact that the
suburbanites who commute to jobs in them use more city services than they
pay for. They use city streets, police enforcement, parks, utilities, water, and
sewer services, but these services cost more than suburbanites contribute in
user fees, sales taxes, and earnings taxes.[25] A study of the Detroit area concluded that, in 1970, suburbanites enjoyed a net subsidy from Detroit of
between $7 and $50 per year for a family of four.[26] A 1986 case study of the
Pittsburgh region concluded that nonresident commuters cost the city of

Pittsburgh 74 percent more than they contributed in tax revenues.[27] The fiscal problems of central cities are also made worse by the disproportionate amount of property in cities that is tax exempt, a consequence of the fact that such cultural and governmental institutions as churches, hospitals, parks, symphony halls, state office complexes, and historic landmarks are disproportionately located in them. The proportion of tax-exempt property in the central cities is about twice that in suburbs.[28]

Central city home owners benefit less from the dynamics of the private housing market than do the people in the suburbs. Studies have shown, for example, that home values appreciate faster in the suburbs than in central cities.[29] Since owning a house is the most important way that American families accumulate savings, it means that the central city residents, who already are disadvantaged, have more roadblocks placed in their way because of where they live. Central city households also bear external costs between $750 and $900 per year greater than costs in an average suburban location because of a higher incidence of air pollution, crime, and inferior public services. Many of the private services left in the cities are substandard. Retail merchants are able to take advantage of the fact that poorer inner-city residents lack the mobility to comparison shop. A study based on a U.S. Department of Agriculture sample of prices found that the inner-city poor pay, on average, 4 percent more for food than do suburbanites.[30] Further, inner-city residents are isolated from expanding job opportunities in the suburbs because a disproportionate share of entry-level service jobs have migrated to the suburbs.[31] More than half of the black and Hispanic households in Boston and Philadelphia in 1980 lacked access to an automobile or a truck. The proportion was about 70 percent in New York.[32] In the absence of adequate public transportation, many central city residents are isolated from expanding job opportunities. Ultimately, governments in central cities must bear some of the costs of the unemployment that results.

In analyzing the effects of governmental fragmentation, it would be misleading to focus solely on the inequalities between core cities and suburbs. There is a great deal of variation among suburbs as well. The conventional image of suburbia as a homogeneous collection of upper-middle-class white residential enclaves is no longer accurate. American suburbs are heterogeneous, though that heterogeneity is generally greater among suburbs than it is within any one suburban jurisdiction. There are working-class, middle-class, and upper-class suburbs.[33] The rich and the poor tend to be segregated in high- and low-income suburbs. Separate suburban governments are advantageous for the rich, but they can become a liability for small jurisdictions that lack a sufficient tax base to finance adequate services. For example, Kinloch, a predominantly black suburb of St. Louis, incorporated in 1948 to gain control of its local schools and to escape harassment from white county police. Since then, the community has been plagued by inadequate streets, sewers, schools, and law enforcement.[34] The disparities in resources are particularly damaging to school children whose parents live in poor suburbs with independent

TABLE 9-2   FINANCIAL DISPARITY AMONG SELECTED ST. LOUIS COUNTY SCHOOL DISTRICTS, 1984–1985

	1985 TAX RATE[a]	ASSESSED VALUATION PER PUPIL	EXPENDITURES PER PUPIL
Clayton	2.40	$193,076	$7,005
Ferguson	3.76	62,634	4,321
University City	3.02	46,253	3,640
Jennings	3.66	40,594	2,726
Wellston	4.13	19,306	2,635
County average (all districts)	2.77	74,076	4,110

[a]Dollars per $100 of assessed valuation.
Source: St. Louis County, Department of Planning, *1986 St. Louis County Data Book* (1986), pp. 66–67, 110–115.

school districts. As shown in Table 9-2, the gap in spending per pupil in wealthy suburbs and poor suburbs is huge.

Suburbanization has allowed many people to escape to tax havens that supply superior services. But it has not worked for everyone. Indeed, the overall effect is to enrich some and impoverish others: "The political incorporation and municipal segregation of classes and status groups in the metropolis tend to divorce fiscal resources from public needs and serve to create and perpetuate inequality among urban residents in the United States."[35] For this reason, one might accurately consider metropolitan fragmentation a redistribution scheme from the poor to the rich.

❖ ZONING FOR EXCLUSION

Over the past half century, zoning has become the central strategy for preserving the racial and social composition of suburban communities. The history of zoning shows that it was born as an exclusionary instrument, and it became popular because it was a subtle, though effective, method of segregating on the basis of income. Through zoning, communities have been able to regulate the uses of land within their jurisdictions, making it difficult or impossible for "undesirables" to cross community boundaries. The list of "undesirables" is often quite lengthy, though it differs from one suburban jurisdiction to the next.

The nation's first zoning law was enacted in New York City on July 25, 1916. By the end of the 1920s, 768 municipalities with 60 percent of the nation's urban population had enacted zoning ordinances.[36] Quick adoption was made possible by the unanimity of real estate interests in advancing the concept that zoning was a useful tool for protecting valuable land against encroaching slums. Promoters of New York's ordinance explained it in this fashion to audiences around the nation: "The small homeowner and the little shopkeeper were now protected against destructive uses next door. Land in the lower Fifth Avenue section, which had been a drag on the market when zoning arrived, was now undergoing so successful a residential improvement that rents were on the rise. 'Blighted districts are no longer produced in New York City.'"[37] The main theme used to promote zoning was that it kept land values high by segregating "better" from "inferior" land uses. In state after state, real estate groups and politicians lobbied for state laws enabling cities to zone their property.

New York City's zoning ordinance was prompted by fears that fashionable sections of Fifth Avenue would be invaded by loft buildings from the Garment District on the West Side. Indeed, there was abundant evidence that such an invasion would occur. From 1850 to 1900, New York's population increased from 661,000 to 3,437,000. Such growth rewarded speculators and entrepreneurs who had been discerning enough to predict the path of the city's expansion. But it was bothersome, too, for upper-class residents who had repeatedly established themselves at the city's periphery, only to be pushed out again by encroaching waves of immigrants and businesses.

By the turn of the century the upper class had established a mansion district and an exclusive shopping area on upper Fifth Avenue. They felt threatened by the teeming masses only a few blocks away. The Garment District, characterized by tall loft buildings in which thousands of poorly paid immigrant seamstresses and carters worked, threatened to destroy the exclusive shopping district. A way—a legal way—had to be found to restrict the uses of land and to protect Fifth Avenue. Fifth Avenue was described (by the rich) as the cultural fulcrum of New York, "a unique place" in "the traditions of this city and in the imagination of its citizens," "probably the most important thoroughfare in this city, perhaps any city in the New World," an area with a "history and associations rich in memories," "the common pride, of all citizens, rich and poor alike, their chief promenading avenue, and their principal shopping thoroughfare."[38] The Fifth Avenue Association, which employed lawyers to invent this kind of rhetoric, pleaded in 1916 that Fifth Avenue was a special area that should be protected from encroachment. Fifty-four years later, the rationale behind zoning had changed little: "We moved out here . . . to escape the city. I don't want the city following me here," explained a Long Island resident.[39]

Between 1913 and 1916, the Fifth Avenue Association, composed of wealthy retail merchants and landowners, lobbied to exclude tall loft buildings from their district. At first they sought restrictions only on building height. In 1916, the Buildings Heights Commission, first appointed in 1913 to investigate the problems of tall buildings in New York City, proposed carving Manhattan into distinct zoned areas to ensure a "place for everything and everything in its place."[40] According to the commission, "the purpose of zoning was to stabilize and protect lawful investment and not to injure assessed valuations or existing uses."[41]

New York's law specified five zones based on different uses and values of land. In the zoning pecking order residential uses assumed first place, even though commercial and industrial land was often more valuable. Next in the hierarchy were commercial business districts, differentiated on the basis of building height (the higher the buildings, the lower the place in the zoning hierarchy). Warehouses and industries were allotted last place.

New York City officials were keen to publicize their law, in part to ensure that it would be widely adopted before courts could challenge its constitutionality. The law contained a tailor-made appeal to real estate interests across the nation. "By the spring of 1918 New York had become a Mecca for pilgrimages of citizens and officials" who wanted to enact a similar ordinance. Within a year after passage of the legislation, more than twenty cities had initiated "one of the most remarkable legislative campaigns in American history."[42] Zoning was literally mass produced; most cities copied the New York ordinance and adopted it with few changes. Zoning soon became the chief weapon used by urban real estate interests to protect land prices. By 1924, the federal government had given zoning its sanction. A committee of the Department of Commerce drafted the Standard State Zoning Enabling Act, which served as a model zoning law for all the nation's cities.

In 1926, the United States Supreme Court reviewed a case from Ohio, *Village of Euclid v. Ambler Realty Co.*, and in a landmark decision declared that zoning was a proper use of the police power of the municipalities.[43] One interesting facet of the case revealed how zoning would be used in the future. Ambler Realty had purchased property in the village of Euclid in hopes that it would become valuable as commercial property. In 1922, the village zoned Ambler's property as residential, thus instantly lowering its value. In bringing suit against the village, Ambler argued that Euclid's zoning law had lowered its property values without due process of law. In its decision the Court set forth a classic statement in defense of restrictive zoning, arguing that the presence of apartment, commercial, or industrial buildings threatened the value of single-family dwellings. There was an assumed hierarchy of uses, which the Court itself enunciated:

> With particular reference to apartment houses, it is pointed out that the development of detached house sections is greatly retarded by the coming of apartment houses . . . the coming of one apartment house is followed by others, interfering by their height and bulk with the free circulation of air and monopolizing the rays of the sun which otherwise would fall upon the smaller homes, and bringing, as their necessary accompaniments, the disturbing noises incident to increased traffic and business, and the occupation, by means of moving and parked automobiles, of larger portions of the streets, thus detracting from their safety and depriving children of the quiet and open

spaces and play, enjoyed by those in more favored localities—until, finally the residential character of the neighborhood and its desirability as a place of detached residences is utterly destroyed.[44]

In its decision the court ruled that separating residential from other land uses was a legitimate use of the city's police power to promote the order, safety, and well-being of its citizens.

If suburbanization was one of the important movements of the 1920s, so was zoning. Because zoning was the best available technique for controlling land use, it was favored by entrepreneurs as a way to protect their investments. With the automobile and the street railway providing the technology for suburban expansion, unregulated urban sprawl seemed more threatening than it had in the past. Zoning provided an alternative to runaway growth and it provided a method for protecting investments made by developers.

Zoning became popular at the same time that well-to-do suburbs proliferated around the large cities—Beverly Hills, Glendale, and a host of other communities outside Los Angeles; Cleveland Heights, Shaker Heights, Garfield Heights outside Cleveland; and Oak Park, Elmwood Park, and Park Ridge outside Chicago. The utility of zoning for these communities was apparent. From its inception to the present, zoning became the legal means to ensure what informal social class barriers might not have been able to ensure—the exclusion of the inner-city Great Unwashed. The possibility that the poor might disperse throughout metropolitan areas threatened people living in exclusive neighborhoods, both in central cities and in suburbs. At the heart of zoning lay the fear of what urban life might become if left unregulated: a hodgepodge of mixed land uses and the mingling of the poor and racial minorities with the owners of property.

Normally, restrictive residential zoning attempted to exclude apartments, to set minimum lot sizes, or to stop new construction altogether. Apartments in the suburbs represented the possibility of class, life-style, or racial changes. The residential character of a tree-lined, curved-street development with individual homes set well back was threatened by apartment buildings, which symbolized the city environment. "We don't want this kind of trash in our neighborhood" was an attitude applied even to luxury apartments. Apartments were seen as potential slums that might attract lower-class white or minority residents. Thus apartments symbolized the coming to suburbia of city problems, with crime, welfare, crowding, and minorities:

> The apartment in general, and the high-rise apartment in particular, are seen as harbingers of urbanization, and their visibly higher densities appear to undermine the rationale for the development of the suburbs, which includes a reaction against the city and everything for which its stands. This is particularly significant, since the association is strong in suburbia between the visual characteristics of the city and what are perceived to be its social characteristics.[45]

Many suburban communities became deeply concerned when apartment projects were proposed. For example, an executive living in Westport, an exclusive suburb in Connecticut, exclaimed:

> Thank god we still have a system that rewards accomplishment, and that we can live in places where we want to live, without having apartments and the scum of the city pushed on us.[46]

Most suburbs excluded the building of apartments entirely. In the 1970s, over 99 percent of undeveloped land zoned residential in the New York region excluded apartments.[47] Although this did not mean apartments could not be constructed, it did require apartment builders to secure zoning variances, which maximized the chances for opposition.[48]

Suburban governments also attempted, in effect, to regulate the social class and incomes of people who occupied single-family homes. Subdivision regulations and building codes made developers go through a costly review process that artificially raised the cost of new houses and gave local residents an opportunity to oppose new developments. But the most common device for raising the minimum cost of new construction was (and is) large-lot zoning.

Large-lot zoning is a device to keep out people with lower incomes. In some upper-class communities this means keeping out the middle class; in some middle-class communities it means excluding the working class. A defender of four-acre lot minimums in Greenwich, Connecticut, said that large-lot zoning is "just economics. It's like going into Tiffany and demanding a ring for $12.50. Tiffany doesn't have rings for $12.50. Well, Greenwich is like Tiffany." Large-lot zoning was defended by a New Jersey legislator as a means of making sure "that you can't buy a Cadillac at Chevrolet prices." An official of St. Louis County, where 90,000 acres were zoned for three-acre lots in 1965, indicated that his suburban county welcomed anyone "who had the economic capacity [to enjoy] the quality of life that we think our county represents . . . be they black or white."[49]

Minimum building size regulations are another popular tool for raising the price of buying into a suburb. Wealthy suburbs frequently mandate a minimum floor space that exceeds what most middle-income home buyers can afford.

Exclusionary zoning often makes room for industrial and commercial investment that will provide more in taxes than it consumes in services. Of course, communities only want certain kinds of industry—industry that does not produce bothersome pollution and traffic. Sy Schulman, a Westchester County (New York) Planning Commissioner, wryly noted that the ideal industry "is a new campus-type headquarters that smells like Chanel No. 5, sounds like a Stradivarius, has the visual attributes of Sophia Loren, employs only executives with no children and produces items that can be transported away in white station wagons once a month."[50] Since the demand for such clean industry exceeds the supply, there is a fierce competition for it. As with other aspects of suburban development, it is the wealthier suburbs that usually win.

❖ THE NATIONAL CHALLENGE TO EXCLUSIONARY ZONING

The importance of zoning is its ability to manipulate the value of land. Thus it cannot be neutral, for it protects some people's investments and costs other people money and opportunity. One measure of its importance is that it is frequently the subject of litigation in the courts. From 1948 to 1963, for example, 52 percent of all litigation in the local courts of suburban New York City involved zoning and land use issues.[51]

As a tool for creating and perpetuating exclusion and privilege, zoning went largely unchallenged in the state and federal courts for nearly half a century.[52] In the 1970s, for a time, it was challenged in the courts. Zoning survived, but local governments learned that they could not use it as a blatant tool to preserve racial segregation. Black Jack, Missouri, found this out when the federal courts overturned their city's zoning ordinance after years of litigation.[53]

On June 5, 1970, the Federal Housing Administration (FHA) granted approval to a federally subsidized housing project to be built near the unincorporated Black Jack subdivision in St. Louis County, just north of the city of St. Louis. The project, to be sponsored by St. Mark's United Methodist Church of Florissant and the United Methodist Metro Ministry of St. Louis, was to contain 210 two- and three-story town houses for middle-income residents. The application for federal funding stated that the project would fill a need in St. Louis County for integrated, moderately priced housing.

On hearing of the proposed project, the residents of the Black Jack area held neighborhood meetings, circulated petitions against the project, and contacted political figures, going so far as to send a delegation to Washington, D.C., to present petitions to federal officials. They complained that the apartment project would overload their schools, crowd their highways, and threaten the value of their homes. Although cautious about saying so in Washington, the delegates and their constituents were mainly concerned that low-income blacks would move into their community. Before they learned to be wary of reporters, residents freely expressed racist sentiments in their first discussions of the housing project. After attending a Black Jack meeting in 1971, a *St. Louis Post-Dispatch* reporter wrote, "The most common statement we heard during the meeting in Black Jack was, 'We don't want those people, we don't want another Pruitt-Igoe in North St. Louis County.'"[54] Pruitt-Igoe was the nationally infamous public housing project built in St. Louis during the 1950s, noted for its crime, broken windows, and urine-stained hallways. It took little insight to guess to whom "those people" referred.

Black Jack residents perceived that they could best protect their interests by creating their own political jurisdiction. As an unincorporated area of St. Louis County, they were subject to the county's zoning laws, which made sixty-seven acres available for apartment construction within the Black Jack area.

In late June 1970, the Black Jack Improvement Association presented petitions to the St. Louis County Council requesting the incorporation of a new city, to be called Black Jack. The proposed boundaries were to include about 2,900 residents, most of them living in recently constructed middle-income housing tracts. On August 6, 1970, incorporation was approved by the County Council, thus terminating the county's zoning authority and passing it to the new Black Jack City Council.

The county's decision to allow incorporation reveals much about the fears not only of Black Jack residents, but of other suburbanites elsewhere. The Black Jack Improvement Association lobbied throughout the North County area, linking the fate of Black Jack with that of other communities. Allowing the project to be built, said the association, "could open the door to similar projects being located almost anywhere in the North County area. By stopping this project, you would lessen the chance of one perhaps appearing in your neighborhood."[55] In the face of overwhelming pressure, the County Council decided it could best get out of the situation by approving incorporation, thus washing its hands of the whole issue.

The Black Jack incorporation ignited a national controversy over zoning. In September 1970, the Park View Heights Corporation (the nonprofit housing corporation formed by the original sponsors of the housing project) filed suit in federal court against the new city of Black Jack, alleging that both the city's incorporation and its proposed zoning ordinance constituted an attempt to use its zoning power to circumvent the Civil Rights Acts of 1866 and 1964, the National Housing Act of 1937, and the Fair Housing Act of 1968. In a brief hearing, Judge Roy W. Harper dismissed the suit and on October 20, 1970, the Black Jack City Council adopted a zoning ordinance that excluded multiunit residential buildings. Judge Harper's decision was appealed.

In the months following the Black Jack incorporation, it seemed unlikely that its zoning ordinance would be allowed to stand. Lawton, Oklahoma, southwest of Oklahoma City, had attempted to use its zoning ordinance to exclude apartments, but the federal appellate court for its circuit ruled that municipalities could not use zoning to exclude minorities or the poor unless they could show a nondiscriminatory intent concerning land-use objectives.[56] In the case of Black Jack, this would be extremely difficult. In April 1971 another case gave even more hope to proponents of suburban integration. The United States Court of Appeals for the Second Circuit rejected an attempt by the city officials of Lackawanna, New York, to block the building of a black housing subdivision in a white neighborhood.[57] Comments in the editorials of the *St. Louis Post-Dispatch* compared the *Lackawanna* suit favorably with the *Black Jack* suit: "The unanimous action indicates that local governments will have legal difficulties if they try to zone out Negroes from white areas. The Lackawanna decision clarifies the fact that misuse of political powers to keep out minority groups is unconstitutional."[58]

The Eighth Circuit Court of Appeals reversed Judge Harper's decision in September 1974. Surprisingly, the court threw out the argument that the Black Jack zoning ordinance was intentionally discriminatory. The court did, however, rule that the ordinance had a discriminatory effect. The potential impact of this ruling on zoning laws everywhere was enormous. If they could be invalidated when courts found a discriminatory effect (not intent), zoning laws across the country could be declared illegal. In June 1975 the Supreme Court refused to review the circuit court's decision, thereby affirming it.

As it turned out, the *Black Jack* ruling was not much of a victory for the Park View Heights Corporation. By the time the litigation was concluded, the housing program that funded the project had lapsed. Worse, the inflated costs of housing materials made the project infeasible for moderate-income families. Black Jack eventually paid a $450,000 settlement to the corporation, but the town houses were never built.

The *Black Jack* case promised to set an important precedent for challenges to exclusionary zoning laws because it ruled that it was not necessary to prove discriminatory *intent,* only racially discriminatory *effect.* In 1977, however, the Supreme Court backed away from this standard. In reviewing the zoning ordinance of Arlington Heights, Illinois, which barred a federally subsidized town house project from being built, the Court declared that the impact of zoning laws could not be used as the only argument against them; rather, they had to be shown to have racially discriminatory intent: "Disproportionate impact is not irrelevant, but it is not the sole touchstone of an invidious racial discrimination."[59] The Supreme Court had already narrowed the jurisdiction of federal courts in exclusionary zoning cases.[60] Thus, challenging exclusionary zoning became very difficult. To be challenged under federal laws, zoning laws must blatantly be drawn up for the express purpose of excluding blacks or other protected groups.

Though the Constitution protects racial minorities from discrimination, such discrimination is usually difficult to prove. Moreover, the courts have consistently held that discrimination on the basis of income or class is not prohibited by the Constitution. If suburbs can show that their zoning laws are designed to protect the tax base and the exclusive residential character of the community, even though they discriminate against poor people, the laws will not be declared unconstitutional. In 1971, for example, the Supreme Court upheld an amendment to the California Constitution, passed in 1950, which required that low-rent housing could not be built without prior approval by a referendum of the voters of the city. While clearly biased against those seeking low-income housing, the Court ruled that discrimination on the basis of income was not unconstitutional under the Fourteenth Amendment.[61]

❖ NEW JERSEY'S CHALLENGE TO EXCLUSIONARY ZONING

Federal courts have been unwilling to use the U.S. Constitution to break down the walls of suburban exclusion. The states, therefore, are left as the main avenue of action for those who want to challenge local zoning laws. Since a large proportion of state legislators answer to suburban voters, it is unlikely that state laws will be changed to limit what local governments can do. Clearly, any challenges to zoning would have to go through state courts. New Jersey is the best example of both the promise and the pitfalls of such an approach.

In 1970, Mount Laurel, located not far from Camden and Philadelphia, was a mostly rural community. The area contained a small black community that had been there since before the Civil War. Quakers had made Mount

Laurel a sanctuary for runaway slaves on the Underground Railroad, and their descendants still resided in the area. Many of them lived in small shacks and converted chicken coops, and when these were condemned by the city of Mount Laurel, black residents feared that they would be forced to move to the slums of Camden. They formed an action committee and applied for federal funds to build a subsidized housing project. In 1970 the committee was turned down by the local Planning and Zoning Board.

The residents then turned to the courts. They found three idealistic lawyers working for the Camden Region Legal Services who agreed to pursue a case to strike down Mount Laurel's zoning laws, which allowed only single-family homes and specified large lots, large building sizes (a minimum of four bedrooms), and substantial setbacks from the street. In 1972, a trial court found that Mount Laurel's zoning laws excluded housing for poor people and therefore violated language in the New Jersey Constitution that guaranteed equal protection of the law for all persons. On appeal, in 1975, the New Jersey Supreme Court upheld the decision, ruling that exclusionary zoning violated the state constitution even though its main intent was economic.[62] It was not necessary for the litigants to prove racial intent. In an important advance, the Jersey court ruled that, in order to meet the constitutional standard, cities had an obligation to meet not just the housing needs of city residents, but, as the court put it, "the municipality's fair share of the present and prospective regional housing need."[63] The court ruled that not only Mount Laurel but all of New Jersey's 567 municipalities had an obligation to provide land uses that would meet regional housing needs. The United States Supreme Court refused to hear the appeal, thus leaving the matter in the hands of the New Jersey courts.

One month after the *Mount Laurel* decision, Governor Brendan Byrne ordered the Department of Community Affairs to prepare a housing quota plan for all of New Jersey's municipalities and threatened to withhold state grants from towns failing to comply with the quotas. The political pressure on Governor Byrne quickly mounted, however, as the suburbs realized that they could be forced to build housing for the state's approximately 1 million poor people. Critics charged that the state government was engaging in "suburban blockbusting." When the housing quota plan came out, Byrne backtracked; he criticized the recommended quotas on the grounds that they interfered with his plans for the revitalization of all of New Jersey's cities. He gave the Department of Community Affairs one year to revise the plan. Conveniently, this pushed any state action to open up the suburbs past the 1977 gubernatorial election (which Byrne won). The new quotas were prepared after the election, but they were quietly tucked away in the State House, with no further attention from the governor's office.

Progress in striking down exclusionary zoning proceeded at glacial speed. Exclusionary laws had to be struck down on a case-by-case basis. Moreover, the *Mount Laurel* decision had ruled that suburbs must provide the opportunity for low-income housing, but they were not required to provide the resources for it. If low-income housing was not profitable, builders would not construct it. It is hardly surprising that little low-income housing was built, even in the communities whose zoning laws had been declared invalid by the courts.

In 1982, the new Chief Justice of the New Jersey Supreme Court, Robert N. Wilentz, heard six cases showing that the city of Mount Laurel was ignoring the original trial court's decision.[64] He combined the six cases into one proceeding, and in 1983 the Court issued a pathbreaking, unanimous 270-page decision, widely know as *Mount Laurel II.* The Court noted that the town of Mount Laurel had made little progress in complying with the original judicial decision: It had simply rezoned 33 of its 14,176 acres, and none of the 515 low-income housing units required to meet the dictates of the decision had been built.[65] In the words of the court, "After all this time, ten years after the trial court's initial order invalidating its zoning ordinance, Mount Laurel remains afflicted with a blatantly exclusionary ordinance. Papered over with studies, rationalized by hired experts, the ordinance at its core is true to nothing but Mount Laurel's determination to exclude the poor."[66] In response to the decision, the mayor of Mount Laurel, Andrew August, said: "We'd just like to see our town develop in a nice way. We should have the right to run our own town."[67]

The justices in *Mount Laurel II* stated that they would have preferred that the legislature address the problem, but "enforcement of constitutional rights cannot await a supporting political consensus."[68] In order to speed up compliance with the decision, *Mount Laurel II* contained additional remedies. First, it required that municipalities not only rezone land for low-income housing, but also that they make low-income housing attractive to developers through such devices as tax incentives and federal subsidies. Second, to encourage builders to pursue lawsuits against exclusionary zoning, it established "builder's remedies," that is, when a town was found to have engaged in exclusionary zoning, a developer would be allowed to construct housing at a higher level of density than otherwise allowed to achieve a ratio of eighty units of higher-priced housing for every twenty units of low- and moderate-income housing. Developers would be able to build only if they followed this formula. If local governments proscribed such projects, builders could themselves initiate challenges to exclusionary zoning. Third, municipalities were given an incentive to cooperate. Once a town was judged to have voluntarily rezoned to accommodate its "fair share" of low-income housing, it would enjoy a six-year grace period against builders' suits. (The "fair share" was based on a complex formula that assigned a certain number of low- and moderate-income units to each municipality in the state.)

As a result of *Mount Laurel II,* New Jersey's suburban municipalities were besieged with lawsuits and politicians were increasingly pressured to do something about it. Republican Governor Thomas H. Kean, who won office in 1981, came out strongly against what he called an "undesirable intrusion on the home rule principle." In a 1984 interview Kean stated, "I don't believe that every municipality has got to be a carbon copy of another. That's a socialistic country, a Communistic country, a dictatorship."[69] Kean advocated an amendment to the New Jersey Constitution that would give local governments exclusive power over zoning policy, beyond review by state courts. On November 5, 1985, 266,000 voters supported such an amendment in nonbinding municipal referenda.

Meanwhile, on July 2, 1985, Kean signed the Fair Share Housing Act, which was designed to move exclusionary zoning cases (at the time there were more than a hundred pending) out of the courts and into arbitration before a nine-member Council on Affordable Housing (COAH), appointed by the governor.[70] The bill included a twelve-month moratorium on builders' remedies to give towns a chance to submit housing plans to the Council that met the requirements of the *Mount Laurel II* decisions. Those towns whose plans were certified by the Council were given a six-year grace period from builders' suits. The Fair Share Housing Act also called for an appropriation of $25 million for a Fair Housing Trust Fund to subsidize efforts to construct affordable housing units. On February 20, 1986, the New Jersey Supreme Court upheld the Act and transferred pending housing cases to the Council.

In order to gain passage, the Fair Share Housing Act incorporated compromises that weakened its ability to achieve the goals of the *Mount Laurel* decisions. Municipalities were allowed, for example, to allot up to 25 percent of their "fair share" to the elderly, and any city was allowed to transfer up to 50 percent of its fair share obligation to another city in the region (if the receiving city approved), along with the funds to help the receiving town pay for the housing. Older central cities, which already contained most low-income housing, were put in the position of competing against one another for subsidies from suburbs so they could obtain funds to meet pressing housing needs. Clearly, this undermined the intent of the *Mount Laurel* decisions.

The results of the long, drawn-out Mount Laurel process have been meager. The original Byrne report called for the construction of 500,000 low- and moderate-income units in New Jersey by 1990.[71] Later, the court estimated that New Jersey needed 277,808 units to meet the *Mount Laurel* guidelines. The Council on Affordable Housing reduced that estimate to 145,707.[72] By May 1990 only about 8,000 housing units had been built,[73] and most of these were moderate-income units, not low-income. In the town of Mount Laurel, by the late 1980s, only twelve families had moved into low-cost mobile homes and twelve more had put down deposits on similar units, and by May 1988, 20 low-cost subsidized condominiums were nearing completion. This was the sum total of low-income housing after seventeen years of litigation.[74]

The New Jersey case illustrates the difficulty of changing local land-use practices by using the courts when a political consensus is lacking. *Mount Laurel* represents the clash between two deeply held American values: equal protection of the law and local home rule. Americans are reluctant to support policies that force powerful middle-class suburban interests to give up their privileges. However, in an era when the federal government has cut housing subsidies drastically, even if local zoning laws could be successfully challenged, this would not insure that low-income housing would be built in the suburbs. Pursuing suits through state courts may be the only way to open up the suburbs in the present political climate, but, if the New Jersey experience is any guide, progress will be slow.

❖ THE SUBURBANIZATION OF AFRICAN AMERICANS

The suburbanization of African Americans stretches back many decades, but the rate at which it occurred did not start to increase substantially until the 1960s. Between 1970 and 1980, the number of blacks who lived in suburbs grew by almost 50 percent, an increase of 1.8 million persons.[75] During this period, one in ten blacks living in central cities in 1970 moved to the suburbs and the percentage of blacks living in suburbs increased from 16 percent to 21 percent.[76] In the 1980s, the trend continued. Though blacks are still far behind whites in their overall rate of suburbanization, they are catching up, and in many metropolitan areas blacks are moving to the suburbs at a faster rate than whites.

As with whites, blacks who move to the suburbs tend to earn higher incomes than blacks who stay behind in the core cities. They move to escape the problems of the inner city and to find a better environment in which to raise children. To some extent, African Americans are able to improve their condition in the suburbs. For example, the rapidly expanding suburban economy provides more job opportunities; controlling for occupation, blacks who live in suburbs earn more money than blacks who live in central cities.[77] Also, suburban public services and schools are sometimes better, and the degree of residential segregation is less in the suburbs than in central cities.

The suburbanization of African Americans, however, cannot be taken as an indication of progress toward integration. It is a misconception that suburbanization by blacks has been a significant vehicle for upward mobility and that it signals the removal of barriers to residential integration. For the most part, suburbanization of blacks "replicates the racial and class disparities found within cities."[78] It does not represent integration, but rather an extension of racially segregated living patterns into the suburbs closest to the central cities. Research shows that the older the suburb, the greater the black population growth. Blacks are moving into older, inner-ring suburbs such as Oak Park outside Chicago, Shaker Heights outside Cleveland, and Yonkers outside New York City.[79] Suburbs tend to be "black" or "white." Most suburban whites have little contact with blacks: 86 percent of suburban whites live in suburbs with an African-American population of less than 1 percent.[80]

Even those suburbs that are racially mixed tend to be highly segregated internally. One index of segregation scores cities and suburbs on a scale from 0 to 100.[81] A uniform distribution of both races across all spatial units yields a score of 0; obversely, complete segregation between blacks and whites would yield a score of 100. While segregation, overall, is lower in suburbs than in central cities, the suburbs are still highly segregated, especially in metropolitan areas with large black populations.[82] A study of the St. Louis metropolitan area in 1980 found that the city of St. Louis had a segregation index of 90.3 and that the three suburban counties with substantial numbers of blacks (St. Louis, Madison, and St. Clair) had segregation indexes of 79.9, 86.5, and 91.4, respectively.[83] A study comparing many urban areas found only one suburban area, outside El Paso, Texas, which could be classified as having "low" segregation in 1980.[84] Another study found little reduction in the degree of suburban residential segregation between 1970 and 1980. Of 18 suburban areas studied, 15 stayed the same, in one segregation increased (Newark), and two showed some decline in the degree of segregation (San Francisco and Houston).[85]

Not only are African Americans segregated in suburbs, but they live in political jurisdictions that have many of the same fiscal problems as the central cities. A study of Philadelphia's suburbs for the period 1977 to 1982 found that predominantly black suburbs had a per capita tax base that was 30 percent less than the average for white or mixed suburbs; in addition, municipal debt per capita in black suburbs was almost twice that in mixed and white suburbs. Indeed, predominantly black suburbs are often worse off than central cities because they lack the diverse tax base that exists in most core cities. In general, predominantly black suburbs tend to have lower tax bases, higher debts, poorer municipal services, lower socioeconomic status, and higher population densities than suburbs that house white residents.[86] One study of 374 suburbs in the New York metropolitan area found that blacks and Hispanics of the same socioeconomic class as non-Hispanic whites typically live in suburbs that have less tax wealth, lower rates of home ownership, and higher property crime rates. These findings show that race is more important than class in determining the suburbs where people live.[87]

Three explanations are commonly offered for the continued segregation of blacks in the suburbs: differences in class background between whites and blacks, personal preferences, and the legacy of past institutional discrimination. The first says that African Americans are segregated not because they are black, but because they are poor. Research has thoroughly discredited this explanation.[88] If households were distributed on the basis of class and not race, most neighborhoods would contain a mixture of whites and blacks. One study of Chicago predicted where people would live according to socioeconomic background. If there were no racial discrimination, it concluded, 151,000 more African-American households would have lived in the suburbs than actually lived there in 1980 (a 226 percent increase). Moreover, if class determined residential location, suburban blacks would be much more evenly distributed among suburbs instead of being concentrated in a small number of suburbs, as they actually are.[89] A study of St. Louis concluded that socioeconomic differences between blacks and whites account for less than 15 percent of the segregation in the suburbs in 1980.[90]

The second explanation is that blacks are segregated because they prefer to live among other blacks, that just as there are Italian and Polish neighborhoods, there are black neighborhoods. The difference is that while there is some ethnic clustering, ethnics tend to live all over metropolitan areas. This is not true of blacks, and, in any case, surveys have consistently found that blacks prefer to live in integrated neighborhoods. A 1969 *Newsweek* poll found that 74 percent of African Americans preferred to live in a neighborhood that contained both blacks and whites; only 16 percent preferred to live in an all-black neighborhood.[91] Moreover, those who express a desire to live in all-black neighborhoods may be expressing not a desire for segregated living but a fear of white hostility.[92]

In general, white resistance to residential integration appears to be declining. The proportion of whites in national surveys who report that they would not be upset if a black with an income and an education similar to their own moved into their block increased from 35 percent in 1942 to 84 percent in 1972.[93] Looked at more closely, however, it is clear that though most whites will accept one or a few African Americans in their neighborhoods, most will refuse to live in neighborhoods that are truly integrated. If a neighborhood reaches a "tipping point," say above 30 percent black, whites usually abandon it. As long as most whites believe that stable integrated neighborhoods with more than a few black families are impossible, they will, indeed, be impossible.[94] Obviously, these white beliefs constitute a self-fulfilling prophecy.

The best explanation of segregated housing patterns is neither the class background of blacks nor black preferences but white racism. And white attitudes toward racial integration have been powerfully shaped by past, and present, institutional discrimination. We saw in the previous chapter how, for decades, the federal government, through the massive FHA and VA loan guarantee programs, made integrated neighborhoods in the suburbs almost impossible. In addition, for much of the twentieth century, local governments engaged in racial zoning and courts enforced restrictive covenants that forbade whites to sell their homes to blacks. Suburban governments still engage in exclusionary zoning, private lenders discriminate against integrated neighborhoods, and real estate agents steer qualified black clients away from white neighborhoods. These powerful institutional practices reinforce the belief that stable integrated neighborhoods are impossible to maintain, thus reinforcing white racism.

❖ YONKERS: SEGREGATED HOUSING IN THE SUBURBS

Yonkers is a city of about 190,000 located just north of New York City on the Hudson River. In the nineteenth century, Yonkers became a thriving manufacturing center as the home for textile factories and the Otis Elevator Company. Beginning in the 1920s, it developed into a commuter suburb with many Irish, Italian, and, years later, black families moving up from the Bronx. After World War II the industrial jobs began to move out, leaving behind pockets of poverty concentrated in the old, southwestern section of the city. By the 1980s, blacks and Hispanics made up 19 percent of the population and lived almost entirely in the southwestern section.

In a legal action that began during the 1970s, the U.S. Department of Housing and Urban Development and the local chapter of the NAACP sued the City of Yonkers for intentionally segregating the city by race. In 1985, following a fourteen-month trial with eighty-four witnesses and thousands of exhibits, Judge Leonard B. Sand of the Federal District Court in Manhattan ruled that Yonkers had intentionally discriminated in education and housing.[95] Judge Sand's six-hundred-page ruling documented a forty-year history of discrimination, including the fact that 97.7 percent of the subsidized housing units were concentrated in the southwestern section of the city in order to maintain segregated housing. Judge Sand's decision was subsequently upheld by the U.S. Court of Appeals.[96]

Yonkers instituted a busing program to comply with the education part of the ruling, but the city refused to implement the court's housing remedies. Judge Sand's order called for 200 units of housing subsidized by the federal government to be dispersed in a number of small, low-rise developments outside the southwestern section of the city. In January 1988, the City Council voted 5 to 2 to implement this part of the plan. Sixty policemen lined up to protect the politicians as more than 800 residents showed up for the meeting and denounced their representatives as "wimps, liars, snakes, and 'masters of deceit.'" Only one woman spoke in favor of the desegregation order. The crowd jeered her so loudly she could barely be heard. "Send her back to Harlem!" one man shouted.[97] Subsequently, Yonkers residents, including some black residents, expressed their opposition to low-income housing by picketing federal government offices in Washington, D.C., and Judge Sand's home in Manhattan.

Judge Sand's order also called for the construction of 800 units of moderate-income housing for families making $14,750 to $35,400 a year. To build this housing, the city would offer incentives to developers in exchange for a requirement that 20 percent of the units be set aside for moderate-income families. On August 1, 1988, the Council refused by a vote of 4 to 3 to amend the city's zoning law to approve the 800 units. The next day Judge Sand imposed a fine on the City of Yonkers of $100 the first day, with the fine doubling every day until the city approved the zoning change. The judge also fined the members of the Council who voted against the plan $500 a day. The fines were suspended pending appeal of the case to the United States Supreme Court. On September 1, 1988 the Supreme Court suspended the contempt fines against the members of the city council but upheld the fines against the city.[98]

Judge Sand warned Council members that they were in violation of provisions of the Constitution guaranteeing equal protection of the law, but they refused to budge. The pressure on the Council to comply mounted as the fines escalated. By September 10, the fines had reached $1 million a day and 630 city employees faced layoffs. The dissenting councilors defended their position by asserting they were standing up for local democracy against an unelected judiciary. One councilor vented his frustration against the judge: "Clearly the blood is on the judge's hands. Judge Sand is a truly evil person, a heinous human being. The revolution has started and working people have to rise up. I hope there is a God up there that will strike him down."[99] Finally, on September 10, 1988, the Council voted 5 to 2 to comply with the order to change the zoning ordinance to allow the 800 units of housing.

The situation in Yonkers demonstrates the limits of residential integration in the suburbs and, as in *Mount Laurel*, shows the difficulty of "balancing the democratic doctrine of majority rule with the constitutional guarantees of minority rights."[100] One of the ironies of the case is that Yonkers was singled out by the federal courts even though it had more low-income housing than any of the surrounding suburban communities. Even though only 25 percent of the population of Westchester County lives in Yonkers, 43 percent of the County's public housing is located there. The nearby communities of Bronxville and Scarsdale have no publicly assisted housing whatsoever; and, since there are few blacks in these communities, they cannot be accused of segregating them and are therefore free from the threat of suits.

❖ THE COSTS OF SUBURBANIZATION

At the beginning of the twentieth century, reformers thought that suburbanization would help to solve many of the problems of poverty-ridden city slums. Writing in 1898, Adna Weber expressed an optimistic view about the effect of suburbs on city life, asserting that "The 'rise of the suburbs' is by far the most cheering movement of modern times. It means an essential modification of the process of concentration of population that has been taking place during the last hundred years and brought with it many of the most difficult political and social problems of our day."[101] Suburbanization did not live up to such hopes. Many suburbs simply reproduced the problems of the central cities. Moreover, most of the poor and racial minorities never had a chance to move to the suburbs; they were trapped in central cities whose social problems remained as debilitating as ever, perhaps worse. Some argue that suburban mobility actually exacerbated the problem of urban poverty by more intensely isolating the poor into the ghettos that still existed.[102]

Suburbanization has imposed costs even on those who reaped its benefits. The problems they moved to escape came with them, a process referred to as the urbanization of the suburbs.[103] Among the costs exacted by the peculiar American pattern of sprawled development are the following.

■ Expensive Infrastructure

As suburbs zone out new housing to retain their exclusiveness, suburbs sprawl even more in what is called "leapfrog development." The cost of roads, water mains, sewers, telephone lines, and other utilities to service leapfrog development has been estimated to be 55 percent higher than in planned communities.[104] Suburban sprawl increases infrastructure costs not only because it often involves a wasteful use of space and materials, but also because it results in the abandonment of sound infrastructure in central cities. Expensive schools are being built in the suburbs at the same time that schools are being closed in the cities.[105] Hundreds of thousands of potentially sound housing units in central cities are abandoned each year, along with their water lines, sewer lines, and other utilities.

▓ Loss of Agricultural Land and Open Space

Suburbs use up tremendous amounts of land. Whereas planned residential development can leave up to 50 percent of the land as undeveloped open space, the typical suburban sprawl uses up nearly all the open space.[106] In 1958, 3,000 acres of countryside per day were being swallowed up by suburban sprawl.[107] Suburban development today is consuming land at an even faster pace. For example, though the New York region's population grew by only 5 percent between 1964 and 1989, the amount of developed land increased by 61 percent. Suburban sprawl consumed 23 percent of the undeveloped land in the region, including forests and farmland, in just twenty-five years.[108]

▓ Mismatch Between Jobs and Housing

Most entry-level jobs in manufacturing, wholesaling, and retailing have been moving to the suburbs. At the same time, the exclusionary practices of suburbs have made it difficult for poor people and minorities in the central cities to follow the jobs. Not only can they not move to follow the jobs, they often cannot travel to them because they do not have access to an automobile or adequate public transit. The result is high unemployment and income deprivation for inner-city minorities.[109]

▓ Mismatch Between Changing Families and Suburban Housing

Suburban single-family homes were designed for the typical 1950s family: a breadwinning father who commuted to work each day and a full-time housewife who stayed home with the kids and dealt with the long distances that need to be traveled in low-density, spread out communities. Obviously, this "typical" family is now much less common, since more than half of all married women are in the labor force[110] and there are increasing numbers of single-parent families and singles in the suburbs. The basic problem is that household members must shop, drop kids off at day-care and pick them up, take family members to the doctor, and, of course, get together with friends. All of this is difficult in low-density suburbs, especially for working women on whom many of these tasks fall.[111] A comparison of Levittown (Pennsylvania) and Vallingby, a moderately high-density suburb of Stockholm, found that the Swedish suburb met the needs of working women much better. In contrast to Levittown, the Swedish suburb had excellent public transportation and nearby public facilities such as day-care centers, play parks, and youth centers. The Swedish suburban homes required lower maintenance and because the journeys to work were shorter, Swedish men could spend more time at home helping with household tasks.[112] The sprawled-out pattern of urban development in the United States requires excessive driving just to meet daily needs for shopping, education, and recreation.

■ Traffic Congestion

Sprawl is an important cause of highway congestion. In 1970 in the United States there were 61 yards of roadway per vehicle; by 1986, there were 39 yards of roadway per car.[113] The number of cars has gone up because people who live in sprawled-out suburbs need them. As more women enter the work force, two- and three-car families are becoming more common. As jobs move out to the urban periphery, cross-commuting is increasing; in 1980 over 40 percent of all work trips in the United States were suburb to suburb and only 20 percent were suburb to central city.[114] Unfortunately, the road system is not geared to this pattern of traffic, and the result is suburban gridlock: "From 1975 to 1985, the share of rush-hour freeway traffic in urbanized areas that flowed under 35 miles per hour [the speed used by freeway engineers to signify freeway congestion] increased from 41 percent to 56 percent."[115]

A main cause of suburban gridlock is the extreme separation of work from residence. Since the decentralization of housing and jobs is almost completely unplanned in the United States, job-holders often live a long distance from work. Oak Park, Illinois, for example, has 35,100 jobs but only 6,600 residents.[116] Exclusionary zoning practices drive up the cost of housing, forcing many people to tolerate long commutes to find affordable housing.

■ High Energy Consumption and Air Pollution

The United States consumes an extraordinarily high amount of energy per capita, and it produces a disproportionate share of the world's pollution. With only about 5 percent of the world's population, the United States produces an estimated 25 percent of the carbon dioxide emissions in the world,[117] which are a principal cause of the greenhouse effect. The country's high energy consumption is not due solely to a prosperous economy. Many European countries that are just as prosperous consume far less energy per capita.[118]

The reliance on the private automobile resulting from unplanned urban sprawl and the inadequacy of public transportation are major causes of high energy consumption and pollution in the United States. Cars have become more efficient and less polluting over the past two decades, but air quality has continued to deteriorate because people drive more. The number of cities that exceeded the federal standards for ground level ozone increased from 64 in 1985–1987 to 101 in 1986–1988. Americans now drive the equivalent of 3 million round trips to the moon each year, up an incredible 50 percent since 1970.[119] American cities consume about four times as much gasoline per capita as European cities.

Within the United States gasoline consumption varies considerably, and a basic factor determining this variation is the degree of sprawl. For example, consumption is 567 gallons per capita in sprawled-out Houston, but only 335 gallons in New York City, whose higher population density facilitates the use of mass transit. (In Manhattan, energy consumption is only 90 gallons per capita.)[120] A study conducted for the federal government on the costs of sprawl compared a typical low-density pattern of suburban development with a high-density planned community having a combination of apartments, town houses, and clustered single-family homes.[121] The authors concluded that the planned community could save up to 44 percent in energy consumption over the typical suburban community and that the pollution from autos would be reduced 20 percent to 30 percent.[122]

As the problem of pollution becomes more urgent, the American pattern of suburbanization will become increasingly anachronistic. This issue is not hypothetical. Los Angeles has tried to regulate automobile emissions for years and treats air pollution as a crisis requiring drastic remedies. The South Coast Air Quality District in Southern California has called for such measures as eliminating gasoline-powered vehicles by the year 2007.[123] The California problem and its remedies are but harbingers of the issues that soon will confront urban areas elsewhere. A preeminent historian of American suburbanization put it this way: "Thus, the United States is not only the world's first suburban nation, it will also be its last. By 2025 the energy-inefficient and automobile-dependent suburban system of the American republic must give way to patterns of human activity and living structures that are energy efficient."[124]

It is important to emphasize again that the pattern in the United States is unique. Here, more than elsewhere, decentralization has resulted in autonomous governmental units that make their own decisions about land use and housing, decentralization has occurred in the absence of planning, and the degree of sprawl has been peculiarly high. The American style of suburbanization, not decentralization of population itself, imposes social costs and creates a politics of racial and social class segregation that fragments metropolitan areas into competing fiefdoms all trying to move the costs of suburbanization, American style, onto somebody else.

CHAPTER
10

THE RISE OF THE SUNBELT CITIES

❖ THE CONCEPT OF THE SUNBELT

The term Sunbelt was popularized as recently as the mid-1970s, but it quickly became almost indispensable in everyday discourse about national development and politics. Even though the geographic boundaries of the Sunbelt are rather vague in most people's minds, the term conveys a distinctly positive image of a part of the country that is prosperous and growing: "When a person hears the term on radio or on television, or reads it in a magazine or book, or sees it in the telephone book or on a firm's letterhead, it is likely to conjure up an image of growing cities and booming economies in Southern or Southwestern cities with pleasant climates."[1] It would be possible to regard the term as merely a "rhetorical ruse," as one scholar called it,[2] or a "public relations coup," as the president of a corporation helping other companies move to the Sunbelt labeled it,[3] if it were not for the fact that the long-term population growth in the region has resulted in a fundamental realignment of political power in the nation. Six of the last seven presidents came from the South or the West. (The exception is Gerald Ford.) Over the past half century, the reapportionment that follows each decennial census has shifted the balance of power in Congress decisively toward the delegations that represent southern and western states. Without doubt, this realignment of power helps to account for the decline in federal aid for the cities since the late 1970s.

Kevin Phillips, the chief political analyst for the 1968 Republican presidential campaign, is generally credited as the person who coined the term Sunbelt. In his book *The Emerging Republican Majority,* published in 1969, Phillips asserted that the United States was going through an electoral realignment that was transforming the Republican party into the nation's majority party. The basis of this national political realignment, he said, was the movement of millions of Americans out of the old industrial cities of the North to the suburbs and to the South and West. Phillips sometimes lumped the South and the West into an area he called the Sunbelt, though he never actually defined its boundaries; indeed, of forty-seven maps in his book, none portrays such a region.[4]

Phillips's prediction that regionalism would become an ascendant influence in national politics turned out to be correct. In 1973, an embargo on the sale of oil organized by the Arab oil-producing nations drove the world price of oil sharply upward. The economies of oil-producing states such as Texas, Louisiana, Oklahoma, and Colorado boomed, and new jobs were created throughout the southern and western states. At the same time, energy-dependent industries and consumers in the northern states were hit hard. In 1974 and 1975, northern states went through an economic depression that saw hundreds of thousands of layoffs in industrial jobs. In the winter of 1975, the mood turned ugly. In the spring of 1975, when New York City asked the federal government for a bailout loan, President Gerald Ford's initial reply was "Get lost!"[5] Voting on legislation in Congress began to reflect sharp regional divisions. A minor civil war had broken out between a prosperous South and West and a declining North.

In the anxious atmosphere of 1975, Kirkpatrick Sale's book *Power Shift* quickly became a national bestseller.[6] Sale, a liberal, described the rise of the political power of the states in the South and West—a region he called the Southern Rim. Trying to find a way to report on the political issues raised by the new regional antagonisms, the popular press revived Phillips' notion of the Sunbelt, and the term soon came into common use. In February 1976, the *New York Times* published a five-part series documenting the demographic and political trends favoring the Sunbelt. In May *Business Week* devoted its feature article to "The Second War Between the States."[7] The regional war became one of the hot topics that helped to sell newspapers and magazines in 1976 and 1977.

Though the concept of the Sunbelt has entered the everyday language of Americans (the term has been included in dictionaries since the late 1970s), the precise boundaries of the region shimmer in the distance like a mirage, changing with each new writer or scholar who writes about it. For example, in a letter to a scholar researching the politics of the Sunbelt, Kevin Phillips defined it as the "territory stretching from the eastern Carolina lowlands down around (and excluding) Appalachia, picking up only the great Memphis area of Tennessee, omitting the Ozarks and moving west to Oklahoma, thence virtually due west," possibly also including Colorado.[8] It is understandable that Phillips would want to draw his boundaries to exclude pockets of poverty in the border

Figure 10-1   The American Sunbelt and Frostbelt

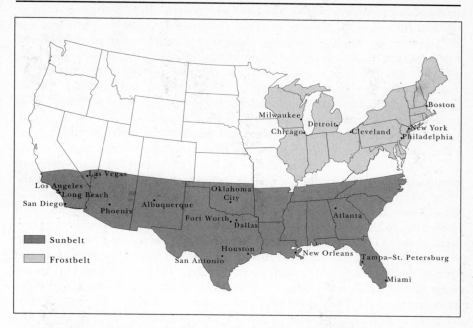

Source: Adapted from Richard M. Bernard and Bradley R. Rice, Eds., *Sunbelt Cities: Politics and Growth Since World War II* (Austin: University of Texas Press, 1985), p. 7.

states, but his description is extremely imprecise. For our purposes in this chapter, we adopt Sale's definition, as shown in Figure 10-1. Sale's Sunbelt encompasses the entire portion of the United States below the thirty-seventh parallel (what he called the Southern Rim), extending across the country from North Carolina to the West Coast, including southern California and a part of southern Nevada.[9] (For statistical purposes, we will include all of California and Nevada.) Thus there are fifteen states in the Sunbelt. The fourteen states of the Northeast and the upper midwest constitute the so-called Frostbelt.

A significant number of scholars are troubled by the concept of the Sunbelt. For one thing, the huge area encompassed by Sale's definition is far from uniformly prosperous. The most rapid economic and population growth has occurred in Florida, parts of Texas, Arizona, southern Nevada, and southern California. Rural areas all across the Sunbelt and many urban areas of the South have remained untouched by the prosperity that is proclaimed as the Sunbelt's principal defining feature, a fact that led two scholars to note that the Sunbelt "has collapsed into only a few 'sunspots.'"[10]

A second problem with the Sunbelt concept is that it assumes that the South and the Southwest are similar enough that they can be lumped together under a single label. Until its image was refurbished by its inclusion in the prosperous Sunbelt, the South was often thought of as a backward, poverty-ridden, violent region with a peculiar caste system. Most political studies of the South focused on issues of race, the enduring effects of the Civil War and Reconstruction, and the dominance of a single, authoritarian party—the elements that made up a conservative political culture that had changed little since the Civil War. The main industries that had located in the South were those associated with low-wage labor. In the 1930s, Franklin Roosevelt and the New Deal administrators looked at federal programs as a way to bring economic development to a backward region.[11]

The image of the West, in contrast, tended to be "urban, opulent, energetic, mobile, and individualistic, a region of economic growth and openness to continual change which matched America's self-image."[12] If the image of perpetual sunshine gave the Sunbelt its name, then certainly this image fit the West better than the South. Since Los Angeles was the home of the movie and television industries, America's popular culture became increasingly identified with western images. Los Angeles itself served as a vision of America's future, with its sprawling suburbs, freeways, and shopping centers and even its smog.

Some scholars have claimed that the idea of the Sunbelt is about dead and that its brief existence was overplayed anyway. They agree with the assessment by *Texas Monthly* editor Nicholas Lemann that "Millions of people were living in the Sunbelt without one of them realizing it. They thought of themselves as Southerners or Texans, or Los Angelenos."[13] They assert that the concept of the Sunbelt is not useful not only because there are so many differences within it, but also because it has become outdated as all regions of the United States have converged. The old industrial states have become less industrial, urban populations have spread out into suburbs in all parts of the country, and a media-based national culture has replaced regional cultural differences: "Just try to find a town anywhere in the United States without a McDonald's or a television happy-news format featuring an anchorperson with an unidentifiable accent."[14]

Despite the obvious problems with the Sunbelt concept, it remains useful in analyzing urban growth and change, in describing the way that economic restructuring has transformed cities, and in explaining why governmental policies have changed so much over the past twenty years.

❖ THE RISE OF THE SUNBELT

For the past half-century population and economic activities in the United States have been dispersing away from older urban areas. There can be no doubt that this dispersal constitutes a historic shift. In the hundred years leading up to the 1930s, the cities of the North had acted as magnets drawing millions of immigrants and migrants to their industrial economies. The North was the most heavily urbanized and prosperous region of the country. With the economic prosperity in the years after World War II, it appeared that northern metropolitan areas—though not necessarily the central cities—would enjoy another sustained period of growth and prosperity. Indeed, through the 1950s and 1960s the manufacturing economies of these regions did well. In 1950, 65 percent of the nation's metropolitan population lived in or near the industrial belt that reached from Boston and New York in the northeast across to the Great Lakes and down to St. Louis.[15] More than two-thirds of the manufacturing jobs and ten of the nation's fourteen urban areas of more than 1 million people were stretched across this industrial zone.[16] By the 1990 census, however, of the country's thirty-seven metropolitan areas of more than 1 million people, twenty were located in the South and West. All through the 1970s and 1980s, northern metropolitan areas struggled to cope with the effects of massive losses in manufacturing jobs.

The decline of the old industrial cities that had been occurring since the 1930s seemed not to affect the metropolitan areas of the industrial belt. Throughout the 1950s and 1960s suburban populations boomed. In the 1970s, however, in an important new development, the rate of suburban growth outside these cities slowed to a crawl (the suburbs of Boston and Pittsburgh actually declined in population). For the first time, metropolitan areas of the Frostbelt, as well as its central cities, experiencd stagnation, though they rebounded somewhat in the 1980s. In contrast, throughout all this period most metropolitan areas in the Sunbelt were still growing rapidly.

A large-scale redistribution of national population to the South and West was occurring. National economic development and population movement favored suburbs, smaller towns, and cities outside the Northeast and Midwest. Between 1970 and 1980 northeastern central cities lost 10.5 percent of their populations and midwestern cities 9 percent. During the same decade, southern central cities grew by almost 9 percent and western cities by 15 percent.[17] Table 10-1 shows the postwar redistribution of the national population.

In nearly all the Sunbelt metropolitan areas shown in Table 10-1, population increases ranged from 20 percent to 50 percent or more in each of the decades since 1950. In the six Frostbelt metropolitan areas shown, population growth was modest in the 1950s and 1960s and population actually declined in several urban areas after 1970.

The redistribution of the national population to the South and West began in the 1940s and gathered speed in the 1950s. Between 1940 and 1990, the population of the fifteen Sunbelt states increased 162.7 percent (to 103,868,000), whereas the population of the fourteen Frostbelt states increased only 48.3 percent (to 92,818,000).[18]

People moved to the Sunbelt mainly for jobs. In the 1930s the South was considered the nation's economic basket case. In subsequent decades conditions have changed dramatically, however, as the older industrial cities have lost business and jobs to the Sunbelt. Table 10-2 shows that in the 1970s the Northeast gained 8.4 percent of the nation's new jobs and the Midwest region gained 13.5 percent. From 1981 to 1989, the Northeast and the Midwest did better, increasing their combined share of employment growth to 34.6 percent. However, from 1981 to 1989 almost two-thirds of the nation's job

TABLE 10-1 POPULATION GROWTH OF SELECTED METROPOLITAN AREAS OF 1,000,000 OR MORE, 1950–1990

METROPOLITAN AREA (RANKED BY GROWTH IN 1970s)	PERCENT INCREASE IN POPULATION			
	1950–1960	1960–1970	1970–1980	1980–1990
Phoenix (MSA)[a]	100.0	45.8	55.3	40.6
Houston (PMSA)	51.6	40.0	45.3	20.7
San Diego (MSA)	85.5	31.4	37.1	34.2
Anaheim (PMSA)	225.6	101.8	35.9	24.7
Denver–Boulder (CMSA)	51.8	32.1	30.7	43.8
Miami (PMSA)	88.9	35.6	28.3	29.0
Atlanta (MSA)	39.9	36.7	27.2	32.5
Dallas–Fort Worth (CMSA)	43.4	39.0	25.1	24.6
Los Angeles–Long Beach (PMSA)	45.5	16.4	6.2	18.5
San Francisco–Oakland (CMSA)	24.0	17.4	4.6	16.5
Chicago (PMSA)	20.1	12.2	1.8	0.2
Detroit (PMSA)	27.7	11.6	−1.9	−1.5
St. Louis (MSA)	19.9	12.3	−2.3	2.8
New York City (PMSA)	11.9	8.2	−4.5	3.3
Boston (NECMA)	7.5	6.1	−4.7	−1.3
Pittsburgh (PMSA)	8.7	−0.2	−5.7	−7.3

[a]Abbreviations refer to different statistical types of metropolitan areas, as defined by the Census Bureau in the 1990 census.
Source: U.S. Bureau of the Census, *1970 Census of Population*, vol. 1, *Characteristics of the Population*, pt. A (Washington, D.C.: Government Printing Office, 1973), p. 171, Table 32; *1980 Census of Population*, Supplementary Reports, *Standard Metropolitan Statistical Areas and Standard Consolidated Statistical Areas*, p. 3, Table 1; U.S. Bureau of the Census, *State and Metropolitan Area Data Book: 1991* (Washington, D.C.: Government Printing Office, 1991), Table A.

growth took place in the South and West. Note that five of the ten fastest growing metropolitan areas listed in Table 10-3 are in Florida and all ten are smaller urban areas of the Sunbelt.

Central cities in the Sunbelt are usually not as isolated within their metropolitan areas as those in the Frostbelt. Many of them have annexed huge amounts of new territory to keep themselves from becoming surrounded by independent suburbs. Oklahoma City, for example, grew from about 51 square miles in 1950 to 636 square miles in 1970. Much of its territory is semi-rural land waiting for new housing tracts. Phoenix expanded from just 17 square miles in 1950 to 277 square miles in 1978. Most Sunbelt cities added substantial territory in the 1950s and 1960s and at least some additional territory in the 1970s and even 1980s.

TABLE 10-2 COMPARISON OF REGIONAL SHARES OF U.S. EMPLOYMENT AND SHARES OF U.S. JOB GROWTH, 1960–1989 (IN PERCENTAGES)

REGION[a]	1960 SHARE OF EMPLOYMENT	1960–1970 SHARE OF JOB GROWTH	1970 SHARE OF EMPLOYMENT	1970–1981 SHARE OF JOB GROWTH	1981 SHARE OF EMPLOYMENT	1981–1989 SHARE OF JOB GROWTH	1989 SHARE OF EMPLOYMENT
Northeast	29.1	18.3	26.4	8.4	21.6	16.2	20.8
Midwest[b]	29.3	25.5	28.3	13.5	25.9	18.4	24.8
South	26.5	35.1	28.7	47.8	32.9	37.4	33.5
West	15.1	21.2	16.6	30.4	19.6	28.4	20.9

[a]Regions defined according to Bureau of the Census definition.
[b]North Central changed to Midwest in 1989.
Source: U.S. Department of Labor, Bureau of Labor Statistics, *Employment and Earnings,* Statistics for March 1960 (vol. 6, no. 9), 1970 (vol. 16, no. 9), 1981 (vol. 28, no. 3), and *Profile of Employment and Unemployment, 1989,* (Washington, D.C.: Government Printing Office, 1990).

TABLE 10-3 THE TEN FASTEST GROWING METROPOLITAN AREAS IN 1970–1980 AND 1980–1990

1970–1980		1980–1990	
METROPOLITAN AREA	PERCENT INCREASE IN POPULATION	METROPOLITAN AREA	PERCENT INCREASE IN POPULATION
1. Fort Myers–Cape Coral, FL[a]	95	1. Naples, FL	77
2. Ocala, FL[a]	77	2. Riverside–San Bernardino, CA	66
3. Las Vegas, NV[a]	69	3. Fort Pierce, FL	66
4. Sarasota, FL	68	4. Fort Myers–Cape Coral, FL	63
5. Fort Collins, CO	66	5. Las Vegas, NV	61
6. West Palm Beach–Boca Raton, FL[a]	64	6. Ocala, FL	59
7. Fort Lauderdale–Hollywood, FL	64	7. Orlando, FL	53
8. Olympia, WA	62	8. West Palm Beach–Boca Raton–Delray Beach, FL	50
9. Bryan–College Station, TX	61	9. Melbourne–Titusville–Palm Bay, FL	46
10. Reno, NV	60	10. Austin, TX	46

[a]Contained in both lists.

Source: U.S. Bureau of the Census, *1980 Census of Population*, Supplementary Reports, *Standard Metropolitan Statistical Areas and Standard Consolidated Statistical Areas* (Washington, D.C.: Government Printing Office, 1981), p. 2, Table C; *Urban News* 5, no. 1 (Spring 1991): 5, as reported by the U.S. Bureau of the Census.

Older industrial cities found it impossible to keep up with new growth mostly because they had already been surrounded by independent suburban municipalities decades earlier. Few of them added significant territory through annexation after 1950. As described in Chapter 9, suburban governments prevented annexation or merger moves. In 1979 there were 1,214 governmental units in the Chicago standard metropolitan statistical area (SMSA), 864 in the Philadelphia SMSA, and 615 in the St. Louis SMSA.[19]

Some older cities in the Sunbelt, like older cities elsewhere, have not been able to expand their boundaries, and these cities contain a disproportionate share of the minority and poverty populations in their regions. Atlanta, for instance, lost 14 percent of its population during the 1970s, but its regional population grew by 46 percent. Denver also lost population (−4.5 percent) while its suburbs gained (+60 percent).

❖ THE CHANGING POLITICAL BALANCE

The rapid rise of Sunbelt cities and the decline of Frostbelt cities has profoundly influenced national urban policy. At the national level, urban policy, in the sense of specific policies to deal with urban problems, was essentially invented by the New Deal of Franklin Delano Roosevelt. Roosevelt was not personally inclined toward cities and in the early years of his presidency supported the back-to-the-land movement.[20] Roosevelt realized, however, that the urban working class was the key to his electoral success and this is one reason he supported programs like public housing and public works employment. The big city vote was decisive in every one of FDR's four presidential election campaigns. The nation's eleven largest cities provided 27.1 percent of his national vote in 1932[21] and a much larger proportion of the vote in the industrial states.

The urban vote continued to be important from the 1940s on. Time after time large pluralities in the big cities balanced out Republican pluralities in the suburbs and small towns, providing the margin of victory in key states with large electoral votes. The Democrats would have lost the presidency in 1940, 1944, and 1948 without the overwhelming pluralities delivered in twelve big cities.[22] The urban vote provided the margin of victory for John F. Kennedy in the close election of 1960. Kennedy beat Nixon by 112,000 votes, a margin of less than one-tenth of 1 percent, but he carried 27 out of the 39 largest cities.[23] In 1964, Lyndon Johnson won by an unprecedented landslide, with the cities topping the national Democratic margins by 10 percent or more.

Democratic successes in presidential elections were bound to end eventually because the Democrats were strongest in the industrial cities which were declining in population. In contrast, the Republicans were strongest in the suburbs, the West, and, after 1964, the South, all of which were growing rapidly. Each decennial census was followed by a reapportionment of seats in the House of Representatives, which, together with the two senators from

Figure 10-2   Electoral Votes and Congressional Representation: Sunbelt and Snowbelt States, 1928–1992

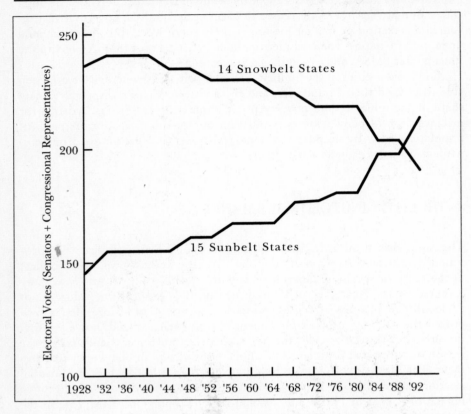

Sources: U.S. Bureau of the Census, *Historical Statistics of the United States, Colonial Times to 1970*, Bicentennial Edition, Part 1 (Washington, D.C.: Government Printing office, 1975), p. 1015; U.S. Bureau of the Census, *Statistical Abstract of the United States: 1989* (Washington, D.C., U.S. Government Printing Office, 1989), p. 241; Felicity Barringer, "Census Bureau Places Population at 249.6 Million," *New York Times* (December 27, 1990).

each state, determines the number of electoral votes each state gets. As Figure 10-2 shows, the Sunbelt states increased their number of congressional representatives and presidential electoral votes every time the country was reapportioned after 1928, and the Frostbelt states lost congressional and electoral votes. The Frostbelt states gradually lost their commanding presence in Congress. The old industrial cities lost influence even faster than the northern states. The number of representatives from six older industrial cities—Boston, New York, Philadelphia, Baltimore, Detroit, and Chicago—fell from 52 in 1923 to only 33 by 1983.[24]

Figure 10-3   Metropolitan Proportion of State Actual Electorate, 1952–1988

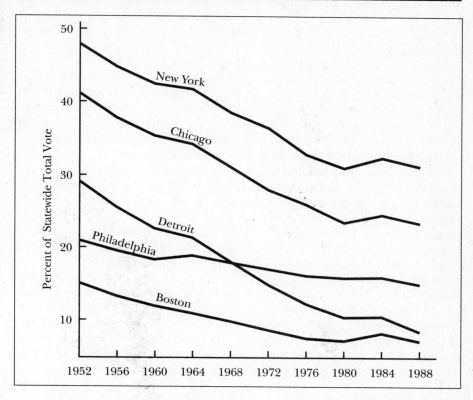

Sources: Richard Scammon, *America Votes* (various issues). Data compiled by Richard Squerzopf.

As shown in Figure 10-3, within the industrial states the number of central city voters declined. In the 1952 presidential election, for example, New York City cast almost half the total votes in the state of New York (47.9 percent), but by 1992 New York City's share of the total state vote had fallen to less than a third (30.9 percent). The declining political voice of central cities was occurring not only because the suburbs were growing so fast, but also because low-income voters in the cities were turning out for elections at a much lower rate than suburban voters.

The changing distribution of population and votes has transformed American national politics. Historically, the South and West have been governed by political elites that have been able to keep political participation low. In the South, business elites defined a good economy as one in which labor was quiescent and cheap. In the West, business elites tended to define the role of government in narrow terms: It was all right to promote business investment and general prosperity through water and dam projects, but otherwise government was to remain out of sight. In short, the political culture of the Sunbelt was, and is, highly individualistic and generally hostile to government action, unless that action is geared toward expanding the private economy. Peter Lupsha and William Siembieda sum up the political orientation in the Sunbelt this way: "The critical elements shaping political forms in the Sunbelt were the values of privatism, individualism, religious fundamentalism, fiscal conservatism, laissez faire, and a view of good government as good business."[25]

By contrast, political participation in Frostbelt cities has historically been more broad-based. Labor unions, blacks, and ethnic groups fought for and expected government to help ordinary citizens. As a consequence, local expenditures on social welfare are much higher in Frostbelt than in Sunbelt cities. In 1970, fifteen Sunbelt cities averaged only $3.77 in per capita for public welfare expenditures, compared to $26.45 in fifteen northern cities.[26]

A generation ago, the influence of urban voters gave the Democratic party an advantage in presidential elections. Between 1932 and 1964 the Republicans lost seven out of nine presidential elections. In the 1960s, building on Sunbelt and suburban growth, the Republican party formed a geopolitical counterweight to the urban strategy of the Democrats. This culminated in Richard Nixon's victory over Hubert Humphrey in the 1968 presidential election. Nixon scorned the eastern establishment that had dominated the Republican party for a century. Born in California and elected Congressman and Senator from that state, Nixon's roots were in the expanding electorate of the Sunbelt and in the new corporate wealth located there. In the 1968 election, Nixon appealed to the white, Protestant and Catholic, white- and blue-collar ethnics of the northern suburbs by promising "law and order," a code phrase for cracking down on inner-city civil disorders; the same message appealed to middle-class whites living in the Sunbelt.[27] Though Nixon did not drastically cut federal spending, his New Federalism shifted resources to Sunbelt and suburban jurisdictions.[28]

The Republican strategy paid off. From the 1968 through 1988 elections the Republicans won five out of six presidential contests. By 1980 the coming of age of the suburban middle class and the Sunbelt gave the Republicans a decisive advantage in presidential elections.[29] Ronald Reagan won the presidency easily in 1980 even though he carried only 35 percent of the big city vote.[30] A large portion of his campaign funds came from independent oil producers in several Sunbelt states.[31] Once in office, Reagan sharply cut programs targeted to older central cities.[32]

By the 1988 presidential election the Democrats also began to abandon the strategy of appealing to central city voters. The Democratic nominee, Michael Dukakis, made little effort to appeal to the central city vote. Instead, Dukakis crafted a southern strategy. He selected a Sunbelt politician, Lloyd Bentsen of Texas, as his running mate and attempted to lure the suburban blue-collar Democrats back to the party by avoiding the word "liberal" and its connotations. According to Democratic pollster Peter Hart, political analysts had determined that there weren't enough votes in the major cities to enable Dukakis to win states.[33] George Bush won the presidency, though he did poorly in the central cities and carried only 8 percent of the African-American vote.[34] By the 1988 election, the central cities accounted for less than 12 percent of the national vote.

❖   WHY THE SUNBELT BOOMED

The causes of the rise of the Sunbelt are many and complex. Economic and technological factors played a major role.[35] The infrastructure of the older Frostbelt cities was geared to the high-density patterns of production and consumption characteristic of the industrial period. Sunbelt cities had an advantage because they could start afresh to build infrastructure suited to the postindustrial economy. The building of a freeway network throughout the nation provided the foundation for a national economy that favored the decentralization of economic activities. The adoption of air conditioning made the Sunbelt more attractive both for living and for white-collar work.[36] The materials used in manufacturing shifted from heavy metals such as iron and steel to lighter materials such as aluminum and plastic, and the newer manufacturing plants could be located on relatively cheap, easily available land in Sunbelt metropolitan areas. Most importantly, the source of energy for industry and for homes shifted from Frostbelt coal to Sunbelt oil. Oil jumped from meeting less than half of the nation's energy needs in 1940 to almost 78 percent by 1975. By the mid-1970s, coal met no more than 17 percent of the nation's energy needs.[37]

The Sunbelt had advantages for new patterns of consumption as well as for new patterns of production. Increased leisure time and more emphasis on recreation encouraged people to seek out warmer climates. After World War II tourism became a major component of the national economy. Major recreational and tourist facilities developed in Florida and California (homes of Disneylands) and in New Orleans and Las Vegas. Whole communities, such as Lake Havasu, Arizona, arose to serve the needs of an expanding class of retired people who preferred Sunbelt life-styles and the lower cost of living found there.

As in the case of suburbanization, however, explanations of Sunbelt expansion that ignore the crucial role played by governments are incomplete. Government policies shaped the environment in which individuals and corporations made their locational decisions. Sunbelt success resulted not only from free market competition, but also from crucial aid from federal and state policies.

The importance of policy factors can be appreciated by looking at the experience of other advanced industrial countries. Other countries have their "sunbelts": in Great Britain, employment has shifted from the industrial north to the south of England, where a high-tech economy is booming along the M-4 motorway between London and Bristol; in Germany, economic power has shifted from the traditional centers of industry in the Ruhr and Saar regions to new centers of high-technology engineering and electronics in the southern states of Hesse, Baden-Wurttemberg, and Bavaria. However, no European country has experienced the extraordinary degree of redistribution of population and production that the United States has undergone since World War II.

A major reason for the lesser degree of redistribution in Europe is that the European countries have enacted explicit regional development policies designed to counteract uneven development. Great Britain began regional policies in the 1930s to restrain the growth of London and to aid the economies of the industrial north to employ laid-off miners and industrial workers. Britain's regional policies were supported by both Labour and Conservative governments, until the accession of Margaret Thatcher in 1979.[38] Support for regional development policies was even stronger in continental Europe, where programs to move jobs to declining regions were inaugurated in Italy (1950), West Germany (1951), the Netherlands (1951), Ireland (1952), France (mid-1950s), Denmark (1958), and Belgium (1959).[39] The effects of these policies are difficult to evaluate, but in a country like France, which made regional development policy an integral part of national economic planning, there is little doubt that national planners wielding construction controls and powerful incentives were able to disperse jobs and population from Paris to "growth poles" in languishing regions.

The United States has always lagged far behind European social democracies in enacting national growth policies. A few abortive regional development policies were begun in the 1960s, such as the creation of the Appalachian Regional Commission in 1962, but these policies were weak, establishing, basically, a few new federal grants for economic development. Overall, the United States has never had comprehensive regional development policies; "Indeed, in treating the geographical distribution of economic activity and population as a matter of market forces, rather than national planning ... the United States stands alone among advanced democratic countries."[40]

The lack of an explicit regional development policy in the United States does not mean that urban development has been determined simply by the market. Though lacking an explicit regional development policy, the United States has had a powerful *implicit* policy embedded in the massive Pentagon budget. Military expenditures, especially military-led industrial innovation, "explain in large part why the United States has had such massive postwar redistribution of productive capacity [largely to the Sunbelt], unlike any other major industrialized nation."[41]

The Great Depression ended in the United States when government spending for military procurement climbed sharply in 1940 in response to the stunning success of the Nazi blitzkrieg in Europe. As military contracting soared, the War Production Board made a policy decision to spread out defense installations and productive capacity to make bombing and a potential invasion more difficult. The South and West had the advantage of favorable weather for aircraft training facilities. Overall, it is estimated that 60 percent of the $74 billion wartime expenditures went into the fifteen states of the Sunbelt at a time when those states contained less than 40 percent of the national population.[42] The metropolitan areas of the South experienced the most rapid growth of any region. World War II pulled the rural poor into the cities in search of relatively well-paid industrial employment, contributing to the rapid urbanization of the South, which had heretofore lagged behind the rest of the country. Between 1940 and 1943, the population of the metropolitan counties of the South grew by 3.9 percent and those of the West by 2.7 percent. By contrast, the metropolitan counties in the upper midwest grew by only 2.0 percent and the northeastern metropolitan areas contracted by 0.6 percent.[43]

Some cities, most located in the Sunbelt, experienced phenomenal growth, as people migrated in search of jobs in booming defense plants. Between April 1940 and October 1941, 150,000 people poured into Los Angeles, increasing the city's population by about a third. During the war years, San Diego grew by 27 percent and Wichita, Kansas, by 20 percent.[44] The wartime boom taxed the housing stock, infrastructure, and public services in these cities to the breaking point.

Near the end of World War II, war production began to shift from heavy industry (tanks and guns) to high-technology electronic weapons (missiles, jet airplanes, sophisticated communications systems). This trend in military weaponry, which accelerated after the war, accentuated the shift from older industrial cities to newer Sunbelt cities. The federal government continued its decentralization strategy during the Korean War. During a nine-month period, $15 billion worth of "certificates of necessity" were issued that allowed new plants to be built, largely in the Sunbelt, out of untaxed profits.[45] During the Cold War, military spending remained high and most of it went to the Sunbelt. One study showed a "definite regional shift" from the Northeast to the Sunbelt between 1950 and 1976 in the awarding of defense contracts.[46] During that period, total defense employees increased by more than 35 percent, but there was a 3 percent decline in these employees in the sixteen northeastern and upper midwestern states.[47] By 1975 the defense budget contributed only 3.8 percent of the personal income in the Northeast, compared to 8.8 percent in the Sunbelt.[48]

Defense spending went to the Sunbelt not simply because the region was the most efficient place for military production. For a long time many Democratic senators and representatives from the South were so secure in their seats because of uncontested one-party elections, that they were able to control key committees in Congress through the seniority system. The southerners used their powerful positions as committee chairs to steer defense spending and major infrastructure investments, such as dams and water projects, to their districts. Perhaps the best example is Mendell Rivers, who represented Charleston, South Carolina, for forty years, from 1930 to 1970. Rivers succeeded in getting the federal government to build in his hometown "an Army depot, a Marine Corps air base, a Marine boot camp, two Navy hospitals, a Navy shipyard, a Navy base, a Navy supply center, a Navy weapons center, a Navy submarine base, a Polaris missile base, two Air Force bases, and a federal housing development."[49] Because senators and representatives from more pluralistic and diverse Frostbelt districts usually served fewer terms in Congress before being defeated for reelection, they were not able to accumulate comparable seniority and congressional clout.[50]

Other federal spending programs also disproportionately benefited the Sunbelt. Extensive federal subsidies for highways favored Sunbelt growth over the Frostbelt, which relied more heavily on railroads and mass transit. Federal grants for new sewer and water systems and for large dams and water projects tended to favor the Sunbelt. Of course, some federal spending programs were biased toward the older industrial cities, such as public employment programs and social welfare spending. The difference is that federal spending oriented to the Frostbelt came often in the form of infusions of urban aid or welfare grants that did little to create sustained economic development. In contrast, federal spending in the Sunbelt created permanent federal payrolls and infrastructure to support whole new industries such as microelectronics. One of the most important ingredients of economic growth is a skilled labor force. The military actively recruited highly trained white-collar workers, engineers, and scientists to areas near Sunbelt military installations: "Every year the Department of Defense pays a number of companies a large sum of money to move college-educated (often at the public expense) engineers and scientists from the Midwest and other regions to the Southwest."[51]

Besides spending, the revenue side of the federal budget also tilted toward the Sunbelt. Provisions in the federal tax code benefited the Sunbelt over the Frostbelt. In 1954, accelerated depreciation allowances deducted from corporate income taxes provided tax breaks for constructing new commercial and industrial structures, but not for rehabilitating old buildings. Accelerated depreciation thus speeded up the flow of capital out of older industrial cities to suburban and Sunbelt locations.[52] Between 1954 and 1980 this subsidy was worth $30 billion in reduced taxes. The Investment Tax Credit, introduced by President Kennedy in 1962, gave a dollar-for-dollar reduction on corporate taxes for new investment in plant and equipment. Thus the federal tax code encouraged companies to abandon older plants and build new ones. The effect was to accelerate the movement of capital out of the older cities of the Frostbelt. Between 1962 and 1981, this subsidy was worth $90 billion.[53] In 1982 alone it was worth $20 billion.[54]

The geographic effects of the federal tax code may have been unintentional. Nevertheless, the tax code had a substantial impact on regional and urban development. For a long period the federal government gave money to distressed central cities through urban renewal and other programs; at the same time, it was underwriting the movement away from those cities.[55] A study of nine tax subsidies that promote the mobility of investment found that they were worth more than twice the total budget of the U.S. Department of Housing and Urban Development.[56] In short, the tax code was, in its effects, a powerful policy that contradicted the urban policies of the federal government.

❖ REGIONAL CONFLICT: SUNBELT VERSUS FROSTBELT

In the 1970s a new regional conflict erupted that *Business Week* called "The Second War Between the States."[57] The conflict was precipitated in part by

President Richard Nixon's efforts to shift urban aid to small cities and the Sunbelt through formulas in block grants, such as the 1974 Community Development Block Grant Act. High-profile articles in the *New York Times, Business Week,* and the influential *National Journal* focused public attention on the issue in 1976.[58] The *Business Week* article warned:

> As long as the migration of industry and population was gradual from what was a relatively rich Northeast to what was a relatively impoverished South and Southwest, it helped unify the nation. But within the past five years the process has burst beyond the bounds that can be accommodated by existing political institutions.[59]

One study calculated "balance of payments" for the regions of the country, comparing how much money each region sent to the federal government in taxes and how much it got back in federal outlays. In fiscal year 1975 the South and West together enjoyed a $22.2 billion surplus, while the Northeast and the Midwest suffered a $30.9 billion deficit.[60]

Regional inequities in federal policy spawned regional lobbying groups. In June 1976, the Coalition of Northeast Governors was organized, and in September 1976 congressional representatives from sixteen states formed the Northeast-Midwest Economic Advancement Coalition. To counter the lobbying of the Frostbelt politicians, the Southern Growth Policy Board, which had been formed in 1971, stepped up its efforts.[61] Regional inequities in federal spending did generally decline between 1975 and 1979,[62] but Ronald Reagan's election in 1980 shifted the momentum once again to the Sunbelt and decisively tilted federal spending away from the Frostbelt.[63] His administration increased spending in programs that benefited the Sunbelt (defense and highways) and cut spending in programs that benefited Frostbelt cities (mass transit, public housing, social welfare, job training). Between 1980 and 1987, for example, grant programs of special importance to cities were cut 47 percent, from $45.3 billion to $21.6 billion.[64]

Not all areas of the Frostbelt were hurt by the new federal spending priorities. Areas along the East Coast, such as Long Island in New York and the suburbs of Boston, received military contracts because of the presence there of major universities and science and computer centers. In fact, the "Massachusetts Miracle," which Michael Dukakis took credit for in his 1988 run for the presidency, was, ironically, stimulated by the Reagan defense buildup.[65] In addition, the collapse of oil prices in 1985 helped the oil-consuming Frostbelt and crippled the oil-producing regions in the Sunbelt. Cities like Houston faced unprecedented fiscal crises, soaring unemployment rates, and tumbling real estate prices.

Considerable evidence suggests, however, that the Sunbelt will continue to dominate growth patterns in the 1990s. The 1990 census revealed that Sunbelt states were the biggest population gainers in the 1980s. The fifteen Sunbelt states grew overall by 18.8 percent between 1980 and 1990, compared to 2.2 percent for the fourteen Frostbelt states. The growth states were

Nevada (+50.1 percent), Arizona (+34.8 percent), Florida (+32.7 percent), and California (+25.7 percent). The only Frostbelt state to show a significant gain was New Hampshire (+20.5 percent), and that state was attracting suburban dwellers working elsewhere in the Northeast urban corridor.[66]

The savings and loan crisis, precipitated in part by the collapse of real estate prices in the mid-1980s, will in the long run boost Sunbelt economies. After deregulation was enacted during the Reagan Administration, savings and loans institutions were allowed to extend loans not only on residential property but also on industrial and commercial ventures. This prompted a wave of real estate speculation throughout the Sunbelt. When land prices fell sharply, hundreds of the savings and loans went broke. The Financial Institution Reform, Recovery, and Enforcement Act of 1989 (FIRREA) authorized the use of federal funds to guarantee depositors' investments in bankrupt institutions. Estimates of the total cost to taxpayers in 1990 dollars at first ranged from $159 billion to well over $200 billion, and may go as high as $500 billion. According to one study, thirty-seven states will be fiscal "losers"—their taxpayers will pay more tax money into the program than investors in these states will receive back. Thirteen states will be "winners." Most of the winners are in the Sunbelt; most Frostbelt states are losers. The net cost of the bailout to the fourteen states of the Frostbelt will be $71.4 billion. In other words, taxpayers who live in the Frostbelt will be sending huge amounts of money over the years to depositors and investors who live in the Sunbelt. The biggest winner is Texas, whose investors will receive 43.2 percent of all the bailout funds—an inflow of $4,775 for every man, woman, and child in the state.[67]

At least for a time, the savings and loan crisis rekindled the regional conflicts of the 1970s. Keith Laughlin, staff director of the Northeast-Midwest Congressional Coalition, charged, "Taxpayers in our region are being stuck with the tab resulting from the irresponsible actions of state-regulated, but federally insured, thrifts in the Southwest." Frostbelt politicians blame the problem on lax regulation of savings and loans by Sunbelt states. In 1991 the Northeast-Midwest Congressional Coalition introduced in Congress the State Thrift Deposit Insurance Premium Act, which would require states with "excessive" bailout costs to pay a premium for federal insurance. Noting the failure of major banks in the Northeast, Sunbelt politicians objected that the problem was national, not regional, and therefore required a national solution.[68]

❖ POLITICS IN SUNBELT CITIES: GROWTH MANIA

Politics in Sunbelt cities has historically been different from politics in Frostbelt cities. Before World War II, many Sunbelt cities were dominated by entrenched political machines based on alliances between machine politicians and conservative businessleaders. Tampa, Florida, and San Antonio, Texas, for example, were governed by corrupt machine politicians until well after World

War II. New Orleans was run by a long-time machine, the Regular Democratic Organization, until de Lesseps S. Morrison was elected mayor in 1946.[69] The old-style machines were ill-prepared for the rapid growth set in motion by the defense buildup in World War II. New political actors appeared on the stage after the war demanding to be part of local politics. In city after city there were "G.I. revolts" in which "bright young candidates marched against corrupt or inept city hall cliques under the banner of progress."[70] Over the long term an informal coalition of white-collar professionals, businessleaders, and growth-oriented city managers and bureaucrats created business-dominated reform machines in many Sunbelt cities.

The twin goals of the new regimes were political reform and economic growth—two goals which were seen as reinforcing one another. The reformers wanted government to be responsive to the imperatives of regional economic growth. They thought that the best way to accomplish this was to put local government in the hands of people who would be reliably sympathetic to the business community. This wave of reform resulted in commission and city manager forms of government, nonpartisan elections held at-large, and city home-rule charters. Business-dominated reform regimes also favored aggressive annexation to acquire the fiscal resources necessary to sustain a public sector that could underwrite growth. Between 1945 and 1955, San Antonio, Houston, and Dallas in Texas; Oklahoma City; Albuquerque, New Mexico; Phoenix, Arizona; and San Jose, California all adopted reform charters or other significant reforms.[71]

San Antonio is a fairly typical example of business-dominated reform regimes. In 1949, A. C. "Jack" White won the mayoralty with the support of good government reformers and the business community. It was not until 1951, however, that reformers put aside their disagreements and voted in a council-manager charter. Subsequently, the Good Government League began endorsing candidates for the city government. From 1955 to 1971, seventy-seven out of San Antonio's eighty-one members of the city council were recruited and endorsed by the League. The Good Government League became the functional equivalent of a political party, a "sort of upper-middle class political machine, officing not in Tammany Hall, but in a savings and loan association, whose electoral wonders are impressive to behold."[72]

The Good Government League succeeded in passing a series of bond referenda to finance infrastructure improvements to facilitate San Antonio's growth. The business-dominated reformers pushed through a massive system of freeways, 98.3 miles by 1986, within the city limits. The League also sponsored revitalization of the central business district through urban renewal and facilitated the construction of the HemisFair tourism and shopping project on 149 acres southeast of the Alamo. The HemisFair was a classic example of civic boosterism, with the public sector providing subsidies to a project that was largely planned and operated by the private sector.[73]

Like other Sunbelt reform organizations, such as the Phoenix Charter Government Committee and the Albuquerque Citizens Committee, San Antonio's Good Government League was dominated by middle- and upper-class, Anglo professionals and businessleaders. The regime was oriented toward investment and growth. Like business-dominated reform regimes throughout the Sunbelt, voter turnout in elections was low.

❖ CHALLENGE TO THE GROWTH REGIMES: THE GROWTH CONTROL MOVEMENT

Though the rapid expansion that Sunbelt cities enjoyed in the postwar period benefited many people, it also entailed social costs. The social costs of urban growth include air pollution, water pollution, water depletion, land subsidence (due to pumping of groundwater), traffic congestion, and overburdened infrastructure, such as inadequate schools and sewers. Sunbelt cities are classic "spread" cities, with single-purpose downtowns and low-density residential and strip commercial development. Developers often find it more profitable to build on cheaper land at the urban fringe, which increases the costs of supplying public services. The costs of these services are borne by taxpayers.

Houston is the quintessential sprawled-out "free enterprise city."[74] Giving free rein to private enterprise, meaning imposing few land controls or regulations, Houston enjoyed average growth each decade from 1950 to 1980 of 66 percent—"probably the most sustained for any city in North America."[75] Its local economy was built around oil production and equipment, but it also developed a diverse manufacturing base in nonelectrical machinery, chemicals, and fabricated metal products. Houston prided itself on being the only major city in the country with no zoning code and having a small public sector.[76] In fact, however, government played a major role in Houston's growth, investing large amounts in the ship channel and the Johnson Space Center. Government invested heavily in the infrastructure of growth but little in dealing with the social costs of growth. Houston's image as "the golden buckle of the Sunbelt" has been tarnished by its vulnerability to oil price declines and the mounting costs of rapid growth.

The social costs exacted by Houston's economy are legion.[77] Toxic waste, largely from the petrochemical industry, is a major threat to the environment. In the mid-1980s, William Ruckelshaus, the head of the federal Environmental Protection Agency (EPA), described Houston as one of the worst hazardous waste disposal areas in the nation, with nine major toxic waste dumps on the Superfund list.

Industrial waste has so polluted water in the Houston ship channel that citizens have sometimes been cautioned not to let it touch their skin. Houston is also plagued by water pollution problems due to inadequate sewage treatment. Over 200 small sewage treatment plants, many meeting only minimal standards, dump 50 million gallons of effluent daily into Lake Houston. Fecal coliform bacteria counts were so high that an environmental specialist advised residents not to swim in Lake Houston. Disturbingly, in the mid-1980s, 140 to 160 million gallons of water were drawn daily from the lake and treated for drinking water. Houston's sewer capacity was so inadequate that a sewer connection moratorium was placed on three-quarters of the city. Before a developer could build, the developer had to obtain a special sewer permit to con- nect into the existing system. Since the number of permits was fixed by the capacity of the system, acquiring the permits was difficult. Reflecting its free market image, the city allowed unused sewer permits to be bought and sold. Locally, this informal trading, called "poop futures," was a thriving business. In the late 1980s, unused permits, even from cemeteries, could be purchased for from $3,000 to $5,000 each.[78]

Another problem related to Houston's rapid growth is ground subsidence and flooding. Drawing so much water from wells caused the clay soils on which Houston sits to become compacted, and the ground started to sink. Some areas of southeast Houston have sunk 6 to 8 feet since 1943. With subsi- dence and increased water runoff due to road building and other development, flooding became routine in many areas. In the 1970s and 1980s, annual costs due to flooding were averaging over $30 million. As with water pollution, though private developers caused the problems the costs of dealing with them fell on the public. In 1984, a Chamber of Commerce task force recommended a $922 million improvement program over twenty-five years to correct the drainage problems.

As a classic low-density Sunbelt city, Houston developed severe traffic problems. Since autos increased at more than twice the rate of the population, highway construction was not able to keep pace with traffic volume. The result was congestion and delays. A mid-1980s study by the Federal Highway Administration found that, of the thirty-seven metropolitan areas studied, Houston had the worst traffic problems. At one point traffic delays triggered a rash of violent incidents by irate motorists involving knives and guns. In the late 1980s, Houston's traffic fatality rate was among the highest in the nation. Not surprisingly, out of ten cities studied, Houston was found to have the highest per capita gasoline consumption in the nation.[79] Along with its bur- geoning petrochemical industry, auto use contributed to a serious air pollu- tion problem. Air pollution is probably one reason Houston has one of the highest lung cancer death rates in the United States.

The government investment in transportation infrastructure was inade- quate. With 1 million to 2 million potholes, Houston became the pothole cap- ital of the country. In the absence of zoning, large buildings were constructed so close to major thoroughfares that the thoroughfares could not be widened, and huge projects blocked crucial cross-streets. In recognition of the serious- ness of the traffic problem, Houston voters approved a 1 percent sales tax in 1978 to improve the bus system and build a light rail transit system. It was not until the 1980s that the city adopted modest restrictions on development to improve traffic flow. In 1990 Mayor Kathy Whitmire came out in favor of zoning; in 1992 zoning came at last to the only major American city without it.[80]

Out of many that could be cited, Houston is only one example of a Sunbelt city that has become increasingly affected by the costs of rapid urban growth. These costs have prompted the mobilization of new constituencies to challenge the business-dominated reform regimes. By 1965 cracks began to appear in the growth coalitions that had dominated Sunbelt cities since World

War II. By 1981 a voter revolt against the business elite, aided by the minority, liberal, and gay communities, brought Kathy Whitmire to the mayoralty of Houston.

Ironically, it was the economic success of the business-dominated reform regimes that undermined their political domination. The economic diversification of Sunbelt metropolitan economies created splits within the business elite. Industrial interests clashed with recreational and tourist interests, and corporations in the central business districts clashed with those in the independent suburban commercial districts.

Rapid economic growth and immigration also created diverse and unruly electorates that were unwilling to defer to the interests of the business reform coalition. Concerned about the destructive effects of rapid growth on the quality of life, professionals and the middle classes increasingly broke ranks with the business interests. They supported a growth control movement that challenged the accepted orthodoxy that growth is good for everybody. In addition, lower-income inner-city residents, mostly African Americans and Hispanics, began to question the costs to their neighborhoods of urban renewal and highway building and demanded that city governments respond to local service needs, as well as to the imperatives of regional growth. In short, the business-dominated reform regimes of the postwar period came under pressure from two movements: the growth control movement and the neighborhood movement.

Growth control is a national movement, but it was pioneered in Sunbelt cities where the costs of rapid growth are most obvious. Measures advocated by the movement include caps on new construction, moratoriums on population growth for fixed periods of time, impact fees (assessing developers for the costs of growth), linkage fees (linking development to related needs such as affordable housing, schools, and day-care), and refusal to provide expanded public facilities, such as schools and water systems, to discourage growth. Growth controls spread rapidly. By 1975 growth controls were in effect in over 300 jurisdictions across the country.[81] A 1973 sample survey of 416 suburbs found that 19.5 percent had enacted growth moratoriums in the previous two years and 26.9 percent had enacted growth limitations, such as placing a limit on the number of new housing units that are allowed to be constructed each year.[82]

The growth control movement is strongest in California. Between 1971 and 1986 more than 150 growth control measures appeared on local ballots; 50 measures appeared on ballots in 1986 alone, with three-quarters of them winning.[83] The growth control movement has been especially active in Southern California, even in politically conservative areas. In 1986, over the objections of Mayor Tom Bradley, Los Angeles voters passed Proposition U, which effectively ended most new office construction in residential neighborhoods on the West Side and in the San Fernando Valley.[84] In the same election voters in Newport Beach in Orange County, a bastion of conservatism, defeated plans for a $400 million mixed-use complex overlooking the harbor. The no-growth forces won even though they were outspent in the campaign by $500,000 to $10,000.[85]

Los Angeles has the most polluted air in the country. In 1988, Los Angeles violated the federal standard for ozone pollution on 176 days—far more than any other city in the country. Much of the pollution is caused by its sprawled-out urban form and almost complete reliance on the automobile. In 1989, regional officials in Southern California voted to impose severe restrictions on everyday activity in order to reduce air pollution. The plan called for a range of measures, some of them quite radical, including limiting the number of cars per family, raising parking fees for cars that carry only one person, banning gasoline-powered lawn mowers, outlawing the use of liquid fire starter, and requiring that all cars be converted to electricity or other "clean" fuels by the year 2007.[86] Whether it is fully implemented or not, the Southern California air quality plan shows that politicians are willing to consider radical measures plans to control the costs of growth and protect the quality of life for voters.

Support for growth controls is strongest in rapidly growing cities, in wealthier cities, and among wealthier individuals.[87] Growth controls have been criticized for driving up the cost of housing and limiting job growth, thus favoring middle- and upper-income residents who already own their own homes and hold well-paying jobs.[88] One study concluded that growth controls push average housing prices as much as 35 to 40 percent higher than communities without growth controls.[89]

Growth controls may have less impact, however, than many believe. Controls by one local government may push development into other areas, thus encouraging leapfrog development. Nonlocal influences on housing prices, such as inflation and interest rates, may overwhelm local growth controls.[90] Growth controls are instituted in most communities only after rapid development has already occurred; growth controls may be, therefore, more of a reaction to growth that has occurred than a set of policies to control it.[91]

Most people are not anti-growth or pro-growth; most favor slow or managed growth that can control the costs while achieving the benefits of growth.[92] However, so long as growth controls are enacted by fragmented suburban jurisdictions, they are likely to come down to being attempts by one jurisdiction to move the costs of growth to another. State-mandated growth standards, or regional planning, would offer better opportunity for more equally distributing the costs and benefits of growth controls.[93]

❖ CHALLENGE TO THE GROWTH REGIMES: THE NEIGHBORHOOD MOVEMENT

Whatever the long-term effects of the growth control movement, Sunbelt urban politics cannot go back to the old business-dominated reform regimes. Along with the growth control movement, the neighborhood organizing movement, led by African Americans and Hispanics, has challenged the business-dominated reform regimes. These groups have refused to be victimized by the costs of growth in the form of displacement by urban renewal and highway building. And they have demanded governments that are more responsive to neighborhood needs.

One of the most significant trends of the recent period is the increasing political influence of blacks and Latinos in American cities. African Americans have become the majority in many cities, especially in older Frostbelt cities. Latinos now are the largest minority group in many metropolitan areas of the Sunbelt. Their numbers are increasing at a much faster rate than non-Hispanic whites or blacks, and some researchers expect Latinos to equal blacks in total national population by the year 2003. Their potential political power is enormous, especially because they are concentrated in fast-growing Sunbelt cities. Latinos constitute about a third of the population of the eight largest Sunbelt cities. (For a discussion of recent migration and immigration patterns, see Chapter 14.) African Americans also make up a large proportion of the population in Sunbelt cities: more than 25 percent in Dallas–Fort Worth, Houston, Miami, and Tampa and over 10 percent in Los Angeles and Denver (see Table 14-3). As in older cities in the Frostbelt, there are significant racial and ethnic disparities in Sunbelt cities. As a result, the tensions that have existed in older cities for more than a century are increasingly being felt in the Sunbelt.

Rioting broke out in Miami in 1989, 1990, and 1991. The most serious riot of the twentieth century occurred in Los Angeles in 1992. The riot was ignited on April 29th when word spread through the city's ghettos and barrios that four white policemen had been acquitted by an all-white suburban jury of violating the law in the brutal beating of a black man, Rodney King. For months the nation had repeatedly seen the 81-second amateur video of the beating. A guilty verdict seemed certain. Reacting in anger, blacks, Latinos, and some whites poured into the streets. By the time the rioting was over, the death toll had reached 53, more than the 43 deaths in the 1967 Detroit riot and the 34 deaths in the 1965 riot in the Watts section of Los Angeles.[94]

Unlike the race riots of the 1960s that swept through northern cities in four consecutive summers, the Los Angeles riot was multiethnic. Between April 30 and May 5, 3,498 Latinos, 2,832 African Americans, and 640 non-Latino whites were arrested. The "rainbow" of participants could be taken as evidence that the causes of the rioting were endemic to the politics and economy of the entire city of Los Angeles, and that people of diverse backgrounds apparently felt cause for anger.

Television series such as *Dallas, Santa Barbara*, and *Knots Landing* convey the impression that the Sunbelt is filled with wealthy, prosperous people. It is true that white residents of Sunbelt metropolitan areas usually make incomes above the national average, and fewer whites are poor than in the nation as a whole.[95] The promise of prosperity is hollow, however, for many Sunbelt residents. Indeed, the gap between the rich and the poor has been greater in the southwestern metropolitan areas than in those of the North.[96] Corporations moved South and West to escape higher labor costs in the North and take advantage of a vast pool of low-wage, nonunionized labor in the Sunbelt. Twelve out of fifteen Sunbelt states have right-to-work laws that discourage unionization and keep wages low.[97] (Right-to-work laws make it more difficult to organize unions because nonmembers can benefit from union contracts without paying union dues.) However, even those parts of the Sunbelt that experienced industrial growth due to low wages, low taxes, and few environmental regulations have suffered in recent years from deindustrialization, as hundreds of footloose industries have fled to even lower-cost production sites in Third World countries. A good example is the migration of microcomputer assembly plants from California's Silicon Valley to Pacific Rim countries.[98] Industrial jobs are important because they provide entry-level positions for blacks and Hispanics with limited education. Research shows that as southern cities move away from industry toward advanced corporate service economies, the black-white income gap widens.[99]

As we have seen, though rates of urban poverty are at least as high in the Sunbelt as in the Frostbelt, Sunbelt cities spend considerably less on public health, welfare, and even basic municipal services than northern cities.[100] But the problems experienced in Sunbelt cities by the poor, especially blacks and Latinos, have been difficult to translate into effective political demands. Blacks and Latinos tend to have low voter turnout rates and often do not feel that they can influence the political system.[101] Over the years, whites used various methods, legal and extralegal, to keep blacks and Latinos from voting. One of the most effective devices was the white primary, which prevented blacks from casting ballots in Democratic primaries. In one-party states like Texas and Georgia this was tantamount to disenfranchisement. In 1944 the United States Supreme Court struck down the white primary as a violation of the Fifteenth Amendment of the Constitution.[102]

Other devices continued to be used to dilute the voting power of blacks and Latinos. Many cities used at-large election districts to deny representation to minority neighborhoods whose votes were overwhelmed in citywide totals. The 1965 Voting Rights Act, however, gave federal judges the power to strike down voting systems when they found that the system systematically reduced minority representation. In 1975 the Act was extended to Latinos. Both Houston and Dallas were forced to modify their at-large systems by providing some wards that would guarantee representation for blacks and Latinos. Likewise, Los Angeles was forced to redraw its ward boundaries. Minority voters helped to pass new city charters that provided for ward voting in San Antonio, Fort Worth, Albuquerque, San Francisco, Atlanta, Richmond, and other cities.[103]

The striking down of legal barriers to voting and electoral influence helped to increase dramatically the number of black and Latino elected officials. Nationwide, the number of black elected officials increased from 1,479 in 1970 to 7,445 in 1991.[104] Blacks have been elected mayor in some of the largest Sunbelt cities, such as Los Angeles, New Orleans, Atlanta, and Birmingham. With about 20,000 Latino immigrants gaining citizenship and the right to vote each year, Latino gains have been especially dramatic in recent years. Nationwide, the number of Latino elected officials increased from 3,128 in 1984 to 4,004 in 1990, a 25 percent jump in only six years.[105]

Latinos have been elected mayor in Miami, Denver, and San Antonio. It should be pointed out, however, that the representation of both blacks and Latinos is still below their proportion in the population.

The surge in minority voter representation in Sunbelt cities was reinforced by a movement to organize neighborhoods to force city governments to address the longstanding grievances of minorities. San Antonio is a good example of the power of the neighborhood movement.[106] For decades the residents of neighborhoods on the west side of San Antonio harbored resentments over inadequate public services. Fire stations were older than elsewhere in the city, parks were less well maintained, and the zoning commission was less willing to protect west side neighborhoods from commercial encroachments. Most importantly, low-lying west side neighborhoods in San Antonio lacked both storm sewers and sanitary sewers. On August 7, 1974, large sections of the west side Mexican-American neighborhoods were flooded by the runoff from Anglo-American highlands. This event proved to be the catalyst that mobilized the Mexican-American electorate.

Communities Organized for Public Service (COPS), a coalition of neighborhood groups, was able to channel resentments into effective political action. Within months of the flood San Antonio passed a $47 million bond issue to implement a drainage plan that had languished on the shelf since 1946. In 1976, COPS endorsed a growth control referendum to deny permission to build a huge shopping mall that threatened to contaminate the groundwater aquifer from which San Antonio drew its water. The mall also would have siphoned off infrastructure funds from the city to new suburban neighborhoods. In coalition with environmental forces, minority voters won a stunning victory by a lopsided margin of 78 percent to 22 percent.

Under pressure from the federal government, the San Antonio city council proposed a new charter that called for a mayor to be elected citywide and each of ten city council members to be elected from districts. Vigorously supported by COPS but opposed by north side Anglo voters, the charter narrowly passed by a 51 percent majority in January 1977. The first election under the new charter resulted in a balanced city council, with five Mexican Americans, one African American, and five Anglos (including the mayor). In one of its first actions, the new city council declared an eighteen-month moratorium on major development in the aquifer recharge zone.

For decades, San Antonio had been run by business-dominated reformers, represented by the Good Government League. The League, however, was unable to adapt to the new issues represented by the growth control movement and the minority neighborhood movement, and it formally dissolved in 1976. The transition was completed in 1981 when a dynamic young Hispanic politician, Henry Cisneros, won 62 percent of the vote to decisively defeat a representative of the downtown business establishment. Though Cisneros garnered strong support in the Latino neighborhoods, most of his programs ended up emphasizing job growth. For example, he pushed high-tech job opportunities by allotting resources to biotechnology development. Booming growth on the far north side, however, did not result in many jobs for poor inner-city neighborhoods. Nevertheless, the tone of San Antonio politics had changed considerably.

❖ CONCLUSION: THE FUTURE OF SUNBELT URBAN POLITICS

A great deal of evidence points to a gradual convergence in the types of political regimes that govern Sunbelt and Frostbelt cities. On the one hand, the economic and demographic profiles of Sunbelt cities are coming to resemble Snowbelt cities. Not surprisingly, many of the problems of the older industrial cities, including rapid immigration, concentrated poverty, and racial and ethnic conflict, have hit Sunbelt cities. New constituencies have been mobilized, in particular growth control and neighborhood and minority constituencies. Over the years many Sunbelt cities effectively used annexation to maintain a dominant middle-class (largely white) electorate within city boundaries. This strategy, however, has lost its effectiveness. Federal courts have disallowed annexations if they have the effect of diluting minority voting strength. In addition, the introduction of ward-based elections has moved Sunbelt cities away from business-dominated reform politics to a more pluralistic politics.

At the same time there is evidence that Frostbelt urban politics is becoming more like the Sunbelt pattern. Older industrial cities have moved aggressively to imitate Sunbelt cities and become more "entrepreneurial" in their pursuit of business investment.[107] Many Frostbelt cities have shifted resources to developmental programs for business.[108] Business-dominated reform coalitions have come to power in many older industrial cities. Efforts to remove decision making from the hands of neighborhood-based politicians and give it to growth-oriented elites with a regional perspective generally do not take the form in Frostbelt cities of proposals for at-large, nonpartisan elections. Instead, functions are moved out of general purpose governments into independent authorities, often supported by user fees, or business techniques of "strategic planning" are applied to urban issues to make them more responsive to growth concerns.[109] The convergence hypothesis is based on the premise that the economies of the various sections of the country will become more alike and that political convergence will follow economic convergence. Whether economic convergence will occur is difficult to predict. Much depends on unpredictable factors such as the price of oil, federal social welfare policies, and the size of the military budget. But even if economic convergence occurs, it is not inevitable that political convergence will follow. Distinctive political cultures persist in different regions of the country and they will continue to influence urban politics.

CHAPTER 11

THE STRUGGLE OVER URBAN POLICY: 1968–1992

❖ POLITICAL SUPPORT FOR URBAN PROGRAMS

During the administrations of Richard Nixon and Gerald Ford, the White House made a concerted effort to consolidate the categorical grant programs that funded social welfare and urban policies. These reforms were justified by a heavy dose of rhetoric about balancing the federal budget by paring the number and size of such programs. Despite the rhetoric, federal social welfare and urban spending continued to rise. Outlays for grants-in-aid to state and local governments, including revenue sharing, increased from $34.4 billion in fiscal 1972 to $71.6 billion in fiscal 1978. The proportion disbursed through less restrictive "block" grants increased from just 2.8 percent to 34.5 percent.[1] It is important to note that the block grant approach represented an attempt to reduce federal oversight of how cities used federal money, but it did not reduce the overall amount of federal spending. That would come years later. By the late 1970s, political support for urban programs had weakened. Funds for social and urban problems began to decline, and when Ronald Reagan won the 1980 presidential contest, it was clear that federal assistance to cities would be reduced. In the ensuing years, federal spending for the cities dropped sharply. All attempts by mayors and other urban interests to resist this trend were to no avail because for the Republican party, city voters had become politically unimportant.

❖ THE REPUBLICAN AGENDA: THE NEW FEDERALISM

As a result of the 1968 election, the Republicans held 62 percent of the governorships and installed a president rhetorically pledged to return "power to the people" through the decentralization of domestic policy and a New Federalism.[2] "The Sixties are ending," observed the Advisory Commission on Intergovernmental Relations, "with substantial support of a 'New Federalism' championed by the Nixon Administration by which increased reliance is placed upon State and local governments to make the multitude of public decisions required in the pursuit of domestic goals."[3]

Immediately following his election victory, President Nixon emphasized his desire to decentralize domestic government programs. In his January 1969 message proposing a revenue-sharing rather than a grant approach, he spoke of the grant programs as producing a "gathering of the reins of power in Washington," which he saw as "a radical departure from the vision of federal-state relations the nation's founders had in mind." He referred to his proposal as "a turning point in federal-state relations, the beginning of decentralized relations of governmental power, the restoration of a rightful balance between the state capital and the national capital."[4] This turned out to be a rather modest summary of a theme he was to return to many times, perhaps most concisely in his October 21, 1972, radio address on "The Philosophy of Government":

> Do we want to turn more power over to bureaucrats in Washington in the hope that they will do what is best for all the people? Or do we want to return more power to the people and to their state and local governments so that people can decide what is best for themselves? It is time that good, decent people stopped letting themselves be bulldozed by anybody who presumes to be the self-righteous moral judge of our society. In the next four years, as in the past four, I will continue to direct the flow of power away from Washington and back to the people.[5]

The president devised a two-fold strategy to achieve his objectives. First, he ordered reviews of the major programs left over from the Johnson Administration. Throughout his first term, he repeatedly attempted to reduce spending on social programs. Second, as a step toward implementing his philosophy, he proposed a new revenue-sharing program through which the federal government would give money to states and localities with few restrictions on how it could be spent. This would, he said,

> reverse the flow of power and resources from the states and communities to Washington, and start power and resources flowing back from Washington to the states and communities, and more important, to the people all across America.
>
> The time has come for a new partnership between the federal government and the states and localities.[6]

Submitted to Congress in 1971, his revenue-sharing proposal promised to give state and local officials substantial freedom to spend federal money according to their own, rather than the federal government's, priorities. The preamble to the revenue-sharing legislation promised:

> to restore balance in the Federal system of government in the United States; to provide both the flexibility and resources for state and local government officials to exercise leadership in solving their own problems; to achieve a better allocation of total public resources and to provide for the sharing with State and local governments a portion of the tax revenues received by the United States.[7]

The revenue-sharing plan was intended to be the centerpiece of domestic policy for the Nixon Administration. The Administration contended that implementation of the plan would go a long way toward addressing the complaints that local officials had expressed about the complexity of the grants-in-aid system. Of the $16.1 billion proposed for distribution under revenue sharing for the first year, $5 billion was to come in the form of general revenue sharing and $11.1 billion was to be allocated to state and local governments through "special" revenue sharing in six functional areas.[8]

The presidential proposal stole the initiative from the Democrats. The idea of revenue sharing had been around for years. It had first been proposed by Walter Heller, chairman of the Council of Economic Advisors in the Kennedy and Johnson administrations. Like so many others, Heller had noticed that the federal government's ability to raise taxes was far superior to that of local governments.[9] The federal income tax structure was such that tax revenues grew at a rate one and one-half times that of the economy—for every 10 percent increase in economic growth, the government registered a 15 percent rise in tax revenues. The result, by 1963, was the prospect that revenues might exceed expenditures in the federal treasury.[10] Heller proposed that the national government share its surplus with the nation's states and cities.

Especially for big cities mayors, the idea that the federal government might "share" its reserves with them would have been very attractive. Revenue sharing, however, was never seriously considered by the Democratic presidents. Instead, a multitude of grant programs to accomplish specific national goals captured their attention. Rather than transfer revenues quietly to state and local governments, policymakers in Washington decided to launch national efforts to eliminate poverty, improve education, help inner-city neighborhoods, and accomplish other social goals.

The Nixon Administration's revenue-sharing proposal received backing from mayors, governors, city managers, county executives, and other state and local public officials. Their main incentive for lobbying for the legislation through the halls of Congress was to gain access to federal resources in order to ameliorate their fiscal problems. Though local officials liked the federal money that flowed to the cities through the numerous grants enacted during the Johnson years, they deplored their loss of control over how the money was spent. Federal administrators dictated what could be done with the new funds. Local officials' control over local politics slipped in other ways, too. The administrators of antipoverty and Model Cities programs protested city hall decisions, and nonprofit housing organizations proposed federally funded housing projects without consulting with city councils or mayors. City officials saw revenue sharing as a way to get federal money flowing directly through city hall without giving up power to federal administrators, community activists, or nonprofit agencies.

The support for revenue sharing was centered in a group of organizations, known as the Big Seven, that represented local government officials. The members of this coalition were the National League of Cities (NLC), the U.S. Conference of Mayors (USCM), the National Governors' Conference, the National Legislative Conference, the Council of State Governments, the National Association of Counties, and the International City Management Association (ICMA). City managers had long defined themselves as trained professionals who rejected political activities as beyond their purview. In the fight for revenue sharing, however, they broke with a fifty-year tradition of neutrality vis-à-vis legislative issues.[11]

With this coalition backing the concept of shared revenues, the ensuing political battle pitted the fiscal interests of local elected officials against the ideological and philosophical concerns of liberals who preferred that the federal government take an activist stance in solving social problems. Many of the groups that had supported the expansion of the federal role in the 1960s now opposed the retreat from specific social concerns implicit in the revenue-sharing proposal. Organized labor, except for the American Federation of State, County, and Municipal Employees (AFSCME) (which correctly perceived that its members would be beneficiaries of revenue sharing) decried the concept. The AFL-CIO opposed the absence of any stated national purpose and federal oversight in the revenue-sharing proposal.[12] The union's executive council articulated its position in February 1971:

> The AFL-CIO urges complete rejection of the revenue sharing proposal. . . . There is no reason to believe that each of the fifty states and 81,000 cities, boroughs, townships and school districts is in a better position to weigh and balance national priority needs, and use Federal Funds to meet them more effectively and efficiently. Moreover, without specified and enforceable federal performance standards, there is no assurance that federal civil rights guarantees and fair labor practices will be applied to projects supported by no-strings federal grants.[13]

Civil rights groups also opposed revenue sharing. They feared that social programs benefiting minorities would be abandoned in favor of funds distributed to states and localities with no federal oversight. Many liberals opposed revenue sharing because they thought it placed too much trust in the competence and intent of local governments. They argued that local governments could not be depended on to respond to social needs:

> Fiscal poverty and poverty of ideas often go together in state government, especially when the programs are designed to help the least affluent and influ-

ential of citizens . . . states are loath to spend additional dollars unless compelled to.[14]

. . . revenue sharing is a cop-out as regards the almost universally admitted inadequacies of state and local governmental structure and financial systems.[15]

Conservatives generally supported revenue sharing because they thought it would eventually replace the programs inherited from the 1960s. Some conservative organizations, however, did not see revenue sharing as an alternative to social programs; they didn't want either. One of the more active groups of this type was the U.S. Chamber of Commerce (USCC). Its opposition to revenue sharing stemmed from its general ideological position opposing expansion of the public sector at any level. It is significant to note, however, that the Chamber's Committee on Urban Problems advocated support of the revenue-sharing proposal within the organization, arguing that it would strengthen local government without adding to federal bureaucracy. The organization's general opposition to all government programs won out in the end, however, and the USCC became an active opponent of any form of revenue sharing—going to the extreme of issuing an "action call" to all its affiliated local chambers to pressure their respective senators and representatives to vote against the proposal.[16]

The Democratic party was deeply split over revenue sharing. On the one hand, social welfare liberals wanted to protect their hard-won social and urban programs and they suspected revenue sharing of being the entering wedge of policies that might eventually replace the programs. On the other hand, Democratic mayors from the big cities strongly supported the proposal. The fiscal crisis of the cities was too pressing for the mayors to oppose any proposal that would increase the flow of federal dollars to the cities. They also welcomed the prospect of new dollars that they could spend as they wished.

A report commissioned by the National League of Cities in 1967 estimated that the nation's cities were facing a gap between revenues and expenditures totaling $262 billion over the decade ending in 1975. Less than half of this staggering figure could be expected to be raised through federal grant programs. Even assuming increased municipal tax rates and more state funding, total city debt could be expected to rise by $63 billion by the mid-1970s.[17] The National Urban Coalition predicted in 1971 that the difference between the revenues and expenditures of the nation's cities would reach $94 billion annually by 1976, even assuming passage of the revenue-sharing bill. The needs of the nation's cities were indeed critical.[18]

The seriousness of the fiscal gap was evidenced by major cutbacks in municipal services. The 1971 National Municipal Survey reported, for example, that:

> Pittsburgh recently closed fourteen fire stations; Philadelphia would soon have to reduce various police support units; Cincinnati was cutting back on school libraries, kindergartens, and teaching staffs; Hamtramck [Michigan, in the Detroit area] was so very near bankruptcy that its mayor requested that HEW stop the flow of federal funds—the city could no longer supply the necessary matching funds; Detroit was forced to lay off 600 municipal employees and keep 2,200 authorized positions vacant due to the lack of suf-

ficient funds, and given the plight of the city's treasury, would need an additional 26 million new dollars to keep from backsliding any further—just to stay even; *New York* had 1 million persons on its welfare rolls—requiring annual welfare outlays of 600 million dollars in that category alone.[19]

Though sympathetic to the cities' plight, Democrats in Congress resisted the pressure to approve revenue sharing. With a national election only a year away, the Democratic legislative leadership did not want to give Nixon any type of domestic victory. Such big-city mayors as Pittsburgh's Peter Flaherty and Cleveland's Carl Stokes considered this attitude an "ill-advised . . . partisan reflex"[20] to what they considered a nonpartisan issue.

The tension between the party's congressional leadership and the mayors came to a head in a March 1971 private meeting between the House leadership and the U.S. Conference of Mayors' Legislative Action Committee:

> As one of those in attendance recalls it, New York's Mayor John V. Lindsay had just gotten up to speak, when Majority Leader Hale Boggs (D-La.) suddenly slammed his fist on the desk and shouted: "You don't need to make any points. Revenue sharing is dead. I'll see that it never passes. So let's get on to something else." Flabbergasted, Lindsay slid back into his seat. There was a moment of embarrassed silence—and then a rolling southern drawl rang out from the back of the room. "Hale," said New Orleans Mayor Moon Landrieu, "that's the rudest treatment I have ever witnessed, and I think you better talk about revenue sharing and you better listen. Because, Hale, if you don't start thinking about helping the cities, I want you to know that you'll never be welcome in the city of New Orleans again." Now it was Boggs' turn to be flabbergasted.[21]

In the aftermath of this heated exchange, the congressional leadership began to reassess its position. Lawrence O'Brien, in his capacity as chair of the National Democratic Committee, worked hard to keep the party together. Finally, Representative Wilbur Mills, the powerful chair of the House Ways and Means Committee, dropped his opposition to the concept of revenue sharing. Being a back-burner presidential aspirant, he proposed a plan of his own, a $3.5 billion emergency aid plan for the cities. His move opened the way for other Democrats to change their minds and support the revenue-sharing concept.[22]

Once it became clear that revenue sharing would be adopted, conflict broke out over details. The principal points of contention among the several groups making up the Big Seven centered on the appropriate formulas for dividing the federal monies. Governors, of course, preferred that all money go to the states, and they were willing to back a provision requiring the states to pass through a portion to the cities. Wilbur Mills's plan, which the mayors liked, would have allocated all the money to the cities, with the states left out completely. After several months of haggling, a compromise was reached. All the money would nominally go to states, but two-thirds of the amount would automatically pass through directly to the cities and other local governments without state review. The one-third being allocated to the state governments might be spent on local governments as well, at the states' discretion.

Having emerged moderately victorious, the groups representing the cities now turned to the formula for apportioning money to different kinds of local governments—municipalities, counties, and townships. In this vital matter there was a direct conflict between urbanized and nonurbanized areas. Reflecting the composition of the House Ways and Means Committee, which drafted the bill, the House proposed a bill with a five-factor formula that supposedly balanced allocation between urban and rural local governments. The Senate disagreed with the House allocation procedure. Again reflecting the makeup of the appropriate substantive committee (the Finance Committee, chaired by Russell Long of Louisiana) and the overall small-state bias of the Senate as a body (each state, regardless of population, has two senators), a bill emerged from the Senate with a three-factor formula that reduced the proportion that would go to local governments in urban areas. The Senate formula allocated a higher proportion of the total funds to local governments in the smaller, poorer, rural states of the South and Southwest.[23]

Mayors and congressional representatives from urban areas watched intently as the two bills were sent to the House and Senate Conference Committees. In the end, an artful compromise was worked out. Both the House and Senate formulas were to be used, with the choice between them left to the individual states.[24]

The passage of the State and Local Fiscal Assistance Act of 1972[25] marked the culmination of four years of intense efforts by big city mayors and other government officials to gain largely unrestricted access to the federal treasury. Revenue sharing was passed as a result of four basic political facts: (1) all the groups concerned, primarily those making up the Big Seven, agreed that it was a high-priority measure; (2) a shaky but essential consensus was hammered out with respect to the division of money between the states and their local governments; (3) the president gave it the highest priority; and (4) the Democratic congressional leadership reluctantly agreed to allow the president a domestic policy victory on this issue.[26]

Officials representing every level of the American political system were present in Philadelphia for the outdoor signing ceremony. After the signing, the copy of the new law was inadvertently left behind as everyone scurried off for cocktails. The State and Local Fiscal Assistance Act of 1972 nearly suffered the windy fate of a candy wrapper as it was left unattended: "[A]fter the great ceremony of signing under the shadow of Independence Hall, nobody picked up the bill. And after everybody else had left, it was still sitting there. One of the policemen picked it up and asked: 'Does anybody want this?'"[27]

❖ THE IMPACT OF THE NEW FEDERALISM

The revenue-sharing legislation gave local officials considerable autonomy in spending federal money. Unlike the grant-in-aid programs of the 1960s, such guidelines as had to be followed were minimal and virtually unenforceable in the face of the limits of government accounting procedures. Because of the lack of detailed federal oversight, revenue-sharing dollars were intermingled with other monies that flowed into the treasuries of the more than 39,000 state, county, township, and municipal governments across the nation. As such, they could not be traced beyond the reports filed with the Treasury Department by local officials. They constituted a largely unrestricted, though small, supplement to the tax revenues of state and local governments. In 1974, the $4.5 billion apportioned among 35,077 local governments accounted for an average of 3.1 percent of their revenues for that year.[28]

Local governments, and big cities in particular, reported that they channeled their revenue-sharing funds into conventional service functions rather than into social services. As shown in Table 11-1, cities during fiscal year 1973 spent the largest portion their revenue-sharing funds, 44 percent, on public safety (that is, police and fire services). The next largest portion of the funds, 15 percent, went to transportation. The fifty-five cities with population over 250,000 put even more, 59 percent, into fire and police services. Townships and counties reported that they spent one-third of their revenue-sharing funds on police and fire services.

It was clear that financially strapped big cities used most of their funds just to keep things going, not to offer a greater array of municipal services and amenities.[29] While cities of all sizes, on the average, spent 56 percent of their revenue-sharing funds on day-to-day operations and maintenance, cities with populations of more than 250,000 reported spending 79 percent on this category. Because of their intractable fiscal problems, the five largest cities—New York, Chicago, Los Angeles, Philadelphia, and Detroit—reported spending virtually all their revenue-sharing funds (97 percent) for operations and maintenance related to basic services.[30]

These figures stand in striking contrast to the expenditures reported by the states. Because police and fire services are traditionally considered local matters, the states spent little, 2 percent of the total in 1973, on public safety. The largest expenditure by the states, completely reversing the cities' priorities, went to education.

The enactment of general revenue sharing resulted in a drop in the share of federal assistance to states and localities devoted to "human resources"— those programs that treat individual needs in housing, health, education, welfare payments, nutrition, and the like. Human resources spending accounted for 69 percent of all federal grant-in-aid outlays in 1972, the last year before revenue sharing, but only 59 percent in 1973.[31] States and localities reported spending 35 percent of their revenue-sharing monies on human resources. As a proportion of federal grants to states and localities, unspecified general government services increased sharply from 2 percent to 8 percent of the total.[32]

Most mayors were pleased with the program. The only substantial criticisms of the program were offered by liberal and civil rights groups who objected to the political implications of policy decentralization. The Reverend Jesse Jackson, a Chicago civil rights activist, typified this sentiment when he decried the bias of general revenue sharing against social spending:

> Most statehouses, county courthouses, and city halls are dominated by the more advantaged sectors of the body politic.

TABLE 11-1 REPORTED USE OF GENERAL REVENUE SHARING FUNDS, JANUARY 1972–JUNE 1973

FUNCTION	STATES (50 STATES AND PUERTO RICO)		ALL CITIES (15,785 CITIES)		CITIES OF 250,000 AND OVER (55 CITIES)	
	AMOUNT (IN MILLIONS)	PERCENT	AMOUNT (IN MILLIONS)	PERCENT	AMOUNT (IN MILLIONS)	PERCENT
Public safety	$ 20.0	2	$434.0	44	$208.9	59
Environment/conservation	7.4	1	126.0	13	40.0	12
Transportation	55.6	5	148.7	15	35.2	10
Health	30.7	3	50.3	5	10.5	3
Recreation/culture	3.7	—[a]	76.6	8	27.8	8
Libraries	—[b]	—[b]	10.4	1	3.8	1
Social services	61.2	6	11.7	1	7.8	2
Financial administration	18.5	2	16.0	2	3.8	1
Education	664.3	65	4.7	—[a]	0.2	—[a]
General government	5.9	1	68.7	7	9.3	3
Housing/community development	1.1	—[a]	14.4	2	1.2	—[a]

TABLE 11-1 (*Continued*)

FUNCTION	STATES (50 STATES AND PUERTO RICO)		ALL CITIES (15,785 CITIES)		CITIES OF 250,000 AND OVER (55 CITIES)	
	AMOUNT (IN MILLIONS)	PERCENT	AMOUNT (IN MILLIONS)	PERCENT	AMOUNT (IN MILLIONS)	PERCENT
Economic development	2.2	—a	7.3	1	3.3	1
Other^c	151.9	15	11.7	1	0.4	—a
Operations and maintenance	959.1	94	546.3	56	277.9	79
Capital expenditures	63.4	6	431.2	44	75.2	21

aLess than 0.5 percent.
bState expenditures for libraries included under "other"; "libraries" not a separate reporting category for states.
cIncludes "social development."
Source: Adapted from U.S. Department of the Treasury, Office of Revenue Sharing, *Revenue Sharing: The First Actual Use Reports*, by David A. Caputo and Richard L. Cole (Washington, D.C.: Government Printing Office, 1974), pp. 4, 10–11, 29.

Revenue sharing funds, in contrast to certain categorical aids targeted on the poor as a group, do not flow in sufficient quantities to help those local governments, particularly the major central cities, with extraordinary concentrations of poor people.[33]

The Democratic leadership in Congress continued to feel uneasy about the program, convinced as they were that it threatened to undermine the policy initiatives of the 1960s.[34] Only months after the first checks were sent out by the Revenue Sharing Office, congressional Democrats began to complain about the manner in which the money was being spent. Representative Shirley Chisholm of New York voiced concern "that the program failed to aid the disadvantaged and minority groups."[35] Other members of Congress expressed concern that revenue-sharing funds were not going to people who needed them the most.[36] Despite the offended ideological and political interests of congressional liberals and the Democratic leadership, however, general revenue sharing was extended in 1976. Again it was the unrelenting political pressure applied by the Big Seven, with big city mayors taking the lead, that prodded Congress to act. The U.S. Conference of Mayors adopted a resolution "supporting reenactment of the general revenue sharing program and promising to make renewal a key local issue in the Congressional campaigns."[37]

The 1976 extension kept funding at the same level. Because of inflation, the level of funding, measured in constant dollars, dropped by 17 percent between 1972 and 1979.[38] Instead of extending the program for five and three-quarter years as proposed by the Ford administration, Congress extended revenue sharing for only three and three-quarter years. In 1980, Congress amended the revenue-sharing legislation to eliminate the states as recipients. Through the first half of the 1980s revenue sharing constituted about 1.5 percent of municipal budgets. Under attack by the Reagan Administration, the program was dropped at the end of fiscal year 1986.

❖ THE HOUSING AND COMMUNITY DEVELOPMENT ACT

The Housing and Community Development Act of 1974, which funded the Community Development Block Grant (CDBG) program, was the most important urban policy initiative of the 1970s, and by the 1990s it was by far the most important survivor of the urban policies enacted since World War II. It has consistently enjoyed bipartisan support in both houses of Congress, probably because it seems to have achieved the two objectives, as stated in the original legislation, of "increased private investment and streamlining of all levels of government programming."[39] Democrats and Republicans have often skirmished over details, but the program survived even the budget cuts of the 1980s.

The enduring popularity of the CDBG program can best be understood against the background of more than two decades of federal urban policy that preceded it. The urban renewal and public housing programs funded by the

1949 Housing Act were targeted to older cities with spreading slums. Cities were required to show a need for federal assistance and to submit detailed plans describing how federal dollars would be utilized. By 1955, 96 cities were participating in the programs, rising to 195 cities by 1962.[40] Urban renewal and public housing accounted for almost all the direct federal aid these cities received. The hundreds of smaller cities and suburbs that did not participate in these programs had little or no direct contact with federal administrators.

Federal-local relationships became dramatically more complex in the 1960s. The number of grant programs escalated, and many of these were directly available to public and private agencies at the local level. Most grants bypassed the states entirely, and many of them also bypassed the cities, going directly to community action or nonprofit agencies. There were so many programs and grants went to so many different public and private agencies that it was impossible for most cities even to track the number of programs coming into the city. In 1966, Oakland's mayor was praised by the chair of a Senate committee for compiling a list of the 140 local programs and projects that received federal dollars.[41] It is doubtful that any other mayor could have made such an accounting.

Many of the programs had overlapping or parallel purposes, and that was one more reason for the increasing complexity of dealing with the programs. In addition, each program required different application procedures. Cities were being buried in an avalanche of red tape. In trying to solve their problems with the help of federal dollars, cities were building whole bureaucracies whose sole function seemed to be filling out forms. In 1973 the mayor of Omaha, Nebraska, noted that a significant portion of the city's employees' time was spent documenting the city's share of its matching contribution on federal grants. He was concerned that the pursuit of federal dollars was undermining the ability of the city to define its own priorities and activities. He asked, "Are we going to wake up some morning and find that only 25 percent of city employees are working on city business?"[42]

Even if the Republicans had failed to win the presidency in 1968, initiatives would have been forthcoming to address the grant-in-aid mess. Congressional Democrats and Republicans and federal and local officials were concerned. In 1967, Walter Heller, the chair of the Council of Economic Advisors in both the Kennedy and Johnson administrations, urged that grants be consolidated into "broader categories that will give states and localities more freedom of choice."[43] Charles L. Schultze, the director of the Bureau of the Budget in the Johnson Administration, wrote in 1968 that "The ability of a central staff in Washington to judge the quality and practicality of the thousands of local plans submitted under federal program requirements and to control their performance is severely limited. . . . I believe that greater decentralization in the government's social programs should and will be made."[44]

What Heller, Schultze, and other advocates of reform had in mind was a system whereby individual categorical and project grants—each with its own specified purposes, guidelines, and application and reporting procedures—

could be bundled together with other grants with similar purposes to make up a "block" grant with one simplified procedure for application, reporting, and accounting. As a device for streamlining administrative practices, the idea was attractive. In 1968, Congress had passed the Law Enforcement Assistance Act which consolidated several law enforcement programs in just this way.

Thus, Nixon's call for a New Federalism "struck a responsive chord among a broader segment of American society" than simply those identified with the Republican party.[45] It is important to note, however, that significant partisan differences remained. As revealed in the wrangling over the revenue-sharing program, Democrats favored relatively more federal oversight than did Republicans. They tended to think that most local governments, left to their own devices, would not have the sufficient political will to address problems associated with racial segregation, poverty, and inequality. Struggles over the New Federalism involved far more than questions about the complexity of the intergovernmental system. What was at stake was the issue of whether the national government would serve as an agent of change in the lives of American citizens.

In January 1971, President Nixon proposed that 129 grant programs be consolidated into 6 block grants. These grants, which he labeled "special revenue sharing" to distinguish them from "general revenue sharing" (which would provide federal dollars for purposes to be defined by the recipient government), were to be distributed for spending within six broad areas—urban community development ($2 billion), rural development ($1 billion), job training ($2 billion), law enforcement ($0.5 billion), education ($3 billion), and transportation ($2.6 billion).[46] Urban renewal, Model Cities, and a few other programs were to be folded into one block grant under the Urban Community Development Revenue Sharing Act of 1971. The funds made available to local governments in each of these categories would be automatically distributed according to a formula. Cities would not be required to submit applications or reports, or even to account for expenditures.

The clash of perspectives that pitted the Administration against those who wanted some federal oversight over how federal dollars were spent was brought into bold relief by Nixon's proposals. George Romney, Secretary of the Department of Housing and Urban Development (HUD), justified the Administration's view by asking, "[W]hat is gained by these requirements? There is simply no good reason why a Federal official should have to approve in advance a local community's decision about the shape a new building will have or where a new street will run or on what corner it will put a new gas station."[47] The Democrats in Congress remained unconvinced by such rhetoric. Even local officials thought the remedy of dropping all federal guidelines was too radical a cure for the ills of the grant system. Representatives of the National League of Cities, the U.S. Conference of Mayors, and the National Association of Housing and Redevelopment Officials expressed opposition to the proposals. The executive director of the National Association of Housing and Redevelopment Officials told a Senate committee:

. . . community development block grants must embody national priorities. The primary development objectives of this program should be related to the physical development and redevelopment of the community; the elimination and prevention of slums and blight; the conservation and rehabilitation of the existing housing stock and non-residential facilities; the increased housing opportunities, especially for low and moderate income families; and, the provision of related public facilities and services.[48]

As revealed by the controversy over general revenue sharing, local officials were happy to endorse unrestricted federal grants, and they wanted congressional Democrats to go along with block grants, but only up to a point—they wanted the block grants in addition to, not in replacement of, existing categorical grants that carried national purposes. They were afraid that the Nixon Administration viewed block grants as a way to reduce the overall amount of funding for urban programs. Their suspicion was somewhat justified.[49]

Partisan wrangling between the Administration and the Democratically controlled Congress, and the unraveling of Nixon's presidency because of the unfolding Watergate scandal, doomed most proposals for special revenue sharing. In addition to the State and Local Fiscal Assistance Act of 1972, only two block grants were enacted, the Comprehensive Employment Training Act of 1973 and the Housing and Community Development Act of 1974.

The Housing and Community Development Act was signed into law by President Gerald Ford in August 1974 and took effect in January 1975. It replaced seven major categorical grant programs with a single block grant authorization, called the Community Development Block Grant (CDBG). Categorical grants for water and sewerage systems, neighborhood facilities, land acquisitions, code enforcement, neighborhood development, urban renewal, and Model Cities were folded into the CDBG. Though cities qualified for the program by meeting a specified formula, they were required to submit an application that detailed how the money would be used and were required to submit quarterly reports to the Department of Housing and Urban Development (HUD).

Of the $8.4 billion authorized by Congress for the first three years, 80 percent was to be distributed to cities within standard metropolitan statistical areas (metropolitan areas with a central city of at least 50,000 population). Aside from the central cities, only cities of at least 50,000 people (meaning large suburbs) qualified for funds. Communities were guaranteed that they would receive at least as much in the first three years as they had under the programs that CDBG replaced. The formula for distributing money to the various entitlement communities (so-called because they were "entitled" to a share of funds if they fit the formula) took into account the population of the city, its poverty level, and its percent of overcrowded housing.

This program was significant to the urban areas of the nation, for it facilitated redistribution of grant funds administered by HUD away from the smaller cities and towns toward the larger cities (see Table 11-2). The average city of over 100,000 population registered a 1 percent to 4 percent net increase in federal funding after CDBG grants became available. The annual amounts

---

TABLE 11-2 COMPARISON OF COMMUNITY DEVELOPMENT BLOCK GRANTS AND HUD CATEGORICAL GRANTS

CITY SIZE[a] (1970 CENSUS)	NUMBER OF CITIES	AVERAGE ANNUAL GRANTS (THOUSANDS OF DOLLARS)		
		CATEGORICAL GRANTS (FY 1968–1972)	COMMUNITY DEVELOPMENT BLOCK GRANTS[b] (FY 1974)	PERCENT CHANGE
500,000 and over	26	23,459	23,776	+1
250,000–199,999	30	9,841	9,981	+4
100,000–249,999	97	3,381	3,722	+4
50,000–99,999	232	1,191	1,149	−4
25,000–49,999	455	954	922	−3
10,000–24,999	1,127	600	554	−8
9,999 and under	16,699	332	207	−38

[a]Data exclude Puerto Rico, the Virgin Islands, and Guam, as well as places not considered incorporated by the Bureau of the Census.
[b]SMSA discretionary funds not included.
Source: Adapted from U.S. Department of Housing and Urban Development, Office of Community Planning and Development, Office of Evaluation, *Housing and Community Development Act of 1974, Community Development Block Grant Program: First Annual Report* (Washington, D.C.: Government Printing Office, 1975), p. 142.

---

of grants-in-aid under HUD-administered programs to cities of smaller size fell sharply, with cities of less than 10,000 persons experiencing an average 38 percent loss.

Ironically, the implementation of the Nixon Administration's philosophy of decentralization penalized the Republican party's natural base of support in "middle America"—in the smaller cities, towns, and suburbs where conservative, pro-Republican sentiments predominated. Balancing this, however, was the fact that since any city of 50,000 or more people qualified for a CDBG grant, many cities in the Sunbelt, including those that did not have significant urban problems, qualified for federal funds for the first time. This gave Sunbelt Republicans an incentive to vote for the program.

Unlike general revenue sharing, local governments were required to apply for community development block grant funds even though they were entitled to receive money if they had 50,000 residents or more. The yearly applications asked for statistics that federal administrators could use for reporting purposes and statements of how the recipients intended to use the funds. In additon to the applications, entitlement cities were required to submit a three-year development plan that, among other things, projected "long-range community objectives," included a housing assistance plan for the poor and elderly, respected equal opportunity and environmental protection guidelines, and, most notably, gave "maximum feasible priority" to low- and moderate-income areas.[50] In addition to the pool of so-called entitlement funds, about 20 percent of the total money authorized for the CDBG program was awarded on a competitive basis and in accordance with specific detailed performance standards and review procedures.[51]

The first few months of implementation were characterized by delays and confusion. HUD was in the midst of a bureaucratic shake-up, which made policy-making extremely difficult. For the first several months the HUD bureaucracy repeatedly changed its mind about almost everything: review requirements, forms, and deadlines.[52] Adding to the confusion was President Ford's express opposition to detailed review of applications by HUD. This helped HUD to streamline procedures. By the end of the program's first year, Secretary Carla Hills reported that HUD had reduced the average review period from two years for the programs that the Housing and Community Development Act replaced to forty-nine days, and that applications averaged 50 pages, compared with an average of 1,400 pages for the old urban renewal applications alone.[53] Until the Carter Administration assumed office in January 1977, no meaningful monitoring of spending by communities took place.

The lack of HUD oversight became an issue as soon as Democrat Jimmy Carter became president. In HUD's first annual report on the program, issued early in 1976, HUD stated that 71 percent of all community development funds were allocated to low- and moderate-income priority areas.[54] A year later, in its second annual report (and the first issued under Carter), HUD revised its calculation to represent the actual proportion of lower-income residents in such areas, rather than counting the number of areas defined by municipalities, often inaccurately, as "low and moderate income." In the cities, the percentage of funds being spent in low- and moderate-income areas as now defined by HUD (as areas in which the median income was 80 percent or less than the metropolitan average) averaged only 44.1 percent.[55]

Evidence indicated that southern cities were allocating far more money to affluent areas than was intended by Congress. According to the Southern Regional Council, "the very mixed achievements of southern cities had shown that local diversions from national purpose are not just occasional abuses, but rather form a pattern inherent in the implementation of the Act."[56] That community development funds would be spent in affluent areas was hardly a surprising turn of events, since local political elites exerted a controlling voice in the allocation process. In most local communities poorer residents had little influence. As a result of this circumstance, Little Rock, Arkansas, for example, spent $150,000 of the city's block grant funds to construct a tennis court in an affluent section of town. When questioned about this use of funds, the director of the local Department of Human Resources unpersuasively claimed that "ninety-nine percent of this money is going to low and moderate income areas." But he revealingly continued: "You cannot divorce politics from that much money. We remember the needs of the people who vote because they hold us accountable. Poor people don't vote."[57]

One strategy that local communities employed to make it appear that funds were flowing to priority (low- and moderate-income) areas was to draw their funding district boundaries in such a way as to include affluent and less affluent people within the same areas. Gulfport, Mississippi, went even further when the city council declared the entire city to be a "renewal" area so that it could spend all of its CDBG funds to improve citywide services. It built a new central fire station with the money, claiming, "When you expand fire protection, everybody in every census tract benefits from lower insurance rates," including, ostensibly, the primary target population of the legislation, the low- and moderate-income residents.[58] Whatever gimmick or tortured logic a city resorted to, the outcome was that federal guidelines were generally ignored. Analyses of a number of individual cities demonstrated higher-than-expected CDBG allocations in more affluent areas. A study by the Brookings Institution examined the distribution of the block grants funds in sixty-two cities and found that only 29 percent of the monies were spent in neighborhoods that had lower-than-median family incomes.[59]

The Carter Administration began to crack down on some communities that flagrantly ignored the congressional intent that funds be targeted to low- and moderate-income areas: "HUD Secretary Patricia R. Harris and Assistant Secretary Robert C. Embry . . . told mayors bluntly that they will have to concentrate their CD [Community Development] programs in poorer areas, instead of scattering projects all over town."[60] The Administration examined the applications of the grant recipients more carefully than did the Ford Administration. The impact of the new commitment was soon felt; for example, "An application by Hempstead, New York, was turned down . . . because of the community's poor record on low-income housing projects in order to save a $400,000 grant."[61]

In May 1979, HUD enforced new regulations that required communities to target 75 percent of their CDBG funds to benefit priority areas. But the way such areas were to be defined was left vague. A study of Denver, Colorado, found that a redistribution of funds to middle-income areas had taken place, with poor areas the biggest losers and better-off areas only modest losers.[62] This was because HUD's definition of "priority" areas as "moderate and low income" was, midway through Carter's term, beginning to give way to a new rhetorical goal of using CDBG funds to leverage private investment in the cities.

Even before passage of the Housing and Community Development Act, Anthony Downs, then president of the Real Estate Research Corporation in Chicago and a consultant for HUD, recommended that urban programs be targeted to maximize their potential for securing private investment in deteriorated neighborhoods.[63] Downs encouraged a "triage" strategy, similar to the system used to treat wounded French soldiers during World War I. Medical personnel classified the wounded into three groups: those who were so badly wounded that they could not be saved, who were given painkillers; those who would die without treatment but would probably live with it, to whom maximum treatment was given; and those who would survive even without or with minimal medical care, who were treated when time and resources allowed. Based on the triage concept, Downs recommended that areas within cities be divided into three categories: deteriorated, transitional (or deteriorating), and healthy. Transitional neighborhoods, which he thought would benefit the most from aid, should receive highly visible federal projects to stimulate private investment.[64] In this way national dollars would be used to exert maximum impact in turning around deteriorating areas, and little money would be spent in deteriorated neighborhoods which seemed too far gone, or in healthy neighborhoods which would survive without aid. Urban consultant Roger Starr took the triage analogy even further.[65] Starr advocated the idea of reducing public services and expenditures in blighted urban areas so that resources, both federal and local, could be concentrated in stronger, viable areas.

Local governments generally denied that they used the triage strategy. To admit that such a policy was in force would surely incite protest from the residents of poorer neighborhoods not receiving assistance. It is clear, however, that the triage approach actually was used in many, perhaps most, cities. In a 1974 report to the city planning commission, a St. Louis consulting firm recommended that the city reduce services and discourage investment in severely blighted areas and allocate most of its resources to neighborhoods it defined as declined but salvageable.[66] Commenting in 1978 on the policy recommendations in the consulting firm's report, one of the report's authors wrote: "The Land Reutilization Authority is increasing its holdings and its land banking property [in severely blighted areas] either by chance or design [and] . . . other parts of the strategy memo are now in the process of being implementec Another researcher showed that a similar triage approach underpinned "Chicago 21" plan for redevelopment of the Loop.[68] Community development funds in Denver also were distributed in conformity with a triage strategy. According to two Denver researchers, it would be surprising indeed if this were not the case in other cities, considering the guidelines established by the federal government.[69]

The Carter Administration tried to pursue two often contradictory goals at once. On the one hand, it tried to enforce the legislative intent that CDBG dollars should go primarily to low- and moderate-income areas. On the other hand, it urged cities to emphasize strategies to stimulate private investment. According to HUD secretary Patricia R. Harris, "The specific intent of action programs will be to stimulate new and increased private investment while establishing private sector confidence that will protect current investment."[70] This goal dictated the federal government's implementation of the Housing and Community Development Act. On March 27, 1978, the White House issued a document entitled "New Partnership to Conserve America's Communities."[71] The first section of the document emphasized the loss of private sector investment in the central cities and the fiscal strain placed on local governments as a result of this loss. Thus, "the loss of private sector activity, and of middle-income households, has eroded the tax base of many urban areas."[72] The logic behind the new partnership—and Carter's policy— was that urban programs should be directed toward leveraging private sector investment.

❖ AMENDMENTS TO THE COMMUNITY DEVELOPMENT ACT

By the end of 1975 there was growing concern, particularly among the representatives of big cities, that older cities in fiscal and social stress were destined to receive a declining share of CDBG funds over time. From a level of nearly 83 percent of the community development monies allocated in fiscal year 1975, the Illinois Bureau of the Budget projected that only 60 percent would go to older cities of the North by 1980.[73] By 1980, Newark would lose over 52 percent of its block grant allocation compared to 1975, Philadelphia nearly 45 percent, Detroit 22 percent, and Rochester, New York, almost 70 percent. The "lost" money would be largely reallocated to the growing cities of the Sunbelt. Dallas would receive a huge 549 percent increase in its CDBG block grant by 1980, Fort Lauderdale 536 percent, and Phoenix 727 percent.[74]

Why was this the case? It turned out that the formula for distributing CDBG funds, as adopted in the 1974 legislation, was unintentionally biased against the declining older cities. The formula distributed money on the basis of three weighted factors: It assigned equal weights for a city's population and the extent of overcrowded housing; plus a double weight for the city's level of poverty. The older cities were going to receive less CDBG money over time simply because they were rapidly losing population. Sunbelt cities, in contrast, would qualify for more money every year because they were growing rapidly. The other factors in the formula could not counterbalance the population factor, since levels of poverty in southern and southwestern cities ran at or above the national average and the extent of housing overcrowding was about the same in the older cities of the Frostbelt and the newer cities of the Sunbelt.

To reverse the bias in the distribution of funds, several groups initiated efforts to have Congress revise the CDBG formula. In response to requests from governors of fourteen northern industrial states who attended the Conference on Federal Economic Policies in October 1976, an Illinois agency designed an alternative formula to benefit the older urbanized areas.[75] Similarly, the Brookings Institution and HUD's Office of Policy Development and Research proposed changes in the allocation criteria to aid the declining Frostbelt cities.[76] The group of representatives who made up the Northeast-Midwest Congressional Coalition in the House lined up behind a new formula that would assign 20 percent weight to the degree of population loss in a city, 30 percent weight to the city's poverty level, and 50 percent weight to the age of the city's housing stock (defined as the percentage of housing built before 1939). Obviously, two of these factors applied only to older cities: They were losing population, and most of their housing had been built before 1939. This formula gave maximum advantage to the Frostbelt cities, and HUD selected it as its recommended replacement for the old formula precisely for that reason.[77]

The introduction of the legislation to revise the formula ignited a bitter political conflict. Two California representatives introduced amendments to retain the old formula because it provided more money to cities in their districts than the new one would.[78] The Southern Growth Policies Board, an organization representing state officials and businesses in the South, mounted a well-organized lobbying campaign against the revision.

Ultimately, the struggle within Congress was resolved by a compromise. The House passed legislation in May 1977 intended to increase dramatically the community development entitlement funds flowing to the distressed cities of the North. Under the HUD-sponsored amendments, New York City stood to receive a 50 percent increase in its entitlement for 1978 and about a 42 percent increase ($100 million) in 1980.[79] Several older cities expected to double their entitlements. To make the increases in northern cities politically palatable, the new entitlements to these cities were allocated from a $1 billion per year addition to appropriations so that the Sunbelt cities would not be total losers. The most important compromise, however, was the acceptance of a "dual formula," whereby cities could select the original 1974 formula or the new one, depending on which brought them more money.

As a further aid to distressed cities, Congress approved the Urban Development Action Grants (UDAG) program. Unlike the entitlement CDBG grants, these funds required applications to accomplish particular projects, and they were explicitly designed to leverage private investments. Over the years, UDAG grants were used to build festival malls such as the Union Station in St. Louis and Harborplace in Baltimore; to expand convention centers; to build public infrastructure that would stimulate business and residential investments (such as improving streets with new lighting, landscaping, and fountains); to repair historic buildings; and to support neighborhood improvements. In July 1977 the community development amendments and the UDAG grants were approved by Congress and sent to the White House for President Carter's signature. As a result of the new legislation, cities in the Northeast received an average 77 percent increase in fiscal year 1980 over the amount of community development funds they would have received under the 1974 formula. Cities in the Midwest received 66 percent more in funding. In contrast, cities of the South were held to an 8 percent increase and cities in the West to a 14 percent increase.[80]

❖ ERODING SUPPORT FOR URBAN PROGRAMS

As a Democratic president, Jimmy Carter could have been expected to respond favorably to the cities of the northern industrial states. Voters in these cities traditionally voted solidly Democratic, and they helped give Carter his margin of victory in several states in the 1976 election. Accordingly, the Carter Administration tried to develop policies responsive to urban constituencies. The President pushed an amendment to the revenue-sharing program through Congress that increased allocations to distressed cities by adding an "excess unemployment" factor to the distribution formula.[81] He successfully sought increases in Community Development Block Grant funding. Large increases were legislated for Comprehensive Employment Training Act (CETA) programs, which gave money to local training centers and to local governments to put people to work repairing parks and public facilities.

The Urban Development Action Grant (UDAG) program of 1977 was a major accomplishment.

Of particular importance to fiscally distressed cities were several counter-cyclical and antirecessionary programs. Democrats were successful in passing the Anti-Recession Fiscal Assistance Act over President Ford's veto in July 1976. The program distributed aid to cities with particularly high unemployment rates and was designed as an emergency measure to help distressed cities avert layoffs, maintain service levels, and avoid tax increases. It was scheduled to end on September 30, 1977, by which time, it was hoped, the recession's impact on these cities would have run its course. But in 1977 the Carter Administration recommended that the Act be extended and funds increased. In the Intergovernmental Anti-Recession Act of 1977, $2.25 billion was added and antirecession assistance to city governments was extended to September 30, 1978.[82]

These programs were heavily weighted in favor of distressed cities. Five cities—New York, Philadelphia, Detroit, Chicago, and Los Angeles—received 13 percent of the Anti-Recession Fiscal Assistance funds. (Together these cities made up 8 percent of the U.S. population.)[83] By far the smallest allocations went to Sunbelt cities. Dallas, for example, received 4 cents per capita through the program and Houston $1.56, compared to Newark's allocation amounting to $39.34 per capita.[84]

The various antirecession and public employment programs reversed the trend begun during the Nixon Administration, whereby programs increasingly benefited Sunbelt cities. This pattern is shown in Table 11-3. Between fiscal years 1972 and 1975, federal grants to eight Frostbelt cities increased by an average 62 percent, while grants to nine Sunbelt cities rose by 238 percent. This happened because revenue sharing and CDBG grants went to cities on the basis of a formula rather than through an application showing "need." Between 1975 and 1978, however, grants went up faster in the Frostbelt cities (133 percent) than in the Sunbelt cities (83 percent). The federal grants to distressed cities were extremely important to their financial well-being. In 1977, because of new federal funds, revenues in twenty-seven of the largest cities exceeded expenditures by 3.2 percent. In contrast, these cities had accumulated an average per city debt of $28.3 million in 1975 and $150.7 million in 1976.[85]

For a variety of reasons, in 1978 President Carter made an about-face in his urban policy. The policy change can be traced to political pressures to curb overall federal spending. In 1978, California voters passed Proposition 13, which sharply reduced local property taxes. The gathering strength of a tax revolt across the nation helped shape a mood of fiscal conservatism in Congress and a go-slow approach in the White House.[86] The most important proposal Carter placed before Congress in 1978 was the National Development Bank, which would have made loans and some limited grants available to depressed urban and rural areas for the purpose of promoting local economic development. In part because of concerns over cost, this proposal failed to make it out of a conference committee after passing the House and Senate in a much amended form.[87]

TABLE 11-3   COMPARATIVE GROWTH OF TOTAL FEDERAL GRANTS TO
SELECTED FROSTBELT AND SUNBELT CITIES, 1972–1978

CITY	PERCENT INCREASE		
	1972–1975	1975–1978	1972–1978
Frostbelt			
Baltimore	146	68	314
Boston	9	81	97
Buffalo	107	154	427
Chicago	75	145	329
Cleveland	184	131	558
Detroit	26	87	136
Philadelphia	59	151	297
St. Louis	123	248	674
Mean for 8 Frostbelt cities	62	133	354
Sunbelt			
Atlanta	269	53	465
Birmingham	346	119	877
Dallas	405	74	777
Houston	267	88	591
Jacksonville	390	34	554
Louisville	68	86	214
New Orleans	209	90	488
Oklahoma City	237	107	599
Phoenix	423	94	689
Mean for 9 Sunbelt Cities	238	83	584

Source: Adapted from Paul R. Dommel, "Block Grants for Community Development:
Decentralized Decision-Making," in *Fiscal Crisis in American Cities: The Federal Response,*
ed. L. Kenneth Hubbell (Cambridge, Mass.: Ballinger, 1979), p. 254. Copyright 1979,
Ballinger Publishing Company. By permission.

In the last year of the Carter Administration, attention turned away from
urban policy toward the problems of the national economy. A decline in manufacturing jobs and an acceleration in foreign investment and imports became
prominent themes in Carter's 1980 campaign speeches. There were no new
urban policy proposals. Indeed, it was beginning to appear that there would
be no further initiatives and, possibly, even a retrenchment. After Carter's
election in 1976 Mayor Kenneth A. Gibson of Newark had spoken for many
Democratic mayors when he remarked that "We have every reason to believe
that this is the beginning of a new relationship between the White House and

the nation's mayors."[88] The new relationship, however, proved to be short-lived. Even if Carter had won the 1980 presidential race, it is doubtful that any significant urban programs would have emerged.

❖ URBAN POLICY IN THE REAGAN ADMINISTRATION

In a press conference held in October 1981, President Ronald Reagan suggested that the residents of cities where unemployment was high should "vote with their feet" and move to more prosperous areas of the country.[89] His remark ignited an instant controversy, but it could well have been (although it probably wasn't) inspired by the recommendations of a presidential commission appointed by his predecessor, Jimmy Carter. In a report issued in 1980 the Presidential Commission on the National Agenda for the Eighties, which had been appointed by Carter to review urban policy and recommend policy changes, urged that the national government stop helping cities. The Commission emphasized that there should be policies to promote national economic growth, but that these should be neutral about the location of that growth:

> It may be in the best interest of the nation to commit itself to the promotion of locationally neutral economic and social policies rather than spatially sensitive urban policies that either explicitly or inadvertently seek to preserve cities in their historical roles.[90]

The commission reasoned that economic processes affecting older cities were irreversible:

> [T]he economy of the United States, like that of many of the older industrial societies, has for years now been undergoing a critical transition from being geographically-based to being deconcentrated, decentralized, and service-based. In the process, many cities of the old industrial heartland . . . are losing their status as thriving industrial capitals. . . .[91]
>
> The historical dominance of more central cities will be diminished as certain production, residential, commercial, and cultural functions disperse to places beyond them.[92]

The Commission recommended that the federal government let this process of decay in some areas and growth in others take its natural course. The Commission noted that cities adapt and change in response to economic and social forces. This process of adaptation, said the commission, should be facilitated, not altered, by governmental policy:

> Ultimately, the federal government's concern for national economic vitality should take precedence over the competition for advantage among communities and regions.[93]

> To attempt to restrict or reverse the processes of change—for whatever noble intentions—is to deny the benefits that the future may hold for us as a nation.[94]

The recommendations by Carter's Commission and the policies subsequently pursued by the Reagan Administration constituted a revolutionary change in philosophy: For the first time since national urban policy began to emerge in the 1930s, the judgment was made that individual cities were not valuable cultural, social, or economic entities *except to the degree* to which they contributed to a healthy national economy. Three University of Delaware researchers characterized the new policies as "a form of Social Darwinism applied to cities as it has been previously applied, with pernicious consequences, to individuals and social classes."[95] Cities would survive if they could manage to regenerate their local economies. Otherwise, they would be allowed to wither away.

The Reagan Administration set about sharply reducing federal urban aid, proclaiming that "the private market is more efficient than federal program administrators in allocating dollars."[96] In line with its ideology and its political base in suburbs and the Sunbelt, the Reagan Administration sought to withdraw from urban policy and restore state control over the urban programs that remained. In Reagan's view, federal urban programs improperly finance

> activities that logically and traditionally have been the responsibilities of state and local governments. . . . Individuals, firms, and state and local governments, properly unfettered, will make better decisions than the federal government acting for them. . . . it is state governments that are in the best position to encourage metropolitan-wide solutions to problems that spill over political boundaries . . . and to tackle the economic, financial, and social problems that affect the well-being of the state as it competes with others to attract and retain residents and businesses.[97]

The Administration intended to devolve the "maximum feasible responsibility for urban matters to the states and through them to their local governments." Cities were instructed to improve their ability to compete in a struggle for survival in which "state and local governments will find it is in their interests to concentrate on increasing their attractiveness to potential investors, residents, and visitors."[98] Thus, urban policy was built on the assumption that free enterprise would provide a bounty of jobs, incomes, and neighborhood renewal, and that such local prosperity would make federal programs unnecessary.

The Reagan Administration moved rapidly to reduce or eliminate all urban policies that tried to help distressed cities. The Community Development Block Grant (CDBG) and Urban Development Action Grant (UDAG) programs won a reprieve from being drastically reduced in the 1983 budget, and so did revenue sharing. Budget Director David Stockman wanted to kill these programs altogether; he had previously attempted to write them out of the budget in 1981. But the Administration, bending to the weakened but still viable urban lobby—represented principally by governors and mayors, quite a few of them Republican—backed off. The urban lobby groups came away relieved that the budget cuts were less drastic than they had feared. Only two years later, however, the Administration was able to eliminate most urban programs.

The Reagan Administration's ability to force budget cuts on a Democratically controlled Congress can be explained by reference to two factors. First, the Administration succeeded in focusing the public debate over domestic policy on tax cuts, decentralization, and economic growth. Second, the growing population of the Sunbelt and the suburbs created a new electoral arithmetic that severely weakened the political influence of city voters and their representatives.

❖ THE FEDERAL RETREAT

On February 18, 1981, President Reagan proposed a massive tax cut to stimulate the economy. This package, which would reduce federal revenues by $54 billion in 1982 alone, called for a 10 percent reduction each year for three years for all individual taxpayers, plus accelerated depreciation of capital assets and other liberalized tax write-offs for corporations. Congress was at first cool to the idea, but it soon became apparent to Democratic lawmakers they could improve their own reelection prospects if they offered "improvements" that would be appealing to corporate campaign contributors and to individual constituents. By the time individual legislators had outbid one another to satisfy their own constituency groups, the revenue losses from the package promised to be so staggering that some White House advisers wanted to kill the bill.[99] Reagan, however, wanted it passed, and he lobbied hard for it, even going on television to appeal for expressions of popular support.[100]

Reagan signed the Economic Recovery Tax Act of 1981 on August 13, 1981, asserting that it was "a turnaround of almost a half a century of . . . excessive growth in government bureaucracy, government spending, government taxing."[101] In its final version the Act reduced individual tax rates by 25 percent over three years and also substantially reduced business tax liability. The revenue losses to the federal treasury were huge. In just the first two years, $128 billion in revenue was lost to the treasury, and the total losses by 1987 amounted to more than $1 trillion.[102] The 1981 tax cuts in combination with increased expenditures for defense accounted for virtually all of the huge budget deficits that dominated debates about domestic policy throughout the 1980s and into the 1990s.

The Tax Reform Act of 1986 further slashed federal revenues and sharply reduced the capacity of governments at all levels to collect increased revenues in step with improvements in the economy. The 1986 legislation was sold as a fundamental "reform" of the tax code. Most Americans had the impression that the main purpose was to simplify a maddeningly complex tax system. This promise was never fulfilled. Instead, Congress collapsed graduated tax rates in the code, which increased as a taxpayer's income went up, to three basic rates: 15 percent, 28 percent, and 32 percent. The tax rates were indexed to inflation, so that over time taxpayers would not slide into a higher tax bracket unless their incomes rose faster than the inflation rate. There were two dramatic effects. First, the new law almost eliminated the feature of the tax code that had historically allowed the federal government to collect increased taxes whenever incomes went up, either in real terms or through inflation. This change had the effect of institutionalizing the tax cuts adopted in 1981 by making it difficult for federal revenues to rise, even in a good economy, to reduce budget deficits. Only cuts in expenditures or increases in tax rates could accomplish that.

The second effect of the Tax Reform Act was that tax rates fell only modestly or not at all for most taxpayers, but plunged drastically for the rich. In subsequent years the constant talk about rising deficits, the savings and loan scandal, and a general perception that taxes hit the middle class more than anyone else helped fuel a tax revolt. George Bush won the presidency in 1988 partly with the phrase, "Read my lips: no new taxes." The political atmosphere for increased federal government spending on pressing social problems such as education, housing, health and welfare was thoroughly poisoned.

Overall domestic spending during the Reagan years rose both in actual and in constant dollars (controlling for inflation), though at a sharply reduced rate from previous decades. While many programs beneficial to the middle class were protected from cuts, those for the poor were hit hard. In February 1981, President Reagan told Congress that a "social safety net of programs" would remain in place for "those who through no fault of their own must depend on the rest of us."[103] This promise was, Reagan's budget director later admitted, a political ploy to build support for program reductions.[104] Broad entitlement programs with middle-class recipients, such as the old-age and survivors' benefits funded through the Social Security Act of 1935, veterans' benefits, and Medicare, were affected only marginally. In contrast, deep cuts and new eligibility restrictions were imposed in public assistance programs for poor people. Medicaid, which was available through the states to welfare recipients, was reduced through tighter eligibility requirements. Enrollment in Aid to Families with Dependent Children (AFDC) fell by half a million. A million people lost food stamps. It became harder to get unemployment benefits; whereas three-fourths of the unemployed received benefits during the recession of 1975, only 45 percent were able to qualify during the 1982–1983 recession.[105]

Since a disproportionate share of people in poverty lived in older cities, reductions in social programs hit the cities particularly hard. The capacity of states and localities to make up for federal cuts was severely curtailed by the fact that federal grants-in-aid to local governments were reduced even more sharply than programs for individuals. From 1982 to 1987 grants-in-aid to

states and localities fell sharply. These were the first reductions of consequence in grants-in-aid expenditures since the 1940s.

As shown in Table 11-4, grant programs fell by more than 14 percent (in
constant dollars) from 1980 to 1984 and by an additional 3.5 percent from
1985 to 1987.[106] The 1981 budget act reduced spending for categorical grants
by 30 percent. In 1982, Reagan persuaded Congress to consolidate seventy-six
categorical grants into nine block grants in health, social services, education,
and community development. In the process funding was reduced by 20 percent. Previously, many of these grants went directly to local governments;
now all of them went to the states, to be distributed as they saw fit. Because
the states tended to spread funds broadly across a great many jurisdictions and
to give little priority to distressed communities, the cities were "one of the
clearest losers of federal funds" under these block grants.[107] A 1982 study by
the Senate Joint Economic Committee showed that distressed cities were not
only losing a larger absolute amount and a higher percentage of federal aid
than the cities that were better off.[108] Cities, whose economies were already in
trouble before the cuts were being compelled to endure the highest proportional reductions in federal assistance.

Major urban programs were drastically reduced and some were eliminated
in the 1980s (see Table 11-5). Overall spending dropped from $6.1 billion in
fiscal year 1981 to $5.2 billion in fiscal year 1984. The $5.2 billion spent in
1984 amounted to a decline in spending of almost 20 percent, when inflation is
taken into account. By the 1989 budget year, money for urban programs was
cut to $4.4 billion—a further reduction of about 40 percent when the effects of
inflation are considered. In fiscal year 1986 the revenue-sharing program
ended, and for the first time since the early 1960s a majority of general-purpose governments in the United States received no direct federal assistance
whatsoever.

Other budget cuts also affected the cities. Most subsidies for the construction of public housing were eliminated. Only 10,000 new units a year were
authorized after 1983, compared with the 111,600 new or rehabilitated units
authorized for 1981 alone.[109] Urban mass transit grants were reduced 28 percent
from 1981 to 1983 and were cut another 20 percent by 1986. The programs of
the Comprehensive Employment and Training Act (CETA) were eliminated
entirely after the 1983 budget. The countercyclical urban aid programs initiated
under President Carter ended early in the Reagan Administration.

❖ REDUCING THE CAPACITY OF STATE AND LOCAL GOVERNMENTS

In the early 1970s, President Nixon conceived his New Federalism as a device
to improve the management of federal programs. Block grants were described
as mechanisms for streamlining and simplifying the grant-in-aid system and
also for giving local governments more flexibility in spending federal dollars.

TABLE 11-4   GROWTH RATES IN FEDERAL AID SPENDING, SELECTED FISCAL YEARS 1955–1987

FISCAL YEAR	CURRENT DOLLARS		1972 DOLLARS	
	AMOUNT (IN BILLIONS)	PERCENT CHANGE	AMOUNT (IN BILLIONS)	PERCENT CHANGE
1955	3.2	—	5.6	—
1959	6.5	103	10.0	79
1960	7.0	—	10.8	—
1964	10.1	44	14.7	36
1965	10.9	—	15.5	—
1969	20.3	86	24.2	56
1970	24.0	—	27.0	—
1974	43.4	82	37.9	40
1975	49.8	—	39.2	—
1979	82.9	66	48.1	23
1980	91.5	10.4	48.2	0.2
1981	94.8	3.6	46.1	−4.4
1982	88.2	−7.0	40.4	−12.4
1983	92.5	4.9	40.7	0.7
1984	97.6	5.5	41.3	1.5
1980–1984	—	6.6	—	−14.2
1985	105.8	8.6	43.1	4.4
1986	112.4	6.1	44.5	3.0
1987	108.4	−3.6	41.7	−6.3
1985–1987	—	2.4	—	−3.5

Sources: Based on U.S. Advisory Commission on Intergovernmental Relations, *Significant Features of Fiscal Federalism, 1985–86*, M-146 (Washington, D.C.: Government Printing Office, 1986), p. 19; U.S. Office of Management and Budget, *Budget of the United States Government, Historical Tables, Fiscal Year 1989* (Washington, D.C.: Government Printing Office, 1990), Table 12.1.

The Reagan Administration had something different in mind when it proposed reforms in the intergovernmental aid system. With his block grants, Reagan was trying to take, in his words, "a step toward total withdrawal of the federal government from education, health and social services programs which . . . are properly the responsibility of state and local governments."[110] Block grants, in other words, were a device not for administrative reform, as

TABLE 11-5   FEDERAL OUTLAYS FOR URBAN AND REGIONAL PROGRAMS TO STATE AND LOCAL GOVERNMENTS, FISCAL YEARS 1981–1988 (IN BILLIONS OF DOLLARS)

	FY 1981	FY 1984	FY 1987 (EST.)	FY 1988 (EST.)
Community Development Block Grants	4.0	3.8	3.1	2.6
Urban Development Action Grants	0.4	0.5	0.4	0.3
Economic Development Administration and Appalachian Regional Commission	0.7	0.5	0.3	0.2
Other community and regional development	1.0	0.4	0.7	0.4
Total	6.1	5.2	4.5	3.6

Source: U.S. Office of Management and Budget, *Budget of the United States Government, Historical Tables, Fiscal Year 1987* (Washington, D.C.: Government Printing Office, 1986), Table 12.3.

they had been during the Nixon Administration, but for a political revolution that would, Reagan hoped, result in the national government's eventually abandoning the responsibilities it had assumed in the New Deal years and in the 1960s and 1970s.

In his State of the Union address of January 27, 1982, President Reagan unveiled a revolutionary "New Federalism" that would, he said, return power to states and communities. The president outlined a ten-year program for turning over to the states $47 billion in federal programs, all to be accomplished by 1991. In fiscal year 1984, Aid to Families with Dependent Children and Food Stamps, at a combined cost of $16.5 billion, would be turned over to the states. As a "bribe," the federal government would in turn assume all costs of the Medicaid program, which could save the states $19.1 billion. From fiscal year 1984 through 1988, the states would go through a voluntary transition period, assuming responsibility for up to forty-three grant programs, including the CDBG, UDAG, and other urban programs. To help them pay for these programs, a trust fund would be established, composed of federal excise taxes on gasoline, tobacco, alcohol, and telephones, plus part of the federal "excess profits" tax on oil. After fiscal year 1988, the trust fund would be phased out over four years, leaving the states with full responsibility to fund and administer the programs, if they saw fit.

David Cohen, the former president of Common Cause, noted that about half of the state legislatures did not have the staff and expertise that were needed for the types of programs they were being asked to assume. Based on all prior experiences, the states would not treat cities well. A 1982 Conference of Mayors report stated, "The history of city-state relations has too often been one of neglect of city needs by the state."[111] A former Atlanta mayor pointed out that "at best, there are only four states—Massachusetts, Michigan, Minnesota, and California—that have shown responsibility on urban issues. The other forty-six have shown either neglect or downright hostility."[112]

Decentralization of programs would have resulted in fewer programs, not a replacement of the federal effort, and this was the result that Reagan actually wanted. Decentralization was a Trojan horse to reduce the scope of government not only at the national but also at state and local levels. He thought that citizen pressure at these lower levels of government would prevent those governments from funding programs at levels comparable to the federal government: "When tax increases are proposed in state assemblies and city councils," he said, "the average citizen is better able to resist and to make his influence felt."[113]

Congress soundly rejected Reagan's New Federalism. Important features of the 1986 Tax Reform Act, however, were expressly designed to make it more difficult for states and localities to support activist government. When the tax rates were reduced to three levels in the federal code, with a 32 percent cap on the highest rate, most states similarly revised their state income tax laws; this change was irresistible since most state tax forms had, in the past, been modeled on the federal forms. Thus, the states almost automatically reduced their taxes when the federal government did. In addition, as originally proposed, the 1986 Act would have eliminated the federal deduction for state and local taxes and eliminated any taxpayer exclusion of interest earned on tax-exempt municipal bonds. The first feature would have resulted in huge pressures on state and local governments to lower tax levels and simultaneously would have increased federal tax revenues (which would, presumably, be used to reduce deficits and finance the arms build-up). The second feature would have radically reduced the capacity of state and local governments to sell tax-exempt bonds (which could be sold to investors at lower interest rates than corporate bonds). Tax exempt bonds had, since before the 1930s, been used to build roads, bridges, schools, airports, water and sewer facilities, and other public infrastructure.

State and local officials furiously lobbied for the removal of these two features. The first was removed, but the elimination of taxpayer deductions for state and local sales and personal property taxes was retained, increasing federal revenues by $17 billion over a five-year period.[114] And a state-by-state cap was imposed on the volume and purposes of tax-exempt municipal bonds. By the early 1990s the effects of federal cutbacks and tax code changes had reverberated throughout the intergovernmental system. State and local governments found themselves deeply in debt, forcing them to slash funding for schools, higher education, and other programs. (We discuss these fiscal crises in more detail in Chapter 12.)

❖ URBAN ENTERPRISE ZONES

Even against this background, it would be inaccurate to say that the Reagan Administration had no urban policy. Indeed, its policy was clear: Cities were instructed to cut taxes and offer tax abatements and other incentives to spur local economic growth. The one specific federal program proposed to help cities do this was urban enterprise zones. In June 1980, two New York representatives, Jack Kemp, a conservative Republican who later served as President Bush's secretary of Housing and Urban Development, and Robert Garcia, a liberal Democrat from New York City, introduced the Urban Jobs and Enterprise Zone Act into Congress. A year later they introduced a revised version of the bill.

The 1980 bill proposed to cut property taxes in designated zones by 20 percent over a four-year period, to allow depreciation of business property over a three-year period (compared to five years elsewhere), to eliminate federal capital gains taxes, to lower corporate taxes, and to reduce employer social security tax contributions. All of this was designed to encourage businesses to locate in depressed urban areas. In 1981 the proposed legislation was amended to require a state and local commitment to lower their tax levels. It also dropped the accelerated depreciation allowance and the social security tax reduction. As a substitute, businesses in the zones were to be allowed up to $1,500 in tax credits for each of their employees.

Deregulation provisions were included in both bills. In the 1981 bill participating cities would be required to waive and relax various building codes, zoning requirements, and other regulations—the specific package to be proposed by each city. The Administration pushed for a waiver of federal minimum wage laws, but Garcia adamantly opposed this recommendation.

Beginning in the fall of 1981, Secretary of Commerce Malcolm Baldridge chaired a study group, composed mostly of HUD and Treasury staff members, with the purpose of modifying the Kemp-Garcia bill. The Administration's own proposal, announced by President Reagan on March 23, 1982, proposed the creation of twenty-five zones a year for three years. Businesses in these zones would have 75 percent or more of their corporate income tax forgiven, would pay no capital gains tax, and would pay no tariffs or duties in areas also designated by the federal government as "free trade zones." Employers in the zones would be given tax credits. No relief from minimum wage laws would be granted. The proposal also required states and localities to reduce regulations and support privatization or contracting out of some neighborhood services, such as refuse and leaf collection.

Enterprise zones hardly constituted a comprehensive new urban policy. First, relatively few zones were proposed—after three years, seventy-five in all. The total cost to the federal government was estimated to be only $310 million in the first year, to peak at $930 million after four years. Perhaps even more significant, the incentives offered to businesses in the zones were actually rather inconsequential. According to Rochelle Stansfield of the *National*

Journal, "federal taxes are far down the list of factors involved about where to locate." The tax relief promised in the zones proposal was expected to help "at the margins."[115] Further, the enterprise zones would not generate additional business volume for the nation; they would only redistribute businesses from one location to another. The President's proposal, it seemed, was more symbolic than substantial.

President Reagan promised to push for passage of urban enterprise zones legislation during the special session of Congress in November and December of 1982. In the press of other business the legislation was not even discussed. Finally, on March 7, 1983, the president sent his Urban Enterprise Zone Act to Congress, claiming that the legislation was a sharp departure from past policy:

> [E]nterprise zones are a fresh approach for promoting economic growth in the inner cities. The old approach relied on heavy government subsidies and central planning. A prime example was the model cities program in the 1960s, which concentrated government programs, subsidies and regulations in distressed urban areas. The enterprise zone approach is to remove government barriers, bring individuals to create, produce and earn their own wages and profits.[116]

No matter what claims the president made, the legislation was not a "fresh approach," but a logical development from past policies, Democratic as well as Republican, that stressed the role of government in subsidizing private investment. All through the Reagan years, the enterprise zones idea surfaced from time to time, but it was never pushed by the Administration. After George Bush's election in 1988, the idea continued to receive an occasional nudge from the President or HUD, but it did not surface as a meaningful item on the President's legislative agenda until after the Los Angeles riot of April 29–May 3, 1992.

Measured by the number of deaths and injuries, property damage, and the response required to reestablish order, the riot was the country's worst episode of civil disorder in the twentieth century.[117] Many people thought that the riot could be used as an opportunity to call attention to the problems of urban America. Election-year politics, however, made such a response difficult. Democratic candidate Bill Clinton initially blamed President Bush for ignoring the cities, but soon muted his criticisms. On Monday, May 5, Bush's press spokesman, Marlin Fitzwater, said the Great Society's programs of the 1960s were to blame. That same day, however, President Bush proposed an emergency aid package. In June, Congress passed $1.3 billion in emergency aid that allocated $500 million for summer jobs, $382 million for loans to businesses damaged or destroyed in the riot areas, and some flood relief for the city of Chicago.

Through the summer and early fall of 1992 Congress worked on a larger, permanent urban aid bill. A version was finally approved by the House on October 6 and the Senate on October 8. The legislation would have created twenty-five urban and twenty-five rural enterprise zones, financed "weed and seed" programs that combined enhanced law enforcement with job training and education programs. The bulk of the legislation, however, was made up of an array of items that had nothing to do with cities. There was a provision for liberalized (tax-free) retirement accounts that would benefit upper-income people and a provision for the repeal of luxury taxes on yachts, furs, jewels, and planes (Democrats backed this amendment as enthusiastically as did Republicans). It was estimated that of the $30 billion that the bill would cost over five years, only $6 billion would be used to help depressed areas in cities.[118]

In the 1992 campaign Bush made a pledge that, if reelected, he would not sign any legislation that raised taxes. Congressional leaders delayed sending the urban aid bill to the White House so that the President could sign it after the election. They pointed out that tax increases in the bill were offset by an equal volume of tax reductions. Nevertheless, Bush vetoed the legislation, asserting that it was contaminated by pork-barrel amendments.

The fate of the urban aid bill revealed the weak political position of cities. The boost given to the urban agenda by the riot proved to be short-lived. Few congressional representatives are elected from districts located wholly within cities. None of the presidential candidates, Bush, Clinton, or H. Ross Perot, paid significant attention to urban issues during the campaign. Despite this fact, cities were certain to receive some important benefits from a Clinton administration. Public works and infrastructure development occupied center stage in Clinton's economic stimulus proposals. The reconstruction of bridges, roads, and other infrastructure would have a significant impact on inner cities because the nation's most severely deteriorated public infrastructure is located there.

❖ THE WANING POLITICAL INFLUENCE OF CITIES

Abandoning urban policy made political sense for the Republicans. Party leaders had long sought to capitalize on white suburbanites' disaffection from Democratic civil rights and antipoverty policies. Reagan took advantage of this sentiment in 1980 and 1984. Jimmy Carter and Walter Mondale carried the vote of large cities by substantial margins, while Reagan won slightly more than a third of the big city vote in each election. Reagan, however, carried the suburban and small city vote by a margin of 53 percent to 37 percent in 1980 and 57 percent to 42 percent in 1984. Since only 12 percent of the 1984 national vote was cast in large cities and 55 percent was cast in suburbs and small cities, the Republican advantage was devastatingly effective.[119] To illustrate, Mondale carried 65 percent of 173,000 votes in the city of St. Louis in 1984, while Reagan carried 64 percent of 308,000 votes in suburban St. Louis County.[120] Coupled with the antitax core of Reagan support, the Administration had strong incentives to abandon forms of urban revitalization that required federal activism or intrusions on suburban autonomy.

Mayors are aware of their rapid decline in influence in both political parties. On February 28 and March 1, 1987, the National Municipal League met in Washington, D.C., to try to amplify their influence in the 1988 presidential elections. They established an "Election "88 Task Force," designed to force candidates to promise programs important to local governments.[121] Their efforts were in vain. Even in the Democratic party, the political influence of central cities has melted away. In 1968, the Democrats used the word city twenty-three times in the party platform adopted at their presidential nominating convention. It did not appear even once in the 1988 platform. The substitute term, clearly a recognition of the power of the suburbs, was "hometown America." At the 1988 GOP convention, rural, but not urban, development rated a subcommittee in the platform debates. The omission of an urban focus in the platform was made official by this language: "Urban America is center stage in our country's future. That is why we address its problems and potential throughout this platform, rather than limiting our concern to a particular section."

As cities have lost population, they also have lost their influence in the White House and in Congress. In 1952, for example, voters in New York City cast 48 percent of their state's share of the presidential vote. By 1992, the city's share had fallen to 31 percent. This has been the experience for other cities as well: Chicago's share of the popular vote in Illinois dropped from 41 percent in 1952 to 22 percent in 1992; St. Louis's share of Missouri's vote fell from 20 percent to 6 percent.[122] Presidents of both parties, therefore, do not now pay as much attention as they once did to city voters or to urban issues. A similar development has occurred in Congress. The number of senators and representatives elected mainly by city voters has declined sharply over the past thirty years. The influence of urban electorates in state legislatures, in Congress, and in presidential politics has eroded to the point that central city voters, on their own, can influence national policies very little. In the 1988 election, George Bush could have carried almost all of the northern industrial states without a single vote from the big cities in those states.

Unlike Ronald Reagan, President Bush did not have an actively hostile relationship with urban leaders. Nevertheless, urban issues were absent from his agenda. Despite his promise to establish a task force on urban affairs, Bush never did so. Bush's Secretary of Housing and Urban Development, Jack Kemp, advocated a federal initiative to create seventy enterprise zones, and five bills to create such zones were introduced into Congress during 1989, but until the Los Angeles riots Kemp had not succeeded in putting the enterprise zones proposal high on the President's or Congress's agenda.

Cities lost even more influence after the redistricting following the 1990 census. The 1990 census revealed that during the 1980s the Sunbelt and suburbs continued to grow at a much faster rate than did the central cities. As of the 1990 census, 48 percent of Americans live in suburbs, and a majority of all the votes cast in the 1992 presidential election were suburban. The number of states with suburban majorities increased from three in 1980 to fourteen in 1990.

Within the Frostbelt states, the suburbs now command majorities in even more congressional districts than before. And in 1992 fifteen congressional seats were reapportioned to the South and West from northern states. One of the few positive trends to counter urban decline was that many cities, for the first time in decades, gained population in the 1980 due to immigration (which we discuss in Chapter 14).

PART FOUR

THE URBAN FISCAL CRISIS: THE RETURN OF THE PRIVATE CITY

CHAPTER
12

THE URBAN FISCAL CRISIS

❖ THE FISCAL CRISES OF THE 1990s

In 1975, when the nation's largest city, New York, teetered on the edge of bankruptcy, urban fiscal crises were much in the news. As cities all over the country experienced budgetary problems, urban officials learned well the art of retrenchment and cutback management. These measures, when combined with the economic upturn after 1983, made it possible for cities to cope with a sharp reduction in federal grants to cities in the 1980s. Urban fiscal crises moved from the headlines to the back pages.

How fast things change! By the early 1990s, American cities were again confronted by historic levels of fiscal stress. According to Mayor Sidney J. Barthelemy of New Orleans, "Cities are facing the toughest times since the Great Depression."[1] Local governments in all regions of the country were raising taxes, laying off employees, slashing services, and postponing infrastructure investments. In August 1990, Mayor Wilson Goode of Philadelphia announced a $73 million shortfall. The announcement prompted an immediate reduction in the city's bond rating. The city slashed its social service programs, but the budget gap steadily widened. Philadelphia's transit system, the fourth largest in the country, teetered on the verge of a total shutdown due to a shortage of money—even though it charged the highest transit fares in the nation.[2] All observers agreed that the city could be saved from financial collapse only if the state legislature stepped in with a plan to market bonds to cover the deficits.

In New York City, David Dinkins, the city's first black mayor, faced a $3 billion deficit for the 1991–1992 budget year. To close the gap, Dinkins proposed a $2 billion cut in city services, involving laying off 20,000 city workers, and a $1 billion tax increase. The first round of service cuts and tax increases, however, was not enough. In November 1991, four months after passing a balanced budget, New York faced a $250 million dollar budget deficit for the 1991 fiscal year and an estimated $7 billion deficit for the following four years.[3]

Not only large cities were suffering fiscal stress. In 1991 Chelsea, an impoverished suburb of Boston, was running an estimated 1991 budget deficit of $9 million out of a $48 million budget. Massachusetts Governor William F. Weld proposed legislation that would place the city of 28,000 into state receivership, ending local home rule.[4] Bridgeport, Connecticut, a city of 141,000 residents in the wealthiest state in the nation (as measured by per capita income), filed a Chapter 9 bankruptcy petition in July 1991 in federal court. According to city officials, property taxes were already so high that any further increases would have disastrous consequences. Bankruptcy was the only way out.[5]

Nor were fiscal problems confined to older industrial cities in the Northeast. The city of New Orleans reported a $91 million budget deficit in 1991. Mayor Tom Bradley of Los Angeles, anticipating a $177 million budget deficit in fiscal year 1992, proposed cutting the police force, library hours, tree trimming, park and recreation programs, traffic signal repairs, and street resurfacing. Sacramento, California, facing a $26 million budget gap for fiscal year 1992, among other measures planned to delay the opening of its new downtown central library for six months, and then only two of the five floors would be opened and only 5 percent of the library's 500,000 books would be available to the public.[6]

Cities of every description—small and large, suburban and central—in every region of the country experienced fiscal problems in the early 1990s. To assess the financial condition of cities, the National League of Cities in the spring of 1991 mailed a questionnaire to a sample of city officials across the country. The survey documented the presence of a widespread urban fiscal crisis:[7]

- 71.5 percent of the cities were less able to meet their financial needs in 1991 than in the previous year.

- 60.9 percent reported that 1991 general fund expenditures were expected to exceed revenues (up from 45.5 percent in 1990).

- The number of cities reporting severe negative imbalances (greater than −5.0 percent) in their general funds increased dramatically to 26.5 percent in 1991. The proportion was higher for western and small cities than for northeastern cities.

- Per capita general fund revenue growth was well below the inflation rate in 1990–1991. Revenue growth stagnated even though 84.6 per cent of all cities raised taxes or fees or imposed new taxes or fees in the preceding 12 months.

- 36.2 percent of the cities froze municipal hiring.

- 43.2 percent of the cities planned cutbacks in capital spending.

Throughout American history, every time the national economy has dipped into a recession or a depression, cities have plunged into financial crisis. As the saying goes, when the national economy gets a cold, cities catch pneumonia. At the beginning of the 1990s, however, the situation was more threatening than it had been for decades, because federal grants to city governments had been greatly reduced and state governments were themselves facing severe budget crises. The situation was similar to the crisis that confronted cities during the Great Depression.

❖ CITY EXPENDITURES

City expenditures depend ultimately on political demands. If citizens are not willing to forgo or reduce public services it is difficult for municipal officials to cut expenditures. In addition, demands for city services are driven by powerful structural forces that are largely beyond the control of local officials and voters. City governments are not sovereign entities. Higher levels of government (state and federal) allocate functional responsibilities to city governments within the intergovernmental system. Equally important, actions of the private sector, both corporations and individuals, create problems and establish needs that city expenditures must address.

There is a limit to reductions city officials can make, since public services are necessary for maintaining the physical well-being of city residents and the viability of the city. City governments provide a wide range of services that people take for granted as essential to a civilized existence: police and fire protection, education, water distribution, sewage collection, parks, highways, museums, libraries. The relative distribution of municipal expenditures among various functional areas for a year typical of the late 1980s is shown in Table 12-1. In 1988–89 America's six cities of over 1 million population spent a large proportion of their funds on education, public welfare, health and hospitals, and police. These services combined accounted for 40 percent of expenditures in these cities. Education and public welfare led the list.

Most smaller municipalities, and even most big cities, do not run the schools within their boundaries; education normally is financed through independent school districts. The exceptions include some older cities, such as New York, Boston, San Francisco, and Baltimore, that built schools before it had become the usual practice to finance education through special districts. Smaller cities spend much less on public welfare and public health than do big central cities. Thus, since they do not finance education, welfare, and public

---

TABLE 12-1   DISTRIBUTION OF REVENUES AND EXPENDITURES FOR SELECTED URBAN GOVERNMENTS, 1988–1989 (IN PERCENTAGES)

	ALL MUNICIPALITIES[a]	CITIES OF 1,000,000 AND OVER (6 CITIES)	CITIES OF 500,000– 999,999 (18 CITIES)
Revenues			
Intergovernmental	28	33	31
State aid	21	27	18
Federal aid	5	4	11
Local	72	67	69
Property taxes	23	19	22
Sales taxes	12	13	11
Income taxes	6	13	8
Expenditures by function			
Education	9	15	12
Public welfare	4	11	5
Health and hospitals	5	7	8
Police protection	9	7	8
Highways	9	5	7
Sewerage	8	5	8
Parks and recreation	5	3	5
Fire protection	6	4	6
Financial administration	3	1	2
Interest on debt	7	7	7
Other	35	35	32

[a]These data are estimates subject to sampling variation.
Source: Calculated from U.S. Bureau of the Census, *City Government Finances in 1988–89,* GF 89, no. 4 (Washington, D.C.: Government Printing Office, 1991), Table 2.

---

health services, a few basic services such as roads and sewers account for a relatively larger share of expenditures.

Collectively, cities spend huge sums of money. In fiscal year 1990, for example, they spent $198.8 billion, which was more than one-third (34.2 percent) of all local government expenditures in the United States. School districts and counties, with 35.9 percent and 22.0 percent respectively, accounted for most of the rest of local government expenditures.[8] In fiscal year 1990 the leading municipal budget by far was New York City's, an astonishing $31.3 billion. Four other cities spent more than $2 billion: Washington, D.C. ($4.1 billion), Los Angeles ($3.2 billion), Chicago ($2.9 billion), and Philadelphia ($2.6 billion).[9]

Per capita expenditures of cities are closely related to city size. Big cities spend more for a variety of reasons: They support a wider array of services, often provide service of better quality (for example, well-trained police officers and firefighters), pay higher salaries to their public employees, and experience the high service costs made necessary by high-density populations, aging buildings and infrastructure, and poverty and unemployment. In 1990, the eight cities with populations exceeding 1 million people spent $2,283 for each of their citizens; the average for all city governments in the United States was less than half that figure, $1,005.[10]

City expenditures have risen sharply in the second half of the twentieth century, not only in total amount but also relative to the economy as a whole, increasing from 4.8 percent of the gross national product (GNP) in 1949–1950 to a high of 9.2 percent in 1975–1976. Municipal expenditures rose sharply throughout the 1960s and up to the recession of 1974–1975. Between 1962 and 1972, per capita spending in the twenty-eight largest cities increased by 198 percent.[11] These cities expanded their budgets at a much faster rate than other local governments, but even the latter increased spending by 142 percent. As indicated in Table 12-2, a steep rate of increase for local governments of all kinds was maintained until 1975.

After the recession of 1974–1975, the brakes were applied to municipal budgets. The six biggest cities increased their budgets 30 percent from 1975 to 1980, but after adjustments for inflation their purchasing power actually dropped 9.7 percent. After adjusting for inflation, cities of all sizes, on the average, did not increase spending at all over the same years. In the 1980s, cities continued to hold the line on spending; between 1980 and 1984 there were no per capita increases, after adjustments for inflation. The six biggest cities increased expenditures by 3.4 percent (after inflation), but cities of 500,000 to 1 million in population reduced expenditures.

Inflation is a main cause of rising local government expenditures. Inflation affects local governments more than it affects the private sector. The cost of state and local government services has consistently risen at a more rapid rate than prices in general over the past twenty-five years. In the seventeen years from 1965 to 1982, prices in the economy as a whole (as measured by the GNP implicit deflator) increased 195.9 percent, while state and local government costs increased 247.2 percent. In the 1980s, inflation slowed down in both the private and public sectors, but the inflation rate for state and local government services still ran ahead of the inflation rate for private sector services. Between 1982 and 1990, the costs of state and local government rose 41.3 percent, but costs in the economy as a whole increased only 31.5 percent.[12]

The high rate of inflation for city governments can be explained, in part, by the fact that most municipal services are labor intensive. Wages of city workers tend to keep pace with wages in the private sector.[13] However, while in the private sector labor costs can be reduced over time through mechanization and computer technologies, such technologies have limited applications for many public services. The need for police officers, for instance, cannot be reduced to any appreciable extent by the use of computers.

TABLE 12-2 CHANGES IN SPENDING FOR CITIES OF DIFFERENT SIZE, 1970–1984

| | GROWTH RATE (PERCENTAGE) | | | | | |
| | 1970–1975 | | 1975–1980 | | 1980–1984 | |
	UNADJUSTED	ADJUSTED FOR INFLATION[a]	UNADJUSTED	ADJUSTED FOR INFLATION[a]	UNADJUSTED	ADJUSTED FOR INFLATION[a]
All municipalities	76	21.6[b]	47	0.02	31	0
Cities of 500,000 to 999,999[c]	76	21.6	45	0.01	26	–3.8
Big six cities	72.5	19.2	30	–9.7	35	3.4

[a]Using GNP implicit price deflator for state and local government purchases, U.S. Bureau of the Census, *Statistical Abstract of the United States: 1986* (Washington, D.C.: Government Printing Office, 1986), p. 470.

[b]Population in 1982.

Sources: U.S. Bureau of the Census, *Local Government Finances in Selected Metropolitan Areas and Large Counties: 1969–70*, GF 70, no. 6 (Washington, D.C.: Government Printing Office, 1971), Table 4; *Local Government Finances: 1974–75*, GF 75, no. 6 (1976); *City Government Finances: 1974–75*, GF 75, no. 5, Table D; *Local Government Finances: 1979–80*, GF 80, no. 5, (1981), Table D; *City Government Finances: 1983–84*, no. 4 (1985), Table 3. U.S. Advisory Commission on Intergovernmental Relations, *Significant Features of Fiscal Federalism, 1980–81* (Washington, D.C.: Government Printing Office, 1981), p. 19.

The labor costs of city government are heavily influenced by the same economic and social forces that influence the price of labor throughout the economy. Wage adjustments in the private sector together with the salary scale of federal employees (especially after the federal government made wage parity with the private sector its official policy in the mid-1970s) raised both the expectations and the aspirations of city workers across the country. Between 1960 and 1975, wages paid to state and local government employees rose from 89 to 98 percent of the earnings of private sector workers.[14] During the second half of the 1970s, however, the ratio of public to private employee wages fell back to 93 percent. After 1975, for the first time since 1955, wage gains in the public sector consistently lagged behind earnings in the private sector,[15] but because of the labor-intensive nature of most municipal services, this did not help cities enough to avert layoffs and service reductions.

During the years of rising labor costs public employee unions were instrumental in securing better wages for local government workers. In the 1960s, labor organizations such as the American Federation of State, County, and Municipal Employees (AFSCME) and the American Federation of Government Employees, both affiliated with the AFL-CIO, grew rapidly. Union membership rose from 1,070,000 in 1960 to 2,318,000 by 1970. At the same time, the unions became more militant. Worker-days lost through work stoppages by state and local employees escalated from 58,000 in 1960 to 1,375,000 in 1970 to 2,299,000 by 1973.[16] Unionization of city workers, which was more widespread in the older northern cities than elsewhere, brought 10 percent to 15 percent higher pay to public employees, and thus it was a significant cause of higher expenditures in the bigger cities.[17]

Few people realize that local governments employ more workers than any other level of government in the United States. In 1990, for example, local governments, including school districts, employed 10.8 million people, far more than the combined total for state governments (4.5 million) and the federal government (3.1 million civilian employees).[18] Since 1970 the rate of growth of local government employment has exceeded state and federal employment growth. Between 1970 and 1990, local government employment rose 38.3 percent, a sharp contrast to the 7.8 percent increase in the "growing federal bureaucracy" so often decried by vote-seeking political candidates. Employment by city governments (municipalities) grew by 17.7 percent during this same twenty-year period.[19]

The local public sector is an important job creator in economically depressed central cities. In the five major cities listed in Table 12-3, for instance, almost 33,000 new public service jobs were created between 1967 and 1972, which helped to offset a decline of 73,000 private sector jobs. Without the rise in public employment, unemployment rates would have risen far higher than they did in the nation's large cities. Budget cutbacks after the mid-1970s reversed this effect, however. Between 1977 and 1983 more than 15,000 public service jobs were lost in these five cities, in addition to the more than 20,000 private sector jobs that disappeared. Cutbacks in federal and state programs aggravated the recession that began in 1980. The same thing happened again in the early 1990s.

TABLE 12-3   CHANGE IN NUMBER OF JOBS IN PRIVATE AND PUBLIC SECTORS IN FIVE CENTRAL CITIES, 1967–1972 AND 1977–1983

	1967–1972		1977–1983	
	PRIVATE SECTOR[a]	PUBLIC SECTOR[b]	PRIVATE SECTOR[a]	PUBLIC SECTOR[b]
Baltimore	−7,000	+3,900	−13,342	−4,617
New Orleans	+7,000	+2,500	+5,349	−2,542
Philadelphia	−53,000	+18,400	−19,705	−4,445
St. Louis	−23,000	+2,300	−29,508	−3,854
San Francisco	+6,000	+5,700	+37,000	+7
Total	−73,000	+32,800	−20,206	−15,451

[a]Jobs covered by Social Security only.
[b]Includes city school district.
Source: Adapted from George E. Peterson, "Finance," in *The Urban Predicament*, ed. William Gorham and Nathan Glazer (Washington, D.C.: Urban Institute, 1976), p. 112, citing U.S. Bureau of the Census, *Compendium of Public Employment, 1967* and *1972; State and Metropolitan Data Book, 1982*, Table A, *1986*, Table A; *County Business Patterns, 1972, 1983*, Table 2 (Washington, D.C.: Government Printing Office).

The ability of cities to maintain expenditure levels is closely related to local economic vitality. All of the four cities that reduced expenditures between 1975 and 1989, as shown in Table 12-4, are located in the Frostbelt. Five of the cities that increased their budgets, however, were also older industrial cities in the Frostbelt, showing that special circumstances (such as ability to raise taxes or find new tax sources) can be important. Seven of the fourteen cities that increased expenditures were in the Sunbelt.

The economic vitality of cities varies tremendously, and the differences are particularly sharp between central cities and their suburbs. In 1960, for a sample of sixty-two cities, the per capita income of central city residents was 105 percent of the income of people living in suburbs; in other words, people living in central cities earned, on the average, slightly more than suburban residents. Clearly, lots of affluent people still lived in the cities, even after more than a decade of suburban flight. By 1989, the income ratio had fallen drastically to 84 percent. In 1989, the poverty rate in central cities was 18.1 percent, but in the metropolitan areas outside central cities it was only 8.0 percent.[20]

High rates of poverty boost the cost and the need for city services. Central cities and older suburbs, therefore, are particularly vulnerable to fiscal stress. Poverty and unemployment are basically national problems, but they are concentrated in central cities and older suburbs, a result of historical patterns of population immigration and of exclusionary policies that keep poor people out of wealthier suburban jurisdictions. The governments of central cities and older suburbs are in no position to reduce poverty and unemploy-

TABLE 12-4   GENERAL GOVERNMENT EXPENDITURES FOR SELECTED LARGE CITIES, 1975–1989 (IN MILLIONS OF 1987 DOLLARS[a])

	FY 1975 EXPENDITURES	FY 1989 EXPENDITURES	PERCENT CHANGE
Cities with declining expenditures			
Baltimore	2,159	1,390	−36
Cleveland	586	473	−19
Boston	1,597	1,412	−12
St. Louis	515	495	−4
Cities with increasing expenditures			
New York	$26,326	$28,254	+7
Pittsburgh	285	314	+10
Denver	718	887	+13
Jacksonville, Fla.	515	552	+1
Washington, D.C.	3,159	3,780	+19
El Paso[b]	121	174	+44
Houston[b]	775	1,429	+84
New Orleans	506	656	+30
Milwaukee	433	515	+19
San Jose	289	583	+102
Dallas[b]	472	956	+98
Detroit	1,343	1,527	+14
Phoenix	435	970	+123
Chicago	2,210	2,722	+23

[a]Adjustments for inflation are calculated using GNP implicit price deflator for state and local government purchases, U.S. Bureau of the Census, *Statistical Abstract of the United States: 1989*, p. 464.
[b]1987 fiscal year data.
Source: U.S. Bureau of the Census, *City Government Finances: 1975–76*, GF 76, no. 4 (Washington, D.C.: Government Printing Office, 1977), Table 5; U.S. Bureau of the Census, *City Government Finances: 1987–88*, GF 88, no. 4 (Washington, D.C.: Government Printing Office, 1990).

ment, but they are disproportionately saddled with these problems. And, sometimes with tragic results, they are the least able of all governments to generate the resources necessary to provide the basic public services that help to ameliorate the problems faced by the poor.

Poverty boosts public spending not only for welfare and social services, but also for a broad range of other services. Central city governments spend money on lead paint poisoning prevention (a problem prevalent in older homes), rat control, and housing demolition. In the 1980s the problems of AIDS, homelessness, and crack cocaine soared in central cities. Courts have ordered cities to provide shelter for the homeless at significant expense to local governments. In 1987, for example, New York City, as required by court order, spent $274 million to provide emergency shelter to its homeless population.[21] Increased violence associated with substance abuse and other aspects of concentrated poverty strains the ability of police to protect the safety of the citizens.[22]

Poverty also drives up the cost of other services. Children from culturally and educationally deprived homes are more difficult to educate than middle-class youngsters. Street cleanliness is more difficult to maintain in ghetto neighborhoods where the streets are used heavily for recreation but infrequently repaired. Costs of fire protection are higher than elsewhere because of deteriorating housing, the high density of building, old and outdated wiring, and a concentration of flammable materials.

Almost all older cities have experienced significant population losses due to the flight of the middle class to the suburbs. As a city's population falls, the cost of providing infrastructure and basic services, such as police and fire, does not decline correspondingly.[23] Cities still have the same sewer and water lines—often old and in need of frequent repair—and the same miles of streets to plow and patrol. Once the middle-class has fled, however, there are fewer taxpayers to pay for these services and the taxpayers who are left make less taxable income and own less valuable property than those in surrounding jurisdictions.

Another factor that drives up the cost of city services is the panoply of expensive mandates forced on cities by higher levels of government. Cities are not mentioned in the U.S. Constitution; legally, city governments are the creatures of state legislatures. Though many cities have home rule charters that allow them to govern themselves internally within broad guidelines, municipal corporations are not fully sovereign. The scope of a city's service responsibilities is beyond its control. State and federal governments can, and frequently do, order cities to provide particular services or meet minimum standards of service provision. Rarely do the cities receive more money to cover the costs of the mandated standards and services.

New York State, for example, is one of the few states in the nation that requires local governments to pay a portion of the costs of welfare (Aid to Families with Dependent Children) and Medicaid. New York City must pick up 20 percent of Medicaid bills for city residents; this program alone costs local taxpayers over $1 billion each year. New York City is an extreme example, but many cities across the country are forced to pay a share of welfare costs. Over the past two decades several states have made an effort to reduce their cities' welfare costs, but the problem still is significant. Cities that still have an expensive welfare burden, despite state and federal welfare programs, include Washington, D.C., Denver, San Francisco, Indianapolis, and all large cities in Virginia.[24]

Unfunded federal mandates imposed on cities have proliferated since the 1960s. In the case of concurrent powers shared by the federal and state governments, Congress has the power to preempt (override) state and local laws. According to the Supremacy Clause (Article VI) of the Constitution, when there is a conflict between a national law and a state (or local) law, the national law prevails. Since 1965, Congress has used its powers of preemption to force city governments to address pressing problems; at the same time, however, Congress has failed to compensate cities for their additional costs. Thus, Congress has been able to take credit for solving problems while foisting the costs of these solutions onto lower levels of government.

The Supreme Court upheld federal preemption in the 1985 *Garcia* decision.[25] In *Garcia* the Court upheld the constitutionality of the 1974 amendments to the Fair Labor Standards Act, which applied minimum-wage and overtime pay provisions to public transit workers in San Antonio, Texas. This decision made it clear that state and local governments are not protected from federal preemption statutes by the Tenth Amendment (which reserves powers not granted to the federal government to the states). Their only protection comes from political pressures they can put on Congress. In 1986, the U.S. Department of Labor estimated that the cost to state and local governments of complying with the new labor standards exceeded $1.1 billion.[26]

Federal mandates to preserve environmental quality have been enormously expensive. The Clean Air Act of 1990, for example, required 100 cities to install antipollution devices on their garbage incinerators, at an estimated average cost of $20 million per incinerator.[27] The U.S. Environmental Protection Agency estimated that the total cost of environmental mandates for local governments increased from $7.7 billion in 1972 to $19.2 billion in 1987. By the year 2000, the costs to local governments are projected to increase to $32.6 billion.[28]

It is easy to say that city officials should limit the soaring costs of local government. As we have seen, however, a variety of economic and political forces beyond the control of local officials drive up the costs of government: inflation in labor-intensive city services, concentrated poverty, and unfunded mandates by higher levels of government. In the next section, we examine the other side of the ledger, revenue. Just as external factors limit the ability of local officials to reduce costs, they also limit the cities' ability to raise money to cope with the squeeze on municipal budgets.

❖ CITY REVENUES

Historically, the property tax has been the principal source of revenue for local governments. The most important and widely used form of property tax is the *ad valorem* real property tax, a levy imposed as a rate percent of the value of land and its improvements. From colonial times through the early years of the republic, real property was taken to be the best indicator of both wealth and the ability to pay taxes. Indeed, this was generally true. Most of the wealth of the era was tied to the land, and fortunes were made in land speculation. A person's wealth was roughly proportional to landholdings. The real property tax, therefore, was relied upon to finance state and local governmental services.[29]

The property tax had several advantages over alternative sources of taxation. Real property was impossible to conceal. And insofar as the tax was levied on the land and not on the taxpayer, the tax could not easily be evaded. Even if the owner were unknown, the tax could be levied and extracted, if need be, by confiscation of the property.

The location of the land and improvements on it determined the value of property. The closer a place of business was to the waterfront, the more valuable the property. If one recalls that early urban services were developed by local entrepreneurs largely out of a concern for the safety of their own businesses and real estate investments, it becomes clear the *ad valorem* levy was a relatively reliable index of the value of public services received by property holders. The owner of a $1,000 property received twice as much benefit from fire protection service as did a neighbor who owned a $500 property; the former had twice as much to lose in a fire and twice as much to gain if the property was saved. It was considered equitable if the levy were proportional to the value of the property.

Taxation of personal (or nonreal) property, that is, assets other than real estate and improvements, evolved steadily as the cities became more complex. As trade and manufacturing grew in importance, more and more wealth became represented in bank accounts, merchandise, patent rights, machinery, capital stock, and corporate assets. Cities (and states) began to levy taxes on such sources of wealth in order to maintain a reliable relationship between individual tax burdens and personal wealth. Such assets were often hard to find and assess, however. Because of this, although the numbers of people with significant personal assets mushroomed after the Civil War, the proportion of the property tax attributable to personal property actually declined.[30]

In 1902, personal and real property taxes accounted for 73 percent of all municipal revenues, with license and franchise fees accounting for most of the rest. These taxes continued to provide approximately three-fourths of all local receipts until the late 1930s and early 1940s, when the proportion began to decline in favor of other revenue sources, especially new municipal sales and income taxes.[31] By 1962, property taxes accounted for barely 50 percent of municipal revenues in the seventy-two largest metropolitan areas (even though the property tax continued to be used to generate almost all the revenue for school districts). In the 1960s, intergovernmental transfers contributed such large amounts to local revenues that the proportion of the revenues derived from property taxes necessarily fell. By fiscal 1975, property taxes accounted for little more than a third (35 percent) of the revenues in the largest metropolitan areas, despite a 130 percent increase in the average per capita levy since the early 1960s.[32] Other sources of local and intergovernmental revenue had increased faster.

Reliance on the property tax dropped to 22 percent of local revenues for municipalities in metropolitan areas by 1987–1988 (refer to Table 12-1); as recently as 1970, this tax had generated 39.1 percent of all municipal revenues.[33] The figure was somewhat higher for all local governments combined, as opposed to municipalities, because school districts and counties continued to rely heavily on the property tax (in 1984, 97 percent in school districts, 76 percent in counties).

Only in rapidly growing cities of the Sunbelt has the property tax been used as an important source of revenue growth since the 1960s. This has been possible because of the sharply escalating value of property in those cities. The value of taxable property rose 251 percent in Phoenix from 1965 to 1973. In contrast, it increased only 2 percent in Newark and 14 percent in Detroit during the same period.[34] But stagnant property values in the industrial cities were only part of the problem. Antiquated assessment procedures in many cities failed to keep the assessed valuations of property in line with their market values in periods of inflation.[35]

The property tax has a number of weaknesses that have prompted cities to search for alternatives. One weakness is the high proportion of tax-exempt property. According to one study, almost one-third of all real property in the United States is subject to some kind of exemption.[36] In 1982, in just twenty-three states and the District of Columbia, there were $15 billion in exempt property for religious institutions, $22 billion for educational institutions, $15 billion for charitable institutions, and $128 billion for government property.[37] Cities must provide services for these properties, including police and fire protection, but the owners pay no taxes. Unfortunately, the burden of tax-exempt property falls most heavily on those cities that are least able to afford it, since "the percentage of property exempt in the central city is generally at least twice the percentage found in the respective suburbs."[38] In 1985, for example, over 51 percent of the real property in Boston was tax exempt, up from 41 percent in 1972.[39] A 1983 article traced a 3.2-mile route through Boston where a walker would not set foot upon a single parcel of taxable property.[40] The situation in New York so incensed one taxpayer that he sued the city tax commission over the "subsidy of religion," going all the way to the United States Supreme Court before finally losing the case.[41]

In recent decades the proportion of tax-exempt property has increased. Many cities have provided tax relief for the aged or people in poverty ("circuit breaker" laws). States and cities have tried to attract or retain businesses and investors by forgiving or reducing their property taxes. Many states have exempted various forms of business property, such as machines and inventory, from taxation without consulting local governments.[42] Another weakness of the property tax as a revenue generator for central cities is that it does not touch suburban commuters and visitors who work and play in the city but do not live there. As we discussed in Chapter 9, commuters cost cities money. Researchers have found that cities with higher proportions of suburban commuters "must spend more per capita on crime protection, traffic control, parking, parks, and other general services to keep up with the flow of people into and through the central city."[43]

One method cities have used to deal with this problem is to levy earnings taxes to be paid by anyone working in the city. Although Charleston, South Carolina, is reported to have levied a tax on income prior to the Civil War, the modern municipal income tax movement began in Philadelphia in 1939. That levy, a flat-rate payroll tax on all earnings of persons who lived or worked in the city, was adopted to relieve financial pressures during the Great Depression. Since that time it has been adopted in thousands of communities, more than 3,500 by 1970. It "was not adopted because cities thought it was in some sense a 'fairer' tax than the property tax, but solely because it was a tax that could generate large amounts of revenue."[44]

The big advantage of the income tax is that it enables cities to tax nonresident commuters. Research demonstrates that the export ratio (proportion of tax paid by nonresidents) is higher for local income taxes than for sales taxes or property taxes.[45] Not surprisingly, except for Ohio and Pennsylvania, where virtually all cities can levy such taxes, suburban-dominated state legislatures have been reluctant to grant cities the power to impose income taxes: Only fifteen out of eighty-six major central cities have the power to impose an earnings tax.[46] As Table 12-1 demonstrates, the income tax is used most extensively by large cities.

The revenue source that saved the cities during the 1960s, allowing them to expand both the level and scope of services, was intergovernmental aid. At that time, the federal government established a direct partnership with city governments that helped to relieve their fiscal stress. Between 1965 and 1974, for example, intergovernmental transfers to all cities rose 370 percent, more than twice the 153 percent increase in municipal expenditures.[47] Direct federal aid to cities peaked in 1978 at over 26 percent of the cities' own-source revenue. Federal aid began to decline during the Carter Administration, and the decline accelerated in the 1980s. By 1984, federal aid had fallen to 14.5 percent of own-source revenues and it has continued to fall since then (Figure 12-1). The federal retreat from the cities has placed them in a tightening vice between costs and revenues.

The Reagan Administration effectively ended the special relationship that had been forged between the federal government and cities in the 1960s. The Reagan approach was generally to maintain spending for programs benefiting individuals (the so-called safety net programs) and to cut grants-in-aid programs targeted to geographic places or governments. Overall, nine grants-in-aid programs of special importance to urban governments were cut 46.7 percent between 1980 and 1987. Officials in the Reagan Administration asserted that grants to individuals are mobile and accommodate the process of economic change and population mobility, while grants to distressed cities interfere with market processes and therefore should be avoided, even if the processes work to the disadvantage of some regions and cities.[48] Thus, general revenue sharing for cities was eliminated in 1986 and the Community Development Block Grant was reduced by 20 percent between 1980 and 1987. Moreover, the targeting of federal grants shifted from distressed to relatively prosperous urban areas.[49] Few cities emerged unscathed. The most distressed cities lost the most.

Figure 12-1 Direct Aid to Cities as a Percentage of Own-Source Revenue, 1965–1986

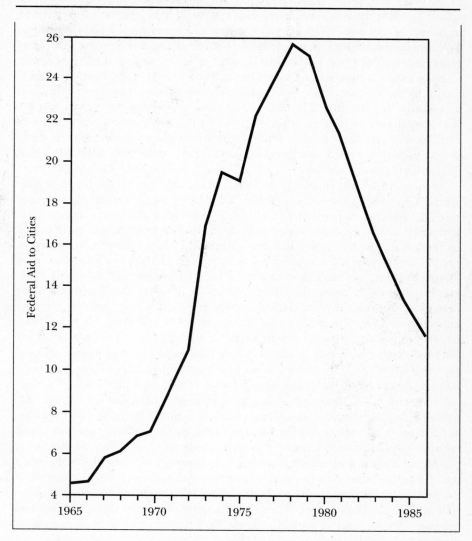

Source: Helen F. Ladd and John Yinger, *America's Ailing Cities: Fiscal Health and the Design of Urban Policy*, updated edition (Baltimore: Johns Hopkins University Press, 1989), p. 270.

Direct federal aid to Chicago fell from $472 million in 1981 to $151 million in 1986. Baltimore's grant volume fell from $220 million to $124 million, Indianapolis's from $125 million to $65 million. Detroit lost $305 million annually, falling from $456 million in 1981 to $151 million by 1986.[50]

Although federal assistance grew at a faster rate than state government aid in the 1960s and 1970s, more intergovernmental assistance still came from the states. In 1974, cities as a whole received nearly $2 in state revenue for each $1 in federal revenue. By 1980 the ratio of state to federal dollars had declined to $1.47 in state funding for each federal dollar.[51] In the 1980s, some state governments, such as New York, Florida, and Oklahoma, stepped in aggressively to compensate for the federal cuts. Others, such as California, responded minimally to the Reagan cuts.[52] State responses overall were not nearly sufficient to make up for the cuts. The share of total local revenues from state sources fell from almost 32 percent at the beginning of the Reagan Administration in 1980 to 29 percent in 1987.[53] With states facing record deficits in the early 1990s, fiscally strapped city governments could expect little relief from that quarter in the near future.

Not surprisingly, cities responded to cuts in aid from higher levels of government by raising taxes. Between 1979 and 1987 locally generated revenues rose 84.4 percent, but still many city governments had trouble balancing their budgets.[54] Moreover, many cities found it difficult to respond to cuts in grants by increasing taxes, for they had not escaped the taxpayer's revolts started in the 1970s. In the 1970s, at least fourteen state legislatures enacted laws that limited property tax rates or spending by local governments.[55] Even more far-reaching, however, were the citizen initiatives. The first well-publicized of these was Proposition 13 in California, which was passed by popular referendum in June 1978. From March to November 1978, sixteen states held initiatives or referenda to limit taxes or spending, though not all were binding on public officials.[56] Thirteen of the citizen initiatives passed. More such proposals were approved after 1978. Consequently, even though cities faced severe fiscal problems, their budgetary options were drastically constricted.

Cities imposed a variety of user fees in lieu of new taxes. In 1991, 73.1 percent of cities increased user fees and 40.0 percent adopted new user fees for at least one city service.[57] Fees for museums, public parking, ice rinks, and swimming pools were increased. In many cities garbage collection became a private service for which each household pays instead of being a public service paid for out of general tax revenues. User fees make services more expensive in proportion to income for low-income households than for better-off households. Since user fees and sales taxes are far more regressive than property and income taxes, the mix of municipal taxes has become steadily more regressive over the past few years.[58]

❖ MUNICIPAL BONDS

If cities had always relied on taxation alone, they would never have been able to build the permanent infrastructure upon which all city life depends. From the mid-nineteenth century to the present cities have issued bonds to private investors as a way of borrowing money. Cities are authorized by state legislation to issue long-term bonds to pay for capital improvements, such as schools, highways, bridges, and hospitals, that will benefit city residents over a long period of time. Though cities in most states can borrow short term to cover operating expenses, unlike the federal government they cannot borrow long term to cover repeated budget deficits. Big cities, especially Chicago and New York, often use short-term notes to increase budgetary flexibility and to improve their cash flow.

Given the continuing need to build and maintain public infrastructure, access to the municipal bond market is essential for the well-being of cities. Cities are directly dependent on the willingness of private sector individuals and institutions to buy their bonds. The municipal bond market is a significant sector of the economy. Borrowings typically represent 20 to 25 percent of all state and local spending.[59] In 1990 cities, counties, and townships issued $43.4 billion in new long-term debt, with total debt outstanding by all local governments amounting to $542.3 billion.[60]

The most important fact about municipal bonds is that they are tax exempt. Because the interest income derived from municipal bonds is not subject to taxation, investors are willing to buy municipal bonds at a lower interest rate than they would pay for corporate bonds. In effect, the federal government provides cities with a subsidy by exempting municipal bonds from taxation. The municipal bond market is effectively limited to corporations and wealthy individuals because the minimum bond size is typically $25,000 or greater. Municipal bonds are purchased by commercial banks, casualty insurance companies, and, increasingly, wealthy individual investors, who find the federal tax exemption especially attractive.[61] Unlike other corporations, commercial banks are taxed at the full corporate tax rate, and therefore they have invested heavily in tax-exempt municipal debt. Because the banks control such a large portion of the outstanding bonds (32 percent in 1984), city finances are heavily dependent on their investment decisions.[62]

Even though municipal bonds have the appeal of being tax exempt, their low interest rate means that cities still have to compete for investors. States and local governments also sell tax-exempt industrial development bonds for the purpose of subsidizing land, sports stadiums, shopping malls, access roads, and even industrial buildings. The competition has increased because, since the mid-1970s, private industry has been allowed to sell nontaxable securities to finance pollution control investments. This type of bond was estimated to have appropriated 25 percent of the tax-exempt market by 1975. The additional cost to cities of having to pay higher interest rates in order to compete for investors was $500 million by 1980.[63]

The federal subsidy to cities through the bond market is relatively inefficient because only part of it, in the form of lower interest rates paid to investors, goes to cities. The rest of the federal subsidy is siphoned off to wealthy taxpayers who avoid paying federal taxes by buying the tax-exempt municipal bonds. Legislation has been proposed, but never passed, to allow municipalities to float bonds at normal interest rates in exchange for a direct subsidy by the federal government.[64] In this way, the subsidy would go entirely to cities and not, indirectly, to investors.

Cities issue two types of long-term bonds: general obligation and revenue bonds. General obligation bonds pledge the "full faith and credit" of the city's taxing powers behind the bonds and generally require voter approval. Revenue bonds are not guaranteed by the issuing government and do not require voter approval; anticipated future revenues from the facilities which are constructed with the bond monies are committed to pay back the bonds. Almost any facilities that can charge user fees—sports stadiums, convention centers, museums, aquariums—are financed through revenue bonds. Local government borrowing through revenue bonds has sharply risen since the 1970s. In the 1960s and through much of the 1970s, general obligation bonds represented about 60 percent of outstanding local long-term debt,[65] by 1988 nonguaranteed revenue bond debt represented 67 percent of all outstanding debt issued by city governments and their dependent agencies.[66]

Cities use revenue bonds, basically, to avoid having to go before the voters. States do not require voter approval because, in theory, the voters' tax dollars are not at risk. However, when revenues are not sufficient to pay bond premiums (and they often are not), local governments must make up the difference. Sports stadiums (for instance the Super Dome in New Orleans) often lose millions of dollars a year, and taxpayers pay these debts.

Revenue bonds permit cities to use their tax-exempt borrowing privileges for private purposes. In the late 1970s, cities began issuing mortgage revenue bonds to subsidize interest rates for middle-income home buyers, although in 1980 Congress restricted this practice with the passage of the Mortgage Subsidy Act. In an attempt to stimulate economic growth, in the 1970s and 1980s cities increasingly issued industrial revenue bonds to subsidize a broad assortment of businesses, including K-Marts, McDonalds, liquor stores, and law offices. Investors found these bonds a convenient way to escape federal taxation; although they were buying tax-exempt bonds, the proceeds actually went to businesses. Congress, noting the hemorrhage of federal tax revenues, restricted the use of industrial revenue bonds by passing the Tax Equity and Fiscal Responsibility Act of 1982 and the Deficit Reduction Act of 1984.[67] The Tax Reform Act of 1986 placed state-by-state limits on what it termed governmentally subsidized "private-activity bonds."[68]

❖ THE RATINGS GAME

The cost of borrowing for a city is basically determined by its bond rating. A bond rating purports to represent the relative credit quality of the issuing municipality, and therefore the rating determines the rate of interest a city must pay. A high rating means a lower interest rate, on the theory that there is less risk for the investor. When a city's bond rating is lowered due to fiscal problems, a bond may be more difficult to sell, and the additional interest paid over the amortized life of the bond can amount to millions of dollars.

Bond ratings are published by two national rating firms: Moody's Investors Service and Standard and Poor's Corporation. Until the late 1960s, both firms routinely rated most bond issues. Since that time, however, the firms have rated municipal bonds only for an annual fee, ranging from $500 to $2,500 or more.[69] Cities have no choice but to seek a rating if they want to be able to market their bonds.

Ratings represent a combination of subjective and objective evaluations. The exact formulas and procedures for making the ratings are unknown, but they almost certainly are rather arbitrary. Both "rating agencies are loath to divulge the particular factors taken into account."[70] One commentator on the rating system noted, "Instead of using systematic and objective measurements, both municipal bond rating agencies emphasize the importance of careful study and [subjective] decisions made by experienced municipal bond analysts and committees."[71] If the amount of time spent is in any way indicative of the quality of analysis, it is interesting to note that though initial ratings typically take a few days, "ratings on subsequent sales of outstanding bonds take only a couple of hours" or less.[72] The rating of municipal bonds has been very inconsistent over time. Accurate duplication of ratings, using objective data about cities' financial conditions, occurs in only 50 to 70 percent of the cases. So-called hidden factors known only to the ratings firms must therefore account for the discrepancies in ratings between otherwise similar communities.[73]

Nevertheless, distinct patterns in ratings can be identified. Cities that were downgraded in their ratings between 1975 and 1980 lost population in the 1970s, while cities whose bonds were upgraded grew. The downgraded cities also experienced slower growth in per capita income.[74] Fiscal factors correlate closely with bond ratings. The cities that became most dependent on intergovernmental resources in the 1960s and 1970s were the most frequently downgraded.[75] All these factors are associated with older cities of the Northeast and Midwest. Table 12-5 makes this relationship obvious, as does a study of larger cities published in 1980.[76] Every one of the seven big cities listed in the table as being downgraded between 1965 and 1978 was an older industrial city noted for its social and economic problems. Of eleven big cities listed as being downgraded from 1978 to 1986, nine were older industrial cities in the Northwest or Midwest. The one Sunbelt city that was downgraded, Houston, was hit hard by a drop in oil prices in the mid-1980s.

Bond ratings are totally unrelated to the likelihood of default. (Default does not mean that the loan was not repaid; it simply means that the payments were not made on time.) The discrepancy in the interest rates between the highest and lowest investment grade bonds is inexplicable on the basis of relative risk.[77] From 1929 to 1933, when 77 percent of all municipal defaults of the twentieth century occurred, the highest-rated bonds recorded the highest incidence of default.[78]

Major cities simply do not fail to pay their debts. True, from the first recorded default in 1838 (Mobile, Alabama) through 1969 there were more

TABLE 12-5   CHANGES IN RATINGS ON GENERAL OBLIGATION BONDS (MOODY'S RATINGS)

RATING DOWNGRADED 1965–1978	RATING DOWNGRADED 1978–1986
St. Louis	St. Louis
Newark	San Francisco
Buffalo	Chicago
New York	Houston
Cleveland	Cleveland
Philadelphia	Detroit
Pittsburgh	Cincinnati
	Columbus
	Toledo
	Milwaukee
	Louisville

Source: Moody's Municipal and Government Manual, 2 vols. (New York: Moody's Investors Service, 1986).

than 6,000 recorded bond defaults by local governments. Fewer than a third of these, however, involved incorporated municipalities (cities); most of the rest were special districts that provided particular services such as irrigation. Seventy-five percent of all such failures occurred between 1930 and 1939. Less than 10 percent occurred after the depression.[79] During the worst period for municipal bonds, 1929 through 1937, only 8 percent of all cities and 19.9 percent of their bonded debt were ever in default.[80] In all but a handful of cases, the debts were eventually paid.

From World War II through early 1970, a total of 431 state and local units defaulted on their obligations. The total principal involved was $450 million, approximately 0.4 percent of the outstanding state and local debt. Three noncity units, the West Virginia Turnpike Commission, the Calumet Skyway Toll Bridge, and the Chesapeake Bay Bridge and Tunnel Commission, accounted for over 74 percent of this amount. Only two of twenty-four major default situations ($1 million or more) involved general obligation bonds.[81] Of 114 defaults by cities during the 1960s, almost all were temporary or technical defaults. Only thirty-four involved general obligation bonds, and in all these cases the cities involved had populations under 5,000 and the amount in default was less than $1 million.[82]

An analysis of cases filed in federal district courts between 1938 and 1971 reveals that nine cities took advantage of federal municipal bankruptcy legislation. With one exception (Saluda, North Carolina), all the cases involved small, rather obscure cities in Texas (Ranger, Talco, Benevides) or Florida (Manatee, Medley, Center Hill, Webster, Wanchula). Only in the case of Benevides (population 2,500) were general obligation bonds of post–World War II origin involved. In all other cases, the defaulted debt was of prewar origin, related to revenue bonds, or unrelated to bonds altogether.[83]

In the rare cases when a city defaulted on its obligations, it has invariably involved only a technical failure to pay on time, and the failure has been temporary. Bondholders have always recovered their money, even though it may have taken longer than they liked. On December 15, 1978, Cleveland became the first major city to default, even in a technical sense, since 1933. On that day the city failed to make payments on $14 million in short-term notes; the city renewed payments a few months later and officially ended default in 1980.[84] There would appear to be little justification for differential rating of city bonds, especially general obligation bonds: "Where the full faith and credit has been pledged . . . there simply has been no record of meaningful risk for forty years."[85]

❖ A TALE OF TWO CITIES: NEW YORK AND CHICAGO

In 1975, financial disaster threatened New York City. Unable to pay the city's debts, city officials asked for a federal loan to avoid bankruptcy. Many people believed that New York had brought its problems on itself through profligate spending. Under the leadership of liberal mayors like John Lindsay (1966 to 1973), New York (it was usually supposed) had enacted a host of expensive social programs for the poor that eventually busted its budget and frightened off its middle-class tax-paying residents. As a city run by the last of the machine bosses, Chicago, in contrast, had an image as "the city that works." Under the leadership of Mayor Richard J. Daley (1955 to 1976), Chicago, supposedly, concentrated on basic services and did not cave in to the demands of special interests. A closer look at New York and Chicago, however, reveals a more complex picture than that portrayed by the conventional wisdom. It also enables us to separate the general factors that affect all cities from the influence of local leadership and political structures.

Economically and socially, New York and Chicago are very much alike; they share the basic characteristics of urban decline. In the two decades between 1960 and 1980, for example, New York's population fell 9.1 percent, and Chicago's dropped 15.4 percent. In both cases the main cause of the population loss was a massive white flight to the suburbs. In twenty years the nonwhite percentage of the total population increased from 15 percent to 39 percent in New York and from 24 percent to 50 percent in Chicago.[86] Both cities suffered substantial job losses in the postwar period, especially in manufacturing. In the ten-year period from 1967 to 1977, New York lost 287,000 manufacturing jobs and Chicago lost 181,000.[87] Both suffered from high unemployment rates, welfare dependency, and concentrated poverty.[88] Clearly, in the 1960s and 1970s New York and Chicago were both cities in decline. Various attempts to measure urban decline all ranked New York and Chicago in the "distressed" category.[89] One study ranked cities according to "standardized fiscal health," measured as the difference between a city's revenue-raising capacity and its expenditure needs based on economic and social trends. In 1972, out of seventy-one cities, Chicago ranked sixty-eighth and New York ranked dead last.[90]

Though their underlying socioeconomic profiles looked quite similar, New York's and Chicago's fiscal conditions diverged dramatically. In the mid-1970s, while New York approached financial collapse, Chicago managed to restrain expenditure growth and avoid going deeply into debt. Chicago did not use short-term debt to cover operating expenses the way New York did. In 1975, New York's per capita short-term debt was $618, compared to only $72 for Chicago. That same year Chicago's long-term per capita debt was about a fourth of New York's.[91] During the 1970s, when New York's bond ratings plummeted and the city lost access to the bond market, Chicago retained high ratings and access to credit. Mayor Daley was viewed almost as a hero by the business community. Why did the financial histories of two cities with similar conditions diverge so greatly, and what can their differences tell us about the politics of urban budgets?

In the case of New York, blame can be apportioned to both politicians and bankers. For years New York spent more than it took in, and by 1975 it had accumulated a $3 billion operating deficit.[92] Politicians tried to avoid the painful remedies that could reduce the debt, namely, lowering spending or raising taxes. Instead, they engaged in some creative accounting. One method of making each year's budget appear balanced when it actually wasn't was to count projected revenue instead of actual revenue received. The flaw in this method was that not all revenue was collectible even in the distant future. From 1970 to 1976 between $2 and $3 billion in city taxes, fees, and fines went uncollected, $1 billion in 1976 alone. Between 1970 and 1975, the delinquency rate for real property taxes rose from 4 percent to 7 percent, totaling $571 million by June 30, 1975.[93] By treating all taxes, fees, and fines as collectible, and therefore as projected income, millions of dollars were added, on paper, to the revenue side of the ledger.

Other creative techniques moved funds around and put off the day of reckoning. The last payday of the year was advanced into the next fiscal year. Some current operating expenses, such as planning and engineering operations, were dumped into the capital expenditures budget, where deficits could be covered by long-term bonds. In 1975–1976 alone, $600 million was thus transferred to long-term debt.[94] Vendors and other creditors were held off until a new fiscal year arrived. Contributions to the city's pension funds were delayed and underfinanced, while the interest on those accounts above the statutory minimum was "borrowed" for the city's current general fund.[95] Present expenses were shifted onto future taxpayers by calling borrowed funds "income" and issuing Revenue Anticipation Notes (RANs) and Tax Anticipation Notes (TANs). These were short-term bonds against which future intergovernmental receipts and taxes were pledged.

All these gimmicks simply papered over the underlying problem: each year expenditures exceeded revenues. New York's accumulated debt continued to rise. The deficits were rolled over from year to year by issuing new short-term bonds to cover debt service on last year's bonds coming due. Short-term debt, which represented the bulk of this accumulated rolled-over debt, grew by over 400 percent in ten years. (On a personal basis, this is like someone who charges living expenses on one credit card, uses a second credit card to cover payments on the first, a third to cover the second, ad infinitum—and never comes up with the cash.)

The politicians could not have resorted to such a clever shell game without cooperation and even enthusiastic encouragement from bankers and lenders. The bankers were making an enormous amount of money underwriting and marketing New York's securities. Between 1965 and 1975, New York issued nearly $58 billion in bonds. Of this total, $48.5 billion was in short-term, high-interest notes used to roll over the accumulating deficit and rectify the cash flow problems of the city. Bankers and brokers made commissions on every bond sale and were able to promote the bonds to investors because of the high interest rates they carried.

The banks and brokers were direct participants in the financial processes of the city through the Bond Counsel and the Comptroller's Technical Debt Advisory Committee. The latter body, which was composed of both public officials and bankers, existed to advise the city on its borrowing strategy. It gave implicit approval to the city's practices by always approving the continuous stream of bonds. William E. Simon, one of the nation's biggest bond brokers, was a member of the committee in 1971 and 1972. As a senior partner in the firm of Salomon Brothers, he "was personally in charge of Salomon's [substantial] municipal and governmental bond sales."[96] One participant in the committee's meetings remarked that "all Simon and some of the other bankers wanted to do was sell bonds, make their profits, and look the other way."[97] This was the same William E. Simon who, as President Gerald Ford's Secretary of the Treasury, advocated a policy of punitive measures against New York when the city asked for a federal loan to avoid default on its debts in 1975. His own culpability in New York's problems did not deter him from observing, when the city asked for help, "We're going to sell New York to the Shah of Iran. It's a hell of an investment."[98]

In the mid-1970s, the United States entered its worst depression in forty years. Ten million workers joined the ranks of the unemployed—11 percent of the work force in New York by March.[99] At the same time the country experienced the worst inflationary rates for "any period of similar length in all of American history."[100] The recession threatened to bring a $25 trillion mountain of debt tumbling down on the nation's financial institutions.[101] By the end of 1974, the large commercial banking institutions had lent out 82 percent of their deposits, a historic level. The highest loans-to-deposits ratio in the seventy years prior to 1970 had been 79 percent (in 1921). Even in the black year of 1929 the ratio had been only 73 percent.[102]

The deteriorating economy and the troubles of many private businesses (such as the failure of the retail chain W. T. Grant, which left banks holding $640 million in debts[103]) led banks to reevaluate their holdings. New York's bonds were doubly threatening. Not only were they deemed marginal, but should the city default, the banks could not control a possible bankruptcy action resolution that might result in a write-down in the value of the bonds. A rapid write-down would translate into huge losses for the banks[104] and would reverberate through the national and world economies. A near panic about the financial viability of the city ensued.

As described in a report issued by a committee of the New York State Legislature, the banks scrambled to save their own profits at the city's expense:

> They began to rapidly and quietly (and perhaps improperly and illegally) unload their New York City bonds and thus saturated the market. You recall, they claimed the market was saturated and hence they could not sell their bonds. This seems to be untrue. In fact it appears that Chase [Manhattan Bank] unloaded two billion dollars' worth of bonds in a very short time!
> . . . Here is where the problem gets sticky for the banks. They had knowledge of the problems ahead, but they kept this knowledge to themselves while unloading their portfolios on others. They created the panic by their heavy sales.[105]

The culpability of the banks in precipitating the fiscal crisis was subsequently documented in a 10-pound, 800-page investigative report issued by the U.S. Securities and Exchange Commission.[106]

New York City's fiscal crisis came to a head in May 1975 when the banks publicly refused to market the city's securities. To resolve the crisis, the state legislature of New York, in response to pressure from the city's banking and business elite, established the Municipal Assistance Corporation (MAC) and the Emergency Financial Control Board (EFCB), both of which essentially took control of city government away from the city's elected officials. Members of the financial community firmly controlled both agencies and through them wielded the power to review annual budgets and borrowing requests.

The bankers were still not satisfied. To get the taxpayers to insure the safety of their investments, they asked the federal government to guarantee MAC bonds issued to cover the city's debts. Initially, President Ford refused to consider any special aid for New York, prompting a *New York Daily News* headline, "FORD TO CITY: DROP DEAD" (October 29, 1975). Eventually, the Ford Administration did support a modified bailout bill that enabled the city to borrow funds at 1 percent above the Treasury borrowing rate. Summing up the federal bailout, one scholar remarked, "Not only did the federal government make money on New York's fiscal crisis but the 'aid' package to the city was actually much less than the Chrysler Corporation bailout and aid given to many Third World nations."[107]

The fiscal retrenchment that followed the crisis had a profound impact on New York. Immediately, 25,000 city workers were fired, with black and Hispanic workers disproportionately losing their jobs. Between 1975 and 1980, city expenditures declined by 21.4 percent (in constant dollars).[108] There were serious reductions in the quantity and quality of municipal services. Within a year of the crisis, the century-old tradition of free tuition at the City University ended. Subway fares were increased three times in the six following years.[109] As New York gradually regained access to the bond market, tax subsidies for economic development were accorded highest priority and social services were pared.[110] Poor people bore most of the burdens of retrenchment.[111]

The 1975 fiscal crisis transformed politics in New York City. Led by Mayor Edward Koch (1978 to 1989), New York formed a "fiscal crisis" regime in which priorities shifted from services for the poor and middle class to tax breaks and other incentives for corporate investors and real estate developers. Koch effectively used the threat of another fiscal crisis to limit demands for public spending.[112]

Following the 1975 crisis, New York enjoyed a decade-long economic boom that enabled the city to balance its budget once again. Between 1978 and 1987 the city's economy gained over 300,000 jobs and tax revenues soared.[113] Even with Mayor Koch's skillful use of the rhetoric of urban fiscal crisis, however, the city failed to restrain its expenditure growth adequately and with the economic downturn that began in 1989 found itself, once again, on the brink of fiscal crisis. In 1991, the city government faced multibillion dollar budget deficits and the Emergency Financial Control Board threatened to again take control of city finances away from elected officials.[114]

Chicago's experience provides an instructive contrast to New York's. Chicago's powerful Democratic machine concentrated on providing basic city services and keeping taxes low. At the center of the electoral coalition were home owners and owners of small businesses who had a direct concern with keeping taxes low.

Following the death of Richard Daley in 1976, Chicago experienced a period of political turbulence that threatened the ruling regime and its budgetary policy. In the early 1980s, Chicago, like other cities, had fiscal problems. Its bonds were downgraded in 1984. However, the city was able to control spending growth and by 1987 Moody's had returned the city's bond rating to an A level.[115] Mayor Daley's son, Richard M. Daley, was elected mayor in 1989 and largely reconstituted the governing coalition that his father ruled so effectively for many years. An editorial in the *Wall Street Journal* praised Daley's responsible management of city government and cited Chicago as an example for other cities, like New York, to emulate.[116]

Though some of the differences between New York and Chicago can be attributed to styles of leadership, it is clear that political leaders in the two cities worked in different institutional contexts. The fragmentation of New York's Democratic party, among other factors, led to a situation in which, by the 1960s, the only way a citywide governing coalition could be held together was for mayors to spend more than they took in. In the absence of party loyalty, politicians had to buy electoral loyalty from individual interest groups with expensive programs. Various groups and constituencies expected concrete programs in exchange for their support.[117] In contrast, because Chicago's machine was able to deliver votes "through its ward-based organization, the machine either suppressed or absorbed most interest group activity in the city."[118]

New York's per capita tax burden was more than four times higher than Chicago's in 1989 (see Table 12-6). New York's high tax rates can be traced to several causes. The fragmented nature of its politics is one cause, but to blame everything on "liberal" politicians who caved in to demands from interest groups is simplistic. New York City was forced to fund a whole series of functions that in Chicago were funded by other governments. A study of sixty-two cities found that New York's functional responsibilities were broader than any other city's.[119] Chicago concentrated on basic housekeeping services, such as police, fire, and street cleaning. In 1975, Chicago spent only $12.18 per capita on public welfare, while New York City spent $365.78 per capita.[120] In Chicago most public welfare functions were the responsibility of Cook County, thus saving Chicago city taxpayers considerable money. To cite another example, in 1974 Chicago formed the Regional Transportation Authority (RTA) that spread funding for mass transit over a six-county area.[121]

New York, on the other hand, had costly responsibilities in welfare, health care, education (including an expensive city university system), public hospitals, public housing, and mass transit. In 1968, New York created the Metropolitan Transit Authority (MTA) to coordinate mass transit policy for the city and seven suburban counties, but the city still carried a substantial financial burden for mass transit.[122] In most cases, there was little the city could do about the added burden of all these responsiblities because it was New York State that determined the city's responsibilities. For example, New York City paid 23 percent of the Medicaid bill for recipients in the city.[123] Because such social programs relied on federal grants, New York became dependent on intergovernmental grants. In 1975, 50 percent of its total revenue came in the form of intergovernmental grants, compared to only 29 percent for Chicago. This left New York far more vulnerable than Chicago to the federal cuts of the 1980s.

The comparison between New York and Chicago shows that local leadership can make a difference in avoiding fiscal crises. However, leaders are constrained by the institutional setting within which they work. New York's mayors lacked the political authority to control spending. Indeed, the costs of many of the social programs the city helped fund were driven by the number of eligible recipients, and thus the city could not really control their costs. Chicago's solution, which was to move such programs into special districts or county or regional authorities, could not be implemented in New York. The suburban-dominated state legislature would never allow it. The lesson is that cities rarely control, to any significant degree, the causes of their fiscal difficul-

TABLE 12-6   PER CAPITA MUNICIPAL TAX BURDEN AND PER CAPITA BONDED DEBT, 1965–1989

	TAX BURDEN		DEBT BURDEN	
	NEW YORK	CHICAGO	NEW YORK	CHICAGO
1965	$ 285.93	$ 83.99	$ 959.00	$ 281.43
1970	382.90	122.76	1,101.00	497.00
1975	614.61	176.63	1,874.00	616.00
1980	948.50	245.00	1,505.00	716.00
1989	2,052.79	478.12	2,486.00	1,848.00

Note: Municipal tax burden = general revenue from own sources ÷ population; bonded debt = city's gross direct debt outstanding for end of fiscal year + overlapping debt.
Source: Adapted from tables in Esther Fuchs, *Mayors and Money: Fiscal Policy in New York and Chicago* (Chicago: University of Chicago Press, 1992), pp. 37–38. U.S. Bureau of the Census, *City Government Finances: 1964–65, 1969–70, 1974–75, 1987–88,* Tables 4, 5, 6, 7. *Moody's Municipal Credit Reports:* December 30, 1965 Chicago, Illinois: February 5, 1990; March 26, 1981; July 9, 1976; August 19, 1966; City Government Finance: New York City. U.S. Bureau of the Census, *Current Population Reports,* census year populations used.

ties or the options available for solving fiscal problems. The manifold social problems besetting central cities are related to national economic and social conditions. When cities try to manage the problems caused by such conditions, they find themselves locked into institutional and political arrangements that leave them little flexibility.

❖ THE POLITICAL SOURCES OF URBAN FISCAL STRESS

The occurrence of fiscal crises in cities of all sizes in all regions of the country suggests that cities are subject to national trends beyond their control. Cities are hemmed in by the actions of the federal government, state governments, and private economic institutions in ways that severely restrict their ability to cope:

> [A] city's fiscal health . . . depends on economic, social, and institutional factors that are largely outside the city's control. Poor fiscal health is not caused by poor management, corruption, or profligate spending, and a city government's ability to alter the city's fiscal health is severely limited.[124]

City officials under fiscal stress find themselves on the horns of a dilemma: They can either raise taxes or cut services, but either alternative can have a negative impact on the long-term fiscal viability of a city. When cities raise taxes, they run the danger of losing the investors and middle-class taxpayers that are so essential to urban revival. By 1981, the tax burdens of central cities, as a percentage of personal income, exceeded suburban tax burdens by more than 50 percent.[125]

Alternatively, when cities reduce the level of services and fail to build and maintain infrastructure, they become less attractive places to live and work. For cities in severe fiscal crisis, a vicious cycle of decline may set in: Deteriorating services chase away business and residents, the tax base deteriorates as a result and revenues decline, services must be cut further, and so on. East St. Louis, Illinois, is a city that long ago reached that point. Between 1960 and 1990, its population fell by 50 percent. Property values plummeted and the tax rate, as a result, quadrupled. East St. Louis shows that it is possible for a city to lose all ability to remain a functional public entity:

> East St. Louis, with its acre upon acre of burned-out hulks that were once houses, its sad tales of backed-up sewers and of police cars that run out of gas, of garbage piled so deep that entire streets are rendered impassable and of books so poorly kept that no one can calculate its debt, has become a textbook case of everything that can go wrong in an American city.[126]

In 1990, in order to satisfy a court judgment, East St. Louis was forced to give its City Hall to a creditor, who then leased the building back to the city. An appeals court subsequently returned City Hall to the city, but this left the creditor's demands still unsatisfied.

Urban fiscal crises are not inevitable. They result from the structure of America's intergovernmental system, which makes each city an autonomous fiscal unit, but also subject to the whims and demands of higher levels of government. Western European cites have no general tendency toward fiscal crisis.[127] A major reason for this is that higher levels of government provide a substantial portion of local revenues, thus limiting the internecine competition among cities for tax base. In 1984, for example, when intergovernmental transfers provided only about 20 percent of local revenues in the United States, they provided 40 percent in Japan, 54 percent in Great Britain, and 80 percent in the Netherlands.[128] Most western European city governments do not have to rely upon private lenders to raise money for capital projects; those are generally financed by national governments. The U.S. arrangement is peculiar: "By not providing capital resources to subnational governments from the central government, the United States stands apart from almost every other advanced capitalist state, even other federal states."[129] All across the country, urban residents live, often very uncomfortably, with this peculiar arrangement.

URBAN ECONOMIC DEVELOPMENT
WHO WINS AND WHO LOSES?

❖ THE URBAN RENAISSANCE

On August 26, 1976, Boston's Mayor Kevin White presided over opening day ceremonies for Quincy Market in downtown Boston. The brainchild of developer James Rouse, who made a fortune developing suburban shopping malls, Quincy Market was housed in three 150-year-old market buildings that were creatively renovated, at a cost of more than $40 million, into a collection of boutiques, gourmet food shops, and restaurants.[1] Located in the center of a declining central city with inadequate parking and no big-ticket items to sell, few expected Quincy Market to succeed. Indeed, six weeks before opening day, the retail complex was less than 50 percent leased. In order to hide the empty stores, Rouse came up with the idea of pushcarts, leased to artists and craftspeople for $50 a day, plus a percentage of the sales. On opening day forty-three pushcarts contributed to a carnival-like atmosphere.

By eleven o'clock only a modest crowd had gathered for the ceremonies. After the speeches were over, Mayor White cut the ribbon and developer Rouse and a company of kilted highland bagpipers led the crowd inside for a champagne reception. At lunch time, the crowd swelled as curious workers poured out of nearby office buildings. By mid-afternoon it was clear that opening day would be a huge success, with police estimating the crowd at 100,000.

Opening day was not a fluke; people never stopped coming to Quincy Market. In its second year of operation the market drew 12 million visitors—more than Disneyland that year. Newspapers reported the market's "instant acceptance" by the public, which delighted in the colorful sights, sounds, and smells of the food and imaginatively displayed merchandise and the festival air created by a liberal sprinkling of magicians, acrobats, and puppeteers. The banks that financed the project were originally highly skeptical; they calculated that Quincy Market would have to produce retail sales comparable to the most successful suburban shopping malls ($150 per square foot) to justify its unusually high development costs. Quincy Market shocked the experts by producing sales of $233 per square foot in its first year, with the pushcarts doing best of all.

The opening of Quincy Market was hailed by the media as a sign of an "urban renaissance." It seemed to disprove the conventional wisdom that the downtowns of American cities were doomed to obsolescence and decline. Quincy Market was soon followed by a number of festival marketplaces, many of them designed by Rouse: the Gallery of Market Street East in Philadelphia, Grand Avenue in Milwaukee, Pike Street Market in Seattle, Horton Plaza in San Diego, Trolley Square in Salt Lake City, Union Station in St. Louis, Harborplace in Baltimore, and many others.

Other cities built sprawling indoor complexes connected by pedestrian bridges and tubes. Architect John Portman pioneered such "cities within cities" when he opened the Peachtree Plaza in downtown Atlanta in 1967. The hotel lobbies and vaulted atriums that make up the complex are dazzling, filled with flowing water and pools, ascending ranks of balconies vanishing toward a skylight, corridors rigged with lights and mirrors, glass elevators outlined in lights. Peachtree Plaza replaced the old downtown Atlanta, which was almost completely razed, with a new, gleaming, enclosed city-within-a-city. Portman built several other complexes, lesser in scale but aspiring to a similar grandeur, in other cities—the Renaissance Center in Detroit, the Hyatt at Embarcadero Center in San Francisco, the Bonaventure Hotel in Los Angeles, and the Marriott Marquis in Times Square, New York City.

Downtown malls helped to boost a downtown retailing boom that began in the mid-1970s. There was also a renaissance in a whole range of downtown real estate developments: corporate offices, hotels, convention centers, sports stadiums, concert halls, and museums. By the middle of the 1980s every mayor's downtown "trophy collection" included at least one luxury hotel (preferably one with a multistory atrium), new sports stadium (usually domed), downtown shopping mall, redeveloped waterfront, or new convention center.[2] The real estate development boom occurred when central business districts became centers of corporate white-collar employment, entertainment, culture, and a burgeoning tourism and convention trade.

The revival of downtown real estate was connected to a change in the methods used by city governments to spur development. The urban renewal and slum clearance programs of the 1950s and 1960s had been based on a massive infusion of federal funds. Urban renewal was replaced by the Community

Development Block Grant (CDBG) and the Urban Development Action Grant (UDAG) programs, which gave cities greater discretion over how federal funds were spent. But as the rules changed, the federal pipeline for urban development gradually dried up. Federal aid fell by almost 80 percent in the 1980s. The Reagan Administration instructed cities to promote local economic growth as a way to make up for declining federal grants.

Cities began to experiment with partnerships between the public and private sectors to promote investment in the local economy. They devoted CBDG and UDAG funds to big downtown projects, floated bonds, offered property tax abatements, built utilities tunnels, constructed sewer lines and water mains, and rerouted and resurfaced streets. In these and other ways cities provided public subsidies to encourage private investment in office towers, malls, and cultural and tourist facilities. The melding of public subsidies and private dollars took place through newly created incorporated entities that oversaw specific projects—a sports authority to build a stadium, for example, or a public development corporation run like a private corporation, established specifically to receive both public subsidies and private investment funds.[3]

As cities aggressively pursued new strategies to replace disappearing federal funds, the dividing line between the public and private sectors became blurred. Public-private partnerships became the talisman of urban economic development. More cities began cutting complex deals with private developers. In exchange for subsidies, some cities took profit-sharing positions in development projects. In the case of Quincy Market, for example, Boston provided $12 million—almost 30 percent of the total cost of the project—and gave the Rouse Corporation a ninety-nine-year lease on the property. In exchange, the city was guaranteed a minimum annual cash payment plus a portion of income from store rents above that minimum.

The skylines of American cities were transformed by forests of new skyscrapers constructed to house the thousands of corporate employees working downtown. Most cities experienced at least some degree of gentrification, the movement of young professionals and businesspeople into older urban neighborhoods. In some cities—Boston, Chicago, Washington, D.C., Philadelphia, San Francisco—there was a massive displacement of the poor and aged from older residential areas. Metropolitan newspapers and city magazines loved to feature the renovation of historic architecture in such neighborhoods as Society Hill in Philadelphia, Park Slope in Brooklyn, and uptown in Chicago. An entire generation of "messiah mayors" led the efforts and took much of the credit for the revival of downtown. As noted by the historian Jon Teaford, "if nothing else the messiah mayors . . . boosted the spirits of many urban dwellers and made them proud of their cities."[4]

It is important to be cautious, however, when evaluating the urban renaissance. Local boosters and media have invariably overstated the extent of the revival. Though central city economies undoubtedly improved in the 1980s compared to the 1970s, they still lagged behind the nation as a whole. Suburban job growth far outpaced job growth in the central cities.[5] In the first half of the 1980s the glitter of new development could not be missed in Baltimore, Philadelphia, and St. Louis and other cities, yet most cities experienced jobs losses and continued decline in many areas. Was the renaissance in such cases a mere "political sleight-of-hand" or an "illusion of success"?[6]

The answer to that question depends on one's point of view and, crucially, on whether one was a beneficiary or a loser in the most recent round of revival. Those who touted the benefits of inner-city renaissance claimed that it created jobs for city residents, raised the tax base for financially strapped city governments, and revived the cities as centers of culture.

There is no doubt that the central business districts of most cities have been resuscitated; some had seemed near death. In most cases, however, the spillover to other business areas and neighborhoods within the cities has been limited. Islands of prosperity have emerged in the cities, but they generally are surrounded by depressed areas that seem no better off because of the urban renaissance. There are at least two reasons for the circumscribed effects of the renaissance. First, the best jobs created in the revived downtown are taken disproportionately by suburbanites, not by people living in the inner cities. Second, in many cases the subsidies given by city governments far exceed the new tax revenues that are generated, and as a result, city taxpayers pay more than they get back. Despite the renaissance, central cities still struggle with fiscal problems so severe they cannot provide adequate services and maintain public infrastructure.

In this chapter we consider the question: Who benefits and who loses from the recent urban renaissance? These questions are especially important for blacks, Hispanics, and the poor who make up a large proportion of the population of older American cities.

❖ THE RATIONALE FOR THE POLITICS OF GROWTH

From the very beginning, European settlement in North America was founded on town promotion and growth. The first colony, Jamestown, founded in 1607, was the risky venture of a group of English entrepreneurs who organized themselves into a joint stock company. Shares sold in London for about $62 in gold. If the colony was successful, investors hoped to make a profit on their investment. Though Jamestown failed, town promotion and civic boosterism became a way of life in the New World as cities competed for the settlers and investors who swept across the continent.

Government subsidies to aid business expansion are as old as the Republic. Alexander Hamilton, Secretary of the Treasury under President Washington, justified subsidies for private businesses as an effective way of promoting growth.

> This has been found to be one of the most efficacious means of encouraging manufactures, and is, in some views, the best. . . . It is a species of encourage-

ment more positive and direct than any other, and for that reason, has a more immediate tendency to stimulate and uphold new enterprises, increasing the chance for profit, and diminishing the risk of loss. . . .[7]

The popular notion that nineteenth-century capitalism developed without government intervention is false. Governments heavily subsidized private turnpike, canal, and railroad companies. Railroads, especially, enjoyed huge subsidies from city governments. Railroad connections were the key to urban growth in the nineteenth century, and consequently, civic boosters did everything in their power to attract railroads to their towns.

Today, although the objects of civic largess have changed from railroads to highways, airports, and white-collar corporate and entertainment facilities, the nature of local boosterism has remained remarkably similar. Public and private leaders still promote local growth, and they do it by claiming that growth brings prosperity to everyone. Because the coalitions promoting growth are so similar from city to city, two urban scholars have called them "growth machines."[8] They are stable coalitions made up of local public officials and influential business leaders, plus, usually, real estate developers, local media, labor leaders, and others who have a stake in the value of local real estate and economic performance. Coalitions like these pushed the urban renewal programs of the 1950s and 1960s and came together behind the new urban renaissance.

It would be misleading to characterize these growth coalitions as cynically pursuing their self-interest at the expense of the city. Most supporters of public subsidies sincerely believe that redevelopment will ultimately benefit everyone living in the city. The members of the downtown coalitions are convinced that the city's survival depends upon local economic vitality. The logic of their argument is as follows: A healthy tax base is necessary to maintain the public services and infrastructure that the local economy and residents rely upon; a healthy tax base, in turn, requires rising land values and business prosperity; in order to attract private investment, a city must offer a good business climate and special incentives that make it less expensive for mobile investors to locate there than in other cities; an increasing volume of private investment begins the cycle all over again, resulting in rising land values, a healthy tax base, better services, and a better business climate.[9] Built into the logic underlying this argument, it should be noted, is the assumption that cities must be actively involved in creating the conditions for growth. This argument, and the assumptions on which it rests, are shown in Figure 13-1.

The reverse of the process shown in Figure 13-1, is the presumed logic of economic decline and fiscal impoverishment, wherein a poor business climate leads to disinvestment, which in turn causes land values to fall. Consequently, the property tax and other sources of revenue decline, causing deterioration in city services. The city then finds it more difficult to borrow funds to improve the infrastructure. Many people would recognize this downward spiral as an all-too-familiar experience for older cities over the past several decades.

Figure 13-1   The Logic of Growth Politics

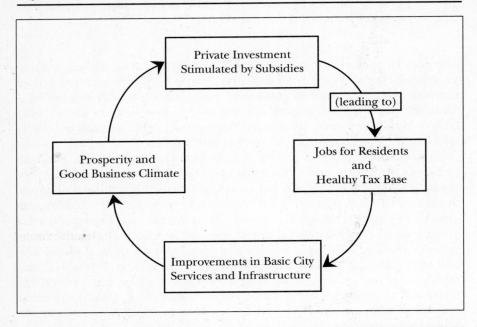

Growth politics at the local level has more frequently been a source of unity than a source of conflict. Considering the degree to which business leaders believe that their own success undergirds everyone else's, it is not surprising that they become infuriated when opponents question their motives and accuse them of feeding at the public trough. Members of local growth coalitions are usually intolerant of opposition, accusing their opponents of weakening the ability of the city to compete. Appeals to unity are frequent, as exemplified by the slogan adopted by a midwestern city in the 1920s:

> United we stick, divided we're stuck.
> United we boost, divided we bust.[10]

Few people would assert that local economic decline is preferable to prosperity. It is not always clear, however, that growth brings the benefits that the proponents of business subsidies claim. Development projects often displace small businesses. Neighborhood gentrification typically drives up rents and housing costs. Growth can also impose what economists call "negative externalities," such as air pollution, water pollution, and traffic congestion. Finally, it is not always clear that new investment provides more in tax revenues than it costs in subsidies and additional city services. As we discuss in the next section, economic change is inevitable in cities. The role that governments assume in promoting growth, however, is not.

❖ THE CHANGING ECONOMIC FUNCTIONS OF CITIES

The distribution of economic activities in the nation has changed fundamentally over the past hundred years. In the late nineteenth and early twentieth centuries, cities prospered as centers of manufacturing production. Railroad connections made it possible to transport raw materials into industrial cities and ship the finished products around the country. Large factories, employing the new energy sources of steam and electricity, reaped the benefits of economies of scale as the new techniques of mass production were perfected. Large factories required thousands of workers. As the center of the nation's economic production, cities, with their growing concentrations of immigrant workers, burst at the seams.

During the 1920s, American cities began to change from centers of goods production, wholesale trade, and retail sales to centers of services, culture, entertainment, and tourism. These trends accelerated after World War II. After 1950, cities lost a large portion (though not all) of their manufacturing jobs. One reason is that manufacturing employment everywhere declined as a percentage of the overall work force. Technological advances in production processes, such as the use of robots for assembly, made it possible to produce goods with far fewer workers than in the past. Between 1970 and 1988, though the volume of production increased, the nation's manufacturing employment remained stable at 19.4 million jobs. During the same period, however, service jobs increased rapidly. There were two distinct tiers of service employment. The upper tier was employment in business and financial services (white-collar professionals such as lawyers, accountants, investment brokers, and computer and communications specialists). The lower tier was employment in food, retail, and personal services (such as those provided in restaurants, stores, laundromats, and barbershops). From 1975 to 1990, there were 30.3 million new jobs created in service industries, which employed 84.4 million people in 1990, compared to only 25.0 million in goods production.[11] Nearly 80 percent of the new jobs created during the 1980s were service jobs.[12] In 1970, manufacturing jobs were the dominant category in metropolitan areas; today service jobs dominate (see Table 13-1).

Another reason the economies of cities changed, in addition to the overall change in the national economy, is that factories moved out of them. The development of highways and truck transportation, heavily subsidized by government policies, enabled factories to move to the periphery of metropolitan areas and beyond, especially to locations with convenient connections to interstate highways. Modern mass production requires large amounts of inexpensive land for one-story, assembly-line production methods. With the range of commuting made possible by the automobile, factories can locate at a distance from residential centers and still be accessible to workers. Manufacturers also moved out of older metropolitan areas entirely to avoid unions and to find a cheaper and more pliant work force.[13] Some companies moved to the Sunbelt for these reasons, but increasingly, manufacturing firms have moved

TABLE 13-1   CHANGE IN JOB CATEGORIES IN SEVEN NORTHEASTERN AND MIDWESTERN METROPOLITAN AREAS,[a] **1970–1991**

	PERCENT EMPLOYED IN EACH CATEGORY[b]				
	1970	1975	1982	1986	1991
Manufacturing	30.1	25.8	22.4	18.5	15.6
Transportation, communications, and public utilities	6.4	6.3	5.9	5.8	5.8
Wholesale and retail	20.8	21.6	21.9	22.5	21.9
Finance, insurance, and real estate	6.4	6.7	7.4	9.1	9.2
Services	18.4	20.6	24.6	27.4	30.6
Government	13.6	15.1	14.5	13.4	13.5

[a]New York City, Chicago, Boston, St. Louis, Cleveland, Detroit, and Pittsburgh.
[b]Columns do not add to 100 percent because they do not include employment in mining and construction.
Source: U.S. Department of Labor, Bureau of Labor Statistics, *Earnings and Employment* (Washington, D.C.: Government Printing Office, 1970, 1975, 1982, 1986, 1991).

to such places as the Caribbean, Latin America, and Asia, where wages are much lower and environmental regulations are lax.[14] Table 13-2 shows the decline in manufacturing in major metropolitan areas from 1977 to 1987, with a less drastic decline in suburbs than in central cities.

Until the 1950s, cities were the centers of wholesale and retail trade within urban areas. The large downtown department stores offered the greatest selection and best prices, and middle-class shoppers took mass transit downtown to shop. Macy's in New York City, Hudson's in Detroit, and Jordan Marsh in Boston were elegant shopping palaces that attracted huge crowds. With a staff of more than 8,000, Marshall Field in Chicago attracted more than a quarter of a million customers in a day.[15]

Downtown shopping was killed in the 1950s by suburbanization and the automobile. By the 1960s, suburban shopping centers had begun to eclipse central business districts. With big parking lots and freeway interchanges nearby, the shopping centers and their later incarnation, the malls, were more convenient for shoppers, who had by now completely abandoned mass transit for the automobile. In 1956, the first enclosed, climate-controlled mall, Southdale, was opened in the Minneapolis suburb of Edina. By making shopping comfortable all year round it was an instant success.[16] Mall owners became proficient at creating a leisurely atmosphere conducive to consumption, including common hours for stores, directories and uniform signs, and benches and landscaping. In comparison, downtown shopping seemed chaotic and inconvenient, and perhaps even menacing.

TABLE 13-2 CHANGES IN FOUR JOB CATEGORIES IN METROPOLITAN AREAS[a] AND CENTRAL CITIES, 1977–1987 (IN THOUSANDS)

	CENTRAL CITIES		PERCENT CHANGE 1977–1987	OUTSIDE CENTRAL CITIES		PERCENT CHANGE 1977–1987
	1977	1987		1977	1987	
Manufacturing	2,027	1,563	−22.9	3,001	2,864	−4.6
Wholesale trade	633	642	+1.4	718	950	+32.3
Retail trade	1,193	1,337	+12.1	1,803	2,474	+37.2
Services	1,129	2,127	+88.4	2,444	5,195	+112.6

[a]Ten largest metropolitan areas (1980 rank): New York, Los Angeles, Chicago, Philadelphia, Detroit, San Jose, Washington, D.C., Dallas–Fort Worth, Houston, Boston; suburbs of New York City not included for reasons of data comparability.
Source: U.S. Bureau of the Census, *State and Metropolitan Area Data Book: 1991* (Washington, D.C.: Government Printing Office, 1991); U.S. Bureau of the Census, *County and City Data Book: 1983* (Washington, D.C.: Government Printing Office, 1983); U.S. Bureau of the Census, *Census of Manufacturing, Census of Wholesale Trade, Census of Retail Trade, Census of Services, Geographic areas series* (Washington, D.C.: Government Printing Office, 1987).

By 1974, 15,000 shopping centers had captured more than 44 percent of the nation's retail sales.[17] Downtown department stores began to close for good. Hudson's, a longtime landmark in downtown Detroit, finally closed its doors in 1981.[18] Few downtowns now are sites for major consumer purchases, such as appliances or furniture. Instead, most downtowns must content themselves with capturing a portion of specialty niche and entertainment shopping that appeals to downtown workers or tourists. Table 13-2 shows that wholesale and retail employment in central cities gained slightly from 1977 to 1987, but declined as a proportion of the overall central city work force. In contrast, employment in wholesale and retail trade surged in the suburbs during this period.

In only three decades the central business districts of cities were transformed from centers of wholesale and retail trade to centers of high-level corporate services. Corporations prefer to concentrate a variety of interdependent activities within small geographic areas, whether those areas are within central cities or in the new edge cities on the periphery of metropolitan areas in which light manufacturing, retail, service, and residential functions cluster.[19] While routine, back-office service jobs that rely primarily on electronic processing and communications technologies (such as check processing and data entry) are dispersing, high-level corporate services, decision making, and skilled information-processing functions (accounting, legal, consulting, computing, and stenographic services) are concentrating in central business districts and edge cities.

By concentrating a mass of skilled service specialists in a geographical area close to restaurants and entertainment, central business districts provide rich hosting environments for corporations. Corporate decision makers have quick access to skilled professionals. Small firms clustered around and in the corporate skyscrapers provide basic secretarial, reproducing, office supply, and maintenance and janitorial services. The bigger and more concentrated the downtown, the more specialized services can become, providing access, for example, to lawyers who specialize in patent law or accountants who are experts in the intricacies of corporate taxes. Downtowns also provide the face-to-face contacts that are essential for effective relationships with key clients and customers.

The skyscrapers that sprout from the downtowns of American cities are the physical manifestation of the new economic functions of central cities. From the 1920s to the 1950s, few office towers were built in downtowns. Between 1950 and 1984, over 40 percent of the nation's gain in office employment and construction was concentrated in the downtowns of the thirty largest urban areas.[20] Between 1960 and 1984, these areas built the equivalent of 250 Empire State Buildings. During this period, central cities maintained a constant share of the nation's office space. During the 1980s office boom, cities even increased their share—a significant feat given the simultaneous boom in suburban office construction.[21]

The whole phenomenon of service sector expansion in cities has taken place within a changing international division of labor. Corporate headquarters cluster most densely in a few global cities such as San Francisco, New York, Paris, London, Hong Kong, Sidney, and Tokyo. Sitting atop the urban hierarchy, these cities house corporate command and control functions that manage production and distribution networks that are truly global. Second-level cities, such as Chicago, Atlanta, Montreal, and Hamburg, for the most part house national corporate systems. Further down the hierarchy, medium-sized cities, such as Cleveland and St. Louis, are the hubs of regional corporate networks. Down the pyramid further still, there are cities that have quite specialized economies. The higher a city is in the urban hierarchy, the more pulling power it has for jobs and investment and the more control it potentially has to shape its economic future.[22]

The changing economic complexion of central cities presents opportunities as well as dangers for downtown economies. The opportunity is that expanding service sector employment will offset the loss of industrial jobs and revive depleted central city tax bases. As Figure 13-2 shows, between 1969 and 1988 New York City, for instance, lost 460,000 manufacturing jobs, but gained 344,000 service jobs. Much of New York's job growth came in export services, which are the most valuable to a local economy, more valuable, certainly, than the low-paying jobs in personal services (e.g., cleaning and laundering, haircutting, waitressing and bartending, and the like). Export services such as accounting and advertising are paid for by consumers who are not located exclusively in the areas where the services are located. Export services pull money into the local economy from elsewhere. The service jobs connected to corporations, because they are more specialized and productive, tend to pay well. A study of fourteen large metropolitan areas in 1987 found that wages of central city jobs averaged 20 percent higher than suburban jobs, and that gap was increasing.[23]

The concentration of high-wage professional jobs in the downtowns of central cities offers an opportunity for spin-off economic development. People who work in the city may decide to live in the city. The housing needs of these affluent new residents can lead to gentrification, that is, investment in older city neighborhoods and the rehabilitation of older, architecturally significant housing stock.

Though the expanding service economy of cities offers many benefits, there is also a downside. The transition from manufacturing to services has created a missing middle in the two-tiered service wage structure. Well-paying manufacturing jobs are being replaced by service jobs that fall into either the high or the low end of the wage scale. One study found that, between 1979 and 1984, almost 60 percent of the new jobs created in the American economy paid less than $7,000 a year.[24] In any case, central city residents are not the chief job-takers. The cities that led the nation in office employment growth from 1950 to 1984 did not, thereby, appreciably reduce their levels of unemployment.[25] The main problem was that most of the jobs went to suburban commuters. In 1984, commuters held 60 percent of the jobs in San Francisco and 70 percent in Boston.[26]

Figure 13-2   Changing Employment in New York, by Sector, 1969–1966
(1969 = 100 Percent)

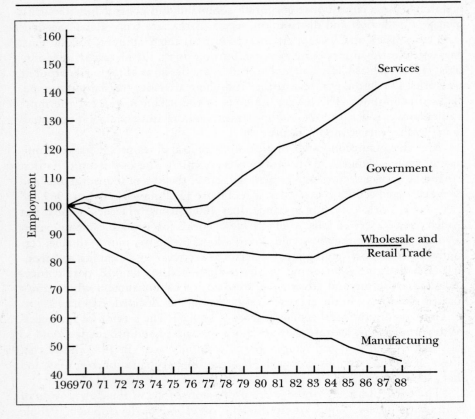

Source: Port of New York and New Jersey, Regional Economic Analysis Group, Office of Business Development, *The Regional Economy: Review 1988 and 1989 for the New York–New Jersey Metropolitan Region* (March 1989), p. 34.

❖ THE CORPORATE CENTER STRATEGY: THE BALTIMORE EXAMPLE

Mayors and development officials in central cities realize that the cities will never regain their dominant position in maufacturing. They accept as well that it is pointless for cities to compete head-to-head with suburbs for certain kinds of wholesaling and retailing. Cities must carve out a niche. The special mix that central cities try to nurture today has been labeled the "corporate center strategy," a stew of financial, administrative, and professional services and "an orientation toward luxury consumption that is appealing to young corporate managers, educated professionals, convention goers, and the tourist trade."[27]

Baltimore is an excellent test case of the corporate center strategy because it is here that the strategy has been applied consistently over an extended period of time to revitalize a depressed downtown. If the strategy is going to succeed anywhere, it should in Baltimore. Writing in *Fortune* magazine, journalist Gurney Breckenfeld praised the close collaboration between government and business in Baltimore: "Their [public and private sector] strategy, established at the outset, has been to convert the heart of the city into a culturally rich, architecturally exciting magnet where both affluent and middle-class families will choose to work, shop, and live."[28] Dubbed the "Cinderella city of the 1980s," Baltimore is one of the nation's most successful examples of the corporate center strategy.[29]

Downtown redevelopment in Baltimore is closely identified with an extraordinary politician, William Donald Schaefer. As the leader of a coalition of government and business, Schaefer served as the energizing force behind redevelopment in Baltimore during his four terms as mayor from 1971 to 1987. Fiercely loyal to Baltimore, Schaefer continued to live with his mother in the same West Side house where he was born. Baltimore was Schaefer's love, politics his obsession. On weekends he would cruise the city in his 1975 Pontiac jotting down the location of uncollected garbage, faulty street lights, and abandoned cars. On Monday morning, department heads would find "mayor's action memos" on their desks, and a few days later mayoral aides would follow up to make sure the problem was solved. Known for his showmanship, Schaefer demonstrated his devotion to Baltimore in sometimes eccentric ways:

> When the new National Aquarium failed to open by the July 4 deadline he (Schaefer) had guaranteed, Willie Don, as they call him, demonstrated his contrition by plunging into the seal pool (temperature 79 degrees) in striped Victorian swimsuit and straw boater, clutching a yellow duck (he is also affectionately known as Donald Duck). His penitential immersion was shared by a voluptuous model done up as a mermaid.[30]

As the head of a strong-mayor system of government in a city characterized by machine politics, Schaefer modeled himself on Chicago's Mayor Daley and, like Daley, he knew how to exercise power. After spending nineteen years on the city council, Schaefer was elected mayor in 1971 and quickly became one of the shrewdest, most powerful mayors in the country. Realizing he wanted to redevelop the downtown as fast as possible, Schaefer devised a strategy that circumvented the slow-moving bureaucratic and democratic processes of city government at the same time that it won the confidence of corporate investors. Schaefer relied on a network of twenty-four quasi-public development corporations that contracted with the city government to direct and implement downtown redevelopment. Schaefer's model for these corporations was the Charles Center Management Office, a development corporation that contracted with the city, beginning in 1959, to implement a $180 million, 33-acre urban renewal project in the middle of downtown. Charles Center became a bustling complex of offices, apartments, and retail shops that convinced investors that downtown could succeed.

In 1964, the city unveiled an even more ambitious $270 million plan for rehabilitating Baltimore's decaying waterfront. When Schaefer was elected mayor in 1971, he enthusiastically embraced a plan to rehabilitate 240 acres in Baltimore's Inner Harbor and staked his political future on aggressive implementation of the plan. Charles Center—Inner Harbor Management, Inc. (CCIHM) was at the center of the network of quasi-public corporations used to redevelop the harbor. The city contracted with CCIHM to plan and implement the Inner Harbor project. More specialized development corporations were established to implement other parts of the plan, such as housing. Though they contracted for public projects (and thus could be called quasi-public), as private entities the development corporations were able to pay higher salaries than public agencies to attract talented executives and could circumvent public regulations concerning such requirements as competitive bidding and affirmative action. Proponents viewed them as "apolitical means for improving the city's development potential by infusing speed, flexibility, and technical expertise into the policy-making process."[31]

The Inner Harbor project was daunting. In an earlier period, the harbor had been a bustling center of commerce, but by the 1960s it was an eyesore—composed of rotting, rat-infested piers, abandoned buildings, and desolate parking lots—perched on a harbor that smelled, in H. L. Mencken's words, "like a million polecats."[32] The audacious idea was to transform the area into a national tourist attraction.

The linchpin of the Inner Harbor plan was Harborplace, two newly constructed, block-long, translucent pavilions situated right on the harbor. Designed by James Rouse, the same person who had designed Boston's Quincy Market, Harborplace offered a dazzling array of specialty shops, ethnic foods, and, above all, sights and sounds, including dancers, clowns, and magicians. Built at a cost of $22 million, Harborplace was designed to be a marketplace that would make the inner city, in Rouse's words, "a warm and human place, with diversity of choice, full of festival and delight."[33] Completed in 1980, Harborplace succeeded beyond anyone's expectations, attracting 18 million visitors the first year (like Quincy Market, it outpulled Disneyland), earning $42 million, and creating 2,300 jobs. In 1981 the National Aquarium was completed, giving the Inner Harbor a major tourist attraction. By 1992 more than 15 million visitors had toured the aquarium's exhibits, including a 64-foot glass pyramid housing a reproduction of a South American rain forest.[34]

The success of Harborplace and the National Aquarium established the Inner Harbor as a tourism and convention center, unleashing a surge of private investment throughout the entire Inner Harbor area. Between 1980 and 1986 the number of tourists and the amount of money they spent tripled; in order to accommodate the increased demand, the number of hotel rooms also tripled. The benefits to the city seemed obvious. The city's manpower programs succeeded in placing 1,300 persons in jobs at Harborplace.[35] More than 40 percent of the Harborplace work force was drawn from minorities.[36] By 1984 a revived convention business was pumping an estimated $52 million annually into Baltimore's economy.[37] Tax revenues from Baltimore's central business district soared from $13.8 million in 1976 to $44.3 million in 1987.[38]

Inner Harbor was a big political winner for Schaefer. The press hailed him as "The Best Mayor in America"; Howard Cosell dubbed him "the genius mayor."[39] Schaefer won reelection three times in succession by overwhelming margins. In November 1986, Schaefer rode the wave of positive publicity about Baltimore's renaissance into the Maryland governor's mansion.

Amidst the hoopla over Baltimore's highly visible downtown revival, however, conditions in the city's deteriorating neighborhoods were often overlooked. Kurt Schmoke, who succeeded Schaefer as Baltimore's first black mayor in 1987, observed, "If you were revisiting Baltimore today after a twenty-year absence, you would find us much prettier and much poorer."[40] While Baltimore's rate of population loss declined in the 1980s, it still showed a loss of more than 50,000 people. In a comparison with eleven Frostbelt cities of similar size in 1979, the per capita income growth of Baltimore residents lagged behind nine of them, and Baltimore showed the highest poverty rate.[41] On an index of urban hardship that ranked fifty-five cities, Baltimore improved only three places between 1970 and 1980, moving from the sixth worst to the ninth worst.[42] Between 1970 and 1980 the poverty rate increased in 90 percent of Baltimore's predominantly black neighborhoods.[43]

How can the apparent paradox between the stunning commercial success of Baltimore's corporate center strategy and the declining conditions in nearby neighborhoods be explained? Studies indicate that the downtown corporate economy has few links with small businesses and job creation in neighborhoods.[44] Central city residents often lack the skills and education to qualify for the knowledge-intensive jobs that locate in central business districts.[45] In 1979, a majority of the employees working in central business districts lived outside the central cities. And the better the jobs paid, the more likely they were to be held by suburbanites; 71 percent of those working downtown and making over $50,000 in 1979 lived in the suburbs.[46] Many of the jobs in the tourist industry that do go to central city dwellers are unpleasant, low-skilled jobs, with few prospects for advancement. Hence, the overall skill level of the resident work force does not improve even if the downtown is new and glittering.[47]

In addition to its failure to bring material benefits to most city residents, Baltimore's corporate center strategy was criticized for sidestepping the democratic process. Located outside of the public sector, the development corporations were not required to give information to the public or to consult with the citizens in making decisions. They operated as private corporations, with their files locked and meetings closed.

It is clear that Baltimore's redevelopment projects involved conflicts and trade-offs that legitimately are the subject of democratic debate. The Inner Harbor development did not induce middle- and upper-income residents to move into the city despite the fact that significant amounts of money were used to build middle-income housing. Area residents adjacent to the valuable Inner Harbor real estate found their tax assessments rising rapidly. Those who were on fixed incomes were forced to sell their suddenly valuable homes or seek tax relief from the city. While downtown development expanded tax revenues, it also absorbed additional city services. Indeed, according to one scholar, "downtown redevelopment in Baltimore annually absorbs around $17 million more in city expenditures than it generates in municipal revenues."[48]

Schaefer's quasi-public development corporations constituted a kind of shadow government that made key decisions about Baltimore's future and yet remained outside the democratic process. The most important quasi-public corporation was the Baltimore City Trustee Loan and Guarantee Program, which, between 1976 and 1986, used public funds to loan or guarantee loans worth $500 million in 239 projects.[49] The trustees were controlled by the mayor, but as a private entity the corporation that ran the program was not required even to provide information to the city council. Downtown projects were given priority by the trustees and numerous loans were awarded to political contributors to Mayor Schaefer's campaigns. Perhaps sensing that the loan program could become an issue in his upcoming gubernatorial campaign, Schaefer abolished the trustees in 1986 and moved the loan portfolio over to the City Finance Department, where it would be subject to public scrutiny.[50]

The corporate center strategy in Baltimore was a great commercial success. However, instead of "a rising tide lifts all boats," the appropriate metaphor to describe Baltimore's renaissance is a "leaky bucket," with most of the benefits leaking out to developers and to suburban residents who took the best white-collar jobs. Relatively few benefits trickled down to the residents of the city. This does not mean that the corporate center strategy directly hurt Baltimore residents; urban decline and continued population loss would have occurred anyway. Certainly, the success of downtown development raised the morale of Baltimore residents—no small feat. The material benefits for Baltimore residents, however, were surprisingly limited.

Baltimore has become, in essence, two cities. One city is populated by office workers, executives, and tourists, who pass the residents of the other city on their way from their homes in the suburbs or on the expressway to the airport. In this regard, the Inner Harbor development has made Baltimore much like other American cities that have successfully implemented a corporate center strategy

❖ WHY CITIES SEEK TOURISTS

Tourism has been a central component of the corporate center strategy in all cities. Aside from the direct benefits to downtown businesses, cities seek tourism trade because it seems uniquely beneficial to all residents, essentially a "free" commodity. It is generally assumed that tourists spend money without taking anything out of the local economy. Tourism frequently has been described as "the industry without a smokestack." As a consequence, there is keen competition among cities for a share of the nation's tourist and recreation business.

A major part of the tourist trade is conventions. One indicator of municipal efforts to attract convention trade is the widespread construction of municipally financed convention centers designed to accommodate larger and more specialized groups. *Aud-Arena Stadium Guide* conducted a survey in 1972 showing that seventy cities ranging in size from Pontiac, Michigan, to New York City had recently opened, had under construction, or had planned multimillion-dollar convention centers designed to enable them to achieve or maintain competitive positions as convention sites.[51] In the late 1980s and early 1990s there was another round of convention center construction.

Since the 1980s, if not before, virtually every major city in the United States has formed a convention bureau whose primary task is to attract and assist convention groups. In the 1960s, about sixty-five cities operated convention bureaus. By 1977, their number had swollen to approximately a hundred and had doubled again by 1983. Convention bureaus compile lists of national, regional, local, and, in some cases, international associations that are regular sponsors of conventions. The bureaus send them promotional literature and, along with the state governor, the city mayor, and the county supervisor, invite them to convene in their city. If the association indicates an interest, the bureau sends sales representatives who stage elaborate promotional presentations to describe the city, its facilities, tourist attractions, and any other features, such as reduced-rent or rent-free convention facilities that the city has to offer. Or, the bureau may bring association members to their city for a complimentary visit. In November 1975, for example, the St. Louis Convention and Visitors Bureau hosted representatives of 227 associations for a weekend tour in an effort to promote its $39 million convention center, which was then under construction.[52]

According to the International Association of Convention and Visitors Bureaus, there were approximately 30,000 conventions in the United States in 1975, and that number was expected to double by 1993.[53] In 1975, conventions were a $7 billion a year business, and ancillary spending, estimated at up to $18 billion, affected the entire American economy.[54] Conventions are considered a growth industry because of the proliferation of specialized groups and associations that feel the need to pull people together periodically to exchange information.

There are five basic types of conventions: the social convention, which is held by groups who share hobbies, recreational activities, or religious, civic, or other interests; the professional or managerial convention, which is held by members of various occupational groups, for example, lawyers, doctors, academics, and business executives; the sales convention, at which businesses promote and sell goods or services directly to the public; the political convention, both regional and national; and the trade convention, at which manufacturers display their merchandise for wholesale sales.

Table 13-3 gives a breakdown of delegate expenditures in eighty-three convention cities during 1985. Delegates to national or international conventions stayed an average of 4.4 days and spent about $105 each day, for a total of $505 for a convention. Most delegates (75 percent to 80 percent) brought their spouses.[55] Large conventions, such as that of the American Dental Association, bring as many as 15,000 delegates to a city. From the expenditures on hotels, restaurants, and retail stores, it is apparent why these businesses so assiduously promote conventions.

Site selection by the sponsoring association is made two to four years in advance. According to a study by the National Tourism Review Commission:

> The key requirements are the availability of specialized facilities such as exhibit space, banquet halls, meeting rooms, with sufficient hotel/motel accommodations at hand, and a site which promises to attract a high level of attendance. Attendance relates to ease of access, a locality around which a high proportion of attendees live, and the appeal of the city to them. Cost is relevant absolutely and as a means of bargaining for better terms from those communities bidding for the conventions.[56]

Tourist appeal is a central consideration in convention site selection. Although many small- and medium-sized cities compete for a share of the business, large cities, with their multitude of entertainment, cultural, and commercial attractions, remain the primary drawing cards for national and international conventions.

Table 13-4 ranks the top thirty-three convention cities by their shares of the convention market for 1981, for meetings with exhibits. New York and Chicago led the nation in the 1970s as magnets for conventions.[57] New York, despite its high prices, attracted 3 million convention visitors in 1975, who brought in $403.5 million in direct spending, roughly one-third of the $1.25 billion spent in the city by all visitors during the year.[58] Atlanta, Las Vegas, and Dallas attracted the most events after New York and Chicago. The convention trade rapidly diminishes as one goes down the list.

The top ten cities accounted for 44 percent of total attendance. The other cities listed in the table fought for the remaining share of convention business. Competition is so keen that none of the secondary cities have much of a chance to improve their positions; they must fight just to stay even. *Successful Meetings,* a magazine that monitors convention trends, identified Atlanta, Houston, and Las Vegas as the fastest-moving cities in the convention trade in the late 1970s.[59]

Development of the convention industry, it is argued, provides jobs for the difficult-to-employ, unskilled segment of the population. Low-skill jobs account for 65 percent of employment in the food service and lodging industries.[60] In addition to providing service jobs for the low-skilled labor force in the urban population, convention trade provides employment in professional, managerial, clerical, and sales categories.

TABLE 13-3 PER DELEGATE PERSONAL EXPENDITURES, NATIONAL AND INTERNATIONAL CONVENTIONS HELD IN 83 CITIES,[a] 1985

BUSINESS	PERCENT OF TOTAL	DAILY EXPENDITURE	TOTAL EXPENDITURES[b]
Hotels and motels	46.8	$ 49.35	$236.50
Eating establishments	24.1	25.41	121.79
Retail stores	11.0	11.60	55.59
Other (night clubs, sporting events, etc.)	18.1	19.09	91.47
Total average expenditures per delegate		$105.45	$505.34

[a]Based on a sample of fourteen conventions held in 1985 in seventy-two cities in the United States and eleven outside the United States.
[b]Average of 4.4 days.
Source: 1985 Convention Income Survey, in *Successful Meetings* (Champaign, Ill.: International Association of Convention and Visitors Bureaus, 1986), p. 12.

TABLE 13–4 CONVENTION TRADE, U.S. CITIES, 1981

TOP 33 CITIES MEETINGS WITH EXHIBITS	PERCENT OF TOTAL ATTENDANCE		PERCENT OF TOTAL ATTENDANCE
1. New York	10.6	21. Louisville	1.1
2. Chicago	6.7	22. Miami Beach	1.1
3. Atlanta	4.4	23. Seattle	1.1
4. Las Vegas	3.8	24. San Diego	1.0
5. Dallas	3.8	25. Denver	1.0
6. Los Angeles	3.7	26. Cleveland	0.8
7. Anaheim, Calif.	3.5	27. Orlando	0.8
8. San Francisco	2.9	28. Phoenix	0.6
9. New Orleans	2.6	29. Cincinnati	0.6
10. Boston	2.3	30. Oklahoma City	0.6
11. Detroit	2.0	31. Memphis	0.5
12. Kansas City	2.0	32. Pittsburgh	0.5
13. Philadelphia	1.7	33. Tulsa	0.3
14. Indianapolis	1.7		

TABLE 13-4 (*Continued*)

TOP 33 CITIES MEETINGS WITH EXHIBITS	PERCENT OF TOTAL ATTENDANCE
15. Houston	1.5
16. St. Louis	1.4
17. Atlantic City	1.3
18. Columbus	1.2
19. Minneapolis	1.2
20. San Antonio	1.1

Source: Successful Meetings Magazine, *Convention and Exhibit Market Profile*, Bill Communication Inc., 1983

The impact of tourism and convention money on local economies is difficult to trace, but some estimates have been made. Roger Bivus, director of the International Association of Convention Bureaus, estimated in 1972 that for every $20,000 that convention visitors spent in an area, a new job was generated.[61] He claimed that 4 million jobs were supported directly and indirectly by the tourist industry.[62] According to Bivus, convention trade pumps "new money" into the local economy, which has the same multiplier effect that any investment does:

> The dollars that a convention-goer spends become income for hotel, restaurant, and other service personnel. Subsequently, these dollars are spent again—on rent, food, and basic necessities. In the process they generate earnings for real estate investors and other investors who may plow back a portion of their profit into plant expansion and new equipment.[63]

In this way, a visitor dollar may be spent several times, filtering into different sectors of the economy until "leakage" payment for goods and services outside the region takes the money out of local circulation.

Even using the roughest of estimates, it is clear that tourist contributions to municipal tax bases are substantial. In most cities hotels and restaurants are subject to special city sales taxes in addition to the regular city or state sales tax. About 75 percent of convention visitors' dollars are spent within city limits.[64] Boston officials estimated in the mid-1970s that the city received 10 percent of its total revenues from visitor-related activities, New Orleans 10 percent, Washington, D.C., 15 percent, and New York 15 percent.[65] The United States Travel Service estimated that 7.2 percent of tourism spending in the United States ended up in federal, state, or local treasuries.[66]

Convention bureau literature, reports in trade publications, and real estate feasibility studies optimistically expound the benefits of tourism. Assumptions of economic prosperity and social improvement are rarely challenged or carefully substantiated. The potential liabilities of economic dependence on the tourist trade are glossed over or ignored by cities and entrepreneurs in their scramble to get their share of the pie. George Young, in his study *Tourism: Blessing or Blight?*, explored those liabilities.[67] Young, a British economist and member of the London Tourist Board and Convention Bureau, maintained that low-wage employment needed to service the tourist and convention industry can be a threat to the local employment structure. He argued that most tourism jobs are low paying and that these jobs do not increase the overall wage income of a city appreciably or provide much income tax revenue. Because the work is unpleasant, offering little incentive for advancement, the turnover is high and the labor force as a whole never improves its skills. Moreover, because wages are minimal and turnover high, it is likely that workers will have trouble supporting their families and will require welfare services from government. Thus, he argues, not only do cities gain little, but they may even wind up subsidizing tourism-generated jobs.

Young's second point was that tourist saturation may sometimes cost more in services than it provides in revenue. Convention trade involves costs to a city because visitors require such services as police and fire protection, transportation, and sewers. An example of residents' awareness of the cost of saturation was the strenuous opposition mounted by the citizens of San Diego to the Republican Convention Site Selection Committee's designation of their city as host city for the 1972 Republican convention. Taxpayers saw the costs of city services required during the convention as an excessive revenue drain.[68]

The debate over the civic and convention center complex proposed as the core of a downtown renewal project in Washington, D.C., in the 1970s illustrates the kinds of trade-offs and controversies that can arise when a city promotes tourism.[69] The proposed complex was to be built on 10 acres of city land that then was occupied by low-income housing, shops catering to local residents, and pleasant open space. City officials argued that redevelopment would stimulate overall improvement by bringing jobs, revenue, and business into the area. They asserted that the facility was badly needed, that the city was losing money because of its lack of a convention center to accommodate larger business group functions, and that the center was vital for maintaining the city's competitive position as a tourist destination.

Opponents called the proposed center one more instance of removal of the poor and claimed that there was insufficient information on the future of convention business to gauge whether or not there was a demand for the facility. They recalled similar arguments that a demand existed for a new sports stadium, which subsequently was built and which cost the city $6.7 million in interest subsidies over twelve years—and which failed to keep the city's major league baseball team from moving to Texas. Even admitting the possibility of a demand, opponents claimed that the convention center would force residents to move at a time of an acute housing shortage, destroy ethnic neighborhoods, and cause many small businesses to close. As land values rose, they asserted, the area would become another enclave for the wealthy. In spite of the opposition the convention center was built.

Reliable information on convention business and its costs is scarce. Most estimates concerning the extent of the convention trade and projections of its economic benefits are based on guesswork rather than on hard economic data. Cities make massive investments in convention centers based on insufficient information, scarce sampling, and sketchy feasibility studies. There is the real possibility that many cities will lose out in the future, since the growing pool of facilities is likely to exceed the demand. As more and more facilities are constructed and as the competition for business grows more intense, cost is increasingly favorable for convention sponsors and unfavorable for individual cities.

Most convention centers lose money,[70] but city officials are so caught up in the competition for tourism that they cannot refrain from spending taxpayers' dollars. According to Ruth Messinger, a member of the City Council of New York, "It's exactly like the international arms race."[71] In the decade between 1976 and 1986, 250 convention centers, sports arenas, community centers, and performing arts halls were constructed or started, with a price tag of more than $10 billion. But in Denver voters rejected bonds for a new center that was pushed hard by downtown business leaders. (The facility was built later through the issuance of revenue bonds, which did not need voter approval.) Expansion of the Moscone Center in San Francisco was the subject of intense political conflict. The final building was mostly constructed underground in order to avoid neighborhood opposition. In the mid-1980s, the Dallas Convention Center made a profit, but Los Angeles's Convention and Exhibit Center was subsidized by construction bonds backed by the city (even though the center itself made money), San Francisco's center lost $2.5 million in 1985, and Washington's center lost $5.9 million.[72]

Competition ensures that all cities cannot be winners in the tourism sweepstakes. If all cities that have 50,000 square feet or more of convention space got an equal share of the trade, each would have less than six bookings a year.[73] Though some cities win, others are bound to lose.

❖ SPORTS POLITICS: THE FRANCHISE RELOCATION GAME

In March 1971, Mayor John Lindsay of New York announced that the city would buy and rebuild Yankee Stadium, at a cost of $24 million, to serve as a permanent home for the Yankees and the football Giants.[74] "The house that Ruth built" was by then almost fifty years old and in need of modernization. Lindsay did not want to be the mayor who lost the Yankees or the Giants to a rival city. (Subsequently, the Giants moved to a new stadium in the Meadowlands in New Jersey, so the only issue became how to keep the Yankees in town.) Yankee Stadium was located in the South Bronx, one of the worst urban ghettos in the nation. In order to sweeten the deal, Lindsay promised $2 million to rehabilitate the neighborhood.

In 1973, George Steinbrenner and seventeen associates purchased the Yankees from CBS. Steinbrenner made rumblings about moving the Yankees to New Jersey and negotiated a highly advantageous lease for the stadium. By the time of the groundbreaking in 1976, the price tag for rebuilding the stadium had escalated to $27 million. From then on the cost overruns continued until the final cost of rebuilding exceeded $100 million. Revenues from the stadium would never come close to covering interest costs added to the city's debt and would cover none of the principal on bonds the city floated.

Even the $100 million figure, however, obscured the actual costs of Yankee Stadium to the taxpayers. By purchasing the stadium, the city gave up $570,000 per year in taxes the Yankees used to pay.[75] The figure did not include 6,900 parking spaces the city agreed to build for the stadium, which were projected to cost $60 million over a 31-year period. And because the garages are publicly owned, the city will lose an estimated $25 million in real estate taxes over the 31-year period.[76] In addition, a new interchange on the

Major Deegan Expressway cost $16 million—paid for mostly by state and federal taxpayers.[77]

One of the few respects in which New York saved money was on its commitment to enhance the surrounding neighborhood. The city simply announced in 1975 that it would not honor its promises. The savings were used to buy extra equipment for the stadium, such as a tarpaulin. The dominant sentiment in the neighborhood was anger and resentment. "We were promised extensive renovations and improvements as part of the rebuilding of Yankee Stadium," said Francisco Lugovina, chairman of the local community board that oversees the area. "What we have gotten are dying maples and sycamores."[78] (Later, in appreciation of sharply increased attendance, the Yankees did commit $35,000 to upgrade baseball fields and paddleball courts in neighboring Macombs Dam Park.[79])

Professional sports franchises occupy an important place in the corporate center strategy. In 1992 there were 102 franchises in the four major sports worth almost $9.5 billion (see Table 13-5). New York City, in the midst of its worst fiscal crisis, spent lavishly on a new sports stadium while ignoring the surrounding neighborhood. Clearly, the city felt that the Yankees were a valuable asset to New York that would pump new money into the local economy and provide jobs for area residents. Even more important, however, was the emotional attachment of New Yorkers to the Yankees. What would New York be without the Yankees? Lindsay's inability to answer this question no doubt motivated him to give away the store to keep them in town. It is the emotional attachment of fans to professional sports teams that makes it so difficult for city officials to know where to draw the line when working to attract and retain sports franchises.

Professional baseball franchises had their origins in amusement parks. Team owners were often real estate speculators who used the teams to attract buyers to their subdivisions.[80] Until the 1950s, however, franchises rarely moved—except occasionally in basketball and football because of intense interleague competition. The first baseball franchise relocation occurred in 1953, when the Boston Braves relocated to Milwaukee.

The franchise relocation game began in earnest in 1957 when Walter O'Malley moved the Brooklyn Dodgers to Los Angeles. Previous moves had been motivated by a desire to turn around an unprofitable franchise, but the Brooklyn Dodgers were one of the most lucrative franchises in baseball, with fanatically loyal fans who packed the bleachers at Ebbets Field. The problem was that O'Malley wanted to build a new stadium, but his plans were thwarted by Robert Moses, who wielded tremendous power in building roads, bridges, and parks throughout the New York region. Any major project involving significant public funds required his approval. To woo the Dodgers, Los Angeles agreed to renovate their minor league stadium at Chavez Ravine, install 22,000 more seats than at Ebbets Field, and then give the stadium to O'Malley. In addition, they offered him 300 acres of prime downtown Los Angeles real estate. O'Malley snapped at the chance to get rich quick and make a profitable franchise even more profitable.[81]

TABLE 13-5 VALUE OF NORTH AMERICAN MAJOR SPORTS FRANCHISES, 1992 (IN MILLIONS OF DOLLARS)[a]

FRANCHISE	VALUE	FRANCHISE	VALUE
Detroit Tigers, MLB	$85	New York Yankees, MLB	$200
Atlanta Braves, MLB	83	Los Angeles Dodgers, MLB	180
New York Knicks, NBA	83	New York Mets, MLB	170
Minnesota Twins, MLB	83	Toronto Blue Jays, MLB	160
Cleveland Cavaliers, NBA	81	Boston Red Sox, MLB	160
Phoenix Suns, NBA	80	Los Angeles Lakers, NBA	150
Seattle Mariners, MLB	79	Miami Dolphins, NFL	150
Portland Trail Blazers, NBA	78	New York Giants, NFL	150
Milwaukee Brewers, MLB	77	Dallas Cowboys, NFL	146
Cleveland Indians, MLB	77	Philadelphia Eagles, NFL	146
Montreal Expos, MLB	75	Baltimore Orioles, MLB	140
Charlotte Hornets, NBA	74	Chicago White Sox, MLB	140
Detroit Red Wings, NHL	70	Chicago Bears, NFL	139
Boston Bruins, NHL	67	San Francisco 49ers, NFL	134
Sacramento Kings, NBA	63	St. Louis Cardinals, MLB	132
Philadelphia 76ers, NBA	63	Chicago Cubs, MLB	132
Golden State Warriors, NBA	63	Seattle Seahawks, NFL	130
San Antonio Spurs, NBA	63	Houston Oilers, NFL	128
New York Rangers, NHL	62	Los Angeles Raiders, NFL	128

TABLE 13-5 *(Continued)*

FRANCHISE	VALUE	FRANCHISE	VALUE
Orlando Magic, NBA	62	Los Angeles Rams, NFL	126
Minnesota Timberwolves, NBA	62	Buffalo Bills, NFL	125
Montreal Canadiens, NHL	62	Cleveland Browns, NFL	125
Houston Rockets, NBA	61	Texas Rangers, MLB	123
Chicago Blackhawks, NHL	61	New Orleans Saints, NFL	123
Dallas Mavericks, NBA	60	Kansas City Chiefs, NFL	123
Miami Heat, NBA	60	Pittsburgh Steelers, NFL	121
Los Angeles Kings, NHL	60	Indianapolis Colts, NFL	121
Atlanta Hawks, NBA	57	Minnesota Vikings, NFL	120
Milwaukee Bucks, NBA	56	Detroit Pistons, NBA	120
Calgary Flames, NHL	55	Phoenix Cardinals, NFL	120
Edmonton Oilers, NHL	55	Atlanta Falcons, NFL	120
New Jersey Nets, NBA	54	Kansas City Royals, MLB	117
Toronto Maple Leafs, NHL	54	Washington Redskins, NFL	117
Los Angeles Clippers, NBA	54	New York Jets, NFL	117
New York Islanders, NHL	53	Philadelphia Phillies, MLB	115
Utah Jazz, NBA	52	Green Bay Packers, NFL	115
Philadelphia Flyers, NHL	51	Cincinnati Bengals, NFL	115
Hartford Whalers, NHL	49	Oakland Athletics, MLB	115
Denver Nuggets, NBA	46	San Diego Chargers, NFL	115

TABLE 13-5 (*Continued*)

FRANCHISE	VALUE	FRANCHISE	VALUE
Washington Bullets, NBA	46	Denver Broncos, NFL	114
Quebec Nordiques, NHL	45	Tampa Bay Buccaneers, NFL	113
Vancouver Canucks, NHL	45	Boston Celtics, NBA	110
Seattle SuperSonics, NBA	45	Detroit Lions, NFL	110
Indiana Pacers, NBA	43	California Angels, MLB	103
New Jersey Devils, NHL	41	New England Patriots, NFL	103
Pittsburgh Penguins, NHL	41	Chicago Bulls, NBA	100
Washington Capitals, NHL	40	San Francisco Giants, MLB	99
Buffalo Sabres, NHL	39	Cincinnati Reds, MLB	98
St. Louis Blues, NHL	39	San Diego Padres, MLB	96
Minnesota North Stars, NHL	34	Houston Astros, MLB	95
Winnipeg Jets, NHL	30	Pittsburgh Pirates, MLB	87

*a*Value is based upon gate receipts, media revenues, stadium revenues, operating income, player salaries, and other operating expenses.

Source: Financial World Magazine, as reported in *New York Times*, June 17, 1992.

Other owners soon followed O'Malley's example. Threats to move became standard weapons for prying more subsidies out of host cities. Between 1980 and 1986 more than half the cities with major league sports franchises were confronted with demands for increased subsidies—with relocation an implied if not always explicit threat hanging over the negotiations.[82] Between 1950 and 1982 there were 78 franchise relocations in the four major professional sports: 11 in baseball, 40 in basketball, 14 in hockey, and 13 in football.[83]

In negotiations with team owners, cities find themselves in a disadvantageous bargaining position. The reason is simple: the demand for major league sports franchises far outstrips the supply. Professional sports leagues are essentially monopolies that can limit the supply of their product. Owners generally oppose increasing the number of teams because a significant increase would cause the value of existing franchises to fall. In 1993, two new professional baseball teams, the Colorado Rockies in Denver and the Florida Marlins in Miami, were added to the National League. The number of big-city markets had expanded enough that a modest expansion did not threaten the investment of other owners. In a few cases newly created teams formed new leagues that successfully competed with the established leagues, eventually merging with them. The best examples are the American Football League (AFL) and the old American Basketball Association (ABA) of Julius (The Doc) Erving fame. This kind of merger is rare, however. If a city wants a team, usually it has to attract a franchise away from another city.

Lest there be any doubt that all franchises are insecure, on August 8, 1992, the owner of the San Francisco Giants announced that he was selling the team to investors who would move the Giants to St. Petersburg, Florida, in time for the 1993 season. Over a six-year period, voters in San Francisco, San Jose, and Santa Clara counties had voted down four referenda that would have committed public monies to construct a new stadium. Ultimately, the Giants stayed.

Robert Isray, owner of the Baltimore Colts, went shopping around for a better deal in 1983. Phoenix offered a new domed stadium. In addition to the Hoosierdome, however, Indianapolis offered guaranteed ticket sales, a $12.5 million low-interest loan, a new training facility, and financial assistance for moving the team. Baltimore scrambled to match the offer, but when the Maryland legislature passed an eminent domain law that might have allowed the city to seize the Colts for public use, Isray acted. To forestall possible legal action, in the middle of the night eleven moving vans pulled into Baltimore and carted the Colts away. Indianapolis wanted the Colts to buttress its corporate center strategy. "It put us on the map to be in the National Football League," said Indianapolis's Mayor William Hudnut[84] even though the Colts were perennial losers.

The demand for major sports franchises is insatiable. Every city wants to be "big league." Following the daring lead of Indianapolis, cities now build stadiums even when they don't have a team. St. Petersburg, Florida (1990 population 238,629), built a $139 million domed stadium in 1988 in the hopes of attracting a baseball team. Since the concerts and tractor pulls staged in the stadium generated relatively little revenue, the taxpayers were paying most of the annual $1.7 million operating cost and the estimated $8 million debt service. For years the city had been the target of derision. Dubbed "heaven's waiting room," St. Petersburg justified the Suncoast Dome as a way of changing the city's image as a doddering retirement community.[85] In the early 1990s, St. Peterburg attempted to attract a number of major league baseball teams, including the Seattle Mariners, the San Fransisco Giants, and a National League expansion team. As of the 1993 baseball season, all efforts had failed.

A significant danger in the franchise relocation game is that it can undermine the fan support that is the foundation of community support for the teams. By playing one city against another, team owners abuse fan loyalty, ultimately producing a backlash. In 1980, the owner of the Oakland Raiders, Al Davis, threatened to move the team to Los Angeles. Angry fans, among the most loyal in professional football, demanded that something be done. In an attempt to stop the move Oakland filed suit, arguing that it had the right to purchase the Raiders under eminent domain law. Cities can assume ownership of private property under eminent domain if the property performs an important "public use." Oakland argued that the team was in the public domain because public money was used to support it and because it was crucial to the community's social and economic well-being. The city's action was upheld by a California lower court in November 1985, but that verdict was overturned by a state appeals court. Subsequently, the United States Supreme Court refused to review Oakland's appeal. In 1982, after thirteen consecutive sold-out seasons, Al Davis moved the Raiders to Los Angeles.

A few years later, Oakland's Mayor Lionel Wilson supported a deal to bring the Raiders back. The deal would have guaranteed the Raiders $602 million in ticket revenues over a fifteen-year period, leaving the city treasury at risk at a time when many of the city's schools and neighborhoods were dangerously deteriorated. Citizens were so outraged by the proposed deal that they went to the polls against Wilson. On June 5, 1990, after thirteen years in office, Wilson was defeated for reelection. Commenting on his defeat, Wilson acknowledged that his support of the proposal "was a negative factor for the politics."[86]

Various reforms have been suggested to limit the ability of team owners to play one city off against another. One proposal is to grant professional sports leagues antitrust immunity that would enable them to veto the relocation of teams if the moves were deemed to be against the interests of the sport. According to a Supreme Court decree, baseball already possesses antitrust immunity, but the owners are understandably reluctant to interfere with the property rights of any of their peers. Another frequently mentioned proposal is to reduce the barriers to league expansion. Also, cities could, in theory, protect their interests by insisting on long-term leases for stadiums, but such an action might well incite an owner to threaten to leave. The most effective but least likely remedy would be public ownership of teams. The Green Bay Packers are owned by 1,789 stockholders, 90 percent of whom live in the Green Bay area. Moving the Packers would require the approval of thousands of loyal fans—an unlikely prospect.

Knowing where to draw the line in giving subsidies to sports franchises depends on knowing how much a sports franchise is worth to a city. Measuring the costs and benefits of franchises, however, is notoriously difficult. Cities typically pay more in subsidies than they get back from professional sports teams. The argument for subsidies hinges on arguments that the intangible benefits to a city far outweigh material costs.

As with any development project, material benefits depend primarily on two factors: how much new consumer spending comes into a city because of the franchise and how much this spending multiplies through the local economy (for example, in money to beverage and food vendors, souvenir sellers, hotels, bars, and restaurants). Optimistic studies done by consultants for their clients, who are invariably local boosters and want optimistic projections, generally inflate the estimated multiplier, often claiming that a dollar multiplies as many as six or seven times before being lost to the local economy. A more realistic multiplier would usually be less than three. The multiplier effect of sports fans' spending on the local economy is difficult to calculate. Clearly, however, the smaller the jurisdiction, the lower the multiplier effect (the more quickly the benefits leak out of the city). A study of two suburbs in Texas (Arlington, home of the Texas Rangers, and Irving, home of the Dallas Cowboys) concluded that the benefit from the professional sports teams was spread over the entire region, and therefore it does not make sense for single cities to shoulder the entire investment and risk.[87]

In light of the inherent difficulties of such calculations, it is not surprising that, according to a leading scholar on the topic, "no comprehensive cost-benefit analysis has been done in any city" on sports franchises.[88] In place of studies, proponents argue that the most important benefits of a major sports franchise are intangible and therefore impossible to measure. The most frequently cited benefit is "image." Cities spend millions of dollars to enhance their image for investors, and it is assumed that nothing improves the image of a city better than a World Series or Superbowl champion. Another factor is civic identity. Americans crave an identity beyond their own individual lives. Sports teams satisfy that craving. A winning franchise can motivate residents to take pride in their community and to identify with the city as a whole.

Perhaps the most important intangible benefit of a sports franchise is its ability to overcome differences and unify a city. Contemporary American cities are riven by class, ethnic, and racial differences. Racial conflicts, in particular, threaten to undermine the quality of life in cities. Professional sports are now fully integrated. Whether rich or poor, black or white, in 1991 Angelenos rooted for Magic Johnson to bring the Los Angeles Lakers another championship. San Antonio's Mayor Henry Cisneros, commenting on his proposal to build a $200 million all-purpose stadium, maintained that, "Those of us who lead cities need all the help we can get in bringing people together, and nothing integrates a city better than major league sports."[89] Cisneros's claim, if nothing else, demonstrates the tremendous symbolic power of sports in American culture. However, as in other elements in the recent economic revitalization of American cities, there are losers as well as winners in the contemporary game that pits city against city.

❖ THE DIVIDED CITIES

As in the railroad era of the nineteenth century, there has been fierce economic competition among cities in the last two decades. In their efforts to outdo one another, cities have offered an array of subsidies to investors, and at the same time they have cut basic services to balance their budgets. The successful cities have undergone a new generation of downtown development, characterized by corporate towers, waterfront recreational development, enclosed shopping malls, new convention centers, and stadiums. The look of this development is strikingly similar from city to city. One effect of the development is also strikingly similar; it has created divided cities split between the affluent and the poor.

In most cities the split has taken the form of an extreme separation between fortress enclaves, which are often privately-owned, and increasingly dangerous public streets. Mirroring the tendency of suburbanites to separate themselves in enclaves, the affluent workers and residents of inner cities also have retreated into protected spaces.[90] Projects like the Peachtree Center in Atlanta, Renaissance Center in Detroit, Water Tower Place in Chicago, and the IDS Center in Minneapolis bring recreation, shopping, and work into an enclosed environment. The multiuse structures make it possible for suburbanites to drive into the city, park in an underground garage, work in an attached office tower, shop in a mall connected by skyways, and perhaps attend a ball game in a domed stadium or attend a concert—all without setting foot on a city street.

John Portman's Peachtree Center in Atlanta is one of the most dramatic examples of enclosure. By the late 1980s, the center was composed of sixteen buildings linked by second-story skyways. At the edges of the sidewalks on the streets below the skyways the walls of the buildings curve upward into space. One can gain access to the center only through a few grand porticos, usually the entrance to hotel lobbies. The fortresslike walls of the buildings give the streets a menacing feeling, and the public sidewalks are often deserted.

Whether located in suburbs or in central cities, whether corporate headquarters, a convention center, or a domed stadium, the new megastructures enclose and segment space. The cities that contain them seem to be glittering symbols of renewal, phoenixes risen from the ashes, but is such development, for all its benefits, a success story? The answer to that question depends considerably upon whether one is a beneficiary or a victim of the most recent brand of inner-city regeneration.

CHAPTER
14

IMMIGRATION, CONCENTRATED POVERTY, AND THE NEW URBAN LEADERSHIP

❖ DIVIDED CITIES AND POLITICAL LEADERSHIP

On April 29, 1992, the news passed quickly through the barrios and ghettos of Los Angeles: The four white policemen who had been accused of beating a black man, Rodney King, had been found not guilty by a jury composed of ten suburban whites, one Latino, and one Asian. Even though the trial had been moved to the white, middle-class suburb of Simi Valley, a guilty verdict had seemed certain. The key piece of evidence was an 81-second amateur videotape showing the officers brutally beating King. The tape had been shown on television news programs over and over for months. Public leaders and police in Los Angeles had not even considered the possibility of a total acquittal and therefore had made no plans for possible disorders.

Within hours, rioting broke out in south-central Los Angeles. Hundreds of buildings were set on fire, cars were turned over and burned, and stores were looted. In the next three days, the rioting spread to much of the legal city of Los Angeles. Before it ran its course, it had become the most violent urban uprising in the twentieth century. Within a week the death toll reached 53. There were 2,383 injuries, 16,291 arrests, over 5,500 fires, and over $700 million in property damage.[1] At one point the smoke was so thick over Los Angeles that air traffic controllers could keep only one runway open at Los Angeles International Airport. The Los Angeles Police Department (LAPD), known for its high-tech weaponry and overwhelming firepower, seemed helpless to stop the rioting. It wasn't until Governor Pete Wilson and President George Bush called in 16,000 state troopers, soldiers of the National Guard, and federal troops that order was finally restored on Sunday, May 3.

Unlike the urban riots of the 1960s, all of which were confined to predominantly black areas, the 1992 Los Angeles riots involved a rainbow of participants. Between April 30 and March 5, 3,498 Latinos, 2,832 African Americans, and 640 non-Latino whites were arrested in the riot areas.[2] The multiethnic nature of the riot, and its range over much of the city, led some observers to label it a rebellion against established authority—a rebellion that could recur not only in Los Angeles, but in other cities as well. In the aftermath of the King verdict there were disturbances in San Francisco, Atlanta, and Las Vegas, and an air of tension lasted for weeks in many cities across the country.

The basic causes of the disorders were similar in every city. Structural changes in the U.S. economy have affected residents of central cities everywhere. Urban economies have experienced a loss of well-paying jobs in manufacturing. They have been replaced by a two-tiered job market of high-paying jobs in high-technology manufacturing and professional services and of minimum-wage jobs primarily in consumer services. The desirable jobs that are available pit whites, blacks, Latinos, and Asians in an intense competition that exacerbates social, racial, and ethnic tensions, such as those that erupted during the Los Angeles riots. Bands of angry looters and arsonists sought out Korean businesses, and some Korean business owners defended their stores with guns. Similar racial and ethnic tensions had exploded into violent confrontations previously in New York City and Miami.

It is clear that the corporate center strategy of economic development, which we described in Chapter 13, has sometimes contributed to rather than reduced social tensions in the inner cities. The new office towers, sports stadiums, and tourist facilities have often taken land that previously supplied affordable housing, and most of the new jobs created by downtown development have been low paying or beyond the skill levels of inner-city residents.

Are there any alternatives to this mode of development? In many cities African-American and Latino leaders have increased their political power, and in some cities they have even gained control of city government. For the most part, minority mayors have pushed conventional economic development policies that concentrate on big downtown projects. Some of them, however, have experimented with a "populist" policy agenda that emphasizes neighborhood empowerment and social issues that advance racial and economic equality. In this chapter, we describe the increasing racial and ethnic complexity of cities, the social tensions that arise from concentrated unemployment and poverty, and, finally, the efforts made by some mayors to pursue policies designed to reduce the tensions and inequalities that characterize today's divided cities.

❖ THE NEW WAVE OF IMMIGRATION

The volume of immigration entering the United States has increased steadily since 1950, and during this period the sources of immigration have shifted from Europe to Asia, Latin America, and the Caribbean (see Table 14-1). Few people realize that the 1980s was the second largest decade of legal immigration in American history, exceeded only by the immigrant flood tide from 1900 to 1910. More immigrants now live in the United States than in any previous period, more than 17 million (though the proportion of immigrants in the population is far less than in the late nineteenth and early twentieth centuries).[3] In addition, an estimated 2.5 million to 4 million illegal aliens reside in the United States.[4]

Recent immigrants have tended to settle in the core cities of major metropolitan areas, mostly moving into neighborhoods already occupied by their own ethnic group. In 1987, less than 7 percent of legal immigrants settled in nonurban areas and more than half located in just ten metropolitan areas. Figure 14-1 shows how the various groups have sorted themselves out on the urban landscape.

Figure 14–1 Composition of Immigrant Flows to Six Major Metropolitan Destinations, 1987

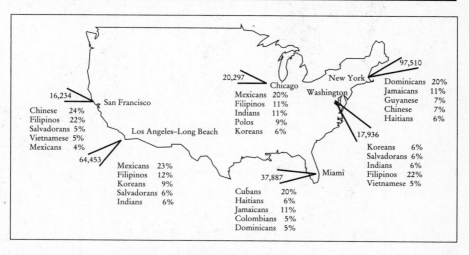

Note: **Chinese include immigrants from mainland China only.**

Source: U.S. Immigration and Naturalization Service, 1987 *Annual Report* (Washington, D.C.: U.S. Government Printing Office, 1988), Table 18; as reported in Alejandro Portes and Ruben G. Rumbaut, *Immigrant America: A Portrait* (Berkeley: University of California Press, 1990), p. 36. Reprinted by permission

TABLE 14-1   IMMIGRANTS, BY PLACE OF ORIGIN, 1820–1989

YEAR	PERCENT OF TOTAL IMMIGRATION						TOTAL NUMBER (THOUSANDS)
	EUROPE	ASIA[a]	CANADA	OTHER WESTERN HEMISPHERE[b]	ALL OTHER[c]		
1951–1960	57.2	6.1	10.9	22.5	3.1		2,515.5
1961–1970	36.9	13.2	8.6	38.9	2.3		3,321.7
1971–1980	18.1	35.9	2.6	40.4	3.1		4,493.3
1981–1989	11.3	41.3	2.3	41.9	3.1		5,801.6

[a]Cambodia, China, Taiwan, Hong Kong, India, Iran, Israel, Japan, Korea, Philippines, Thailand, Vietnam, and "other Asia."
[b]Mexico, Caribbean, Central America, South America.
[c]Africa, Australia, New Zealand.
Source: U.S. Department of Justice, Immigration and Naturalization Service, Statistical Yearbook of the Immigration and Naturalization Service, 1989 (Washington, D.C.: Government Printing Office, 1990), pp. 2–5.

The immigration laws in effect from the 1920s to the mid-1960s reflected xenophobic fears that foreigners might overwhelm the country. The National Origins Immigration Act of 1924 set quotas for immigrants based on the foreign-born population in 1890, allowing into the United States each year 2 percent of the base population of each nationality group already residing in the United States. The quota formulas accomplished their intended goal of drastically reducing immigration by all groups except those from northern Europe. Immigration by Slavs, Jews, Italians, Greeks, and other supposedly "inferior" peoples, most of whom entered the country after 1890, was severely limited.

Immigration laws continued to rely on national-origin quotas until passage of the Hart-Celler Act of 1965. This Act essentially put immigrants from all countries on equal footing. Hart-Celler put a high priority on family reunification. Expanded by special provisions for political refugees from socialist and communist countries, the volume of immigration soared well beyond expectations, and the ethnic composition of the immigrants changed radically. Between 80 and 85 percent of the new immigrants came from the Caribbean, Central and South America, and Asia.[5]

In 1980, Mexican Americans constituted 60 percent of all Latinos in the United States (see Table 14-2). Mainland Puerto Ricans made up about 14 percent of the total, with more than half (61 percent) of the Puerto Ricans concentrated in New York City and northern New Jersey. About 25 percent of Latinos were recent immigrants from Cuba, the Caribbean, and Central and South America. Over half of all the Latinos in the United States and 73 percent of all Mexican Americans lived in just two states, California and Texas.[6]

In the early 1990s, most Latinos lived in metropolitan areas: about 80 percent of Mexican Americans and more than 98 percent of Puerto Ricans, Cubans, and South and Central Americans. As shown in Table 14-3, Latinos constituted one-third of the population of eight large cities in 1990 (up from one-fourth of the population in those cities in 1980). All of these cities are located in the South or West. The Latino population is increasing at a much faster rate than non-Latino whites and African Americans, and some researchers predict that Latinos will equal African Americans in national population by the year 2003. In several cities they are certain to become the dominant social and political ethnic group.

Almost as many immigrants came from Asia in the 1980s as came from all the countries of the Western Hemisphere south of the U.S. border. Asian Americans are the fastest-growing racial group in the country, with the metropolitan areas of Los Angeles (1,339,000), San Francisco (927,000), and New York (873,000) having the largest Asian communities.

Immigration is rapidly changing the face of urban America. The ethnic enclaves in many American cities seem little different from their counterparts in the immigrants' countries of origin. Koreatown in Los Angeles is a thriving enclave of immigrant businesses that advertise their wares in brightly colored signs in both English words and Korean characters. Walking along Calle Ocho (S.W. 8th Street) in Miami, the heart of "Little Havana," there is the ever-present smell of Cuban coffee and cigars. Bolsa Avenue in Westminster

TABLE 14-2 REGIONAL SETTLEMENT PATTERNS FOR PERSONS OF HISPANIC ORIGIN

STATE OR REGION	NUMBER	PERCENT OF REGION'S TOTAL POPULATION	PERCENT OF NATIONAL HISPANIC-ORIGIN POPULATION	NATIONAL BACKGROUND
New York State	1,657,417	9.4	11.4	59.4% Puerto Rican; 2.3% Mexican
New York City (SMSA)	1,492,559	16.4	10.2	
Five southwestern states	8,776,660	19.6	60.2	82.2% Mexican
California	4,538,360	19.2	31.1	80% Mexican
Texas	2,983,111	21.0	20.4	92.2% Mexican
Arizona, New Mexico, Colorado	1,255,189	18.2	8.6	66.9% Mexican origin; 33.1% other
Florida	860,403	8.8	5.9	54.8% Cuban; 25% Latin American
Miami (SMSA)	580,927	35.7	4.0	
Remainder of United States	3,294,396		22.6	
Total United States	14,588,876	6.4	100.0	59.8% Mexican; 13.8% Puerto Rican; 5.5% Cuban; 20.9% other

Source: U.S. Bureau of Census, *1980 Census of Population,* Supplementary Reports, *Persons of Spanish Origin by State 1980* (Washington, D.C.: Government Printing Office, 1981).

TABLE 14-3 BLACK AND HISPANIC POPULATION IN SELECTED SUNBELT CITIES AND METROPOLITAN AREAS, 1990

METROPOLITAN AREA	PERCENT BLACK IN LARGEST CENTRAL CITY	PERCENT HISPANIC IN LARGEST CENTRAL CITY	PERCENT BLACK IN METROPOLITAN AREA	PERCENT HISPANIC IN METROPOLITAN AREA	PERCENT MINORITIES[a] IN CENTRAL CITIES
Los Angeles–Anaheim–Riverside (CMSA)	14.0	39.9	8.5	32.9	64.2
San Diego (MSA)	9.4	20.7	6.4	20.4	42.5
Phoenix	5.2	20.0	3.5	16.3	28.8
Dallas–Fort Worth (CMSA)	29.5	20.9	14.3	13.4	53.1
Houston–Galveston–Brazoria	28.1	27.6	17.9	20.8	60.1
Miami–Fort Lauderdale (CMSA)	27.4	62.5	18.5	33.3	90.7
Tampa–St. Petersburg–Clearwater (MSA)	25.0	15.0	9.0	6.7	41.7
Denver–Boulder (CMSA)	12.8	23.0	5.3	12.2	39.4
San Antonio (MSA)	7.0	55.6	6.8	47.6	64.1
Mean for eight cities	16.3	33.2	8.0	24.1	56.3

[a]Includes Asians, Pacific Islanders, American Indians, Eskimos, and Aleuts.

Source: U.S. Bureau of the Census, *Statistical Abstract of the United States, 1991,* 111th ed. (Washington, D.C.: Government Printing Office, 1991), Tables 37, 38, 40.

(Orange County), California, called the Vietnamese capital of America, is lined with restaurants selling Oriental food. Chinatown on the island of Manhattan in New York City grew so fast that it burst its seams and spread across the river into Flushing in the borough of Queens. The new Chinatown across the river bustles with Asian tourists and is rapidly becoming famous for its Chinese restaurants.

The new immigrant communities are often quite diverse, not unlike the immigrant communities of a century ago. Though there are areas (mostly in inner cities) where only the poorest immigrants live, there are even more neighborhoods that are made up of immigrants of different backgrounds and occupations.

The economic well-being of each immigrant group is closely related to its reasons for moving to the United States. Immigration is provoked by both push and pull factors. Poor economic conditions and political repression in the home country have pushed most of the new immigrants to American shores. The basic pull factor is economic opportunity in the United States. The minimum wage in the United States, for example, is approximately six times the prevailing wage in Mexico, where wages are higher than in most other Latin American countries.[7] While many immigrants work in poorly paid jobs, quite a few come into the country to work in professional and technical occupations. Indeed, the proportion of immigrants with professional and technical backgrounds who work in this country consistently exceeds the average for U.S. workers as a whole.[8]

The experience of different immigrant groups varies. For the most part, Asian immigrants have done well, quickly achieving educational credentials and succeeding at small businesses.[9] Latinos, as a group, have not fared as well. Latinos fall well below the general U.S. population on all indicators of economic well-being. Their median family income in 1985 ($19,027) was only 65 percent of the median income for non-Hispanic whites (see Table 14-4). Latinos lag far behind on educational attainment: More than 75 percent of all non-Latino whites had completed high school in 1984, compared with 47 percent of Latinos. A small proportion of Latinos, 8.2 percent, had earned a college degree. Lagging educational qualifications have meant that Latinos also occupy lower rungs on the job ladder. Though 39 percent of the non-Latino white work force held relatively high status white-collar jobs in 1984, only 17 percent of Latinos held such jobs. Only a small minority of people of Latino descent have entered the middle class in income, education, and occupational status. Blacks lag behind Latinos on many indicators of social and economic well-being. Despite the fact that African Americans have, as a group, a higher level of educational attainment than Latinos, blacks have lower family incomes and higher unemployment rates than Latinos.

Together, blacks and Hispanics make up almost half of the population in many large Sunbelt cities (see Table 14-3). Sunbelt cities are now subject to the same kinds of social tensions that have plagued older cities in the North for decades, and there is reason to believe that social tensions will escalate in southern and western cities in the years ahead. Since the early 1970s, neither blacks nor Hispanics have made significant gains in comparison with non-

TABLE 14-4   ECONOMIC STATUS OF WHITE, BLACK, AND HISPANIC-ORIGIN AMERICANS, 1984, 1985

ECONOMIC INDICATOR	WHITE	BLACK	HISPANIC ORIGIN
Education			
Percentage who completed 4 years of high school (among those 25 years or older)	75.0	58.5	47.1
Percentage who completed 4 years of college (among those 25 years or older)	19.8	10.4	8.2
Income and employment			
Median family income (1985)	$29,152	$16,786	$19,027
Percentage white collar	39.4	22.7	21.6
Unemployment rate (1985)	6.2	15.1	10.5
Percentage below the poverty level	11.4	31.3	29.0

Source: U.S. Bureau of the Census, *Money Income and Poverty Status of Families and Persons in the United States: 1985 (Advanced Report),* Current Population Reports, Series P 60, no. 154 (Washington, D.C.: Government Printing Office: 1986); Current Population Reports, Series P 60, no. 151, *Money Income of Household, Families, and Persons in the U.S.: 1984,* p. 154, Table 38; *U.S. Statistical Abstract: 1986,* pp. 133–135; and *Employment and Earnings,* 1985.

Hispanic whites. Table 14-5 shows that, in 1969, black median income was 61 percent of white median income (up from 52 percent in 1959). By 1989 blacks were making only 56 percent as much as whites. The ratio of Hispanic income to non-Hispanic white income also worsened, dropping from 71 percent to 65 percent between 1972 and 1989.

There have been rising tensions in recent years among Asians, Latinos, and African Americans. Riots erupted in black neighborhoods in Cuban-dominated Miami four times during the 1980s, beginning with the Liberty City disorders in May 1980. Each of the riots was associated with the killing of a black man by Latino or non-Latino white police officers.[10] Rioting erupted in Washington, D.C., when a black female police officer attempted to arrest some Latino men and when a Salvadoran immigrant was shot by police. Ethnic tension reached a breaking point in Brooklyn in 1991–1992, with a boycott by the African-American community of a Korean greengrocer and violent street confrontations between African Americans and Hasidic Jews. In the 1992 Los Angeles riots 30 percent of the approximately 4,000 businesses destroyed were Latino-owned,[11] but Korean-owned businesses were especially singled out by looters and arsonists.[12]

TABLE 14-5   RATIOS OF BLACK AND HISPANIC INCOMES TO WHITE INCOMES

| YEAR | MEDIAN FAMILY INCOME RATIOS | |
	BLACK TO WHITE	HISPANIC-ORIGIN TO WHITE
1959	.52	—
1964	.54	—
1969	.61	—
1972	.59	.71
1975	.62	.67
1978	.59	.68
1981	.58	.67
1982	.55	.66
1985	.58	.65
1989	.56	.65

Source: Adapted from James Heilbrun, *Urban Economics and Public Policy*, 3rd ed. (New York: St. Martin's Press, 1987), p.244. Copyright 1987 by St. Martin's Press, Inc. Reprinted by permission of the publisher; and U.S. Bureau of the Census, *Current Population Reports, Population Profile of the United States* P 23, no. 80 (1979), Table 14; P 60, no. 154 (August 1986), Table 2 (Washington, D.C.: Government Printing Office, 1982), pp. 49–50; U.S. Bureau of the Census, *Current Population Reports, Money Income and Poverty Status in the United States, 1989,* P 60, no. 168, Table A (Washington, D.C.: Government Printing Office, 1990), p. 3.

Illegal immigration has exacerbated the competition among African Americans and the new immigrants for scarce jobs. Undocumented aliens, whose numbers peaked in 1986 at 3 to 5 million, are willing to take jobs at below the minimum wage and often end up in sweatshops working under abysmal conditions. Frequently led across the border by professional smugglers, called "coyotes" for their predatory habits, illegal aliens live at the bottom of U.S. society, doing the dirty work that few other are willing to do. Because they live in constant fear of detection by the Immigration and Naturalization Service (INS), they are in no position to bargain with employers.

To deal with the problem of illegal immigrants, Congress enacted the Immigration Reform and Control Act (IRCA) in 1986, which established stiff penalties for employers who knowingly hire illegal aliens. At the same time, the law made it possible for illegals who had already entered the country to achieve citizenship by registering with the INS. Since passage of the IRCA, approximately 2.5 million formerly illegal aliens have attained legal status,[13] and the INS has stepped up efforts to find employers who violate the law. One of the unintended effects of the 1986 reform is that many employers discriminate against anyone who looks or sounds foreign for fear of sanctions. A report by the General Accounting Office (GAO) found that at least 227,000 employers refuse to hire persons who appear foreign.[14]

In 1990, Congress again reformed the immigration laws, increasing the number of legal immigrants allowed into the country by 40 percent, to 700,000 per year. The law more than doubled the number of visas granted to immigrants with job skills needed in the United States.[15] The United States now admits more legal immigrants than all the rest of the nations of the world put together.[16] In the years ahead, immigration will continue to reshape America's urban areas, and urban politics will become increasingly complex.

❖ CONCENTRATED POVERTY

At the same time that the cities have had to absorb millions of new immigrants, they have also had to deal with the effects of concentrated poverty. The problems of the urban poor are magnified by the fact that they live in neighborhoods that have been abandoned by the middle and working classes. More and more, the poor live only with other poor people. In 1959, 56 percent of the nation's poor lived in rural areas, 27 percent in central cities, and 17 percent in suburbs.[17] By 1985, these percentages had reversed themselves; 29 percent of poor lived in rural areas, 43 percent in cities, and 28 percent in suburbs. Though the population of the fifty largest cities fell by more than 5 percent between 1970 and 1980, the poverty population in these cities rose by nearly 12 percent.[18] Sixty-one percent of all the poor people in the nation now live in central cities and in inner-ring suburbs.

Within central cities a large proportion of poor people live in neighborhoods in which almost everyone is poor. Though the poverty population in the five largest cities increased 22 percent between 1970 and 1980, the number of people living in "extreme-poverty areas" (areas with a poverty rate of at least 40 percent) increased by an incredible 161 percent.[19] The trend continued in the 1980s. The Census Bureau estimated that the percentage of central city residents in poverty who lived in "poverty neighborhoods" (areas with a poverty rate that exceeds 20 percent) increased from 39.9 percent in 1980 to 56.8 percent in 1986.[20]

The intensified segregation of the poor interacts with the segregation of minorities and recent immigrants to create hypersegregation in urban areas.[21] Little progress has been made in reducing racial segregation in housing since passage of the 1968 Civil Rights Act, which outlawed most forms of discrimination in residential real estate. An analysis of sixty metropolitan areas found that the degree of residential segregation changed little between 1970 and 1980, with blacks being twice as segregated as Latinos and Asians.[22] In 1989, 71 percent of low-income, black, central city residents lived in poverty neighborhoods, compared to only 40 percent of low-income, white, central city residents.[23] Whites in poverty can often escape the ghetto and move into working-class or even middle-class neighborhoods, but blacks in poverty find it very difficult, due to racial discrimination in housing, to find affordable housing outside racially segregated areas.

The concentration of poverty brings with it a concentration of other problems. Media accounts and some scholars have tended to assume a causal relationship between poverty and some of these problems, such as family breakdown, drug use, and crime. There has been a lively and often contentious debate over whether an urban "underclass" is perpetuated through personal conduct and social interactions that keep people from obtaining educational credentials, job skills, and values that lead to economic betterment. In the 1992 presidential campaign, the Republican vice-presidential candidate Dan Quayle presented such a theory under the label of "family values." Perhaps because the term underclass has turned out to be as difficult to define as "family values," most scholars have now abandoned it, though it continues to be used, however ill-defined or vague, by the popular media.

As we point out in Chapter 15, many of the problems ascribed to people in poverty, such as family breakdown and substance abuse, also affect the white middle-class in the suburbs. The impact of such problem is magnified for poor people, however, because they are often forced to live in neighborhoods where everyone is poor. As a result, they are distant from most jobs, and they have little access to quality schools and services such as child-care centers, family counselors, and treatment programs. The sociologist William Julius Wilson refers to the harmful effects that result from concentrating the poor in the inner cities as "concentration effects."[24] Some of the problems that typically confront the poor in the inner cities are unemployment and low-paying jobs, family breakdown, poor health, substance abuse, deteriorating housing, homelessness, and crime.

The movement of jobs to the suburbs, combined with pervasive and continuing racial discrimination in hiring, has meant that many of the inner-city poor have become disconnected from the economy. Since the 1950s the number of jobs that undereducated inner-city residents can qualify for has fallen rapidly. Between 1953 and 1984, for example, New York City, Philadelphia, Baltimore, and St. Louis lost 1,082,000 manufacturing jobs. At the same time, these cities gained 1,013,000 jobs in services. As we have seen before, the best of these jobs are in skilled or professional fields out of reach of the inner-city poor.[25] In 1980 the unemployment rate in high-poverty areas was 29.6 percent, but this statistic counted only people who were looking for work and could not find it. Only 20 percent of the adults in these areas actually held jobs.[26]

Poverty is closely correlated with family structure. In 1983 the median family income of female-headed households was only 43 percent of the median family income of households with a husband and a wife.[27] Middle-class families have been able to maintain high living standards mainly because there are two wage-earners. For both the poor and the nonpoor, family income is negatively affected when there is only one female earner. This is because women, on average, make less than men in the same jobs, and in addition many of the jobs that are traditionally female are lower paying than jobs men usually get. Many women in poverty areas are forced to stay home to take care of their children and try to make ends meet on welfare. If women manage to find jobs, they usually have to pay for child care. In 1983, 46 percent of black children under the age of 18 lived in families whose incomes fell below the poverty level, and three-quarters of those were in families headed by women.[28]

In recent years another trend has become apparent: the rise of zero-parent households. About 10 percent of American children in 1990 lived in households not headed by any parent at all—up from 6.7 percent in 1970. There may be a need to bring back an institution that disappeared decades ago: the orphanage. Orphanages arose in the nineteenth and early twentieth centuries in response to the rash of orphans created by epidemics of diphtheria, influenza, and tuberculosis.[29] Today a big problem is AIDS.

Health and health care in inner-city poverty areas have deteriorated sharply since the late 1970s. Chronic illnesses and contagious diseases are common. The poor lack health insurance and often do not have access to even the most basic health care. The United States has among the worst infant mortality rates in the industrialized world: approximately 40,000 infants in this country never see their first birthday each year.[30] While the overall national rate is about 10 deaths for every 1,000 live births, the rate for inner-city poverty neighborhoods approaches levels in Third World countries. In 1988–1989, for example, the infant mortality rate for Central Harlem was 23.4 per 1,000 births, about the same as in Malaysia.[31] A large proportion of women in poverty have babies without having any prenatal care. The result is underweight babies with diminished chances for survival. There is currently an epidemic of AIDS among babies born in inner-city poverty areas. An inner city hospital in Newark estimated that 1 in every 46 babies delivered in 1988 was born infected with the AIDS virus.[32]

Since the first case of AIDS was reported in the United States in 1981, it has become a modern plague. AIDS is primarily an urban disease; with only one-eighth of the nation's population, ten metropolitan areas had five-eighths of the nation's caseload in 1988.[33] Within metropolitan areas AIDS is becoming concentrated in the poorest neighborhoods. Previously in this country, AIDS was primarily a disease of homosexuals, but dramatic alteration in gay sexual behavior has limited its spread within the gay community. In the early 1990s, the disease was spreading most rapidly among poor black and Latino intravenous drug users and their sex partners and offspring. The evidence suggests that "the future composition of AIDS cases will consist primarily of poor, urban minorities."[34] The cost of AIDS threatens to overwhelm the health care systems of several cities.

Substance abuse is another destructive problem in poverty neighborhoods. "Crack" cocaine first appeared on the streets of America's cities in the mid-1980s. Previously, cocaine was a preferred drug of the rich. Free-based cocaine gave a sharper, more pleasurable rush, but the process was expensive and dangerous—resulting in explosions like the one that hospitalized comedian Richard Pryor. Crack was developed as a way of producing the intense high of free-based cocaine at a lower cost. Crack is produced by boiling down cocaine into crystals that can be smoked (the name comes from the crackling sound made when it is smoked). It brings about a rush of sensations, followed quickly by a crash that leaves the user desperate for more. In effect, crack was a breakthrough in mass marketing, a stroke of genius: Cocaine, the "champagne" of drugs, was made available at jug wine prices, less than $10 a hit.

Crack has devastated inner-city poverty neighborhoods across the country. Young, well-armed gangs fight one another to control the lucrative business.[35] The crack trade offers people who have few other opportunities the chance to attain the material goods constantly advertised in a consumer culture and the social status that goes with success. Unlike heroin, crack reinforces feelings of power and aggression. Because the drug is so addictive, users will do almost anything to get another fix. Burglary, car theft, and robbery help to support the habit. Women who become crack addicts often turn to prostitution to support their habit; casual sex in crack houses is a major factor in the AIDS epidemic. Each year thousands of babies are born addicted to crack, costing the nation an estimated $2.5 billion annually by the early 1990s.[36]

Inadequate housing is another effect of concentrated poverty. Housing conditions in urban ghettos have deteriorated markedly over the past two decades. Unsafe, overcrowded conditions are frequently matched with high rents that tax household budgets. The worst form of housing deprivation, of course, is homelessness. In the 1980s, the number of homeless people multiplied and the composition of the homeless population changed. The homeless are now made up of a broad cross section of the American population: single women with children, temporarily unemployed people of every social, ethnic, and racial group, families, mentally and emotionally impaired people. By the very nature of their condition, the homeless are difficult to count; estimates vary from a low of 250,000 to 350,000 to as high as 3 to 4 million.[37]

The homeless are concentrated in older central cities, usually near and in downtown areas. They huddle in doorways, sleep in parks and under bridges, and construct temporary shelters. As the supply of affordable housing dwindled, many families, an estimated 3 million families nationwide, were forced to double up.[38] With a projected loss of 3.5 million low-rent units by the year 2003, the United States will face a several-fold increase in homelessness by the turn of the century.[39]

Fueled by drugs, gangs, and the easy availability of guns, violent crime soared in American cities in the late 1980s and 1990s.[40] In 1990, New York City set a record with 2,262 murders, yet its per capita homicide rate ranked it only slightly above average for the country's twenty-five largest cities.[41] Violent death has reached pandemic proportions among young black and Latino males in inner-city areas. Gangs have proliferated, no doubt because young people find in them a sense of acceptance and personal validation, albeit in a street culture of crime and violence.[42]Citing the fact that homicide was the leading cause of death for black males ages 15 to 24 in 1990, the federal Centers for Disease Control stated that the casualty rate was approaching that of war. According to a study in the *New England Journal of Medicine,* young men in Harlem, primarily because of high homicide rates, were less likely to survive to the age of 40 than their counterparts in Bangladesh.[43] Inner-city youngsters now live with the ever-present danger of violent crime. A survey of schoolchildren in Chicago found that an astonishing 24 percent of them had personally witnessed a murder.[44]

❖ A NEW GENERATION OF LEADERSHIP

Suburban white flight has left many American cities with majority African American and Hispanic populations. This has led to impressive increases in the number of minority elected officials in cities. In 1973, there were 48 African-American mayors in the United States, most of them representing small towns and cities in the South. By 1991, there were 316.[45] Not a single American city with a population over 50,000 in 1960 was governed by a black or Hispanic mayor. In 1967, Richard Hatcher (Gary, Indiana) and Carl Stokes (Cleveland) broke the ice, becoming the first African-American mayors of major American cities. By 1985, there were twenty-seven African American and three Hispanic mayors of cities over 50,000.[46] A survey of eleven large cities found that 47.6 percent of the city council seats were filled by African Americans or Latinos. With the election of Kurt Schmoke as the first black mayor of Baltimore in 1987, every city over 100,000 with a majority black population had elected an African-American mayor. In the early 1990s, the two largest American cities were governed by African-American mayors—David Dinkins in New York and Tom Bradley in Los Angeles.

Statistics documenting growing numbers of minority mayors does not answer a most important question: Have they made a difference? Most central cities may have so few resources and so few options that minority mayors may find that they are able to make few changes. Reflecting on middle-class flight and the loss of jobs and tax revenues in central cities, one analyst suggested that blacks, having struggled for so long to achieve political power in the cities, may have only succeeded in capturing a "hollow prize."[47] This idea was posed in 1969, before there was much basis for making a reliable judgment about what minority mayors might be able (or choose) to accomplish with their inheritance. There are now, however, two and a half decades of experience to examine.

According to political scientist Adolph Reed, Jr., most black mayors have succumbed to a pro-growth, downtown-oriented economic development agenda.[48] Most have worked closely with downtown business leaders to promote local economic growth, hoping that some benefits will trickle down to their black constituents. Detroit provides an example. Since being elected as Detroit's first black mayor in 1973, Coleman Young has aggressively pursued corporate investment. The Renaissance Center has been supported with millions of dollars in tax abatements and federal subsidies. In the early 1980s Detroit engaged in one of the nation's most controversial urban development projects, involving the clearing of 465 acres of land in a working-class, ethnic, and black area known as Poletown in an attempt to keep a General Motors Cadillac plant in the city. Mayor Young accepted the necessity of competing with other cities for outside investment: "This suicidal outthrust competition [between cities] has got to stop but until it does, I mean to compete. It's too bad we have a system where dog eats dog and the devil takes the hindmost. But I'm tired of taking the hindmost."[49]

The history of African-American mayors in Atlanta reveals the enormous pressures that can be brought to bear on a mayor to conform to a strategy of promoting big downtown projects. In 1973, Maynard Jackson became the first African-American mayor of Atlanta, with the support of an electoral coalition of the black community and neighborhood activists, who were predominantly white. Jackson came into office with a strong social reform agenda, explicitly rejecting what he termed "slavish, unquestioning adherence to downtown dicta."[50] What set Jackson apart from previous mayors was that he insisted that business elites "come to City Hall to meet in his office and to ask for his support, rather than simply to inform him of their needs and assume his compliance."[51]

Over time, however, Jackson was pulled toward accommodation with downtown business elites. He supported all the major redevelopment projects favored by downtown business, including construction of the MARTA (Metro Atlanta Rapid Transit Authority) system that mainly connected downtown to the Atlanta airport. In order to accomplish complex projects that he could take credit for when he ran for reelection, Jackson needed the support of the business community. Jackson's successor, civil rights activist Andrew Young, continued Jackson's unqualified support of downtown development. Commenting on his partnership with the business elite, Young said, "Politics doesn't control the world. Money does."[52]

It is important to note that though Jackson and Young gave priority to downtown development, they nevertheless diverted some of the benefits of growth to their African-American black constituents. Over strong opposition, for example, Mayor Jackson insisted that a minority business enterprises (MBE) program be established to set aside a 25 percent (later 35 percent) share of government-generated contracts for minority businesses. Between 1973 and 1980, affirmative action hiring in city government increased the proportion of African Americans in Atlanta city government from 41.5 percent to 60.7 percent of the total government work force, with black professionals in the government increasing even more dramatically, from 19 percent to 47 percent. The percentage of African Americans on the police force increased from 9 percent in 1967 to 33 percent in 1978.[53]

The election of black mayors, even when they wholeheartedly support the corporate center strategy of economic development, makes a difference. On the whole, African Americans support higher levels of social welfare spending and government services than do whites, and black city administrations reflect these priorities. Studies confirm that cities with black mayors and council members support higher levels of social welfare expenditures than cities without black leadership.[54] A study in ten California cities concluded that the incorporation of minorities into local governmental structures makes a difference in local public policy: "When liberal coalitions composed of minorities and whites (typically Democrats) gained control of city councils, city employment of minorities increased, police review boards were created, more minorities were appointed to commissions, more minority contractors were utilized by the cities, and minority-oriented programs were established."[55]

Significant gains in city hiring and contracting have often followed the election of black mayors; indeed, the redistribution of public sector jobs and contracts constitutes the most visible evidence that these mayors have made a difference. The public employment strategy is limited in most cities, however, by stagnating local tax bases and shrinking federal funds. Public sector jobs can support no more than 6 to 8 percent of the total black population of central cities.[56] Moreover, affirmative action public employment programs are frequently criticized for benefiting middle- and upper-income blacks without helping the "truly disadvantaged."[57] Mayor Jackson claimed that the minority set-asides for the airport expansion created twenty-one black millionaires, but the broad benefits to the black community were more difficult to identify.[58]

❖ A POPULIST ALTERNATIVE: CHICAGO'S HAROLD WASHINGTON

Beginning in the 1970s, populist alternatives to the corporate center strategy were tried, usually briefly, in several cities. Basically, the new populism is an outgrowth of a neighborhood organizing movement that began in the 1950s, based on the ideal of decentralizing power to neighborhood and nonprofit organizations. In the 1960s, neighborhood activists began moving into local electoral politics. The new urban populists called for increased participation by ordinary people in running their cities, including decentralized neighborhood planning and coproduction of city services by community organizations. Coproduction meant that neighborhood residents would assist in preventing crime, renovating homes, and so forth. The city would provide grants to neighborhood organizations providing such services.

The new populists argued persuasively that decentralized programs would benefit the unemployed and underemployed, including members of disadvantaged minority groups. Cities such as Burlington, Vermont; Santa Monica, California; and Hartford, Connecticut, were strongly influenced by populist ideas.[59] Major American cities have been led by mayors with urban populist appeals and programs, such as Ray Flynn in Boston and Art Agnos in San Francisco.

Harold Washington, mayor of Chicago from 1983 to 1987, is an especially interesting case because he carried the populist message to the black community. Washington began his political career in a conventional way, working his way up through the Chicago Democratic machine. Son of a minister and lawyer who was a precinct captain in the Chicago machine, Washington served as an assistant precinct captain while in law school and took over the post when his father died in 1954. His precinct work gave him access to government jobs, including a term as assistant city prosecutor. From 1965 to 1977, Washington served in the Illinois legislature. During this time Washington showed evidence of political independence, participating in a movement from 1971 to 1975 to break away from the Democratic machine, which had dominated Chicago politics since Mayor Richard Daley's election in 1953. After Daley's death in 1976, Washington ran in the special 1977 mayoral election. He garnered only 11 percent of the vote, but won the respect of many people as a charismatic campaigner. In 1980 he easily won election to the U.S. Congress over the handpicked machine candidate.

During the administration of Mayor Jane Byrne (1979 to 1983), the African-American community felt increasingly estranged. A survey sponsored by black leaders found that Washington was the top choice of black voters to run for mayor. A coalition of African-American political leaders contacted Washington and asked him to run. He told them that he would, if two conditions could be satisfied: "There has to be a war chest of at least $250,000 to $500,000 and you have to go prove that you can get a number of people registered, at least fifty thousand."[60] Eventually more than 100,000 people were registered and Washington agreed to run.

Washington's victory in the 1983 election was remarkable not only because he beat the machine and he became the first African-American mayor of Chicago, but because his campaign motivated hundreds of people to actively participate in local politics. The campaign transformed grass roots associational life throughout Chicago. Before the Washington campaign most blacks accepted the maldistribution of city services that systematically discriminated against black areas. With Washington's candidacy and election, blacks no longer accepted the old politics. New radio stations, community organizations and newspapers, and nonprofit organizations were formed. Voter turnout in black wards almost doubled, increasing from 34.5 percent in the 1979 primary election to 64.2 percent in 1983.[61]

With African Americans making up only about 40 percent of the city's population, Washington recognized that he would have to build a multiracial coalition. He was successful in knitting together an unlikely coalition of African Americans, Latinos, and affluent white liberals to win the 1983 Democratic primary over the incumbent, Jane Byrne, and Richard Daley, Jr. The mobilization of this coalition provoked a countermobilization by white politicians. Machine Democrats even abandoned their party to back the Republican mayoral candidate, Bernard Epton. Epton ran an overtly racist campaign, claiming that if Washington won, white neighborhoods would be invaded by public housing projects and drugs. His supporters freely used scare tactics and racial slurs, at one point circulating a campaign button with a watermelon pictured on it. Between the 1982 and 1983 general elections, turnout in white wards increased from 54.0 percent to 67.2 percent.[62] Washington narrowly defeated Epton, winning 51.7 percent of the vote.

In April 1983, about two weeks before the mayoral election, the Washington campaign released a fifty-two-page document called The Washington Papers. The document was produced by a remarkable process involving more than 150 volunteers with roots in the neighborhood movement and the black community.[63] They gathered facts, debated issues, produced position papers that defined city policy priorities in urban populist terms and collected the papers into the central policy document of the campaign. The Washington Papers provided the philosophic and strategic underpinning for the lengthy, detailed Chicago Development Plan, published by the city in May 1984 under the title "Chicago Works Together." The five development goals of the plan were:

> Goal I: Increased job opportunities for Chicagoans
>   Targeted business investment in support of job development
>   Local preference in buying and hiring
>   Skilled labor force development
>   Infrastructure development for job development
>   Affirmative action
> Goal II: Promote balanced growth
>   Balanced growth between downtown and neighborhoods
>   Public and private partnerships
>   Strengthened tax base
>   Equitable distribution of the tax burden
> Goal III: Assist neighborhoods to develop through partnerships and
>   coordinated investment
>   Neighborhood planning
>   Linked development
> Goal IV: Enhance public participation in decision making
>   Increased citizen access to information
>   Increased opportunities for citizen involvement
> Goal V: Pursue a regional, state, and national legislative agenda

How much was Washington able to accomplish? First, it must be acknowledged that Washington was hampered throughout most of his first term by the so-called council wars. Led by Edward Vrdolyak, a longtime machine Democrat, white machine politicians, who held a majority on the City Council, did everything possible to thwart Washington's agenda. In 1985, the courts ordered new city council elections based on a reapportionment lawsuit brought in 1982. Washington, a congressman at the time, had been a chief plaintiff. As a result of the new districts ordered by the courts, Washington was able, in 1986, to win a tenuous majority on the Council. In 1987, Washington won reelection and was able to consolidate his control of the City Council. On the brink of being able to wield sufficient political authority to implement sweeping policies, however, Washington fell dead in his office, the victim of a heart attack. It is impossible to know what he might have accomplished in his second term.

His first term does offer, however, some opportunity to evaluate Washington's accomplishments. One of Washington's first acts as mayor was to agree to a federal court decree that sharply reduced hiring outside the civil service system. Critics contended that Washington subsequently created a new patronage system to replace the one that was dismantled. The Washington Administration nurtured a network of 350 agencies that were involved in implementing city policies.[64] Many of these agencies received city funding. Indeed, the city shifted $13 million in Community Development Block Grant money from city agencies and reallocated it to neighborhood organizations.[65] The system differed from the old patronage system in that the city was not directly creating patronage jobs, but it still cemented political support.

Washington also took steps to create a more open and participatory atmosphere in city government. He issued a freedom of information executive order that gave ordinary citizens the right to information held by city bureaucracies.[66] For the first time, community organizations were brought into the governance structure and invited to consult with city officials concerning economic development, housing, and social policies. This caused some problems when city officials became bogged down in frequent meetings and many community associations found it difficult to move from protest to program participation. Nevertheless, there was a flowering of democratic participation that never could have happened under the old Democratic machine.

What remains unknown is whether the Washington Administration would have been able to implement an alternative approach to economic development that demonstrated solid benefits for city residents. By the time of Washington's death, the plans were promising, but the results were limited. Big projects, such as a new stadium for the White Sox and a new central public library, proceeded pretty much as they would have under any mayor, although with more attention to negotiating public concessions. Washington was forced to compromise his neighborhood agenda in order to keep the White Sox in town. Opposition to the new stadium by residents of South Armour Square, who would be forced out of their homes by the new stadium, was vocal and emotional. Washington pushed for a favorable settlement for those who would be displaced, but with the White Sox threatening to move to St. Petersburg, Washington was forced to cave in to the demands of the White Sox owners.[67]

The Washington Administration's preference was for smaller projects that could have significant community input. To accomplish this, the administration funded more than 100 "delegate agencies," mostly neighborhood and nonprofit groups and agencies, to provide economic development services in the neighborhoods. It is difficult, however, to evaluate the overall accomplishments of these groups.

One of the top priorities of Washington's economic development strategy was to retain the industrial jobs that still existed in Chicago. When Hasbro Industries threatened to close its Playskool toy factory in Chicago, the city took an unusual approach, suing Hasbro on the grounds that it was violating an industrial revenue bond agreement to create 400 jobs in exchange for the tax-free borrowing privilege. The city reached a settlement with Hasbro that did not stop the closing but did provide a number of benefits, including offering a $500 bonus to employers who provided jobs to workers laid off from Playskool, establishing a $50,000 emergency fund for Playskool workers, and helping the city to find a successor firm for the plant.[68] The Playskool approach, however, was clearly a defensive action by the city.

The city also attempted a more aggressive approach to promote new industrial jobs in the city. One of the big causes of industrial job loss was displacement of factories due to the expansion of downtown and the construction of upper-income real estate projects. The city developed a proposal for planned manufacturing districts that would restrict conversion of industrial facilities in certain areas. Passed after Washington's death, the proposal required that properties in the core areas would have to be marketed in a good faith manner for manufacturing or it would have to be shown that the new uses did not negatively affect industry.[69] It appears that the Washington Administration was able to aid industrial retention, but no overall evaluation has been conducted of the costs and benefits of the program.

Harold Washington held out the promise of a new populist approach to urban governance, but many constraints limited what he could accomplish. Besides the political constraints of racial conflict, there was opposition from entrenched bureaucrats within the government. In every city department a few Washington appointees, often only two or three, occupied the top positions. The majority of city employees were there long before his election, and they were secure in their jobs. According to the mayor, some of these employees acted as outright saboteurs: "We'd get reports of people calling to ask a question and getting a snotty answer, on purpose. Or they'll say, 'You don't like it? The Mayor did it. You elected him,' and hang up. Or some inspector will harass someone and say it's on orders of the Mayor. We're weeding it out, but we can't control it."[70]

But beyond these problems lies the question of just how much one city can do. Washington operated in a city that was surrounded by suburbs that held a disproportionate share of the region's affluent taxpayers and desirable jobs. Moreover, Washington served as mayor of Chicago during the Reagan years, when federal aid to cities plummeted. Between 1981 and 1986, annual federal aid to Chicago fell from $472 million to only $151 million—a 68 percent drop.[71] Like other cities, Chicago was working hard just to make up for the federal retreat.

❖ PUBLIC POLICY AND THE URBAN CRISIS

Local leadership can make a difference in the quality of life for many urban residents. Police forces can be made more responsive to neighborhoods, and the incidence of police abuses of power can be reduced. Minorities can be guaranteed a fair chance at public employment and contracting opportunities. And, importantly, when minorities hold public office, it signals to their constituents that political participation can be translated into real gains.

Mayors are not, however, in a position to work miracles. Virtually all of the intractable social problems that beset cities have national, not local, causes. Mayors cannot influence rates of immigration, unemployment, and poverty or social changes in family structure. Cities may influence levels of crime and health, but what they can accomplish is limited. The solutions, if there are any, are to be found in regional, state and federal policies and in national economic performance. We discuss these larger forces and their impact on cities in the concluding chapter.

CHAPTER 15

IS THERE A REMEDY TO THE POLITICS OF SECESSION?

❖ SEPARATION AND SEGREGATION

Twenty-five years after the National Commission on Civil Disorders warned, "Our nation is moving toward two societies, one black, one white—separate and unequal,"[1] the Los Angeles rebellion served as a reminder that the conditions that provoked the riots of the 1960s persist. What is different about the 1990s is that metropolitan areas have now fractured not just into two societies, but into many. African Americans, Latinos, Asians, and non-Hispanic whites live mostly in separate neighborhoods, and each of these groups is, in turn, increasingly sorted into separate income groups.

In America's metropolitan areas enclave politics has very nearly eclipsed a politics of accommodation, bargaining, and compromise. By taking refuge in homogeneous communities, affluent Americans have chosen to sever the bonds that connect them to others. As a way of dealing with urban problems, geographical mobility is a way of opting out of a metropolitan community that forces citizens to recognize reciprocal rights and responsibilities. Americans fought a bloody civil war over the right of secession, and the principle was established that states do not have the right to unilaterally leave the political community, but must instead work to change policies from within. Exit is not an option. In urban politics, by contrast, secession has evolved into a sophisticated art.

In this concluding chapter we consider whether there are ways to moderate the tendencies toward separation and segregation. It seems unlikely that the governmental fragmentation within metropolitan areas will be reduced. Almost all attempts to create metropolitan-wide governments have come to naught; people have a deep attachment to the idea of small, local units of government. In any case, it is doubtful that local governments, of whatever scope and however organized and financed, could do much (even if they wished) to reduce the inequalities within metropolitan areas. Effective policies must be national in scope. If the national government were to adopt policies designed to reduce overall levels of inequality and unemployment, improve health care, make child care and other family services more easily available, and make funds available for the repair of urban infrastructure, local governments would be in a better position to direct their resources toward the problems that are truly within their scope and power to address.

❖ THREE MYTHS

The movements toward separation and segregation have been driven by misconceptions and stereotypes. To the degree that urban residents retreat into separate enclaves, they develop simplistic and distorted images of what it is outside their enclaves. There are three particularly common myths.

Myth 1: Unlike the suburbs, cities are havens for social chaos and crime. Of all the misconceptions and distorted images that people have developed, this one is the most influential and pernicious. Affluent residents of suburban (and central city) enclaves view inner-city ghettos as places inhabited by people who would rather rob, pillage, and plunder than work. In the late 1960s, a leading urban scholar wrote a book based on just such a stereotype.[2] Such descriptions of a supposed subculture of crime and social chaos are often thinly veiled attacks on inner-city blacks. Local media rely heavily on sensationalized accounts of crime and violence to maintain their ratings. Approximately 20 percent of front page news stories and local news broadcasts focus on violent crime.[3] Studies have shown that television viewing is related to heightened fear of crime, even for people living outside urban settings.[4] The constant lurid portrayals in the media create the inevitable impression that inner-city residents, and especially blacks and Latinos, are devoid of civilizing influences. In response to such images, affluent people try to insulate themselves from potential harm: "The more vulnerable we feel, the more we fragment into smaller living and working units, or whatever it takes to create the feeling of insulation and safety and home."[5]

The media constantly conflate "inner city," "poverty," "minorities," and "crime" into a bundle of interchangeable images. Discourse on the inner cities has become "our current national morality play," a play that unremittingly presents "black and brown violence, crime, laziness, and sexual profligacy."[6] These behaviors are typically ascribed to an urban "underclass," a term laden with a multitude of meanings. Reporters and social scientists have applied the term to "residence (inner city), employment and housing status (illegal only; tenements, shelters, or the streets), reproductive status (illegitimate children, missing fathers), criminal status (non–white collar only), and drug use (preferably crack cocaine)."[7] So loosely applied and ill-defined, "underclass" loses all meaning except as the bogeyman of the urban morality play.

The script of the urban morality play constantly draws hard-and-fast distinctions between suburbs and inner cities. The term inner city becomes synonymous with dilapidated neighborhoods, blacks and Latinos, and the "underclass." Central cities are, in fact, internally complex; like the suburbs they are fragmented among various income, ethnic, and racial groups. These groups are, in turn, sociologically and economically complex. Most African Americans and Latinos do not live in so-called underclass neighborhoods; according to one estimate, only 6 percent of the black population reside in areas of high crime or drug use.[8] It would be impossible, however, to derive such an impression from the nightly news.

A more important reason for discarding the distinctions between suburbs and inner cities and the language of the underclass is that social behaviors commonly attributed to the poor, wherever they live, are also present among other groups. Instability in the traditional nuclear family has affected all income, racial, and ethnic groups. Married couples are declining among middle-class whites and single-parent families are increasing. In 1991, women headed 19 percent of white families with children, up significantly since 1970.[9] One scholar has demonstrated that while a higher proportion of black families are headed by women, the rate of increase in female-headed families among whites has been almost identical to the rate of increase among blacks. Indeed, the rate of out-of-wedlock births has been rising faster among whites than among blacks.[10]

Though crack cocaine use has not hit middle-class families as hard as it has hit poor families in core cities, substance abuse is a major problem in even the most affluent suburbs, with alcohol now the drug of choice. The distribution of other problems, too, defies the usual distinctions of middle-class versus poor and suburban versus inner city. Though crime is clearly higher in central cities, for instance, it is rising faster in many suburban areas than anywhere else.[11] The residents of Green Valley, Nevada, a gated community of more than 20,000 affluent residents on the outskirts of Las Vegas, are learning that problems have a way of following people. A rash of crimes has been committed within the community, all by affluent residents who have moved there, demonstrating that crimes of rape, child molestation, burglary, teenage gang fights, and murder are not the exclusive province of the poor. Even the Green Valley Community Association president was arrested for burglary. One resident commented, "People are coming here from all over the place and bringing their problems with them."[12]

Myth 2: Affluent taxpayers subsidize the poor in the inner cities. A popular notion is that urban welfare programs are a huge drain on the federal budget and that these programs are disproportionately paid for by the taxes of the suburban middle class. Thomas Byrne Edsall, a reporter for the *Washington Post,* has written two influential books (one co-authored with Mary Edsall) tracing the Democratic presidential losses in 1980, 1984, and 1988 to white voters' resentments of federal programs that seemed to benefit blacks and the poor disproportionately.[13] When running for the presidency in 1992, Bill Clinton went to great pains to talk about the "forgotten middle class."

Over the years conservatives have been effective in selling a message that "special interests," that is, minorities and poor people, have primarily benefited from federal programs. Actually, however, people who live in suburbs have been some of the most favored beneficiaries. Programs through which money flowed principally to central cities constitute only a trickle compared to the massive flow of federal tax breaks and spending programs that have benefited suburbanites and wealthy taxpayers.

In Chapter 8 we described the national policies that subsidized suburbanization. One of these policies was the $123 billion interstate highway program, which displaced hundreds of thousands of inner-city residents in the cause of building highways to primarily serve suburban commuters. Nearly all FHA and VA federal loan guarantees underwrote mortgages for homes built in suburban subdivisions. The federal tax code, which allows home owners to deduct mortgage interest and property taxes from their federal income tax, provided a huge boost to suburban (and vacation home) construction. Subsidies for nonpoor home owners vastly exceed housing subsidies for the poor, both in total amount and per recipient. From 1980 to 1988, annual federal outlays for low-income housing fell two-thirds, to less than $8.6 billion by 1988. Over the same period annual home owner tax deductions soared to $43.6 billion.[14] By the late 1980s, public housing accounted for less than 2 percent of the nation's housing units, and only about one-fifth of the poor lived in units subsidized by the federal government or local governments.[15] The numbers of subsidized units built each year lagged far behind the growing numbers of the poor. In the late 1970s, the number of subsidized units was increasing by 300,000 units a year. A decade later, the number of units added each year fell to less than 30,000.[16] The rate of increase in tax subsidies for the nonpoor was rising much faster than the cost of low-income subsidized units.

The volume of political rhetoric aimed at welfare is grossly out of proportion to the cost of these programs. They take a surprisingly small portion of the federal budget. In 1989, all public assistance expenditures totaled about 4.2 percent of federal outlays. In 1992, the average state spent just 3.4 percent of its budget on welfare.[17] The total of all federal public aid spending, including Medicaid and food stamps (and it should be noted that a large proportion of food stamps go to people with incomes above the poverty line), accounts for 7.0 percent of federal outlays.[18] Public benefits paid out to the nonpoor are exponentially higher. In 1989, Social Security entitlements (including pensions and disability benefits) and Medicare took 36.6 percent of federal outlays.[19] Neither of these programs are targeted to the poor.

While welfare spending is highly visible and always controversial, policies that benefit the middle- and upper-classes are often hidden in the tax code.

When the federal government gives tax breaks to any group, the policy is equivalent to taking the amount of money lost to the treasury and giving it to that group. If this were the way these policies were actually implemented, they would be far more visible, and they would be far more controversial and politically unpalatable. Imagine, for example, that instead of allowing home owners to deduct interest and local property taxes from their federal tax bill, the federal government appropriated money and sent checks to home owners (more than $40 billion in 1988). To conform to its present policies, as accomplished through tax deductions, Congress would have to allocate the largest amounts of money to wealthy home owners, modest amounts to middle-income home owners, practically nothing to those who owned less expensive homes, and, of course, nothing at all to renters. Made visible in this way, one suspects that the policies used to promote home ownership would be far less popular. Indeed, they might look like a way of providing welfare for the rich.

One author has referred to tax subsidies, nearly all of which benefit upper-income taxpayers disproportionately (since they have the highest potential tax exposure), as "fiscal welfare."[20] For example, the deduction of employer contributions to pension plans and to medical insurance rose from $7.7 billion in 1974 to an astonishing $113.9 billion in 1992.[21] Most of the benefits, in the form of more generous pensions and health coverage, went to professional and managerial employees working for large corporations and governments. The fiscal welfare state, composed of all tax write-offs and deductions, grew at a much faster rate than the welfare state funded through appropriations, but there was almost no public debate about its drain on the federal budget.

Defense expenditures accounted for 20.8 percent of federal outlays in 1992, and taxpayers in the central cities contributed far more to defense than they got back in federal defense spending.[22] In this way the taxpayers of New York City, for example, lost $8.4 billion in 1990, taxpayers of Chicago $3.1 billion, and taxpayers of Houston $1.7 billion. For New York City alone this represented a subsidy by city taxpayers of 250,000 full-time jobs elsewhere in the country.[23] Many of those jobs were located in the Sunbelt.

There are, to be sure, federal programs that especially benefit central cities as municipalities. Compared to military spending and entitlement programs, such as Medicare and Social Security, these programs have always been relatively small. In the 1960s and early 1970s they grew rapidly, but in the 1980s they suffered much deeper cuts than the programs that benefit individuals. For example, federal aid to municipalities as a percentage of federal outlays fell from 2.2 percent in 1978 ($10.2 billion) to 1.0 percent in 1986 ($9.8 billion).[24]

Myth 3: The core cities are obsolete; the suburbs are better off without them. In 1991, *Newsweek* magazine ran a story entitled, "Are Cities Obsolete?" quoting an expert in urban land use as saying, "The basic problem is that cities are no longer functional. . . . We don't need them anymore."[25] *New York Times* polls showed that residents of the suburban counties outside of New York City no longer felt significantly connected to the city. The percentage of respondents who said that events in the city had "hardly any impact" on their daily lives increased from 39 percent in 1978 to 51 percent in 1991.[26] The implication of this view is that those who secede from the city into suburbs are deserting a sinking ship whose fate is of little concern to them.

If core cities were somehow to disappear tomorrow, suburbanites might quickly notice interdependencies they had overlooked. Central cities still perform essential functions in the American economy, and they are pivotal to the health of metropolitan areas. Downtown business districts bring together a rich mixture of business services that improve productivity. They are centers of highly innovative and sophisticated information processing. They are essential for keeping a metropolitan area competitive in the global marketplace; in 1990, central cities in the United States contributed $23 billion more in services to the world economy than they took in.[27] The clustering of highly skilled workers in downtown office buildings explains why the earnings of workers in central cities are higher than the average earnings of those who work in the suburbs.[28]

Central cities are uniquely suited to be locations for tourism and leisure because of their historic architecture, public monuments, redeveloped waterfronts, renovated neighborhoods, symphony halls, parks, zoos, and ethnic restaurants and neighborhoods. The old industrial cities have a particular advantage. Convention centers and most sports stadiums are located within the core cities. As the fastest-growing sectors of the American (and world) economies, tourism and leisure are extremely important to the economic future of metropolitan areas.

Suburbanites take a lion's share of the jobs in the downtown corporate towers and tourist facilities. For example, 46 percent of all earnings of suburban residents of San Francisco were earned in the central city in 1989; the figure was 41 percent for the Denver metropolitan area and 39 percent for New Orleans.[29] Without the economic contribution of their central cities, in most metropolitan areas 40 percent or more of suburbanites would find themselves without a job.

Many nations recognize the importance of core cities to their economies by investing large amounts of money in mass transit and other infrastructure to make them work more efficiently. In the 1980s, Japan embarked on a fifteen-year, $8 trillion infrastructure investment program that was largely concentrated on cities. Central governments in all the major industrial nations provide much higher levels of support than does the United States government for local government budgets, thus alleviating urban fiscal crises.[30] In a competitive global marketplace, no nation is in a position to squander the investments in physical infrastructure and human capital that are located in central cities.

Cities are engines of growth that constantly spin off new ideas and businesses. Cities assimilate masses of new immigrants who bring their energy, skills, and international connections to metropolitan economies. Suburbanites cannot escape from the problems of central cities because if cities decline, eventually the surrounding suburbs will come down with them. When cities grow and prosper, their suburbs grow and prosper. Metropolitan areas with the greatest disparities between cities and suburbs have the lowest rates of economic growth.[31] The fates of central cities and their suburbs are intertwined.

❖ POLICIES THAT UNITE RATHER THAN DIVIDE

About 48 percent of the U.S. population lived in suburbs when the 1990 census was taken. Because they turn out for elections at a higher rate than rural and central city voters, suburban voters cast a majority of the votes in the 1992 presidential election. Central cities now hold only 29 percent of the nation's population.[32] The media characterized the 1992 presidential election as a contest for the "swing" suburban vote made up of the so-called Reagan Democrats, primarily white working-class voters who had become disaffected with Democratic policies targeted to central cities, blacks, and the poor.

Bill Clinton made an effort to appeal to suburban voters. He distanced himself from Jesse Jackson and the urban wing of the Democratic party. He called for a get tough approach to welfare reform. His bus tours were replete with suburban and small town imagery. Clinton's claim that he represented a new Democratic party that would pay attention to the concerns of the middle class was politically shrewd. Republicans had been effective in driving a wedge between suburban and central-city voters, between the middle and working classes and the poor, and between white and minority voters. Clinton's victory in the presidential election was generally credited to the success of his suburban strategy.

The urban policies of the 1960s were targeted to depressed cities and the inner-city poor. Clinton advocated broader policies designed to appeal to voters of almost every income group (except for the very rich). He often said that the problems of a stagnant economy, soaring health care costs, affordable housing, crime, and drugs affect all Americans. No doubt these claims are a bit overdrawn (not all Americans are affected similarly), but they have considerable political appeal. It is likely that the some of the national policies pushed by the Clinton Administration will, if enacted, have a considerable impact on urban America. Three examples illustrate their potential.

■ An Infrastructure Employment Program

Though experts debate the magnitude of the problem, nearly everyone agrees that the United States has been seriously underinvesting in its public infrastructure for some time. Government investment in public infrastructure declined from 2.3 percent of GNP in 1960 to 1.1 percent in 1985.[33] Urban transportation systems are overloaded, often dangerously dilapidated and need to be redesigned. Roads and bridges are in need of repair. Water mains, many of them installed decades ago, are causing some streets to subside and collapse in older cities. To forestall massive leaks, older cities must repair and replace entire grids of water mains. Waste water treatment facilities must be improved if a major contamination of rivers and lakes is to be avoided.

The Clinton Administration has emphasized the importance of public infrastructure investment to productivity and the economy. An infrastructure program would be expensive, with estimates of annual spending ranging from $37.8 billion to $140.5 billion.[34] A federal infrastructure block grant program would allow considerable flexibility for local governments. Cities would necessarily receive a large proportion of the federal funds because they have so much of the older infrastructure that needs reconstruction and repair. It makes economic sense to maintain existing infrastructure in cities rather than start from scratch and build anew. A massive investment in infrastructure would also represent an opportunity to lower the unemployment rate using a strategy similar to the public works programs of the 1930s.

During the 1992 campaign, Clinton promised big city mayors a $20 billion a year infrastructure investment program that would link the physical revitalization of the cities with national economic revitalization.[35] A public works employment program would provide employment for people in all parts of the country, but since unemployment rates are higher in most core cities than elsewhere, it would especially benefit the urban poor.

▣ A Family Support Program

Since the mid-1960s the United States has made tremendous progress in reducing poverty among the elderly. In 1959, 35.2 percent of the elderly were poor; by 1986, only 12.6 percent of the elderly fell below the poverty line.[36] The Social Security trust funds and Old Age Benefits, plus Medicare and some other programs, brought about this stunning result. Entitlement programs for the elderly are highly popular and well protected politically because they benefit a large segment of the population that has been able to exert political muscle.[37] Few politicians dare to even discuss cutting Social Security.

Programs for families and children, on the other hand, have fared poorly, with the result that the poverty rate for children has soared since the early 1980s. By 1989, one child in five lived in poverty.[38] The United States lacks comprehensive policies for supporting families. Almost every other developed country provides child allowances—a cash payment to families for each child.[39] Such an entitlement program in the United States, say $1,000 for each child, would go a long way toward lifting children out of poverty and would be politically popular because it would benefit the suburban middle class as well as the inner-city poor.

Over the past two decades a revolution in the work force has taken place. Most women with children now work, making it impossible for them to be with their children at all hours of the day. Despite this revolution, day-care and after-school services are erratically available in the United States, in many areas they are hardly available, and regulation is almost absent in most states. Day-care salaries are low and services are expensive. "Latchkey" children have become an issue in recent years; frequently, even in middle-class families, there is no one at home when children get out of school.

With a system of social support services for families, it is probable that families would be better able to withstand economic pressures, juvenile delinquency would decline, and children would perform better in school. As with infrastructure needs, family support issues transcend the boundaries between income groups and between central cities and suburbs.

▦ A National Health Insurance Program

A national health insurance program, as promised by the Clinton Administration, would have particularly dramatic effects in urban areas. In older metropolitan areas public health facilities are in danger of being overrun. Increased funding and administrative attention to the AIDS epidemic would, all by itself, provide huge relief to metropolitan, and especially inner-city, health facilities. A national health insurance program might also come in time to prevent epidemics of contagious diseases, many of which are spreading once again because of inadequate public health systems. A virulent strain of tuberculosis, for example, is spreading in several of America's largest cities. Tuberculosis was once a scourge in cities because it spreads easily in crowded conditions. It knows no boundaries between rich and poor—anyone riding a bus, going to school, or entering a hospital can be exposed through a cough or sneeze. By the post-World War II era tuberculosis in the U.S. almost vanished, as did facilities to treat it. Its reappearance is shocking. By 1992, there were more than 4,000 cases of tuberculosis in New York City, but fewer than 75 hospital beds assigned for patients and only 9 mostly run-down, overcrowded chest clinics. In 1967, the last time there were as many as 4,000 cases in the city, more than 1,000 hospital beds were reserved for tuberculosis patients.[40]

❖ THE URBAN FUTURE

Secession politics is rooted in the stark inequalities that characterize America's urban areas. In the absence of policies that reduce such inequalities, urban residents will continue to choose separation and segregation. Their choice is not irrational. By choosing a political jurisdiction and neighborhood carefully, they can lower their taxes, gain access to high-quality public services and amenities (or private services and amenities), and to some degree escape the social problems that are inevitably associated with inequality, poverty, and want.

Policies to alleviate inequalities can be enacted at the metropolitan level. In December 1992, the county supervisor of St. Louis County, which contains ninety-two suburbs of St. Louis, proposed a plan whereby wealthier communities would share some of their tax base with poorer communities.[41] It was a courageous political move. In the St. Louis area, as elsewhere, some towns and suburbs hit the jackpot when malls, shopping centers, or other large businesses decided to locate within their boundaries. Areas that were losers in the competition were less able to raise money to provide adequate basic services. Some towns and suburbs have rutted streets that have not been paved in years. Some pay their police officers miserly salaries, and some collect most of their revenues from traffic tickets (with all the abuses that this combination of circumstances would produce). A "share the tax wealth" program would improve the quality of life for all but the most cloistered urban residents. This kind of program would have a similar effect in most metropolitan areas.

Metropolitan-wide solutions, however, are unlikely in the present political climate. What cities can do by themselves is limited. Cities can, for instance, provide shelters or camping space for their homeless, but few have the resources to permanently house the homeless. National economic and social policies have far-reaching effects. National policies that would reduce social and economic inequalities would allow local governments to concentrate on addressing the problems that lie realistically within their resources and governmental powers.

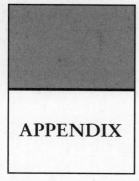

APPENDIX

TOP 100 METROPOLITAN AREAS, 1980-1990

Source: U.S. Bureau of the Census, *State and Metropolitan Area Data Book: 1991* (Washington, D. C.: Government Printing Office, 1991); U.S. Bureau of the Census, *Statistical Abstract of the United States: 1991*, 111th ed. (Washington, D. C.: Government Printing Office, 1991).

POPULATION OF TOP 100 METROPOLITAN AREAS AND THEIR LARGEST CENTRAL CITY, 1980–1990 (IN THOUSANDS)

METROPOLITAN AREA (LARGEST CENTRAL CITY IN ITALICS)	METROPOLITAN AREA			LARGEST CENTRAL CITY		
	1980	1990	PERCENT CHANGE, 1980–1990	1980	1990	PERCENT CHANGE, 1980–1990
1. *New York*–northern New Jersey–Long Island, NY–NJ–CT (CMSA/NECMA)	17,412	17,953	+3.1	7,072	7,323	+3.5
2. *Los Angeles*–Anaheim–Riverside, CA (CMSA)	11,498	14,532	+26.4	2,969	3,485	+17.4
3. *Chicago*–Lake County, IL–IN–WI (CMSA)	7,937	8,066	+1.6	3,005	2,784	–7.4
4. *San Francisco*–Oakland–San Jose, CA (CMSA)	5,368	6,253	+16.5	679	724	+6.6
5. *Philadelphia*–Wilmington–Trenton, PA–NJ–DE–MD (CMSA)	5,681	5,899	+3.9	1,688	1,586	–6.1
6. *Detroit*–Ann Arbor, MI (CMSA)	4,753	4,665	–1.8	1,203	1,028	–14.6
7. *Washington*, DC–MD–VA (MSA)	3,251	3,924	+20.7	638	607	–4.9
8. *Dallas*–Fort Worth, TX (CMSA)	2,931	3,885	+32.6	905	1,007	+11.3
9. *Boston*–Lawrence–Salem–Lowell–Brockton, MA (NECMA)	3,663	3,784	+3.3	563	574	+2.0
10. *Houston*–Galveston–Brazoria, TX (CMSA)	3,100	3,711	+19.7	1,595	1,631	+2.2
11. *Miami*–Fort Lauderdale, FL (CMSA)	2,644	3,193	+32.6	347	359	+3.4
12. *Atlanta*, GA (MSA)	2,138	2,834	+32.5	425	394	–7.3
13. *Cleveland*–Akron–Lorain, OH (CMSA)	2,834	2,760	–2.6	574	506	–11.9
14. *Seattle*–Tacoma, WA (CMSA)	2,093	2,559	+22.3	494	516	+4.5
15. *San Diego*, CA (MSA)	1,862	2,498	+34.2	876	1,111	+26.8
16. *Minneapolis*–St. Paul, MN–WI (MSA)	2,137	2,464	+15.3	371	368	–0.7
17. *St. Louis*, MO–IL (MSA)	2,377	2,444	+2.8	453	397	–12.4
18. *Baltimore*, MD (MSA)	2,199	2,382	+8.3	787	736	–6.4
19. *Pittsburgh*–Beaver Valley, PA (CMSA)	2,423	2,243	–7.4	424	370	–12.8

POPULATION OF TOP 100 METROPOLITAN AREAS AND THEIR LARGEST CENTRAL CITY, 1980–1990 (IN THOUSANDS) (Continued)

METROPOLITAN AREA (LARGEST CENTRAL CITY IN ITALICS)	METROPOLITAN AREA			LARGEST CENTRAL CITY		
	1980	1990	PERCENT CHANGE, 1980–1990	1980	1990	PERCENT CHANGE, 1980–1990
20. *Phoenix, AZ (MSA)*	1,509	2,122	+40.6	790	983	+24.5
21. *Tampa–St. Petersburg–Clearwater, FL (MSA)*	1,614	2,068	+28.2	272	280	+3.1
22. *Denver–Boulder, CO (CMSA)*	1,618	1,848	+14.2	493	468	−5.1
23. *Cincinnati–Hamilton, OH–KY–IN (CMSA)*	1,660	1,744	+5.1	385	364	−5.5
24. *Milwaukee–Racine, WI (CMSA)*	1,570	1,607	+2.4	636	628	−1.3
25. *Kansas City, MO–KS (MSA)*	1,433	1,566	+9.3	161	150	−7.1
26. *Sacramento, CA (MSA)*	1,100	1,481	+34.7	276	369	+34.0
27. *Portland–Vancouver, OR–WA (CMSA)*	1,298	1,478	+13.9	368	437	+18.8
28. *Norfolk–Virginia Beach–Newport News, VA (MSA)*	1,160	1,396	+20.3	267	261	−2.2
29. *Columbus, OH (MSA)*	1,244	1,377	+10.7	565	633	+12.0
30. *San Antonio, TX (MSA)*	1,072	1,302	+21.5	786	936	+19.1
31. *Indianapolis, IN (MSA)*	1,167	1,250	+7.1	701	731	+4.3
32. *New Orleans, LA (MSA)*	1,257	1,239	−1.4	558	497	−10.9
33. *Buffalo–Niagara Falls, NY (CMSA)*	1,243	1,189	−4.3	358	328	−8.3
34. *Charlotte–Gastonia–Rock Hill, NC–SC (MSA)*	971	1,162	+19.6	315	396	+25.5
35. *Hartford–New Britain–Middletown–Bristol, CT (NECMA)*	1,052	1,124	+6.9	136	140	+2.5
36. *Orlando, FL (MSA)*	700	1,073	+53.3	128	165	+28.4
37. *Salt Lake City–Ogden, UT (MSA)*	910	1,072	+17.8	163	160	−1.9
38. *Rochester, NY (MSA)*	971	1,002	+3.2	242	232	−4.2
39. *Nashville, TN (MSA)*	851	985	+15.0	456	488	+6.9
40. *Memphis, TN–AR–MS (MSA)*	913	982	+7.5	646	610	−5.5

METROPOLITAN AREA (LARGEST CENTRAL CITY IN ITALICS)	METROPOLITAN AREA			LARGEST CENTRAL CITY		
	1980	1990	PERCENT CHANGE, 1980–1990	1980	1990	PERCENT CHANGE, 1980–1990
41. *Oklahoma City*, OK (MSA)	861	959	+11.4	404	445	+10.1
42. *Louisville*, KY–IN (MSA)	956	953	−0.4	299	269	−9.9
43. *Dayton–Springfield*, OH (MSA)	942	951	+1.0	194	182	−5.9
44. *Greensboro–Winston-Salem–High Point*, NC (MSA)	851	942	+10.6	156	184	+17.9
45. *Providence–Pawtucket–Woonsocket*, RI (NECMA)	866	916	+5.8	157	161	+2.5
46. *Birmingham*, AL (MSA)	884	908	+2.7	284	266	−6.5
47. *Jacksonville*, FL (MSA)	772	907	+25.5	541	635	+17.9
48. *Albany–Schenectady–Troy*, NY (MSA)	836	874	+4.6	102	101	−0.6
49. *Richmond–Petersburg*, VA (MSA)	761	866	+3.9	219	203	−7.4
50. *West Palm Beach–Boca Raton–Delray Beach*, FL (MSA)	577	864	+49.7	63	68	+6.9
51. *Honolulu*, HI (MSA)	763	836	+9.7	365	365	+0.1
52. *New Haven–Waterbury–Meriden*, CT (NECMA)	761	804	+5.6	126	130	+3.5
53. *Austin*, TX (MSA)	537	782	+45.6	346	466	+34.6
54. *Las Vegas*, NV (MSA)	463	741	+60.1	165	256	+56.9
55. *Raleigh–Durham*, NC (MSA)	561	735	+31.2	150	208	+38.4
56. *Scranton–Wilkes Barre*, PA (MSA)	729	734	+0.7	88	82	−7.2
57. *Worchester–Fitchburg–Leominster*, MA (NECMA)	646	710	+9.8	162	170	+4.9
58. *Tulsa*, OK (MSA)	657	709	+7.9	361	367	+1.8
59. *Grand Rapids*, MI (MSA)	602	688	+14.4	182	189	+4.0
60. *Allentown–Bethlehem*, PA–NJ (MSA)	635	687	+8.1	104	105	+1.3
61. *Fresno*, CA (MSA)	515	667	+29.7	217	354	+62.9

POPULATION OF TOP 100 METROPOLITAN AREAS AND THEIR LARGEST CENTRAL CITY, 1980–1990 (IN THOUSANDS) (Continued)

METROPOLITAN AREA (LARGEST CENTRAL CITY IN ITALICS)	METROPOLITAN AREA			LARGEST CENTRAL CITY		
	1980	1990	PERCENT CHANGE, 1980–1990	1980	1990	PERCENT CHANGE, 1980–1990
62. *Tucson, AZ (MSA)*	531	667	+25.5	331	405	+22.6
63. *Syracuse, NY (MSA)*	643	660	+2.6	170	164	-3.7
64. *Greenville–Spartanburg, SC (MSA)*	570	641	+12.4	58	58	+0.1
65. *Omaha, NE–IA (MSA)*	585	618	+5.7	314	336	+7.0
66. *Toledo, OH (MSA)*	617	614	-0.4	355	333	-6.1
67. *Knoxville, TN (MSA)*	566	605	+6.9	175	165	-5.7
68. *Springfield, MA (NECMA)*	582	603	+3.6	152	157	+3.1
69. *El Paso, TX (MSA)*	480	592	+23.3	425	515	+21.2
70. *Harrisburg–Lebanon–Carlisle, PA (MSA)*	556	588	+5.7	53	53	-1.7
71. *Bakersfield, CA (MSA)*	403	543	+34.8	106	175	+65.5
72. *Baton Rouge, LA (MSA)*	494	528	+6.9	220	220	-0.4
73. *Little Rock–North Little Rock, AR (MSA)*	474	513	+8.1	159	176	+10.5
74. *Charleston, SC (MSA)*	430	507	+17.8	74	80	+9.0
75. *New Bedford–Fall River–Attleboro, MA (NECMA)*	475	506	+6.7	98	100	+1.5
76. *Youngstown–Warren, OH (MSA)*	531	493	-7.3	116	96	-17.1
77. *Wichita, KS (MSA)*	442	485	+9.7	280	304	+8.6
78. *Stockton, CA (MSA)*	347	481	+38.4	150	211	+42.3
79. *Albuquerque, NM (MSA)*	420	481	+14.4	332	385	+15.6
80. *Mobile, AL (MSA)*	444	477	+7.5	200	196	-2.1
81. *Columbia, SC (MSA)*	410	453	+10.6	101	98	-3.1
82. *Johnson City–Kingsport–Bristol, TN–VA (MSA)*	434	436	+0.6	46	49	+8.2

POPULATION OF TOP 100 METROPOLITAN AREAS AND THEIR LARGEST CENTRAL CITY, 1980–1990 (IN THOUSANDS)
(Continued)

METROPOLITAN AREA (LARGEST CENTRAL CITY IN ITALICS)	METROPOLITAN AREA			LARGEST CENTRAL CITY		
	1980	1990	PERCENT CHANGE, 1980–1990	1980	1990	PERCENT CHANGE, 1980–1990
83. *Chattanooga*, TN–GA (MSA)	426	433	+1.6	170	152	−10.1
84. *Lansing–East Lansing*, MI (MSA)	420	433	+3.1	130	127	−2.4
85. *Flint*, MI (MSA)	450	430	−4.4	160	141	−11.8
86. *Lancaster*, PA (MSA)	362	423	+16.7	55	56	+1.5
87. *York*, PA (MSA)	381	418	+9.6	45	42	−5.4
88. *Lakeland–Winter Haven*, FL (MSA)	322	405	+26.0	54	71	+29.7
89. *Saginaw–Bay City–Midland*, MI (MSA)	422	399	−5.3	78	70	−10.3
90. *Melbourne–Titusville–Palm Bay*, FL (MSA)	273	399	+46.2	18	63	+237.5
91. *Colorado Springs*, CO (MSA)	309	397	+28.3	215	281	+30.7
92. *Augusta*, GA–SC (MSA)	346	397	+14.7	48	45	−6.2
93. *Jackson*, MS (MSA)	362	395	+9.2	203	197	−3.1
94. *Canton*, OH (MSA)	404	394	−2.6	93	84	−9.6
95. *Des Moines*, IA (MSA)	368	393	+6.9	191	193	+1.2
96. *McAllen–Edinburg–Mission*, TX (MSA)	283	384	+35.4	67	84	+25.0
97. *Daytona Beach*, FL (MSA)	259	371	+43.3	57	62	+9.4
98. *Modesto*, CA (MSA)	266	371	+39.3	113	165	+46.1
99. *Santa Barbara–Santa Maria–Lompoc*, CA (MSA)	299	370	+23.7	74	86	+15.0
100. *Madison*, WI (MSA)	324	367	+13.5	171	191	+12.1

Source: U.S. Bureau of the Census, *State and Metropolitan Area Data Book: 1991* (Washington, D.C.: Government Printing Office, 1991); U.S. Bureau of the Census, *Statistical Abstract of the United States: 1991*, 111th ed., (Washington, D.C.: Government Printing Office, 1991).

NOTES

CHAPTER 1

1. Lawrence J. R. Herson and John M. Bolland, *The Urban Web: Politics, Policy, and Theory* (Chicago: Nelson-Hall, 1990), p. 43.

2. Sam Bass Warner, Jr., *The Private City: Philadelphia in Three Periods of Its Growth* (Philadelphia: University of Pennsylvania Press, 1968), p. 4.

3. Frederic Harrison, quoted in James A. Clapp, *The City: A Dictionary of Quotable Thoughts on Cities and Urban Life* (New Brunswick, N.J.: Center for Urban Policy Research, Rutgers University, 1984).

4. Quoted in *ibid.*, p. 66

5. Fellini's film *Roma* opens with scenes of a subway excavation that results in a dramatic archeological discovery.

6. Quoted in *ibid.*, 210.

7. *Ibid.*

8. Quoted in *ibid.*, p. 148.

9. Quoted in *ibid.*, pp. 128–129.

10. Herson and Bolland, p. 46.

11. Eric Nordlinger, *On the Autonomy of the Democratic State* (Cambridge, Mass.: Harvard University Press, 1981).

12. Todd Swanstrom, "Semisovereign Cities: The Politics of Urban Development," *Polity* 21, no. 1 (Fall 1988): 83–110.

13. Martin Shefter, *Political Crisis/Fiscal Crisis: The Collapse and Revival of New York City* (New York: Basic Books, 1985).

14. Robert C. Wood, *Suburbia: Its People and Their Politics* (Boston: Houghton Mifflin, 1958).

15. Clarence N. Stone, *Regime Politics: Governing Atlanta 1946–1988* (Lawrence: The University Press of Kansas, 1989), p. 3.

CHAPTER 2

1. London proper had 957,000, but the greater London area had 1,117,000 people.

2. Brian R. Mitchell, *European Historical Statistics, 1750–1970* (New York: Columbia University Press, 1975), p. 76 (population of major cities).

3. Defined as settlements with at least 5,000 population.

4. "The Inevitability of City Growth," reprinted from *Atlantic Monthly,* April 1985, in *City Life, 1865–1900: Views of Urban America,* ed. Ann Cook, Marilyn Gittell, and Herb Mack (New York: Praeger, 1973), p. 17.

5. From Table 2, "Populations of Principal U.S. Cities, 1790 to 1839," in Blake McKelvey, *American Urbanization: A Comparative History* (Glenview, Ill.: Scott, Foresman, 1973), p. 24.

6. U.S. Department of Commerce, Bureau of the Census, *Historical Statistics of the United States, Colonial Times to 1970,* pt. 1, Bicentennial ed. (Washington, D.C.: Government Printing Office, 1975), p. 11.

7. Eric H. Monkkonen, *America Becomes Urban: The Development of U.S. Cities and Towns 1780–1980* (Berkeley: University of California Press, 1988), p. 78.

8. *Historical Statistics of the United States, Colonial Times to 1970,* pt. 1, p. 11.

9. Richard C. Wade, *The Urban Frontier: Pioneer Life in Early Pittsburgh, Cincinnati, Lexington, Louisville, and St. Louis* (Chicago: University of Chicago Press, 1959), p. 103.

10. David M. Gordon, "Class Struggle and the Stages of American Urban Development," *The Rise of the Sunbelt Cities,* ed., David C. Perry and Alfred J. Watkins (Beverly Hills, Calif.: Sage, 1977), p. 64.

11. George Rogers Taylor, *The Transportation Revolution, 1815–1860* (New York: Holt, Rinehart and Winston, 1951), p. 52.

12. Carter Goodrich, *Government Promotion of American Canals and Railroads, 1800–1890* (New York: Columbia University Press, 1960), pp. 266–267.

13. Wade, *The Urban Frontier,* p. 70.

14. McKelvey, *American Urbanization,* p. 31.

15. U.S. Department of Commerce, Bureau of the Census, *Historical Statistics of the United States, Colonial Times to 1970,* pt. 2, Bicentennial ed. (Washington, D.C.: Government Printing Office, 1975), pp. 728, 731.

16. McKelvey, *American Urbanization,* pp. 25–26.

17. *Ibid.*

18. Alfred D. Chandler, *The Railroads: The Nation's First Big Business* (New York: Harcourt Brace Jovanovich, 1965).

19. Henry W. Broude, "The Role of the State in American Economic Development, 1820–1890," *United States Economic History: Selected Readings,* ed. H. N. Scheiber (New York: Knopf, 1964).

20. David Chalmers, *Neither Socialism Nor Monopoly* (Philadelphia: Lippincott, 1976), p. 4.

21. Samuel P. Hays, *The Response to Industrialism, 1885–1914* (Chicago: University of Chicago Press, 1957), p. 8.

22. *Ibid.,* p. 8.

23. Paul Kantor with Stephen David, *The Dependent City: The Changing Political Economy of Urban American* (Glenview, Ill.: Scott, Foresman and Co., 1987), pp. 499–500.

24. Goodrich, *Government Promotion,* p. 241. Goodrich estimates that up to 1860 local governments provided 29 percent of total public subsidies (p. 268). The proportion of local contributions increased significantly after the Civil War. In his study of New York from 1826 to 1875, Harry Pierce concludes that three-quarters of the subsidy came from local governments and one-quarter from the state. See Harry H. Pierce, *The Railroads of New York: A Study of Government Aid, 1826–1875* (Cambridge, Mass.: Harvard University Press, 1953).

25. *Ibid.*

26. In 1849, for example, the voters of Cleveland approved a $100,000 subscription to stock in the Cleveland and Pittsburgh Railroad by a vote of 1,157 to 27. Despite the enthusiasm of the voters, the stock never paid any dividends and eventually sold at far below par. Charles C. Williamson, *The Finances of Cleveland* (New York: Columbia University Press, 1907), pp. 218–220.

27. Goodrich, *Government Promotion,* p. 42.

28. *Ibid.,* p. 272. One study gave the following figures for New York: "Only 52 of the 297 municipalities that bought stock in a railroad disposed of their securities at par or better, 162 held stock with no market value." (Pierce, *The Railroads of New York,* p. 273.)

29. A. M. Hillhouse, *Municipal Bonds: A Century of Experience* (Englewood Cliffs, N.J.: Prentice-Hall, 1936), p. 39.

30. Goodrich, *Government Promotion,* pp. 268–271. Repudiation goes beyond default, which is simply a failure to pay the debt on time. Repudiation declares an unwillingness to *ever* repay the debt.

31. Alberta Sbragia, "Governance Through Debt: Law and Market in Urban Capital Investment" (Unpublished ms., first draft), chap. 5, p. 4.

32. Carter Goodrich, "The Revulsion Against Internal Improvements," *Journal of Economic History* 10, no. 2 (1959): 145–169; also Sbragia, "Governance Through Debt," chap. 5.

33. Lawrence Goodwyn, *The Populist Movement* (New York: Oxford University Press, 1978).

34. Eric Lampard, "Historical Aspects of Urbanization," in *The Study of Urbanization,* ed. Philip M. Hauser and Leo F. Schnore (New York: Wiley, 1965), p. 523.

35. Allan R. Pred, *The Spatial Dynamics of Urban-Industrial Growth, 1800–1914* (Cambridge, Mass.: M.I.T. Press, 1966), p. 103.

36. Howard P. Chudacoff, *The Evolution of American Urban Society* (Englewood Cliffs, N.J.: Prentice-Hall, 1975), p. 26.

37. Edwin J. Perkins, *The Economy of Colonial America* (New York: Columbia University Press, 1980), p. 157.

38. Philip Foner, *History of the Labor Movement in the United States* (New York: International, 1975), pp. 13–18.

39. Sam Bass Warner, Jr., *The Private City; Philadelphia in Three Periods of Its Growth* (Philadelphia: University of Pennsylvania Press, 1968), p. 21.

40. Pred, *The Spatial Dynamics,* p. 16.

41. *Ibid.,* p. 170.

42. *Ibid.,* pp. 68–69.

43. Chartered by the states, limited-risk corporations allowed the selling of shares to investors whose liability in case of corporate failure was limited to their direct investment. In partnerships the partners were liable for all debts incurred by the company, and these could easily exceed the partners' own assets. The corporate form of business organization thus made it easier to raise capital, for investors risked less than in other forms of business investment.

44. U.S. Department of the Interior, Census Office, *Census Reports of 1900,* vol. 7, *Manufacturers,* pt. 1: "United States by Industries" (Washington, D.C.: Government Printing Office, 1902), pp. 503–509.

45. William Miller, "American Historians and the Business Elite," *Journal of Economic History* 9 (1949), pp. 184–208.

46. The skyscraper boom on Fifth Avenue between 1900 and 1915 was largely fueled by the desire of rich individuals to outdo one another in pretentious architecture. See Seymour I. Toll, *Zoned American* (New York: Grossman, 1969), chap. 2.

47. Hays, *The Response to Industrialism,* p. 73.

48. Kenneth Jackson, *Crabgrass Frontier: The Suburbanization of the United States* (New York: Oxford University Press, 1985), p. 35.

49. George Rogers Taylor, "Building an Intra-Urban Transportation System," *The Urbanization of America: An Historical Anthology,* ed. Allen M. Wakstein (Boston: Houghton Mifflin, 1970), p. 137.

50. Glen E. Holt, "The Changing Perception of Urban Pathology: An Essay on the Development of Mass Transit in the United States," *Cities in America,* ed. Kenneth

T. Jackson and Stanley K. Schultz (New York: Knopf, 1972), p. 327.

51. Taylor, "Building an Intra-Urban Transportation System," p. 139.

52. C. G. Kennedy, "Commuter Services in the Boston Area, 1835–1860," *Business History Review* 26 (1962), pp. 277–287.

53. Jackson, *Crabgrass Frontier,* p. 41.

54. David Ward, *Cities and Immigrants: A Geography in Nineteenth-Century America,* (New York: Oxford University, Press, 1971), p. 4.

55. Jackson, *Crabgrass Frontier,* p. 108.

56. *Ibid.*

57. Gary A. Tobin, "Suburbanization and the Development of Motor Transportation: Transportation and Technology and the Suburbanization Process," *The Changing Face of the Suburbs,* ed. Barry Schwartz (Chicago: University of Chicago Press, 1975), p. 99.

58. "The Smell of Cincinnati," *Enquirer* (Richmond, Va.), November 15, 1874, cited in *City Life,* p. 143.

59. Ward, *Cities and Immigrants,* chap. 3.

60. Blake McKelvey, *The Urbanization of America, 1860–1915* (New Brunswick, N.J.: Rutgers University Press, 1963), p. 54.

61. U.S. Bureau of the Census, *The Growth of Metropolitan Districts in the United States: 1900–1940,* by Warren S. Thompson (Washington, D.C.: U.S. Government Printing office, 1947).

62. Hays, *The Response to Industrialism,* p. 14.

63. Ward, *Cities and Immigrants,* p. 52.

64. Thomas Monroe Pitkin, *Keeper of the Gate: A History of Ellis Island* (New York: New York University Press, 1975), p. ix.

65. Ward, *Cities and Immigrants,* p. 56.

66. *Ibid.,* p. 52.

67. John Higham, *Strangers in the Land: Patterns of American Nativism, 1860–1925* (New Brunswick, N.J.: Rutgers University Press, 1955), pp. 54–55.

68. Stephen Thernstrom, *The Other Bostonians: Poverty and Progress in the American Metropolis, 1880–1970* (Cambridge, Mass.: Harvard University Press, 1973), p. 160.

69. *Ibid.*

70. Charles N. Glaab and A. Theodore Brown, *A History of Urban America* (New York: Macmillan, 1967), p. 160.

71. Moses Rischin, *The Promised City, New York's Jews 1870–1914* (Cambridge, Mass.: Harvard University Press, 1962), p. 87.

72. Gerald M. Caters, Jr., "Yellow Fever in Memphis in the 1870s," in *The City in American Life, From Colonial Times to the Present,* ed. Paul Kramer and Frederick L. Holborn (New York: Capricorn Books, 1970), pp. 180–185.

73. Glaab and Brown, *A History of Urban America,* p. 86.

74. Richard Hofstadter, *Social Darwinism in American Thought,* rev. ed. (New York: Braziller, 1955), p. 5.

75. *Ibid.,* p. 7.

76. Quoted in Robert Green McCloskey, *American Conservatism in the Age of Enterprise, 1865–1910* (New York: HarperCollins, 1951), p. 49.

77. *Ibid.,* p. 27.

78. Quoted in *ibid.,* p. 50.

79. Nelson M. Blake, *Water for the Cities: A History of the Urban Water Supply Problem in the United States* (Syracuse, N.Y.: Syracuse University Press, 1956), p. 6.

80. *Ibid.,* pp. 102–103.

81. *Ibid.,* p. 6.

82. Sam Bass Warner, Jr., *The Private City: Philadelphia in Three Periods of Its Growth* (Philadelphia: University of Pennsylvania Press, 1968), pp. 107–109.

83. Arthur N. Schlesinger, "A Panoramic View: The City in American Life," in *The City in American Life, From Colonial Times to the Present,* ed. Paul Kramer and Frederick L. Holborn (New York: Capricorn Books, 1970), p. 23.

84. Stanley K. Schultz, *Constructing Urban Culture: American Cities and City Planning, 1800–1920* (Philadelphia: Temple University Press, 1989), p. 120.

85. *Ibid.*

86. Edgar W. Martin, *The Standard of Living in 1860* (Chicago: University of Chicago Press, 1942), pp. 44–47, 89–112.

87. McKelvey, *The Urbanization of America,* p. 13.

88. *Ibid.,* p. 13.

89. *Ibid.,* p. 90.

90. McKelvey, *American Urbanization,* p. 44.

91. McKelvey, *The Urbanization of America,* p. 90.

92. Stephen Thernstrom, *Poverty and Progress: Social Mobility in a Nineteenth-Century City* (Cambridge, Mass.: Harvard University Press, 1964), p. 39.

93. Warner, *The Private City.*

94. James F. Richardson, "To Control the City: The New York Police in Historical Perspective," in Kenneth T. Jackson and Stanley K. Schultz, eds., *Cities in American History* (New York: Knopf, 1972), pp. 272–289.

95. Warner, *The Private City,* chap. 7.

96. Fred M. Wirt, *Power in the City* (Berkeley: University of California Press, 1974), p. 110.

97. Richardson, "To Control the City," p. 278.

98. Bayrd Still, *Milwaukee: The History of a City* (Madison: State Historical Society of Wisconsin, 1984), chap. 10.

99. Warner, *The Private City,* p. 86.

100. Sbragia, "Governance Through Debt," chap. 4, p. 23.

101. *Ibid.*

102. *Ibid.*

103. *Ibid.,* chap. 4, p. 14.

104. Jon Teaford, *The Unheralded Triumph: City Government in America, 1870–1900* (Baltimore: Johns Hopkins University Press, 1984), chap. 8.

105. *Ibid.,* p. 222.

106. *Ibid.,* p. 221.

107. Schultz, *Constructing Urban Culture,* p. 174.

108. Teaford, *The Unheralded Triumph,* p. 247.

109. *Ibid.,* p. 246.

110. McKelvey, *The Urbanization of America,* p. 90.

111. Alexander Callow, Jr., *The Tweed Ring* (New York: Oxford University Press, 1966).

112. Teaford, *The Unheralded Triumph,* p. 17.

113. *Ibid.,* p. 18.

114. *Ibid.,* p. 20.

115. *Ibid.,* p. 45.

116. *Ibid.,* p. 68.

117. *Ibid.,* p. 76.

118. *Ibid.,* p. 47.

119. *Ibid.,* p. 10.

120. See *Dartmouth College v. Woodward,* 4 Wheat. 518 (1819).

121. *City of Clinton v. Cedar Rapids and Missouri River Railroad Co.,* 24 Iowa 455 475 (1868).

122. Schultz, *Constructing Urban Culture,* p. 73.

123. *Ibid.,* p. 69.

124. Mark I. Gelfand, *A Nation of Cities: The Federal Government and Urban America, 1933–1965* (New York: Oxford University Press, 1975), p. 11.

125. *Ibid.,* p. 11.

126. *Baker v. Carr,* 369 U.S. 189 (1962).

127. *Reynolds v. Sims,* 377 U.S. 533 (1964).

128. Higham, *Strangers in the Land.*

CHAPTER 3

1. As quoted in Edward McChesney Sait, "Political Machines," *Encyclopedia of the Social Sciences,* ed. Edwin R. A. Seligman (New York: Macmillan, 1933), p. 657. We will use the terms *machine* and *boss,* but in doing so we are not implying any moral judgment.

2. Raymond Wolfinger makes the distinction that we draw here between machine politics and a centralized machine. Wolfinger, "Why Political Machines Have Not Withered Away and Other Revisionist Thoughts," in *Readings in Urban Politics: Past, Present, and Future,* ed. Harlan Hahn and Charles H. Levine (New York: Longman, 1984), p. 79. See also Roger W. Lotchin, "Power and Policy: American City Politics Between the Two World Wars," *Ethnics, Machines and the American Urban Future,* ed. Scott Greer (Cambridge, Mass.: Schenkman, 1981), p. 9.

3. M. Craig Brown and Charles N. Halaby, "Machine Politics in America, 1870–1945," *Journal of Interdisciplinary History* 17, no. 3 (Winter 1987): 598. In order to qualify as a dominant political machine, a machine-style party had to control both the executive and the legislative branches of the city for an uninterrupted series of three elections.

4. One of the last classic machines, the O'Connell machine in Albany, New York, is finally losing its grip. See Todd Swanstrom and Sharon Ward, "Albany's O'Connell Organization: The Survival of an Entrenched Machine" (Paper delivered at the American Political Science Association Convention, Chicago, Ill., September 1987).

5. For the definitive treatment of this question, see Steven P. Erie, *Rainbow's End: Irish-Americans and the Dilemmas of Urban Machine Politics, 1840–1985* (Berkeley: University of California Press, 1988). President Lyndon Johnson's National Advisory Commission on Civil Disorders linked the 1960s urban riots to the "demise of the historic urban political machines." *Report of the National Advisory Commission on Civil Disorders* (New York: Bantam Books, 1968), p. 287.

6. William N. Chambers, "Party Development and the American Mainstream," in *The American Party System: Stages of Political Development,* 2d ed., ed. William Nisbet Chambers and Walter Dean Burnham (New York: Oxford University Press, 1975), p. 12.

7. Alan DiGaetano, "The Rise and Development of Urban Political Machines," *Urban Affairs Quarterly* 24, no. 2 (December 1988): 247, Table 3. For more information on the expansion of city governments in the late nineteenth century, see Jon C. Teaford, *The Unheralded Triumph: City Government in America, 1870–1900* (Baltimore: Johns Hopkins University Press, 1984); Eric H. Monkkonen, *America Becomes Urban: The Development of U.S. Cities and Towns, 1780–1980* (Berkeley: University of California Press, 1988).

8. Terrence J. McDonald and Sally K. Ward, "Introduction," *The Politics of Urban Fiscal Policy,* ed. Terrence J. McDonald and Sally K. Ward (Beverly Hills: Sage, 1984), p. 14.

9. Jon M. Kingsdale, "The 'Poor Man's Club': Social Functions of the Urban Working-Class Saloon," *The Making of Urban America,* ed. Raymond A. Mohl, (Wilmington, Del.: Scholarly Resources, 1988), p. 123.

10. *Ibid.*

11. *Ibid.*

12. *Ibid.,* p. 130.

13. "He [the boss] does not seek social honor; the 'professional' is despised in 'respectable society.' He seeks power alone, power as a source of money, but also power for power's sake." Max Weber, "Politics as a Vocation," in *From Max Weber: Essays in Sociology,* ed. H. H. Gerth and C. Wright Mills (New York: Oxford University Press, 1946), p. 109.

14. William L. Riordan, *Plunkitt of Tammany Hall* (New York: Dutton, 1963), p. 50.

15. Dayton McKean, *The Boss* (Boston: Houghton Mifflin, 1940), p. 132.

16. Milton Rakove, *Don't Make No Waves . . . Don't Back No Losers: An Insider's Analysis of the Daley Machine* (Bloomington: Indiana University Press, 1975).

17. *Ibid.,* pp. 114–115.

18. *Ibid.,* p. 115.

19. *Ibid.,* p. 120.

20. *Ibid.,* p. 122.

21. The information presented here on the Pendergast machine comes from Lyle W. Dorsett, *The Pendergast Machine* (New York: Oxford University Press, 1968). Only direct quotations from Dorsett are cited by page in subsequent notes.

22. *Ibid.,* p. 14.

23. *Ibid.,* p. 21.

24. *Ibid.,* p. 41.

25. *Ibid.,* p. 26.

26. Sait, "Political Machines," p. 658. See also Robert M. Merton, *Social Theory and Social Structure* (New York: Free Press, 1949), pp. 126–127. For decades Merton's functional analysis of political machines was widely accepted, but it has been seriously challenged in recent years. See Erie, *Rainbow's End;* DiGaetano, "The Rise and Development of Urban Political Machines"; M. Craig Brown and Charles N. Halaby, "Functional Sociology, Urban History, and the Urban Political Machine: The Outlines and Foundations of Machine Politics, 1870–1945," (Albany: Department of Sociology, State University of New York at Albany, n.d.)

27. DiGaetano, "The Rise and Development of Urban Political Machines," pp. 257–262. See also M. Craig Brown and Charles N. Halaby, "Bosses, Reform, and the Socioeconomic Bases of Urban Expenditure, 1890–1940," in *The Politics of Urban Fiscal Policy,* ed. Terrence S. McDonald and Sally K. Ward (Beverley Hills, Sage), p. 90.

28. DiGaetano, "The Rise and Development of Urban Political Machines," p. 261. Urban politics is often portrayed as a "morality play" in which reformers are pitted against machine politicians. In fact, machines often used reforms to consolidate their power and put reformers on the ballot in order to legitimate their rule. On the other side, reformers often created their own type of political machines. For a critique of the dichotomy between bosses and reformers, see David P. Thelen, "Urban Politics: Beyond Bosses and Reformers," *Reviews in American History* 7 (September 1979): 406–412. For an example of a reformer who created a new type of political machine, see Robert Caro's masterful biography of Robert Moses, *The*

Power Broker: Robert Moses and the Fall of New York (New York: Vintage Books, 1974), p. 354..

29. M. Craig Brown and Charles N. Halaby, "Bosses, Reform and the Socioeconomic Bases of Urban expenditure, 1890–1940," p. 87. Interestingly, Brown and Halaby found that machine cities, after reform, such as the establishment of a city manager form of government, spent more than other cities, p. 89.

30. Lotchin, "Power and Policy," p. 11.

31. Stanley K. Schultz, *Constructing Urban Culture: American Cities and City Planning, 1800–1920* (Philadelphia: Temple University Press, 1989).

32. There are many sources of information on the Tweed Ring. The two books used here are Alexander Callow, Jr., *The Tweed Ring* (New York: Oxford University Press, 1966), and Seymour J. Mandelbaum, *Boss Tweed's New York* (New York: Wiley, 1965). For a provocative, yet ultimately unpersuasive, defense of Tweed, see Leo Hershkowitz, *Tweed's New York: Another Look* (Garden City, N.Y.: Anchor Books, 1977).

33. Martin Shefter, "The Emergence of the Political Machine: An Alternative View," in *Theoretical Perspectives on Urban Politics,* ed. Willis D. Hawley, *et al.* (Englewood Cliffs, N.J.: Prentice-Hall, 1976), p. 21.

34. The information presented here on Abraham Reuf's machine is taken from Walter Bean, *Boss Reuf's San Francisco* (Berkeley: University of California Press, 1952; reprinted 1972). Only direct quotations from Bean are cited by page in subsequent notes.

35. *Ibid.,* pp. 93–94.

36. Paul Kantor, with Stephen David, *The Dependent Citys, The Changing Political Economy of Urban America* (Glenview, Illinois: Scott Foresman, 1988), p. 104.

37. Ernest S. Griffith, *A History of American City Government: The Conspicuous Failure, 1870–1900* (New York: Praeger, 1974), p. 183.

38. Zane Miller, *The Urbanization of Modern America: A Brief History* (New York: Harcourt Brace Jovanovich, 1973), p. 121.

39. Ester R. Fuchs and Robert Y. Shapiro, "Government Performance as a Basis for Machine Support," *Urban Affairs Quarterly* 18, no. 4 (June 1983): 537–550.

40. Merton, *Social Theory and Social Structure,* p. 130.

41. Robert A. Dahl, *Who Governs? Democracy and Power in an American City* (New Haven, Conn.: Yale University Press, 1961) p. 34.

42. See Doris Kearns Goodwin, *The Fitzgeralds and the Kennedys: An American Saga* (New York: Simon and Schuster, 1987).

43. The discussion of mobilizing versus entrenched machines relies heavily on Erie's "life cycle" theory of political machines in *Rainbow's End.*

44. Erie, *Rainbow's End,* p. 69.

45. Terry Nichols Clark, "The Irish Ethic and the Spirit of Patronage," *Ethnicity* 2 (1975), pp. 341–342.

46. Martin Shefter, "Political Incorporation and the Extrusion of the Left: Party Politics and Social Forces in New York City," *Studies in American Political*

Development, vol. 1, ed. Karen Orren and Stephen Skowronek (New Haven, Conn.: Yale University Press, 1986), p. 55.

47. Caro, *The Power Broker,* p. 354.

48. For a useful review of the relationships between African Americans and political machines, see Hanes Walton, Jr., *Black Politics: A Theoretical and Structural Analysis* (Philadelphia: Lippincott, 1972), chap. 4.

49. Erie, *Rainbow's End,* p. 165.

50. Thomas M. Guterbock, *Machine Politics in Transition: Party and Community in Chicago* (Chicago: University of Chicago Press, 1980).

51. See Paul Kleppner, *Chicago Divided: The Making of a Black Mayor* (DeKalb: Northern Illinois University Press, 1985).

52. Michael Johnston, "Patrons and Clients, Jobs and Machines: A Case Study of the Uses of Patronage," *American Political Science Review* 73, no. 2 (June 1979): 385–398.

53. Erie, *Rainbow's End,* p. 218.

54. *Ibid.,* pp. 48, 242.

55. For a discussion of the role of political clubs in the evolution of Tammany Hall, see Shefter, "The Emergence of the Political Machines," p. 35.

56. Erie, *Rainbow's End,* pp. 102–103.

57. Kenneth D. Wald argues that ethnics supported machines not so much in response to socioeconomic disadvantage, but out of an awareness of their social marginality and in the belief that machines would defend them from external pressures; see his "The Electoral Base of Political Machines: A Deviant Case Analysis," *Urban Affairs Quarterly* 16, no. 1 (September 1980), pp. 3–29.

58. It would be misleading to say that such practices simply reflected the desires of poor immigrants. Irish family life was disrupted by the easy availability of illicit entertainment. Catholic priests and a significant proportion of the immigrant population opposed vice activities.

59. Harold Zink, *City Bosses in the United States* (Durham, N.C.: Duke University Press, 1930).

60. Wolfinger, "Why Political Machines Have Not Withered Away," p. 70.

61. Allan Rosenbaum, "Machine Politics Class Interest and the Urban Poor," Paper Delivered at the American Political Science Association Annual Meeting (Sept. 4–8, 1973). pp. 25–26.

62. *Ibid.,* p. 26.

63. John D. Buenker, *Urban Liberalism and Progressive Reform* (New York: Scribner, 1973). Joseph J. Huthmacher also provided evidence of machine legislators' support for reform; see his "Urban Liberalism and the Age of Reform," *Mississippi Valley Historical Review* 44 (September 1962), pp. 231–241.

64. For the distinction between social and structural reformers, see Melvin G. Holli, *Reform in Detroit: Hazen S. Pingree and Urban Politics* (New York: Oxford University Press, 1969), chap. 8. In this chapter we discuss the social reformers; in the next chapter we will discuss the structural reformers.

65. Martin J. Schiesl, *The Politics of Efficiency: Municipal Administration and Reform in America, 1880–1920* (Berkeley: University of California Press, 1977), pp. 80 ff.

66. Quoted in Holli, *Reform in Detroit*, p. 42.

67. Quoted in *ibid.*, p. 92.

68. *Ibid.*, p. 195.

69. Peter Marris and Martin Rein, *Dilemmas of Social Reform* (New York: Atherton Press, 1967), p. 7.

70. Kantor, *The Dependent City*, pp. 117–118. Machine politicians appealed to voters on the basis of where they lived (their ethnic identification), not on the basis of where they worked (their class identification). Thus, machine politics confirmed the "city trenches" that have divided the American political landscape into community politics and workplace politics and have blunted political action by the working class. See Ira Katznelson, *City Trenches: Urban Politics and the Patterning of Class in the United States* (New York: Pantheon, 1981).

71. See James C. Scott, "Corruption, Machine Politics, and Political Change," *American Political Science Review* 63 (December 1969): 1142–1158; Clarence N. Stone, Robert K. Whelan, and William J. Murin, *Urban Policy and Politics in a Bureaucratic Age*, 2d ed. (Englewood Cliffs, N.J.: Prentice-Hall, 1986), chap. 7.

72. Lotchin, "Power and Policy," p. 17.

73. Kenneth R. Mladenka, "The Urban Bureaucracy and the Chicago Political Machine: Who Gets What and the Limits to Political Control," in *Readings in Urban Politics: Past, Present, and Future*, ed. Harlan Hahn and Charles H. Levine (New York: Longman, 1984), p. 114. A later study of Chicago found that the local party structure did influence the provision of one service: building code enforcement. See Bryan D. Jones, "Party and Bureaucracy: The Influence of Intermediary Groups on Urban Public Service Delivery," *American Political Science Review* 75, no. 3 (September 1981), pp. 688–700.

74. Erie, *Rainbow's End*.

75. By ending the dependence of the urban poor on political machines for favors, many argued that the rise of the New Deal welfare state undermined political machines. See Rexford Tugwell, *The Brain Trust* (New York: Viking, 1968), pp. 366–371. Historical research has shown, however, that many machines were able to use the welfare state to strengthen their organizations. See Bruce M. Stave, *The New Deal and the Last Hurrah: Pittsburgh Machine Politics* (Pittsburgh: University of Pittsburgh Press, 1970); Lyle W. Dorsett, *Franklin D. Roosevelt and the City Bosses* (Port Washington, N.Y.: Kennikat Press, 1977); Wolfinger, "Why Political Machines Have Not Withered Away," pp. 85–88; Erie, *Rainbow's End*.

76. H. Paul Friesema, "Black Control of Central Cities: The Hollow Prize," *Journal of the American Institute of Planners* 35 (March 1969), p. 75.

77. Melvin G. Holli and Paul M. Green, *Bashing Chicago Traditions: Harold Washington's Last Campaign* (Grand Rapids, Mich.: Eerdmans, 1989), p. 120.

78. Dennis R. Judd and Randy L. Ready, "Entrepreneurial Cities and the New Policies of Economic Development," in *Reagan and the Cities*, ed. George E. Peterson and Carol W. Lewis (Washington, D.C.: The Urban Institute Press, 1986), pp. 232–233.

CHAPTER 4

1. William L. Riordon, *Plunkitt of Tammany Hall* (New York: Dutton, 1963), p. 17.

2. James Bryce, *The American Commonwealth,* 3rd rev. ed., vol. 1 (New York: Macmillan, 1924), p. 642.

3. H. E. Deming, *The Government of American Cities: A Program of Democracy* (London and New York: Putnam, 1909), p. 194.

4. Quoted in Michael B. Katz, *School Reform: Past and Present* (Boston: Little, Brown, 1971), p. 169.

5. Josiah Strong, *Our Country,* ed. Jurgen Herbst (Cambridge, Mass.: Belknap Press, Harvard University Press, 1963; first published in 1886), p. 55.

6. James Weinstein, *The Corporate Ideal in the Liberal State, 1900–1918* (Boston: Beacon Press, 1968).

7. Melvin G. Holli, "Urban Reform in the Progressive Era," in *The Progressive Era,* ed. Louis L. Gould (Syracuse, N.Y.: Syracuse University Press, 1974), p. 137.

8. Frank Mann Stewart, *A Half Century of Municipal Reform: The History of the National Municipal League* (Berkeley: University of California Press, 1950), chap. 1.

9. Samuel Haber, *Efficiency and Uplift: Scientific Management in the Progressive Era, 1890–1920* (Chicago: University of Chicago Press, 1964), p. 99.

10. Andrew D. White, "City Affairs Are Not Political," originally titled "The Government of American Cities," *Forum,* December 1890, pp. 213–216; reprinted in Dennis Judd and Paul Kantor, eds., *Enduring Tensions in Urban Politics: A Regime Perspective* (New York: Macmillan, 1992), pp. 205–208.

11. Amy Bridges, "Winning the West to Municipal Reform," *Urban Affairs Quarterly* 27, no. 4 (June 1992).

12. Arthur T. Hadley, *The Empty Polling Booth* (Englewood Cliffs, N.J.: Prentice-Hall, 1978), p. 61.

13. Alexander B. Callow, Jr., ed., *The City Boss in America* (New York: Oxford University Press, 1976), p. 158.

14. William T. Stead, *If Christ Came to Chicago* (Chicago: Laird and Lee, 1894), pp. 56–57.

15. Lloyd Wendt and Herman Kogan, *Bosses in Lusty Chicago* (Bloomington: Indiana University Press, 1967), p. 169.

16. Lyle W. Dorsett, *The Pendergast Machine* (New York: Oxford University Press, 1968), p. 59.

17. *Ibid.,* p. 60.

18. Allan F. Davis, *Spearheads for Reform* (New York: Oxford University Press, 1967), pp. 156–162.

19. William D. Miller, *Mr. Crump of Memphis* (Baton Rouge: Louisiana State University Press, 1964), p. 74.

20. Bruce M. Stave, *The New Deal and the Last Hurrah: Pittsburgh Machine Politics* (Pittsburgh: University of Pittsburgh Press, 1970), p. 77.

21. Ernest S. Griffith, *A History of American City Government, 1900–1920* (New York: Praeger, 1974), p. 71.

22. *Ibid.*

23. Richard S. Childs, *Civic Victories: The Story of an Unfinished Revolution* (New York: Harper and Brothers, 1952), p. 299. In this passage Childs was referring to the short ballot reform in conjunction with nonpartisanship. The short ballot reformers felt that there should be fewer elected officials so that voters would not be confused, and to make it possible for voters to hold elected officials accountable.

24. Edward C. Banfield, ed., *Urban Government: A Reader in Administration and Politics* (New York: Free Press, 1969), p. 275. Selection from Brand Whitlock, *Forty Years of It*, preface by Allen White (New York and London: Appleton, 1925; first published 1914).

25. Haber, *Efficiency and Uplift*, pp. 99–101.

26. White, "City Affairs Are Not Political," pp. 206–207.

27. Griffith, *A History of American City Government*, p. 130.

28. *Ibid.*, p. 131.

29. Willis D. Hawley, *Nonpartisan Elections and the Case for Party Politics* (New York: Wiley, 1973), p. 14. Subsequent information on the use of nonpartisan elections is from Hawley, pp. 15–18.

30. Weinstein, *The Corporate Ideal*, p. 109. Subsequent information on the Dayton election is from Weinstein.

31. Samuel P. Hays, "The Politics of Reform in Municipal Government in the Progressive Era," in *Social Change and Urban Politics: Readings*, ed. Daniel N. Gordon (Englewood Cliffs, N.J.: Prentice-Hall, 1973), pp. 107–127.

32. Quoted in Holli, "Urban Reform in the Progressive Era," p. 144.

33. Frederick Winslow Taylor, *The Principles of Scientific Management* (New York: Harper and brothers, 1919; first published 1911).

34. *Ibid.*, p. 140.

35. *Ibid.*, p. 7.

36. Haber, *Efficiency and Uplift*, p. 56.

37. Harold A. Stone, Don K. Price, and Kathryn H. Stone, *City Manager Government in the United States: A Review After Twenty-five Years* (Chicago: Public Administration Service, 1940), p. 5.

38. Henry Bruerè, *The New City Government: A Discussion of Municipal Administration Based on a Survey of Ten Commission-Governed Cities* (Englewood Cliffs, N.J.: Prentice-Hall, 1912).

39. *Ibid.*, p. v.

40. *Ibid.*, pp. 27–29.

41. Robert A. Caro, *The Power Broker: Robert Moses and the Fall of New York* (New York: Oxford University Press, 1969), p. 75.

42. Taylor, *The Principles of Scientific Management*, p. 20.

43. Melvin B. Holli, *Reform in Detroit: Hazen S. Pingree and Urban Politics* (New York: Oxford University Press, 1969), p. 167.

44. Haber, *Efficiency and Uplift*, p. 115.

45. Stone, Price, and Stone, *City Manager Government*, p. 4.

46. Martin J. Schiesl, *The Politics of Municipal Reform: Municipal Administration and Reform in America, 1880–1920* (Berkeley: University of California Press, 1977), pp. 134–135.

47. Quoted in Weinstein, *The Corporate Ideal*, p. 96.

48. Clinton R. Woodruff, ed., *City Government by Commission* (Englewood Cliffs, N.J.: Prentice-Hall, 1911), pp. 293–294.

49. Childs, *Civic Victories*, p. 138.

50. Hays, "The Politics of Reform," p. 116.

51. Weinstein, *The Corporate Ideal*, p. 99.

52. Childs, *Civic Victories*, p. 137.

53. *Ibid.*

54. Stone, Price, and Stone, *City Manager Government*, p. 5.

55. Griffith, *A History of American City Government*, p. 167.

56. *Ibid.*, p. 166; Schiesl, *The Politics of Municipal Reform*, pp. 175–176.

57. Weinstein, *The Corporate Ideal*, pp. 115–116.

58. Quoted in Stone, Price, and Stone, *City Manager Government*, p. 27.

59. *Ibid.*, p. 37.

60. *Ibid.*, p. 43.

61. Hays, "The Politics of Reform," p. 111.

62. Griffith, *A History of American City Government*.

63. Mowry, *The Era of Theodore Roosevelt*, 1900–1912 (New York: Harper and Row, 1958), p. 86. Mowry claims the reformers represented the "solid middle class," but his own data belie this classification.

64. Griffith, *A History of American City Government*, p. 21. Subsequent information on studies of reforms is from Griffith.

65. Though most historians have labeled the reformers middle class, research uniformly documents upper-class occupations, incomes, and educational status. It defies common sense to think that middle-class people would have had the time or the personal resources to participate in politics as active reformers. Middle-class bank clerks, accountants, small business owners, sales clerks, school teachers, small-town lawyers, and college professors normally worked sixty-hour weeks. Their salaries were little above that of working-class skilled laborers. If college educated (and most were not), their degrees were usually granted by small, unprestigious private colleges or state schools. Then as now, only a small percentage of the middle class participated in politics at any level. Much of the problem with the historians' labeling is that they have rarely provided careful definitions of social class. Often the term middle class seems to cover everyone except immigrant unskilled laborers.

66. Hays, "The Politics of Reform," p. 111.

67. *Ibid.;* Weinstein, *The Corporate Ideal,* pp. 99–103.

68. Weinstein, *The Corporate Ideal,* pp. 103–105; Stone, Price, and Stone, *City Manager Government,* pp. 32–50.

69. Weinstein, *The Corporate Ideal,* pp. 106–109.

70. Edward C. Hays, *Power Structure and Urban Policy: Who Rules in Oakland?* (New York: McGraw-Hill, 1972), p. 11.

71. *Ibid.,* pp. 13–14.

72. Stone, Price, and Stone, *City Manager Government,* pp. 35–36. Several other case studies in this book reveal a similar bias.

73. Quoted in Weinstein, *The Corporate Ideal,* pp. 106, 107.

74. Samuel P. Hays, "The Politics of Reform," p. 116.

75. James Q. Wilson, *Negro Politics: The Search for Leadership* (New York: Free Press, 1960), p. 26.

76. *Ibid.,* p. 27.

77. Alan DiGaetano, "Urban Political Reform: Did It Kill the Machine?" *Journal of Urban History,*

78. *Ibid.*

79. *Ibid.*

80. *Ibid.*

81. *Ibid.*

82. *Ibid.*

83. *Ibid.*

84. Steven P. Erie, *Rainbow's End: Irish-Americans and the Dilemmas of Urban Machine Politics, 1840–1985* (Berkeley: University of California Press, 1988).

85. Robert L. Lineberry and Edmond P. Fowler, "Reformism and Public Policies in American Cities," *American Political Science Review* 61 (September 1967); Chandler Davidson and George Korbel, "At-Large Elections and Minority Group Representation: A Re-examination of Historical and Contemporary Evidence," *Journal of Politics* 43 (November 1981): 982–1005; Jerry L. Polinard, Robert D. Wrinkle, and Tomàs Longoria, Jr., "The Impact of District Elections on the Mexican American Community: The Electoral Perspective," *Social Science Quarterly* 71, no. 3 (September 1991): 608–614; Richard L. Engstrom and Michael D. McDonald, "The Effect of At-Large versus District Elections on Racial Representation in U.S. Municipalities," in Bernard Grofman and Arend Liphart, eds., *Electoral Laws and Their Political Consequences* (New York: Agathon, 1986), pp. 203–225; W. E. Lyons and Malcolm E. Jewell, "Minority Representation and the Drawing of City Council Districts," *Urban Affairs Quarterly* 23 (1988): 432–447; Delbert Taebel, "Minority Representation on City Councils: The Impact of Structure on Blacks and Hispanics," *Social Science Quarterly* 59 (1982): 729–736; Jeffrey S. Zax, "Election Methods, Black and Hispanic City Council Membership," *Social Science Quarterly* 71 (1990), pp. 339–355.

86. *City of Mobile v. Bolden*, 446 U.S. 55 (1980).

87. *Thornburg v. Gingles*, 106 S.Ct. 2752 (1986).

88. C. Robert Heath, "Thornburg v. Gingles: The Unresolved Issues," *National Civic Review* 79, no. 1 (January–February 1990), pp. 50–71.

89. *Dillard v. Crenshaw County*, 649 F.Supp. at 289 (C.O. Ala. 1986).

90. *McNeal v. Springfield*, 658 F.Supp. at 1015, 1015, 1022 (C.D. Ill. 1987).

91. *McNeal v. Springfield Park District*, 851 F.2d at 937 (7th Cir. 1988).

92. *Derrickson v. City of Danville*, 87-2007 (C.D. Ill. 1987).

93. Joseph F. Zimmerman, "Alternative Local Electoral Systems," *National Civic Review* 79, no. 1 (January–February 1990), 23–36.

94. Heath, "Thornburg v. Gingles," pp. 51–53.

95. *Ibid.*, pp. 54–55.

96. *Ibid.*, pp. 55–59; Charles S. Bullock III, "Symbolics or Substance: A Critique of the At-Large Election Controversy," *State and Local Government Review* 21, no.3 (Fall 1989), pp. 91–99.

97. Scott Armstrong, "Minorities Seek More Clout on the Bench," *Christian Science Monitor,* October 1, 1991, pp. 1, 2.

98. International City Management Association, *Baseline Data Report: Municipal Election Processes: The Impact on Minority Representation* 19, no. 6 (November–December 1987): 3–4.

99. *Ibid.*, pp. 6–9; Polinard, Wrinkle, and Longoria, "The Impact of District Elections," pp. 608–614.

100. Tim O'Neil, "Blacks Want Half of City's Wards in Redistricting," *St. Louis Post Dispatch,* June 8, 1991, p. 3A.

CHAPTER 5

1. W. B. Munro, *The Government of American Cities* (New York: Macmillan, 1913), p. 27.

2. For a discussion of suburbanization before World War II, see Chapter 8.

3. Francis E. Rourke, "Urbanism and the National Party Organizations," *Western Political Quarterly* 18 (March 1965), p. 150.

4. Wilfred E. Binkley, *American Political Parties: Their Natural History* (New York: Knopf, 1943), p. 285.

5. *Ibid.*, pp. 285–286.

6. Robert A. Caro, *The Power Broker: Robert Moses and the Fall of New York* (New York: Knopf, 1974), pp. 118–119.

7. William E. Leuchtenburg, *The Perils of Prosperity, 1914–1932* (Chicago: University of Chicago Press, 1958), pp. 213–214.

8. Robert K. Murray, *The 103rd Ballot: Democrats and the Disaster in Madison Square Garden* (New York: Harper and Row, 1976), p. 9

9. Kenneth T. Jackson, *The Ku Klux Klan in the City, 1915–1930* (New York: Oxford University Press, 1967).

10. Murray, *The 103rd Ballot,* p. 7.

11. *Ibid.*

12. *Ibid.,* p. 103.

13. For good accounts of the 1924 convention, see Murray, *The 103rd Ballot;* Edmund A. Moore, *A Catholic Runs for President: The Campaign of 1928* (New York: Ronald Press, 1956); Arthur M. Schlesinger, Jr., *The Crisis of the Old Order, 1919–1933* (Boston: Houghton Mifflin, 1956).

14. John D. Hicks, *Republican Ascendancy, 1921–1933* (New York: Harper and Brothers, 1960), p. 212.

15. John Kenneth Galbraith, *The Great Crash, 1929,* rev. ed. (Boston: Houghton Mifflin, 1979; first published 1961), p. 99.

16. Lester V. Chandler, *America's Greatest Depression, 1929–1941* (New York: HarperCollins, 1970), p. 5.

17. *Ibid.*

18. *Ibid.,* p. 35.

19. William E. Leuchtenburg, *Franklin D. Roosevelt and the New Deal, 1932–1940* (New York: Harper and Row, 1963), p. 19.

20. *Ibid.,* p. 1.

21. Chandler, *America's Greatest Depression,* p. 19.

22. *Ibid.,* p. 57.

23. Arthur M. Schlesinger, Jr., *The Coming of the New Deal* (Boston: Houghton Mifflin, 1957), p. 3.

24. Leuchtenburg, *Franklin D. Roosevelt,* p. 18.

25. Most relief was given by local public and private agencies. Though many states had programs for relief to designated categories of people—dependent children, the blind, and the disabled—few of these were actually funded.

26. Arthur E. Burns and Edward A. Williams, *Federal Work, Security, and Relief Programs* (New York: Da Capo Press, 1971), pp. 1–2; first published as Research Monograph 24 (Washington, D.C.: Works Progress Administration, Division of Social Research, 1941).

27. James T. Patterson, *The New Deal and the States: Federalism in Transition* (Princeton, N.J.: Princeton University Press, 1969), p. 30.

28. *Ibid.,* p. 15.

29. *Ibid.*

30. Mark I. Gelfand, *A Nation of Cities: The Federal Government and Urban America, 1933–1965,* Urban Life in America Series (New York: Oxford University Press, 1975), p. 35.

31. Leuchtenburg, *Franklin D. Roosevelt*, p. 11.

32. *Ibid.*, p. 39.

33. *Ibid.*

34. *Ibid.*, p. 40.

35. For a thorough account of New Deal programs, see Burns and Williams, *Federal Work.*

36. Leuchtenburg, *Franklin D. Roosevelt*, p. 174.

37. Burns and Williams, *Federal Work*, pp. 29–36.

38. Leuchtenburg, *Franklin D. Roosevelt*, pp. 122–123.

39. *Ibid.*, p. 133.

40. Josephine Chapin Brown, *Public Relief, 1929–1939* (New York: Holt, Rinehart and Winston, 1940), p. 249.

41. Quoted in Binkley, *American Political Parties*, p. 284.

42. *Ibid.*, pp. 380–381.

43. Patterson, *The New Deal and the States*, p. 26.

44. Calculated from James A. Maxwell, *Federal Grants and the Business Cycle* (New York: National Bureau of Economic Research, 1952), p. 23, Table 7.

45. *Ibid.*

46. Gelfand, *A Nation of Cities*, p. 49.

47. Maxwell, *Federal Grants and the Business Cycle*, p. 29.

48. U.S. Department of Commerce, Bureau of the Census, *Historical Statistics on State and Local Government Revenues, 1902–1953* (Washington, D.C.: Government Printing Office, 1955), p. 12.

49. Maxwell, *Federal Grants and the Business Cycle*, p. 27, Table 11.

50. *Ibid.*, p. 24, Table 8.

51. Gelfand, *A Nation of Cities*, p. 31.

52. *Ibid.*, p. 32.

53. *Ibid.*, p. 36.

54. *Ibid.*

55. *Ibid.*, p. 34.

56. Patterson, *The New Deal and the States*, p. 39.

57. *Ibid.*, p. 40.

58. *Ibid.*

59. *Ibid.*, p. 44.

60. *Ibid.*, p. 47.

61. *Ibid.*, p. 40.

62. Brown, *Public Relief*, pp. 72–96.

63. *Ibid.*

64. George C. S. Benson, *The New Centralization: A Study in Intergovernmental Relationships in the United States* (New York: Holt, Rinehart and Winston, 1941), pp. 104–105.

65. Gelfand, *A Nation of Cities,* p. 34.

66. Robert G. Dixon, Jr., *Democratic Representation: Reapportionment in Law and Politics* (New York: Oxford University Press, 1968), p. 174.

67. *Ibid.,* pp. 71–75, 80, 86–87.

68. Patterson, *The New Deal and the States,* p. 45.

69. Leuchtenburg, *Franklin D. Roosevelt,* p. 52.

70. *Ibid.,* p. 136.

71. Guy Rexford Tugwell, quoted in *ibid.,* p. 35.

72. Quoted in Gelfand, *A Nation of Cities,* p. 66.

73. U.S. Department of the Interior, National Resources Committee, Urbanism Committee, *Our Cities: Their Role in the National Economy* (Washington, D.C.: Government Printing Office, 1937).

74. Philip J. Funigiello, "City Planning in World War II: The Experience of the National Resources Planning Board," *Social Science Quarterly* 53 (June 1972): 91–104.

CHAPTER 6

1. U.S. Department of the Interior, National Resources Committee, Urbanism Committee, *Our Cities: Their Role in the National Economy* (Washington, D.C.: Government Printing Office, 1937). Quotes are from the letter of transmittal to President Franklin D. Roosevelt.

2. Joint Resolution 52-22, 52d Cong. (1892); refer also to U.S. Congress, House, *Your Congress and American Housing—The Actions of Congress on Housing,* 82d Cong., 2d sess., 1952, H. Doc. 82-532, p. 1.

3. Public Law 65-102, 65th Cong. (1918); refer also to Congressional Quarterly Service, *Housing a Nation* (Washington, D.C.: Congressional Quarterly Service, 1966), p. 18; Edith Elmer Wood, *Recent Trends in American Housing* (New York: Macmillan, 1931), p. 79.

4. *Housing A Nation,* pp. v, xiii.

5. Public Laws 65-149 and 65-164, 65th Cong. (1918); refer also to Twentieth Century Fund, *Housing for Defense* (New York: Twentieth Century Fund, 1940), pp. 156–157; Congressional Quarterly Service, *Housing a Nation,* p. 18.

6. Refer to the Emergency Relief and Reconstruction Act, Public Law 72-302, 72d Cong. (1932).

7. The only other loan made under this authorization was $155,000 for rural housing in Ford County, Kansas.

8. Edwin L. Scanton, "Public Housing Trends in New York City" (Ph.D. thesis, Graduate School of Banking, Rutgers University, 1952), p. 5.

9. Public Law 73-67, 72d Cong. (1933).

10. From a statement by Harold L. Ickes, Secretary of Interior and Public Works Administrator, quoted in Bert Swanson, "The Public Policy of Urban Renewal: Its Goals, Trends, and Conditions in New York City" (Paper delivered at the American Political Science Association Meeting, New York, September 1963), p. 10.

11. *U.S. v. Certain Lands in City of Louisville, Jefferson County, Ky., et al.,* 78 F.2d 64 (1935).

12. *U.S. v. Certain Lands in City of Detroit, et al.,* 12 F.Supp. 345 (1935).

13. Refer to Glen H. Boyer, *Housing: A Factual Analysis,* drawings by Zevi Blum (New York: Macmillan, 1958), p. 247.

14. Richard D. Bingham, *Public Housing and Urban Renewal: An Analysis of Federal-Local Relations,* Praeger Special Studies in U.S. Economics, Social, and Political Issues (New York: Praeger, 1975), p. 30.

15. Nathaniel S. Keith, *Politics and the Housing Crisis Since 1930* (New York: Universe Books, 1973), p. 29.

16. Public Law 75-412, 75th Cong. (1937). Also found in U.S. Congress, House Committee on Banking and Currency, *Basic Laws and Authorizations on Urban Housing,* 91st Cong., 1st sess., 1969, p. 225.

17. Roscoe Martin, "The Expended Partnership," in *The New Urban Politics: Cities and the Federal Government,* ed. Douglas Fox (Pacific Palisades, Calif.: Goodyear, 1972), p. 51.

18. Mark Gelfand, *A Nation of Cities: The Federal Government and Urban America, 1933–1965,* Urban Life in America Series (New York: Oxford University Press, 1975), p. 199.

19. Keith, *Politics and the Housing Crisis,* p. 33.

20. Speech delivered before the Fourth Annual Meeting of the National Public Housing Conference, New York, December 1935, cited in ibid., pp. 32–33.

21. The restriction limiting participation to low-income families, seen from a comparative perspective, is a root cause of the failure of public housing in America. See Arnold J. Heidenheimer, Hugh Heclo, and Carolyn Teich Adams, *Comparative Public Policy: The Politics of Social Choice in Europe and America* (New York: St. Martin's Press, 1975), pp. 69–96.

22. Charles Abrams, *The Future of Housing* (New York: Harper and Brothers, 1946), p. 260.

23. Public Law 76-671, 76th Cong. (1940), relating to defense housing needs; Public Law 80-301, 80th Cong. (1946), suspending cost limitations for some low-income housing projects.

24. U.S. Housing and Home Finance Agency, *Fourteenth Annual Report* (Washington, D.C.: Government Printing Office, 1961), p. 380.

25. U.S. Congress, Senate Special Committee on Post-War Economic Policy and Planning, *Housing and Urban Development: Hearings Pursuant to S. Res. 102,* Senate, 79th Cong., 1st sess., 1945, pp. 1228–1237.

26. U.S. Congress, Senate Special Committee on Post-War Economic Policy and Planning, *Housing and Urban Development,* pp. 1228–1237; also see John H. Haefner, *Housing in America: A Source Unit for the Social Studies,* Bulletin no. 14 (Washington, D.C.: National Council for the Social Studies, 1934), p. 6.

27. Refer to Robert B. Navin, *An Analysis of a Slum Area in Cleveland* (Cleveland: Cleveland Metropolitan Housing Authority, 1934), p. 6.

28. U.S. Congress, Senate Committee on Banking and Currency, *General Housing Act of 1945: Hearings,* 79th Cong., 1st sess., 1945, pp. 837–838.

29. U.S. Congress, Senate Committee on Banking and Currency, *General Housing Act of 1945,* p. 754.

30. Gelfand, *A Nation of Cities,* p. 112; refer also to pp. 112–118 for a discussion of aspects of the NAREB plan.

31. U.S. Congress, House Select Committee on Lobbying Activities, *Housing Lobby: Hearings Pursuant to H. Res. 288,* 81st Cong., 2d sess., 1950, Exhibit 349, p. 11.

32. Refer to Gelfand, *A Nation of Cities,* p. 14.

33. U.S. Congress, House Select Committee on Lobbying Activities, *Housing Lobby,* p. 11; also see Leonard Freedman, *Public Housing: The Politics of Poverty,* Public Policy Studies in American Government (New York: Holt, Rinehart and Winston, 1969), pp. 58–75; Keith, *Politics and the Housing Crisis,* pp. 35–39.

34. For one explication of this policy, see Guy Greer and Alvin Hansen, *Urban Redevelopment and Housing: A Program for Post-War,* Planning Pamphlets Series no. 10 (Washington, D.C.: National Planning Association, 1941).

35. Housing Act of 1949, Public Law 81-171, Preamble, sec. 2, 81st Cong. (1949).

36. International Union, United Automobile, Aircraft, and Agricultural Implement Workers of America, *Memorandum on Post War Urban Housing* (Detroit: International Union, United Automobile, Aircraft, and Agricultural Implement Workers of America, 1944), p. 94 (original text italicized throughout).

37. Wilson W. Wyatt, quoted in Congressional Quarterly Service, *Housing a Nation,* p. 6.

38. See Keith, *Politics and the Housing Crisis,* pp. 41–100.

39. See Chester Hartman et al., *Yerba Buena: Land Grab and Community Resistance in San Francisco* (San Francisco: Glide, 1974); John H. Mollenkopf, "The Post-War Politics of Urban Development," in *Marxism and the Metropolis: New Perspectives in Urban Political Economy,* ed. William Tabb and Larry Sawers (New York: Oxford University Press, 1978), pp. 117–152.

40. Martin Meyerson and Edward C. Banfield, *Politics, Planning, and the Public Interest* (New York: The Free Press, 1955).

41. Freedman, *Public Housing,* p. 55.

42. Robert H. Salisbury, "The New Convergence of Power in Urban Politics," *Journal of Politics* 26 (November 1964): 775–797.

43. Mollenkopf, "The Post-War Politics of Urban Development," p. 138.

44. Quoted in Institute of Housing, "Proceedings" (University College, Washington University, St. Louis, March 21–22, 1952, Mimeograph), p. 18. For studies of the coalition in other cities, see Harold Kaplan, *Urban Renewal Politics: Slum Clearance in Newark* (New York: Columbia University Press, 1963); Meyerson and Banfield, *Politics, Planning and the Public Interest;* Peter H. Rossi and Robert A. Dentler, *The Politics of Urban Renewal—the Chicago Findings* (New York: The Free Press, 1961). Refer also to Jewel Bellush and Murray Hausknecht, "Entrepreneurs and Urban Renewal: The New Mean of Power," *Journal of the American Planning Institute* 32 (September 1961); George S. Duggar, "The Relation of Local Government Structure to Urban Renewal," in *Urban Renewal: People, Politics and Planning,* ed. Jewel Bellush and Murray Hausknecht (Garden City, N.Y.: Doubleday, Anchor Books, 1967), pp. 179–187, 200–208, as reprinted from *Law and Contemporary Problems* 26 (Winter 1961); Herbert Kay, "The Third Force in Urban Renewal," *Fortune,* October 1964.

45. Quoted in Robert A. Dahl, *Who Governs: Democracy and Power in an American City* (New Haven, Conn.: Yale University Press, 1961), p. 136. See also Jewel Bellush and Murray Hausknecht, "Urban Renewal and the Reformer," in *Urban Renewal: People, Politics and Planning,* ed. Jewel Bellush and Murray Hausknecht (Garden City, NY: Doubleday, Anchor Books, 1967), pp. 189–197, for another insightful example of the use of urban renewal by political entrepreneurs.

46. Dahl, *Who Governs,* p. 135.

47. Quoted in *ibid.,* pp. 135–136.

48. Quoted in *ibid.,* p. 136.

49. Quoted in Institute of Housing, "Proceedings," p. 18.

50. Gelfand, *A Nation of Cities,* p. 161.

51. Mollenkopf, "The Post-War Politics of Urban Development," p. 140.

52. *Ibid., p. 138.*

53. Herbert J. Gans, *The Urban Villagers: Group and Class in the Life of Italian-Americans* (New York: The Free Press, 1962), chap. 13.

54. John H. Mollenkopf, "On the Causes and Consequences of Neighborhood Political Mobilization" (Paper delivered at the Annual Meeting of the American Political Science Association, New Orleans, September 4-8, 1973).

55. Quoted in Clarence N. Stone, *Economic Growth and Neighborhood Discontent: System Bias in the Urban Renewal Program of Atlanta* (Chapel Hill: University of North Carolina Press, 1976), pp. 48–49.

56. Quoted in *ibid.,* p. 66.

57. The following material on the Yerba Buena controversy draws on Chester Hartman's excellent book *Yerba Buena.* In most cases citations are limited to quotations or specific data.

58. *Ibid.,* p. 159.

59. *Ibid.,* p. 31.

60. *Ibid.,* p. 48.

61. *Ibid.,* p. 19.

62. *Ibid.,* p. 190.

63. *Ibid.,* p. 73.

64. *Ibid.,* p. 128.

65. Arthur I. Blaustein and Geoffrey Faux, *The Star-Spangled Hustle,* foreword by Ronald V. Dellums (Garden City, N.Y.: Doubleday, Anchor Books, 1973), p. 71.

66. See Martin Anderson, *The Federal Bulldozer: A Critical Analysis of Urban Renewal, 1949–1962* (Cambridge, Mass.: MIT Press, 1964), p. 65; compare Rossi and Dentler, *The Politics of Urban Renewal,* p. 224.

67. Chester Hartman, "The Housing of Relocated Families," in *Urban Renewal: The Record and the Controversy,* ed. James Q. Wilson (Cambridge, Mass.: MIT Press, 1966), p. 322, as reprinted from *Journal of the American Institute of Planners* 30 (November 1964): 266–286.

68. Anderson, *The Federal Bulldozer.*

69. Bernard Frieden and Marshall Kaplan, *The Politics of Neglect: Aid from Model Cities to Revenue Sharing* (Cambridge, Mass.: MIT Press, 1975).

70. Anderson, *The Federal Bulldozer,* pp. 65–66.

71. Mollenkopf, "The Post-War Politics of Urban Development," p. 140.

72. Keith, *Politics and the Housing Crisis,* p. 120.

73. Refer to Anderson, *The Federal Bulldozer,* pp. 65–66. Also see Bellush and Hausknecht, "Urban Renewal and the Reformer," p. 13.

74. Anderson, *The Federal Bulldozer,* p. 105.

75. Freedman, *Public Housing,* p. 140.

76. Arnold J. Heidenheimer, Hugh Heclo, and Carolyn Teich Adams, *Comparative Public Policy: The Politics of Social Choice in America, Europe, and Japan,* 3rd ed. (New York: St. Martin's Press, 1990), chap. 4.

77. Freedman, *Public Housing,* p. 105. The points in the following discussion of public housing borrow from Freedman's treatment at pp. 105–122.

78. Lawrence M. Friedman, *Government and Slum Housing: A Century of Frustration* (Chicago: Rand McNally, 1968), p. 121.

79. Freedman, *Public Housing,* p. 111.

80. Friedman, *Government and Slum Housing,* p. 123.

81. James Baldwin, *Nobody Knows My Name* (New York: Dial Press, 1961), p. 63., quoted in Freedman, *Public Housing,* p. 117.

82. Friedman, *Government and Slum Housing,* p. 121.

83. Lee Rainwater, *Behind Ghetto Walls: Black Families in a Federal Slum* (Chicago: Aldine, 1970).

84. National Commission on Urban Problems, *Building the American City* (New York: Praeger, 1969), p. 153. This commission, appointed by the president, was established in January 1967 and headed by former Illinois senator and long-time urban policy advocate Paul H. Douglas.

85. National Commission on Urban Problems, *Building the American City,* pp. 164–165.

86. Housing and Urban Development Act of 1968, Public Law 90-448, 90th Cong. (1968).

87. John C. Weicher, *Urban Renewal: National Program for Local Problems,* Evaluative Studies Series (Washington, D.C.: American Enterprise Institute for Public Policy Research, 1972), p. 6, citing unpublished HUD statistics: 538,044 housing units had been demolished as a result of urban renewal activities through 1971.

88. U.S. Department of Housing and Urban Development, *1974 Statistical Yearbook of the U.S. Department of Housing and Urban Development* (Washington, D.C.: Government Printing Office, 1976), p. 104.

CHAPTER 7

1. A brief but excellent account of these movements may be found in Stanley B. Greenberg, *Politics and Poverty: Modernization and Response in Five Poor Neighborhoods* (New York: Wiley, 1974), pp. 15–27.

2. Stewart E. Tolnay and E. M. Beck, "Rethinking the Role of Racial Violence in the Great Migration," in *Black Exodus: The Great Migration from the American South,* ed. Afrerdteen Harrison (Jackson: University Press of Mississippi, 1991), p. 20.

3. Nicholas Lemann, *The Promised Land: The Great Migration and How It Changed America* (New York: Vintage Books, 1991), p. 6.

4. See Greenberg, *Politics and Poverty,* pp. 15–27; Leo Grebler, Joan W. Moore, and Ralph C. Guzman, *The Mexican-American People* (New York: Free Press, 1970), p. 113.

5. *Night Comes to the Cumberlands* (Boston: Little, Brown, 1962) is Harry M. Caudill's account of the political and social decay of the Cumberland plateau.

6. Robert B. Grant, ed., *The Black Man Comes to the City: A Documentary Account from the Great Migration to the Great Depression, 1915–1930* (Chicago: Nelson-Hall, 1972), p. 27. See pages 16 to 30 for a complete set of statistics on black migration from 1890 to 1930. These data are used throughout this section.

7. *Ibid.,* p. 22.

8. *Ibid.,* p. 23.

9. Winfred P. Nathan, *Health Conditions in North Harlem, 1923–1927,* Social Research Series no. 2 (New York: National Tuberculosis Association, 1932), pp. 44–45, excerpted in Grant, *The Black Man Comes to the City,* pp. 59–61.

10. *Chicago Defender,* reprinted in Grant, *The Black Man Comes to the City,* pp. 31–40.

11. Tolnay and Beck, "Rethinking the Role of Racial Violence," p. 27.

12. *Memphis Commercial Appeal,* October 5, 1916, reprinted in Grant, *The Black Man Comes to the City,* pp. 43–44.

13. *Chicago Defender*, August 12, 1916, reprinted in Grant, *The Black Man Comes to the City*, p. 45.

14. Herbert Northrup, *Organized Labor and the Negro* (New York: Kraus Reprint, 1971).

15. These statistics are from several sources excerpted in Grant, *The Black Man Comes to the City*, pp. 58–61.

16. See Elliott M. Rudwick, *Race Riot at East St. Louis, July 2, 1917* (Carbondale: Southern Illinois Press, 1964) for a discussion of this event.

17. Chicago Commission on Race Relations, *The Negro in Chicago: A Study of Race Relations and a Race Riot* (Chicago: University of Chicago Press, 1922), p. 122.

18. Grant, *The Black Man Comes to the City*, p. 71.

19. U.S. Department of Commerce, Bureau of the Census, *Census of Population 1970: General Social and Economic Characteristics* (Washington, D.C.: Government Printing Office, 1972), pp. 448–449, Table 3.

20. Quoted in Theodore H. White, *The Making of the President, 1964* (New York: Atheneum, 1965), p. 165.

21. John Hope Franklin, "History of Racial Segregation in the United States," *Annals of the American Academy of Political and Social Science* 304 (March 1956): 6.

22. *Ibid.*, pp. 1–9.

23. *Ibid.*; John Hope Franklin, *From Slavery to Freedom: A History of American Negroes*, 2d ed. (New York: Knopf, 1956). See also C. Vann Woodward, *The Strange Career of Jim Crow*, rev. ed. (New York: Oxford University Press, 1965).

24. White, *The Making of the President, 1964*, p. 171.

25. Reported in the *New York Times*, December 1, 1959, p. 27, quoted in Mark I. Gelfand, *A Nation of Cities: The Federal Government and Urban America*, Urban Life in America Series (New York: Oxford University Press, 1975), p. 295. Also see John F. Kennedy, "The Great Unspoken Issue," *Proceedings, American Municipal Congress 1959* (Washington, D.C.: American Municipal League, n.d.), pp. 23–28; John F. Kennedy, "The Shame of the States," *New York Times Magazine*, May 18, 1958.

26. Quoted in Theodore H. White, *The Making of the President, 1960* (New York: Atheneum, 1961), p. 206. Nixon's strategy, which White contends was no strategy at all, was a "national" one, in which he committed himself to visit all fifty states; Kennedy, on the other hand, used an "urban" strategy centered on the industrial states (see pp. 267, 352).

27. John C. Donovan, *The Politics of Poverty*, 2d ed. (New York: Bobbs-Merrill, Pegasus, 1973), p. 19.

28. *Ibid.*, p. 225.

29. *Ibid.*, p. 104.

30. Nelson W. Polsby and Aaron Wildavsky, *Presidential Elections: Contemporary Strategies of American Electoral Politics*, 7th ed. (New York: The Free Press, 1988). The statistics given are for "nonwhite" voters.

31. White, *The Making of the President, 1960*, p. 354.

32. *Ibid.*

33. Lemann, *The Promised Land*, p. 117.

34. For good recent summary accounts, see *ibid.;* James A. Morone, *The Democratic Wish: Popular Participation and the Limits of American Government* (New York: Basic Books, 1990), chap. 6.

35. Quoted in Richard Blumenthal, "The Bureaucracy: Antipoverty and the Community Action Programs," in *American Political Institutions and Public Policy,* ed. Allan P. Sindler (Boston: Little, Brown, 1969), p. 149.

36. Message of the President to Congress, reprinted in *Congressional Quarterly Weekly Report* 32, no. 2 (January 11 1964).

37. *Congress and the Nation, 1945–1964* (Washington, D.C.: Congressional Quarterly Service, 1965), p. 1379.

38. U.S. Office of Management and Budget, *Special Analyses: Fiscal Year 1975*, (Washington, D.C.: Government Printing Office,), 1976 p. 207.

39. U.S. Advisory Commission on Intergovernmental Relations, *Eleventh Annual Report* (Washington, D.C.: Government Printing Office, 1970), p. 2.

40. U.S. Congress, Senate Committee on Government Operations, *Catalogue of Federal Aids to State and Local Governments*, 88th Cong., 2d sess., April 15, 1964.

41. U.S. Congress, Library of Congress, *Number of Authorizations for Federal Assistance to State and Local Governments,* by I. M. Labovitz (Washington, D.C.: Legislative Reference Service, 1966).

42. Michael Reagan, *The New Federalism* (New York: Oxford University Press, 1972), p. 55. In 1971 and 1972, there was virtually no growth in the number of grant programs, largely because of presidential vetoes. Nixon vetoed sixteen bills in 1972. See U.S. Advisory Commission on Intergovernmental Relations, *Fourteenth Annual Report: Striking a Better Balance* (Washington, D.C.: Government Printing Office, 1973), p. 12.

43. U.S. Office of Management and Budget, *1979 Catalog of Federal Domestic Assistance* (Washington, D.C.: Government Printing Office, 1980).

44. Refer to Daniel J. Elazar, *The American Partnership: Intergovernmental Cooperation in the Nineteenth Century United States* (Chicago: University of Chicago Press, 1962).

45. Manpower Development and Training Act of 1962, Public Law 87-415, 87th Cong. (1962); emphasis added.

46. Economic Opportunity Act of 1964, Public Law 88-452, 88th Cong. (1964); emphasis added.

47. Demonstration Cities and Metropolitan Development Act of 1966, Public Law 89-754, 89th Cong. (1966); emphasis added.

48. See James L. Sundquist and David W. Davis, *Making Federalism Work: A Study of Program Coordination at the Community Level* (Washington, D.C.: Brookings Institution, 1969), pp. 3–5.

49. Alexander P. Lamis, *The Two Party South* (New York: Oxford University Press, 1984).

50. Kathleen Hall Jamieson, *Packaging the Presidency: A History and Criticism of Presidential Campaign Advertising* (New York: Oxford University Press, 1984), pp. 202–203.

51. Joseph McGinniss, *Selling the President, 1968* (New York: Trident Press, 1969).

52. Numan V. Bartley and Hugh D. Graham, *Southern Politics and the Second Reconstruction* (Baltimore: Johns Hopkins University Press, 1975), pp. 126–127; Everett Carl Ladd, Jr., "The Shifting Party Coalitions—1932–1976," *Emerging Coalitions in American Politics* ed. Seymour Martin Lipset (San Francisco: Institute for Contemporary Studies, 1978), p. 98; A. James Reichley, *Conservatives in an Age of Change: The Nixon and Ford Administrations* (Washington, D.C.: Brookings Institution, 1981), p. 145.

53. Reichley, *Conservatives in an Age of Change*, p. 186. For a general discussion, see David B. Robertson and Dennis R. Judd, *The Development of American Public Policy: The Structure of Policy Restraint* (Glenview, Ill.: Scott, Foresman, 1989), pp. 190–197.

54. Theodore H. White, *America in Search of Itself: The Making of the President, 1956–1980* (New York: Harper and Row 1982), p. 381.

55. D. Lee Bawden and John L. Palmer, "Social Policy: Challenging the Welfare State," in *The Reagan Record* ed. John L. Palmer and Isabel V. Sawhill (Cambridge, Mass.: Ballinger, 1984), p. 200.

56. See Daniel Hellinger and Dennis R. Judd, *The Democratic Facade* (Pacific Grove, Calif.: Brooks/Cole, 1991), pp. 74–77.

57. Quoted in Lemann, *The Promised Land*, p. 134.

58. U.S. Office of Economic Opportunity, *Community Action Program Guide* (Washington, D.C.: Government Printing Office, 1965).

59. Frances Fox Piven and Richard A. Cloward, *Regulating the Poor: The Functions of Public Welfare* (New York: Pantheon, 1971).

60. *Ibid.*, p. 295.

61. U.S. Advisory Commission on Intergovernmental Relations, *Fiscal Balance in the American Federal System*, vol. 1 (Washington, D.C.: Government Printing Office, 1967), p. 169.

62. Lemann, *The Promised Land*, p. 188.

63. Demonstration Cities and Metropolitan Development Act of 1966, Public Law 89-754.

64. R. Douglas Arnold, *Congress and the Bureaucracy: A Theory of Influence* (New Haven: Yale University Press, 1979), p. 160.

65. *Ibid.*, p. 168.

66. Stuart Butler and Anna Kondratas, *Out of the Poverty Trap: A Conservative Strategy for Welfare Reform* (New York: Free Press, 1987), pp. 7–25.

67. Lyndon B. Johnson, "Total Victory over Poverty," Message to Congress, March 15, 1964, reprinted in *The Failure of American Liberalism: After the Great Society*, ed. Marvin E. Gettleman and David Mermelstein (New York: Vintage Books, 1970), p. 181.

68. See George Gilder, *Wealth and Poverty* (New York: Basic Books, 1981); Charles Murray, *Losing Ground: American Social Policy 1950–1980* (New York: Basic Books, 1984).

69. U.S. Department of Commerce, Bureau of the Census, *Statistical Abstract of the United States: 1980* (Washington, D.C.: Government Printing Office, 1980), p. 464.

70. John E. Schwarz, *America's Hidden Success: A Reassessment of Public Policy from Kennedy to Reagan*, rev. ed. (New York: Norton, 1988), p. 24.

71. Quoted in Jeffrey L. Pressman and Aaron Wildavsky, *Implementation: How Great Expectations in Washington Are Dashed in Oakland: Or, Why It's Amazing That Federal Programs Work at All. This Being a Saga of the Economic Development Administration as Told by Two Sympathetic Observers Who Seek to Build Morals on a Foundation of Ruined Hopes*, 3rd ed. (Berkeley: University of California Press, 1984).

72. Irving Lazar, *Summary: The Persistence of Preschool Effects*, Community Services Laboratory, New York State University College of Human Ecology at Cornell University, October 1977, quoted in Schwarz, *America's Hidden Success*, pp. 217–218.

73. Schwarz, *America's Hidden Success*, pp. 38–39.

74. Joe Feagin and Harlan Hahn, *Ghetto Revolts* (New York: Macmillan, 1937), p. 102.

75. *Report of the Advisory Commission on Civil Disorders* (New York: Bantam Books, 1968), p. 9.

76. *Ibid.*, p. 22.

77. Quoted in Bob Adams, "The Great Society Programs of '60s and '70s Under Attack," *St. Louis Post-Dispatch*, May 10, 1992, p. 1B.

78. Quoted in "Schlesinger Accepts Award, Assails Bush," *St. Louis Post-Dispatch*, May 10, 1992, p. 13C.

CHAPTER 8

1. Barry Checkoway. "Large Builders, Federal Housing Programs, and Postwar Suburbanization," in *Marxism and the Metropolis: New Perspectives in Political Economy*, ed. William K. Tabb and Larry Sawers (New York: Oxford University Press), p. 156.

2. Population growth on the outskirts probably exceeded population growth in the center before the 1920s. However, before 1920, annexation of suburban land by central cities obscured the statistical trend. See John D. Kasarda and George V.

Redfearn, "Differential Patterns of City and Suburban Growth in the United States," *Journal of Urban History* 2, no. 1 (November 1975), p. 53.

3. For a comparative analysis of suburbanization in advanced industrial countries, see Donald N. Rothblatt and Daniel J. Garr, *Suburbia: An International Assessment* (New York: St. Martin's Press, 1986); Christopher M. Law, *The Uncertain Future of the Urban Core* (London: Routledge, 1988). Kenneth T. Jackson identifies Brooklyn in 1815 as the first suburb in the United States; see Jackson, *Crabgrass Frontier: The Suburbanization of the United States* (New York: Oxford University Press, 1985), chap. 2.

4. Cities in the former West Germany have a population density of about 6,000 per square mile; urbanized areas in the United States have a population density of about half of that (3,327 per square mile). See James A. Dunn, Jr., *Miles to Go: European and American Transportation Policies* (Cambridge, Mass.: MIT Press, 1981), p. 68. Canadian cities, which have experienced extensive suburbanization, still have densities that are about twice that of American cities. See Barry Edmonton, Michael A. Goldberg, and John Mercer, "Urban Form in Canada and the United States: An Examination of Urban Density Gradients," *Urban Studies* (1985), p. 213.

5. "According to the 1980 census, the typical American worker traveled 9.2 miles and expended twenty-two minutes each way in reaching his place of employment at an annual cost of more than $1,270 per employee." Jackson, *Crabgrass Frontier*, p. 10.

6. Nick Buck and Norman Fainstein, "A Comparative History, 1880–1973," in *Divided Cities: New York and London in the Contemporary World*, ed. Susan S. Fainstein, Ian Gordon, and Michael Harloe (Cambridge, Mass.: Blackwell, 1992), p. 37.

7. Jackson, *Crabgrass Frontier*, chap. 1.

8. Quoted in James A. Clapp, ed., *the City: A Dictionary of Quotable thoughts on Cities and Urban Life* (New Brunswick, N. J.: Center for Urban Policy Research, Rutgers University, 1984), p. 129.

9. Robert Fishman, *Bourgeois Utopias: The Rise and Fall of Suburbia* (New York: Basic Books, 1987), p. 62. Fishman's account stresses the role of changing cultural values and family life in the rise of suburbs. See also Jackson, *Crabgrass Frontier*, chaps. 3, 4.

10. Jackson, *Crabgrass Frontier*, pp. 25–30. Robert Fishman dates the first true suburb somewhat earlier, in the 1790s in Clapham and other villages outside London. See Fishman, *Bourgeois Utopias*, p. 53.

11. The phrase "scattered buildings in a park" is Lewis Mumford's; see his *The City in History: Its Origins, Its Transformations, and Its Prospects* (New York: Harcourt, Brace & World, 1961), p. 489.

12. For accounts of railroad suburbs and land speculation, see Jackson, *Crabgrass Frontier*, chap. 5; Fishman, *Bourgeois Utopias*, chap. 5; Harry C. Binford, *The First Suburbs: Residential Communities on the Boston Periphery, 1815–1860* (Chicago: University of Chicago Press, 1985).

13. Peter O. Muller, *Contemporary Suburban America* (Englewood Cliffs, N.J.: Prentice-Hall, 1981), p. 28.

14. Our account of Huntington relies on Robert M. Fogelson, *The Fragmented Metropolis: Los Angeles, 1850–1930* (New York: Cambridge, 1967), pp. 89–92; Jackson, *Crabgrass Frontier,* p. 122; Fishman, *Bourgeois Utopias,* pp. 159–160.

15. Gary A. Tobin, "Suburbanization and the Development of Motor Transportation: Transportation Technology and the Suburbanization Process," in *The Changing Face of the Suburbs,* ed. Barry Schwartz (Chicago: University of Chicago Press, 1976), p. 100. See also U.S. Bureau of the Census, *Industrial Districts: 1905, Manufactures and Population,* Bulletin 101 (Washington, D.C.: Government Printing Office, 1909), pp. 9–80: U.S. Bureau of the Census, *Census of Manufactures: 1914, vol. 1, Reports by States with Statistics for Principal Cities and Metropolitan Districts* (Washington, D.C.: Government Printing Office, 1918), pp. 564, 787, 1292.

16. These data are cited in Tobin, "Suburbanization and the Development of Motor Transportation," pp. 102, 103, and are also available in National Industrial Conference Board (NICB), *The Economic Almanac 1956: A Handbook of Useful Facts about Business, Labor and Government in the United States and Other Areas* (New York: Crowell for the Conference Board, 1956).

17. Tobin, "Suburbanization and the Development of Motor Transportation," pp. 102, 103.

18. *Ibid.*

19. Jackson, *Crabgrass Frontier,* pp. 174, 184.

20. The birthrate (the number of live births per 1,000 population) increased from 18.4 in 1936 to 26.6 in 1947. U.S. Bureau of the Census, *Historical Statistics of the United States, Colonial Times to 1970, Bicentennial Edition, Part 2* (Washington, D.C.: Government Printing Office, 1975), p. 49.

21. Jackson, *Crabgrass Frontier,* p. 232.

22. *Ibid.,* p. 233.

23. Checkoway, "Large Builders, Federal Housing Programs, and Postwar Suburbanization," pp. 155–156.

24. U.S. Bureau of the Census, *Historical Statistics of the United States, Colonial Times to 1970, Bicentennial Edition, Part 1* (Washington, D.C.: Government Printing Office, 1975), p. 646.

25. For criticisms of the 1950s stereotype of suburbia, see Bennett M. Berger, *Working-Class Suburb: A Study of Auto Workers in Suburbia* (Berkeley: University of California Press, 1968); Herbert J. Gans, *The Levittowners: Ways of Life and Politics in a New Suburban Community* (New York: Pantheon, 1967).

26. Thomas M. Guterbock, "The Push Hypothesis: Minority Presence, Crime, and Urban Deconcentration," in *The Changing Face of the Suburbs,* ed. Barry Schwartz (Chicago: University of Chicago Press, 1976), p. 26.

27. National Advisory Commission on Civil Disorders, *Report of the National Advisory Commission on Civil Disorders* (New York: Bantam Books, 1968), p. 1.

28. James Heilbrun, *Urban Economics and Public Policy,* 2d ed. (New York: St. Martin's Press, 1981), p. 48.

29. Muller, *Contemporary Suburban America,* p. 123.

30. David M. Gordon, "Capitalist Development and the History of American Cities," in *Marxism and the Metropolis: New Perspectives in Urban Political Economy,* 2d ed., eds. William K. Tabb and Larry Sawers (New York: Oxford University Press, 1984), p. 41.

31. George E. Peterson, "Federal Tax Policy and Urban Development," in *Central City Economic Development,* ed. Benjamin Chinitz (Cambridge, Mass.: Abt Books, 1979), pp. 67–78.

32. Robert Cevero, "Unlocking Suburban Gridlock," *Journal of the American Planning Association* (Autumn 1986), p. 389.

33. Brian J. L. Berry, *The Open Housing Question: Race and Housing in Chicago, 1966-—1976* (Cambridge, Mass.: Ballinger, 1979).

34. Joel Garreau, *Edge City: Life on the New Frontier* (Garden City, N.Y.: Doubleday, 1991), p. 6.

35. Muller, *Contemporary Suburban America,* p. 180.

36. See Mark Gottdiener, *Planned Sprawl: Private and Public Interests in Suburbia* (Beverly Hills, Calif.: Sage, 1977).

37. The term community builders is taken from a book by Mark Weiss, *The Rise of the Community Builders* (New York: Columbia University Press, 1987).

38. J. C. Nichols, "The Planning and Control of Outlying Shopping Centers," *Journal of Land and Public Utility Economics* 2 (January 1926): 22. By concentrating stores in one location and using leasing policy to determine the store "mix," "Nichols created the idea of the planned regional shopping center." Jackson, *Crabgrass Frontier,* p. 258.

39. Gwendolyn Wright, *Building the Dream, A Social History of Housing in America* (Cambridge, Mass.: MIT Press, 1981), p. 202.

40. Mark H. Rose, "There Is Less Smoke in the District": J. C. Nichols, "Urban Change and Technological Systems," *Journal of the West* (January 1986): 48. Rose adds, "as late as 1917, no more than five Jewish families resided in the district, the result of resales."

41. "Up from the Potato Fields," *Time,* July 3, 1950, p. 70.

42. *Ibid.*

43. "The Most House for the Money," *Fortune,* October 1952, p. 156.

44. Jackson, *Crabgrass Frontier,* p. 234.

45. Wright, *Building the Dream,* p. 252.

46. "Up from the Potato Fields," p. 71.

47. Jackson, *Crabgrass Frontier,* p. 234.

48. "Up from the Potato Fields," p. 68.

49. Quoted in Gans, *The Levittowners,* p. 372.

50. Jackson, *Crabgrass Frontier,* p. 241.

51. Gans, *The Levittowners,* pp. 8–9.

52. Joe R. Feagin and Robert Parker, *Building American Cities: The Urban Real Estate Game,* 2d ed. (Englewood Cliffs, N.J.: Prentice-Hall, 1990), p. 211.

53. Robert Goldston, *Suburbia: Civic Denial* (New York: Macmillan, 1970), p. 68.

54. *New York Times,* March 31, 1953. Notes 56 through 60 refer to advertisments that appeared in the *Times.*

55. *New York Times,* March 22, 1953.

56. *Ibid.*

60. *New York Times,* January 6, 1962.

58. *New York Times,* October 26, 1952. Emphasis in the original.

59. *New York Times.*

60. *New York Times,* May 26, 1968.

61. *Ibid.*

62. *St. Louis Post-Dispatch,* April 16, 1972. Notes 64 through 67 refer to advertisements that appeared in the *Post-Dispatch.*

63. *St. Louis Post-Dispatch,* August 18, 1974.

64. *St. Louis Post-Dispatch,* July 5, 1970.

65. *Ibid.*

66. National Association of Real Estate Boards, *Code of Ethics* (1924), art. 34.

67. Harry Grant Atkinson and L. E. Frailey, *Fundamentals of Real Estate Practice* (Englewood Cliffs, N.J.: Prentice-Hall, 1946), p. 34, quoted in Evan McKenzie, *Privatopia* (In Press), pp. 105–106. Forthcoming, Yale University Press (1994).

68. *Shelly v. Kraemer ,* 334 U.S. 1 (1948). The Court had struck down racial zoning some thirty years earlier in *Buchanan v. Warley,* 245 U.S. 60 (1917).

69. McKenzie, "Privatopia," p. 36.

70. Evan McKenzie, "Morning in Privatopia," *Dissent,* Spring 1989, p. 257.

71. Richard Louv, *America II* (New York: Penguin Books, 1985), p. 85.

72. *Ibid.,* p. 115.

73. From *New York Times* advertising supplement, November 18, 1990, p. 13.

74. *Ibid.*

75. Stephen David and Paul Peterson, eds., *Urban Politics and Public Policy: The City in Crisis* (New York: Praeger, 1973), p. 94.

76. Charles Abrams, *The Future of Housing* (New York: HarperCollins, 1946), p. 213.

77. Bureau of National Affairs, *The Housing and Development Reporter* (Washington, D.C.: Bureau of National Affairs, 1976).

78. *Ibid.*

79. Calculated from data in Congressional Quarterly Service, *Housing a Nation* (Washington, D.C., Congressional Quarterly Service, 1966), p. 6.

80. U.S. Department of Housing and Urban Development, *1974 Statistical Yearbook of the Department of Housing and Urban Development* (Washington, D.C.: Government Printing Office, 1976), pp. 116–117.

81. U.S. Bureau of the Census, *Historical Statistics, Part I,* p. 646.

82. Jackson, *Crabgrass Frontier,* p. 205.

83. For a discussion of this phenomenon, see Murray Edelman, *The Symbolic Uses of Politics,* 7th ed. (Champaign: University of Illinois Press, 1976), pp. 44–76. We are indebted to Jeffrey Gilbert for several of the ideas contained in this section.

84. Michael Stone, "Reconstructing American Housing" (Unpublished manuscript), quoted in Chester W. Hartman, *Housing and Social Policy,* Prentice-Hall Series in Social Policy (Englewood Cliffs, N.J.: Prentice-Hall, 1975), p. 30.

85. Quoted in Berry, *The Open Housing Question,* p. 9.

86. Quoted in *ibid.,* pp. 9, 11.

87. Luigi M. Laurenti, "Theories of Race and Property Value," in *Urban Analysis: Readings in Housing and Urban Development,* ed. Alfred N. Page and Warren R. Seyfried (Glenview, Ill.: Scott, Foresman, 1970), p. 274.

88. Charles Abrams, quoted in Norman N. Bradburn, Seymour Sudman, and Galen L. Gockel, *Side by Side: Integrated Neighborhoods in America* (Chicago: Quadrangle Books, 1971), p. 104.

89. Mark Gelfand, *A Nation of Cities: The Federal Government and Urban America, 1933—1965* (New York: Oxford University Press, 1975), p. 221.

90. Nathan Glazer and David McEntire, eds., *Housing and Minority Groups* (Berkeley: University of California Press, 1960), p. 140.

91. Public Law 90-284, 90th Cong. (1968), Title VIII ("Fair Housing"), sec. 805.

92. D.C. Public Interest Research Group (DCPIRG), Institute for Self-Reliance, and Institute for Policy Studies, *Redlining: Mortgage Disinvestment in the District of Columbia* (Washington, D.C.: DCPIRG, Institute for Local Self-Reliance, and Institute for Policy Studies, 1975), p. 3.

93. See Daniel Seering, "Discrimination in Home Finance," *Notre Dame Lawyer* 68 (June 1973): 5 ff; U.S. Commission on Civil Rights, *The Federal Civil Rights Enforcement Effort: Summary,* Clearinghouse Publication 31 (Washington, D.C.: Government Printing Office, 1971); U.S. Commission on Civil Rights, *The Federal Civil Rights Enforcement Effort: One Year Later,* Clearinghouse Publication 34 (Washington, D.C.: Government Printing Office, 1972).

94. DCPIRG, Institute for Self-Reliance, and Institute for Policy Studies, *Redlining,* p. 2.

95. *Ibid.,* p. 3. See also "Nondiscrimination Requirements in Real Estate Loan Activities," *Federal Register,* February 8, 1973, pp. 3586–3587.

96. *St. Louis Post-Dispatch,* April 29, 1977.

97. DCPIRG, Institute for Self-Reliance, and Institute for Policy Studies, *Redlining,* p. 4.

98. *Ibid.,* p. 5. See also U.S. Commission on Civil Rights, *Mortgage Money: Who Gets It? A Case Study in Mortgage Lending Discrimination in Hartford, Connecticut,* Clearinghouse Publication 48 (Washington, D.C.: Government Printing Office, 1974).

99. Public Law 93-495, 93rd Cong. (1974), Title V, amendments.

100. Public Law 94-200, 94th Cong. (1975), Title III.

101. Public Law 95–128, 95th Cong. (1977), Title VIII.

102. Calvin Bradford, *Community Reinvestment Agreement Library* (Des Plaines, Ill.: Community Reinvestment Associates, 1992), as cited in *From Redlining to Reinvestment: Community Responses to Urban Disinvestment*, ed. Gregory D. Squires (Philadelphia: Temple University Press, 1992), p. 2.

103. Mitchelle Zuckoff, "Study Shows Racial Bias in Lending," *Boston Globe* (October 9, 1992).

104. Dunn, *Miles to Go,* p. 59.

105. John R. Meyer and Jose A. Gomez-Ibanez, *Autos Transit and Cities* (Cambridge, Mass.: Harvard University Press, 1981), pp. 23, 28, 34.

106. Henry Ford, quoted in J. Allen Whitt and Glenn Yago, "Corporate Strategies and the Decline of Transit in U.S. Cities," *Urban Affairs Quarterly* 21, no. 1 (September 1985): 61.

107. Dunn, *Miles to Go,* p. 116.

108. Whitt and Yago, "Corporate Strategies and the Decline of Transit in U.S. Cities," p. 52.

109. Dunn, *Miles to Go,* p. 116. Many policy analysts question whether earmarked gasoline taxes pay for the full costs of highways, including the costs of air and noise pollution and the expenses associated with traffic accidents. See Meyer and Gomez-Ibanez, *Autos Transit and Cities*; and Glenn Yago, *The Decline of Transit* (New York: Cambridge University Press, 1984), p. 195.

110. Bradford C. Snell, "American Ground Transport," in *The Urban Scene*, 2d ed., ed. Joe R. Feagin (New York: Random House, 1979), p. 247.

111. *Ibid.,* p. 248.

112. Quoted in *ibid.,* p. 249.

113. Alan Lupo, Frank Colcord, and Edmund P. Fowler, *Rites of Way: The Politics of Transportation in Boston and the U.S. City* (Boston: Little, Brown, 1971), p. 184.

114. Mark Rose, *Interstate Express Highway Politics, 1941–1956* (Lawrence: The Regents Press of Kansas), p. 97.

115. A local participation agreement is required before public housing can be built in a jurisdiction. Suburban governments simply refuse to negotiate such agreements and therefore exclude all conventional public housing from their locality.

116. Quoted in Leavitt, *Superhighway—Superhoax* (Garden City, N.Y.: Doubleday, 1970), p. 53.

117. Robert A. Caro, *The Power Broker: Robert Moses and the Fall of New York* (New York: Random House, 1974), p. 19.

118. For example, between 1951 and 1974, 89 percent of the 10,000 households displaced by public projects in Baltimore were black. Anthony Downs, *Urban Problems and Prospects* (Chicago: Marsham, 1970), pp. 204–205.

119. *Ibid.,* p. 223.

120. Meyer and Gomez-Ibanez, *Autos, Transit, and Cities,* p. 177. Boston is now embarked on a multibillion dollar project to demolish part of the Fitzgerald Expressway and rebuild it underground in order to eliminate its negative effects. Jennifer A. Kingson, "Highway Project: A 10-Year Plague?" *New York Times,* August 2, 1988.

121. By 1970 there were 400 struggles underway by community groups to oppose highway construction. Harry C. Boyte, *The Backyard Revolution: Understanding the New Citizen Movement* (Philadelphia: Temple University Press, 1980), p. 11.

122. H. Josef Hebert, "Billions Needed to Fix Interstates," *Albany Times Union,* April 5, 1987.

123. Jackson, *Crabgrass Frontier,* p. 250.

124. Reynolds Farley, "Suburban Persistence," in *North American Suburbs,* ed. Kramer, pp. 82-96.

125. Robert Wood, "Suburban Politics and Policies: Retrospect and Prospect," *Publius, The Journal of Federalism* 5 (Winter 1975), p. 51.

CHAPTER 9

1. U.S. Bureau of the Census, *Statistical Abstract of the United States, 1992,* 112th ed. (Washington, D.C.: Government Printing Office, 1992), p. 278.

2. Kenneth Newton, "American Urban Politics: Social Class, Political Structure and Public Goods," in *Readings in Urban Politics: Past, Present and Future,* 2d ed., ed. Harlan Hahn and Charles H. Levine (New York; Longman, 1984), p. 350.

3. Sam Bass Warner, *Streetcar Suburbs: The Process of Growth in Boston, 1870–1900* (Cambridge, Mass.: Harvard University Press, 1962), pp. 164–165.

4. Data cited in Robert C. Wood, *Suburbia: Its People and Their Politics* (Boston: Houghton Mifflin, 1958), p. 69, and in National Municipal League, Committee on Metropolitan Government, *The Government of Metropolitan Areas in the United States,* prepared by Paul Studenski with the assistance of the Committee on Metropolitan Government (New York: National Municipal League, 1930), p. 26.

5. Robert Park, Ernest W. Burgess, and Roderick D. McKenzie, *The City* (Chicago: University of Chicago Press, 1925), p. 109.

6. Quoted in Peter J. Schmitt, *Back to Nature: The Arcadian Myth in Urban America* (New York: Oxford University Press, 1969), p. 180; original quotation found in Ernest Groves, "The Urban Complex," *Sociological Review* 12 (Fall 1920): 74, 76.

7. A more complete list of titles can be found in Schmitt, *Back to Nature.*

8. Editorial, *Independent,* February 27, 1902, p. 52.

9. Weldon Fawcett, "Suburban Life in America," *Cosmopolitan,* July 1903, p. 309.

10. Advertisement in *Country Life in America,* November 1906, p. 3.

11. Advertisement in *Country Life in America,* March 1908, p. 474.

12. See Anwar Syed, *The Political Theory of American Local Government* (Clinton, Mass.: Random House, 1966).

13. Jon C. Teaford, *City and Suburb: The Political Fragmentation of Metropolitan America, 1850–1970* (Baltimore: Johns Hopkins University Press, 1979), p. 6.

14. *Ibid.,* p. 31.

15. Gary J. Miller, *Cities by Contract: The Politics of Municipal Incorporation* (Cambridge, Mass.: MIT Press, 1981), p. 12.

16. *Ibid.*

17. Teaford, *City and Suburb,* p. 18.

18. C. B. Glasscock, *Lucky Baldwin: The Story of an Unconventional Success* (Indianapolis, Ind.: Bobbs-Merrill, 1933), p. 140.

19. Teaford, *City and Suburb,* pp. 18–19.

20. Charles Hoch, "City Limits: Municipal Boundary Formation and Class Segregation," in *Marxism and the Metropolis: New Perspectives in Urban Political Economy,* 2d ed., ed. William K. Tabb and Larry Sawers (New York: Oxford University Press, 1984), pp. 101–119.

21. Miller, *Cities by Contract,* pp. 49–50. Another good example of an industrial suburb is Teterboro, New Jersey, which in 1977 had only 24 residents, but employed 24,000 nonresidents. Michael N. Danielson and Jameson W. Doig, *New York: The Politics of Urban Regional Development* (Berkeley: University of California Press, 1982), p. 92.

22. Ann R. Markusen, "Class and Urban Social Expenditure: A Marxist Theory of Metropolitan Government," in *Marxism and the Metropolis: New Perspectives in Urban Political Economy*, 2d ed., ed. William K. Tabb and Larry Sawers (New York: Oxford University Press, 1984), p. 92. The American system contrasts with that of Great Britain where the central government retained control over the organization of local government. "English law did not allow every race track promoter, tax evading industrialist, or community of teetotalers to create its own community." Teaford, *City and Suburb,* p. 70.

23. Richard P. Nathan and Charles F. Adams, Jr., "Four Perspectives on Urban Hardship," *Political Science Quarterly* 104, no. 3 (Fall 1989): 483–508. The study also found that the greater the city-suburban disparity, the worse the region as a whole did economically.

24. U.S. Advisory Commission on Intergovermental Relations (ACIR), *Fiscal Disparities: Central Cities and Suburbs, 1981* (Washington, D.C.: Government Printing Office, 1984), p. 23.

25. For analyses of the "suburban exploitation" hypothesis, see Amos Hawley, "Metropolitan Population and Municipal Government Expenditures in Central Cities," *Journal of Social Issues* 7 (1951); Harvey Brazer, *City Expenditures in the United States* (New York: National Bureau of Economic Research, 1959); Julius Margolis, "Metropolitan Finance Problems: Territories, Functions, and Growth," in James Buchanan, ed., *Public Finances: Needs, Sources, and Utilization* (Princeton, N.J.: Princeton University Press, 1961), pp. 229–293.

26. William B. Neenan, "Suburban-Central City Exploitation Thesis: One City's Tale," *National Tax Journal,* June 1970, pp. 117–139; Kenneth Green, William Neenan, and Claudia Scott, *Fiscal Interactions in a Metropolitan Area* (Lexington, Mass.: Lexington Books, 1974), pp. 147–206.

27. David K. Hamilton and Jim Turner, "Fiscal Implications of Suburbanites on the Central City: A Case Study" (Paper presented at the Urban Affairs Association Conference, Fort Worth, Tex., March 7 1986).

28. John M. Quigley and Debra Stinson, *Levels of Property Tax Exemption* (Monticello, Ill.: Council of Planning Librarians, 1975), p. 31. See also Gregory H. Wassall, *Tax-Exempt Property: A Case Study of Hartford, Connecticut* (Hartford, Conn.: John C. Lincoln Institute, 1974), pp. 62–64.

29. Matthew Edel demonstrated the differential appreciation of homes in the suburbs and the central city in the Boston metropolitan area. "The Distribution of Real Estate Value Changes: Metropolitan Boston, 1870–1970," *Journal of Urban Economics* 2 (1975): 366–387. For studies of Cleveland, see Todd Swanstrom, *The Crisis of Growth Politics: Cleveland, Kucinich, and the Challenge of Urban Populism* (Philadelphia: Temple University Press, 1985), pp. 69–70; Edward W. Hill and Thomas Bier, "Economic Restructuring: Earnings, Occupations, and Housing Values in Cleveland," *Economic Development Quarterly* 3, no. 2 (May 1989): 140.

30. The study is cited in Mark S. R. Suchecki, "Poor Pay More for Big-City Living: Study Cites Suburban Edge," *Albany Times Union,* August 14, 1988. See also David Caplovitz, *The Poor Pay More* (New York: The Free Press, 1967).

31. John D. Kasarda, "Urban Change and Minority Opportunities," in *The New Urban Reality,* ed. Paul E. Peterson (Washington, D.C.: Brookings Institution, 1985), pp. 33–67; Keith R. Ihlanfeldt and David L. Sjoquist, "The Impact of Job Decentralization on the Economic Welfare of Central City Blacks," *Journal of Urban Economics* 26 (1989): 110–130.

32. Kasarda, "Urban Change and Minority Opportunities," p. 56.

33. John R. Logan, "Growth, Politics, and the Stratification of Places," *American Journal of Sociology* 84, no. 2 (1978): 404–416.

34. John Kramer, "The Other Mayor Lee," *North American Suburbs: Politics, Diversity, and Change,* ed. John Kramer (Berkeley, Calif.: Glendessary Press, 1972), pp. 192–198.

35. Richard Child Hill, "Separate and Unequal: Governmental Inequality in the Metropolis," *American Political Science Review* 68, no. 4 (December 1974): 1567.

36. Seymour I. Toll, *Zoned America* (New York: Grossman, 1969), p. 193.

37. *Ibid.,* p. 197.

38. *Ibid.,* p. 159.

39. Quoted in Michael N. Danielson, *The Politics of Exclusion* (New York: Columbia University Press, 1976), p. 54.

40. Toll, *Zoned America,* p. 183.

41. *Ibid.,* pp. 182–183.

42. *Ibid.,* p. 187.

43. "Police power" refers to the implied powers of government to adopt and enforce laws necessary for preserving and protecting the immediate health and welfare of citizens. The meaning of this is, of course, subject to a wide variety of interpretations.

44. *Village of Euclid v. Ambler Realty Co.,* 272 U.S. 365, 47 S.Ct. 114, 71 L. Ed. 303 (1926).

45. Quoted in Danielson, *The Politics of Exclusion,* pp. 53–54.

46. "The End of the Exurban Dream," *New York Times,* December 13, 1976.

47. Danielson, *The Politics of Exclusion,* p. 53.

48. Because of the fears concerning apartment developments, the planning process involving their construction is complicated, requiring petitions for zoning variances, public hearings, and lengthy review proceedings. For an excellent account of these complexities, see Daniel R. Mandelker, *The Zoning Dilemma: A Legal Strategy for Urban Change* (Indianapolis, Ind.: Bobbs-Merrill, 1971).

49. Quoted in Danielson, *The Politics of Exclusion,* p. 60.

50. Quoted in Merrill Folson, "Westchester Finds Influx of Business a Worry," *New York Times,* April 18, 1967; cited in Danielson and Doig, *New York,* p. 90.

51. Kenneth M. Dolbeare, "Who Uses the State Trial Courts?" in *The Politics of Local Justice,* ed. James R. Klonoski and Robert I. Mendelsohn (Boston: Little, Brown, 1970), p. 69.

52. A detailed discussion of the legal status of zoning is not included in this section. For further information, the following sources are especially useful: Danielson, *The Politics of Exclusion;* Richard F. Babcock, *The Zoning Game* (Madison: University of Wisconsin Press, 1969); Richard F. Babcock and Fred P. Bosselman, *Exclusionary Zoning: Land Use Regulation and Housing in the 1970s* (New York: Praeger, 1973); Daniel R. Mandelker, *Managing Our Urban Environment* (Indianapolis, Ind.: Bobbs-Merrill, 1971); Randall W. Scott, ed., *Management and Control of Growth,* vol. 1 (New York: Urban Land Institute, 1975); and David Listokin, ed., *Land Use Controls, Present Problems and Future Reform* (New Brunswick, N.J.: Rutgers University, Center for Urban Policy Research, 1975).

53. The following account draws upon many sources, including articles in the *St. Louis Globe-Democrat* and *St. Louis Post-Dispatch;* Donald F. Kirby, Frank deLeeuw, and William Silverman, "Residential Zoning and Equal Housing Opportunities: A Case Study in Black Jack, Missouri" (Washington, D.C.: Urban Institute, 1972); *Park View Heights Corp. v. City of Black Jack,* 467 F.2d (1972), reversing: 335 F.Supp. 899 (1971); *U.S. v. City of Black Jack,* Civ. Action No. 71; "Confrontation in Black Jack," in *Land-Use Controls Annual* (Chicago: American Society of Planning Officials, 1972); Danielson, *The Politics of Exclusion.*

54. Jack Quigley, *St. Louis Post-Dispatch,* June 15, 1971.

55. Quoted in William K. Reilly, ed., *The Use of Land: A Citizen's Guide for Urban Growth* (New York: Crowell, 1973), p. 90.

56. *Dailey v. City of Lawton,* 425 F.2d 1037 (1970).

57. *Kennedy Park Homes v. City of Lackawanna,* 436 F.2d 108 (1971).

58. Editorial, *St. Louis Post-Dispatch,* April 5, 1971.

59. Quoted in *St. Louis Globe-Democrat,* January 11, 1977.

60. In 1975, the Supreme Court made it more difficult to challenge exclusionary zoning in federal courts by "refusing standing"—dismissing a case on the grounds that the plaintiffs had no right to sue. Those who want to challenge an exclusionary ordinance must prove "distinct and palpable injury"; a suit cannot be based on general injury to those who do not live in the town, but want to live there. See *Warth v. Seldin,* 442 U.S. 490, 1975.

61. See *James v. Valtierra* 91 S.Ct. 133 (1971) and *Shaffer v. Valtierra,* 402 U.S. 137 (1971).

62. *Southern Burlington County NAACP v. Township of Mount Laurel,* 67 N.J. 151, 336 A.2d 713, cert. denied, 423 U.S. 808 (1975).

63. Quoted in Ronald Sullivan, "Jersey's Zoning Laws Are Upset," *New York Times,* March 25, 1975.

64. Joseph F. Sullivan, "Restless Seeker for Justice," *New York Times,* January 22, 1983; Anthony DePalma, "N.J. Housing Woes Are All Over the Map," *New York Times,* April 17, 1983.

65. Robert Hanley, "After 7 Years, Town Remains Under Fire for Its Zoning Code," *New York Times,* January 22, 1983.

66. *Southern Burlington County NAACP v. Township of Mount Laurel,* 92 N.J. 158, 456 A.2d 390, 410 (1983).

67. Quoted in Hanley, "After 7 Years."

68. Quoted in DePalma, "N.J. Housing Woes."

69. Robert Hanley, "Some Jersey Towns, Yielding to Courts, Let in Modest Homes," *New York Times,* February 29, 1984.

70. 1985 N.J. Sess. Law Serv. 222 (West).

71. Joseph F. Sullivan, "Byrne Is Displeased by a Report on Housing Quotes in the Suburbs," *New York Times,* December 9, 1976.

72. Anthony DePalma, "Mount Laurel: Slow, Painful Progress," *New York Times,* May 1, 1988.

73. Anthony DePalma, "Subsidized Housing Hurt in Ailing Market," *New York Times,* May 15, 1990.

74. DePalma, "Mount Laurel."

75. John F. Kain, "Housing Market Discrimination and Black Suburbanization in the 1980's," in *Divided Neighborhoods: Changing Patterns of Racial Segregation,* ed. Gary A. Tobin (Newbury Park, Cal.: Sage, 1987), p. 68.

76. Thomas A. Clark, "The Suburbanization Process and Residential Segregation," in *Divided Neighborhoods: Changing Patterns of Racial Segregation,* ed. Gary A. Tobin (Newbury Park, Cal.: Sage, 1987), p. 115; Larry Long and Diane Deare,

"The Suburbanization of Blacks," *American Demographics* 3 (1981), cited in Douglas S. Massey and Nancy A. Denton, "Suburbanization and Segregation in U.S. Metropolitan Areas," *American Journal of Sociology* 94, no. 3 (November 1988): 592–626.

77. James Heilbrun, *Urban Economics and Public Policy,* 2d ed. (New York: St. Martin's Press, 1981), p. 330. Researchers at Northwestern University found that poor black women who moved to the suburbs of Chicago were more likely to find jobs than those who moved to another neighborhood in the city. Reported in Dirk Johnson, "Move to the Suburbs Spurs the Poor to Seek Work," *Albany Times Union,* May 1, 1990.

78. John R. Logan and Harvey L. Molotch, *Urban Fortunes: The Political Economy of Place* (Berkeley: University of California Press, 1987), p. 195.

79. John M. Stahura and Richard C. Hollinger, "Black and White Population Growth Since World War II: A Comparison of Interdecade Models," *Journal of Urban Affairs* 9, no. 3 (1987): 245.

80. Logan and Molotch, *Urban Fortunes,* p. 194.

81. For discussion of how the segregation index is calculated, see John E. Farley, "Metropolitan Housing Segregation in 1980: The St. Louis Case," *Urban Affairs Quarterly* 18, no. 3 (March 1983), p. 349.

82. For evidence on this point, see Clark, "The Suburbanization Process and Residential Segregation"; Massey and Denton, "Suburbanization and Segregation in U.S. Metropolitan Areas."

83. Farley, "Metropolitan Housing Segregation," p. 351.

84. Massey and Denton, "Suburbanization and Segregation in U.S. Metropolitan Areas," p. 605.

85. Clark, "The Suburbanization Process and Residential Segregation," p. 135.

86. For citations of the literature on all these points, see Massey and Denton, "Suburbanization and Segregation in U.S. Metropolitan Areas," pp. 595–594.

87. John Logan and Richard Alba, "Locational Returns to Human Capital," State University of New York at Albany (April 1990). Interestingly, Asians tend to live in *more* desirable suburbs than their class position would predict.

88. For a summary of the evidence against the class theory of segregation, see Joe T. Darden, "Choosing Neighbors and Neighborhoods: The Role of Race in Housing Preference," in *Divided Neighborhoods: Changing Patterns of Racial Segregation,* ed. Gary A. Tobin (Newbury Park, Cal.: Sage, 1987), pp. 16–17.

89. Kain, "Housing Market Discrimination," p. 77.

90. John Farley, *Segregated City, Segregated Suburbs: Are They Products of Black-White Socioeconomic Differentials?* (Edwardsville: Southern Illinois University, 1983), cited in Darden, "Choosing Neighbors and Neighborhoods," p. 16.

91. Thomas F. Pettigrew summarizes the survey evidence on residential preferences: "Attitudes on Race and Housing: A Social Psychological View," in *Segregation in Residential Areas,* ed. Amos H. Hawley and V. P. Rock (Washington, D.C..: National Academy of Sciences, 1973).

92. Darden, "Choosing Neighbors and Neighborhoods," p. 25; Thomas F. Muller, *Contemporary Suburban America* (Englewood Cliffs, N.J.: Prentice-Hall), p. 95; Reynolds Farley et al., "Chocolate City, Vanilla Suburbs: Will the Trend Toward Racially Separate Communities Continue?" in *Cities and Urban Living,* ed. Mark Baldassare (New York: Columbia University Press, 1983), pp. 302–303.

93. P. B. Sheatsley, "White Attitudes Toward the Negro," *Daedalus* 95 (1966): 217–238, and National Opinion Research Center, *National Data Program for the Social Sciences,* General Social Survey (Chicago: National Opinion Research Center, University of Chicago, 1972), both cited in Farley et al., pp. 294–295.

94. Farley et al.

95. *United States v. Yonkers Board of Education,* 624 F. 54 pp. 1276 (1985).

96. *United States v. Yonkers,* 837 F. 2d 1181 (1987).

97. Sarah Rimer, "Council Backs Housing Order in Yonkers," *New York Times,* January 29, 1988.

98. *Spallone v. United States,* 110 s. Ct. 625 (1990).

99. Edward J. Fagan, quoted in James Feron, "Tempers Flare at a Hearing in Yonkers Fund Transfer," *New York Times,* September 9, 1988.

100. J. Anthony Lukas, "Beyond Yonkers: Cracking Gilded Ghettos," *New York Times,* August 23, 1988.

101. Adna Weber, "Annexation—Legal Adjustment to Suburban Growth," *North American Review* (May 1898), excerpted in *Urban America: A History with Documents,* ed. Bayrd Still (Boston: Little, Brown, 1974), p. 258.

102. William Julius Wilson, *The Truly Disadvantaged: The Inner City, the Underclass, and Public Policy* (Chicago: University of Chicago Press, 1987).

103. Louis H. Masotti and Jeffrey K. Hadden, eds., *The Urbanization of the Suburbs* (Beverly Hills, Calif.: Sage, 1973).

104. Real Estate Research Corporation, *The Costs of Sprawl* (Washington, D.C.: Government Printing Office, 1974), p. 3.

105. John Herbers, *The New Heartland: America's Flight Beyond the Suburbs and How It Is Changing Our Future* (New York: Times Books, 1986), p. 159.

106. Real Estate Research Corporation, *The Costs of Sprawl,* p. 2.

107. William H. Whyte, Jr., "Urban Sprawl," in *The Exploding Metropolis,* ed. The Editors of *Fortune* (Garden City, N.Y.: Doubleday, 1958), p. 115.

108. Regional Plan Association, *Annual Report, 1990* (New York: Regional Plan Association, 1989), p. 3.

109. Kasarda, "urban Change and Minority Opportunities," Ihlanfeldt and Sjoquist, "The Impact of Job Decentralization."

110. Dolores Hayden, *Redesigning the American Dream: The Future of Housing, Work, and Family Life* (New York: Norton, 1984), p. 50.

111. Ann R. Markusen, "City Spatial Structure, Women's Household Work, and National Urban Policy," in *Women and the American City,* ed. Catherine R. Stimson et al. (Chicago: University of Chicago Press, 1980), pp. 20–41.

112. A study of 825 households in San Jose, California, found that high-density residential areas provided higher levels of satisfaction for women than conventional low-density suburban developments. Donald N. Rothblatt, Daniel J. Garr, and Jo Sprague, *The Suburban Environment and Women* (New York: Praeger Holt, 1979).

113. Matthew L. Wald, "How Dreams of Clean Air Get Stuck in Traffic," *New York Times,* March 11, 1990.

114. Robert Cervero, "Unlocking Suburban Gridlock," *Journal of the American Planning Association* (August 1986): 389.

115. J. A. Lindley, "Urban Freeway Congestion: Quantification of the Problem and Effectiveness of Potential Solutions," *ITE Journal* 57 (1987): 27–32, cited in Robert Cervero, "Jobs-Housing Balancing and Regional Mobility," *Journal of the American Planning Association* (Spring 1989): 136.

116. Cervero, "Jobs-Housing Balancing," p. 140. Only 2.5 percent of the people who work in Oak Park live there.

117. Craig R. Whitney, "Scientists Warn of Dangers in a Warming Earth," *New York Times,* May 26, 1990.

118. James A. Dunn, Jr., *Miles to Go: European and American Transportation Policies* (Cambridge, Mass.: MIT Press, 1981), p. 150.

119. Wald, "How Dreams of Clean Air Get Stuck in Traffic."

120. Peter G. Newman and Jeffrey R. Kenworthy, "Gasoline Consumption and Cities," *Journal of the American Planning Association* (Winter 1989), p. 26–27.

121. Real Estate Research Corporation, *The Costs of Sprawl,* p. 2.

122. *Ibid.,* pp. 4, 5.

123. Gregory P. Nowell, *A Crack in the Empire of Oil: The Plan to Phase Out Gasoline and Diesel Fuels in the South Coast Air Quality Management District* (Cambridge, Mass.: International Motor Vehicle Program, Massachusetts Institute of Technology, 1990).

124. Jackson, *Crabgrass Frontier,* p. 304.

CHAPTER 10

1. Bradley R. Rice, "Searching for the Sunbelt," in *Searching for the Sunbelt: Historical Perspectives on a Region,* ed. Raymond A. Mohl (Knoxville: University of Tennessee Press, 1990), p. 217.

2. David R. Goldfield, *Cotton Fields and Skyscrapers: Southern City and Region, 1706–1980* (Baton Rouge: Louisiana State University Press, 1982), p. 192, cited in Rice, "Searching for the Sunbelt," p. 218.

3. Sam Allis, "Regions," *Wall Street Journal,* April 14, 1981, cited in Rice, "Searching for the Sunbelt," p. 218.

4. Kevin P. Phillips, *The Emerging Republican Majority* (New Rochelle, N.Y.: Arlington House, 1969).

5. *New York Daily News,* "Ford to City: Drop Dead!" (October 29, 1975), p. 1.

6. Kirkpatrick Sale, *Power Shift: The Rise of the Southern Rim and Its Challenge to the Eastern Establishment* (New York: Random House, 1975).

7. "The Second War Between the States," *Business Week,* May 17, 1976.

8. Carl Abbott, *The New Urban America: Growth and Politics in Sunbelt Cities* (Chapel Hill: University of North Carolina Press, 1987), p. 6.

9. Sale, *Power Shift,* p. 11.

10. Bernard Weinstein and Harold Gross, interview quoted in Abbott, *The New Urban America,* p. 4.

11. Bruce J. Schulman, *From Cotton Belt to Sunbelt: Federal Policy, Economic Development, and the Transformation of the South, 1938–1980* (New York: Oxford University Press, 1991), chap. 2.

12. Abbott, *The New Urban America,* p. 22.

13. David R. Goldfield and Howard N. Rabinowitz, "The Vanishing Sunbelt," in *Searching for the Sunbelt: Historical Perspectives on a Region,* ed. Raymond A. Mohl (Knoxville: University of Tennessee Press, 1990), p. 224.

14. *Ibid.,* p. 231.

15. William H. Frey, "Metropolitan America: Beyond the Transition," *Population Bulletin* 45, no. 2 (July 1990), p. 14.

16. *Ibid.*

17. U.S. Bureau of the Census, *1980 Census of Population,* Supplementary Reports, *Standard Metropolitan Statistical Areas and Standard Consolidated Statistical Areas* (Washington, D.C.: Government Printing Office, 1981), p. 49, Table 3.

18. U.S. Bureau of the Census, *Statistical Abstract of the United States, 1980,* 101st ed., (Washington, D.C.: Government Printing Office, 1981), p. 10; U.S. Bureau of the Census, *Statistical Abstract of the United States, 1992,* 112th ed., (Washington, D.C.: Government Printing Office. 1992), p.22.

19. U.S. Bureau of the Census, *Local Government Finances in Selected Metropolitan Areas and Large Counties: 1970–1980* (Washington, D.C.: Government Printing Office, 1980), p. 2.

20. Phillip J. Funigiello, *The Challenge to Urban Liberalism: Federal-City Relations During World War II* (Knoxville: University of Tennessee Press, 1978), pp. xi–xii.

21. Samuel J. Eldersveld, "The Influence of Metropolitan Party Pluralities in Presidential Elections Since 1920: A Study of Twelve Key Cities," *American Political Science Review* 43, no. 6 (December 1949), p. 1200.

22. *Ibid.,* p. 1201.

23. John Mollenkopf, *The Contested City* (Princeton, N.J.: Princeton University Press, 1983), p. 83.

24. R. Cohen, "Task for Politicians: Keeping Up with the Votes," *National Journal,* 1981, p. 2037, cited in Robert B. Bradley, "The Changing Political Realities for National Urban Policy in the Eighties," in *Transition to the 21st Century: Prospects and Policies for Economic and Urban-Regional Transformation,* ed. Donald A. Hicks and Norman J. Glickman (Greenwich, Conn.: JAI Press, 1983).

25. Peter A. Lupsha and William J. Siembieda, "The Poverty of Public Services in the Land of Plenty: An Analysis and Interpretation," in *The Rise of the Sunbelt Cities* ed. David C. Perry and Alfred J. Watkins (Beverly Hills, Calif.: Sage, 1977), p. 185.

26. Lupsha and Siembieda, "The Poverty of Public Services," p. 174.

27. Mollenkopf, *The Contested City,* p. 123.

28. *Ibid.,* p. 131.

29. Kevin Phillips predicted this trend in 1968; see *The Emerging Republican Majority.*

30. *New York Times*/CBS News Poll; *New York Times,* November 8, 1984, cited in Gerald Pomper, "The Presidential Election," in Gerald Pomper, ed., *The Election of 1984: Reports and Interpretations* (Chatham, N.J.: Chatham House, 1985), pp. 68–69.

31. "It is the convergence of the interests of the Sunbelt business community and the ideological right-wing that has resulted in the sharpest growth for the Republican party, following the shift of the financial heartland of the GOP South from Wall Street and from downtown Chicago to Houston, Dallas, and Tulsa." Thomas Byrne Edsall, *The New Politics of Inequality* (New York: Norton, 1985), p. 101.

32. Harold Wolman, "The Reagan Urban Policy and Its Impacts," *Urban Affairs Quarterly* 21, no. 3 (March 1986), pp. 311–336.

33. Gerald F. Seib and Alex Kotlowitz, "The Urban Poor Feel Generally Neglected in Presidential Race," *Wall Street Journal,* November 4, 1988.

34. Tom Wicker, "White Flight, Again," *New York Times,* November 18, 1988.

35. For a thorough analysis of the growth of the Sunbelt that emphasizes economic and technological factors, see John D. Kasarda, "The Implications of Contemporary Redistribution Trends for National Urban Policy," *Social Science Quarterly* 61, no. 3 (December 1980), pp. 373–400.

36. Raymond Arsenault, "The End of the Long Hot Summer: The Air Conditioner and Southern Culture," in *Searching for the Sunbelt: Historical Perspectives on a Region,* ed Raymond A. Mohl (Knoxville: University of Tennessee Press, 1990), pp. 176–211.

37. Kirkpatrick Sale, "Six Pillars of the Southern Rim," in *The Fiscal Crisis of American Cities,* ed. Roger E. Alcaly and David Mermelstein (New York: Random House, Vintage Books, 1977), p. 174.

38. For a brief discussion of British regional policies, see James L. Sundquist, *Dispersing Population: What America Can Learn from Europe* (Washington, D.C.: Brookings Institution, 1975), chap. 2.

39. David Pinder, *Regional Economic Development and Policy: Theory and Practice in the European Community* (London: Allen & Unwin, 1983), pp. 13–14.

40. Sundquist, *Dispersing Population,* p. 241.

41. Ann R. Markusen, *Regions: The Economics and Politics of Territory* (Totowa, N.J.: Rowman and Littlefield, 1987), p. 113.

42. Sale, "Six Pillars of the Southern Rim," p. 170.

43. Funigiello, *The Challenge to Urban Liberalism,* pp. 12–13.

44. Abbott, *The New Urban America,* p. 103.

45. Richard O. Boyer and Herbert M. Morais, *Labor's Untold Story* (New York: United Electrical, Radio & Machine Workers of America, 1977), p. 362.

46. Maureen McBreen, "Regional Trends in Federal Defense Expenditures: 1950–76," in *Selected Essays on Patterns of Regional Change: The Changes, the Federal Role, and the Federal Response,* submitted by Senator Henry Bellmon to the Senate Committee on Appropriations (Washington, D.C.: Government Printing Office, 1977), p. 527.

47. A report issued by the Northeast-Midwest Economic Advancement Coalition, cited in Edward C. Burks, "16 Northeast and Midwest States Find Inequities in Defense Outlays," *New York Times,* September 22, 1977.

48. Richard S. Morris, *Bum Rap on America's Cities: The Real Causes of Urban Decline,* (Englewood Cliffs, N.J.: Prentice-Hall, 1978), pp. 148–149.

49. Sale, *Power Shift,* p. 149.

50. Since the early 1970s, exceptions to the seniority rule have been permitted by both parties, and the power of committee chairs has been reduced.

51. Ann R. Markusen, "Regional Planning and Policy: An Essay on the American Exception," Working Paper no. 9 (Center for Urban Policy Research, Rutgers–The State University, Piscataway, N.J., July 1989).

52. See George Peterson, "Federal Tax Policy and Urban Development," in *Central City Economic Development,* ed. Benjamin Chinitz (Cambridge, Mass.: Abt Books, 1979), pp. 67–78.

53. Michael I. Luger, "Federal Tax Incentives as Industrial and Urban Policy," in *Sunbelt/Snowbelt: Urban Development and Regional Restructuring,* ed. Larry Sawers and William K. Tabb (New York: Oxford University Press, 1984), pp. 204–205.

54. John F. Witte, "The Growth and Distribution of Tax Expenditures," in *The Distributional Impacts of Public Policies* ed. Sheldon H. Danziger and Kent E. Portney (New York: St. Martin's Press, 1988), p. 179.

55. For further evidence on the regional bias of the federal tax code, see Roger J. Vaughan, *The Urban Impacts of Federal Policies,* vol. 2, *Economic Development* (Santa Monica, Calif.: Rand Corporation, 1977); Morris, *Bum Rap on America's Cities.*

56. Peter Marcuse, "The Targeted Crisis: On the Ideology of the Urban Fiscal Crisis and Its Causes," *International Journal of Urban and Regional Research* 5, no. 3 (1981): 339.

57. "The Second War Between the States," p. 92.

58. See five-part series in the New York Times, February 8, 9, 10, 11, 12, 1976; "The Second War Between the States"; *Business Week,* May 17, 1976; pp. 92–113; "Federal Spending: The North's Loss Is the Sunbelt's Gain," *National Journal,* June 26, 1976, pp. 878–890.

59. "The Second War Between the States," p. 92.

60. "Federal Spending," p. 881.

61. See Markusen, *Regions,* chap. 8. The Southern Growth Policy Board relinquished its federal monitoring activities to the Congressional Sunbelt Council in January 1981.

62. "Neutral Federal Policies Are Reducing Frostbelt-Sunbelt Spending Imbalances," *National Journal,* February 7, 1981, pp. 233–236.

63. For evidence on the Sunbelt bias of direct federal military expenditures during the Reagan Administration, see the data compiled in *New York Times,* December 20, 1983, cited in Michael Peter Smith, *City, State, and Market: The Political Economy of Urban Society* (New York: Blackwell, 1988), p. 57.

64. Peggy L. Cuciti, "A Nonurban Policy: Recent Public Policy Shifts Affecting Cities," in *The Future of National Urban Policy,* ed. Marshall Kaplan and Franklin James (Durham, N.C.: Duke University Press, 1990), p. 243.

65. David L. Warsh, "War Stories: Defense Spending and the Growth of the Massachusetts Economy," in *The Massachusetts Miracle,* ed. David R. Lampe (Cambridge, Mass.: PERMIT Press, 1988).

66. U.S. Bureau of the Census, *Statistical Abstract of the United States,* 1992, p. 22

67. Figures on the regional effects of the bailout are based on the work of Edward W. Hill. See "The S&L Bailout: Some States Gain, Many More Lose," *Challenge,* May-June 1990, pp. 37–45; "The Regional Tilt in the S&L Bailout," *Center for Urban Policy Research Report* 1, no. 3 (Fall 1990), p. 2.

68. Laurie Ledgard, "Sunbelters Say Bank Problems Are National," *Albany Times Union,* January 14, 1991.

69. See Gary Mormino, "Tampa: From Hell Hole to the Good Life," in *Sunbelt Cities: Politics and Growth Since World War II,* ed. Richard M. Bernard and Bradley R. Rice, (Austin: University of Texas Press, 1983), pp. 138–161; Abbott, *The New Urban America.*

70. Abbott, *The New Urban America,* p. 247.

71. Amy Bridges, "Politics and Growth in Sunbelt Cities," in *Searching for the Sunbelt: Historical Perspectives on a Region* ed. Raymond A. Mohl, (Knoxville: University of Tennessee Press, 1990), p. 2.

72. Robert L. Lineberry, *Equality and Urban Policy: The Distribution of Municipal Public Services* (Beverly Hills, Calif.: Sage, 1977), pp. 55–56, quoted in Abbott, *The New Urban America,* p. 139.

73. Our account of San Antonio's business-dominated reform movement relies on Abbott.

74. Joe R. Feagin, *Free Enterprise City: Houston in Political and Economic Perspective* (New Brunswick, N.J.: Rutgers University Press, 1988).

75. *Ibid.,* p. 7.

76. On the relatively small size of the local public sector in Houston, see Ted Robert Gurr and Desmond S. King, *The State and the City* (Chicago: University of Chicago Press, 1987), chap. 3.

77. The following account of the social costs of growth in Houston relies on Feagin, *Free Enterprise City,* chap. 8.

78. Wayne King, "Houston Spawns a Thriving Underground Market in Sewer Rights," *New York Times,* November 26, 1983.

79. Peter W. G. Newman and Jeffrey R. Kenworthy, "Gasoline Consumption and Cities: A Comparison of U.S. Cities with a Global Survey," *Journal of the American Planning Association,* Winter 1989, p. 26.

80. Lisa Belkin, "Now That City's Grown, They Plan," *New York Times,* February 10, 1991.

81. D'vera Cohn, "Big Is No Longer Beautiful for Many U.S. Communities," *Santa Barbara News-Press,* March 4, 1979, cited in John R. Logan and Harvey L. Molotch, *Urban Fortunes: The Political Economy of Place* (Berkeley: University of California Press, 1987), p. 159.

82. John R. Logan and Min Zhou, "The Adoption of Growth Controls in Suburban Communities," *Social Science Quarterly* 71, no. 1 (March 1990) p. 122.

83. Mark Baldassare, "Suburban Support for No-Growth Policies: Implications for the Growth Revolt," *Journal of Urban Affairs* 12, no. 2 (1990): 198.

84. Robert Reinhold, "Growth in Los Angeles Poses Threat to Bradley," *New York Times,* September 22, 1987.

85. Charles Lockwood and Christopher B. Leinberger, "Los Angeles Comes of Age," *Atlantic Monthly,* January 1988, p. 48.

86. Robert Reinhold, "Southern California Takes Steps to Curb Its Urban Air Pollution," *New York Times,* March 18, 1989.

87. See David E. Dowell, "An Examination of Population-Growth-Management Communities," *Policy Studies Journal* 9 (1980), pp. 414–427; Richard Maurer and James Christenson, "Growth and Nongrowth Orientations of Urban, Suburban, and Rural Mayors: Reflections on the City as a Growth Machine," *Urban Affairs Quarterly* 17 (1982), pp. 350–358; William Protash and Mark Baldassare, "Growth Policies and Community Satisfaction: A Test and Modification of Logan's Theory," *Urban Affairs Quarterly* 18 (1983), pp. 397–412.

88. See Bernard J. Frieden, *The Environmental Protection Hustle* (Cambridge, Mass.: PERMIT Press, 1979).

89. Jane H. Lillydahl and Larry D. Singell, "The Effects of Growth Management on the Housing Market: A Review of the Theoretical and Empirical Evidence," *Journal of Urban Affairs* 9, no. 1 (1987), p. 71. See also M. Bruce Johnson, ed., *Resolving the Housing Crisis: Government Policy, Decontrol, and the Public Interest* (Cambridge, Mass.: Ballinger, 1982).

90. John I. Gilderbloom and Richard P. Appelbaum, *Rethinking Rental Housing* (Philadelphia: Temple University Press, 1988), chap. 6.

91. Logan and Molotch, *Urban Fortunes,* pp. 159–162; John R. Logan and Min Zhou, "Do Suburban Growth Controls Control Growth?" *American Sociological Review* 46 (1989), pp. 175–186.

92. Baldassare, "Suburban Support for No-Growth Policies"; Ronald K Vogel and Bert E. Swanson, "The Growth machine versus the Antigrowth Coalition: The Battle for Our Communities." *Urban Affairs Quarterly* 25, no. 1 (1989), pp. 63–85.

93. See Robyne S. Turner's discussion of Florida's 1985 Growth Management Act, "New Rules for the Growth Game: The Use of Rational State Standards in Land Use Policy," *Journal of Urban Affairs* 12, no. 1 (1990), pp. 35–47.

94. James H. Johnson, Jr., Cloyzelle K. Jones, Walter C. Farrell, and Melvin L. Oliver, "The Los Angeles Rebellion," *Economic Development Quarterly* 6, no. 4 (November 1992), pp. 356–372.

95. U.S. Bureau of the Census, *Census of Population,* Supplementary Reports, *General Social and Economic Characteristics by Race and Spanish Origin: 1980* (Washington, D.C.: Government Printing Office, 1981), p. 2.

96. Mollenkopf, *The Contested City,* p. 247.

97. Robert Goodman, *The Last Entrepreneurs: America's Regional Wars for Jobs and Dollars* (New York: Simon and Schuster, 1979), p. 42. Only one out of fourteen Frostbelt states (Iowa) has a right-to-work law.

98. Smith, *City, State, and Market,* p. 104. See also Peter Applebome, "Economic Boom in the South Ebbs as Advantages Diminish," *New York Times,* August 11, 1989.

99. Charles Jaret and Lyn Meyers, "Black-White Income Inequality and the Urban System of the South," *Journal of Urban Affairs,* 10, no. 2 (1988), pp. 95–118.

100. Lupsha and Siembieda, "The Poverty of Public Services in the Land of Plenty."

101. Clifton McCleskey and Bruce Merrill, "Mexican American Political Behavior in Texas," *Social Science Quarterly* 53 (March 1973), pp. 785–798; Susan Welch, John Comer, and Michael Steinman, "Political Participation Among Mexican Americans: An Exploratory Examination," *Social Science Quarterly* 53 (March 1973), pp. 799–813.

102. *Smith v. Allwright,* 321 U.S. 649 (1944). See the discussion in V. O. Key, *Politics, Parties, and Pressure Groups,* 5th ed. (New York: Crowell, 1964), p. 607.

103. Abbott, *The New Urban America,* p. 217.

104. U.S. Bureau of the Census, *Statistical Abstract of the United States, 1992,* 112th ed. (Washington, D.C.: Government Printing Office, 1992), p. 226.

105. Seth Mydans, "California Expects Hispanic Voters to Transform Politics," *New York Times,* January 27, 1991.

106. For more information on the neighborhood organizing movement, see Harry C. Boyte, *The Backyard Revolution* (Philadelphia: Temple University Press, 1980); Robert Fisher, *Let the People Decide: Neighborhood Organizing in America* (Boston: Twayne, 1984). The following account of the neighborhood movement in San Antonio relies heavily on Abbott, *The New Urban America,* chap. 9.

107. Peter K. Eisinger, *The Rise of the Entrepreneurial State: State and Local Economic Development Policy in the United States* (Madison: University of Wisconsin Press, 1988).

108. For evidence of the shift, see Kenneth K. Wong, *City Choices: Education and Housing* (Albany: State University of New York Press, 1990), p. 16.

109. See Roger Friedland, Frances Fox Piven, and Robert R. Alford, "Political Conflict, Urban Structure, and the Fiscal Crisis," in *Comparing Public Policies,*

ed. Douglas E. Ashford (Beverly Hills, Calif.: Sage, 1978), pp. 197–225; Todd Swanstrom, "The Limits of Strategic Planning for Cities," *Journal of Urban Affairs* 9, no. 2 (1987), pp. 139–157.

CHAPTER 11

1. U.S. Office of Management and Budget, *Special Analyses, Budget of the United States Government: Fiscal Year 1978* (Washington, D.C.: Government Printing Office, 1979), p. 276.

2. Donald H. Haider, *When Governments Come to Washington: Governors, Mayors, and Intergovernmental Lobbying* (New York: The Free Press, 1974), p. 109.

3. U.S. Advisory Commission on Intergovernmental Relations, *Eleventh Annual Report,* (Washington, D.C.: Government Printing Office, 1970), p. 1.

4. Michael Reagan, *The New Federalism* (New York: Oxford University Press, 1972), p. 97.

5. Quoted in Timothy B. Clark, John K. Iglehart, and William Lilley III, "New Federalism 1: Return of Power to States and Cities Looms as Theme of Nixon's Second-Term Domestic Policy," *National Journal,* December 16, 1972, p. 1911.

6. U.S. Congress, House Committee of the Whole on the State of the Union, *The State of the Union, Address of the President of the United States*, House, 92d Cong., 1st sess., January 1971, pp. 4–5.

7. H. Res. 4185, 92d Cong., 1st sess., 1971.

8. U.S. Office of Management and Budget, *Special Analyses, Budget of the United States Government: Fiscal Year 1972* (Washington, D.C.: Government Printing Office, 1973), p. 237.

9. W. W. Heller, *New Dimensions in Political Economy* (Cambridge, Mass.: Harvard University Press, 1967), p. 129.

10. Richard E. Thompson, *Revenue Sharing: A New Era in Federalism* (Washington, D.C.: Revenue Sharing Advisory Service, 1973), p. 20.

11. *Ibid.*, pp. 4, 45. For discussions of the politics of passing the legislation, see also Paul R. Dommel, *The Politics of Revenue Sharing* (Bloomington and London: Indiana University Press, 1974); Richard P. Nathan, Allen D. Manvel, Susannah E. Caulkins, et al. *Monitoring Revenue Sharing* (Washington, D.C.: Brookings Institution, 1975).

12. U.S. Congress, Joint Committee on Internal Revenue and Taxation, *Summary of Testimony on General Revenue Sharing at Public Hearings, June 2 to June 28, 1971, Held by the Committee on Ways and Means on the Subject of General Revenue Sharing* (committee print), 92d Cong., 1st sess., 1971, pp. 2, 14; Thompson, *Revenue Sharing*, pp. 55–56.

13. Statement of the AFL-CIO Executive Council on Revenue Sharing, Bal Harbour, Fla., February 15, 1971, pp. 2–3, cited in Thompson, *Revenue Sharing*, p. 67. Dommel cites this opposition by organized labor as a major contributing factor to

Lyndon Johnson's lack of enthusiasm for the revenue-sharing concept (*The Politics of Revenue Sharing*, p. 51).

14. Reagan, *The New Federalism*, p. 117.

15. *Ibid.*, pp. 130–131.

16. U.S. Congress, Joint Committee on Internal Revenue and Taxation, *Summary of Testimony*, p. 8; Thompson, *Revenue Sharing*, p. 103.

17. National League of Cities, U.S. Conference of Mayors, and International City Management Association, *The Fiscal Plight of American Cities* (National League of Cities and ICMA, 1974) reprinted in Thompson, *Revenue Sharing*, p. 145.

18. Robert S. Benson and Harold Wolman, eds., *The National Urban Coalition Counterbudget: A Blueprint for Changing National Priorities, 1971–1976,* foreword by Sol M. Linowitz (New York: Praeger, 1971), p. 129.

19. National League of Cities, U.S. Conference of Mayors, and the International City Management Association, *The Fiscal Plight of American Cities,* reprinted in Thompson, *Revenue Sharing*, pp. 130–132.

20. *Washington Post,* March 22, 1971, cited in Thompson, *Revenue Sharing,* p. 69.

21. *Newsweek,* May 24, 1971, p. 94.

22. Thompson, *Revenue Sharing,* p. 72.

23. *Ibid.*, pp. 114–116.

24. *Ibid.*, p. 118.

25. Public Law 92-15, 92d Cong. (1972).

26. Haider, *When Governments Come to Washington,* p. 64.

27. Senator Howard Baker (Republican from Tennessee), quoted in Thompson, *Revenue Sharing,* p. 120.

28. U.S. Department of the Treasury, Office of Revenue Sharing, *Reported Uses of General Revenue Sharing Funds 1974-1975: A Tabulation and Analysis of Data from Actual Use Report 5* (Washington, D.C.: Government Printing Office, 1966), p. 5.

29. U.S. Department of the Treasury, Office of Revenue Sharing, *Revenue Sharing: The First Actual Use Reports,* by David A. Caputo and Richard L. Cole (Washington, D.C.: Government Printing Office, 1974), pp. 10, 12, 29.

30. Ibid., p. 25.

31. *Ibid.,* pp. 4–5.

32. *Ibid.*

33. Quoted in U.S. Department of the Treasury, Office of Revenue Sharing, *Renewal of Revenue Sharing* (Washington, D.C.: Government Printing Office, 1975), p. 11.

34. For a discussion of this topic, see Richard P. Nathan, Charles F. Adams, Jr., et al., with the assistance of Andre Juneau and James W. Fossett, *Revenue Sharing: The Second Round* (Washington, D.C.: Brookings Institution, 1977), pp. 1–23.

35. *Congressional Record,* February 20, 1973, p. 746, cited in *ibid.*, p. 2.

36. See, e.g., *Congressional Record,* February 22, 1973, p. 987; *Congressional Record,* March 1, 1973, p. 1160.

37. *Revenue Sharing Bulletin,* July 1973, p. 2.

38. Nathan, Adams, et al., *Revenue Sharing,* p. 171.

39. Housing and Community Development Act of 1974, sec. 101.

40. Michael J. Rich, "Federal Aid to Cities: Patterns of City Participation and Funding Distributions, 1950–1986," *Urban Resources* 5, no. 2 (Winter 1989), p. 7.

41. Michael J. Rich, "National Goals and Local Choices: Distributing Federal Aid to the Poor" (Unpublished ms., October 1991), p. 27.

42. Quoted in Deil S. Wright, *Understanding Intergovernmental Relations,* 2d ed. (Monterey, Calif.: Brooks/Cole, 1982), p. 59.

43. Walter Heller, *New Dimensions in Political Economy* (Cambridge, Mass.: Harvard University Press, 1967), p. 142.

44. Charles L. Schultze, *The Politics and Economics of Public Spending* (Washington, D.C.: Brookings Institution, 1968), p. 105.

45. Timothy Conlan, *New Federalism: Intergovernmental Reform from Nixon to Reagan* (Washington, D.C.: Brookings Institution, 1988), p. 9.

46. U.S. Office of Management and Budget, *Special Analyses: Fiscal Year 1972,* p. 237.

47. Quoted in Rich, "National Goals and Local Choices," p. 33.

48. Quoted in *ibid.*

49. *Ibid.,* p. 66.

50. Housing and Community Development Act of 1974, sec. 104(a).

51. Most of the funds are allocated to entitlement cities with populations of 50,000 or more, SMSA central cities, and certain urban counties. Jurisdictions that participated in the previous categorical programs folded into the Housing and Community Development Act also received "hold-harmless" grants under which their level of funding could not decline for a three-year period. About 20 percent of the monies are distributed without regard to the entitlement formulas. These funds represent the competitive portion of the program.

52. See the Community Development Monitor series, *Housing and Development Reporter,* 1976.

53. "New Directions Cited in First Annual Block Grant Reports," *Housing and Development Reporter,* January 12, 1976, p. 761.

54. U.S. Department of Housing and Urban Development, Office of Community Planning and Development, Office of Evaluation, *Housing and Community Development Act of 1974, Community Development Block Grant Program: First Annual Report* (Washington, D.C.: Government Printing Office, 1975), p. 38.

55. Reported in *Housing and Development Reporter,* January 10, 1977, p. 684.

56. Quoted from the Report of the Southern Regional Council in *Housing and Development Reporter,* April 5, 1976, p. 1051.

57. Interview by Sharon Cribbs (investigator for the Southern Governmental Monitoring Project) with Nathaniel Hill, Director, Department of Human Resources, Little Rock, Arkansas (Summer 1975), quoted in Southern Governmental Monitoring Project, *A Time for Accounting: The Housing and Community Development Act in the South,* A Monitoring Report by Raymond

Brown with Ann Coil and Carol Rose (Atlanta: Southern Regional Council, 1976), p. 53.

58. *Ibid.*, p. 51.

59. For a review of this and other studies, see Carl E. Van Horn, "Decentralized Policy Delivery" (Paper presented at the Workshop on Policy Analysis in State and Local Government, State University of New York–Stonybrook, May 22–24, 1977); Carl E. Van Horn, *Policy Implementation in the Federal System* (Lexington, Mass.: Lexington Books, 1979).

60. "Grants with Strings Attached," *St. Louis Post-Dispatch,* August 6, 1977, p. 4A; reprinted from the *Washington Post.*

61. *Ibid.*

62. Dennis R. Judd and Alvin H. Mushkatel, "Inequality of Urban Services: The Impact of the Community Development Act," in *The Politics of Urban Public Services,* ed. Richard Rich (Lexington, Mass.: Lexington Books, 1981).

63. See M. Leanne Lachman, "Planning for Community Development: A Proposed Approach," *Journal of Housing* 32, no. 2 (February 1975): 58.

64. *Ibid.*, p. 58.

65. Roger Starr, "Making New York Smaller," in *Revitalizing the Northeast,* ed. George Sternlieb and James W. Hughes (New Brunswick, N.J.: Rutgers University Press, 1978).

66. Jerome Pratter, "How Cities Can Grow Old Gracefully," *House Committee on Banking, Finance, and Urban Affairs Report* (Washington, D.C.: Government Printing Office, 1978).

67. *Ibid.*

68. James L. Greer, "Urban Planning and Redevelopment in Chicago: The Political Economy of the Chicago 21 Plan" (Paper presented at the Annual Meeting of the Midwest Political Science Association, Chicago, April 19–21, 1979).

69. Alvin H. Mushkatel and Howard Lasus, "Geographic Targeting of Community Development Funds in Denver: Who Benefits?" (Paper presented at the Annual Meeting of the Western Social Science Association, Albuquerque, N.M., April 23–26, 1980).

70. Quoted in Robert L. Joller, "HUD Secretary Quiets Critics," *St. Louis Post-Dispatch,* April 18, 1977, p. 38.

71. Reprinted in Roy Bahl, ed., *The Fiscal Outlook for Cities: Implications of a National Urban Policy* (Syracuse, N.Y.: Syracuse University Press, 1978), pp. 111–127.

72. *Ibid.*, p. 112.

73. State of Illinois, Bureau of the Budget, Federal Relations Unit, *Equity in Federal Funding: A First Step* (Springfield: State of Illinois, Bureau of the Budget, 1976), p. 2.

74. Rochelle L. Stansfield, "Federalism Report: Government Seeks the Right Formula for Community Development Funds," *National Journal,* February 12, 1977, p. 242.

75. See State of Illinois, Bureau of the Budget, Federal Relations Unit, *Equity in Federal Funding,* p. 32.

76. Refer to Stansfield, "Federalism Report."

77. Ann R. Markusen, "The Urban Impact Analysis: A Critical Forecast," in *The Urban Impact of Federal Policies,* ed. Norman Glickman (Baltimore: Johns Hopkins University Press, 1979). Also see discussion by Ann R. Markusen, Annalee Saxenian, and Marc A. Weiss, "Who Benefits from Intergovernmental Transfers?," in *Cities Under Stress: The Fiscal Crises of Urban America,* ed. Robert W. Burchell and David Listokin (New Brunswick, N.J.: Center for Urban Research, 1981), p. 656; Stansfield, "Federalism Report."

78. See Stansfield, "Federalism Report"; Joel Havemann, Rochelle L. Stansfield, and Neal R. Pierce, "Federal Spending: The North's Loss Is the Sunbelt's Gain," *National Journal,* June 1976, p. 1031.

79. Robert Reinhold, "More Aid on Way for Older Cities," *St. Louis Post-Dispatch,* May 9, 1977, p. 3C, reprinted from the *New York Times.*

80. Calculated from Richard DeLeon and Richard LeGates, "Beyond Cybernetic Federalism in Community Development," *Urban Law Annual* 15 (1978): 31. Also see Paul R. Dommel, "Block Grants for Community Development: Decentralized Decision-Making," in *Fiscal Crisis in American Cities: The Federal Response,* ed. L. Kenneth Hubbell (Cambridge, Mass.: Ballinger, 1979), pp. 236–241.

81. Ann R. Markusen and David Wilmoth, "The Political Economy of National Urban Policy in the U.S.A.: 1976–81," *Canadian Journal of Regional Science* (Summer 1982.)

82. John P. Ross, "Countercyclical Revenue Sharing," in *Fiscal Crisis in American Cities: The Federal Response,* ed. L. Kenneth Hubbell (Cambridge, Mass.: Ballinger, 1979), pp. 256–261.

83. *Ibid.,* p. 266.

84. *Ibid.,* pp. 266–267.

85. U.S. Department of Housing and Urban Development, "The Urban Fiscal Crisis: Fact or Fantasy (A Reply)," in *Cities Under Stress: The Fiscal Crises of Urban America,* ed. Robert W. Burchell and David Listokin (New Brunswick, N.J.: Center for Urban Research, 1981), p. 151.

86. Markusen and Wilmoth, "The Political Economy of National Urban Policy," p. 15.

87. *Ibid.,* p. 15.

88. "Washington Update: Administration Officials, Mayors Have Love Fest," *National Journal,* January 29, 1977, p. 189.

89. *New York Times,* October 23, 1981.

90. President's Commission for a National Agenda for the Eighties, *A National Agenda for the Eighties* (Washington, D.C.: Government Printing Office, 1980), p. 66.

91. *Ibid.*

92. *Ibid.,* p. 67.

93. *Ibid.,* p. 4.

94. *Ibid.,* p. 66.

95. Timothy K. Barnekov, Daniel Rich, and Robert Warren, "The New Privatism, Federalism, and the Future of Urban Governance: National Urban Policy in the 1980s," *Journal of Urban Affairs* 3, no. 4 (Fall 1981): 3.

96. U.S. Department of Housing and Urban Development, *The President's National Urban Policy Report* (Washington, D.C.: Government Printing Office, 1982), pp. 2, 23.

97. *Ibid.,* pp. 54–57.

98. *Ibid.,* p. 14.

99. Conlan, *New Federalism,* p. 137.

100. *Ibid.*

101. *Ibid.,* p. 135.

102. *Ibid.,* p. 138.

103. Quoted in Sar A. Levitan and Clifford M. Johnson, *Beyond the Safety Net: Reviving the Promise of Opportunity in America* (Cambridge, Mass.: Ballinger, 1984), p. 155.

104. *Ibid.*

105. David B. Robertson and Dennis R. Judd, *The Development of American Public Policy: The Structure of Policy Restraint* (Glenview, Ill.: Scott, Foresman, 1989), p. 233.

106. Conlan, *New Federalism,* p. 153.

107. George E. Peterson et al., *The Reagan Block Grants: What Have We Learned* (Washington, D.C.: Urban Institute, 1986), p. 21.

108. U.S. Congress, Joint Economic Committee, *Emergency Interim Survey: Fiscal Condition of Forty-eight Large Cities,* (Washington, D.C.: Government Printing Office, 1982), p. 6.

109. Henry J. Aaron and Associates, "Nondefense Programs," *in Setting National Priorities: The 1983 Budget,* ed. Joseph A. Pechman (Washington, D.C.: Brookings Institution, 1982), p. 119.

110. Quoted in Conlan, *New Federalism,* p. 224.

111. Quoted in *New York Times,* January 21, 1982.

112. Quoted in *ibid.*

113. Conlan, *New Federalism,* p. 224.

114. *Ibid.,* p. 147.

115. Quoted in Rochelle L. Stansfield, "New Federalism: A Neatly Wrapped Package with Explosives Inside," *National Journal,* February 27, 1982, p. 359.

116. White House press release, March 7, 1983.

117. James H. Johnson, Jr., Cloyzelle K. Jones, Walter C. Farrell, Jr., and Melvin L. Oliver, "The Los Angeles Rebellion: A Retrospective View," *Economic Development Quarterly* 6, no. 4 (November 1992): 356–372.

118. Clifford Krauss, "Congress Passes Aid to Cities," *New York Times,* June 9, 1992, p. A20.

119. Gerald Pomper, "The Presidential Election," in *The Election of 1984: Reports and Interpretations,* ed. Gerald Pomper (Chatham, N.J.: Chatham House, 1985), pp. 68–69.

120. State of Missouri, *Official Manual, 1985–1986* (Jefferson City: State of Missouri, 1986).

121. "Mayors Plot to Regain Influence," *St. Louis Post-Dispatch,* March 2, 1987, p. 12A.

122. Richard Scammon, *American Votes,* various editions (Washington, D.C.: Elections Research Center, Congressional Quarterly).

CHAPTER 12

1. Quoted in Michael deCourcy Hinds, "Cash Crises Force Localities in U.S. to Slash Services," *New York Times,* June 3, 1991.

2. Michael deCourcy Hinds, "Philadelphia Transit Officials Warn of a Shutdown," *New York Times,* April 16, 1991.

3. Josh Barbanel, "Dinkins Outlines Fiscal Crisis Plan with Drastic Cuts," *New York Times,* May 5, 1991; Todd S. Purdum, "Dinkins Woos Rohatyn's Aid on Budget Gap," *New York Times,* November 7, 1991.

4. Fox Butterfield, "Insolvent Boston Suburb Faces Threat of Takeover," *New York Times,* September 8, 1991.

5. George Judson, "In Bridgeport, Higher Taxes Add Injury to Insult," *New York Times,* June 10, 1991; "Bridgeport Declares It Can't Go It Alone," *New York Times,* June 16, 1991.

6. For general accounts of urban fiscal crises, see David Rosenbaum, "States and Cities with Budget Deficits May Slow Rebound," *New York Times,* May 31, 1991; Michael deCourcy Hinds, "Cash Crises."

7. Michael A. Pagano, *City Fiscal Conditions in 1991* (Washington, D.C.: National League of Cities, 1991).

8. Bureau of the Census, *Statistical Abstract of the United States, 1992,* 112th ed. (Washington, D.C.: Government Printing Office, 1992), pp. 154, 280, 297, 298.

9. *Ibid.,* p. 299.

10. *Ibid.,* p. 302.

11. George E. Peterson, "Finance," in *The Urban Predicament,* ed. William Gorham and Nathan Glazer (Washington, D.C.: Urban Institute, 1976), p. 41.

12. *Business Statistics: 1961–88, Survey of Current Business,* March 1991, cited in Roy Bahl et al., "The Fiscal Conditions of U.S. Cities at the Beginning of the 1990s" (Paper presented Urban Institute Conference on Big City Governance and Fiscal Choices, Los Angeles, Calif., June 6–7, 1991), Table 12.

13. This is known as "Baumol's disease," after the economist who first fully analyzed the problem. William Baumol, "The Microeconomics of Unbalanced Growth," *American Economic Review* 57 (June 1967), pp. 415–526.

14. U.S. Advisory Commission on Intergovernmental Relations, *Significant Features of Fiscal Federalism, 1985–86 Edition* (Washington, D.C.: Government Printing Office, 1986), p. 71. These data exclude school district employees. If they were included, public employee earnings would be 104.7 percent of private wages in 1975.

15. U.S. Advisory Commission, *Significant Features, 1980–81,* p. 71.

16. *Ibid.,* p. 19.

17. See Roger W. Schmenner, "The Determination of Municipal Employee Wages," *Review of Economics and Statistics* 60 (February 1973), pp. 83–90; Orley Ashenfelter, "The Effect of Unions on Wages in the Public Sector: The Case of Fire Fighters," *Industrial and Labor Relations Review* 24 (January 1971), pp. 191–202; George E. Peterson, "Finance," pp. 108–109.

18. U.S. Bureau of the Census, *Statistical Abstract of the United States, 1992,* p. 304.

19. *Ibid.*

20. Larry C. Ledebur and William R. Barnes, *City Distress: Metropolitan Disparities and Economic Growth* (Washington, D.C.: National League of Cities, 1991), pp. 2, 6. Figures based on the 85 largest metropolitan areas.

21. Jonathan Kozol, *Rachel and Her Children: Homeless Families in America* (New York: Crown, 1988), p. 14.

22. "Homicide Records Set in 3 Big Cities," *New York Times,* January 3, 1992.

23. Bahl et al., "The Fiscal Conditions of U.S. Cities," pp. 5–6.

24. Helen F. Ladd and John Yinger, *America's Ailing Cities: Fiscal Health and the Design of Urban Policy,* updated ed. (Baltimore: Johns Hopkins University Press, 1989), p. 180.

25. *Garcia v. San Antonio Metropolitan Transit Authority,* 469 U.S. 528 (1985).

26. Employment Standards Administration, *Minimum Wage and Maximum Hours Standards Under the Fair Labor Standards Act* (Washington, D.C.: U.S. Environmental Protection Agency, 1986), pp. 110–111; U.S. Congress, House Committee on Education and Labor, *Report to Accompany H.R. 3530, 99th Cong., 1st sess., 1985.* H. Rept. 99-331, p. 30; both cited in Joseph F. Zimmerman, "Federally Induced State and Local Governmental Costs" (Paper presented at the Annual Meeting of the American Political Science Association, Washington, D.C., August 29–September 1, 1991), p. 14.

27. Todd Sloane, "Clean Air Act Likely to Burn Many Municipalities," *City & State,* November 19, 1990, p. 2, cited in Zimmerman, "Federally Induced State and Local Government Costs," p. 12.

28. *Environmental Investments: The Cost of a Clean Environment: A Summary* (Washington, D.C.: U.S. Environmental Protection Agency, 1990), pp. 2–6, cited in Zimmerman, "Federally Induced State and Local Governmental Costs," p. 14.

29. Refer to Richard T. Ely, *Taxation in American States and Cities* (New York: Crowell, 1888), pp. 109–113; Sumner Benson, "A History of the General Property Tax," in *The American Property Tax: Its History, Administration, and Economic Impact,* ed. C. G. Benson, S. Benson, H. McClelland, and P. Thompson (Claremont, Calif.: College Press, 1965), p. 24.

30. E. R. A. Seligman, *Essays in Taxation,* 9th ed. (New York: Macmillan, 1923), p. 24.

31. U.S. Bureau of the Census, *Historical Statistics of the United States: Colonial Times to 1970,* part 2, Bicentennial ed. (Washington, D.C.: Government Printing Office, 1975), p. 1133.

32. Calculated from the data in U.S. Bureau of the Census, *Local Government Finances in Selected Metropolitan Areas and Large Counties: 1969–70,* GF 70, no. 6 (Washington, D.C.: Government Printing Office, 1970), p. 7; U.S. Bureau of the Census, *Local Government Finances in Selected Metropolitan Areas and Large Counties: 1974–75,* GF 75, no. 6 (Washington, D.C.: Government Printing Office, 1976), p. 7.

33. U.S. Bureau of the Census, *Government Finances in 1978–79,* GF 79, no. 5 (Washington, D.C.: Government Printing Office, 1980), p. 64.

34. Peterson, "Finance," p. 52.

35. *Ibid.,* p. 53.

36. Alfred Balk, *The Free List—Property Without Taxes* (New York: Russell Sage Foundation, 1971), pp. 10–12.

37. J. Richard Aronson and John L. Hilley, *Financing State and Local Governments,* 4th ed. (Washington, D.C.: Brookings Institution, 1986), p. 136.

38. Gregory H. Wassall, *Tax-Exempt Property: A Case Study of Hartford, Connecticut* (Hartford, Conn.: John C. Lincoln Institute, 1974), p. 27.

39. Todd Swanstrom, *Capital Cities: Challenges and Opportunities* (Albany, N.Y.: Rockefeller Institute of Government), p. 17.

40. Michael J. Barrett, "The Out-of-Towners," *Boston Globe Magazine* (August 7, 1983).

41. *Walz v. Tax Commission of the City of New York,* 397 U.S. 664. See also Boris I. Bittker, "Churches, Taxes and the Constitution," *Yale Law Review* 78 (July 1969): 1285–1310.

42. Ladd and Yinger, *America's Ailing Cities,* pp. 129–130; see also Michael Wolkoff, *Municipal Tax Abatement: A Two-Edged Sword,* New York Case Studies in Public Management no. 4 (Albany, N.Y.: Rockefeller Institute of Government, 1984).

43. Ladd and Yinger, *America's Ailing Cities,* p. 87.

44. Christopher H. Gadsen and Roger W. Schmenner, "Municipal Income Taxation," in *Local Public Finance and the Fiscal Squeeze: A Case Study,* ed. John R. Meyer and John M. Quigley (New York: Ballinger, 1977), p. 70.

45. Ladd and Yinger, *America's Ailing Cities,* p. 54. Surprisingly, local sales taxes have an even worse export ratio than property taxes.

46. *Ibid.,* p. 293.

47. Eric A. Anderson, "Changing Municipal Finances," *Urban Data Services Reports* 7, no. 12 (Washington, D.C.: International City Manager Association, December 1975), p. 2.

48. See U.S. Department of Housing and Urban Development, *The President's National Urban Policy Report* (Washington, D.C.: Government Printing Office,

1982), esp. p. 23. See also U.S. Congress, Joint Economic Committee, *Urban and Economic Adjustment to the Post-Industrial Era,* report prepared by Donald A. Hicks, 97th Cong., pt. 2, 1982, p. 585.

49. Peggy L. Cuciti, "A Nonurban Policy: Recent Public Policy Shifts Affecting Cities," in *The Future of National Urban Policy,* ed. Marshall Kaplan and Franklin James (Durham, N.C.: Duke University Press, 1990), pp. 243–244. See also Hal Wolman, "The Reagan Urban Policy and Its Impacts," *Urban Affairs Quarterly* 21, no. 3 (1986), pp. 311–335.

50. Richard L. Cole, Delbert A. Taebel, and Rodney V. Hissong, "America's Cities and the 1980s: The Legacy of the Reagan Years," *Journal of Urban Affairs* 12, no. 4 (1990): 348.

51. U.S. Advisory Commission, *Significant Features, 1980–81,* p. 59.

52. Richard P. Nathan and Fred C. Doolittle, *Reagan and the States* (Princeton, N.J.: Princeton University Press, 1987), p. 19.

53. Ledebur and Barnes, *City Distress,* p. 10.

54. *Ibid.,* p. 11.

55. John L. Mikesell, "The Season of Tax Revolt," in *Fiscal Retrenchment and Urban Policy,* ed. John P. Blair and David Nachmias (Beverly Hills, Calif.: Sage, 1979), p. 109.

56. *Ibid.,* p. 109.

57. Pagano, *City Fiscal Conditions in 1991,* p. 24.

58. Cole, Taebel, and Hissong, "America's Cities and the 1980s," p. 352.

59. Twentieth Century Fund Task Force on Municipal Bond Credit Ratings, *The Rating Game,* with a background paper by John E. Peterson (New York: Twentieth Century Fund, 1974), p. 25.

60. U.S. Bureau of the Census, *Statistical Abstract of the United States, 1992,* 112th ed. (Washington, D.C.: Government Printing Office, 1992), p. 285. Amounts are estimates subject to sampling variation.

61. Alberta Sbragia, "Finance Capital and the City," in *Cities in Stress: A New Look at the Urban Crisis* ed. M. Gottdiener (Beverly Hills, Calif.: Sage, 1986), p. 210.

62. Aronson and Hilley, *Financing State and Local Governments,* p. 174.

63. Cited by National League of Cities, *The Tax System: Consequences for Urban Policy,* 2d ed., National League of Cities Working Paper (Washington, D.C.: National League of Cities, 1975), p. 4.

64. See Robert Huefner, *Taxable Alternatives to Municipal Bonds,* Research Report no. 53 (Boston: Federal Reserve Bank of Boston, 1972); *Building a Broader Market: Report of the Twentieth Century Fund Task Force on the Municipal Bond Market,* with a background paper by Ronald W. Forbes and John E. Peterson (New York: McGraw-Hill, 1976).

65. Elaine B. Sharp, "The Politics and Economics of the New City Debt," *American Political Science Review* 80, no. 4 (December 1986), pp. 1271–1288.

66. U.S. Bureau of the Census, *Statistical Abstract of the United States, 1991,* p. 285.

67. Thomas A. Pascarella and Richard D. Raymond, "Buying Bonds for Business: An Evaluation of the Industrial Revenue Bond Program," *Urban Affairs Quarterly* 18 (September 1982): 73–89.

68. Dephane A. Kenyon and Dennis Zimmerman, "Private-Activity Bonds and the Volume Cap in 1990," *Intergovernmental Perspective* (Summer 1991), pp. 35-37.

69. Twentieth Century Fund Task Force, *The Rating Game*, p. 55.

70. *Ibid.*, p. 78.

71. George H. Hempel, *Measures of Municipal Bond Quality*, Michigan Reports no. 53 (Ann Arbor: Bureau of Business Research, Graduate School of Business Administration, University of Michigan, 1967), p. 124.

72. Twentieth Century Fund Task Force, *The Rating Game*, p. 83.

73. *Ibid.*, p. 107; Allen J. Michel, "Municipal Bond Ratings: A Discriminant Analysis Approach," *Journal of Financial and Quantitative Analysis* 12 (November 1977), pp. 587–598; W. T. Carleton and E. M. Lerner, "Statistical Credit Scoring and Municipal Bonds," *Journal of Money, Credit and Banking* 1 (November 1969): 750–764; Larry K. Hastie, "Determinants of Municipal Bond Yields," *Journal of Financial and Quantitative Analysis* 7 (June 1972), pp. 1729–1748.

74. Jesse F. Marquette, R. Penny Marquette, and Katherine A. Hinkley, "Bond Rating Changes and Urban Fiscal Stress: Linkage and Prediction," *Journal of Urban Affairs* 4 (Winter 1982), p. 92.

75. *Ibid.*, p. 93.

76. John E. Peterson, "Changing Fiscal Structure and Credit Quality: Large U.S. Cities," in *Fiscal Stress and Public Policy*, ed. Charles H. Levine and Irene Rubin (Beverly Hills, Calif.: Sage, 1980), pp. 179–202.

77. Thomas Geis, "Municipal Credit and Bond Rating System" (Paper presented at the Municipal Officers Association Meeting, Denver, Colo., May 31, 1972), pp. 5–6.

78. *Ibid.*

79. U.S. Advisory Commission on Intergovernmental Relations, *City Financial Emergencies* (Washington, D.C: Government Printing Office, 1971), p. 10.

80. *Ibid.*, p. 12.

81. *Ibid.*, p. 16.

82. *Ibid.*, p. 17.

83. *Ibid.*, pp. 81–82.

84. Todd Swanstrom, *The Crisis of Growth Politics: Cleveland, Kucinich, and the Challenge of Urban Populism* (Philadelphia: Temple University Press, 1985), chap. 7.

85. Twentieth Century Fund Task Force, *The Rating Game*, p. 117. See also Geis, "Municipal Credit and Bond Rating System"; Hempel, *Measures of Municipal Bond Quality*, p. 74.

86. U.S. Bureau of the Census figures as compiled by Ester R. Fuchs, *Mayors and Money: Fiscal Policy in New York and Chicago* (Chicago: University of Chicago Press, 1992), pp. 22–23. For our comparison of New York and Chicago, we rely heavily on Fuchs's insightful account.

87. U.S. Bureau of the Census, *Census of Manufacturing*, selected years (Washington, D.C.: Government Printing Office, 1950 and 1981), as compiled by John D. Kasarda, "Urban Change and Minority Opportunities," in *The New Urban Reality*, ed. Paul Peterson (Washington, D.C.: Brookings Institution, 1985), p. 44.

88. See William Julius Wilson, *The Truly Disadvantaged: The Inner City, the Underclass, and Public Policy* (Chicago: University of Chicago Press, 1987).

89. See Robert W. Burchell et al., "Measuring Urban Distress: A Summary of the Major Urban Hardship Indices and Resource Allocation Systems," in *Cities Under Stress: The Fiscal Crises of Urban America* ed. Robert W. Burchell and David Listokin (Piscataway, N.J.: Center for Urban Policy Research, 1981), p. 219; Katherine L. Bradbury, "Urban Decline and Distress: An Update," *New England Economic Review*, July-August 1984, p. 43.

90. Ladd and Yinger, *America's Ailing Cities*, p. 121.

91. Fuchs, *Mayors and Money*, pp. 30, 32.

92. Martin Shefter, *Political Crisis/Fiscal Crisis: The Collapse and Revival of New York City* (New York: Basic Books, 1985), p. 106.

93. Jack Newfield and Paul DuBrul, *The Abuse of Power: The Permanent Government and the Fall of New York* (New York: Viking, 1977), p. 31.

94. Fred Ferretti, *The Year the Big Apple Went Bust* (New York: Putnam, 1976), p. 46.

95. Peterson, "Finance," p. 65.

96. Ferretti, *The Year the Big Apple Went Bust*, p. 45.

97. Roger E. Alcaly and Helen Bodian, "New York's Fiscal Crisis and the Economy," in *The Fiscal Crisis of American Cities*, ed. Roger E. Alcaly and David Mermelstein (New York: Random House, 1977), p. 288.

98. Ferretti, *The Year the Big Apple Went Bust*, p. 6.

99. Newfield and DuBrul, *The Abuse of Power*, p. 12; U.S. Congress, Congressional Budget Office, "New York City's Fiscal Problem," a background paper prepared by Robert D. Reischauer, Peter K. Clark, and Peggy, L. Cuciti, as edited and published in *The Fiscal Crisis of American Cities*, ed. Alcaly and Mermelstein, p. 288.

100. Robert Zevin, "New York City Crisis: First Act in a New Age of Reaction," in *The Fiscal Crisis of American Cities*, ed. Roger E. Alcaly and David Mermelstein (New York: Random House, 1977), p. 12. The annual inflation rate reached 12 percent in 1974.

101. See "Never Enough Money for the States," *Business Week*, October 12, 1974, p. 106.

102. Harry Magdoff and Paul M. Sweezy, "Banks: Skating on Thin Ice," *Monthly Review* 26 (February 1975):1–21.

103. Alcaly and Bodian, "New York's Fiscal Crisis and the Economy," p. 53.

104. Edward J. Kane, "Why 'Bad Paper' Worries Economic Policies," *Bulletin of Business Research*, July 1975, cited in *ibid.*, pp 53–54.

105. From a confidential memorandum from William Haddad, director of the Office of Legislative Oversight and Analysis, to George Cincotta, chairman of the New York Assembly Banking Committee, July 7, 1976; quoted in Newfield and DuBrul, *The Abuse of Power,* p. 42.

106. *CBS Evening News,* August 26, 1977.

107. Fuchs, *Mayors and Money,* p. 91.

108. Raymond D. Horton and Mary McCormick, "Services," in *Setting Municipal Priorities, 1981,* ed. Charles Brecher and Raymond D. Horton (Montclair, N.J.: Allanheld Osmun, 1980), p. 89.

109. Shefter, *Political Crisis/Fiscal Crisis,* p. 135.

110. Charles Brecher and Raymond D. Horton, "Retrenchment and Recovery: American Cities and the New York Experience," *Public Administration Review* 45 (March-April 1985): 270.

111. Shefter, *Political Crisis/Fiscal Crisis,* p. 148.

112. Fuchs, *Mayors and Money,* p. 10.

113. Robert F. Wagner, Jr., *New York Ascendant: The Report of the Commission on the Year 2000* (New York: HarperCollins, 1987), p. 1.

114. Todd S. Purdum, "A Sense of Fiscal Doom," *New York Times,* June 23, 1991.

115. Fuchs, *Mayors and Money,* p. 8.

116. *Wall Street Journal,* May 15, 1991, cited in *ibid.*

117. Shefter, *Political Crisis/Fiscal Crisis,* p. 105.

118. Fuchs, *Mayors and Money,* p. 275.

119. Terry N. Clark, Lorna Ferguson, and Robert Shapiro, "Functional Performance Analysis: A New Approach to the Study of Municipal Expenditures and Debt," *Political Methodology* 8, no. 2 (1982), pp. 87–123.

120. Fuchs, *Mayors and Money,* pp. 112, 119.

121. *Ibid.,* pp. 194–196.

122. *Ibid.,* p. 205.

123. Wagner, *New York Ascendant,* pp. 93–94.

124. Ladd and Yinger, *America's Ailing Cities,* p. 291.

125. U.S. Advisory Commission on Intergovernmental Relations, *Fiscal Disparities: Central Cities and Suburbs, 1981* (Washington, D.C.: Government Printing Office, 1984), cited in *ibid.,* p. 297. See also James Heilbrun, *Urban Economics and Public Policy* (New York: St. Martin's Pros, 1974), p. 484.

126. Isabel Wilkerson, "Ravaged City on Mississippi Floundering at Rock Bottom," *New York Times,* April 4, 1991.

127. L. J. Sharpe, "Is There a Fiscal Crisis in Western European Local Government? A First Appraisal," in *The Local Fiscal Crisis in Western Europe,* ed. L. J. Sharpe (London: Sage, 1981), pp. 5–28.

128. Arnold J. Heidenheimer, Hugh Heclo, and Carolyn Teich Adams, *Comparative*

Public Policy: The Politics of Social Choice in America, Europe, and Japan, 3rd ed. (New York: St. Martin's Press, 1990), p. 278.

129. Thomas H. Boast, "A Political Economy of Urban Capital Finance in the United States" (Ph.D. diss., Cornell University, 1977), p. 114.

CHAPTER 13

1. The following account of Quincy Market is based on Bernard J. Frieden and Lynn B. Sagalyn, *Downtown, Inc.: How America Builds Cities* (Cambridge, Mass.: MIT Press, 1989), and Jon C. Teaford, *The Rough Road to Renaissance: Urban Revitalization in America, 1940–1985* (Baltimore: Johns Hopkins University Press, 1990).

2. Frieden and Sagalyn, *Downtown, Inc.,* p. 43.

3. These arrangements are described in Peter K. Eisinger, *The Rise of the Entrepreneurial State: State and Local Economic Development Policy in the United States* (Madison: University of Wisconsin Press, 1988).

4. Teaford, *The Rough Road to Renaissance,* p. 307.

5. *Ibid.,* p. 296.

6. *Ibid.,* p. 307.

7. Alexander Hamilton, *The Works of Alexander Hamilton,* vol. 3, ed. John C. Hamilton (New York: Trow, 1950), p. 246, quoted in Norman Krumholz, "Recovery of Cities: An Alternative View," in *Rebuilding America's Cities: Roads to Recovery,* ed. Paul R. Porter and David C. Sweet (New Brunswick, N.J.: Center for Urban Policy Research, 1984), p. 182.

8. John R. Logan and Harvey L. Molotch, *Urban Fortunes: The Political Economy of Place* (Berkeley: University of California Press, 1987).

9. For an influential defense of the theory behind growth politics, see Paul E. Peterson, *City Limits* (Chicago: University of Chicago Press, 1981).

10. Quoted in Robert S. Lynd and Helen Merrill Lynd, *Middletown* (New York: Harcourt Brace and world, 1929), p. 487. The Lynds' monumental study of Muncie, Indiana, is a classic sociological analysis of local booster culture.

11. U.S. Bureau of the Census, *Statistical Abstract of the United States, 1992,* 112th ed. (Washington, D.C.: Government Printing Office, 1992), p. 397.

12. Robert B. Reich, *The Work of Nations* (New York: Random House, Vintage Books, 1991), p. 86.

13. David Gordon, "Capitalism and the Roots of the Urban Crisis," *The Fiscal Crisis of American Cities,* ed. Roger E. Alcaly and David Mermelstein (New York: Random House, Vintage Books, 1977), pp. 102–103.

14. Barry Bluestone and Bennett Harrison, *The Deindustrialization of America* (New York: Basic Books, 1982).

15. Frieden and Sagalyn, *Downtown, Inc.,* p. 9.

16. *Ibid.,* p. 65.

17. *Ibid.,* p. 69.

18. Kenneth T. Jackson, *Crabgrass Frontier: The Suburbanization of the United States* (New York: Oxford University Press, 1985), p. 261.

19. Joel Garreau, *Edge City: Life on the New Frontier* (Garden City, N.Y.: Doubleday, 1991).

20. Alexander Ganz, "Where Has the Urban Crisis Gone?" *Urban Affairs Quarterly* 20, no. 4 (June 1985): 456.

21. Frieden and Sagalyn, *Downtown, Inc.,* pp. 265–266.

22. Norman J. Glickman, "Cities and the International Division of Labor," in *Enduring Tensions in Urban Politics,* ed. Dennis Judd and Paul Kantor (New York: Macmillan, 1992), pp. 493–513.

23. Joseph Persky, Elliot Sclar, and Wim Wiewel, *Does America Need Cities?* (Washington, D.C.: Economic Policy Institute, 1991), p. 12; Thomas M. Stanback, Jr., *The New Suburbanization: Challenge to the Central City* (Boulder, Colo.: Westview Press, 1991), p. 45.

24. Barry Bluestone and Bennett Harrison, *The Great American Job Machine: The Proliferation of Low Wage Employment in the U.S. Economy* (Washington, D.C.: Joint Economic Committee, 1986), p. 17.

25. Frieden and Sagalyn, *Downtown, Inc.,* p. 288.

26. *Ibid.*, pp. 288–289.

27. Richard Child Hill, "Crisis in the Motor City: The Politics of Economic Development in Detroit," in Norman Fainstein, Richard Child Hill, Dennis Judd, and Michael Peter Smith, *Restructuring the City: The Political Economy of Urban Redevelopment* (New York: Longman, 1983), p. 105.

28. Gurney Breckenfeld, "It's Up to the Cities to Save Themselves," *Fortune,* March 1977, p. 196.

29. Neal R. Pierce, Robert Guskind, and John Gardner, "Politics Is Not the Only Thing That Is Changing America's Big Cities," *National Journal,* November 26, 1983, p. 2480.

30. "He Digs Downtown," *Time,* August 24, 1981, p. 47.

31. Robert P. Stoker, "Baltimore: The Self-Evaluating City?" in *The Politics of Urban Development,* ed. Clarence N. Stone and Heywood T. Sanders (Lawrence: University Press of Kansas, 1987), p. 248.

32. Quoted in Tony Hiss, "Annals of Place: Reinventing Baltimore," *New Yorker,* April 29, 1991, p. 62.

33. Quoted in "He Digs Downtown," p. 42.

34. Christopher Corbett, "What's Doing in Baltimore," *New York Times,* February 23, 1992.

35. Bernard L. Berkowitz, "Rejoinder to Downtown Redevelopment as an Urban Growth Strategy: A Critical Appraisal of the Baltimore Renaissance," *Journal of Urban Affairs* 9, no. 2 (1987), p. 129.

36. "He Digs Downtown," p. 47.

37. Marc V. Levine, "Downtown Development as an Urban Growth Strategy," *Journal of Urban Affairs* 9, no. 2 (1987), p. 110.

38. Berkowitz,"Rejoinder to Downtown Redevelopment," p. 130.

39. Richard Ben Cramer, "Can the Best Mayor Win?" *Esquire,* October 1984, p. 58.

40. Quoted in Hiss, "Annals of Place," p. 41.

41. Levine, "Downtown Redevelopment," pp. 111–112.

42. Richard P. Nathan and Charles F. Adams, "Four Perspectives on Urban Hardship," *Political Science Quarterly* 104, no. 3 (Fall 1989), p. 488.

43. Levine, "Downtown Redevelopment," p. 112.

44. *Ibid.,* p. 116.

45. John D. Kasarda, "Urban Change and Minority Opportunities," *The New Urban Reality,* ed. Paul E. Peterson (Washington, D.C.: Brookings Institution, 1985); William Julius Wilson, *The Truly Disadvantaged: The Inner City, the Underclass, and Public Policy* (Chicago: University of Chicago Press, 1987).

46. Levine, "Downtown Redevelopment," pp. 113–114.

47. Dennis R. Judd, *The Politics of American Cities: Private Power and Public Policy,* third edition (HarperCollins Publishers, 1988), p. 393.

48. Marc V. Levine, "Response to Berkowitz," *Journal of Urban Affairs* 9, no. 2 (1987), p. 136.

49. Levine, "Dowtown Redevelopment," p. 108.

50. Richard C. Hula, "The Two Baltimores," in *Leadership and Urban Regeneration,* ed. Dennis Judd and Michael Parkinson (Newbury Park, Calif.: Sage, 1990), pp. 199–200.

51. Cited in Governmental Research Unit, "Economic Benefits to St. Louis of the Proposed Convention Hall and Plaza" (Unpublished report, 1972), pp. 4–6.

52. *St. Louis Globe-Democrat,* November 9, 1975, Sunday Magazine, p. 8.

53. Cited in *New York Times,* February 17, 1976, p. 8.

54. *New York Times,* October 21, 1974, p. 38.

55. *New York Times,* January 25, 1976, p. 6.

56. U.S. National Tourism Resources Review Commission, *Destination U.S.A.* 2: 45.

57. *New York Times,* March 17, 1976, p. 43.

58. *New York Times,* October 8, 1976, p. 45.

59. *Ibid.,* p. 46.

60. U.S. National Tourism Resources Review Commission, *Destination U.S.A.* 1: 106.

61. "The U.S. Seeks a Bigger Slice of the World's Convention Business," *Commerce Today,* July 10, 1972, p. 12.

62. *Ibid.,* p. 14.

63. *Ibid.,* p. 12.

64. Governmental Research Unit, "Economic Benefits to St. Louis," p. 14.

65. *New York Times,* June 21, 1976, p. 43.

66. "Each Tourist Dollar Found to Be Producing More Than 7 Cents in Tax Revenues," *Commerce Today,* March 14, 1974, p. 14.

67. George Young, *Tourism: Blessing or Blight?* (Harmondsworth, England: Penguin, 1973).

68. "President Picks a Place: San Diego, California," *Time,* August 2, 1971, pp. 15–16.

69. *Washington Post,* October 4, 1972, p. A1.

70. Chester Hartman, *Yerba Buena: Land Grab and Community Resistance in San Francisco.* (San Francisco: Glide Publications, 1974), p. 165.

71. "Convention Centers Spark Civic Wars," *U.S. News and World Report,* February 10, 1986, p. 45.

72. *Ibid.*

73. Hartman, *Yerba Buena,* p. 175.

74. Peter Kihss, "Stadium Project Put at $57 Million," *New York Times,* July 17, 1975.

75. John L. Hess, "Stadium's Costs Now Seen As Loss," *New York Times,* April 15, 1976.

76. Martin Waldron, "Yanks Get Windfall As City Shifts Plans," *New York Times,* December 1, 1975.

77. Hess, "Stadium's Costs."

78. Quoted in Traway Gupte, "Residents Near Yankee Stadium Say City Reneged on Renovation Promise," *New York Times,* August 21, 1976.

79. "Yankees to Donate $35,000 to Upgrade City Park in Bronx," *New York Times,* July 7, 1976.

80. Logan and Molotch, *Urban Fortunes,* p. 79.

81. Neil J. Sullivan, *The Dodgers Move West* (New York: Oxford University Press).

82. Arthur T. Johnson, "Economic and Policy Implications of Hosting Sports Franchises: Lessons from Baltimore," *Urban Affairs Quarterly* 21, no. 3 (March 1986): 411.

83. Arthur T. Johnson, "The Sports Franchise Relocation Issue and Public Policy Responses," in *Government and Sport: The Public Policy Issues,* ed. Arthur T. Johnson and James H. Frey (Totowa, N.J.: Rowman & Allanheld, 1985), p. 232.

84. Quoted in David Morris, "Let Sports Fans Own Their Teams," *New York Times,* September 29, 1986.

85. Ronald Smothers, "No Hits, No Runs, One Error: The Dome," *New York Times,* June 15, 1991.

86. Quoted in "Support for Pro Football Contract Costs Mayor of Oakland His Job," *New York Times,* June 7, 1990.

87. Mark S. Rosentraub and Samuel R. Nunn, "Suburban City Investment in Professional Sports," *American Behavioral Scientist* 21, no. 3 (January–February 1978): 393–414.

88. Arthur T. Johnson, "Municipal Administration and the Sports Franchise Relocation Issue," *Public Administration Review,* November–December 1983, p. 524.

89. Quoted in "San Antonio Plans for a Sports Dome," *New York Times,* December 28, 1986.

90. For more details about the enclosure and privatization of space in urban areas, see Dennis R. Judd, "The Rise of the New Walled Cities," in *Representing the City,* ed. Helen Liggett and David C. Perry (Newbury Port Calif.: Sage, 1994).

CHAPTER 14

1. James H. Johnson, Jr., Cloyzelle K. Jones, Walter C. Farrell, Jr., and Melvin L. Oliver, "The Los Angeles Rebellion: A Retrospective View," *Economic Development Quarterly* 6, no. 4 (November 1992), pp. 356–372.

2. *Ibid.*

3. "Immigration Reform: Recent Trends and Legislative Responses," *The Urban Institute Policy and Research Report,* Winter/Spring 1991, p. 12.

4. Rodman D. Griffin, "Illegal Immigration," *CQ Researcher* 2, no. 16 (April 24, 1992): 364.

5. Louis Winnick, *New People in Old Neighborhoods* (New York: Russell Sage Foundation, 1990), p. xvi.

6. U.S. Bureau of the Census, *Current Population Reports, Persons of Spanish Origin in the United States: March 1977,* P 20, no. 3239 (Washington, D.C.: Government Printing Office, 1978), p. 2.

7. Alejandro Portes and Ruben Rumbent, *Immigrant America: A Portrait* (Berkeley: University of California Press, 1990), p. 10.

8. *Ibid.*

9. See Min Zhou, *Chinatown: The Socioeconomic Potential of an Urban Enclave* (Philadelphia: Temple University Press, 1992).

10. Christopher L. Warren, John G. Corbett, and John F. Stack, Jr., "Hispanic Ascendancy and Tripartite Politics in Miami," in *Racial Politics in American Cities,* ed. Rufus P. Browning, Dale Rogers Marshall, and David H. Tabb (New York: Longman, 1990), p. 166.

11. Jack Miles, "Blacks vs. Brown," *Atlantic,* October 1992, pp. 41–68. See also Mike Davis, "In L.A., Burning All Illusions," *Nation,* June 1, 1992, pp. 743–746.

12. Tim Rutten, "A New Kind of Riot," *New York Review of Books,* June 11, 1992, pp. 52–54.

13. "Immigration Reform," p. 13.

14. Reported in Charles Kamasaki and Paul Yzaguirre, "Black-Hispanic Tensions: One Perspective" (Paper delivered at the Annual Meeting of the American Political Science Association, Washington, D.C., August 29–September 1, 1991), p. 5.

15. Robert Pear, "Major Immigration Bill Is Sent to Bush," *New York Times,* October 29, 1990.

16. Griffin, "Illegal Immigration."

17. The official poverty line is established by the U.S. Department of Health and Human Services (HHS) and is based on the amount of money HHS calculates is required to purchase an "emergency" diet (a diet that provides adequate nutrition) for one person for a year. That amount is multiplied by three to arrive at the income below which an individual is deemed to be at a poverty level. The definition makes the assumption, challenged by virtually all researchers, that all other necessities can be covered by an amount no more than twice the amount spent for food. In 1990, the poverty line for a family of four was set at $12,293.

18. William W. Goldsmith and Edward J. Blakely, *Separate Societies: Poverty and Inequality in U.S. Cities* (Philadelphia: Temple University Press, 1992), p. 46.

19. William Julius Wilson, *The Truly Disadvantaged: The Inner City, the Underclass, and Public Policy* (Chicago: University of Chicago Press, 1987), p. 46.

20. Based on estimates from the U.S. Bureau of the Census, *Current Population Reports, Poverty in the United States: 1986,* P 60, no 160 (Washington, D.C.: Government Printing Office, 1988), Table 16, cited in Richard P. Nathan and Charles F. Adams, Jr., "Four Perspectives on Urban Hardship," *Political Science Quarterly* 104, no. 3 (Fall 1989), p. 503.

21. Douglas S. Massey and Nancy Denton, "Hypersegregration in U.S. Metropolitan Areas: Black-Hispanic Segregation Along Five Dimensions," *Demography,* August 1989. See also Douglas S. Massey and Nancy Denton, *American Apartheid: Segregation and the Making of the Underclass* (Cambridge, Mass.: Harvard University Press, 1993).

22. Douglas S. Massey and Nancy Denton, "Trends in the Residential Segregation of Blacks, Hispanics, and Asians: 1970–1980," *American Sociological Review* 52, pp. 802–825.

23. Goldsmith and Blakely, *Separate Societies,* p. 48.

24. Wilson, *The Truly Disadvantaged,* p. 58.

25. *Ibid.,* p. 102. For further information on the mismatch between the geographic location of inner-city blacks and available jobs, see John Kasarda, "Urban Change and Minority Opportunities," in *The New Urban Reality,* ed. Paul E. Peterson (Washington, D.C., Brookings Institution, 1985), pp. 33–67; John D. Kasarda, "Urban Employment Change and Minority Skills Mismatch," in *Creating Jobs, Creating Workers: Economic Development and Employment in Metropolitan Chicago,* ed. Lawrence B. Joseph (Chicago: Center for Urban Research and Policy Studies), pp. 65–89, reprinted in *Enduring Tensions in Urban Politics,* ed. Dennis Judd and Paul Kantor (New York: Macmillan, 1992), pp. 605–615.

26. Goldsmith and Blakely, *Separate Societies,* pp. 51–52.

27. Wilson, *The Truly Disadvantaged,* p. 27.

28. *Ibid.*

29. Jane Gross, "Collapse of Inner-City Families Creates America's New Orphans," *New York Times,* March 29, 1992.

30. Sonia L. Nazario, "High Infant Mortality Is a Persistent Blotch on Health Care in U.S.," *Wall Street Journal,* October 19, 1988.

31. Lisa W. Foderaro, "In Harlem, Children Reflect the Ravages U.N. Seeks to Relieve," *New York Times,* September 30, 1990.

32. Lena Williams, "Inner City Under Siege: Fighting AIDS in Newark," *New York Times,* February 6, 1989.

33. Walter J. Jones and James E. Johnson, "AIDS: The Urban Policymaking Challenge," *Journal of Urban Affairs* 11, no. 1 (1989), p. 85.

34. *Confronting AIDS: Update 1988* (Washington, D.C.: National Academy Press, 1988), p. 52.

35. Michael Massing, "Crack's Destructive Sprint Across America," *New York Times Magazine,* October 1, 1989.

36. "Crack," Editorial, *New York Times,* May 29, 1989.

37. Jonathan Kozol, *Rachel and Her Children: Homeless Families in America* (New York: Crown, 1988), p. 9.

38. *Ibid.,* p. 11.

39. Philip L. Clay, *At Risk of Loss: The Endangered Future of Low-Income Rental Housing Resources* (Washington, D.C.: Neighborhood Reinvestment Corporation, 1987), p. 4.

40. Michael deCourcy Hinds, "Number of Killings Soars in Big Cities Across U.S.," *New York Times,* July 18, 1990.

41. Robert D. McFadden, "New York Leads Cities in Robbery Rate, but Drops in Murders," *New York Times,* August 11, 1991.

42. See James Diego Vigil, *Barrio Gangs: Street Life and Identity in Southern California* (Austin: University of Texas Press, 1988).

43. Seth Mydans, "Homicide Rate Up for Young Blacks," *New York Times,* December 7, 1990.

44. Ronald Kotulak, "Study Finds Inner-City Kids Live with Violence," *Chicago Tribune,* September 28, 1990.

45. Huey L. Perry, "Deracialization as an Analytical Construct in American Urban Politics," *Urban Affairs Quarterly* 27, no. 2 (December 1991), p. 181.

46. Rufus P. Browning, Dale Rogers Marshall, and David H. Tabb, "Can Blacks and Latinos Achieve Power in City Government? The Setting and the Issues," in *Racial Politics in American Cities,* ed. Rufus P. Browning, Dale Rogers Marshall, and David H. Tabb (New York: Longman, 1990), p. 5.

47. H. Paul Friesema, "Black Control of Central Cities: The Hollow Prize," *American Institute of Planners Journal* 35, no. 2 (March 1969), pp. 75–79.

48. Adolph Reed, Jr. "The Black Urban Regime: Structural Origins and Constraints," *Comparative Urban and Community Research* 1, no. 1 (1987), pp. 138–189.

49. Quoted in William Greider, "Detroit's Streetwise Mayor Plays Key Role in City's Turn Around," *Cleveland Plain Dealer,* July 3, 1978.

50. Maynard Jackson, quoted in Clarence N. Stone, *Regime Politics: Governing Atlanta, 1946–1988* (Lawrence: University Press of Kansas, 1988), p. 87.

51. Adolph Reed, Jr., "A Critique of Neo-Progressivism in Theorizing About Local Development Policy: A Case from Atlanta," in *The Politics of Urban Development,* ed. Clarence N. Stone and Heywood T. Sanders (Lawrence: University Press of Kansas, 1987), p. 206.

52. Quoted in Stone, *Regime Politics,* p. 136.

53. Peter K. Eisinger, "Black Mayors and the Politics of Racial Economic Advancement," in *Readings in Urban Politics: Past, Present, and Future* 2d ed., ed. Harlan Hahn and Charles H. Levine (New York: Longman, 1984), p. 252.

54. Albert K. Karnig and Susan Welch, *Black Representatives and Urban Policy* (Chicago: University of Chicago Press, 1980).

55. Rufus P. Browning, Dale Rogers Marshall, and David H. Tabb, *Protest Is Not Enough: The Struggle of Blacks and Hispanics for Equality in Urban Politics* (Berkeley: University of California Press, 1984), p. 250.

56. Eisinger, "Black Mayors and the Politics of Racial Economic Advancement," p. 258.

57. Wilson, *The Truly Disadvantaged,* p. 115.

58. Stone, *Regime Politics,* p. 145.

59. For background on urban populism, see Todd Swanstrom, *The Crisis of Growth Politics: Cleveland, Kucinich, and the Challenge of Urban Populism* (Philadelphia: Temple University Press, 1985); Pierre Clavel, *The Progressive City: Planning and Participation, 1969–1984* (New Brunswick, N.J.: Rutgers University Press, 1986); Mark E. Kann, *Middle Class Radicalism in Santa Monica* (Philadelphia: Temple University Press, 1986); W. J. Conroy, *Challenging the Boundaries of Reform: Socialism in Burlington* (Philadelphia: Temple University Press, 1990).

60. Quoted in Robert T. Starks and Michael B. Preston, "Harold Washington and the Politics of Reform in Chicago: 1983–1987," in *Racial Politics in American Cities.* ed. Rufus P. Browning, Dale Rogers Marshall, and David H. Tabb (New York: Longman, 1990), p. 95.

61. Paul Kleppner, *Chicago Divided: The Making of a Black Mayor* (DeKalb: Northern Illinois University Press, 1985). p. 149.

62. *Ibid.*

63. Rob Mier and Kari J. Moe, "Decentralized Development: From Theory to Practice," in *Harold Washington and the Neighborhoods: Progressive City Government in Chicago, 1983–1987,* ed. Pierre Clavel and Wim Wiewel (New Brunswick, N.J.: Rutgers University Press, 1991), p. 71.

64. Wim Wiewel and Pierre Clavel, "Conclusion," in *ibid.,* p. 278.

65. Doug Gills, "Chicago Politics and Community Development: A Social Movement Perspective," in *ibid.*, p. 54.

66. John Kretzman, "The Affirmative Information Policy: Opening Up a Closed City," in *ibid.*, pp. 199–220.

67. John P. Pelissero, Beth M. Henschen, and Edward I. Sidlow, "Urban Policy Agendas and Sports Franchises: The Case of Chicago" (Paper presented at the Annual Meeting of the American Political Science Association, San Francisco, August 30–September 2, 1990), pp. 9–10.

68. Robert T. Giloth and Robert Mier, "Spatial Change and Social Justice: Alternative Economic Development in Chicago," in *Economic Restructuring and Political Response,* ed. Robert A. Beauregard (Newbury Park, Calif.: Sage, 1989), pp. 188–199.

69. *Ibid.,* pp. 194–196.

70. Quoted in B. Kelly, "Harold Washington's Balancing Act," *Chicago Magazine,* April 1985, p. 206.

71. Richard L. Cole, Delbert A. Taebel, and Rodney V. Hissong, "America's Cities and the 1980s: The Legacy of the Reagan Years," *Journal of Urban Affairs* 12, no. 4 (1990): 348.

CHAPTER 15

1. *Report of the National Advisory Commission on Civil Disorders* (New York: Bantam Books, 1968), p. 1.

2. Edward C. Banfield, *The Unheavenly City: The Nature and the Future of Our Urban Crisis* (Boston: Little, Brown, 1970).

3. Margaret T. Gordon and Claudette Guzan Artwick, "Urban Images in the Mass Media" (Research proposal, Urban University Research Consortium, June 17, 1991), p. 2.

4. Linda Heath and John Petraitis, "Television Viewing and Fear of Crime: Where Is the Mean World?" *Basic and Applied Social Psychology* 8 (1987), pp. 97–112.

5. Richard Louv, *America II* (New York: Penguin Books, 1985), p. 34.

6. Micaela di Leonardo, "White Lies/Black Myths: Rape, Race, and the Black Underclass," *The Village Voice,* September 22, 1992, p. 31.

7. *Ibid.*

8. Elizabeth V. Sawhill, "The Underclass: An Overview," *Public Interest* 96 (Summer 1989), pp. 3–15.

9. Robert Suro, "For Women, Varied Reasons for Single Motherhood," *New York Times,* May 26, 1992.

10. Andrew Hacker, "The Myths of Racial Division," *New Republic,* March 23, 1992, p. 21.

11. Josh Barbanel, "From L.I. Teller Machines to Gas Stations, Suburban Robberies Are on the Rise," *New York Times,* February 18, 1992.

12. David Guterson, "No Place Like Home: On the Manicured Streets of a Master-Planned Community," *Harper's,* November 1992, p. 63.

13. Thomas Byrne Edsall, *The New Politics of Inequality* (New York: Norton, 1984);

Thomas Byrne Edsall and Mary D. Edsall, *Chain Reaction: The Impact of Race, Rights, and Taxes on American Politics* (New York: W.W. Norton, 1991).

14. Elizabeth A. Roistacher, "Housing Finance and Housing Policy in the United States: Legacies of the Reagan Era," in *Government and Housing: Developments in Seven Countries,* Urban Affairs Annual Reviews, vol. 36, ed. Willem van Vliet and Jan van Weesep (Newbury Park, Calif.: Sage, 1990), p. 161.

15. Peter Dreier, "Bush to Cities: Drop Dead," *The Progressive* 56, no. 7 (July 1992): 21.

16. *Ibid.*

17. Jason DeParle, "Why Marginal Changes Don't Rescue the Welfare System," *New York Times,* March 1, 1992.

18. U.S. Bureau of the Census, *Statistical Abstract of the United States, 1992* (Washington, D.C.: Government Printing Office, 1992), p. 355.

19. *Ibid.*

20. Michael Peter Smith, *City, State, and Market: The Political Economy of Urban Society* (Oxford, England: Blackwell, 1988).

21. *Ibid.,* p. 47; U.S. Bureau of the Census, *Statistical Abstract of the United States, 1992,* p. 321.

22. *Ibid.,* p. 336.

23. *Report to the Boston Redevelopment Authority by Employment Research Associates,* Lansing, Mich., cited in Peter Dreier, "America's Urban Crisis: Symptoms, Causes, Solutions," *North Carolina Law Review* 71, no. 5 (1993). Also see Ann R. Markusen, Peter Hall, Scott Campbell, and Sabine Deitrick, *The Rise of the Gunbelt: The Military Remapping of Industrial America* (New York: Oxford University Press, 1991); Andrew Kirby, *The Pentagon and the Cities,* Urban Affairs Annual Reviews (Newbury Park, Calif.: Sage, 1992).

24. Robert D. Reischauer, "The Rise and Fall of National Urban Policy, The Fiscal Dimension," in Marshall Kaplan and Franklin James (eds.), *The Future of National Urban Policy* (Durham, N.C.: Duke University Press, 1990), p. 227; U.S. Bureau of the Census, *Statistical Abstract of the United States, 1992,* p. 315.

25. Quoted in Tom Morgenthau and John McCormack, "Are Cities Obsolete?" *Newsweek,* September 9, 1991, p. 42.

26. Elizabeth Kolbert, "Region Around New York Sees Ties to City Faltering," *New York Times,* December 1, 1991; William Blaberson, "For Many in the New York Region, the City Is Ignored and Irrelevant," *New York Times,* January 2, 1992.

27. Joseph Persky, Elliot Sclar, and Wim Wiewel, *Does America Need Cities?* (Washington, D.C.: Economic Policy Institute, 1991), p. 4.

28. "In a sample of fourteen large metropolitan areas, the wages of central city jobs in 1987 averaged 20 percent higher than those of suburban jobs." *Ibid.,* p. 12.

29. *Ibid.,* p. 13.

30. Arnold J. Heidenheimer, Hugh Heclo, and Carolyn Teich Adams, *Comparative Public Policy: The Politics of Social Choice in America, Europe, and Japan,* 3rd ed. (New York: St. Martin's Press, 1990), p. 278.

31. H. V. Savitch, Daniel Sanders, and David Collins, "The Regional City and Public Partnerships," in *In the National Interest: The 1990 Urban Summit,* ed. Ronald Berkman et al. (New York: Twentieth Century Fund, 1992), pp. 65–77; Larry C. Ledebur and William R. Barnes, *Metropolitan Disparities and Economic Growth,* A Research Report of the National League of Cities (Washington, D.C.: National League of Cities, 1992).

32. William Schneider, "Rule Suburbia," *National Journal,* September 28, 1991, p. 2335.

33. National Council of Public Works Improvement, *Fragile Foundations* (Washington, D.C.: National Council of Public Works Improvement, 1988), p. 47, cited in Michael A. Pagano, "Urban Infrastructure and City Budgeting: Elements of a National Urban Policy," in *The Future of National Urban Policy,* ed. Marshall Kaplan and Franklin James (Durham, N.C.: Duke University Press, 1990), p. 131.

34. The studies of infrastructure needs are reviewed in Marshall Kaplan, "Infrastructure Policy: Repetitive Studies, Uneven Response, Next Steps," *Urban Affairs Quarterly* 25, no. 3 (March 1990), pp. 371–388.

35. D. Drummond Ayres, "Mayors Applaud Clinton's Promise to Remake American Economy," *New York Times,* June 23, 1992. For a discussion of Clinton's inclusive approach to the problems of cities, see the campaign book he wrote with his running mate Albert Gore, *Putting People First: How We Can All Change America* (New York: Times Books, 1992), esp. pp. 52–62.

36. Leonard Silk, "Now, to Figure Why the Poor Get Poorer," *New York Times,* December 18, 1988.

37. Margaret Weir, Ann Shola Orloff, and Theda Skocpol, "Understanding American Social Politics," in *The Politics of Social Policy in the United States,* ed. Margaret Weir, Ann Shola Orloff, and Theda Skocpol (Princeton, N.J.: Princeton University Press, 1988), pp. 3–27.

38. William W. Goldsmith and Edward J. Blakely, *Separate Societies: Poverty and Inequality in U.S. Cities* (Philadelphia: Temple University Press, 1992), p. 33.

39. Heidenheimer, Heclo, and Adams, *Comparative Public Policy,* p. 214.

40. Michael Specter, "Neglected for Years, TB Is Back with Strains That Are Deadlier," *New York Times,* October 11, 1992, pp. 1, 20.

41. Virgil Tipton, "Westfall Offers Plan to Share Tax Wealth," *St. Louis Post-Dispatch,* December 9, 1992, pp. 1, 9.

INDEX